FLORENCE NIGHTINGALE

MISS NIGHTINGALE WITH HER TAME OWL ATHENA, *circa* 1850
After a drawing by Parthenope Lady Verney

CECIL WOODHAM-SMITH

FLORENCE NIGHTINGALE
1820–1910

CONSTABLE LONDON

First published in Great Britain 1950 by
Constable and Company Ltd
3 The Lanchesters, 162 Fulham Palace Road
London W6 9ER
Copyright © 1950 Cecil Woodham-Smith
Reprinted nine times
Paperback edition 1982
Reprinted 1991, 1996
ISBN 0 09 475810 7
Printed in Great Britain by
St Edmundsbury Press Ltd
Bury St Edmunds, Suffolk

A CIP catalogue record for this book
is available from the British Library

To

G. I. W.-S.

INTRODUCTION

Cecil Woodham-Smith's biography of Florence Nightingale was first published in September 1950. It was widely acclaimed and has been reprinted nine times in hardback and three times in paperback. This new edition bears witness to its enduring popularity and relevance.

Cecil Woodham-Smith was neither an academic historian nor a known writer. The ambiguity of her name was useful at a time when history, especially military history, was seen as an unlikely subject for a woman to tackle. When *The Reason Why*, her account of the charge of the Light Brigade, was published in 1953 she was amused by reports of military men asking what regiment this Woodham-Smith chap was from. She was in fact called Cecil after a relation in the hope of an inheritance. Though this was not forthcoming she never resented the unusual name which suited her rebellious character.

Cecil Blanche FitzGerald was anglo-Irish and proud of her kinship to Lord Edward FitzGerald who led the rebellion of 1798 against the English. Her mother was related to Sir Thomas Picton, Wellington's general who was killed at Waterloo. Cecil was sent to the Royal School Bath for the Daughters of Officers of the British Army until she was expelled for impertinence and for playing truant to visit the National Gallery. She finished her schooling at a French convent and went up to St Hilda's College, Oxford, graduating in 1917 with a second class degree in English. Her failure to gain a first class degree may have been due in some part to her being sent down for a term for joining in an Irish street demonstration. Identification with her Irish roots would surface again in her powerful book on the tragic consequences of the potato famine of 1846–49.

The exam result frustrated Cecil FitzGerald's plans to pursue an academic career as an archaeologist. Instead she joined Benson's, the advertising agency, as a copywriter, leaving in 1928 to marry a London solicitor, George Woodham-Smith. There were two children of the marriage. While they were young, she wrote a number of popular novels and serials under the pseudonym Janet Gordon. It was only in 1941, when the children were of boarding school age, that she could contemplate a serious literary project.

What led her to Florence Nightingale? Significantly, her father Colonel James FitzGerald had served in India in the years following the Crimean War and had developed an admiration for Miss Nightingale's achievements, particularly her work to improve the conditions of the army in the sub-continent. When her friend Michael Sadleir, senior partner in Constables, advised her to pick a subject with 'star quality', the choice was easy.

Cecil Woodham-Smith felt she 'had been given the opportunity of presenting . . . a complete picture of Miss Nightingale for the first time.' Sir Edward Cook had published his official *Life of Florence Nightingale* in 1913, just three years after Florence Nightingale's death. In the intervening years the social climate had changed and many of those concerned had died, allowing Woodham-Smith to probe more deeply into Florence Nightingale's relationships with her family, friends and suitors. Access to family papers held in private archives was particularly important in this respect and there were also the Nightingale papers of the British Library to consult. This collection of over 10,000 items had been sent to Wales for safekeeping for the duration of the Second World War. Cecil Woodham-Smith found herself staying in a hotel in Aberystwyth full of billeted soldiers and as she worked through the archive she reflected that 'Florence Nightingale would have been at home in this atmosphere'.

Her working method was slow: 'I find that to handle letters, to read them as they were written and not as extracts or copies, and to visit the places where they were written is essential if I am to be able to understand and sympathise with the people I am trying to write about.' She drafted and re-drafted her text using an ancient portable typewriter. She clung to 'this old friend' despite her husband's offers of a new machine, feeling that 'my erratic portable knows my difficulties'. Meanwhile there were family and social obligations, and Cecil Woodham-Smith's daughter remembers that her mother envied Florence Nightingale's ability to isolate herself from social demands in order to devote herself single-mindedly to her work.

In September 1950 a scale model of Miss Nightingale's Crimean carriage, complete with two mules, was the centrepiece of a window display at Harrods. Nine years' work (and five re-writes) were finally over and Cecil Woodham-Smith's first major work was launched in grand fashion. It received laudatory reviews from the literary press and went on to win the James Black Tate Memorial Prize. In the new field of Victorian Studies the reception was also positive: Asa Briggs hailed Woodham-Smith's as 'one of the best modern nineteenth-century biographies'. Cecil Woodham-Smith enjoyed the success of her book, which did not come as a great surprise: it had not occurred to her that it would be otherwise.

Woodham-Smith's presentation of Florence Nightingale still remains the best introduction for general readers to this extraordinary woman and her time. The pace of the narrative never falters; descriptions of conditions in the Barrack Hospital at Scutari are emotionally searing; her portrayal of Miss Nightingale in old age is particularly evocative. Woodham-Smith joked that her gift for fast narrative and human detail was learnt at the feet of 'Janet Gordon', but this is undoubtedly the book's great strength.

Readability is achieved at the expense of comprehensive referencing, which hides some more serious flaws. Woodham-Smith has, as the editors of a selection of Florence Nightingale's letters found out, 'an irritating habit of quoting a letter without dating it correctly, or of eliding different sections or even different letters as if they formed one continuous thought.' The historians Greenleaf and Baly have drawn attention to factual errors and imbalanced assessment in their respective fields of expertise: the Crimean War and the history of nursing. The book was never intended as an academic treatise and these limitations certainly do not detract from its standing as a classic biography.

Woodham-Smith challenges the myth that had grown up around Florence Nightingale's personality by revealing the complexity of her character. We know from the thousands of visitors who come to the Florence Nightingale Museum at St. Thomas' Hospital that she has deepened the popular understanding of Florence Nightingale, and we owe her an immense debt of gratitude.

Dr Susan Thornton, Florence Nightingale Museum

With many thanks to Elizabeth Bonython (née Woodham-Smith), Miss Patricia Mowbray and Dr Monica Baly.

NOTE OF ACKNOWLEDGEMENT

IN WRITING this biography I have been given the opportunity of presenting what I believe to be a complete picture of Miss Nightingale for the first time.

When Sir Edward Cook wrote his admirable official life immediately after Miss Nightingale's death, there was a large body of material which, for family and personal reasons, was either not available to him or he was asked not to use. He did not, for instance, see the Verney Nightingale papers; he saw only part of the collection I have described as the Herbert papers; and there was a great deal of other correspondence of which he was asked to make only a limited use. I have been fortunate enough to be given access to this material.

My thanks are due, first and foremost, to Sir Harry Verney, Bart., who most generously placed at my disposal the very important Verney Nightingale papers comprising the domestic correspondence and private papers of Miss Nightingale's mother, Frances, her sister Parthenope, Lady Verney, and the Nightingale family circle. I am deeply indebted to Lord Herbert for allowing me to use unpublished material from the Herbert papers, establishing, among other important points, the true nature of the relationship between Miss Nightingale and Lord and Lady Herbert of Lea. I should like to thank the late Mrs. Salmon, Sir Harry Verney's sister, for unpublished letters and private information, and I owe very much to the late Lady Stephen, not only for unpublished letters and reminiscences, but for her kindness, too, in procuring me access to family papers.

I am indebted to Sir Ralph Verney, Bart., for the correspondence of his father, Mr. Frederick Verney, with Miss Nightingale; to Sir Maurice Bonham-Carter for permission to make use of family papers; and to Mr. Leigh Smith for information of importance from the Leigh Smith papers. Sir Shane Leslie has allowed me to use two letters from his biography of Cardinal Manning, and Messrs. Hodder and Stoughton have kindly given me permission to quote extracts from letters published in Miss Elizabeth Haldane's *Mrs. Gaskell and Her Friends*. I should like also to thank Mr. James Pope-Hennessy and Mrs. Vaughan Nash. I owe, as every biographer of Miss Nightingale must owe, a debt to Sir Edward Cook, who in his official life first performed the task of tracing a path through the mass of the Nightingale papers—the enormous collection of private and official letters and documents left by Miss Nightingale at her death and deposited at the British Museum in 1940. I should like to thank the Museum authorities, through whose co-operation I was enabled to examine the Nightingale papers at the National Library of Wales when, during the war, it was not possible to see manuscripts in London. Finally I should like to record my obligation to Mr. Michael Sadleir, without whose support, criticism and constant assistance this book could not have been written.

LONDON 1949

ix

LIST OF ILLUSTRATIONS

*The Claydon photograph and the pen-and-ink
drawing reproduced on page 9 are included by
kind permission of Sir Harry Verney, Bart.*

I IT WAS SOMETHING NEW to call a girl Florence. Within fifty years there would be thousands of girls all over the world christened Florence in honour of this baby, but in the summer of 1820, when Fanny Nightingale fixed on the name for her daughter, it was new.

Novelty was the fashion in 1820. Europe was still rejoicing in the liberty which followed the end of the Napoleonic wars. Years of restriction had bred a longing for change, and now that freedom to travel had returned, the roads and cities of Europe were thronged with travellers. No nation welcomed freedom more heartily than the English, who for a generation had been confined to their island; and in the years following Waterloo an army of English travellers flocked across the channel to enjoy Europe once more.

Fanny and William Nightingale had been travelling in Europe since their marriage in 1818. They already had one daughter, born in Naples in 1819 and christened by the Greek name for her birthplace, Parthenope. For her second confinement Fanny chose Florence. She loved gaiety, and Florence had the reputation of being the gayest city in Europe. The Nightingales took a large furnished villa, the Villa Colombaia near the Porta Romana, where a second girl was born on May 12th, 1820. Fanny decided she too should be named after her birthplace, and on July 4th, 1820, she was christened Florence in the drawing-room of the villa.

It would have been better if Florence had been a boy. Though William Edward Nightingale, or as he was always called, W. E. N., was rich, there were complications attached to his property. He had inherited from an uncle, and, under his uncle's Will, if W. E. N. should have no son, the property passed on his death to his sister and next to her eldest son. However, the Nightingales felt no anxiety. Not all W. E. N.'s fortune was involved. He had inherited when a minor; a lead mine discovered on the property had greatly increased its value, and during his minority a large sum had been invested on his behalf which was absolutely his. The Nightingales had been married for two years, and Fanny had already had two healthy children. The next baby would be a boy.

I

Though they were both handsome, agreeable and intelligent they were not a well-matched couple. Only a few months before their engagement Fanny had been anxious to marry another man; and she was six years older than W. E. N. In 1820 she was thirty-two, extremely beautiful, generous and extravagant. She had great vitality, was indefatigable in the pursuit of pleasure, never tired unless bored, always good natured unless thwarted, always kind unless her obstinacy were aroused. In the art of making people comfortable, in the arrangement of a house, the production of good dinners, she possessed genius. She intended, when she returned to England, to make herself a position as a hostess.

She came from a remarkable family. Her grandfather, Samuel Smith, had been a well-known character, celebrated for the riches he had amassed as a London merchant and for his humanitarian principles. He had come to the assistance of Flora Macdonald when she was a penniless prisoner in the Tower in spite of the fact that he was a strong Hanoverian. To show his sympathy with the struggle of the American colonists for freedom in the War of Independence he had relinquished his title to a large part of the city of Savannah. His son William Smith, Fanny's father, devoted his wealth to collecting pictures and fighting lost causes. For forty-six years he sat in the House of Commons fighting for the weak, the unpopular and the oppressed. He was a leading Abolitionist, he championed the sweated factory workers; he did battle for the rights of Dissenters and Jews. Among his intimate friends were Wilberforce, Charles James Fox, Francis Baring, Philip Francis, reputed author of *Junius*, Sir Joshua Reynolds and John Opie.

His children did not inherit his altruism. At Parndon Hall in Essex, in his London house in Park Street, his political and humanitarian activities were carried on against a background of ceaseless junketings. With tireless energy the young Smiths danced, went on pleasure parties and picnics, played parlour games, got up amateur theatricals. There were ten children, five sons and five daughters, all good looking, all with immense zest for living and amazing health. William Smith himself at eighty wrote that he had " no recollection whatever of any bodily pain or illness ". None of his ten children died before the age of sixty-nine, six lived to be over eighty and Fanny lived to be ninety-two. Looking back on her youth fifty years later Fanny described family life as a " hurly burly ". " We Smiths never thought of anything all day long but our own ease and pleasure ", she wrote.

Fanny was the beauty of the family; yet Fanny did not marry. Her sister, Anne, married an immensely rich Mr. Nicholson of Waverley Abbey near Farnham, the house which gave Scott the title for the Waverley novels; her sister, Joanna, married Mr. Bonham Carter, eldest son of a well-known Hampshire family, and settled near Winchester. Fanny remained at home with Patty and Julia who held " advanced " views and suffered from nerves. Association with her father's friends had left its mark on Fanny; she had acquired a passion for good conversation, " had a preference for clever elderly gentlemen, and was comparatively indifferent to gay young ones "; and despised the junketings of Parndon. She had already " arrived at the age when the world acquits those parents who suffer their daughters to act for themselves ", when, in 1816, she fell in love with the Honourable James Sinclair, a younger son of the Earl of Caithness. His character was allowed to be good and his intentions disinterested, but he possessed no income beyond the pay of a captain in the Ross-shire Militia, and no expectations. In immense letters, full of worldly wisdom, kindness and unanswerable common sense, William Smith pointed out the absurdity of a woman of Fanny's habits contemplating life on an income of scarcely four hundred a year and declined, in justice to his other children, to assume the support of her future family. Fanny pleaded in vain that her affections were entirely given away, that she daily felt no difficulties could inflict half the pain that she must suffer under a disappointment, and that losing James would quite break her down. By 1817 the affair was at an end.

Fanny was now nearly thirty and William Edward Nightingale was nearly twenty-four. She had known him since he was a boy; he had been at school with her younger brother Octavius and had been coming to the house for years, an awkward lanky schoolboy, immensely tall, immensely thin, with a habit of always standing upright propped against mantelpieces and doors because he disliked folding himself into a chair.

3

Originally his name had been Shore, but at twenty-one, when he came into the fortune left him by his uncle, he changed his name to Nightingale. He went up to Cambridge with an income of between seven and eight thousand a year, and Cambridge transformed him. He proved, though lazy, to be clever. He gained a reputation for wit. His looks improved, his height and a remote and gentle manner gave him distinction. He developed into a dilettante, rich, appreciative, indolent, charming.

It was an unexpected result. Wild blood ran in W. E. N.'s veins. The uncle, his mother's brother, from whom he inherited, had been an eccentric sporting squire, known throughout Derbyshire as mad Peter Nightingale. Peter Nightingale had been a dare-devil horseman, a rider in midnight steeplechases, a layer of wagers, given to hard drinking and low company.

In 1817 W. E. N. became engaged to Fanny. He was very much in love. Fanny's rich beauty warmed his reserved temperament, and for a short time he thawed. The period was brief. Normally, as Fanny wrote later, " Mr. Nightingale is seldom in the melting mood ".

Fanny's family did not approve. They were fond of W. E. N., but they had no faith in his character. He was clever but he was indolent, hated making up his mind, hated taking action—he was not the husband for Fanny. Within six months they were married and had gone abroad.

Fanny believed she would be able to mould W. E. N. She intended him to become one of the prosperous, cultivated and liberal-minded country gentlemen who played an important part in English public life. They would have a beautiful house, a fine library, maintain an interest in the arts and entertain.

After nearly three years in Italy Fanny began to feel it was time they came home. W. E. N., she wrote, would have been content to idle in Italy for the rest of his life. As long as he had books and conversation he was indifferent to other pleasures. He loved quietness, leisure, long hours in which to read and reflect. If he had these he did not care whether he was in a palace or an attic, wearing a new coat or an old. However, Fanny prevailed, and in 1821, when Florence was a year old, the Nightingales returned to England.

4

The first necessity was to house themselves. The Night-ingales had no family place. Peter Nightingale had inhabited a tumbledown building, half manor, half farm, totally inadequate for the needs of Fanny, W. E. N. and two babies accompanied by maids, footmen, valet, coachman and cook.

Before they left Italy W. E. N. had decided to abandon the old house and had made a flying trip to England to have work started on a new house on higher ground. He was an amateur architect and himself produced the designs from which the plans were drawn. He gave his house mullions, a steep pitched roof, a vaguely Gothic air. The effect is not unpleasing and the situation of the house is unrivalled. Lea Hurst stands high above a rolling country, terraced gardens fall steeply away on every side, and the view from the windows is immensely wide, so that the house, as Mrs. Gaskell wrote, seems to be floating in air.

But no sooner was Lea Hurst finished than Fanny realised she had made a mistake. As a family place Lea Hurst was inadequate, as a house in which to entertain it was impossible. The only attraction was a wonderful view. The situation was isolated, inaccessible from London, the shooting was poor, the house cold and in winter uninhabitable. The Nightingales attempted one winter there, and both children got bronchitis. Above all, Lea Hurst was much too small.

Fanny's standards of accommodation descended to her daughter. Twenty years later at a dinner-party Florence denied that Lea Hurst was anything but a small house. "Why," she said, "it has only fifteen bedrooms."

By 1823 Fanny had convinced W. E. N. that Lea Hurst, except in summer, was impossible. Certainly they would keep up a property where the Nightingales had been rooted for generations, but they must also have another house, a larger house, and in a warmer part of the country than Derbyshire.

Two years of house-hunting followed. Fanny became impatient, W. E. N. despaired. " *Where* is the country which is inhabitable for twelve months in the year? " he asked her in 1824. In 1825 W. E. N. bought Embley Park, near Romsey, in Hampshire, on the borders of the New Forest. It was a good-sized plain square house of the late Georgian period, the situation warm and sheltered, the gardens very large and exceptionally fine. The shooting was good, London was reasonably near, and Fanny's two married sisters, Mrs. Nicholson at Waverley Abbey near Farnham, and Mrs. Bonham Carter at Fairoaks near Winchester, were within easy reach. Above all, in contrast to the uncivilised remoteness of Lea Hurst, Embley was in the centre of a " good neighbourhood ".

By the time Florence was five the pattern of the Nightingales' life was fixed. The summer was passed at Lea Hurst, the remainder of the year at Embley Park, and twice a year during the spring and autumn seasons a visit was paid to London. Fanny would have liked a house in London but W. E. N. refused.

He did, however, proceed to turn himself into an English country gentleman. He shot, he fished, he hunted. " Papa is gone a'hunting the fox ", wrote his younger daughter in one of her earliest letters. He did a great deal for his tenants, supported a free school at great expense near Lea Hurst, and in Hampshire took an active part in local politics. He was High Sheriff for Hampshire in 1829, and Fanny looked forward to the day when he would stand for Parliament. W. E. N. was a Whig and in favour of Parliamentary Reform. " How I hate Tories, all Beer and Money ", he wrote to Fanny in 1830.

Fanny's life ran smoothly. If she fretted after the son who failed to appear she did not record it. The only shadow was cast by Florence. Florence was not an easy child.

The two little girls were not called by their full names. Florence was shortened to Flo, Parthenope to Parthe or Pop. Flo was much the prettier. Neither of the girls inherited their mother's outstanding beauty, but Flo promised to grow up more than ordinarily good looking. She was lightly built, singularly graceful, with thick bright chestnut hair and a delicate complexion.

Both Fanny and W. E. N. loved children. All the closely related families of the Nightingale circle—Smiths, Shores, Nicholsons, Bonham Carters—delighted in children. A stream of cousins spent their holidays at Embley and Lea Hurst, and almost invariably Fanny had a couple of family babies in the house, enjoying a change of air and being fed up on country

6

butter and eggs and cream. " Kiss all babies for me " is a frequent ending to the first letters Flo wrote home. Her childhood was filled with gardens to play in, ponies to ride, and a succession of dogs, cats and birds to be looked after.

In 1827 at Fairoaks, the Bonham Carters' house near Winchester, the children were allowed to build themselves a play-house of boughs. Flo filled a long letter to W. E. N.'s mother with a description of its beauties. There was a door you could really walk in by, and the big boys had made them couches of boughs which you could really sit on, and they had a larder stocked with play provisions. Flo explained the nature of play provisions and listed them in two neat columns. " Pine cones = peaches. Smaller pine cones = nectarines. Beech-nuts = strawberries and gooseberries." A dead bird was found and given a state funeral. Flo wrote the epitaph.

> Tomtitty bird ! Why art thou dead
> Thou who dost bear upon thy head
> A crown ! But now thou art on thy death bed.
> My Tom Tit.

The following year the Bonham Carters and Nicholsons came up to Lea Hurst, and the children had a craze for collecting moths. Three or four times the families united in August to take two houses at Seaview, in the Isle of Wight, and the children bathed and sailed. Christmas was generally spent with the Nicholsons at Waverley Abbey, where the children had a ball of their own and acted a play.

And yet Flo was not happy. If she had been an ordinary naughty child Fanny would have understood her, but she was not naughty. She was strange, passionate, wrong-headed, obstinate and miserable.

In an autobiographical note Miss Nightingale records that as a very young child she had an obsession that she was not like other people. She was a monster. That was her secret which might at any moment be found out. Strangers must be avoided, especially children. She worked herself into an agony at the prospect of seeing a new face, and to be looked at was torture. She doubted her capacity to behave like other people, and refused to dine downstairs, convinced she would betray herself by doing something extraordinary with her knife and fork.

Realisation of the gulf which separated her from everyone round her came hand in hand with the dawnings of conscious thought. At first she was overwhelmed with terror and guilt. Surely she ought to be like everyone else? What might not people do to her if they found out the truth? But almost before she had grown out of babyhood, guilt and terror were succeeded by discontent. She wrote that as early as the age of six she was aware that the rich smooth life of Embley and Lea Hurst was utterly distasteful to her. She ceased to be terrified, she resisted, disliked and despised it.

She began, like many imaginative children, to escape into dreams. She told herself stories in which she played a heroine's part, and for hours at a time transferred herself completely to a dream world.

Though she shrank from meeting people she was not self-sufficient. She was a child who craved for sympathy and attached herself with embarrassing vehemence to anyone whom she felt to be sympathetic. Her childhood was a series of passions—for her governess Miss Christie, for W. E. N.'s younger sister Mary, "Aunt Mai", for a beautiful older cousin. When Miss Christie left, when Aunt Mai married, when the beautiful cousin got tired of her devotion, the violence of her feelings made her physically ill.

She did not attach herself to her mother. As a child Miss Nightingale was a copious letter-writer, and her letters show how early she was conscious of a want of sympathy in Fanny. When she writes to her grandmother, her aunts, to W. E. N., her pen flies on, with a total disregard of spelling, telling them of the adventures of Nelson the dog, of a local suicide, a good crop of apples, a piece of monstrous injustice on the part of one of her uncles who accused the children of upsetting a cart in the garden which they had never even touched, and Aunt Mai's new baby. " Aunt Mai calls her new baby the Thing, don't you think that is very disrespectful ? " Writing to Fanny, the flow is checked. She is on the defensive, her letters are carefully written, formal and short. Even at ten years old she is anxious to appease. She assures her mother that she is wearing the boots to strengthen her ankles, she is endeavouring to improve her spelling, she is trying to be more good-natured.

8

The companion of her childhood was W. E. N. Among the Verney Nightingale papers is preserved a sketch by Julia Smith, Fanny's unmarried younger sister, of W. E. N. and the two little girls. The trio have their backs to the artist. W. E. N., in frock-coat and top-hat, is in the middle, tall and thin as a hop pole, the two children, one on each side, wear pantalettes and broad-brimmed hats. Parthe, as Aunt Julia points out

in a note scribbled below the sketch, clings to her father's coat-tail while Flo " independently stumps along by herself ".

W. E. N. was a man to enchant a child. He loved the curious and the odd, and he loved jokes ; he had a mind stored with information and the leisure to impart it. He had great patience and he was never patronising. Partly as a result of marrying Fanny, partly by temperament, he was a lonely man, and it was with intense pleasure he discovered intellectual companionship in his daughters. Both were quick, both were unusually responsive, both learned easily, but the more intelligent, just as she was the prettier, was Flo.

It was a difficult situation for Parthe. She was the elder, the plainer, the less intelligent, the less remarkable. Flo, strange, passionate, uncomfortable little thing, had something about her which struck people as exceptional. When Flo was still a child, an old friend of the Smith family, Miss Fanny Allen of Prescelly, a remarkable woman and a blue-stocking, wrote that she found Flo for some reason extraordinary. Parthe was far from being unattractive—it was only in contrast with Flo she paled. Flo dominated. Flo led and Parthe followed, but Parthe followed resentfully. She was possessive towards Flo, she adored Flo, wanted Flo's entire devotion, could not bear Flo to have another friend, but she was bitterly envious of Flo.

Fanny made a practice of sending the children to stay with their relatives separately. In 1830 Flo wrote to Parthe from Fair Oaks: " Pray dear Pop, let us love each other better than we have done. It is the will of God and Mamma particularly desires it."

It was impossible for the two children to be the devoted pair of little sisters Fanny desired. The temperamental differences between them were too deep.

Florence had a passion for neatness, method and order and was irritated because Parthe was careless. " Dear Pop," she wrote in 1830, " I have not put your scrap book anywhere, but one day I saw it in the drawer of the music room next to the bow window and I think it *very* odd you did not think of looking for it there ! ! ! " In her next letter she asked for wool, " of which there is plenty in my cabinet, my sand bottles are wrapped up in it. Please empty the contents of the box into one of the *empty* top drawers, as I do *not* wish them to be mixed."

Accuracy, neatness, perseverance were impossible to Parthe. In opposition to her sister she dramatised herself as irresponsible, childlike, joyous. She loved to think of herself dancing into a room, scattering her possessions gaily, turning off reproof with a trill of laughter and a dart into the sunshine. Florence accepted Parthe's valuation of herself. When the girls were twelve and thirteen they agreed to get up early every morning and teach Bessie, their nursery maid, to read and write. Parthe embarked on the scheme readily, but she did not carry it out. One morning she did not get up, another morning she sat and read the *Arabian Nights* to herself, a third morning the sun was shining and she ran out. Florence, writing to W. E. N., remarked it was necessary to remember that Parthe could not be judged by ordinary standards or expected to observe ordinary rules of life.

The final division between the girls was brought about by W. E. N.'s plan for their education. To find a governess proved impossible. The world did not contain a woman who united the intellectual equipment required by W. E. N. with the standard of elegance and breeding demanded by Fanny. In 1832 he determined to teach the girls himself. A governess was engaged for music and drawing, and the girls learnt Greek, Latin, German, French, Italian, history and philosophy from their father. The time-table was formidable and W. E. N. exacting; the girls were required to work long hours, and Parthe rebelled. She left her sister struggling with Greek verbs and joined her mother or escaped into the garden.

Miss Nightingale and her father were deeply in sympathy. Both had the same regard for accuracy, the same cast of mind at once humorous and gloomy, the same passion for abstract speculation.

Parthe did not want to toil at Greek, but she resented the companionship between her father and sister, and in the summer of 1834 she wrote him a protest. He replied in a characteristic letter—involved, vague and curiously reminiscent of a soliloquy in a poetic drama. " My dear Pop—not one word . . . among my waking dreams I sometimes fancy that you and I have not made half as much of each other's society as we might have done. . . . I have more subjects than one in hand, or in mind, which are likely enough to lend themselves to our future intercourse. In the meantime I feel that you are satiating yourself (*perhaps* usefully) with many matters which suit your infantine and merry days of 15—or is it 16?—and, thro' a nervousness of interfering with them, I curtail my letter to a simple expression of my rejoicing at your merriments and your happiness.—W. E. N."

Change of subject did not produce power to concentrate in Parthe. She continued to be bored, resentful and cross, and

W. E. N. became angry with her. In 1835 Parthe wrote to him when he was in London. " Flo in bed, coughing, told me all . . . so exonerate her pray. . . . I really did not know I was laying the ban on my own happiness by such heedlessness of other people's feelings. I am properly punished for it, if you knew how very bitterly I feel your messages through her and your acknowledgment in your own letter, that you have ceased to care enough for my society, to be sorry I behave so ill."

To send messages of reproof to an elder sister through a younger did not make the elder less jealous, and it made the younger self-righteous. At fifteen Florence could be sanctimonious. " I hope our matutinal moments may not have been quite unprofitably spent, though we may not have improved our minds as we ought", she wrote to Fanny from the Isle of Wight in 1835. Her correspondence tended to be a record of her own good deeds. She had learnt to eat sandwiches, which was an effort ; she had practised curling her hair, as her mother desired ; she had been devoting most of her spare time to looking after a baby cousin—" Dear little Robert I am sure I never love him the less for being ugly ". By the time Florence was sixteen the family had divided. She was W. E. N.'s companion in the library, Parthe was Fanny's companion in the drawing-room. Fanny was always busy, there were flowers to arrange, an increasing number of friends to be entertained and innumerable letters to be written to the vast circle of the Nightingale family's connections.

On Florence's fourteenth birthday W. E. N. calculated she had already twenty-seven first cousins and nearly two dozen aunts and uncles by blood and marriage. In the centre of this circle were the energetic handsome Smiths, who had the strongest possible family feelings. As each married, the circle was enlarged by the addition of a whole new family. Husbands of aunts, wives of uncles brought in their brothers and sisters and their wives and husbands ; even the brothers and sisters of grandmothers with their train of children and grandchildren were corresponded with, visited, kept informed, consulted. With the single exception of Fanny's eldest brother, who maintained domestic arrangements which were described as decidedly improper, not one of the huge clan was anything but respectable and prosperous. Enormous numbers of letters were written. Not only major events, weddings, births, deaths, but the choice of a place for a holiday, the advisability of taking a holiday at all, the dismissal of a coachman or cook, the selection of a dress or a carpet provoked correspondence and consultations with aunts, uncles, cousins and grandmothers.

To Miss Nightingale letters and consultations were an intolerable waste of time. " I craved ", she wrote, " for some regular occupation, for something worth doing instead of frittering time away on useless trifles." Parthe had a large correspondence and numerous intimate friends among her cousins ; but to Florence only three families were of importance —the Nicholsons of Waverley Abbey, the Bonham Carters of Fairoaks, and the family of Aunt Mai, now Mrs. Sam Smith of Combe Hurst, Surrey.

Aunt Mai was a person of importance to the Nightingales. She was W. E. N.'s sister ; and, should he have no son, the property would pass to her. In 1827 she married Fanny's younger brother, Sam Smith. It was then seven years since the birth of Florence, Fanny was nearly forty and there was no sign of another child. It was almost certain that, if Aunt Mai had a son, he would eventually inherit Embley and Lea Hurst, and the marriage which linked the two families more closely together was welcomed. In 1831 a son was born, and Fanny, in whom all hope of another child must now have died, behaved admirably. The situation was not easy for her. Not only was Aunt Mai mother of the heir Fanny had failed to produce, she was also the object of the extravagant devotion of Fanny's difficult little daughter Flo. Nevertheless, Fanny's affectionate relations with Aunt Mai were unclouded. Aunt Mai's son was accepted as the heir and given a privileged position in the Nightingale family. Florence was known to have a special gift with babies, and when he was a few days old he was laid in her arms : " My boy Shore ", the eleven-year-old Flo proudly called him. Shore was recognised as being her special property, and devotion to Shore, pride in him, and Shore's devotion to her grew into one of the most important relationships in her life.

So Florence grew into girlhood in a life that seemed all smoothness and peace. At Embley and Lea Hurst there were comfort, security and affection, there were intelligence and companionship. And yet beneath the surface there was no peace; Florence was brought up in a hot-house of emotion.

It was the result of a literary fashion. The wave of romanticism which had swept Europe had penetrated English domestic life, and ordinary wives and mothers were reproducing the behaviour of the heroines of Byron and Chateaubriand. Since a rigid respectability governed their behaviour, their emotions had to be expended on the commonplace events of everyday life. The naughtiness of a child, a misunderstanding between friends, the non-arrival of a letter, called forth tears, explanations, faintness. News of the death of a distant and aged cousin, the engagement to marry of a friend, necessitated smelling salts, a darkened room, a soothing draught. Women prided themselves on being martyrs to their excessive sensibility, and " delicacy " was universal. Fanny, Parthe and Florence were all considered " delicate ", though Fanny lived to be ninety-two, Florence ninety and Parthe seventy-five.

Miss Nightingale grew up in this age and was indelibly impressed by it. Though her extraordinary mind owed its quality to uncompromising clarity and realism, her character contained the contradiction that she was also emotional, prone to exaggeration and abnormally sensitive. The atmosphere in which she was brought up prevented her from achieving balance; throughout her life, when feelings were in question, she entered another world—violent, exaggerated and unreasoning.

In the summer of 1834 she and Parthe were at Cowes with their governess, and W. E. N. wrote to tell them he had been invited to stand for Parliament as candidate for the Andover division. The girls' emotion approached hysteria. " What extraordinary news you have sent us ", wrote the young Flo. " It quite convulsed our quiet little world. . . . Parthe, after a deep reading of the letter in which she neither saw nor heard anything which passed around, screamed out ' Papa is going to be M.P. for Andover!' Miss White and I stood aghast! I could not believe my ears and Parthe said a dozen times ' I wish I were at home, I wish I had seen the deputation.' I could not sleep after it. I slept so lightly that I had the feeling on my mind that something very extraordinary, or dreadful, had happened and kept starting up to find out what it was."

W. E. N.'s candidature for Andover proved a turning-point in the Nightingales' lives. He was a fervent supporter of the Reform Bill of 1832, and had refused to enter political life until the Bill became law, when he believed a new age of political integrity would dawn. The election, in 1835, was the first to be held at Andover under the new franchise, and he entered the contest full of enthusiasm and hope. Fanny saw her plans maturing. They were to have a house in London.

He was not only defeated but profoundly disillusioned. The seat was lost because he refused to bribe the voters. A main object of the Reform Bill had been to end the purchase of votes, but the newly enfranchised electors of Andover took the view that the possession of a vote had always meant hard cash and that the extended franchise merely brought what had been the perquisite of a few within reach of the many. W. E. N.'s first contact with practical politics left him disgusted, and he resolved never to be persuaded to attempt an entry into political life again.

Fanny was defeated. W. E. N. ceased to adapt himself to the character she had planned. He gave up hunting, and took long ambling rides in the New Forest; avoided political meetings and attended congresses of learned societies; spent more time teaching Florence and took to passing the greater part of each day in his library. An immensely tall desk was made for him, and he read standing up, he wrote standing up, he meditated standing up, contemplating for hours at a stretch such abstract subjects as the nature of moral impulses, the relation of ethics to aesthetics and the proofs of the existence of an immortal soul in mortal man.

He would have been content to pass his life in tranquillity, allowing day after day to slide gently by. His natural home, he was fond of saying, was in " the quiet and the shadows ". But life in the quiet and the shadows was unbearable to Fanny. She had been forced to give up her plans for W. E. N., she had had to accept the fact that she would never be a member's wife, never have a house in London. But she did not resign herself. She transferred her plans and her ambitions to her daughters.

15

They were sixteen and seventeen. Next year, or the year after at latest, they must " come out ". Since there was to be no house in London, everything must be done from Embley. Entertaining was necessary to launch the girls in society—house-parties, dinners, balls. At Embley, as Embley stood at present, suitable entertaining could not be done. The history of Lea Hurst repeated itself. The house was discovered to be entirely inadequate. Six more bedrooms must be added, new kitchens built, the exterior remodelled, the interior completely redecorated.

W. E. N. was tempted. He had made a certain reputation with Lea Hurst and was frequently consulted by friends and relations who wished to " improve " their houses, " usually effecting something pretty good in that way ", wrote one of her sisters to Fanny in 1838. He contemplated with pleasure the task of getting out designs to convert the Georgian plainness of Embley to a fashionable Gothic outline. Bow windows were to be replaced by mullions, gables and turrets erected, a terrace with stone griffins planned in the manner of Hampton Court. The expense was bound to be considerable, and Fanny proposed that, while the alterations were carried out, they should make an extended tour abroad. It would do the girls good to see something of the world before they were presented. They could hear music, practise their languages, go to a few parties, buy clothes in Paris. Europe was so cheap that the tour would be an economy. There was no need to keep up an establishment either at Embley or Lea Hurst. W. E. N. agreed. He loved travelling, loved Europe, had many friends in Italy and France. He got out his own design for a travelling carriage, the alterations to Embley were started at once, and the Nightingales fixed a date to leave in September 1837.

At this moment, in the midst of bustle, plans, discussions, Miss Nightingale received a call from God.

It is possible to know a very great deal about Miss Nightingale's inner life and feelings because she had the habit of writing what she called " private notes ". She was unhappy in her environment, she had no one to confide in, and she poured herself out on paper. She hoarded paper (every odd scrap, every half sheet was preserved), and a very large number of her private notes exists. She wrote them on anything that came to her hand—on odd pieces of blotting-paper, on the backs of calendars, the margins of letters ; sometimes she dated them, sometimes not. Sometimes they cover several foolscap pages, sometimes consist of one sentence. Occasionally she used a private note as the basis of a letter. Frequently she repeated a note several times at different dates with only a slight variation in wording. From time to time she also kept diaries ; but it was in her private notes, written from girlhood to old age, that she recorded her true feelings, her secret experiences and her uncensored opinions.

Her experience was similar to that which came to Joan of Arc. In a private note she wrote : " On February 7th, 1837, God spoke to me and called me to His service ". It was not an inward revelation. She heard, as Joan of Arc heard, an objective voice, a voice outside herself, speaking to her in human words.

She was not quite seventeen and she was already living largely in a dream world, which was often more actual to her than the real world. But the voices which spoke to her were not a phenomenon of adolescence. Nearly forty years later, in a private note of 1874, she wrote that during her life her " voices " had spoken to her four times. Once on February 7th, 1837, the date of her call ; once in 1853 before going to her first post at the Hospital for Poor Gentlewomen in Harley Street ; once before the Crimea in 1854 ; and once after Sidney Herbert's death in 1861.

Her path was not made clear. The voices which spoke to Joan told her to take a definite course of action ; Miss Nightingale was told nothing definite. God had called her, but what form that service was to take she did not know. The idea of nursing did not enter her mind. She doctored her dolls, she nursed sick pets, she was especially fond of babies. Her protective instincts were strong, but they had not yet led her to the knowledge that God had called her to the service of the sick.

Meanwhile she knew herself to be God's, and she was at peace. Her call had filled her with confidence and faith. God had spoken to her once; presently He would speak to her again.

On September 8th, 1837, the Nightingales crossed from Southampton to Le Havre. They took with them Fanny's maid, a courier and the girls' devoted, disapproving old nurse, Mrs. Gale. W. E. N. refused to take his valet.

II THE TRAVELLING CARRIAGE W. E. N. had designed was enormous. Five years later, when he lent it to Fanny's sister, it held Mrs. Bonham Carter and six of her daughters, besides a tutor and a maid. The inside was fitted with devices of his own invention for eating, resting, reading and writing in comfort. On the roof were seats for servants and for the family to enjoy the air and admire the scenery in fine weather. Six horses drew the carriage, ridden by postillions.

On the morning of September 9th the Nightingales left Le Havre to travel through France to Italy. W. E. N. intended to leave the beaten track and explore the south of France. The weather was brilliant, the girls sat on the roof, the postillions laughed, sang and cracked their long whips as the carriage lumbered down the straight roads of France.

Florence was in transports of delight. She kept a diary of the tour and recorded that at Chartres she sat all night at her window enchanted by the beauty of moonlight on the cathedral. Her head was full of legends, and she turned romantic land-scapes into the background for imaginary dramas. As they approached Narbonne a lurid sunset flamed in the sky and the city, half hidden by strangely shaped rocks, seemed sinister. She shuddered, and imagined herself a traveller entering a city stricken by plague.

Yet for all her rhapsodies she remained precise. Each day she noted in her diary the exact hours of departure and arrival and the exact distance covered. Her letters to her favourite girl cousin, Hilary Bonham Carter, were not merely transports, for she was capable of mature observation. When they went over the castle at Blaye, she was struck by the fact that the custodian, a Napoleonic veteran, " seemed to have fought everyone but to feel rancune against none ". At Bosuste, a village on the French-Spanish border which had had the mis-fortune to become a battleground in the Carlist war, she was impressed not by the horrors of war but by " the indifference which misery brings ". She observed that, though the people were starving and the land going to ruin, the truly dangerous and shocking symptom was the universal apathy. The population would no longer exert themselves even to save their own lives. " Suffering has made these people indifferent even to their own destruction."

W. E. N.'s explorations were not a success. The roads proved almost impassable, the food uneatable, the beds verminous; and it was with relief that on December 15th, 1837, the Nightingales drove into the gay and pretty town of Nice. Fanny wrote to her sister, Mrs. Bonham Carter, that the accommodation reserved for them at the Hôtel des Étrangers was splendid, the landlord most attentive, and that, even before their boxes were unpacked, she was receiving complimentary visits from the best families in the town. She had stayed at Nice on her wedding-tour twenty years ago, and was remembered. There was a large English colony at Nice, an English Protestant church, balls, concerts.

With startling suddenness cathedrals, moonlight and scenery vanished from Florence's diary and letters. She developed a passion for dancing and wrote to Hilary Bonham Carter that at the biggest ball of the season she danced every quadrille. Her letters took on a new tone, she began to attempt witticisms and to coin phrases.

When the time came to leave Nice, on January 8th, 1838, she was heart-broken. As they climbed up the Corniche she would not look at the famous view or admire the gold and silver lights over the sea. She sat inside the carriage shedding tears. " The worst of travelling is that you leave people as soon as you have become intimate with them, often never to see them again ", she wrote in her diary.

Her tears dried themselves with remarkable speed. The Nightingales reached Genoa on January 13th, and on the 17th Florence wrote to Hilary Bonham Carter that of all towns in the world Genoa was the one she liked best. It was " like an Arabian Nights dream come true ". In 1838 Genoa was still one of the richest and most splendid cities in Europe. Its palaces and gardens, its opera and theatres, its fountains and statues, had earned it the name of " Genova la Superba ".

Florence went to more balls, and at " the most splendid ball of the season " she had so many partners that she became confused. An officer came up and challenged her " in a rage " because, after refusing to dance with him, she sat out with someone else and there was an " embrouillement ".

On February 14th, after giving a large evening party, the Nightingales left Genoa for Florence. They halted at Nervi (described by Florence in one of her phrases as " a town of palaces inhabited by washerwomen "), and again at Pisa, where they went to a ball given by the Grand Duke of Tuscany and a morning entertainment which included luncheon and an inspection of the Grand Duke's camels. On February 27th they reached Florence.

In 1838, thanks to the liberal policy of the Grand Duke, Florence was the intellectual capital of Italy. Fashion and learning united. There were parties for Fanny, learned conversaziones for W. E. N., educational opportunities for the girls. The Nightingales settled in a handsome suite at the Albergo del Arno, near the Ponte Vecchio. They had a salon fifty feet long, a dining-room with a terrace overlooking the Arno, and bedrooms which were magnificently (Mrs. Gale, the girls' old nurse, said indecently) frescoed. Fanny wrote in March 1838 to her sister Julia Smith that the Grand Duke was " exceedingly distinguishing and polite ", the balls at the Grand Ducal Palace " exceedingly fine ", cards had been sent by the Grand Duke not only for public functions but for private entertainments, and Florence had been " much noticed ".

The days flitted by gaily and lightly. Florence had a special link with the brilliant little city, had she not been born there, was she not a Florentine? Her letters became ecstatic, a medley of galleries, pictures, palaces, statues, new frocks and quadrilles. The season proved exceptionally lively. She went to balls, to the opera, to concerts and, as spring came, to fêtes at outlying villas with music under the trees. Fanny gave " at homes " attended by fashionable marchesas and contessas. Long mornings with notebooks were spent in galleries and museums with W. E. N., and every day there were lessons. The best masters in Florence taught the girls Italian, the piano, singing and " perspective ". Florence drew indifferently but conscientiously, Parthe extremely well. Florence had a pretty singing voice, Parthe had none.

Florence became (as she told Hilary Bonham Carter) " music mad ". The opera in Florence was one of the best in

Europe. Grisi and Lablache, the two most famous singers of the day, performed there. Florence lived for opera, persuaded Fanny to take her three times a week, and declared she would like to go every night. She heard most of the operas of Mozart and Donizetti, *Norma* and *La Somnambule*. Mozart was her favourite. She preferred listening to the operas of Mozart to anything else on earth. But she did more than go into transports. With laborious patience she kept a book in which she made a detailed comparison, in the form of a table, of the score, libretto and performance of every opera she heard. Instinctively she reached out for facts. Transports, ecstasies, were not enough. Her mind demanded something hard to bite on, and the romantic extravagance of her emotion crystallised surprisingly into figures.

Italy not only gave her music : in Florence she learnt an enthusiasm for the cause of Italian freedom. Italy had been handed over to Austria, the military despot of Europe, by the Congress of Vienna and was being crushed into subjection. Travelling through Italy she had seen the misery of the country, and in Florence, a free city, she had been able to read the books which were sounding the trumpet call of Italian nationalism—Gurazzi's *Siege of Florence*, which described the great defence of the republican city under Michelangelo, Sismondi's *History of the Italian Republics*. She was just eighteen—imaginative, generous-minded, talented—and, like thousands of her contemporaries, she was seized with a passion for Italy and Italian freedom as violent as falling in love. To Florence Nightingale, as to the Brownings and to George Meredith, the cause of Italian freedom was more than a political conviction, it was a religion, a faith, the embodiment of the struggle of good against the powers of darkness. W. E. N. and Fanny had friends in England intimately connected with the inner circle of Italian patriots. Through these friends the Nightingales were brought into the heart of the movement to set Italy free.

Since childhood Fanny had known a remarkable family, the Allens of Ciesselly, in Pembrokeshire. Fanny Allen was one of the intellectual women who were the advance guard of the feminist movement. Her niece Emma married Charles Darwin. Her sister Jessie married the Italian historian Sismondi. W. E. N. and Sismondi were introduced by the Allens,

A friendship sprang up, and it was agreed that, after leaving Florence and making a tour of the Italian lakes in July and August, the Nightingales would visit Geneva, where, for reasons of prudence, Sismondi was living as an exile.

They reached Geneva in the first week of September 1838 and found the city overflowing with political refugees. The Austrian Government was determined to crush independent thought in Italy; every man of talent felt himself in danger, and a horde of doctors, scientists, educationists, scholars, writers and poets poured across the frontier to safety in Geneva. The refugees found themselves penniless. Everything they owned had been left behind in Italy, and men of first-rate talent, bearing names honoured throughout Europe, lived from hand to mouth, earning a precarious living by teaching.

The change was startling. The world which the Nightingales entered was a world of poverty, learning and sacrifice. Florence instantly responded, and balls and palaces passed from her mind. She became the disciple of Sismondi. He was very short, almost a dwarf, and extremely ugly—so ugly that his wife had hesitated before marrying him—but his nature was charming and his conversation enchanting. He could not bear to see unhappiness or to cause pain to any living creature, fed the mice in his study while he worked, and in Italy had a crowd of 300 beggars permanently encamped outside his door. Sismondi took Florence for long walks while he poured out information on Italian history, economics and theories of government. Through Sismondi she met well-known figures of the Italian movement: Ugoni and Madame Calandrini, who had been ruined and exiled for opening progressive schools; Ricciardi, a young nobleman whom the Austrians had shut up among lunatics with the object of destroying his mind; Confalioneri, who had been practically buried alive for fifteen years—" he still walks as if he had chains on his legs ", wrote Florence—and the exiled poetess Madame Ferucci and her husband.

The Feruccis distressed Florence; she could not understand how anyone could be at once so noble, so unfortunate and so untidy. Madame Ferucci, handsome, gifted and a victim to nerve-storms, earned the family income by giving Italian lessons to the Swiss; her husband, " a magnificently handsome man like a Veronese ", did nothing ; and there was a small spoilt daughter whom no one could control. At intervals the Swiss stolidity and the accent of her pupils became unendurable to Madame Ferucci. She went into hysterics, and with shrieks of " Grandi Asinoni " drove them from the house. Then retiring to her bedroom she spent an hour or two declaiming poems to Florence, while her husband wandered helplessly in and out, her daughter bellowed, and from the kitchen came the sound of breaking crockery. Their servants were invariably incompetent and badly behaved, but in spite of servants and financial difficulties the Feruccis gave a great many parties.

On September 12th the Nightingales were at an evening party at Sismondi's house when news came that the new young Emperor of Austria, Ferdinand I, was celebrating his coronation in Milan by proclaiming a political amnesty. The effect on the exiles was overwhelming. Some burst into tears of joy, some began to laugh and could not stop laughing. Sismondi elbowed his way through the excited throng and, climbing on a table (" pour dominer ", he said, since his height did not allow him to be seen above an ordinary man's shoulder), delivered a brilliant oration on the glories of Italy.

Alas, the following day joy turned to despair. It transpired that a condition of the amnesty was the giving of an undertaking never to conspire against Austria again. The exiles unanimously agreed that to give such an undertaking was impossible, and with many tears the hope of seeing homes and friends once more was relinquished.

Florence was deeply moved. Here was life lived as she had dreamed it might be, with high purpose and uncompromising integrity, and she poured out passionate hero-worship on the martyrs of Italian freedom.

W. E. N. would have stayed indefinitely in Geneva. He had found society which suited him among the Italian exiles and the professors of the University of Geneva to whom he had been introduced by Sismondi, and he had struck up a friendship with de Candolles, the celebrated botanist. But, without warning, a crisis arose in Europe, and it seemed inevitable that a war would be fought in Switzerland. Louis Napoleon Bonaparte, afterwards Napoleon III, had been deported by the

French Government to America after the failure of the Strasbourg conspiracy. He returned to Switzerland to attend the death-bed of his mother, Queen Hortense. The French Government demanded his surrender. The Swiss, maintaining their right of asylum, refused. The French issued an ultimatum; the Swiss refused to give way, and French troops began to march on the frontier. The Swiss mobilised, trenches were dug in the streets, war seemed only a few days distant, and the Nightingales hastily prepared to leave for Paris. As they packed, every man and woman in Geneva was toiling at erecting barricades in the streets. Madame Ferucci was provisioning her house for a siege and exhorting her husband to prepare himself to fight to the death.

To leave Geneva was not easy. There were no horses. The vast carriage stood loaded, but every horse in Geneva had been requisitioned for artillery. W. E. N. scoured the town for horses while Fanny and the girls sat in the salon forbidden to go out, listening to the sound of barricades being erected in the street. Next day he managed to obtain inferior horses at an exorbitant price, and the Nightingales left. Sismondi saw them off, bursting into tears when he said farewell.

A few days later the crisis ended. The English Government mediated, Louis Napoleon voluntarily left Switzerland, and the French Government accepted the suggestion that he should be allowed to live in England. By the time the Nightingales reached Paris the troops had marched back into France, and the Genevese, hysterical with relief, were singing, dancing and embracing each other in the streets. The experience made a deep impression on Florence. There were realities in Europe to which England, safely entrenched behind the Channel, was indifferent and blind. "At home in England changes and revolutions are like storms one only hears", she wrote to Hilary Bonham Carter in November 1838.

W. E. N. proposed to spend four months in Paris and had taken an apartment in the Place Vendôme. It was, wrote Fanny, "extremely splendid". The rooms were vast and richly decorated, the dining-room had gilt mirrors, velvet draperies and carved chairs, the salon crimson satin and ebony cabinets. The windows framed a view of Napoleon's statue on the Vendôme column.

Fanny intended if possible to enter intellectual society and had an introduction, given her by her sister Patty, of which she had great hopes; it was to one of the most celebrated women in Paris—Miss Mary Clarke.

Without money, influence or beauty, Mary Clarke had made herself a major figure in the political and literary world of Paris. In 1838 French politics were dominated by men of letters—Chateaubriand, Victor Hugo, de Vigny, Thiers, Guizot—and the political world had assumed an intellectual tone. Banquets were out of fashion and discussions were the rage. Mary Clarke had remarkable gifts not only for conversing herself but for stimulating others to conversation. In her hands the *salon* was revived, and every Friday night Cabinet Ministers, Dukes of France, English peers, bishops, scholars and writers of international reputation crowded the drawing-room of her apartment in the former hotel of the Clermont-Tonnerre family, 120 rue du Bac.

Mary Clarke was not a Bohemian. She loved society, the great world, great houses and great people. Her family connections were excellent. The Clarkes were an old Scottish Jacobite family, Lord Dalrymple was her cousin, and her sister married Mr. Frewen Turner, a Member of Parliament and owner of the famous Elizabethan mansion of Cold Overton in Leicestershire. Her personal appearance was odd. She was very small, with the figure and height of a child; her eyes were startlingly large and bright, and at a period when women brushed their hair smoothly she wore hers over her forehead in a tangle of curls. Guizot, who was devoted to her, said that she and his Yorkshire terrier patronised the same *coiffeur*. Yet though she had no ordinary feminine attractions, men were devoted to her, and many men wished to marry her. Ampère, son of the celebrated electrician and her intimate friend, wrote: " Her great charm lay in the absence of it. I never knew a woman so devoid of charm in the ordinary sense of the word and yet so fascinating. She was hardly a woman at all." Her effect on her friends was very great. No one, wrote Miss Nightingale, ever had so much influence in forming character, but her candour sometimes took her friends aback. " She had never a breath of posing or of ' edifying ' in her presentation of herself," added Miss Nightingale, " even when it would

have been almost desirable. . . . She was always undressed—naked in full view. A little clothing would have been decent."
Mary was launched on her career by Madame Récamier. About 1830 her mother, who suffered from bronchitis, was forbidden ever to go into fresh air again; the whole of Mrs. Clarke's life must be spent indoors, and Madame Récamier who admired her character and attainments invited her to come and live in her house, the Abbaye-aux-Bois. (Mrs. Clarke obeyed these instructions and lived to be ninety-two.)

Madame Récamier was now fifty-four and her life had narrowed to a single object—the diversion of Chateaubriand, upon whom ennui had seized with the frightful effect of an incurable disease. Mary was invited to meet him. Her freshness amused him, she was invited again and conquered him completely. He declared he " delighted in her ". " *La jeune Anglaise* is like no one else in the world. Boredom is impossible where she is."

Mary became Madame Récamier's close friend, visited her daily, was always present at her evenings; and when in 1838 the Clarkes moved to 120 rue du Bac the intimacy continued.

She entered another distinguished circle through her close friendship with Claude Fauriel, the mediaeval scholar to whom the preservation of old French and Provençal literature is largely due. In 1837 Mary and Fauriel had been on terms of closest intimacy for more than fifteen years. They met daily, they travelled together, he dined with her almost every night, was invariably present at her parties and behaved as master of the house; he had great respect for her mind, always read her his poems to criticise, and had left her his manuscripts in his will. Their intimacy was unconcealed and accepted; yet Mary's reputation was unblemished; she was the friend of bishops and deans, her *salon* was " serious ", and she refused to receive George Sand on account of her irregular life.

There was in fact no cause for scandal. They were friends, not lovers. But friendship was Fauriel's choice, not Mary's. He was devoted to her but he had never fallen in love with her. He could have married her, but he had never asked her to marry him. She was in love with him, and jealousy tormented her.

Fauriel was one of the most charming men in Paris, and his love affairs were celebrated. Madame de Staël's infatuation for him had been notorious. When Mary knew he was engaged on a new love affair she suffered agonies. Shutting herself up alone, she refused to see anyone and wept for days on end, soothing her feelings by lavishing caresses on numerous cats of whom she was extravagantly fond.

While Mary Clarke was in love with Fauriel, who had only devoted friendship to give her, Fauriel's great friend Julius Mohl was hopelessly in love with Mary, who felt only friendship for him. M. Mohl was as much at home in the rue du Bac as Fauriel and, like him, dined with Mary almost every night. The younger son of a well-known German aristocratic family, he had become a naturalised Frenchman because he loved Mary Clarke and wished to live near her in Paris. When Queen Victoria asked him why he had given up his native country for France, " Ma foi, madame, j'étais amoureux ", he told her. He was an Oriental scholar of very great distinction. " M. Mohl ", wrote Miss Nightingale, " was a Wurtemberger who learnt all the Oriental languages he could in order to write some sort of history of religion. He was consulted, tho' a staunch Protestant, by the Jesuit Missions Étrangères in Paris as an authority superior to their own." In addition to collecting material for a history of religion he was engaged on a translation of the Persian epic *Shah Nameh* by Firdausi, for which he received a yearly grant from the French Academy. His character was charming, and he was a celebrated conversationalist. Nassau Senior, the American scholar, selected his conversation to record in one of *Senior's Conversations*. Sainte-Beuve described him as " the best of Germany passed through the filter of England ". He spoke and wrote English perfectly, and passionately admired English political principles. Like Mary Clarke he loved cats and had imported a genuine Persian cat from Persia. He lived with Ampère in rooms where books stood in piles on the floor and on every table and chair. Both of them were indifferent to the ordinary comforts of life and never noticed when the rooms became thick with dust and the carpets wore into holes, or even when the house caught fire. Ampère, who kept his money in his stockings, dropped it all over the floor when he put them on, and once mislaid one of a pair which contained his month's income.

The Nightingales were not the kind of connection which appealed to Mary Clarke. She did not care for young ladies; in fact, she did not care for women at all. " I don't like young ladies ", she wrote to a friend who had asked permission to make an introduction to her, " I can't abide women. Why don't they talk about interesting things? Why don't they use their brains? My dear, they have no manners. I can't abide them in my drawing-room. What with their shyness and their inability to hold their tongues, they ain't fit for decent company. If your friend is a man, bring him without thinking twice about it, but if she is a woman—think well." She was, however, " absurdly fond " of children and regularly gave children's parties, and she acknowledged Fanny's letter of introduction by inviting the Nightingales to a " children's soirée ".

One afternoon near Christmas they drove up to 120 rue du Bac. No servants were visible, but a clamour came from above. They walked up into a front drawing-room crowded with dancing, singing children, no one took any notice of them, and they went through to the back drawing-room, where two impressive and eminent-looking gentlemen were boiling a large black kettle over a log fire. One was Claude Fauriel, the other Julius Mohl.

In the midst of the children, dancing, singing and clapping her hands, was a strange little figure no bigger than a child herself, whom Florence realised must be the celebrated Miss Mary Clarke. The children began to play blind man's buff, and without further ado Florence picked up her skirts and joined in. It was the happiest possible introduction. She was never so unself-consciously gay as with children—indeed, all the Nightingales were past-masters in the art of amusing the young.

Immediately after the children's soirée Mary Clarke invited the Nightingales to one of her celebrated Friday evenings. She had fallen in love with the whole family, most of all with Florence, but also with W. E. N.'s remote charm, Fanny's rich beauty and over-flowing kindness, and Parthe's elegance. They christened her " Clarkey ", and she turned their stay in Paris into a carnival. They met almost every day and, as

Florence wrote to Hilary Bonham Carter, " tore about " together. Clarkey went everywhere and knew everyone. She took the girls to private parties, to studios, to galleries and concerts, to the opera, to the theatre, to receptions and balls. She introduced them to Madame Récamier. They were asked several times to Abbaye-aux-Bois, met Chateaubriand, and were paid the very great compliment of being invited to hear Chateaubriand read his memoirs. And so when the famous readings from the *Mémoires d'outre-tombe* were given by Chateaubriand at the Abbaye-aux-Bois in January 1839, Florence Nightingale was in the audience.

She was wildly happy. She had a " passion " for Clarkey, she was beginning an important friendship with Julius Mohl, and for the first time in her life she was breathing the air of freedom.

Fanny smiled on her infatuation. She wanted Clarkey to be the family's intimate friend. Clarkey was to be the source from which she intended to collect notabilities to add lustre to her parties at Embley. Clarkey was unconventional, but Clarkey was accepted by the best society, and Fanny was satisfied. But the young Florence was receiving impressions of which Fanny never dreamed. One of the deepest was the impression made by Clarkey's friendship with Claude Fauriel. She observed that Clarkey and Fauriel met daily, that they were devoted and made no secret of their devotion, that Fauriel had the greatest possible respect for Clarkey's mental powers and treated her as an equal, above all, that this close intimacy was accepted without disapproval by everyone, even by so conventional a woman as her mother.

She acquired a belief in the possibility of a daily intimacy, a close friendship between a man and a woman on terms which did not include passion, and which did not provoke scandal. It was a belief she never lost and one which regulated her conduct throughout her life.

The Nightingales had now been abroad for eighteen months, and the alterations to Embley were due to be finished by June. Before they went down to the country Fanny wished to spend part of the season in London and have the girls presented.

In April 1839 the family left for London. Fanny was well satisfied. The tour had shown her that in Florence she possessed a daughter who promised to be exceptional. Florence's success in the intellectual world of Paris pleased her as much as her success at balls. It augured well for the kind of future she planned that so young a girl should be warmly liked by Clarkey, by Fauriel and by Julius Mohl. She began to concentrate on Florence. Her pride in her was immense, her hopes for her brilliant.

They were doomed. Florence's conscience was awake, and the brief halcyon period was over. It was two years since God had spoken to her. Why had He not spoken again? The answer was evident—she was not worthy. She had forgotten God in the pleasure of balls and operas, in the vanity of being admired. She loved pleasure too much, she loved society too much, she must school herself to turn her back on it. In March 1839, before she left Paris, she wrote in a private note that, to make herself worthy to be God's servant, the first temptation to be overcome was " the desire to shine in society ".

III WITH THE RETURN of the Nightingales to London
      the first great struggle of Miss Nightingale's life
      began. It was divided into two stages and lasted
fourteen years. First she groped within herself for five years
before she reached the certainty that her " call " was to nurse
the sick; next a bitter conflict with her family followed, and
nine more years passed before she was able to nurse.

In April 1839 Fanny and William Nightingale had no
inkling of Florence's secret life of agony, aspiration and despair.
They congratulated themselves on the possession of a charming
and gifted young daughter destined for a brilliant social success.
She was graceful, witty, vividly good-looking. Among the
Verney papers are two small oblong packets, carefully wrapped
in several thicknesses of black paper, which contain two tresses
of hair tied with silk and labelled in Fanny's writing " Flo 1839 "
and " Parthe 1839 ". The hair has been so well protected that
it might have been cut yesterday. Florence's hair is of unusual
beauty, bright chestnut in colour, thick, glossy and wavy. In
middle age her hair became dark, but at nineteen it was
golden-red. Parthe's hair has less life and colour; it is light
brown, fine, soft and straight.

The Nightingales reached London on April 6th. W. E. N.
went down to Embley and found the alterations would not be
finished by June; Fanny then decided to spend the whole
season in London. Her sister, Mrs. Nicholson, was bringing
out her two elder girls, and the families united to take a floor
of the Carlton Hotel. On May 24th Florence and Parthe were
presented at the Queen's birthday Drawing Room. Florence,
wearing a white dress bought in Paris, looked, wrote Fanny,
" very nice ", and " was not nearly as nervous as she expected ".

The girls were caught up in a whirl of gaiety. Wherever
the Nicholsons went they met hosts of friends, carpets were
rolled up for dancing, the air rang with screams of laughter,
servants ran about, impromptu meals appeared. W. E. N.
called it the " Waverley Saturnalia ". " The *piano* ", he
remarked, " is not their *forte*."

Once more her " call " vanished from Florence's mind,

once more she became absorbed in parties and dresses and partners and balls. Her letters were filled with society gossip, she went a great deal to the opera, her parents gave a series of dinners and evening parties, she attended a second Drawing Room. The summer was hot, the hotel noisy; she was exhausted, deliriously happy, perpetually excited.

She had been seized by a " passion ", the most serious of all her " passions ", for her cousin, Marianne Nicholson. " I never loved but one person with passion in my life and that was her ", she wrote in 1846. Marianne was dazzlingly beautiful—" that brilliant face is almost as the face of an angel ". She had exceptional musical gifts, an exquisite soprano voice, and possessed a confidence in her own charm which enabled her to dare anything. She would even take hold of W. E. N. and shake him. " I was internally screaming with laughter ", wrote Florence to Hilary Bonham Carter. " I should think no one ever shook my Papa's sacred person before."

But to love Marianne was dangerous. Her moods were unpredictable, she was angel and devil, pointlessly cruel, pointlessly kind, generous or mean, malicious or good-natured, truthful or a liar without reason or motive. Yet Florence could not resist her. " The truth is I was afraid of her ", she wrote in a private note.

Marianne's capacity to love was reserved for her family. She adored her brothers and sisters. All the Nicholsons adored each other and stood by each other through thick and thin, and of all her family the one Marianne loved best was her brother Henry.

By an unhappy chance Henry fell in love with Florence. She did not love him, but she encouraged him because he brought her closer to Marianne.

At the end of July Embley was still unfinished, and the Nightingales went north to Lea Hurst. They took Henry Nicholson with them. He was going up to Cambridge in the autumn and was to work at mathematics with Florence.

Henry and Florence passed August almost alone. Parthe was unwell after the exertions of the season, Fanny was absorbed in refurnishing Embley, W. E. N. spent his time travelling between Lea Hurst and Embley, where the builder was profuse in false promises. By the end of August Henry was desperately in love, while Florence had become "absorbed in mathematics". Mathematics, she told Clarkey in August, gave her a sense of "certainty". She did not mention Henry.

In September W. E. N. decided that, finished or not, Embley must be occupied. Parthe, still unwell, was sent to Harrogate with the Bonham Carters, and Fanny, W. E. N. and Florence came south. The move was a series of disasters. They arrived to find men still working in the house, and retreated to one of the lodges. Several days passed in discomfort. At last the move was fixed. That day a hurricane broke, the worst storm of a stormy autumn. The Nightingales waited all the morning, but not a soul appeared. W. E. N. went up to the house to "do housemaid", and late in the afternoon Fanny and Florence determined to follow. The drive was under water and they waded to the house. It was deserted, the servants had failed to arrive. W. E. N. lighted a fire in the servants' hall, and hungry and shivering they peered into the larder. It contained nothing but joints of raw meat. Darkness fell and still no one came. At last the sound of wheels was heard. Florence rushed out. It was a cart containing "a man in a cloak carrying a looking glass". W. E. N. took a candle from a carriage lamp and stuck it on a spike, and they sat by its glimmering light. W. E. N. was in excellent spirits —he found their situation diverting. When the servants at last appeared their explanations were unsatisfactory. The steward spoke "with tears in his eyes", but the truth was that the servants refused to start until they had had their tea, and there was a further difficulty because Mrs. Gale thought it beneath her dignity to be conveyed in a cart.

Embley was now a handsome house, "able to receive five able bodied females with their husbands and belongings", wrote Florence to Clarkey in October 1839. The house had been redecorated. Fanny's descriptions of the drawing-room mention fawn-coloured walls "pale and cool with gold mouldings", a blue ceiling "as skiey as possible", "purple silk cushions ornamented with gold fleur de lys" and a set of chairs in tapestry "with a blue and white ground but worked in a variety of colours with red predominating in the groups of flowers or figures". The sofas were covered in red silk damask. The carpet was "green of a yellowish tint" and considered "a

great prize ". Fanny had fallen in love with the " veloutés "
she had seen in Paris and had had a carpet specially woven at
Axminster in the same design ; this carpet is now in the Victoria
and Albert Museum. W. E. N. had the library enlarged and
put in new shelves of oak elaborately carved in a Gothic style
with each section divided by a caryatid. On top of the shelves
stood antique busts, and the windows were hung with heavy
crimson curtains intricately draped and looped.

Straightening the house and settling the servants filled the
next two months. Fanny had a large family house-warming
at Christmas to which all the Nicholsons came, all the Bonham
Carters and Aunt Mai and her husband, Uncle Sam Smith.
It was not until the New Year that Florence could draw
breath.

She was deeply, furiously discontented with life and with
herself. Her infatuation for Marianne was perpetual torture.
She had let Henry fall more in love with her than ever.
Towards making herself worthy, towards justifying her " call "
she had done nothing. Her life at home was hateful; impossible that God should have bestowed the gift of time on His
female creatures to be used as Fanny wished her to use it,
sitting nicely dressed in the morning-room doing worsted
work, having a little rest, going for a little drive, doing the
flowers, practising quadrilles. " Faddling twaddling and the
endless tweedling of nosegays in jugs ", Clarkey called it.

After the society of Clarkey, Julius Mohl and Fauriel,
Hampshire county society was inexpressibly boring. Idiotic
local agitations were the only interest. At the moment there
was an agitation about the orthodoxy of the new Vicar of
Wellow since, forsooth, he had been presented to his living by
W. E. N., who was a Unitarian. Oh for Paris, wrote Florence
to Clarkey in December 1839, oh to be driving from the Place
Vendôme to see dearest Clarkey in the rue du Bac. Her
letters became so bitter that Clarkey complained of her " nailed
tongue ".

Miserable, irritable, bored, she became unwell. She was
rescued by Aunt Mai, whose visit at Christmas had transformed their relationship. They were now devoted friends,
no longer fond aunt and adoring little niece but equals revelling
in closest intimacy. Aunt Mai was W. E. N.'s sister and

possessed many of his qualities—intellectual curiosity, humour, interest in abstract speculation. She, too, had a leaning towards the metaphysical and the transcendental, and her love for Florence had a mystical quality. In spite of their difference in age she worshipped Florence with the worship of a disciple for a master. Affection was poured out with the lavishness and extravagance for which Florence hungered, but the core of Aunt Mai's devotion was mystical faith. She placed Florence above ordinary humanity, above the claims even of her husband and her children, and became her protector, interpreter and consoler. Aunt Mai's tact, her energy, her flow of words were inexhaustible, and in innumerable letters, almost always undated, written on flimsy paper with a thin pen, criss-crossed on every page, she endeavoured in a flood of apologies, explanations, excuses, to make life easier for Florence. In January 1840 she persuaded Fanny that "Flo would be all the better for a little change" and, at the end of the month, Florence was allowed to pay a visit to Combe Hurst.

At once her spirits soared. London was buzzing with gossip of Queen Victoria's wedding, she went sightseeing, saw Prince Albert "in the clothes which no doubt he borrowed to be married in ", and wrote a lively account of the ceremony on February 10th. "There were but 3 Tories there. Ld Melbourne pressed the Queen to ask more, told her how obnoxious it was. Queen said 'It is MY marriage and I will only have those who can sympathise with me'. She asked D. of Wellington as a public character. Ld Liverpool and the Jenkinsons as her private friends and Ld Ashley because he married a Cowper—but not even the Duchess of Northumberland. . . . Mr. Harcourt told Lord Colchester that there was a great levee to receive the Prince and they were all standing with the Queen ready to receive him. When his carriage was announced she walked out of the room. Nobody could conceive what she was going to do and before anyone could stop her, she had run downstairs and was in his arms."

Florence went to several dinners and to the opera, received a flattering number of Valentines and spent a great deal of her time with Aunt Mai's children and took them to the dentist— " a struggle was expected but Puff with the most dignified calm had three teeth out, the last a double one, but when we came home and not till then we discovered that the whole of the fangs were left in, and the old traitor had never told ", she wrote to Fanny in March. On the surface she was happy enough, charming enough, gay enough, but beneath the surface was agony and despair. It was three years since she had been " called " and she still did not know to what. That was the frightful dilemma—what had she been called to do? The first necessity was to improve herself, to become worthy. God was waiting for her to become worthy before He could give her instructions. But how was she to make herself worthy?

She had written to Clarkey that mathematics gave her certainty: mathematics required hard work, and perhaps she would find life more satisfactory, be more satisfactory herself, if she studied mathematics. She confided in Aunt Mai and they began to work together, getting up before it was light to avoid disturbing the routine of the house. She became wildly happy. If only her parents would let her have lessons, if only they could be persuaded to let her study mathematics instead of doing worsted work and practising quadrilles.

In March 1840 Aunt Mai wrote Fanny a cautious letter. " Flo and I have a good deal of talk about the employment of time and so forth. I am much impressed with the idea that hard work is necessary to give zest to life in a character like hers, where there is great power of mind and a more than common inclination to apply. *So* I write to ask you if you in any way object to a mathematical master, if one can find a clean middle aged respectable person . . . of course shall not do anything without your permit. . . . I feel that if Flo were my own daughter I should be very restless to see her hard at work. Those industrious tendencies which she spends on music and needlework would, I think, make a strong interest for life, if devoted to mathematics."

Fanny did not approve, home duties were not to be neglected for mathematics. Aunt Mai hastened to assure her there was no neglect: " Flo and I have begun getting up at 6, lighting our fire and sitting very comfortably at our work, and I think if she had a subject which required *all* her powers and which she pursued regularly and vigorously for a couple of

37

hours she would be happier all day for it . . . she is disappointed at her want of success in music. . . . I allow her quadrille playing is bad."

Her daughter's destiny, Fanny answered, was, she sincerely hoped, to marry, and what use were mathematics to a married woman? " If she throws up her mathematics ", Aunt Mai replied, " in the more active and interesting pursuits of future life in which I hope I may live to see her powers engaged, whatever she may have done in that line will have benefited her character." In a burst of sincerity she added a postscript: " I don't think you have any idea of half that is in her."

Fanny would not give way. Letters flew backwards and forwards. Where were Florence's lessons to be given? If at her grandmother's in Bedford Square there would be a problem about Aunt Patty. Patty was getting peculiar. There were " outbreaks " and it would not be suitable for Florence to meet her. Fanny's brother, Mr. Octavius Smith, offered the use of his library. Fanny raised difficulties about the master. Would it not be more suitable to have a clergyman, was the master proposed a married man, was there not a class, who would be present during the lessons? Aunt Mai persevered, soothing, reassuring, producing a married man, a clergyman, one accustomed to teaching young ladies, a chaperone. W. E. N. then entered the correspondence with an entirely new consideration. " Why Mathematics? I cannot see that mathematics would do great service. History or philosophy, natural or moral, I should like best." In reply Aunt Mai reported a dialogue. " I told Flo this preference." " I don't think I shall succeed so well in anything that requires quickness as in what requires only work." " Then you prefer mathematics? " " Yes."

All Aunt Mai could obtain was a compromise. She enlisted the aid of the Octavius Smiths. Mrs. Octavius Smith had been ill and asked that Florence, whose gift for managing children was well known, should be allowed to come and stay with her and help with the children. Fanny agreed that she might go for a month, and during part of April and May 1840 she stayed with the Octavius Smiths and had a lesson in mathematics twice a week in their library. In the middle of May she went back to Embley and the mathematics lessons came to an end.

In the summer of 1840 Fanny had a series of house-parties at Embley. Clarkey came for a long visit, and Fauriel and Julius Mohl. Fanny's circle had lately been extended by a friendship with the Palmerstons. In 1839 Lord Palmerston married Lady Cowper, the widow of Earl Cowper and sister of Lord Melbourne, and settled at Broadlands, near Romsey, a few miles from Embley. The Palmerstons took a fancy to the Nightingales and a friendship sprang up. " The Palmerstons ask us to dine *en famille,* I mention this merely to show how friendly they are ", W. E. N. had written to Florence in April. During the summer the Palmerstons were constantly at Embley, bringing with them their son-in-law Lord Ashley, better known by his subsequent title of Lord Shaftesbury, the reformer and philanthropist, founder of the Ragged School Union.

And still Florence was not satisfied. The previous autumn she had complained that she had no one to talk to ; now she complained she had too many people to talk to. She had said she must have intelligent conversation and exchange of ideas, now she said she must have time for study.

She worked at mathematics in her bedroom, and rose in the small hours to read philosophy and study Greek. She was discontented with life, even more discontented with herself. She blamed herself for her bad temper at home, for her unworthiness before God. She suffered agonies on account of Marianne, her conscience smote her on behalf of Henry. Months slipped by and still no revelation came, still she did not know what God had called her to do.

Among her cousins her most intimate friend was Hilary Bonham Carter, eldest of the six daughters of Fanny's sister Joanna. Hilary, who was a year younger than Florence, had been devoted to her from childhood. She was unusually pretty and had a talent for painting ; a self-portrait shows a charming little pointed face framed in heavy bands of soft hair, a wide forehead, large eyes under delicate brows, a sensitive mouth and an expression of intelligence and sweetness. When in 1838 her father had died she had become the support of her mother, a nervous, unpractical woman overwhelmed by the

39

responsibility of bringing up a large family unaided. Florence was passionately attached to Hilary. " Only think dearest ", she wrote in 1838, " it is now really how long since I have seen you . . . six months, tho' it seems more like six years. The more I write, the more I want to see you." She made Hilary the confidante of her difficulties, pouring out her soul in enormous letters, telling almost all—but not all. The story of her " call " on February 7th, 1837, she confided to no one.

By 1841, after nearly two years at home, she had achieved nothing but desperate unhappiness. She loathed life at Embley, but what to substitute for it she had no idea. To solve her problem she must have time—time to grope in her own mind. At Embley she never had a moment to herself: every day was filled with trifling commissions, trifling requests, the performance of endless needless tasks which provoked the asking of endless needless questions. She had a feeling of oppression, she felt herself pursued by servants, guests, relations in a clutching, demanding horde. " There are hundreds of human beings always crying after ladies ", she wrote to Hilary Bonham Carter in 1841. " Ladies' work has always to be fitted in, where a man is, his business is the law." She wrote the phrase again in a private note : " Hundreds of human beings always crying after ladies ", and added, " I must have some leisure to find out a few things ".

She had no leisure. Christmas 1841 was spent at Waverley. Fanny described the festivities in a letter to W. E. N., who had refused to leave home, as " awesome ". Eighty people slept in the house. There was a huge masked ball which went on until five o'clock in the morning, succeeded the following night by an amateur performance of *The Merchant of Venice.* Henry played Shylock, rushed up to London where Macready was performing the part, interviewed him in his dressing-room and secured directions for the interpretation of the part. He had come down from Cambridge, was preparing to be called to the Bar, and was still desperately in love with Florence. In March the Nightingales went to London for the season and took rooms at the Burlington Hotel, Old Burlington Street.

Florence was very gay. Though she was only twenty-two she was becoming a figure in intellectual society. Her demure exterior concealed wit. She danced beautifully yet possessed a surprising degree of learning, had great vitality and was an excellent mimic. She had acquired a light touch and wrote of a dull party at Strathfieldsaye, at which the Queen and Prince Albert were present, that " the only amusement was seeing Albert taught to miss at billiards ", she described the first Lady Ashburton at a London dinner with a " a raspberry tart of diamonds on her head worth seeing " ; and told Parthe, who was not well and had returned to Embley, how " Papa and I went dowagering off in the coach to a formal dinner where Mr. Gerard Noel and I were very thick ".

She was " very much noticed ", Fanny wrote, by the new Prussian ambassador, the Chevalier Bunsen and his wife. The Bunsens united intellect, good breeding and wealth. The Chevalier (he was created Baron in 1857) was a Biblical scholar of European reputation who shared with his friend Lepsius the credit of being the world's leading Egypto-logist ; he had married an Englishwoman of good family, was extremely rich, and had a house in Carlton House Terrace besides a place in Sussex. The Bunsens were close friends of the Queen and Prince Albert, and were liberal Evangelicals. Florence, who went constantly to their house, was addressed by the Chevalier as " My favourite and admired Miss Nightin-gale " ; he lent her books and discussed archaeology and religion with her.

She had achieved a success, and could not help feeling satisfaction, yet she reproached herself bitterly. " All I do is done to win admiration ", she wrote in a private note. She observed that she found herself becoming resentful if she were not the centre of attention in a group. She cared too much for lights, pretty clothes, glitter, the allurements she called in her private notes " the pride of life ". Over and over again she told herself that before she could hope to be worthy enough for God to reveal the path of service the temptation to shine in society must be conquered.

In the summer of 1842 the temptation to shine was greatly increased. In May the Nightingales returned to Embley, and shortly afterwards, at a dinner-party given by the Palmerstons at Broadlands, Florence was introduced to Richard Monckton Milnes. In 1842 Richard Monckton Milnes was thirty-three. He was the only son of Mr. Richard Pemberton Milnes and heir to the estate of Fryston in Yorkshire. He had achieved a brilliant success in London society and had a promising political career.

He wrote talented poetry himself but had an even greater talent for discerning poetic genius. In 1848 he was responsible for the collection and publication of the first collected edition of the poems of Keats. Brought up in Italy, he preserved Italian picturesqueness in his appearance and manners. " Conceive the man," wrote Carlyle to Emerson in 1840, " a most bland, smiling, semi-quizzical, affectionate, high bred, Italianised little man, who has long olive blonde hair, a dimple, next to no chin and flings his arms round your neck when he addresses you in polite society." The breakfasts he gave in his rooms in Pall Mall were famous. He invited everyone in the public eye whether famous or notorious, whether known to him or not. Carlyle, when asked what he thought would be the first thing to happen if Christ came to earth again, said : " Monckton Milnes would ask him to breakfast."

He diffused amiability. " He always put you in a good humour with yourself ", said Thackeray ; and his wit was never malicious—life was his target, not humanity. Life, he was fond of saying, is a jest not witty but humorous. Of failure he said : " The worst part of failure in life is the envy of the successful. It is almost impossible to be just at once to them and to ourselves." Of persecution : " Is it to be wondered that persecution fascinates and obscures the minds of the best of men ? Fancy the united pleasures of the exercise of cruelty and the satisfaction of the love of truth." His kindness and generosity were based on love for his fellow men. " No one who knew Richard ever hesitated to ask him a favour ", wrote one of his friends. He was " a good man to go to in distress ", wrote another. " He treated all his fellow mortals as if they were his brothers and sisters ", said Florence.

His humanity expressed itself in philanthropic work. He loved children and worked for many years, against ceaseless opposition, to improve the treatment of young criminals. It was largely owing to his efforts that juvenile offenders ceased to be sent to jail with adult criminals and were sent to reformatories instead. Children instinctively trusted him. After his death Miss Nightingale wrote : " He had the same voice and

42

manner for a dirty brat as for a duchess . . . once at Redhill, the Reformatory, where we were with a party, and the chiefs were telling us the system in the middle of the courtyard, a mean, stunted, villainous looking boy crept across the yard (quite out of order) and stole his dirty paw into Mr. Milnes' hand. He stayed quite quiet and contented if he could touch his benefactor."

But he had another side to his character. The humane lover of children, the connoisseur of literature was also the man who introduced Swinburne to the works of the Marquis de Sade.

During the summer Richard Monckton Milnes came several times to Embley. He was falling in love with Florence, and he made himself the friend of Fanny, Parthe and W. E. N. By the end of July, when the Nightingales went north to Lea Hurst, he was treated as one of the family.

Fanny had connections in northern society; earlier in the year she had been introduced to the Duke of Devonshire and asked to dine. Now she, W. E. N. and the two girls were invited to stay at Chatsworth to meet H.R.H. the Duke of Sussex. All the society of the north assembled, and in honour of the royal guest the huge house was crammed with " Howards, Cavendishes, Percys, Greys, all in gala dress with stars, garters, diamonds and velvets ", wrote Fanny to Clarkey in August 1842. The entertainment was planned on an enormous scale. Mr. Joseph Paxton, later designer of the Crystal Palace, was head gardener at Chatsworth, and he had erected a vast glasshouse in the Park. " An omnibus ", wrote Fanny, " plied at the gates of Chatsworth every evening to take those who could not walk so far to the monster conservatory, which covers an acre of ground, and where groves of palms and bananas are making all haste to grow to their natural size." One evening the huge glasshouse was brilliantly lit for a " promenade ". Another evening there was a magnificent ball to open a new banqueting hall.

Florence was indifferent to the splendours of Chatsworth; the devotion of Richard Monckton Milnes left her unmoved. Some time in the summer of 1842 she had taken the first step towards the fulfilment of her destiny. She had become conscious of the world of misery, suffering and despair which lay outside her little world of ease and comfort.

Eighteen forty-two was a terrible year for the people of England. The country was in the grip of what has passed into history as "the hungry forties". In villages, as in towns, there were starvation, sweated labour, ignorance and dirt. Diseased scarecrows swarmed not only in the airless, undrained courts of London, but in the "black filth" of rural cottages; workhouses, hospitals and prisons were overflowing. When Florence was at Lea Hurst she visited the cottages in the Holloway, the village adjoining Lea Hurst. Fanny was generous with soup and half-crowns, and it was considered improving for the girls to see that the world contained young women less fortunate than themselves. In the summer of 1842 Florence wrote in a private note: "My mind is absorbed with the idea of the sufferings of man, it besets me behind and before, a very one-sided view, but I can hardly see anything else and all that poets sing of the glories of this world seems to me untrue. All the people I see are eaten up with care or poverty or disease."

She had progressed. She knew now that her destiny lay among the miserable of the world, but what form that destiny was to take she still had no idea.

In the autumn of 1842 she called on the Bunsens, and Baroness Bunsen, in her Memoir of her husband, records that she asked him a question couched more or less in these words. "What can an individual do towards lifting the load of suffering from the helpless and miserable?" The Chevalier mentioned the work of Pastor Fliedner and his wife at Kaiserswerth, on the Rhine, where Protestant Deaconesses were trained in the hospital of the Institution to nurse the sick poor. Florence's attention was not arrested, she had not yet begun to think of nursing.

Meanwhile her mother steadily progressed to social success, and at Embley party followed party. "Pray send him a sly line that he will find *notabilities* here on the 24th", wrote W. E. N. to Clarkey in October 1843, arranging a visit from Ranke the historian, "—to wit the Speaker [Shaw Lefèvre], the Foreign Secretary [Palmerston], the Catholic Weld [future owner of Lulworth and nephew of the Cardinal of that Ilk] and mayhap a Queen's Equerry or two, a Baron of the Exchequer [Rolfe] an Inspector, or rather Engineering Architect,

44

of the new Prisons, and a couple of Baronets. He should think well on this. Yours quizzically but faithfully, W. E. N." Florence scribbled a postscript: " Papa is quizzing the baronets who are not wise ones. Provided *you* come I care for nobody, no not I, and shall be quite satisfied. As M. de Something said to the Staël ' Nous aurons à nous deux de l'esprit pour quarante ; vous pour quatre et moi pour zéro '."

She had formed her own circle. She saw Richard Monckton Milnes constantly, and had become interested in his philanthropic work. She had a new friend, Miss Louisa Stewart Mackenzie, later the second wife of Lord Ashburton. The Palmerstons were devoted to her and she was very friendly with Lord Ashley.

But when, at the end of July 1843, the Nightingales once more went north to Lea Hurst, her whole being was concentrated on the poor and sick in the cottages. There, with the village of Holloway near the house, it was easier to be among the poor than at Embley, where East Wellow village lay a considerable distance away, or in London, where the Nightingales lived in a hotel.

The Holloway was not a purely agricultural village, for it contained a large number of weavers, and she met the evils of nineteenth-century industrialism—drunkenness, overcrowding, brutality. The horrors she saw preyed on her mind. She began to spend the greater part of her day in the cottages, began to badger her mother in and out of season for medicines, food, bedding, clothes, to beg her to undertake schemes of rebuilding and education. Fanny, who was generous in distributing charity, felt Florence was unreasonable. " Perhaps if we got a Sœur de Charité Flo would let us rest in some peace ", she wrote to W. E. N. during the summer of 1843.

When the time came to go to Embley, Florence wanted to stay behind at Lea Hurst. She yearned after the sick, the miserable and the bereaved. How could she hope to accomplish anything when she was forced to be continually on the move ? Seven times, eight times a year, she wrote in a private note, they changed their place of abode. Lea Hurst, Embley, London, Embley again, then back to London and back to Embley. Everything was to be snatched at, everything was to be abandoned after a few weeks. Fanny would not hear of her remaining, and she had to come south. "It breaks my heart to leave Lea Hurst", she wrote to Aunt Mai in September 1843.

When her mother had succeeded in getting Florence away fresh difficulties arose. In the previous year one of her friends, Hope Richardson, had married Henry Reeve, the political writer who later edited the Greville Memoirs. In October Hope died in childbirth, leaving a daughter. Florence demanded permission to cancel her engagements, give up London for the autumn season and go to live with Hope's sister and look after the baby. When Fanny refused she fretted herself into an illness. Forced to give way, Fanny compromised by allowing her to go and look after the baby for a few weeks—at the height of the season when she should have been in London going to parties. Fanny was bitterly disappointed. Florence was perverse, and her mother found it difficult not to blame her. Fanny, generous, good-humoured and affectionate, was also obstinate and unreasonable; her daughter had aroused her obstinacy, and misery resulted on both sides.

Florence's misery was a thousand times increased by a terrifying discovery. She records in a private note that in the autumn of 1843 she suddenly realised the extent to which the habit she called "dreaming" had enslaved her. On the tour abroad there had been "too much time for dreaming", and during the four years she had spent at home consoling visions had come to occupy more and more of her time. She fell into "trance-like" states in the midst of ordinary life, while, for instance, she was making conversation with the Ashburtons at Sir William Heathcote's dinner. She could not control herself, and she gave way with the shameful ecstasy of the drug-taker.

The whole world went wrong for her in the winter of 1843. Henry Nicholson was pressing her to become engaged to him, Marianne was beginning to be angry with her for not accepting him. When Christmas came and she found herself at Waverley with Henry and Marianne the strain became too great, and she broke down. As she lay in bed listening to the sounds of revelry floating up from downstairs, heartbroken by Marianne's unkindness, ashamed of her secret self, frustrated in her destiny, she despaired. Was there nothing for her but dreaming?

46

Had she better close her eyes and find what satisfaction she could in a false paradise of consoling visions? And then, she wrote in a private note, " an acquaintance with a woman to whom all unseen things seemed real and eternal things near, awakened me."

Miss Hannah Nicholson, sister of Mr. Nicholson of Waverley, called Aunt Hannah by the Nightingales, was a deeply religious woman with the gentleness, purity and limited vision of a nun. She did not understand Florence; there were depths, violences, capacities in her she was unable to grasp, but she knew Florence was ill, not on good terms with her family, and unhappy. She believed she could provide the solution. Union with God would bring reconciliation with earthly life. Aunt Hannah was a mystic sharing the sense of the eternal in temporal life which Florence described in a letter to Clarkey in August 1846. " I always believe . . . in the old Italian pictures which have a first story, where the Unseen live *au premier*, with a two pair back where the *Père Éternel's* shadow is half seen peeping out, and a ground floor where poor mortals live, but still have a connexion with the establishment upstairs. . . . I always believe in a multitude of spirits inhabiting the same house with ourselves; we are only the entresol. . . . We are like the blind men by the wayside and ought to sit and cry, Lord that we may receive our sight! And, when we *do* receive it, we shall perhaps find that we require no transporting into another world . . . what we require is sight not change of place I believe."

A close intimacy sprang up. Days were spent discussing the life of the soul and the way of the soul to God, there were long confidences, endless explanations, retrospections. Florence had an enormous amount of unexpended affection which longed for an outlet. In another private note, written at this time, she speaks of " those I love—and no-one knows *how* I love ". She adored Aunt Hannah, became her disciple, and found relief in self-abasement, in expressing her consciousness of sin. " You do not know what it is when one has sinned with such aggravation as I have . . . no one has so grieved the Holy Spirit ", she wrote in March 1844. " No one has had such advantages and I have sinned with all these."

There was, however, an essential difference between them

which Miss Nicholson did not appreciate. Though Florence sought union with God, she did not seek that state as an end in itself. Union with God was a necessary qualification for the performance of God's work, a preparation for action, not submission. Aunt Hannah believed that once Florence's soul was one with God she would be reconciled to the state of life to which it had pleased Him to call her.

In January 1844 Florence went back to Embley and began to write Aunt Hannah letters of enormous length. " When I write the floodgates of my egotism are opened by your sympathy." She was lonely, and she clung to Miss Nicholson. " Your whole life seems to be love, and you always find words which without the pretensions of enlightening yet are like a clearing up to me." She called her letters " my outpourings ". But she did not write either of her " call " or of her dreams, and at the very moment when she seemed to be most thoroughly under Aunt Hannah's influence she took a secret decision of the greatest importance entirely opposed to everything Miss Nicholson hoped.

Some time in the spring of 1844 the knowledge came to her that her vocation lay in hospitals among the sick. At last, seven years after her " call ", her destiny was clear. " Since I was twenty-four ", she wrote in a private note thirteen years later, ". . . there never was any vagueness in my plans or ideas as to what God's work was for me."

In June Dr. Gridley Howe, the American philanthropist, and his wife Julia Ward Howe, later to become celebrated as the author of the " Battle Hymn of the American Republic ", came to stay at Embley. He had founded an institute for the blind in Boston which was the first of its kind and had formulated a scheme to make medicine and nursing available, without payment, to any American citizen who was aged or ill. Dr. Howe's daughter describes in a book of reminiscences how after dinner on the night of his arrival Florence came up to him in the drawing-room. Would he meet her privately in the library for a few moments before breakfast? Dr. Howe consented. When husband and wife were alone Mrs. Ward Howe reminded him that they had heard the younger Miss Nightingale described as an exceptional girl likely to make an exceptional career for herself, though her mother would prefer

her to lead a more conventional life. In the library next
morning Florence went straight to the point: " Dr. Howe, do
you think it would be unsuitable and unbecoming for a young
Englishwoman to devote herself to works of charity in hospitals
and elsewhere as Catholic sisters do? Do you think it would
be a dreadful thing?" He gave a sincere answer: " My dear
Miss Florence, it would be unusual, and in England whatever
is unusual is thought to be unsuitable; but I say to you ' go
forward ', if you have a vocation for that way of life, act up to
your inspiration and you will find there is never anything unbecoming or unladylike in doing your duty for the good of
others. Choose, go on with it, wherever it may lead you and
God be with you."

She had reached the turning-point of her life, the most
important moment she had yet lived—but she confided in no
one. The word hospital had not yet been uttered to her
family; she was well advised to hesitate before introducing it;
it was a dread word. She must think out some method by
which her parents might be brought to consent to their daughter
entering a hospital. Throughout the summer she meditated
in secret. " I dug after my little plan in silence ", she wrote.

It was an unsatisfactory summer. Marianne and Henry
Nicholson came to stay; Marianne was cold and the visit was
not a success. Claude Fauriel died in July and Clarkey did
not feel equal to paying her usual visit to Embley, to Florence's
deep disappointment. The illness of the previous winter,
misery over Marianne, the weight of the shameful secret of her
" dreams ", the perpetual frustration of her life at home,
brought her low, and she wrote Clarkey an unhappy, disconnected, incoherent letter. " Oh do not say that ' you will not
cloud young people's spirits '. Do you think young people
are so afraid of sorrow, or that if they have lively spirits, which
I often doubt, they think these are worth anything, except
in so far as they can be put at the service of sorrow? . . .
When one thinks there are hundreds and thousands of people
suffering . . . when one sees in every cottage some trouble
which defies sympathy—and there is all the world putting
on its shoes and stockings every morning all the same—and
the wandering earth going its inexorable treadmill through
those cold hearted stars, in the eternal silence, as if nothing

were the matter;—death seems less dreary than life at that rate."

That summer when she went north to Lea Hurst there was scarlet fever in the cottages, and she was forbidden to go near them. In October she coached William Nicholson, Henry's younger brother, in mathematics for an examination at Sandhurst, which led to a family unpleasantness. Parthe indiscreetly boasted that Flo was coaching William, and the indiscretion was repeated to Mr. Nicholson; he was furious and told Florence that William would be laughed out of Sandhurst if it got about that he had been coached by a girl. In the manner of her family circle which Florence found unbearably provoking, the incident produced a flood of letters; followed by consultations, interviews, explanations, apologies, tears.

All through the autumn she was ailing and when, at Christmas, Fanny and Parthe went to Waverley she was too ill to go. She stayed in bed at Embley pouring out letters, notes, analyses, plans; striving to find a way to escape from home to a hospital; striving to find a solution to her relations with Marianne; striving to achieve the state of union with God in which Aunt Hannah assured her all difficulties would vanish. She heaped self-reproaches on her own head. Why could she not make herself " worthy " ? All her troubles came from her sinfulness and unworthiness. It was not God's fault that her life was so difficult—it was her own fault. If she were one with God then difficulties would disappear, Fanny would allow her to look after the cottagers, she would be able to find a way to work in hospitals, Marianne would be kind and Parthe would no longer criticise her.

On New Year's Eve 1844 she was unable to leave her room and sat writing late at night with " a little black tea pot on the hob ". Outside it was freezing hard with a brilliant moon. She watched three hares playing on the whitened grass of the lawn; in the stillness the world seemed to be dead except for those three hares. At Waverley at this moment there was a ball. She sighed after the ball and the dress she had been going to wear, a pink dress with black lace flounces, ruefully aware that the " pride of life " was by no means dead. " I am convinced of it when I think of my black lace flounces ", she wrote to Aunt Hannah.

In a fortnight or so she was convalescent, and Hilary Bonham Carter came to stay. She was another victim of family life. In the previous year the Bonham Carters had gone to Switzerland in the Nightingales' enormous travelling carriage. On the way out the younger children had had measles one after the other at Versailles; the party had been delayed for six weeks; and Hilary had met Clarkey. With Clarkey she had attended an atelier, and was pronounced to have genuine talent. Clarkey had rushed down to Versailles to persuade Mrs. Bonham Carter to let Hilary come back to Paris at the earliest possible moment to work seriously. Mrs. Bonham Carter had been most grateful to dear Miss Clarke. But Hilary had not returned—she could not be " spared ". Now she was spending her life housekeeping, teaching her younger sisters, doing the flowers and, as a concession, attending a " ladies' atelier " in London where lessons were taken " when social engagements permitted ".

The girls were alone for two days, the weather was fine and still, and they made long expeditions into the New Forest, walking from breakfast until sunset, and talking all day. Florence poured out her heart on the subject of Marianne, but she spoke neither of her determination to work in hospitals nor of the shameful secret of her " dreams "—that ever-growing terror. During the forced inaction of her illness and the idleness of her convalescence she had found herself more enslaved than ever before, and she was beginning to fear for her mental balance.

That February Aunt Mai's son Shore, " my boy Shore ", the heir to Embley, now aged fourteen, came to convalesce at Embley after measles. She looked after Shore entirely and had a month of freedom from shameful visions. " While he is with me all that is mine is his ", she wrote to Aunt Hannah in February 1845, " my head and hands and time." With Shore she took little walks on the gravel paths, hunted for snow-drops, read aloud and had " a great deal of conversation about dogs ". At night, when she had put him to bed and given him his medicine, they had serious talks. She " warned him against lying long in bed, and the temptations of the world, liking to be praised and admired and a general favourite more than anything else and we were both very much affected ".

In March, Shore went home and the Nightingales started once more on their round, up to London, back to Embley for parties in June, up to the North for July and August, back to Embley again for the shooting, up to London in November, back again to Embley at Christmas-time. And as week followed week Florence became more wretchedly unhappy; in vain had she dug after a plan which could conceivably result in her going to work in hospitals. Nearly a year had passed since her interview with Dr. Howe, and she was no farther forward; eight years had passed since her " call ", and not merely had she accomplished nothing, she had slipped backwards—she had lost the sense of walking with God. In private notes, in enormous letters to Aunt Hannah, she reproached herself with frantic bitterness. Again the strain was too great. Though she went with her family to London in February, as soon as she arrived she was ill. On March 1st, 1845, she was in bed in the Burlington Hotel, suffering from bronchitis, unable to go anywhere and writing to Clarkey in deep depression. Outside was thick yellow fog, candles were lighted though it was only two in the afternoon, but in spite of them and a large fire the fog hung in the room. Clarkey had suggested that she should express herself through writing, but she had no desire to write. She wanted to act, to work, to perform deeds. " You ask me why I do not write something. . . . I had so much rather live than write—writing is only a substitute for living. . . . I think one's feelings waste themselves in words, they ought all to be distilled into actions and into actions which bring results. . . . Do you think anyone ever did anything, who did not go to it with a directness of purpose which prevented him from frittering away his impressions in words? " She had become indifferent to pleasure, she was not disappointed to be ill. Her only regret was for a new dress, " a beautiful new violet ", which she was to have worn when she went " to do blue at a lecture given by Faraday to expound his new discoveries about electricity ".

Before she left London in the spring of this year she received a shattering blow : Henry Nicholson proposed and insisted on a definite answer. She refused him. Henry was heartbroken and the Nicholsons were furious. Florence had, they said with justice, encouraged Henry—and Marianne ended her friendship with Florence. Fanny and W. E. N. supported their daughter: they disapproved of the marriage of first cousins, and Fanny had always been slightly contemptuous of the gaieties of Waverley. A family coldness resulted, and the Nightingales and the Nicholsons ceased to be intimate.

To Florence the loss of Marianne was a catastrophe; through the summer she suffered tortures. " I have walked up and down all these long summer evenings in the garden ", she wrote to Hilary in July, " and could find no words but ' My God, my God, why hast thou forsaken me '. . . . *Je ne comprends rien à la vie.* I have no idea why we suffer so from such insufficient causes . . . only this that there are strange punishments here for those who have made life consist of one idea and that one not God." " She has broken my faith in immortality ", she wrote. " Oh if I could for one moment show the consequences of death in one's own heart (which one never believes except from one's own experience) to those whose hearts are still young. If anyone would know, what are the miseries of indulging the diseased cravings of the heart, or how weary, flat, stale and unprofitable seem all the uses of the world after it. . . . Last night I said to myself that the earth wandered through these suns, themselves changing and burning out, and all would die and pass away, but that on this wandering earth my love to her could never change, no unkindness could affect it and that it was, without any effort of mine, a love of which I could say ' for ever .'" She did not blame Marianne, she wrote no recriminations, she blamed only herself. It was her weakness, her wrongdoing in indulging an affection she knew to be unworthy which had provoked the catastrophe. Because she herself behaved imperfectly she provoked imperfect behaviour in others and drew suffering on her head. " I was not a worthy friend for her. I was not true either to her or to myself in our friendship. I was afraid of her: that is the truth. . . . M. Mohl said of M. Fauriel ' Il n'aime que les gens qui lui plaisent ' as the highest praise he could give him—alack how much more one loves the people one tries to please than those who please one."

Embley was especially full of visitors during the summer. At Whitsuntide Fanny had had a large party, " the picked and chosen of society assembled ", she wrote triumphantly to

Clarkey. The Palmerstons had given a ball, in July Fanny gave a large garden-party, there were dinners, morning visits. Florence, heartbroken and miserable, moved in a dream. Richard Monckton Milnes, who was helping her to find a publisher in London for Fauriel's poems, stayed both at Embley and at Broadlands with the Palmerstons during the summer, but she was hardly conscious of him. Nothing was real to her but her suffering over Marianne.

She was approaching a mental collapse when two serious illnesses in the family saved her.

In August she went with her father to visit her grandmother, Mrs. Shore, found her seriously ill, and was allowed to stay and nurse her. The house was solitary, empty except for the servants; to avoid giving trouble W. E. N. went to Lea Hurst, and she was blessedly alone. Hardly was Mrs. Shore convalescent when Mrs. Gale, the girls' old nurse, was taken ill at Lea Hurst. Fanny behaved with the utmost kindness. Florence was allowed to nurse Gale, and when she seemed too ill to be moved to Embley at the end of the summer Fanny prepared to give up her winter gaieties and stay at Lea Hurst in order that the old nurse might not be separated from " her children ". Gale insisted, however, on being taken to Embley, and there, a week or so later, she died, sitting upright in her chair with Florence beside her holding her hand.

For a short time Florence and her mother drew closer; her heart was melted by Fanny's kindness, and one of the few intimate letters she ever wrote to her mother described Gale's death: " Did I tell you one night she was very suffering and I was doubting whether I should speak to her, something good about the weary and heavy laden, when she said quite distinctly ' Oh I was so well, quite well till now, but I've been sadly off my teas and breakfasts of late '. Oh my dear Mum, life is nothing so much as profoundly ridiculous after all. Is that what the eternal spirit is talking about, when it is communing in its dream with the unspeakable presence, and perhaps with the other invisible spirits on the eve of becoming like them? " The old nurse's last words, Florence wrote to Hilary, were to say sharply, " Hannah, get to your work ". The details of her funeral had been discussed fully by Gale during her illness. She was to be carried across the common,

" *not* over the stiles " ; everyone on the estate came in a clean smock, and Mr. Hogg, the steward, said he was sure Mrs. Gale would have enjoyed it very much.

These two episodes brought a certain amount of emancipation. Florence had proved herself entirely capable in nursing her grandmother and Gale, and it was difficult to forbid her to continue to nurse. In the autumn there was an unusual amount of sickness in the village of Wellow, and she took an active part. She mentions being present at two deathbeds and a difficult birth.

And now she moved forward another step—she realised the necessity of training in nursing. The discovery came as a shock. Neither she herself nor anyone else she had ever met had been taught how to nurse. It was universally assumed that the only qualification needed for taking care of the sick was to be a woman. Ignorance was complete and its consequences disastrous. " I saw a poor woman die before my eyes this summer because there was nothing but fools to sit up with her, who poisoned her as much as if they had given her arsenic ", she wrote to Hilary Bonham Carter in December 1845.

In 1844, when she first knew with certainty that her vocation lay among the sick in hospitals, she had not had the actual practice of nursing in her mind. She had spoken to Dr. Howe of " devoting herself to works of charity in hospitals ". She too had thought that the qualities needed to relieve the misery of the sick were tenderness, sympathy, goodness and patience. Now her short experience had already shown her that only knowledge and expert skill brought relief; and her destiny, which was to lighten the load of suffering, could be fulfilled only if she were armed with knowledge. She must learn how to nurse. How could she learn? There was perhaps one avenue by which she might succeed.

The idea was bold, but since she had achieved a little independence she had been becoming bolder. Her plan was to persuade her parents to allow her to go for three months to Salisbury Infirmary to learn nursing : Salisbury was only a few miles from Embley, the Infirmary was a well-known hospital, and the head physician, Dr. Fowler, was an old friend. He held advanced views, and she thought he might support her

Through the autumn she persuaded herself of the advantages of the scheme—she would be near home, she could live with the Fowlers, she would be in the Infirmary only three months.

In December 1845 the Fowlers came to stay at Embley, and Florence proposed her plan. A storm burst. " Mama was terrified ", she wrote to Hilary. The reason was " not the physically revolting parts of a hospital but things about the surgeons and nurses which you may guess ". Parthe had hysterics. Florence persisted, and her mother's terror passed into furious anger. Writing twenty years later, Miss Nightingale described a series of scenes. Fanny accused her of having " an attachment of which she was ashamed ", a secret love affair with some " low vulgar surgeon ". " My mother was so afraid I should hear indecencies. I heard far more indecencies from the daughters of her evangelical friends to whom I had to play hostess in the nursery." In floods of tears Fanny wept that Florence wanted to " disgrace herself ".

The Fowlers, embarrassed, " threw cold water ". W. E. N., coldly disgusted, went away to London. Was it for this he had educated a charming daughter? Was this to be the end of the Latin and the Greek, the poetry and the philosophy, the Italian tour and the Paris frocks? Hilary described meeting him at a dinner-party a few days later. It had been hoped he would give them inside political news—there was a Cabinet crisis and he was known to have seen Palmerston. But he was morose and would talk of nothing but spoilt and ungrateful daughters and forecast the very worst future for a race at the mercy of the modern girl. Florence was left defeated, helpless, hopelessly depressed. " No advantage that I can see comes of my living on, excepting that one becomes less and less of a young lady every year ", she wrote to Hilary Bonham Carter. " You will laugh, dear, at the whole plan I daresay; but no one but the mother of it knows how precious an infant idea becomes; nor how the soul dies, between the destruction of one and the taking up of another. I shall never do anything and am worse than dust and nothing. . . . Oh for some strong thing to sweep this loathsome life into the past."

IV IT WAS NOT SURPRISING that the Nightingales were horror-struck. In 1845 hospitals were places of wretchedness, degradation and squalor. "Hospital smell", the result of dirt and lack of sanitation, was accepted as unavoidable, and was commonly so overpowering that persons entering the wards for the first time were seized with nausea. Wards were usually large, bare and gloomy. Beds were crammed in, fifty or sixty, less than two feet apart. Even decency was impossible. Fifteen years later, when some improvement had been made, Miss Nightingale wrote in *Notes on Hospitals* :

> The floors were made of ordinary wood which, owing to lack of cleaning and lack of sanitary conveniences for the patients' use, had become " saturated with organic matter, which when washed give off the smell of something quite other than soap and water". Walls and ceilings were "of common plaster" also "saturated with impurity". Heating was supplied by a single fire at the end of each ward, and in winter windows were kept closed for warmth, sometimes for months at a time. In some hospitals half the windows were boarded up in winter. After a time the smell became "sickening", walls streamed with moisture, and "a minute vegetation appeared". The remedy for this was "frequent lime washing with scraping", but the workmen engaged on the task "frequently became seriously ill".

The patients came from the slum tenements called "rookeries", from hovels, from cellars where cholera lurked. Gin and brandy were smuggled into the wards and fearful scenes took place, ending by half-dying creatures attacking each other in frenzy or writhing in fits of the "screaming horrors". In certain hospitals it was not unknown for the police to be called in to restore order.

The sick came into hospital filthy and remained filthy. In 1854 Miss Nightingale wrote: "The nurses did not as a general rule wash patients, they could *never* wash their feet—and it was with difficulty and only in great haste that they could have a drop of water, just to *dab* their hands and face. The beds on which the patients lay were dirty. It was common practice

57

to put a new patient into the same sheets used by the last occupant of the bed, and mattresses were generally of flock sodden and seldom if ever cleaned." In 1860 Colonel Clark Kennedy noted with surprise that at the French Military Convalescent Hospital at Vincennes " no article, however short a time in use, is ever reissued without being thoroughly cleansed".

Yet physically disgusting conditions were not the real obstacle to her scheme; the insuperable objection was the notorious immorality of hospital nurses. In 1845 it was practically unknown for a respectable woman to become a hospital nurse. The conditions under which a hospital nurse lived were such that no respectable woman could endure them. " It was *preferred*", wrote Miss Nightingale, " that the nurses should be women who had lost their characters, i.e. should have had one child." It was common for nurses to sleep in the wards they nursed, and not unknown for nurses of male wards to sleep in the wards with the men. In a letter written on May 29th, 1854, she described the sleeping accommodation provided for nurses in one of London's most famous hospitals. " The nurses . . . slept in wooden cages on the landing places outside the doors of the wards, where it was impossible for any woman of character to sleep, where it was impossible for the Night Nurse taking her rest in the day to sleep at all owing to the noise, where there was not light or air." The nurse had no other home than the ward; there she lived, slept and frequently cooked her meals. Discipline and supervision were almost non-existent. A very large number of patients were under the charge of one nurse—in one case a single night nurse had charge of four wards. The level of decency among the patients was almost unbelievably low.

Drink was the curse of the hospital nurse, as of the patients. " The nurses are all drunkards, sisters and all," said the physician of a large London Hospital in 1851, " and there are but two nurses whom the surgeons can trust to give the patients their medicine." In 1854 the head nurse of a London hospital told Miss Nightingale that " in the course of her large experience she had never known a nurse who was not drunken, and there was immoral conduct practised in the very wards, of which she gave me some awful examples ".

Miss Nightingale herself nursed a nurse who alternated

nursing with prostitution.   Mrs. Gaskell, writing to Catherine
Winkworth on October 20th, 1854, repeated the story.   " F. N.
undressed the woman, who was half tipsy and kept saying, ' You
would not think it Ma'am but a week ago I was in silk and
satins dancing at Woolwich.   Yes Ma'am for all I am so dirty
I am draped in silk and satins sometimes.   Real French silk and
satins.'   This woman was a nurse earning her five guineas a
week nursing ladies."

   One of the extraordinary features of Miss Nightingale's
life is the passage of time.   She starts with a " call " in 1837.
But what has she been called to do ?   What is her vocation to
be ?   Eight years pass before, in 1845, she finds out.   Even then
she is only half-way.   Eight more years pass before she gains
freedom in 1853 to pursue her vocation.   Sixteen years in all,
sixteen years during which the eager susceptible girl was slowly
hammered into the steely powerful woman of genius.   The
last eight years, the years after her failure in 1845, were
years in which suffering piled on suffering, frustration followed
frustration, until she was brought to the verge of madness.
   Yet she endured year after year.   She had the capacity to
assert herself, but she did not.   It was evident that she had
within her enormous powers.   Dr. Howe, after seeing her only
once, was so deeply impressed that when a daughter was born
to him he insisted that she be christened Florence.   Yet she
allowed herself to be frustrated.   The bonds which bound her
were only of straw, but she did not break them.   Her temperament held her a prisoner.   She could act only when she felt
moral justification, and she felt no moral justification.   Her
sense of guilt trapped her.   She was convinced that the
difficulties which confronted her were God's punishment for
her sinfulness ;   she was unworthy, and by being unworthy she
had brought her sufferings on her own head.   If she were
worthy her light would so shine forth that her parents could
not fail to perceive it, and would hasten to release her to do
God's work ;   if they were blind she was to be blamed because
her light shone too feebly to be seen.   " Bless me, too, as poor
Esau said ", she wrote to Aunt Hannah on Christmas Eve
1845.   " I have *so* felt with him and cried with an exceeding

bitter cry ' Bless me, even me also, Oh my father ', but he never has yet and I have not deserved that He should."

She was in disgrace, forbidden by Fanny to mention her shameful desires, her day filled with home duties performed under Fanny's eye. W. E. N. spoke contemptuously of " this folly of nursing ". In his opinion her head had been turned and she must " forever be trying to be different from other people ".

At the end of 1845 she " went down into the depths. My misery and vacuity were indescribable." Humiliated, snubbed, lonely, she found relief in writing private notes. On page after page, in tens of thousands of words, she poured out her wretchedness, her fear and her frustration. " This morning I felt as if my soul would pass away in tears, in utter loneliness in a bitter passion of tears and agony of solitude." " I cannot live—forgive me, oh Lord, and let me die, this day let me die." " The day of personal hopes and fears is over for me, now I dread and desire no more." " The sorrows of Hell compass me about, pray God He will not leave my soul in Hell." " The plough goes over the soul."

She spent her nights sleepless, wrestling with her soul, seeking with tears and prayers to make herself worthy to receive the kindness of God ; she spent her days performing the duties of the daughter at home.

" My life was not painful, but tiresome," she wrote in a reminiscence thirty years later. W. E. N. liked his two daughters to sit with him in the library after breakfast while he went through *The Times*, reading aloud anything that struck him as good. " To hear little disjointed bits read out to us out of book or newspaper ! Now for Parthe the morning's reading did not matter ; she went on with her drawing ; but for me, who had no such cover, the thing was boring to desperation." " What is my business in this world and what have I done this fortnight ? " she wrote on July 7th, 1846. " I have read the ' Daughter at Home ' to Father and two chapters of Mackintosh ; a volume of Sybil to Mamma. Learnt seven tunes by heart. Written various letters. Ridden with Papa. Paid eight visits. Done Company. And that is all."

" Dreaming " enslaved her more and more. While W. E. N. was reading *The Times*, while she was making conversation with visitors or taking " a little drive " with Fanny, she escaped into a dream world. Her dreams centred upon Richard Monckton Milnes. She imagined herself married to him, performing heroic deeds with him. Dreaming was easier than the struggle to make herself worthy. Dreams encroached on her prayers, and she feared she was committing the sin against the Holy Ghost.

Throughout the winter she was unwell, and to be unwell at Embley was to have life made unendurable by Fanny's fussing. " Oh if one has but a toothache," she wrote in a private note of 1846, "what remedies are invented! What carriages, horses, ponies, journeys, doctors, chaperones, are urged on one; but if it is something the matter with the *mind* . . . it is neither believed nor understood."

Yet, in spite of her wretchedness, she was making progress. The philosophy which told her to submit did not tell her to relinquish her determination; indeed, it gave her strength to persist, since she believed that as soon as she had attained a worthy state she would be released from submission. She began to equip herself with knowledge against that day.

At Lord Ashley's suggestion she started to study Blue Books and hospital reports—during the past few years the first Blue Books dealing with public health had been published. In 1838 Dr. Southwood Smith, Dr. Arnott and Dr. Kay presented their report on the condition of the poor in East London to the Poor Law Commissioners. Two years later the Select Committee presented their first report on the Health of Towns. In 1842 the first report on the Sanitary Condition of the Labouring Classes was published, and in 1844 the first report of the Health of Towns Commission.

She worked in secret. She got up before dawn and wrote by candlelight, wrapped in a shawl. Notebook after notebook was filled with a mass of facts, compared, indexed and tabulated. She wrote privately for reports to M. Mohl in Paris, she procured information on hospitals in Berlin from the Bunsens. In the cold dark mornings she laid the foundation of the vast and detailed knowledge of sanitary conditions which was to make her the first expert in Europe. Then the breakfast-bell rang and she came down to be the Daughter at Home.

61

Fanny had put her in charge of still-room, pantry and linen-room. " I am up to my chin in linen, glass and china," she wrote to Clarkey in December 1846, "and I am very fond of housekeeping. In this too highly educated, too-little-active age, it is at least a practical application of our theories to some-thing—and yet in the middle of my lists, my green lists, brown lists, red lists, of all my instruments of the ornamental in culinary accomplishments, which I cannot even divine the use of, I cannot help asking in my head, ' Can reasonable people want all this ? ' . . . ' And a proper stupid answer you'll get ', says the best Versailles service, ' so go and do your accounts ; there is one of us cracked.' "

Among the Verney Nightingale papers is a good-sized box filled with the " green lists, brown lists, red lists ". They are notebooks, kept in minute detail, relating to plate, china, linen and stores. Twice a year she went through linen-room, plate-chest, china and glass cupboard and storeroom, checking, listing damage, replacements and repairs. In the still-room she supervised preserving, and she wrote to Hilary Bonham Carter in September 1846 that after a hard day's work she was " surveying fifty-six jam pots with the eye of an artist ".

So month followed month—it seemed without progress or event, but in her character a profound change was taking place. "I feel", she wrote in a private note of 1846, "as if all my being were gradually drawing together to one point." She decided that her longing for affection, her susceptibility, were too powerful for safety. How much energy, how much strength had she not expended on Marianne, on Henry Nicholson, on Richard Monckton Milnes, on Hilary Bonham Carter, which should have been devoted to the struggle for fulfilment? She began deliberately to detach herself from human relationships. Love, marriage, even friendship, must be renounced. So in September 1846 she wrote to Hilary Bonham Carter : " Are not one's earthly friends too often Atalanta's apple, thrown in each other's way to hinder that course, at the end of which is laid up the crown of righteous-ness ? So, dearest, it is well that *we* should not see too much of each other. . . . Farewell my beloved one." In a private note she wrote : " Oh God, no more love. No more marriage O God."

In July the Nightingales had gone north to Lea Hurst, and in the cottages she found peace. In a private note written on July 16th she wrote : " Rubbed Mrs. Spence for the 2nd time. I am such a creeping worm that if I have anything of the kind to do I can do without marriage or intellect or social inter-course or any of the things people sigh after. . . . It satisfies my soul. It supplies every want of my heart and mind. It heals all my disease. It saves my soul from destruction. I want nothing else, my heart is filled. I am at home."

In October the Chevalier Bunsen sent her the Year Book of the Institution of Deaconesses at Kaiserswerth. Four years earlier he had mentioned Kaiserswerth, but she had not then reached the knowledge that nursing was her vocation. Now with overwhelming joy she realised that Kaiserswerth was what she had been seeking. There she could have training in nursing, and the objections raised against English hospitals did not apply. The religious atmosphere, the character of the deaconesses and pastors who formed the staff, the close super-vision and ascetic discipline—these things placed the nurses above suspicion. On October 7th she wrote in a private note : " There is my home, there are my brothers and sisters all at work. There my heart is and there, I trust, will one day be my body."

The Year Book became her treasure, but she did not dare mention Kaiserswerth to her mother. Fanny was busier, more successful than ever, and Embley was filled for autumn parties ; and so, she wrote in a private note, whenever she wanted " refreshment in the midst of this table d'hôte of people at Embley " she went upstairs and secretly read the Year Book of the Deaconesses of Kaiserswerth.

In the spring of 1847 the Nightingales went to the Burling-ton Hotel for the season. Fanny gave a number of breakfasts and dinners, and on almost every occasion Richard Monckton Milnes was present. At Whitsun he was at Embley and when, in June, the Nightingales went to Oxford for the meeting of the British Association, he went with them. Two astronomers, Adams, an Englishman, and Leverrier, a Frenchman, had simultaneously discovered the planet now called Neptune. The French demanded that Adams's discovery should be dis-regarded and the planet named after Leverrier. Feeling between France and England ran high, but a settlement was reached, the planet was named neither Adams nor Leverrier, but Neptune, and the British Association fêted both astronomers. Florence reported to Clarkey that they sat " on either side of the President like two turtle-doves, cooing at their joint star ".

The weather was perfect, the flowering acacias out everywhere, and she told Clarkey that she had " never imagined so much loveliness and learning ". She strolled through college gardens and cloisters with Richard, and in New College cloister she picked a white rose to press " for a remembrance ". They made up a " set " with Prince Napoleon Bonaparte, afterwards the Emperor Napoleon III, Henry Hallam, a Cambridge scholar and brother of the Arthur Hallam whose early death was commemorated by Tennyson in *In Memoriam*, and an elderly admirer of Florence, Sir Robert Inglis, a Tory politician celebrated for his learning. Bonaparte named a new variety of bat after Sir Robert Inglis, " Inglisia Benevolens ". Henry Hallam announced that the Beast 666 mentioned in Revelation was Gladstone—" It came to him by inspiration one day in the Athenaeum after he had tried Pusey and Newman and found they wouldn't do ", wrote Florence to Clarkey. And they went to lunch at Christ Church with Professor Buckland, the famous naturalist, who kept animals at liberty in his rooms. Florence " invited a Bear of 3 months old in to lunch, who climbed like a squirrel for the butter on the table . . . which went to his head and he became obstreperous. Mr. Buckland put on his cap and gown and rebuked it, at which it became violent and was carried out in disgrace. . . . When we came out it was still walking and storming and howling on its hind legs—gesticulating and remonstrating. I spoke to it but Papa pulled me away, fearing it would bite. I said 'Let alone, I'm going to mesmerise it'. Mr. Milnes followed the suggestion and in $\frac{1}{2}$ minute the little bear began to yawn, in less than 3 min. was stretched fast asleep on the gravel."

From Oxford W. E. N. and Florence went on to pay visits to Lord and Lady Sherborne and Lord and Lady Lovelace. Lady Lovelace, who was Byron's daughter, had a " passion " for Florence, and handed round a set of verses she had written in praise of her "soft and silver voice", her "grave and lucid eye".

What more did Florence want? It was extremely irritating to Fanny that she persisted in being steadily more miserable. The old story repeated itself: she feared success because she enjoyed it too much; "vanity, love of display, love of glory" were still her besetting sins. "Everything I do is poisoned by the fear that I am not doing it in simplicity and godly sincerity", she wrote.

In September Clarkey married Julius Mohl; and Ampère, who attended the wedding, was instructed by the bride to blow his nose loudly when the moment came for her to declare her age so that the fatal figure should be inaudible. The following month Florence wrote Clarkey a long confused letter on the subject of marriage: ". . . We must all take Sappho's leap, one way or other, before we attain to her repose—though some take it to death and some to marriage and some again to a new life even in this world. Which of them is the better part, God only knows. Popular prejudice gives it in favour of marriage. . . . In single life, the stage of the Present and the Outward World is so filled with phantoms, the phantoms, not unreal tho' intangible, of Vague Remorse, Tears, dwelling on the threshold of every thing we undertake alone, Dissatisfaction with what is, and Restless Yearnings for what is not . . . love laying to sleep those phantoms (by assuring us of a love so great that we may lay aside all care for our own happiness . . . because it is of so much consequence to another) gives that leisure frame to our mind, which opens it at once to joy."

Her destiny may have demanded that marriage should be put behind her, but the desire to be loved died hard. She could not rid her heart of longing for "a love so great that we may lay aside all care for our own happiness . . . because it is of so much consequence to another". Nor could she bring herself to face losing Richard Monckton Milnes. Month after month she temporised, evading the moment when she must give him a definite answer. Fanny passed from impatience to anger, accusing her of godless ingratitude, perversity and conceit.

At this point Florence found consolation in a new friend. The previous autumn, through Clarkey, she had met Selina

65

Bracebridge, wife of Charles Holte Bracebridge, of Atherstone Hall, near Coventry. Selina understood her. In a retrospect Miss Nightingale wrote : " She never told me life was fair and my share of its blessings great and that I *ought* to be happy. She did not know that I was miserable but she felt it; and to me, young, strong and blooming as I then was, to me, the idol of the man I adored, the spoilt child of fortune, she had the heart and the instinct to say—' Earth, my child, has a grave and in heaven there is rest '."

Selina Bracebridge was a remarkable woman, beautiful in a regal style (Clarkey described her as " a tall, stately, irresistible, line of battle ship "), intellectual, artistic and possessing an extraordinary warmth of character. " She was totally unlike anyone I have ever known," wrote Miss Nightingale thirty years later, " as unlike as a picture of a sunny scene is to sunshine with its light and warmth; or as this February lamp we call the sun is to her own sun of the East in Palestine."

The Bracebridges were well-known travellers. Charles Bracebridge had an enthusiasm for the cause of Greek freedom, had taken part in a revolt against the Turks, and owned property in Athens. Generous, impetuous, irascible, he combined intense family pride (the Bracebridges liked to trace their descent from Lady Godiva), with a passion for liberty. He dressed picturesquely in wide hats and flowing cloaks, and had brought back Arab horses from the East which he bred at Atherstone Hall. He was " the kindest of friends and one of the best and noblest of men," Miss Nightingale wrote. " All his life he was fighting battles against cruelty and oppression."

Like Fanny, Selina Bracebridge prided herself on collecting interesting people, and in particular young writers. The Bracebridges were rich, had no children, and entertained a great deal both in London and at Atherstone Hall. Fanny warmly encouraged the friendship. Selina was twenty years older than Florence, a very happily married woman and a declared believer in matrimony. Selina might induce Florence to accept Richard Monckton Milnes, and perhaps through Selina's literary connections she might turn to writing. Selina and her husband became family friends, and she was given a pet name by the Nightingales, the Greek character " sigma "—

Σ—partly in compliment to the Hellenic traits of her character, partly in reference to her love for Greece.

The importance of Selina to Florence was overwhelming. Florence was drowning and she was the lifebelt. Florence was dying of thirst and she was the draught of cool water. Selina never doubted that the struggles in Florence's soul were the long agonies through which something of immense importance would eventually be born. She made Florence the main object of her life, pouring out on her an extraordinary affection, partly worship, partly maternal love. " I wonder if she knows the difference she has made to my life," wrote Florence in a private note of November 1846. " The very fact of there being one person by whom one's thoughts are not pronounced fit only for a dream, not worth disputing, who does not look on one as a fanciful spoilt child . . . that mere fact changes the whole aspect of things to one."

Through the spring of 1847 she had a new dream. She imagined Σ was always with her, always waiting for her, beautiful, kind and loving. She wrote imaginary dialogues in which she put down Σ's part in the conversation as well as her own. The dialogues were never sent, they were too private to be read even by Σ. She feared again for her mental balance. All round her she could see the effects of enforced idleness and frustration—" I see so many of my kind who have gone mad for want of something to do. People who might have been so happy, Aunt Evans, Aunt Patty," she wrote. Would she wake up one day to find she was elderly and mad and subject, like Aunt Patty, to " outbursts " ?

In the autumn of 1847 she broke down completely. For the past eighteen months she had been ailing. The morning hours of secret toil were a physical strain, her life in public, repressed and in disgrace, a continual irritation; she grew thin, slept badly. The autumn months at Embley always brought commotion—Clarkey wrote that the Nightingales " lived in a state of endless faddle which wore poor Flo out ". There were shooting parties and a visit to London for the autumn season to be arranged. In September she wrote to Clarkey that she could not face " the prospect of three winter months of perpetual row ". She collapsed, took to her bed, coughed.

She was rescued by the Bracebridges, who were going to spend the winter in Rome; Σ persuaded Fanny to let them take Florence. The fuss was enormous : the clothes she was to take, the books she was to read, the sights she was to see, were separately the subject of consideration, reconsideration, letters, interviews, advice from uncles, aunts, grandmothers and cousins. Solemn farewells were said. Parthe was overcome at the idea of separation, and for the last few days Fanny and W. E. N. withdrew from Embley and left the two sisters alone. " It seems to me a great event," wrote Parthe in October 1847 to Hilary Bonham Carter, " the solemn first launching of her into life, and my heart is very full." But Florence was apathetic. " Dreaming " had enslaved her even further during her illness, and she was terrified. In a private note she wrote : " I see nothing desirable but death ".

On October 27th the party left England, going overland to Marseilles and thence by sea to Civita Vecchia, the port for Rome. " Oh how happy I was ! I never enjoyed any time in my life as much as my time in Rome," Miss Nightingale wrote. Once more as soon as she left home she was transformed. With Σ she was free. They wandered about Rome on foot, eating meals of vegetables and bread in small restaurants and practising their Italian ; they bought chestnuts from a street vendor, filled their handkerchiefs with them and walked all the way to the Villa Mellina, talking and eating ; they stayed at the Villa Mellina to watch the sunset, running all the way home and being late for dinner. And no one scolded.

Florence became devoted to Mr. Bracebridge : he had been ill, he required looking after, and he shared her enthusiasm for Italian emancipation. The winter of 1847 saw Pio Nono's brief ascendancy, and in common with most of Europe, the English visitors regarded him as the champion of Italian freedom. One evening the tricolour of Italy was hoisted in the Capitol. A torchlight procession formed, everyone in Rome illuminated their windows as a demonstration of sympathy and those who did not got them broken. Hearing the roll of a drum, they rushed out to see the procession, and Florence, convinced she was witnessing the dawn of Italian liberty, burst into tears. When they discovered that their own windows were shamefully not illuminated they seized stones and broke a pane, while a huge crowd halted and cheered the English milord and miladi.

Miss Nightingale was intoxicated with Rome. Fifty years later she could still describe every street, every turning, every building in minute detail. One of the great moments of her life was her first sight of the Michelangelo ceiling in the Sistine Chapel. " I did not think I was looking at pictures but straight into Heaven itself ", she wrote to Parthe on December 17th, 1847. She remained alone in the Sistine for the whole of one day, and for the rest of her life had prints of the Sistine frescoes hanging in her room.

She danced out the old year of 1847 into 1848, and it was " the happiest New Year I have ever spent ". In January she wrote : " This is the most entire and unbroken freedom from dreaming that I ever had ". Her health recovered and she was well all the six months she was in Rome.

And in Rome, during the winter of 1847, she met Sidney Herbert. Their strange and fatal intimacy began in picture galleries and churches ; during strolls in the Borghese gardens and sightseeing expeditions to Tivoli. Each was destined to exercise an extraordinary influence on the other, each in meeting the other had met their fate ; but no portent indicated that this was the most important moment of their lives. The acquaintance opened with Florence's introduction by Σ to Sidney Herbert's wife, a remarkably beautiful girl who until August 1846 had been Miss Elizabeth à Court, daughter of General Charles Ashe à Court ; Liz à Court was a close friend, "almost like a daughter", to Σ. She had married Sidney Herbert, half-brother and heir-presumptive of the Earl of Pembroke, and they were now wintering in Rome in the course of a postponed wedding tour. She was immediately attracted by Florence and they became intimate friends.

Liz was a woman of great charm. She was beautiful, with brilliant dark eyes and a glowing olive skin. She had a childlike eagerness, a simple power of enjoyment which made her a delightful companion. After knowing her for a few weeks Miss Nightingale wrote in a private note of " the great kindness, the desire of love, the magnanimous generosity " which distinguished her character.

Fate had heaped blessing upon blessing on Sidney Herbert's

head. He was astonishingly good-looking—"a tall and graceful figure surmounted by a face of such singular sweetness as to be unforgettable", wrote Gladstone. His hair was thick, waving and dark chestnut in colour, his eyes dark and shaded with long lashes. Tall, broad-shouldered yet graceful, he was a superb shot, a remarkably good horseman and an ardent rider to hounds. He had great wealth, he lived at Wilton, one of the most beautiful houses in England which he would eventually inherit, he had a house in Belgrave Square, and vast estates in Ireland in addition. He was brilliantly clever, his wit and social talents were famous, yet he secretly belonged to an association the members of which were pledged to give away a large part of their incomes in private charity.

Years later Miss Nightingale scribbled a sheet of rough notes on Sidney Herbert's character. " Great eloquence, unequalled social fascination. The gentlest man, strong as gentle, did not confront abuses with perhaps honest anger and fervent indignation, but with winning gentleness, subdued far more resistance, and achieved far greater triumphs for his country, than by the spirit of anger and wrath. Modesty, humility. Never said ' I did that ', never referred to it. Eager and enthusiastic in duty, cared little for the reward, and not at all for the credit. No assertion of self; purity of nature and high principle. It was well known that he could do with the House of Commons and the Cabinet what no one else could."

And yet—with so much goodness, brilliance and beauty he was without zest for life. Parliamentary success and philanthropic achievements were dust and ashes in his mouth, and in spite of his gifts, his capacity for bestowing happiness and his good fortune, he would have preferred never to have lived at all. He longed only for quiet—the peace of Wilton. " There is not a spot about Wilton which I do not love as if it were a person ", he wrote. " If one had nothing to do but consult one's own taste and one's own ease I should be too glad to live down here a domestic life."

It was impossible. Fate heaped on him glittering prize after glittering prize. Riches, high office, power, responsibility, descended on him. He found the burden almost intolerable and turned for consolation to religion—both Sidney Herbert and his wife were devout Christians who consecrated their lives to philanthropic works. He built a new church at Wilton, he worked to improve the condition of the poor, he was in process of building and endowing a convalescent home, he was interested in a plan for emigrating sweated workers, and into these and other plans Liz threw herself heart and soul, worshipping her husband and desiring to share his every activity and thought.

In Rome the Herberts had a small circle of friends who met almost daily. One was Doctor Manning, Archdeacon of Chichester, who was wintering in Rome to improve his health, which had broken down under the stress of religious doubts; another was Mary Stanley, sister of Doctor Stanley, then Canon of Canterbury, later famous as Dean Stanley of Westminster. It was the time when the Oxford Movement was shaking the Church of England to its foundations, and the Herberts and their friends belonged to the reforming High Church party, popularly called Puseyites. Would the path which they were following lead them to the Roman Catholic Church? To help them decide this point they had come to Rome. Miss Nightingale, however, was indifferent. She formed a friendship with Mary Stanley because Mary Stanley was interested in nursing and had visited hospitals in England and Europe, and Mary Stanley developed a " passion " for her. With Manning and with Sidney Herbert she discussed social work and schemes of philanthropy. Religious doctrines or the claims of one church against another meant nothing to her.

Nevertheless, while she was in Rome the Roman Catholic Church gave her an experience which profoundly influenced the subsequent course of her life.

On February 6th, 1848, while she was attending Benediction at St. Peter's, her attention was caught by a beautiful little girl of five. She smiled at the child, the smile was returned, and when Benediction was over they walked about St. Peter's together. The child's name was Felicetta Sensi; she was an orphan and miserably poor. Since her first day in Rome Miss Nightingale's heart had been wrung by the beautiful infants who swarmed in the gutters of Rome, doomed to a life of poverty, misery and disease. Against the advice of the

Herberts and the Bracebridges, she determined to rescue Felicetta. She interviewed a woman alleged to be the child's aunt and offered to make herself responsible for Felicetta's education. A few days later she received a message asking her to call on Madre Santa Colomba at the convent of the Trinità de' Monti. She was assured by her friends that she would be fortunate to escape with a rebuke—priests and nuns in Rome did not care for interference from foreigners and Protestants. So she went to the convent, " shaking in my shoes ".

As soon as she saw Madre Santa Colomba she was conscious of her profound sympathy. It was agreed that Felicetta should be placed in the convent school and that Florence should pay for her out of her dress allowance. (For many years her accounts contain notes of " money sent for my little Felicetta ".) She passed the afternoon and evening with Madre Santa Colomba, returning again next day; and for the remainder of her stay in Rome this remarkable woman, who combined an intense mystical life with practical efficiency, ruled her life. The orphanage school at the convent was one of the most advanced in Italy, the children were encouraged to voice their opinions freely even if criticism of their teachers was involved, and the teachers were trained not to startle the children by sudden movements or harsh words.

Madre Santa Colomba instructed her to submit herself completely to the will of God. Like Aunt Hannah, she directed her to purify and tranquillise herself so that God's will might be revealed, and she forbade her to struggle against her environment. During the last two months of her stay in Rome Miss Nightingale went to the convent almost daily, writing down the Madre's sayings when she came back. " It is useless ", she was told, " to separate oneself from people to try and do the will of God. . . . What does it matter even if we are with people who drive us frantic if we are doing the will of God? " The Madre arranged for her to make a retreat at the Convent. At the end of the retreat she had a mystical experience. She received what she believed to be a direct revelation from God. She was instructed to surrender her will completely, to submit to everyone and everything. " He calls you to a very high degree of perfection," the Madre told her; " if you resist you will be very guilty."

In April 1848 she left Rome. The city was in arms again; the Pope had blessed the Army of Freedom, friars were preaching Italian emancipation in the Forum, the flag of United Italy waved over the Capitol and Garibaldi was riding into Rome to defend the city against the Austrians. She heard with indignation the suggestion that Rome should be surrendered without a blow in order that its monuments might be preserved. "They must carry out their defence to the last", she wrote to Clarkey. "I should like to see them fight the streets, inch by inch, till the last man dies at his barricade, till St. Peter's is level with the ground, till the Vatican is blown into the air. . . . If I were in Rome I should be the first to fire the Sistine . . . and Michael Angelo would cry ' Well done' as he saw his work destroyed."

She reached home buoyed up by the experience of her retreat and determined to submit. The summer was largely occupied by the excitement and fuss of a family wedding: Laura Nicholson, Marianne's youngest sister, married Jack Bonham Carter, Hilary's eldest brother. The celebrations, in the Waverley manner, were colossal. Good-will was in the air and differences forgotten. Florence and Parthe were brides-maids. Fanny, busy and excited, was less exacting; Florence, sustained by ecstasy, more cheerful.

Her friendship with the Herberts, a source of profound satisfaction to Fanny, grew closer. As soon as they returned to London in May, she dined with them. The next month she went with them to the opening of their convalescent home at Charmouth, staying at Wilton on her way back. She met a circle of intelligent, socially impeccable, extremely influential people intensely interested in hospital reform. Public opinion was awakening, the Herberts and their friends were eager for information, and Miss Nightingale, who had now been working for more than five years collecting facts on public health and hospitals, had an enormous mass of detailed information at her finger-tips. She gradually became known as an expert on hospitals.

The Herberts knew of her plan to go to Kaiserswerth and approved, and the Bunsens were thinking of sending their daughter there. Once more the fulfilment of her desires seemed within the range of possibility. Who could object to

Kaiserswerth? Who could disapprove of what the Herberts and the Bunsens approved? Surely her mother must allow herself to be convinced. But it was necessary to proceed cautiously—the very word hospital might be fatal.

In September 1848 a heaven-sent opportunity offered. Parthe was ordered to take a cure at Carlsbad and the Nightingales planned to go on to Frankfurt, where Clarkey and her husband M. Mohl were staying. Frankfurt was M. Mohl's native city, and he wished to introduce W. E. N. to learned society there. Kaiserswerth being near Frankfurt, Florence's plan was to leave her family for a week or two to " visit the deaconesses and perhaps fit in a little training ".

But 1848 was the year of revolution in Europe. When disorders broke out in Frankfurt, W. E. N. thought it wiser to stay in England; and the Nightingales went to Malvern instead of Carlsbad. " I am not going to consign to paper for your benefit all the cursings and swearings which relieved my disappointed feelings," Miss Nightingale wrote to Clarkey in October, " for oh! what a plan of plans I had made out for myself. All that I most wanted to do at Kaiserswerth lay for the first time within reach of my mouth, and the ripe plum has dropped."

Her reaction was violent. Her mother was not concerned, for Fanny knew nothing of the scheme. It was God Himself who had prevented her. God who had cut her off from Kaiserswerth, perhaps for years. The old reasoning tortured her. This misfortune had come upon her because she was sinful. God wanted her to go to Kaiserswerth, but He could not let her go until she had reached a greater state of worthiness. She went down into the depths of depression; the short period of comparative happiness was over. She " hated God to hear her laugh as if she had not repented of her sin ". The winter season at Embley lay before her. " My God what am I to do ", she wrote in a private note of October 1848. " Teach me, tell me. I cannot go on any longer waiting till my situation should change, dreaming what the change should be."

She succumbed to " dreaming " helplessly, shamefully. She dreamed of fame, of Richard Monckton Milnes. To escape from " dreaming " she sought relief in nursing the poor of Wellow, the village near Embley, and Fanny and Parthe became irritated: it was unnecessary for Florence to go into the " black filth " of the cottages, actually touching sick people and even making their beds ; she would bring an infectious disease into the house and kill her sister. And she was always late for dinner. She visited her sick in secret, hurrying down the back drive so that she should not be seen from the house, running back breathless through the muddy lanes to be in time for dinner. W. E. N., who hated dirt, disease and ugliness, was disgusted. He told Florence she was being theatrical ; if she wanted something to do, let her work in the school at Wellow. She did for a time, trying to put into practice some of the new ideas she had learned at Madre Santa Colomba's school. But she failed. " I was disgusted with my utter impotence ", she wrote in a private note. " I made no improvement. I obtained no influence. . . . Why should I ? . . . Education I know is not my genius."

Round and round her mind travelled the weary obsession. She was not submitting, and submission was the first exaction of God. She had been told in Rome that God called her to submit her will to everything. Madre Santa Colomba had said that she herself would joyfully give up her religious life if it were the will of God that she should do so. But she could not give up nursing. She was sinful, guilty, utterly wretched and cast away.

Aunt Hannah wrote soothingly that anything, even a house-party or a dinner, can be done to the glory of God. " How can it be to the glory of God ", answered Florence, " when there is so much misery in the world which we might be curing instead of living in luxury." Aunt Hannah, who did not pay her usual visit to Embley in 1848, did not answer : Florence was becoming known as a rebel daughter, and Aunt Hannah could not countenance that. The following year she wrote that she found it necessary with " advancing years and delicate health " to " confine herself to visits to near relatives ", and her correspondence with Florence ceased.

In March 1849 the Nightingales went to London for the season. Miss Nightingale was in a mounting delirium of misery and frustration. She had been driving herself remorselessly through the winter, and long hours of concentration in the cold dark mornings were becoming increasingly difficult.

Again and again she scribbled on the margins of papers and private notes, " *Why* cannot I get up in the morning? "

She was consoled by the affection of Shore, now an undemonstrative lad of eighteen, though on one occasion " he actually sat with astonishing coolness on the arm of my chair, I may say stroked my velvet with a composure amounting to audacity ", she wrote. She now taught at a Ragged School at Westminster, in which one of her uncles was interested, and wished to take up slum visiting, but her mother frustrated her. Florence must conform to the usages of a carefully brought-up young lady and not go out without a footman to attend her— " it would never do for a young woman in her station in life to go out in London without a servant ". The addition of a footman put an end to slum visiting.

She was drawing towards a mental crisis. " Dreaming " became uncontrollable. She fell into trances in which hours were blotted out, she lost sense of time and place against her will. In daily life she moved like an automaton, could not remember what had been said or even where she had been. Agonies of guilt and self-reproach were intensified by the conviction that her worst fears were being realised and that she was going insane.

Again and again she made resolutions to end dreaming, to " tear the sin out ", to " stamp it out "—but they were always broken. She turned on herself with savagery, hating herself, despising her weakness. Nights were spent walking up and down her room. She would have killed herself if she had not thought it mortal sin. On June 7th, 1849, she determined at whatever cost to herself to " crucify " her sin. The 7th of each month was devoted to self-examination because she had received her " call " on February 7th. In this wretched state another blow fell on her. Richard Monckton Milnes would be put off no longer. He insisted on a definite answer—would she marry him or not? She refused him.

It was an act which required extraordinary courage. She was deeply stirred by him, she called him " the man I adored "; and she renounced him for the sake of a destiny which it seemed impossible she would ever fulfil. Her future had never looked more hopeless.

In a private note she analysed her reasons. She wrote

several versions, she began it, broke off, returned to it again before she could clarify her emotions. " I have an intellectual nature which requires satisfaction and that would find it in him. I have a passionate nature which requires satisfaction and that would find it in him. I have a moral, an active, nature which requires satisfaction and that would not find it in his life. Sometimes I think I will satisfy my passional nature at all events, because that will at least secure me from the evil of dreaming. But would it? I could be satisfied to spend a life with him in combining our different powers in some great object. I could not satisfy this nature by spending a life with him in making society and arranging domestic things."

But she could not always be rational. She wrote again with a pencil that trembled, hesitated and dug itself into the paper. " I do not understand it. . . . I am ashamed to understand it. . . . I know that if I were to see him again . . . the very thought of doing so quite overcomes me. I know that since I refused him not one day has passed without my thinking of him, that life is desolate without his sympathy." At night she dreamed of him. He came and told her that he had arranged for her to go to Kaiserswerth. And yet desperately as she longed for him she would not give way. " I know I could not bear his life," she wrote," that to be nailed to a continuation, an exaggeration of my present life without hope of another would be intolerable to me—that voluntarily to put it out of my power ever to be able to seize the chance of forming for myself a true and rich life would seem to me like suicide."

Fanny was severely disappointed and furiously resentful. Her obstinacy hardened, she determined that Florence should not have her own ungrateful way, and what had begun as genuine maternal solicitude for her daughter's welfare turned into a contest of wills in which love and kindness were forgotten.

By the autumn Miss Nightingale's mental and physical state was pitiable. Fanny and Parthe nagged her unceasingly, and she adopted a policy of silence, which they found intensely provoking. Clarkey, who had stayed at Embley during the summer, wrote from Paris exhorting her to " stand up for herself ". She was too proud, she held her tongue, " suffering much and saying little ", she wrote in a private note. She was far from well and fainted on several occasions ; sometimes

77

her mind became a blank and she looked at people wildly and vaguely, not hearing what was said to her.

Σ once more intervened. The Bracebridges were going to Egypt and then to Greece, and they persuaded Fanny to let them take Florence. But the Nightingale circle disapproved. " I think you are all martyrs for having consented ", wrote Ellen Tollet, Parthe's favourite cousin. " I suppose really large minded people think less of space and distance than we do ", commented another. Aunt Patty Smith wrote acidly that " it was to be hoped that change of air and the satisfaction of doing her duty would do Flo good ".

Miss Nightingale herself commented to Hilary Bonham Carter that as Rome had done her some good the family were going to send her farther afield in the hopes that that would be even better.

A journey to Egypt was an adventure in 1849. But she was in a state when Egypt, the desert, even the brilliant landscapes of the Nile itself meant as little as scenes painted on a back-cloth. She was on the verge of mental collapse. Outwardly she performed the functions expected of the well-known, elegant and cultivated Miss Nightingale. She borrowed from Bunsen a pile of learned tomes written by himself and his friend Lepsius, and worked through them with meticulous thoroughness, making tables of dynasties, elaborate plans of temples and notes of inscriptions. She wrote her family immensely long letters, ornate and picturesque in style. The letters were greatly admired and privately printed. The Bracebridges, as travellers of importance, were entertained by governors, chief consuls, ambassadors. She astonished a party by conversing with the abbot of a monastery in Latin.

Yet secretly she was in agony, torn to pieces by incessant mental conflict, sleepless, physically broken and on the edge of catastrophe. The party went up the Nile by dahabiah, and on their return crossed by sea to Athens, where Mr. Brace-bridge had business connected with his property.

In a small black notebook she recorded her secret agonies ; the entries are scribbled in pencil, in phrases which repeat themselves, in writing which wavers and becomes all but indecipherable. The weight of guilt laid on her conscience by " dreaming " was driving her insane.

Jan.	26.	Went with party to Jenab . . . but I spoiled it all with dreaming. Disappointed with myself and the effect of Egypt on me. Rome was better.
Feb.	16.	Where was I all the while—dreaming. Karnak itself cannot save me now.
Feb.	22.	God spoke to me again, sitting on the steps of the portico at Karnak.
Feb.	28.	God called me—with my Madre's words.
March	3.	Ill. Did not get up in the morning.
March	7.	God called me in the morning and asked me would I do good for Him, for Him alone without the reputation.
March	8.	Thought much upon this question. My Madre said to me " Can you hesitate between the God of the whole world and your little reputation ? "
March	9.	During half an hour I had by myself in my cabin, settled the question with God.
March	10.	Every day during the $\frac{1}{4}$ of an hour I had by myself after dinner and after breakfast in my own cabin, read some of my Madre's words " Can you give up the reputation of suffering much and saying little ? " they cried to me.
March	15.	God has delivered me from the great offence and the constant murderer of all my thoughts.
March	21.	Undisturbed by my great enemy.
April	1.	Not able to go out but wished God to have it all His own way. I like Him to do exactly as He likes without even telling me the reason.
May	7.	(In Athens) I have felt here the suspension of all my faculties, I could not write, could not read. . . .
May	9.	I cannot even draw a pattern for a few minutes without turning faint.
May	12.	To-day I am 30—the age Christ began his mission. Now no more childish things. No more love. No more marriage. Now Lord let me think only of Thy Will, what Thou willest me to do. Oh Lord Thy Will, Thy Will.
May	18.	To-morrow is Sacrament Sunday ; I have read over all my history, a history of miserable woe, mistake and blinding vanity, of seeking great things for myself.
May	19.	Whit Sunday. Oh how happy I am to be away from the scene of temptation on this day. I thank Thee Father, three Whitsuntides have I spent torn

with temptation and overcome. Here I am not safe. God I place myself in Thy Hands . . . if it be Thy Will that I should go on suffering let it be so.

May 21. (Ill) Now I am 30, the year when I thought I should have accomplished my Kaiserswerth mission . . . let me only accomplish the Will of God, let me not desire great things for myself.

June 7. I thought I would go up the Eumenides cave and ask God there to explain to me what were these Eumenides which pursued me. I would not ask to be released from them—Welcome Eumenides—but to be delivered from doing further wrong. . . . This day twelve months ago June 7th 1849 I made that desperate effort, that crucifixion of the sin, in faith that it would cure me. Oh what is crucifixion—would I not joyfully submit to crucifixion, Father, to be rid of this. But this long moral death, this failure of all attempts to cure. I think I have never been so bad as this last week, when Plato's plane tree, riding in the Academy, living intercourse could not recall my attention to actual things. And I thought when I was 30 I should be cured. 8 months . . . and not a day has passed without my committing it. I went and sat in the cave of the Eumenides alone and thought how they pursued me —and how could it end and wretched that I am, who shall deliver me from the body of this death? What does it signify to me now whether I see this or do that? I never can be sure of seeing it. I may see nothing but my own self practising an attitude. I shall be in just the same state on June 7th 1851 according to human calculation as I am now.

June 10. The Lord spoke to me; He said "Give five minutes every hour to the thought of Me. Couldst thou but love Me as Lizzie loves her husband, how happy wouldst thou be." But Lizzie does not give five minutes every hour to the thought of her husband, she thinks of him every minute, spontaneously.

June 12. To Megara. Alas it little matters where I go—sold as I am to the enemy—whether in Athens or in London, it is all one to me.

June 17. After a sleepless night physically and morally ill and broken down, a slave—glad to leave Athens. I had no wish on earth but to sleep. . . .

June	18.	I had no wish to be on deck. I let all the glorious sunrises, the gorgeous sunsets, the lovely moonlights pass by. I had no wish, no energy, I longed but for *sleep*. . . . My enemy is too strong for me, everything has been tried. . . . All, all is in vain.
June	21.	Two delightful days in Corfu. My enemy let me go, and I was free. I lived again both in body and mind. Oh to-day how lovely, how poetic it was—and I was *free*.
June	22.	Began to sleep.
June	24.	Here too (Trieste) I was free.
June	29.	Four long days of absolute slavery.
June	30.	[Written faintly and shakily] I cannot write a letter, can do nothing.
July	1.	I lay in bed and called on God to save me.

Again Σ saved her. Egypt was doing Florence no good; if she continued to be thwarted, she would go out of her mind. Σ acted on her own responsibility. They were to travel home by land; she chose a route through Prague and Berlin and suggested that she and her husband should spend a fortnight at Düsseldorf while Florence visited Kaiserswerth.

Miss Nightingale was too exhausted, too wretched to be grateful. " On the brink of my accomplishing my greatest wish," she wrote, " with Σ positively planning it for me, I seemed to be unfit, unmanned for it, it seemed to be not the calling for me. . . . I did not feel the spirit, the energy, to do anything at Kaiserswerth." As they travelled from Trieste to Prague and on to Berlin she wrote that she was " lost and past redemption, a slave that could not be set free ".

She found relief in the companionship of animals. On the Nile she had had two little chameleons which slept on her bed and had been " so sorry to part with them, they were such company ". She was travelling now with two tortoises, called Mr. and Mrs. Hill in honour of two missionaries at Athens, a cicada named Plato, and Athena, a baby owl, which she had rescued from some Greek boys at the Parthenon. Athena was fierce and Miss Nightingale had had to mesmerise her according to Richard Monckton Milnes's method before she could be persuaded to enter a cage, but she became devoted to her mistress and travelled everywhere in her pocket. At Prague Athena ate Plato.

When Miss Nightingale reached Berlin she was still miserably depressed. " I had 3 paths among which to choose ", she wrote on July 10th, 1850. " I might have been a married woman, or a literary woman, or a hospital sister. And now it seemed to me as if quiet with somebody to look for my coming back were all I wanted."

But in Berlin she began visiting hospitals and charitable institutions, and her spirits instantly revived. " All at once I felt how rich life was ", she wrote on July 15th. On July 31st she reached Kaiserswerth. "With the feeling with which a pilgrim first looks on the Kedron I saw the Rhine dearer to me than the Nile." She had with her Trout, her personal maid, who was fiercely disapproving—again and again during the journey she wrote : " Dreadful fights with Trout ". The first night at Kaiserswerth was spent at the inn; next day she went to see Pastor Fliedner, who offered to take her into the Institution. Trout was then sent to the Bracebridges at Düsseldorf.

She stayed a fortnight at Kaiserswerth. It was a visit of inspection, and she did not nurse but was shown the work of the Institution and helped with the children. She noted that the hospital was free from the " disgusting hospital smell " accepted in England as inevitable. The apothecary was a woman, no male doctors were in residence, and the physical wants of the male patients were attended to by male nurses. No sister at Kaiserswerth was " called on to do anything for a man patient that a lady might not do for her brother in a private house ".

On August 13th she left Kaiserswerth " feeling so brave as if nothing could ever vex me again ". She was well, brimming with vitality, her powers of concentration had returned and she performed the feat of dashing off a pamphlet of thirty-two pages in less than a week ; telling the unwanted women kept in " busy idleness " in England, the women she saw on all sides " going mad for the want of something to do", of work, happiness and comradeship waiting for them at Kaiserswerth. She was not used to consideration, and mentioned with surprise that the Bracebridges "staid at Ghent actually for me to finish my M.S." On August 19th " Mr. Bracebridge corrected it and sent it off ". It was printed in 1851 " by the inmates of the Ragged Colonial School at Westminster " and issued anonymously under the title *The Institution of Kaiserswerth on the Rhine for the Practical Training of Deaconesses, under the direction of the Rev. Pastor Fliedner, embracing the support and care of a Hospital, Infant and Industrial Schools, and a Female Penitentiary.*

On August 21st she reached Lea Hurst and " surprised my dear people, sitting in the drawing-room, with the owl in my pocket. Sat with Mama and Parthe in the nursery. Rode with Papa." Happiness lasted only a few hours. Fanny was furiously angry, the visit to Kaiserswerth was not to be spoken of, was shameful, a disgrace. The old resentments broke out, the old accusations were repeated. Parthe had hysterics, Fanny raged and wept. Florence must be forced to do her duty, made to stay at home and engage in the pursuits proper to her upbringing and station.

Five years had passed since her attempt to enter Salisbury Infirmary; she was no longer a girl but a woman of thirty, and she had accomplished nothing. Only her determination persisted. "Resignation!" she had written in 1847, "I never understood that word!" A new struggle began, more bitter, more unhappy than ever before.

V THE CONFLICT changed its character for the worse. Fanny had begun by sincerely wishing for Florence's happiness, sincerely believing what she wished to do would ruin her life. That point was passed. There was justification for Miss Nightingale's sense of guilt : she did evoke the worst from each one of her family ; normally kind, normally generous, they behaved to her as to no one else. Fanny's obstinacy, Parthe's possessiveness, W. E. N.'s hatred of unpleasantness, became mania. The struggle had become entangled with their secret disappointments, longings and griefs, and reason and humanity were forgotten as they fought to impose their wishes on Florence. The most furious opposition came from Parthe. For the past few years Parthe had been difficult. She showed an extraordinary dislike of growing older. She had invented a character called " Miss Pop ", and talked and wrote of herself as " Miss Pop ". " Miss Pop " was curiously small, a " wee " fairy princess, who sat on a " wee " chair, wrote " wee " letters, was fond of sending her friends " wee " presents of water-lilies or coloured leaves. But Parthe was thirty-one, and the truth was that she had achieved only moderate success ; the successes, the lovers, the popularity were Florence's, not hers. The Sidney Herberts, the Bunsens, Richard Monckton Milnes, Clarkey and M. Mohl, the Ashleys, the Lovelaces, were Florence's friends. " I want to see you," wrote Clarkey to Florence, " you know I don't care so much about Parthe." Maiden aunts and less prosperous girl cousins formed Parthe's admirers.

She cast herself for the part of Florence's second self, the adoring indispensable sister who could not be left out. " Her sense of existence is lost in Florence ", wrote Mrs. Gaskell. " I never saw such adoring love." " Your own Flo ", wrote W. E. N. to Parthe in 1849. " Your idolatrised wondrous Flo. . . ." Florence's growing celebrity and success were to be shared, but what if, instead of creating a brilliant, interesting life for Parthe, she went off to lead a sordid existence of her own ? The possibility drove Parthe frantic.

Before Miss Nightingale had been back from Kaiserswerth

a fortnight there was a scene. She worked daily in an Adult School for Girls which she had started in the village adjoining Lea Hurst. Parthe demanded that she give the school up and spend all her time at home, and, when Florence refused, Parthe had hysterics. Fanny and W. E. N. accused Florence of heartlessness : for nearly a year she had been away, at great expense, doing exactly what she pleased ; Parthe had been left behind to mope, and her health had suffered. They demanded that she should devote herself entirely to Parthe for the next six months. " To this ", wrote Miss Nightingale in a retrospect, "I acceded. And when I committed this act of insanity had there been any sane person in the house he should have sent for Connolly to me." Dr. Connolly special-ised in diseases of the brain.

Until the spring of 1851 she was to be Parthe's slave. Parthe triumphed. She made little scenes and was coaxed out of them, she sketched with Florence, sang with Florence, wandered with her in the garden, chattered of poetry and art. The effect on Miss Nightingale was devastating. She had left Kaiserswerth feeling " so brave as if nothing could ever vex me again " ; within a few weeks she was sunk in the old miseries. " Dreaming " returned, and never had she been so hopelessly enslaved. Once more nights were spent in agonised self-reproach, once more stupid with misery and frustration she was carried on Fanny's merry-go-round from Lea Hurst to Embley, Embley to London and back to Embley again.

In October the Nightingales received tragic news. Henry Nicholson had been drowned in Spain. Miss Nightingale was profoundly shocked. Henry had been so young, so handsome, so kind. " Who has not lost a friend in Henry ", wrote Aunt Julia. It was with " deepest relief " that Florence received a summons to Waverley ; Henry's mother wished for the presence of the girl Henry had loved. The house was in a hubbub, swarming with mourners as it had so often swarmed with revellers. Marianne and Mrs. Nicholson were prostrated, and she took charge, accompanying Mrs. Nicholson to Henry's chambers in London and packing his possessions. The Nicholsons besought her to stay on, but Parthe insisted she should return. She wrote asking for " an extension of leave ", but was allowed only a week-end. " Thank you,

thank you dear Mum for letting me stay until Tuesday",
she wrote.

After three months she was in despair. "My present life
is suicide", she wrote on December 31st, 1850. "Slowly I have
opened my eyes to the fact that I cannot now deliver myself
from the habit of dreaming which, like gin drinking, is eating
out my vital strength. Now I have let myself go entirely.
Temporary respite only I have. Henry's death and Waverley
was one. . . . My God what will become of me? . . . I have
no desire but to die. There is not a night that I do not lie
down on my bed, wishing that I may leave it no more. Un-
consciousness is all I desire. I remain in bed as long as I can,
for what have I to wake for?" Three months of subjection to
Parthe had still to run. "Oh, how am I to get through this
day, to talk all through this day, is the thought of every
morning", she wrote in January 1851. ". . . This is the
sting of death. In my thirty-first year I see nothing desirable
but death."

She did not reproach Parthe—"she is a child playing in
God's garden", she wrote on January 7th, 1851, "and delight-
ing in the happiness of all his works, knowing nothing of life
but the English drawing-room, nothing of struggle in her own
unselfish nature". The reproaches were heaped on her own
head. "What is to become of me", she wrote. "I can hardly
open my mouth without giving dear Parthe vexation—everything I say or do is a subject of annoyance to her." "Oh
dear good woman", she wrote of Fanny, "when I feel her disappointment in me it is as if I were going insane . . . what
a murderer am I to disturb their happiness. . . . What am I
that their life is not good enough for me? Oh God what am
I? The thoughts and feelings that I have now I can remember
since I was six years old. It was not I that made them. Oh
God how did they come? . . . But why, oh my God cannot
I be satisfied with the life that satisfies so many people? I
am told that the conversation of all these good clever men
ought to be enough for me. Why am I starving, desperate,
diseased on it? . . . What is the cause of it. . . . Oh what do
books know of the real troubles of life. Death, why its a
happiness. . . . My God what am I to do?"

In the spring of 1851 she unexpectedly met Richard

Monckton Milnes at a party given in London by Lady Palmerston. She had not seen him since the day she refused him, and she was shaken. He came across to her and said lightly: " The noise of this room is like a cotton mill ". She was deeply wounded—how could he speak as if she were an ordinary acquaintance? On March 16th, 1851, she met him again. " Last night I saw him again for the second time," she wrote in a private note; " he would hardly speak. . . . I was miserable. . . . I wanted to find him longing to talk to me, willing to give me another opportunity, to keep open another decision; or perhaps I only wanted his sympathy. . . . He was not ready with it. He did not show indifference but avoidance. No familiar friendship. No confidence such as I felt towards him."

She did not want to recognise the fact that her refusal of Richard was final. But he had waited for her decision for nine years. She had refused him and he would not reopen the subject. Some weeks later he became engaged to Miss Annabel Crewe.

In April the six months of slavery to Parthe ended and Florence went immediately to Wilton to stay with Liz Herbert, who was expecting another child. Liz had begged to have her earlier, but Parthe refused until the promised six months were over. Though Miss Nightingale was thirty-one she had no power to arrange her own life; when she wished to stay on at Wilton it was necessary for Liz to approach Fanny " with a fresh petition for a few more days of dear Florence ". The petition was granted, she stayed with Liz until her confinement was over, and when she returned to Embley took with her Dr. Elizabeth Blackwell, one of the first women to become a doctor. Dr. Elizabeth was the daughter of a Bristol merchant who had emigrated and become a citizen of the United States. She had contrived to get herself accepted as a medical student at the University of Geneva in the State of New York, had taken a medical degree and was now studying medicine in Europe. Her experiences confirmed Fanny's worst fears. She had been training at " La Maternité ", the State School of Midwifery in Paris, where life was " infernal ". It seemed that the female pupils were " pretty generally the mistresses of the students ", and Dr. Blackwell's younger sister was going

to Paris in " male attire " to " avoid improper advances ".
Finally, Dr. Blackwell had contracted purulent ophthalmia at
" La Maternité " and lost an eye.

One afternoon Dr. Elizabeth admired the façade of Embley.
" Do you know what I always think when I look at that row of
windows ? " said Miss Nightingale. " I think how I should
turn it into a hospital and just where I should place the beds."

That summer her attitude to life began to change. The
absurdity of her six months' slavery to Parthe, Richard
Monckton Milnes' decisive action, the encouragement of the
Herberts forced her eyes open. In a private note she wrote :
" There are knots which are Gordian and can only be cut ".
She began to realise she must act, that she was justified in acting.
Her sense of guilt lessened, and at long last she saw herself as
the victim not the criminal. On June 8th, 1851, she wrote a
private note on her family in a new vein. " I must expect no
sympathy or help from them. I have so long craved for their
sympathy that I can hardly reconcile myself to this. I have
so long *struggled* to make myself understood—been sore, cast
down, insupportably fretted, at not being understood (at this
moment I feel it even when I retrace these conversations in
thought) that I must not even try to be understood. I know
that they *cannot*. . . . I must *take* some things, as few as I can,
to enable me to live. I must *take* them, they will not be given
to me. . . . I have so long been treated as a child, and have
so long allowed myself to be treated as a child."

A fortnight later she had arranged to go to Kaiserswerth.

Opinion had changed since her attempt to enter Salisbury
Infirmary in 1845. Interest in hospitals was in the air, Fanny
could no longer assert that a plan approved by the Herberts,
the Bunsens and the Bracebridges was shameful. Forced
to yield, she gave way with the worst grace. Everything was
to be done in secret. Parthe was ailing—Fanny declared that
worry over Florence was making her ill—and had been ordered
a three months' cure at Carlsbad. Florence was to leave
England with Fanny and Parthe, go on to Kaiserswerth, and
join them again to come home. Fanny forbade her to tell
anyone where she was going or to write any letters from
Kaiserswerth—she was not to tell Shore on any account,
because young men were so carelessly indiscreet. " With

regard to your fear of what people will say," Miss Nightingale wrote on July 16th, 1851, "the people whose opinion you most care about, it has been their earnest wish for years that I should come here. . . . However I have not mentioned to anyone where I am."

W. E. N. stayed at home. He was beginning to find the perpetual conflict in his family unbearable, and he " retreated into the shadows ". "You may think me absurd," he wrote to Fanny from Lea Hurst in the summer of 1851, " but I really am spellbound and cannot make up my mind to rush into the world." He read, surveyed Nature, enjoyed silence and peace. " I feel myself too much asking—Why ? What for ? What is God's intention ? " he wrote. "I would rather if I could encourage sentiment, contemplate forms of beauty, the pure and the sublime."

Parthe was transported with fury. She railed, but Florence was silent. " It is better to be silent," she wrote in a private note of 1851, " even when appealed to. . . . How do I do with Shore ? I do not seek his sympathy. I know that he cannot give it to me. I never ask for it. It is just as impossible for Parthe to give me her sympathy as it is for Shore. Let me never seek it. . . . Let me observe what are Parthe's subjects. The owl—music—literature—art (including my dress and appearance). Let me sympathise with these."

Against her silence Parthe dashed herself into frenzy. Scene followed scene, reaching a climax in the hotel at Carlsbad the night before Miss Nightingale left. "My sister ", wrote Miss Nightingale in a retrospect, " threw my bracelets which I offered her to wear, in my face and the scene which followed was so violent that I fainted." The following evening she reached Kaiserswerth.

In 1833 a young pastor named Theodore Fliedner and his wife placed a bed and a chair in a summer-house in their back garden and converted it into a refuge for a single destitute discharged prisoner. From this beginning grew the Kaiserswerth Institution.

In 1851 it included a hospital with a hundred beds, an infant school, a penitentiary, an orphan asylum and a normal school for training school mistresses. The Institution was staffed by a hundred and sixteen deaconesses of whom ninety-four were "consecrated" by "a solemn blessing in the church without vows of any kind"; the remainder were on probation. Twenty-seven of the "consecrated" deaconesses were permanently at Kaiserswerth and sixty-seven were sent out to other parts of Germany.

Life was Spartan, work rigorously hard, the food such as was eaten by peasants. "Until yesterday", wrote Miss Nightingale to Fanny in July 1851, "I never had time even to send my things to the wash. We have ten minutes for each of our meals, of which we have four. We get up at 5; breakfast ¼ before 6. The patients dine at 11; the Sisters at 12. We drink tea (i.e. a drink made of ground rye) between 2 and 3, broths at 12 and 7; bread at the two former, vegetables at 12. Several evenings in the week we collect in the Great Hall for a bible lesson. . . . I find the deepest interest in everything here and am so well in body and mind. This is life. Now I know what it is to live and to love life, and really I should be sorry now to leave life. . . . I wish for no other earth, no other world than this."

She slept in the orphan asylum and worked with the children and in the hospital. She was present at operations, which was considered almost indecent. "The operation to which Mrs. Bracebridge alludes", she told Fanny, "was an amputation at which I was present, but which I did not mention to Parthe, knowing that she would see no more in my interest in it than the pleasure dirty boys have in playing in the puddles round a butcher's shop."

Prayer accompanied every incident at Kaiserswerth. Twenty years later Miss Nightingale told Sir Harry Verney: "We were all taught to pray aloud extempore before the whole community whenever it was called for. And, at all the little fêtes or whenever he appeared Fliedner and his wife did this themselves about *everything*. It was all prayed out loud to God before everybody. If a child did wrong it was recommended to God before all the others. . . . We should all have thought it wrong not only to allege shyness but to feel shyness. . . . For the children there were perpetual birthdays . . . *every* birthday was fêted, there was dressing up, with flowers, telling stories, singing, every birthday child asked its own guests and I was always asked. My bad German and foreign stories amused them. . . . There was of course popping down on the knees and praying in the fête."

Miss Nightingale always denied she had been "trained" at Kaiserswerth. "The nursing there was nil," she wrote in 1897, "the hygiene horrible. The hospital was certainly the worst part of Kaiserswerth. But never have I met with a higher tone, a purer devotion than there. There was no neglect. It was the more remarkable because many of the Deaconesses had been only peasants—none were gentlewomen (when I was there)."

She became the close friend of Herr Fliedner, and was godmother to one of his children born during the time she was at Kaiserswerth. After his death in 1864 she educated her godchild at her own expense.

Towards the end of her stay the Herberts visited her, and Herr Fliedner told them that " no person had ever passed so distinguished an examination, or shown herself so thoroughly mistress of all she had to learn as Miss Nightingale". She was completely satisfied, completely happy, her heart overflowed and she made one last effort to be reconciled with her mother and Parthe. On August 31st, 1851, she wrote a long humble beseeching letter setting out her point of view once again. She repeated what she had tried to explain a hundred times before but never so gently, so affectionately. " Give me time, give me faith. Trust me, help me. Say to me ' Follow the dictates of that spirit within thee '. . . . My beloved people I cannot bear to grieve you. Give me your blessing ", she wrote.

Neither Fanny nor Parthe responded—she never appealed to them again.

Clarkey became alarmed. " Where *is* Flo ? " she wrote to Hilary Bonham Carter. On September 23rd, 1851, Hilary wrote from Embley that she had " Uncle Nightingale's permission to divulge to you this state secret, so please Clarkey darling keep it a secret, even though you may not perceive *why* it should be one. I really believe you thought Flo had stayed behind in England. She went with them . . . left them to visit an Institution at Kaiserswerth." " I did nothing but fidget ", replied Clarkey, " to know where she was. . . . I could almost regret she is not more commonplace, still there **must be burnt offerings and these fine spirits are the chosen** victims, their horns are gilt, they *will* go to the altar."

On October 8th, 1851, Miss Nightingale joined her mother and sister at Cologne, to be treated as if she had "just come out of prison". They were furiously resentful—"They would hardly speak to me", wrote Miss Nightingale in a retrospect. "I was treated as if I had come from committing a crime."

A miserable party travelled towards England. Parthe "talked at" Florence, was angry if she answered, angry if she did not. Parthe's health had not improved: the cure had failed, because, she said, she had been so anxious while her sister was at Kaiserswerth. Fanny made light of Parthe's condition, but fussed herself into a state of nervous exhaustion over bandboxes. For her part, Miss Nightingale was seething with plans. Kaiserswerth had whetted her appetite. She was wild to train in earnest. She wanted a larger hospital, one of the great London hospitals.

Once more her plans were doomed—fate caged her in a new trap. She arrived at Embley to find W. E. N. in pain from inflamed eyes. Hilary reported that he had suffered a great deal but would not do anything the doctor told him. An oculist ordered him at once to Umberslade, in Warwickshire, for a course of cold-water treatment, but he would not go unless Florence went with him. It was impossible for her to refuse, but at the eleventh hour she developed measles.

W. E. N. went alone to Umberslade, but Hilary told Clarkey, on December 5th, 1851, that he "would not stay at the water cure alone, came home after 7 or 8 days and fell into the weakness of calling in a doctor who at once prescribed blue pill. He breaks out into not manly laments, makes faces like a naughty child, but he is so very gentil you know that. Flo is going with him to amuse him when she is better. Parthe is better."

Miss Nightingale could not escape. Parthe was better because her sister was at home. W. E. N. would only undergo his treatment if she were with him; her sense of obligation was enormous, and if the claims of family affection were strong the claims of suffering were stronger. She entered the cage, gave up all she had gained, and submitted once more.

"O weary days—oh evenings that seem never to end—for how many years have I watched that drawing-room clock and thought it never would reach the ten! and for twenty, thirty years more to do this!" she wrote in a private note of 1851. She was nearly thirty-two, no longer the eager, loving girl who had been so ready to reproach herself ten years ago, but fiercely rebellious. In a long private note headed " Butchered to make a Roman Holiday " she wrote a furious indictment of family life. " Women don't consider themselves as human beings at all. There is absolutely no God, no country, no duty to them at all, except family. . . . I have known a good deal of convents. And of course everyone has talked of the petty grinding tyrannies supposed to be exercised there. But I know nothing like the petty grinding tyranny of a good English family. And the only alleviation is that the tyrannised submits with a heart full of affection.

" I hold my tongue.

" Because I know it would be of no use to speak. A man ought to do it. Or a mother.

" A mother who were to say : Well I DON'T think there is NOTHING to do in the world for these four grown-up daughters except to attend on an old woman like me or to marry ; would be listened to. But—and very justly I think—a daughter would be suspected of personal rebellion. . . . What I complain of the Evangelical party for is the degree to which they have raised the claims upon women of ' Family '—the idol they have made of it. It is a kind of Fetichism. There is no duty, no right, no happiness for a woman beyond her Fetich. They acknowledge no God, for all they say to the contrary, but this Fetich. . . . It is only in the lives of the upper classes that you see this. And I think the ' upper classes ' far more ' bourgeois ' than the lower, and this is one reason. There is nothing bourgeois in one woman of a family earning the bread of the others in it and being sacrificed for it. But it is nothing but bourgeois the way in which women of the upper classes are sacrificed."

She was not only furious for herself : Hilary Bonham Carter was being sacrificed, betrayed by her unselfishness, gentleness and sweetness. " Oh Hilly," wrote Clarkey, " thou art like wool ; kind, warm, comfortable and lain on by everybody." In 1850 Hilary had spent almost a year in Paris living with Clarkey and working in a studio ; though her talents were pronounced remarkable she had never returned. She " could not be spared ", her mother " could not be left alone ", she was " needed at home ". Clarkey wrote her letter after letter on a rising note of irritation. " Will you come now ", she wrote in February 1852, " or not at all . . . don't undertake small things in England . . . have character and sense enough to make sacrifice of small things to a large one. . . . You will answer, I must teach drawing to Gertrude whose governess has a cold and I must pack up so and so's trunk and I must go and see Laura whose children have the measles and help nurse them. Poor thing! She is the most fortunate of wives and mothers, she has plenty of money, very good health and can afford servants in abundance, poor dear, how can I neglect my brother's wife so shamefully. Thus and thus life slips through your fingers. . . ."

The uselessness of the sacrifice drove Miss Nightingale frantic. A career was wrecked, talents wasted—for the sake of what? To maintain a life which Clarkey called " one long faddle ".

In 1852, under the title *Cassandra*, Miss Nightingale wrote a description of the life of a girl in a prosperous comfortable home. Cassandra is herself, Cassandra's family the Nightingales. On May 7th, 1861, in a letter to Clarkey, she mentions " my MS. about the family ". *Cassandra* was not published, but a number of copies were printed privately. She takes Cassandra through a day. The morning is spent " sitting round a table in the drawing-room, looking at prints, doing worsted work and reading little books ". " Everybody reads aloud out of their own book or newspaper and every five minutes something is said. And what is it to be ' read aloud to ' ? The most miserable exercise of the human intellect. It is like lying on one's back with one's hands tied and having liquid poured down one's throat." The afternoon is passed " taking a little drive ". " We can never pursue any object for a single two hours for we can never command any solitude ; and in social and domestic life one is bound, under pain of being thought sulky to make a remark every two minutes. . . . One must keep oneself ever on the alert ' to say something '." When night comes, Cassandra declares, women " suffer—even physically . . . the accumulation of nervous energy, which has had nothing to do during the day, makes them feel every

94

night, when they go to bed, as if they were going mad; they are obliged to lie long in bed in the morning to let it evaporate and keep it down. . . . Some are only deterred from suicide because it is in the most distinct manner to say to God ' I will not do as Thou would'st have me'." The vacuity and boredom of this existence are sugared over by false sentiment. " Women go about maudling to each other and preaching to their daughters that ' women have no passions ' . . . if the young girls of the ' higher classes ' who never commit a false step, whose justly earned reputations were never sullied even by the stain which the fruit of the mere ' knowledge of good and evil ' leaves behind, were to speak and say what are their thoughts employed on, their *thoughts* which alone are free, what would they say? . . . They seek a companion for their every thought . . . they see themselves engaged with him in stirring events . . . fancy compensates itself by endless interviews and sympathies . . . and you say ' She is not susceptible, women have no passion '."

Cassandra describes how girls " dream ". " Is not one fancying herself the nurse of some new friend in sickness, another engaging in romantic dangers with him . . . another undergoing unheard of trials under the observation of one whom she has chosen as the companion of her dream? " One of the most painful incidents of Cassandra's life is an episode which reproduces Miss Nightingale's meeting with Richard Monckton Milnes at Lady Palmerston's. " How cruel are the revulsions which high minded women suffer! There was one who loved in connexion with great deeds, noble thoughts, devoted feelings. They met after an interval. It was at one of those crowded parties of Civilization which we call Society. His only careless passing remark was ' The buzz to-night is like a manufactory '. Yet he loved her."

Finally, Cassandra, " who can neither find happiness in life nor alter it, dies ", slain by her family. " My people were like children, playing on the shore of the eighteenth century. I was their hobby horse, their plaything; and they drove me to and fro, dear souls! never weary of the play themselves, till I, who had grown to woman's estate and to the ideas of the nineteenth century lay down exhausted, my mind closed to hope, my heart to strength, ' Free—free—

oh ! divine freedom, art thou come at last ?   Welcome beautiful death !' "

Miss Nightingale never suffered more acutely than at the period when she wrote *Cassandra*, but the change which had begun before she went to Kaiserswerth was now complete. Her suffering was no longer despair, it was rebellion.   In herself she was free.

Though once more the months ground slowly by, though it was six months, seven months, eight months, nearly a year since she had come back from Kaiserswerth, and nothing had been accomplished, the interminable years of inward struggle were over.   " Dreaming " tortured her no longer.   " I have come into possession of myself ", she wrote in a private note of 1852. On her thirty-second birthday she wrote to W. E. N. : " I am glad to think that my youth is past and it never never can return—that time of disappointed inexperience when a man possesses nothing, not even himself ".   She possessed herself now and she was at peace.   Fanny and Parthe frantically prolonged the struggle for another year, but victory had in fact been won when she went to Kaiserswerth.

W. E. N. became uneasy, for it was borne in on him that his wife and daughter were treating Florence badly.   While Fanny and Parthe were at Carlsbad Hilary Bonham Carter had stayed with him, and he had written Florence long, half-humorous, half-melancholy letters, more confidential than any he had written to her for years.   He had even gone so far, in the summer of 1851, as to enquire from the physician of a Brighton hospital whether it was conceivably possible that a young gentlewoman could become a hospital nurse, and had received an answer decidedly in the negative.   In the early spring of the following year Florence went with him to Umberslade for his eye treatment.   When they returned he was secretly her ally ; she had always been his favourite, and he was a lonely man.   Thirty-three years of marriage had accentuated the differences between Fanny and himself. " Seest thou thy father and mother ", wrote Miss Nightingale in a private note.   " They have lived together more than all thy life and they understand each other not a bit more than they did the first day they came together.   The planes of their orbits never cross."

Disappointment made Fanny more extravagant, more unreasonable, more voluble, and W. E. N. withdrew. He was called to Lea Hurst " on business ", he went to London at odd times for " meetings ", he went down to Embley about "tenants ". During the summer of 1852 he indicated that as Fanny required all letters to be handed round it might " avoid enquiry " if Florence wrote to him at the Athenaeum instead of at home.

March of this year brought the Nightingales to London for the season once more, and the restrictions imposed on Miss Nightingale reached absurdity. She was treated as a schoolgirl, her movements controlled, her letters read, her invitations supervised ; yet she was a woman of over thirty with a distinguished circle of her own. Among her friends in 1852 were Elizabeth Barrett Browning, George Eliot, Lord Shaftesbury, Lord Palmerston, Arthur Stanley, later Dean Stanley, and his sister Mary Stanley, who was her slavish admirer. She did social work, continued her teaching in the Ragged School, and a year earlier had inspired a passionate admiration in the poet Arthur Hugh Clough.

She was held prisoner by her belief in Parthe, by her affection for W. E. N., by her sense of duty. To please her family she gave up her plan of training in a large London hospital, but she would not renounce nursing. Where was there an outlet for her, where in all England was there an opportunity for a woman of her class with her vocation ?

In the summer of 1852 it seemed as if she might find what she sought in the Roman Catholic Church. At this time Manning was a priest of the Roman Church remarkable for his devoted work in the poorest districts of the East End and for his conversions of members of the English nobility and gentry to Rome. In the course of a charitable investigation Miss Nightingale came on a child of fourteen who was being forced into prostitution, tried to rescue the girl, but found no organisation in the Church of England would receive her. The child was Irish and, as far as she had any religion, Catholic. Miss Nightingale applied to Manning, who acted instantly, taking the child under his protection and placing her in the Convent of the Good Shepherd.

She was deeply impressed, and a friendship sprang up which

produced a vast correspondence. She confided her family difficulties to Manning, he consoled and advised her, " writing endlessly ". She avowed freely that she had " Catholic yearnings ", she signed her letters " your weary penitent ". She was fascinated by the organisation of the Church of Rome. She recalled the outstanding capabilities of Madre Santa Colomba and the excellence of the school at Trinità de' Monti. In the Roman Church her talents could be admirably employed.

In the autumn of 1852 Dr. Stanley, alarmed at the prospect of his sister's conversion to Catholicism, wrote asking Miss Nightingale to use her influence to persuade Mary to remain in the Church of England. In reply she summarised her experience of the Anglican Church. " The church of England has for men bishoprics, archbishoprics, and a little work. . . . For women she has—what ? I had no taste for theological discoveries. I would have given her my head, my hand, my heart. She would not have them. She did not know what to do with them. She told me to go back and do crochet in my mother's drawing-room ; or, if I were tired of that, to marry and look well at the head of my husband's table. You may go to the Sunday School if you like it, she said. But she gave me no training even for that. She gave me neither work to do for her, nor education for it." To Manning Miss Nightingale wrote : " If you knew what a home the Catholic Church would be to me ! All that I want I should find in her. All my difficulties would be removed. I have laboriously to pick up, here and there, crumbs by which to live. She would give me daily bread. The daughters of St. Vincent would open their arms to me. They have already done so, and what should I find there. My work already laid out for me instead of seeking it to and fro and finding none ; my home, sympathy, human and divine." Again she wrote : " . . . You do know now, with all its faults, what a Home the Catholic Church is. And yet what is she to you, compared to what she would be to me ? No one can tell, no man can tell what she is to women. . . . What training is there (in the Church of England) compared to that of the Catholic nun ? There is nothing like the training which the Sacred Heart or Order of St. Vincent gives to women." Finally she asked : " Why cannot I enter the Catholic Church at once, as the best form of truth I have ever known, and as cutting the Gordian knot I cannot untie ? "

But though she seemed on the brink of conversion to Catholicism she was engaged on a line of thought totally at variance with Catholic teaching. During the summer of 1852 she embarked on an enquiry into the cause of the decline of religious faith among the working class. She had contrived to acquire friends outside her world who held advanced and even revolutionary views. Through her work in the Holloway she had " some acquaintance with the operatives in the North of England among those of what we called 'Holyoake's party'." Jacob Holyoake was an Owenite Socialist and freethinker. In London during 1852 a mysterious " West End lady " called repeatedly at Edward Truelove's bookshop—he was a publisher of freethinking literature, and his shop was described as a fortress of prohibited thought—and held long conversations on the type of book read by intelligent working men. The "West End lady " was Miss Nightingale, and her friendship with the Trueloves, in spite of Edward Truelove's subsequent prosecution, lasted for more than twenty years.

Manning asked her opinion of " the attitude of working men towards the Christian faith ", and she told him, " the most thinking and conscientious of the artizans have no religion at all " ; in the great manufacturing towns the intelligent working men had " almost entirely gone over to Atheism " and would not open a book with a word about religion in it " unless it were *against* the Bible ".

During the summer of this year she began an attempt to formulate " a new religion for the Artizans of England ", aiming at demonstrating that free thought is not incompatible with belief in God. She had learned from conversations with working men that when speaking of religion the name of " God " must be avoided " or no one would listen ". She described God as the Absolute, the Perfect, the Spirit of Truth, and re-stated the case for the existence of a divine Providence in the scientific and philosophical terms popular in the mid-nineteenth century. The moral world, she contended, was ruled by laws as fixed in their operation as those which science had recently discovered ruled the physical world. She did not touch on the Christian doctrines of salvation, redemption and the incarnation of Christ. She was not drawn to the figure of Jesus. Her God was God the Father, not God the Son. Aunt Mai worked with her on the manuscript, and extracts were sent to intimate friends and read aloud to " intelligent artizans ".

When Manning read her manuscript he decided that she was not in the requisite state of mind for admission into the Church of Rome. She craved an opportunity to exercise her powers, but she was very far from submission; indeed, she had no conception of submission in the Catholic sense—it was an idea utterly foreign to her. Submission to her meant endurance, not yielding. In the essence of her character she was a chooser, a heretic, and he refused to accept her as a convert.

Nevertheless, he continued to be her friend, and his friendship proved of enormous importance. In spite of the fact that she was a Protestant he arranged for her to enter a Catholic hospital where the nurses were nuns, and therefore " moral danger " did not exist. In the summer of 1852 he told her she could be received either by the Sisters of Mercy in Dublin or by the Sisters of Charity in the rue Oudinot, Paris. She wished to do both, to go first for a short time to Dublin, later for a longer time to Paris.

Once again there was a storm. Fanny and Parthe had hysterics. All the old arguments and reproaches were revived, Parthe's health, Florence's heartlessness, Parthe's devotion, Florence's ingratitude. Once more she was forced to abandon her plans.

Her friends became alarmed. Fanny's treatment of her younger daughter was beginning to look like mania. Was Florence's life to be ruined, her remarkable talents wasted because Fanny had an obsession? Aunt Mai and Mrs. Bracebridge thought it their duty to interfere, interviewing Fanny separately and together. Fanny, with her world against her, bombarded with what the Herberts thought, the Bunsens thought, the Shaftesburys thought, took refuge in a new policy. She vacillated, she " could not make up her mind to a definite step ". She would discuss the question of Florence's future, agree to a plan, and next day behave as if she had never heard

of any such suggestion in her life before. Still Aunt Mai
persevered, and Fanny was induced to admit that Florence
could not be asked to stay at home for ever : at some future
date she should be free—perhaps in four years. Aunt Mai set to
work to build on this. In July 1852, after Florence had
been back from Kaiserswerth for ten months, Aunt Mai wrote
suggesting a method of coaxing Fanny. " After 10 months of
wearisome frittering could you not say to your people ' In 4
years (was it not so ?) you think I ought to be free to follow
what course I myself think right, but I shall then be unpre-
pared. . . . I wish therefore to visit Institutes where I may
learn. I must go to Dublin in October, and at a future time to
Paris. . . . On the question of home I will do all I can. . . . It
is an impossibility for me to give my heart always to the mode
of employment I have at home. . . . For love of you all, I
would gladly give a portion of time, happy in the thought that
I pleased and satisfied you.' . . . I really do not see that your
people *could* refuse this."

Fanny did refuse and flatly denied she had ever mentioned
releasing Florence at any date. Mrs. Bracebridge and Aunt
Mai saw her again, and Aunt Mai wrote : " Your mother has
in the most express manner said she thought you might at that
future unspecified age be left uninterfered with. She desired
me to write so to Mrs. Bracebridge. Mrs. B. asked me whether
I could get a written agreement from your mother for this. I
did not attempt it. I thought having—from her—written
this to Mrs. B. would answer the purpose better. To Mrs. B.
I could always refer. Your poor mother, even if she forgot it,
could not deny this evidence."

Fanny still clung desperately to the hope that Florence
would marry, shutting her eyes to the fact that her daughter
was thirty-two and had refused all her admirers. In August
1852 Aunt Mai wrote : " I believe in all conscience she would
be most willing that you undertook a mission like Mrs. Fry or
Mrs. Chisholm, but she thinks it necessary for your peace and
well being that there should be a Mr. Fry or Captain Chisholm
to protect you and in conscience she thinks it right to defend
you from doing anything which she *thinks* would be an impediment to the existence of Mr. F. or Captain C."

During the summer of that year Miss Nightingale wrote an

imaginary speech to her mother. She wrote gaily, she was not suffering as she had suffered in the past. "Well, my dear, you don't imagine that with my 'talents', and my 'European reputation', and my 'beautiful letters', and all that, I'm going to stay dangling about my mother's drawing-room all my life! . . . You must look at me as your vagabond son. . . . I shan't cost you nearly as much as a son would have done. I haven't cost you much yet, except for my visits to Egypt and Rome. Remember, I should have cost you a great deal more if I had been married or a son. . . . Well, you must now consider me married or a son. You were willing enough to part with me to be married."

W. E. N. had become wretched. "Your poor father", wrote Aunt Mai in July, "talked to me in a way that made my heart bleed, as usual said your mother would only live in the drawing-room or the carriage—that she and Parthe so agreed on every subject that silence and solitude must be his lot, for even to enunciate anything seemed to unite them to oppose. . . . He expressed most strongly his feeling of your dependence . . . he had evidently been reflecting whether he could arrange so that you could take up any money you wanted, deducting same from his will." Aunt Mai had pointed out that this would be most unfair to Florence as "he had the considerable expense of maintaining your mother and Parthe which cost them nothing".

Parthe was growing steadily worse: in almost daily scenes she attacked Florence with violent reproaches. Florence refused to answer and Parthe drove herself into hysterical frenzies in which she screamed abuse at her sister until she collapsed. She declared she was dying—Florence's behaviour was killing her. She complained of suffering agonies from mysterious pains. She was taken to see the Queen's physician, Sir James Clark,[1] who was a personal friend of the Nightin-

[1] Sir James Clark has passed into history in connection with the case of Lady Flora Hastings, which temporarily destroyed the popularity of Queen Victoria in the second year of her reign. The growth of an abdominal tumour led to a rumour that Lady Flora, an unmarried woman, was pregnant. Sir James Clark, called in as physician in ordinary to the Court, gave a wrong diagnosis, a serious scandal resulted, and the Hastings family demanded an official medical examination with a second doctor in attendance. At this examination Sir James was alleged to have behaved with brutal rudeness; however, both doctors then signed a certificate completely clearing Lady Flora, who died shortly afterwards

gales, and he diagnosed "rheumatic headaches", adding that she was "nervous, fanciful and unstable", but that he could find "no physical disease". She did not improve, and in August 1852 he arranged to have her for some weeks under observation at his house in Scotland, Birk Hall, near Ballater.

Miss Nightingale gained a temporary release and managed to get "permission for absence" from Fanny to go with Dr. and Mrs. Fowler, who in 1845 had been concerned in her attempt to enter Salisbury Infirmary, to the meeting of the British Association in Belfast. From Belfast the party was going on to Dublin, where she intended to use Manning's introduction and enter the hospital of the Sisters of Mercy.

But she was disappointed. "The hospital has got a whole holiday and is being repaired so there's nothing to be seen", wrote Hilary Bonham Carter to Clarkey. "As she thus loses Dublin, Clarkey dear, she will certainly have leave to come to you. I should not wonder—as they had given her permission for absence now at this time—that if really you still hold out the Hand of Helpfulness and the Roof of Shelter she might come to you in the autumn." Nevertheless, while Miss Nightingale was in Dublin in August 1852 she had, in some hospital, an experience of great importance. She speaks in a "Memorandum of 1852" of a "terrible lesson learned in Dublin", and her inclination towards Roman Catholicism vanished.

She was called from Dublin by Sir James Clark. Parthe had had a mental breakdown. There were "delusions", "some degree of chronic delirium" and "extreme irritability". Sir James, a friend of the Bunsens and the Herberts, admired Miss Nightingale, and he told her that she must separate herself from her sister. Parthe's only chance of regaining normal health and balance was to learn to live without her; for Parthe's sake she must, at any rate for a time, leave home.

Ten years later Miss Nightingale wrote: "A very successful and justly successful physician once seriously told a sister who

in July 1839, the course of her disease having been hastened by her mental sufferings. Her family, infuriated, demanded Sir James Clark's dismissal; Queen Victoria refused, and public opinion turned violently against her. In fact, Sir James Clark deserves to be remembered as one of the earliest and most important supporters of Miss Nightingale and as a benefactor to the British Army.

was being Devoured that she must leave home in order that the Devourer might recover health and balance which had been lost in the process of devouring. This person was myself." In a private note she described Sir James Clark's talk to her as " a terrible lesson which tore open my eyes as nothing less could have done. My life has been decided thereby."

On September 20th Sir James wrote W. E. N. a letter of grave warning. Parthe showed "alarming indications" of " extreme irritability, total absorption in self, some degree of chronic delirium " which might end, "I state this as a possible thing not a *probable* thing ", in " aberration of mind . . . nervous feelings have been, I venture to say, fostered by over-indulgence ". He prescribed " more exercise out of doors, less lying in bed and more care for the welfare of her fellow creatures ". He recommended that Parthe should be separated from her family and placed in the care of " some judicious kind relative in the family connection with whom she could reside for some time ".

Fanny's reply was to declare that Sir James was making a fuss about nothing. On October 12th Hilary Bonham Carter wrote to Clarkey from Embley: " Aunt Fanny does not like Parthe's illness made much of. She says ' One need not talk much about a little bilious attack '." None of Sir James's recommendations were followed, and Hilary wrote that Embley was filled with " an immense amount of company ! "

After Miss Nightingale had brought Parthe back from Scotland, she stayed only a few days at Embley, then went to Umberslade with W. E. N. while he took a further course of eye treatment. Afterwards instead of going back to Embley, she went to stay first with Aunt Mai and then with the Herberts. The burden of her responsibility for Parthe had been removed, the last chain which held her had been broken, and she began quietly to separate herself from home. She was making plans to go to Paris, and by the end of October she had obtained, once more through Manning's help, an authorisation from the Council of the Sisters of Charity in Paris allowing her to work in their hospitals and institutions.

She did not wish to go to Paris without Fanny's consent. There was a financial difficulty, W. E. N. was nervous, and she shrank from a quarrel; Fanny must be brought round.

Clarkey was called in to try her hand at persuasion. She did not sympathise with Miss Nightingale's "craving after sisters of charity and hospitals", but it was her philosophy that "everyone should do as they please and be agreeable about it". " I think Flo has as good a right to do foolish things as anyone else ", she wrote to Hilary Bonham Carter in July 1852. " Flo should be perfectly free to do her own foolishness, or her own wickedness, if she likes," she repeated in August, "it is only by knocking their heads that brats learn not to knock them . . . you know my passion for freedom." She wrote off a letter full of confidence, but in a short time she was complaining that Fanny was " so very inexplicit, says not a word in answer to mine, in fact don't seem to have read it . . . talks about politics and Lord Palmerston ". Clarkey wrote again, but Fanny did not answer ; she wrote a third and fourth time, and still there was " no word from Mrs. N." After three months Clarkey had come to the conclusion she had better not interfere. " I think I had better not meddle in the family," Clarkey wrote to Hilary on January 9th, 1853, "as making a coolness between the Mama and me would do no good to Flo and vex me much . . . tell me what I can do to make it up with Aunt F."

Though Fanny fought obstinately she could not continue to fight. Once more the opinion of her world was against her, once more she was persuaded, implored, advised by the Herberts, the Bunsens, by the Bracebridges, by Aunt Mai. She retreated, contesting every inch of the way. How, for instance, was Florence to travel to Paris ? She refused to allow Florence to be accompanied only by her maid. "We are looking about for some good person for her to go with," wrote Hilary to Clarkey from Embley on October 12th, 1852, "and the opportunity once found will be one step towards bringing the matter to a decision. There will be no good in plotting escapes. We *must* find a proper opportunity—one that will satisfy—aye and please the Aunt Fanny. Do you know when Lady Augusta Bruce will return to Paris ? " It turned out that Lady Augusta Bruce was going to Paris in the second week of November and would be delighted to have Miss Florence Nightingale as a travelling companion.

Manning wrote to his friend the Abbé des Genettes in Paris

announcing her arrival; Miss Nightingale, who was in London staying with the Herberts, began to pack her trunks.

At this stage Fanny suddenly spoke as if the visit to Paris was an entirely new idea. " Flo is thinking of some new expedition perhaps to Paris ", she wrote to Aunt Mai. " I cannot make up my mind to it." One evening W. E. N. unexpectedly appeared in the Herberts' drawing-room. He was distraught, saying that life at Embley was unendurable. Parthe was ill and in hysterics and Fanny at her wits' end. A large party of visitors was expected—how could Fanny manage all alone? Florence must leave London and come home.

Before Miss Nightingale could make a decision Great Aunt Evans was taken ill. The journey to Paris was cancelled and she went to Cromford Bridge House to nurse Great Aunt Evans through her last illness. From Cromford Bridge she went to Tapton to break the news to W. E. N.'s mother, who was aged ninety-five and extremely deaf: her chief pleasure was to have the psalms " howled at her every morning to the edification of Thomas in the kitchen ". On New Year's Eve Miss Nightingale was back at Embley writing her " Memorandum for 1852 ". " I am so glad this year is over; nevertheless it has not been wasted I trust. . . . I have re-modelled my whole religious belief. . . . I have re-cast my social belief. . . . I have learnt to know Manning. . . . Have been disappointed in my Dublin Hospital plan. Formed my Paris one. . . . Lastly all my admirers are married . . . and I stand with all the world before me. . . . It has been a baptism of fire this year."

She determined to go to Paris in February, when Hilary Bonham Carter was returning to Clarkey at last. But Fanny and Parthe were not yet defeated; Fanny discovered she could not bear the idea that Florence was going abroad, and suggested a new scheme. Florence had once said she wanted to found a sisterhood. Very well, let her found a sisterhood now, in Aunt Evans's empty house at Cromford Bridge. Everything should be provided—money, furniture, equipment. She declined. Parthe then suggested Forest Lodge, a vacant house on the Embley estate, which Miss Nightingale described as the only place on earth more unsuitable for the purpose than Cromford Bridge House. She declined again.

She had now been at home for some weeks and Fanny must have seen for herself how her presence exasperated Parthe. She gave way—partially. Florence might go to Paris for a short time on a visit to Clarkey, but the horrid name of the Sisters of Charity was not to be mentioned. Fanny spoke of dressmakers and wrote to Hilary enjoining her to make sure that while Florence was in Paris she bought clothes for the coming season. Parthe was furious, possessiveness and jealousy consuming her with a twin flame. On January 29th, 1853, she wrote angrily to Clarkey: " Truth is a good thing and the history of the last year (the others much like it) is one month with the Fowlers in Ireland, three . . . in London, three . . . at Harrogate and Cromford Bridge, three at the water cure and Grandmamma's . . . so that I hope she has passed a very pleasant year, but meantime these eternal poor have been left to the mercies of Mamma and me, both very unwell and whose talkey talkey broth and pudding she holds in very great contempt. . . . I believe she has little or none of what is called charity or philanthropy, she is ambitious— very and would like well enough to regenerate the world with a grand coup de main or some fine institution, which is a very different thing. Here she has a circle of admirers who cry up everything she does or says as gospel and I think it will do her much good to be with you, who, though you love and admire her, do not believe in the wisdom of all she says because SHE says it. I wish she could be brought to see it is the intellectual part which interests her, not the manual. She has no esprit de conduite in the practical sense. When she nursed me everything which intellect and kind intention could do was done but she was a shocking nurse. Whereas her influence on people's minds and her curiosity in getting into varieties of minds is insatiable. After she has got inside they generally cease to have any interest for her."

Yes, there was, in spite of the gentleness, the sympathy, the charming intelligence, something about Florence which chilled. Impossible to move her, or to influence her by a personal appeal. She did not know what personal feelings were, in a private note she wrote that never in her life did she recollect being swayed by a personal consideration. She lived on a different plane, out of reach, frighteningly, but also infuriatingly, remote.

On February 4th Miss Nightingale arrived at 120 rue du Bac. She was like a child out of school. Anna von Mohl, a young niece of M. Mohl, described her as being " so thankful to drop being ladylike ". She would not take cabs but went everywhere in omnibuses. Anna, fascinated, wrote she was " on the point of falling in love with Florence ". Her plan was to stay for a month with Clarkey and make a survey of all the hospitals in Paris. M. Mohl had procured a permit from the Administration Générale de l'Assistance Publique which gave her the right to enter any hospital. She then intended, thanks to Manning, to enter the Maison de la Providence, the hospital of the Sisters of Charity in the rue Oudinot, as a postulante to undergo a training in nursing. She was to wear the convent dress, " the dress of a nun ", and " render all necessary service to the sick " under the direction of the sisters, but she was to eat and sleep in a separate cell and not enter the dormitories or the refectory of the sisters.

She spent a month visiting hospitals, infirmaries, almshouses and institutions, watching doctors examine patients and witnessing operations. She made elaborate tabulations in which she compared the organisation and accommodation of different hospitals; she drew up a detailed questionnaire which she circulated to hospitals in France, Germany and England; she accumulated an enormous collection of reports, returns and statistics illustrating hospital organisation and nursing arrangements in hospitals throughout Europe. To assemble, collate and digest this mass of information in a single month was a remarkable feat. Her long hours of toil in the chilly dawn bore fruit—already she was not a student but an expert. Eight years had been spent in keeping her away from hospitals but she was as much at home in them as if she had lived in hospitals all her life.

She also enjoyed herself. She went to a number of receptions and dinners and several times to the opera. Besides holding her celebrated evening every Friday, Clarkey twice gave " a little dancing " in her honour.

The day of her entry into the Maison de la Providence approached and final arrangements were made. She presented herself to the Reverend Mother, was approved, and an hour was fixed for her admission. She had almost come to her last day in the rue du Bac—when Fate struck again. Her grandmother, to whom she had howled the psalms, was taken ill, and she was recalled to England. Once more the arrangements with the Sisters of Charity were cancelled, and she hurried to Tapton, arriving in time to nurse her grandmother through her last days. " I can never be thankful enough that I came ", she wrote to Hilary Bonham Carter on March 26th. " I was able to make her be moved and changed and to do other little things which perhaps soothed the awful passage and which perhaps would not have been done as well without me."

At Tapton she was joined by Aunt Mai. A family difficulty had arisen on account of Arthur Hugh Clough. Miss Nightingale had introduced Clough to Aunt Mai's daughter, Blanche, and they had fallen in love and were determined to marry. Blanche's family disapproved. Arthur Clough, though one of the finest minds of his day and a poet of distinction, was almost penniless and held religious views which had earned him notoriety. After a brilliant career at Oxford he had been elected a fellow of Oriel, the highest academic distinction Oxford at that time had to offer, but had resigned because he could no longer conscientiously teach the doctrines of the Church of England. He was then appointed Head of University Hall in London and held this post when he first met Miss Nightingale in 1851, but this appointment, too, his religious scruples had forced him to resign. His poetry did not bring him in an income, and he was looking for a post which would enable him to support a wife. Miss Nightingale was greatly attached to Clough, and in the evenings at Tapton she worked out detailed budgets showing what Clough and Blanche absolutely required to live on, including a scale of provision for children, basing her calculations on the frequency at which they would be likely to arrive at the average birth-rate, and with the aid of these figures succeeded in persuading Aunt Mai to approve the engagement.

After Tapton she did not go to Embley, where Fanny and Parthe were in the midst of packing to go to London for the season, but to Lea Hurst. She intended the separation from her family to be final, and before she went to Paris she had decided to take a post when her training was completed; her friends were in her confidence, and were looking for work which would suit her. Early in April 1853 Liz Herbert wrote that through Lady Canning she had heard of what might prove a suitable opening. The Institution for the care of Sick Gentlewomen in Distressed Circumstances, described by Miss Nightingale as " a Sanitarium for Sick Governesses run by a Committee of Fine Ladies ", had got itself into difficulties. It was to be reorganised and moved from its premises in Chandos Street. The committee, of which Lady Canning was chairman, were looking for a Superintendent to undertake the reorganisation. Liz Herbert suggested Florence, and Lady Canning, after consulting her committee, wrote describing the post and its requirements. On April 8th Miss Nightingale wrote to Clarkey: ". . . It is no use my telling you the history of the negotiations which are enough to make a comedy in 50 acts. . . . My people are now at 30 Old Burlington Street, where I shall be in another week. Please write to them there, and if you can do a little quacking for me to them, the same will be thankfully received, in order that I may come in, when I arrive, not with my tail between my legs but gracefully curved round me, in the old way which Perugino's devil wears it, in folds round the waist. I am afraid I *must* live at the place. If I don't, it will be a half and half measure which will satisfy no one. . . . I can give you no particulars, dearest friend, because I don't know any. I can only say that, unless I am left a free agent and am to organise the thing myself, and not they, I will have nothing to do with it. . . . But there are no Surgeon Students or Improper Patients there at all, which is, of course, a great recommendation in the eyes of the Proper. I am to have the choosing of the house, the appointment of the Chaplain and the management of the funds . . . *at present*. But Isaiah himself could not prophesy how they will be minded at 8 o'clock this evening."

Clarkey advised her to be sure to " trample on the Committee and ride the Fashionable Asses rough shod round Grosvenor Square ".

On April 18th there was an interview, and Lady Canning wrote the same day to Mrs. Herbert: " I write a line in great haste to say that I was delighted with Miss N's quiet sensible manner. In one short acquaintance I am sure she must be a most remarkable person. It is true that Miss Nightingale looks very young but that need not matter and I hope the old matron or housekeeper will in point of outward appearance supply the young Miss N's deficiencies in years." Miss Nightingale had suggested she should bring, as her personal attendant, a "superior elderly respectable person" at her own expense.

When the news was broken to Fanny and Parthe sickeningly familiar scenes took place. Parthe wept, raged, worked herself into frenzy, collapsed and had to be put to bed. Fanny stormed, lamented and had to be given sal volatile. Meals were sent away untouched. Ordinary life was at an end. W. E. N. took refuge in the Athenaeum. Among the Verney Nightingale papers are two sheets of Athenaeum notepaper scribbled back and front in W. E. N.'s strange difficult hand—he always used a quill and abhorred "great Iron Spikes":

Memorandum April 20th

I have this day reached the conclusion that Parthe can no more control or moderate the intensity of her interest in Flo's doings than she can change her physical form, and that her life will be sacrificed to the activity of her thoughts, unless she removes herself from the scene immediately—the only question being where to go.

The above conclusion is arrived at quite as much by observing the *manner* in which she furthers Flo's plans, as that in which she objects to them.

Having come to the resolution that it is entirely beyond your mental strength to give up interference in your sister's affairs and being equally sure that your health cannot stand the strain we advise you to retire from London and take to your books and country occupations till her proceedings are settled.

23rd April

I doubt my own thoughts.

24th April

Retirement might do more harm than good—what then? Having made up our minds that your future existence depends upon your surrender of all interference (even mental) so far as regards your sister's plans and proceedings, we propose to you a retirement from London till the decision has taken place.

Reconsidered.

Matters might be worse if I were alone in mediation—Query then, is the case hopeless?

He did nothing. Parthe was not sent to the country but remained in London, passing from fit to fit of hysterics, while Miss Nightingale conducted her negotiations with the committee. W. E. N. did, however, take one vital step—he decided to allow Miss Nightingale £500 a year. Fanny was extremely angry and insisted that since Florence was independent she should pay her share of the bill at the Burlington. She paid and subsequently discovered that Fanny had charged her more than her fair share.

Negotiations with the committee, " those Fashionable Asses with their ' offs ' and ' ons ' poor fools ! " were trying. Their hesitations centred upon her social position. She was a young lady in society—was it not peculiar for a young lady to wish for such a post ; could a lady take orders, even from a committee of other ladies ; should a lady, even in these days of strange mingling of ranks, nurse one who was not a lady ; was it nice for a lady to be present at medical examinations and, worse still, at operations?

The deciding factor in the situation was a family quarrel. The Nicholsons disapproved of Florence. Resentment between Waverley and Embley, in spite of the reconciliation of two years ago, still simmered. "Very unkind things" were said of Florence. She was said to be " going into service ", her conduct " could not be looked on in a charitable light ". It happened that one of the committee knew Marianne, and this lady, referred to as " The Committee Lady ", asked Marianne if Miss Nightingale's parents approved the step she proposed to take. Marianne drew a dramatic picture of Florence in opposition to her family : Parthe prostrated, Fanny in tears. The " Committee Lady ", horrified, rushed to other members and in " a great scrimmage " it was decided to have nothing more to do with Miss Nightingale. A letter was written on behalf of the committee informing her that as she had not her parents' sanction negotiations must be broken off.

Marianne did not stop there. Hastening back from her interview with the " Committee Lady ", she had fresh gossip, which was eagerly broadcast. Florence had not been asked to accept the post at all. She had offered her services, and, when they were refused, had pressed them on the committee. Miss Nightingale settled the committee by writing a letter which was sent by W. E. N. informing them that she had his official sanction. She ignored the gossip.

However, Fanny and Parthe completely changed front. Though they might disapprove they were not going to have Florence attacked by Marianne, and Parthe rushed to her defence. Her tongue was sharp and she said unpleasant things about Marianne. Some of them were repeated to her brother Lothian Nicholson, who promptly lost his temper. He wrote angrily to Parthe and received an angry reply. Finally, he wrote to Miss Nightingale setting forth that a lady had been " deputed " by the committee to ask Marianne about the attitude of Miss Nightingale's family; he suggested with some justice that Fanny and Parthe had provoked gossip about her by their own conduct, but because poor Marianne had the reputation of talking, everything was laid at *her* door; finally, he was unable to resist a dig at the broken friendship with Marianne—" if the deputed lady had known our families better she would have known M. N. [Marianne] was the *last* person to be conversant with the facts ".

Miss Nightingale replied with a masterpiece of tact. " Dear friend ", she began, and apologised for an " overwhelming quantity of work " which prevented her from replying sooner. She praised Lothian's attachment to his sister, he was quite right to defend her; but she preferred " not to go into the matter with him. I hope you will come and see me ' in service ' when you have a day to spare in London. Finally, dear Lothian, one word, our old—and I hope real—friendship encourages me to say it. Do not engage in any paper wars. You will convince nobody and arrive at no satisfaction yourself." They remained friends, and fifteen years later were still meeting.

Despite everything, by the end of April she had successfully completed her negotiations. She was to receive no remuneration and she was to bear all the expenses of the Matron she brought with her to compensate for her youthful appearance, but she was to be in complete control not only of the management of the Institution but of its finances. Her duties were to begin as soon as new premises could be found. In the interval she proposed to go back to Paris and at last accomplish her training with the Sisters of Charity.

There was an explosion from Fanny and Parthe. What, when Florence was preparing to leave home, would she not devote the few weeks that were left to her mother and sister? She would not. They were forced to give way, but they refused to be resigned. Every trifling event brought a reminder of her departure and provoked an outburst of grief. In a memorandum of April 25th W. E. N. wrote, with a gloomy extravagance of emotion remarkable even for the Nightingales: " To linger here during the awful interval between the resolving and the acting the mighty deed is slow torture . . . to see before her a severance from everyday life, from relations which are becoming painful or fictitious and to have the expectancy lasting over hours and weeks is perhaps beyond endurance. To go there is to begin at once the deed, the first act in the great Tragedy. To stay here is a strain on all the forces which the mind possesses, to go there is to let loose the energies of body and soul (for good or ill), right or wrong, as may be the futurity . . . to go or not to go is no question with her I imagine—*how* to go with least disruption or disturbance her only thought. Emancipation her only vision . . . Away, away her only motto. . . . I am off to my own home thanks that I am there at rest is my motto."

Miss Nightingale went to Paris on May 30th, and on June 8th she entered the Maison de la Providence, letting neither her family nor her committee know she was entering a convent. As both strongly disapproved of Roman Catholics she thought it better not to " proclaim her intention ". On June 5th she wrote to Lady Canning: " I am afraid my committee will greatly disapprove of my being in Paris in the enemy's camp. . . . With the fear that they would not be as grateful to me as they ought I did not proclaim my intention of going to Paris."

For the third time she attempted to train at the Maison de la Providence, and for the third time she was defeated, for after a fortnight in the convent she developed measles, " une rougeole intense ". "And, of all my adventures of which I have had many and queer, as will be (never) recorded in the Book of my Wanderings, the dirtiest and queerest I have ever had has been a measles in the cell of a Sœur de la Charité ", she wrote to Clarkey on June 28th. " It is like the Mariage de Mademoiselle ; who could have foreseen it ? . . . It's evident that Providence, who was always in my way, and who, as the Supérieure said is *très admirable* (meaning wonderful) in having done this, does not mean me to come to Paris nor to the Sœurs. . . . For me to come to Paris, to have the measles a second time, is like going to the Grand Desert to die of getting one's feet wet. . . ."

Clarkey was in England, but as soon as Miss Nightingale was convalescent M. Mohl, "in his kind paternity ", brought her to the rue du Bac and put her to bed in the back drawing-room, the same room in which she had seen M. Mohl and Fauriel boil the kettle for tea on a January afternoon sixteen years ago. Her convalescence was spent in conversation with him. " Her gentle manner ", he wrote to W. E. N., " covers such a depth and strength of mind and thought." Before she came home she went to the dressmaker and was fitted for a " great panjandrum of black velvet ". On July 13th she reached London, but she would not join Fanny and Parthe. She took rooms in Pall Mall. She wanted a place of her own in which to meet her friends and spend her free Sundays, and it was as well that the patients of the Institution should not be " scandalised " by discovering that she did not go to church.

These rooms in Pall Mall caused fresh lamentations. Even Clarkey, who was staying at Embley, was moved to write to suggest that she might spend her free time at least with her family. " I have not taken this step Clarkey dear ", wrote Miss Nightingale in August 1853, " without years of anxious consideration. It is the result of the experience of years and of the fullest deepest thought ; it has not been done without advice, and it is a step which, being the growth of so long, is not likely to be repented of or reconsidered. I mean the step of leaving them. I do not wish to talk about it—and this is the last time I shall ever do so. . . . I *have* talked matters over (' made a clean breast ' as you express it) with Parthe, *not once but thousands of times*. Years and years have been spent in doing so. It has been, therefore, with the deepest consideration and with the fullest advice that I have taken the step of leaving home, and it is a fait accompli. . . . So farewell, Clarkey dear, don't let us talk any more about this. It is, as I said before a fait accompli."

From July 13th to August 12th she was in London with Aunt Mai supervising the alterations to the new premises chosen for the Institution. Fanny refused to give her blessing—" it would be useless upon what I consider as being an impossible undertaking ". On August 12th, 1853, she went into residence in the new premises, number 1 Harley Street.

VI "I AM LIVING in an ideal world of lifts, gas, baths and double and single wards ", wrote Miss Nightingale to Hilary Bonham Carter in the summer of 1853. She was moving in her natural element. From Paris, first from her cell at the Maison de la Providence, then from her convalescent couch at 120 rue du Bac, she had kept a firm hand on her committee, issuing precise instructions to them in long, enormously detailed letters.

Her requirements were not merely exacting, they were revolutionary. She had a scheme for saving work by having hot water " piped up to every floor ". She wanted a " windlass installation ", a lift to bring up the patients' food. On June 5th, 1853, she wrote to Lady Canning: " . . . The nurse should never be obliged to quit her floor, except for her own dinner and supper, and her patients' dinner and supper (and even the latter might be avoided by the windlass we have talked about). Without a system of this kind, the nurse is converted into a pair of legs. *Secondly*, that the bells of the patients should all ring in the passage outside the nurse's door *on that story* and should have a valve which flies open when its bell rings, and *remains* open in order that the nurse may see who has rung."

Her committee became dazed. Forced to answer the innumerable questions raised in her letters, sent out on expeditions to unknown parts of London to view " windlass installations ", and new systems of bells with valves, they had the sensation of having unknowingly released a genie from a bottle. They were, she said, " children in administration ". In fact, they had never been called on to administer anything before. The Institution had been managed by two committees, a Ladies' Committee and a Gentlemen's Committee. The Gentlemen had transacted all the business and paid the bills. Miss Nightingale returned from Paris to find nothing had been accomplished. On August 20th she wrote to Clarkey: " I have had to prepare this immense house for patients in ten days—without a bit of help but only hindrance from my committee. I have been 'in service' ten days and

117

have had to furnish an entirely empty house in that time. We take in patients this Monday and have not got our workmen out yet. From Committees, Charity and Schism, from the Church of England, from philanthropy and all deceits of the devil, Good Lord deliver us."

The accounts of the Institution were in confusion. "I am seriously uneasy about our funds ", she had written to Hilary Bonham Carter on July 24th. " . . . The Committee are wholly regardless of money. £1200 we had in the funds they have taken out for the alteration and furniture of this house, and spent every penny of it. I find we cannot possibly live in this house under £1600 a year. We have therefore £700 a year more to raise in subscriptions."

The administration of the Institution was also in confusion. The two committees quarrelled with each other and among themselves, the doctors did the same. "There is as much jealousy in the Committees of one another and among the medical men of one another as ever what's his name had of Marlborough ", she wrote to W. E. N. on December 3rd, 1853. "Lady Canning I continue to like exceedingly ", she told Hilary Bonham Carter. "But to say any of the others is a ' help to me ', is adding insult to injury as the parrot said."

During the first week of her appointment Miss Nightingale and her committee had a serious difference. She was determined the Institution should be non-sectarian, the committee was determined it should be Church of England. On August 20th she wrote to Clarkey : " My Committee refused me to take in *Catholic* patients, whereupon I wished them good morning, unless I might take in Jews and their Rabbis to attend them. So now it is settled, and *in print* that we are to take in all denominations whatever, and allow them to be visited by their respective priests and Muftis, provided *I* will receive (in any case *whatsoever* that is *not* of the Church of England) the obnoxious animal at the door, take him upstairs myself, remain while he is conferring with his patient, make myself *responsible* that he does not speak to, or look at, *anyone else*, and bring him downstairs again in a noose, and out into the street. And to this I have agreed ! And this is in print ! Amen."

She gained her point, but there was disapproval. Some members of the committee were shocked, and an opposition formed against her. Her friends, however, were powerful. Lady Canning, Lady Inglis, Lady Monteagle, Lady Cranworth took her part, and Liz Herbert joined the Ladies' Committee for the express purpose of supporting her. In October Liz wrote offering to come up from Wilton for a committee meeting: " I thought some wicked cats might be there who would set up their backs and if so I would like to set mine up too ".

Miss Nightingale was not what her committee had expected. Her genius was of an unromantic character. She perceived that unorganised devotion, unorganised self-sacrifice were useless. To bring about the installation of a row of bells " with valves that flew open " when the patient called was more effectual than to turn oneself into a devoted nurse, toiling endlessly up and down stairs because no such bells existed. To put in the best possible kitchen stove, to descend into the coal cellar and rake over the coal to ensure the coal merchant had not delivered an undue proportion of dust, to check stores and linen and provide patients with clean beds and good food were more effectual than to sit through the watches of the night cheering the dying moments of the patient expiring from scurvy and bed sores. But it was not so picturesque.

She gave devotion generously, and she did an immense amount of practical nursing in the Institution herself, but she was always aware that its success was impossible without a balanced expenditure and a proper system of keeping accounts.

She set herself to manage the committee. By December she had learned how to get her own way. " When I entered ' into service ' here ", she wrote to W. E. N., " I determined that, happen what would, I NEVER would intrigue among the Committee. Now I perceive that I do all my business by intrigue. I propose, in private, to A, B, or C, the resolution I think A, B, or C, most capable of carrying in Committee, and then leave it to them, and I always win. . . . Last General Committee I executed a series of Resolutions . . . and presented them as coming from the Medical Men . . . these I proposed and carried in Committee, without telling them that they came from *me*, and not from the Medical Men ; and, then, and not till then, I showed them to the Medical Men, without telling *them* that they were already passed in Committee. It was a bold stroke. . . . The Medical Men have had two meetings on them, and approved them all *nem. con.*, and thought they were their own ! "

With cautious diplomacy she proceeded to exercise financial control. She asked that the bills should be paid weekly instead of monthly. The Treasurer refused. She acquiesced, but pointed out that she was personally responsible for any deficiency, and could not undertake responsibility for the large sum that would accumulate if the bills were allowed to run for a month. The Gentlemen must therefore please sign a statement each week, which she would prepare and bring at any time convenient. The Treasurer had intended to save himself trouble by monthly payments, but she showed him he was mistaken. He gave way and the bills were paid weekly.

She went down into the kitchen and herself turned out cupboards and store-rooms, finding, she wrote to Clarkey in August 1853, that while there were no brooms, brushes or dusters, jam at 1s. a pot had been ordered in " £2 worth at a time ". She had 52 pots of jam made in the kitchen of the Institution at a cost of 3½d. a lb. The grocer's boy had been calling " two or three times a day and bringing everything by the ounce ". She gave out contracts to the best firms—one of her contracts was with Fortnum and Mason—and secured wholesale prices.

The bed linen and furniture of the Institution, she told Clarkey, were " dirty and neglected. Table linen and kitchen linen ragged and filthy. Everything except a few good sheets rat eaten. Chairs with covers, not washable, but put on with nails and soaked with dirt. Blankets and pillows rotted, by being used for certain cases without rubber protection. Saucepans deficient." As the committee had already spent more money than the Institution possessed she had to make the best of what was at her disposal. She enlisted Fanny's help and " had odd pieces of linen washed at home and patched together . . . pieced out carpets, contrived bed covers out of old curtains ".

The original staff from Chandos Street did not long survive. The housekeeper left after a single interview, the house surgeon resigned after a month. She secured a successor who " dispensed the medicines in the house, saving our bill at the druggist's of £150 per annum ".

She was in tremendous spirits. On October 20th she wrote Fanny a letter, which was bursting with gaiety, asking for a pair of comfortable old boots—she was spending all day and most of the night on her feet: "Oh my boots! My boots! dearer to me than the best French polished, my brother boots. Where are ye, my boots. I never shall see your pretty faces more. My dear I *must* have them boots. . . . More flowers, more game, more grapes."

Within six months opposition had collapsed. On December 3rd she wrote to W. E. N.: "I am now in the heyday of my power. . . . Lady —— who was my greatest enemy is now, I understand, trumpeting my fame through London. And all because I have reduced their expenditure from 1s. 10d. per head per day to 1s. . . . I have carried my point of having good harmless Mr. X. as chaplain instead of a curate (who by parenthesis was far too young and foolish) to have spiritual flirtations with my young ladies."

Within the Institution she put "more power into the hands of the Medical Men ". No nurse was to be engaged "without their approbation ", treatments were only to be carried out under their instructions and with their approval. She set up a system by which patients could complain directly to her if they had a grievance. A rule was laid down which forbade any patient to remain in the Institution more than two months, except in the case of the dying.

The unfortunate governesses who formed the greater part of the patients showed a disposition to remain because, she wrote to W. E. N., "it is the cheapest lodging they can find with the added luxury of taking medicine and sympathy. All *must* go at the end of 2 months, except those dying. Otherwise there is no incentive to get well."

The unpleasant task of enforcing this rule was left to Miss Nightingale. In the spring of 1854 she wrote to W. E. N.: "My Committee have not the courage to discharge a single case. *They* say the Medical Men must do it. The Medical Men say *they* won't, although the cases they say *must* be discharged. And I *always* have to do it, as the stop gap on all occasions."

She did not lead an easy life. She had disappointments. She had to struggle with suspicion and inefficiency. "The

chemists ", she had told W. E. N. in December 1853, "sent
me a bottle of ether labelled Spirits of Nitre, which, if I had
not smelt it, I should certainly have administered, and should
have an inquiry into poisoning." The builders did not carry
out her orders properly. " The whole flue of a new gas stove
came down the second time of using it, which, if I had not
caught in my arms would certainly have killed a patient."
The patients were ungrateful ; she complained that " my whole
life is spent in managing their unmanageable tempers ".
Medically there were heartbreaking failures. " We have had
an awful disappointment ", she wrote to W. E. N. in the spring
of 1854, "in a couching for a cataract, which has failed. The
eye is lost . . . and I am left, after a most anxious watching,
with a poor blind woman on my hands, whom we have blinded,
and a prospect of insanity. I had rather ten times have killed
her."

Fanny and Parthe continued to disapprove, though Fanny
with ineradicable generosity sent regular weekly hampers of
flowers, vegetables, game and fruit from Embley for the patients.
Miss Nightingale had her own sitting-room at Harley Street
where she gave her friends tea out of special blue cups. Parthe
was persuaded to accept an invitation but collapsed in hysterics
as she crossed the threshold of the Institution. There was friction
over money. Fanny was as unmethodical as she was generous
and her accounts were always in confusion. In January 1854
Miss Nightingale was forced to write to W. E. N. saying she
would only pay bills sent direct to herself. When she had
financial transactions with her mother she found she " always
paid twice ". Fanny looked at her daughter's £500 as if it
were £50,000 a year, and never ceased complaining that she
could not imagine what Florence spent so much money on.
Nevertheless, Miss Nightingale could write in a private note
of January 1, 1854 : " I have never repented nor looked back,
not for one moment. And I begin the New Year with more true
feeling of a happy New Year than I ever had in my life."

By the spring she had achieved " complete success ". " Her
power of conducting an institution exceeds what she or others
could have appreciated until she had tried ", wrote Aunt Mai
to Fanny.

Yet she found time to go to parties, and in the season of

1854 received invitations from Lady Beresford, Lady Canning, Lady Cranworth, Lady Palmerston. Gay little notes went round by hand to Harley Street from frivolous friends. " Lock up your young ladies, leave someone else to stir the gruel and cab round to me." " Dearest do come to an evening party, it will be rather a squeeze." "Don't get too radical, sceptical and querical my Flo." With the Herberts she was on a footing of closest intimacy. " Dearest ", " My dearest ", " Dearest old Flo ", Liz Herbert wrote.

She inspired a number of " passions ". " I always expected the sanatorium would be a hook in my back, for mad women to hang themselves on," she wrote to Hilary Bonham Carter in August 1854, " but I never expected mad women would come over from Germany! . . . This woman, very handsome . . . cousin to one of the Bunsen attachés, actually arrives upon me in London, without writing, without enquiry and says she is going to join me. . . . She says she saw me in Germany. I have not the least recollection of her. Poor fool ! It is very touching." Her patients in Harley Street worshipped her, writing innumerable adoring letters : " My dearest kind Miss Nightingale. I send you a few lines of love." " I felt so lonely when I saw you going away from me." " All your affectionate kindness to me comes before me now and causes me many tears." " I am your affectionate, attached and grateful." " Thank you, thank you darling Miss Nightingale." " You are our sunshine . . . were you to give up all would soon fade away and the whole thing would cease to be."

Hilary Bonham Carter told Clarkey that the devotion of the patients was tiresome. Mrs. Gaskell was told by Fanny that one patient used to get out of bed and stand on the cold hearthstone in the hope that when Miss Nightingale came round and found her feet were cold she would rub them.

Her sympathy with impoverished struggling women penetrated into every detail of their lives. She understood their loneliness, their perpetual financial difficulties, the burden of other relatives even poorer than they. She sent a poor governess to Eastbourne at her own expense and arranged that she should be visited and taken for drives. " I know not how to thank you my dear dear Miss Nightingale. I cannot even express how much indebted I am to you ", wrote the patient.

Often she sent financial help. "How gratefully I accept your offer of defraying my poor aunt's expenses. My mother has unfortunately no means of settling it herself." She wrote when patients were too ill to write themselves : "Many many thanks for your kindness in writing while my sister was with you". She saved women whose savings had been exhausted from going straight from a bed of sickness to a new post. Again and again a letter runs : "I cannot thank you enough for this extra rest". At Harley Street her correspondence was very large. The patients wrote, their relatives wrote, poor friendless women who were complete strangers were "emboldened by your very great kindness to my afflicted friend" to confide their fears of dreaded secret ailments.

The pitiful sordid story was repeated over and over again. "The patients", Miss Nightingale told Dr. Pincoffs in 1857, "were chiefly governesses and the cases, while I was there, almost invariably hysteria or cancer. I gained a very curious experience while there in managing the former class of case. I had more than one lunatic. I think the deep feeling I have of the miserable position of educated women in England was gained while there (or rather of half educated women). But I would not undertake it again. I would begin much nearer the source. For the *fancy* cases I had were to organic cases as 4 to 1. Physicians were of little help to me, they rather made the matter worse (though all first rate). For the patients looked upon medical attendance as a luxury."

In December 1853 Richard Monckton Miles, after staying at Embley, had written to his wife : "They talk quite easily about Florence, but her position does not seem to be very suitable". She had enjoyed the period of reorganisation, but as soon as the Institution was running smoothly she became restless. By January 1854 she was speaking of "this little mole hill".

In the spring of that year she began to visit hospitals and collect facts to establish a case for reforming conditions for hospital nurses. On May 29th Liz Herbert wrote : "Sidney has begged me to write and ask you whether you can give him any facts in writing as to abuses which exist in —— Hospital. Sidney says if he could get some authentic information on the subject of the nurses, their bad pay and worse lodging he could get the evil more or less remedied and public attention at any rate turned that way."

Soon letters were passing almost daily, Miss Nightingale submitting reports and Sidney Herbert asking for " additional information . . . as soon as possible ".

Reform was difficult. Within the hospitals there was jobbery. Hospital appointments were often held as the result of bribery or nepotism, and the official who supported reform found his appointment in danger. " I have seen one of the most useful and independent officials of —— today but he retracted almost all he had ever said before through fear of its being made use of," wrote Miss Nightingale on June 1st. ". . . I believe it is almost useless to see people officially because they ask ' What are you going to make of this ? ' and will never stand to their words. I have tried it a hundred times."

Outside the hospitals there was indifference; their conditions were accepted as a necessary horror. The number of the enlightened who, like the Herberts, pressed for improved conditions and a better type of nurse was very small. Most people agreed with Lady Palmerston. " Lady Pam thinks . . . the nurses are very good now; perhaps they do drink a little, but . . . poor people it must be so tiresome sitting up all night ", wrote Lord Granville.

In any case, where was a better type of nurse to come from ? If better nurses should be wanted how were they to be produced? Superior nurses did not exist. In June 1854 a doctor who had met Miss Nightingale in Paris wrote asking her to recommend two reliable skilful nurses to act as matrons in colonial hospitals. She had to reply that she knew none : " Alas I have no fish of that kind ". It was absurd to create a demand which could not be supplied. Before any scheme of nursing reform was embarked upon a training school capable of producing a supply of respectable, reliable, qualified nurses must be brought into existence. Her first task must be to produce a new type of nurse.

She confided in Dr. Bowman, one of the best-known surgeons of his day, surgeon to the Institution, and her devoted admirer. He had performed a difficult cancer operation at Harley Street, under the new anaesthetic, chloroform, and she had acted as his nurse; he had witnessed her reorganisation of the Institution and had told her she was " wasting her great powers ". King's College Hospital, where he held a senior appointment, was being reorganised and rebuilt, and his influence would be sufficient to obtain her the post of Superintendent of Nurses, where she would have scope for training a new type of nurse. He pressed her to consider it, and Mrs. Bracebridge and Mrs. Herbert also urged her to leave Harley Street. Rumours reached Embley, and Fanny and Parthe broke into lamentations: the suggestion of a hospital post struck them with horror as fresh as if it had been a new idea. The old objections came forward—improper students, unmentionable diseases, immoral companions, disgusting surroundings; the old ground was traversed once more, there were tears, hysterics, reproaches.

But Miss Nightingale was not at home to be reproached in person; she would not go home, she remained in Harley Street. In June 1854 Clough and Blanche Smith, Aunt Mai's daughter, were married on the strength of an ill-paid examinership he had obtained in the Education Office, and she went to stay with Aunt Mai for the wedding. Parthe wrote to Aunt Mai, reviving a long rejected suggestion. Could not Florence give up disreputable hospitals and take up Education? "My dearest Parthe", replied Aunt Mai, "I am sure I feel for your anxieties and your dear mother's. . . . I did say that I wished her line had been education, she said that she felt utterly unable to take any interest in teaching children . . . there is no doubt she has had complete success at Harley Street. . . . It seems to me we must let this ardent spirit pursue its way. To stop its course is quite beyond one. . . ."

The change was complete. The eager, susceptible, over-affectionate girl had become the elegant, composed, independent woman of genius. It was now beyond anyone to stop Miss Nightingale in her course. She continued her negotiations with Dr. Bowman, and, down at Embley, Fanny's reproaches and Parthe's hysterics sank to ineffectual flutterings. They wrote her letters imploring her to nurse babies, to found a penitentiary; she ignored them, and their voices trailed into silence and were heard no more.

In the summer of 1854 cholera broke out in London, particularly in the miserable, undrained slums round St. Giles, to the west of Drury Lane. The hospitals were overcrowded, many nurses died, many, afraid of infection, ran away. In August Miss Nightingale went as a volunteer to the Middlesex Hospital to " superintend the nursing of cholera patients ". From the Middlesex Hospital she went to Lea Hurst, where Mrs. Gaskell was staying. In a long letter to Emily Winkworth, Mrs. Gaskell repeated Miss Nightingale's account of the epidemic. The authorities at the Middlesex Hospital were " obliged to send out their usual patients in order to take in the patients brought in every half hour from the Soho district, Broad Street, etc., . . . chiefly fallen women of the district. . . . The prostitutes came in perpetually—poor creatures staggering off their beat ! It took worse hold of them than of any." Miss Nightingale was " up day and night, undressing them . . . putting on turpentine stupes, etc., herself, to as many as she could manage ". The women were filthy and drunken, crazed with terror and pain, and the rate of mortality was very high. All through the night wretched shrieking creatures were being carried in. From Friday afternoon until Sunday afternoon she was never off her feet.

Mr. Sam Gaskell, a relative, had been prejudiced by what he had heard of Miss Nightingale ; he had spoken very contemptuously of her and called her " your enthusiastic young friend ", but when they did meet he was " carried off his feet ". And Mrs. Gaskell herself continued in a letter to Catherine Winkworth dated October 20th : " Oh Katie ! I wish you could see her. . . . She is tall; very slight and willowy in figure; thick shortish rich brown hair ; very delicate colouring ; grey eyes which are generally pensive and drooping, but which when they choose can be the merriest eyes I ever saw ; and perfect teeth, making her smile the sweetest I ever saw. Put a long piece of soft net, say $1\frac{1}{4}$ yards long and half a yard wide, and tie it round this beautifully shaped head, so as to form a soft white framework for the full oval of her face (for she had the toothache and so wore this little piece of drapery) and dress her up in black silk high up to the long white round throat, and a black shawl on and you may get NEAR an idea of her perfect grace and lovely appearance. . . . She has a great deal of fun, and is carried along by that, I think. She mimics most capitally; mimics for instance the way of talking of some of the poor Governesses in the Establishment, with their delight at having a man servant, and at having LADY Canning and LADY Mounteagle to do this and that for them."

And yet a week later Mrs. Gaskell was chilled. She too had discovered that Florence was intimidating. Beneath the fascination, the sense of fun, the gentle hesitating manner, the demure wit, there was the hard coldness of steel. On October 27th Mrs. Gaskell wrote: " She has no friend—and she wants none. She stands perfectly alone, half-way between God and his creatures. She used to go a great deal among the villagers here, who dote upon her. One poor woman lost a boy seven years ago of white swelling in his knee, and F. N. went twice a day to dress it. . . . The mother speaks of F. N.—did so to me only yesterday—as of a heavenly angel. Yet the father of this dead child—the husband of this poor woman—died last 5th of September and I was witness to the extreme difficulty with which Parthe induced Florence to go and see this childless widow ONCE whilst she was here; and, though this woman entreated her to come again, she never did. She will not go among the villagers now because her heart and soul are absorbed by her hospital plans, and, as she says, she can only attend to one thing at once. She is so excessively gentle in voice, manner, and movement, that one never feels the unbendableness of her character when one is near her. Her powers are astonishing. . . . She and I had a grand quarrel one day . . . she said if she had influence enough not a mother should bring up a child herself; there should be creches for the rich as well as the poor. If she had twenty children she would send them all to a creche, seeing, of course, that it was a well managed creche. That exactly tells of what seems to me THE want—but then this want of love for individuals becomes a gift and a very rare one, if one takes it in conjunction with her intense love for the RACE; her utter unselfishness in serving and ministering . . . but she is really so extraordinary a creature that anything like a judgment of her must be presumptuous. . . . F. N. has very seldom told her family of her plans until they pretty well matured. . . . I saw a little instance of this while she was here. She had the toothache,

and an abscess in her mouth and Mrs. N. was VERY anxious
about her as she was evidently not strong. On Monday she
said 'I am going tomorrow'. This took them quite by
surprise, as she evidently was still very poorly; and Mrs. N.
remonstrated. But it turned out she had written and made
so many arrangements depending on her presence, before she
had even spoken about it to her family, that they had nothing
to do but yield. . . .''

One day Fanny and Mrs. Gaskell were alone. Fanny
spoke of Florence " with tears in her eyes ", telling Mrs.
Gaskell, " We are ducks who have hatched a wild swan ".
But it was not a swan they had hatched : in the famous phrase
of Lytton Strachey's essay—it was an eagle.

The summer of 1854 marked the end of a chapter. The
long agonising apprenticeship was over and the instrument
uniquely fitted for its purpose was forged. In the world outside Harley Street a catastrophe was taking shape. In March
1854 England and France had declared war on Russia. In
September the Allied armies landed in the Crimea. Harley
Street, with its unreasonable committee, its " deficient "
saucepans, its ragged linen, had been a dress rehearsal. Now
the curtain was about to go up on the play.

VII TO THE BRITISH PEOPLE the invincibility of the British Army was an article of faith. Waterloo was a recent memory, and it was taken for granted that the nation which had beaten Napoleon could not be defeated. But since Waterloo forty years of economy had run their course and the army which had won Wellington's victories had ceased to exist. In 1852 the artillery of the British Army consisted of forty field-pieces, many officially described as defective. In 1854, when the army was mobilising for the Crimea, volunteers had to be drafted into the battalions selected for active service to raise their numbers to the regulation 850. The departments of the Army which dealt with supply had been cut to the bone. The Duke of Wellington's great waggon train had been broken up, and the Army was without land transport. The staff of the supply departments had been reduced to a few clerks, who were overwhelmed by the demands of mobilisation. Before the Army sailed the processes by which the troops were to receive food and clothing, to be maintained in health and cared for when wounded or sick, had already fallen into confusion.

An enormous amount of information exists on the Crimean War. While it was in progress four Parliamentary Commissions of Enquiry investigated its disasters. Three of them went to the Crimea, the fourth, which sat in London, examined civil servants and officials in Government service as well as witnesses from the seat of war. The resulting mass of evidence fills a shelf of Blue Books in whose innumerable pages, from which the stench of misery and filth and despair seems palpably to rise, the Crimean War lies embalmed.

But in the spring of 1854 confidence was complete. The Guards were a magnificent body of fighting men as they marched through London to embark. The Grenadiers marched through Trafalgar Square with band playing, the Scots Fusilier Guards swung out of the courtyard of Buckingham Palace with a line of little drummer boys drumming at their head. The crowds which cheered them did not know that behind these splendid troops, the flower of the British Army, were no reserves. They were doomed to perish, and when they perished their ranks were filled with raw recruits made " pretty perfect in drill in sixty days ".

The first operation was not to be in the Crimea. The British Army was to relieve Silistria, in Roumania, then a Turkish province, where the Russians were besieging the Turks. A base was established at Scutari, a large village on the Asian shore of the Bosphorus, and in June 1854 the British Army disembarked at Varna, in Bulgaria. Nothing was accomplished. A cholera epidemic broke out; the site chosen for the British camp, " the beauteous scenery of the Lake of Devna ", was a notorious breeding-ground of cholera; the army became an army of invalids, and the Turks raised the siege of Silistria on their own account. The Allies then proceeded to the true objective of the war, the destruction of the great naval base recently constructed by the Russians at Sebastopol.

Though the plan of a descent on Sebastopol was an open secret and had been discussed in the Press, it had never been officially intimated to the supply departments; consequently no preparations had been made. When the British Army embarked at Varna for the Crimea there were not enough transports to take both the army and its equipment across the Black Sea. Thirty thousand men were crammed in, but pack animals, tents, cooking equipment, hospital marquees, regimental medicine chests, bedding and stores had all to be left behind. Twenty-one waggons only were brought for 30,000 men going into action. On September 14th the army disembarked at a cove with the sinister name of Calamita Bay. " My God ", exclaimed Dr. Alexander, 1st class Staff Surgeon to the Light Division, " they have landed this army without any kind of hospital transport, litters or carts or anything." Cholera still raged, and over 1000 cholera cases were sent back to Scutari.

A week later, the British and the French won the hard-fought battle of the Alma, and the wounded paid the price of the abandonment of the army's hospital equipment. There were no bandages, no splints, no chloroform, no morphia. The wounded lay on the ground or on straw mixed with manure in a farmyard. Amputations were performed without anaesthetics, the victims sat on tubs or lay on old doors, the surgeons worked by moonlight because there were no candles or lamps. And another 1000 cholera cases were sent back to Scutari.

Of this the British public knew nothing. They thrilled with pride at the ferocious courage with which British troops had stormed the heights of the Alma, marching under withering fire in ranks as solid as if they were parading in Hyde Park. The public knew nothing of what had been endured afterwards. Nor did they know what awaited the wounded and the sick when they reached the base at Scutari.

At Scutari were enormous barracks, the headquarters of the Turkish artillery. These barracks and the hospital attached had been handed over to the British, and the British authorities assumed that the hospital, known as the General Hospital, would be adequate. It was already equipped to some extent, and additional stores had been sent, but the unexpected disaster of the cholera epidemic produced total disorganisation. The first 1000 cholera cases sent back after the landing at Calamita Bay filled the hospital to overflowing; drugs, sanitary conveniences, bedding, doctors were insufficient. While Dr. Menzies, senior Medical Officer, was struggling with the crisis, he was notified that many hundreds of battle casualties from the Alma and another 1000 cholera cases were on their way. Since the General Hospital was filled, he was ordered to convert the artillery barracks into a hospital. It was an impossible task. The vast building was bare, filthy and dilapidated. There was no labour to clean it; there was no hospital equipment to put in it.

Meanwhile the sick and wounded were enduring a ghastly journey across the Black Sea. They were conveyed in " hospital ships " which figured well on paper but in fact were ordinary transports equipped "with some medicines and medical appliances ". They were packed far beyond their capacity. One, the *Kangaroo*, fitted to receive 250 sick, received between 1200 and 1500. Cholera cases, battle casualties, were crammed in together. Too weak to move, too weak to reach the sanitary conveniences, they fell on each other as the ship rolled and were soon lying in heaps of filth. Men with amputations were flung about the deck screaming with pain.

When the men arrived at the Barrack Hospital there were

no beds. They lay on the floor wrapped in the blankets saturated with blood and ordure in which they had been lying since they left the battlefield. No food could be given them because there was no kitchen. No one could attend to them because there were not sufficient doctors. Some of them lay without even a drink of water all that night and through the next day. There were no cups or buckets to bring water in. There were no chairs or tables. There was not an operating table. The men, half naked, lay in long lines on the bare filthy floors of the huge dilapidated rooms.

Such scenes of horror were nothing new in our military annals: similar miseries had been endured by the British Army many times before. Smollett, who was present as a surgeon, recorded the ghastly sufferings of the troops at the siege of Carthagena in 1741. During the winter of 1759 outside Quebec, outside Havana in 1762, during the retreat to the Ems in 1797 worse miseries were endured than in the Crimea. In the disastrous Walcheren expedition of 1809 a whole army was lost through sickness. Men died in thousands in the general hospitals of the Peninsula, the Guards were so reduced by sickness that they had had to fall out of the campaign from November 1812 to June 1813. After Talavera the Duke of Wellington himself had had to face a complete breakdown of supply.

But these horrors had remained unknown. England rang with the story of Scutari because with the British Army was the first war correspondent, William Howard Russell of *The Times*.

"By God, Sir, I'd as soon see the devil," said General Pennefather to Russell when they met in the Crimea; but Pennefather did not order Russell home. The Crimea was a casual war. Numbers of tourists, known to the army as "T.G's", "Travelling Gentlemen", came out and camped with the troops. "We wish to pitch our tent in your camp— the 18th," said the author of *Our Tent in the Crimea* to the officer commanding the regiment. "Very well", he answered, "I'll see to getting you some ground." Private philanthropists came out at their own expense to work among the troops. Though Russell and his paper were abominated by the army authorities—*The Times* under the editorship of

Delane was a Radical newspaper—he was never obstructed. He penetrated into the trenches before Sebastopol, talked to men on guard, walked into hospitals, boarded sick transports. The military aristocrats of the high command were content to ignore him. "Lord Raglan", wrote Russell, "never spoke to me in his life. . . . I was regarded as a mere camp follower, whom it would be impossible to take more notice of than you would of a crossing sweeper, without the gratuitous penny."

Russell was an Irishman with an Irishman's capacity for indignation, and in despatches published on October 9th, 12th and 13th he furiously described the sufferings of the sick and wounded. " It is with feelings of surprise and anger that the public will learn that no sufficient preparations have been made for the care of the wounded. Not only are there not sufficient surgeons . . . not only are there no dressers and nurses . . . there is not even linen to make bandages. . . . Can it be said that the battle of the Alma has been an event to take the world by surprise? Yet . . . there is no preparation for the commonest surgical operations! Not only are the men kept, in some cases for a week, without the hand of a medical man coming near their wounds, not only are they left to expire in agony, unheeded and shaken off, though catching desperately at the surgeon as he makes his rounds through the fetid ship, but now . . . it is found that the commonest appliances of a workhouse sick ward are wanting, and that the men must die through the medical staff of the British Army having forgotten that old rags are necessary for the dressing of wounds."

The revelation burst on the nation like a thunderclap, and on October 13th Sir Robert Peel, the third baronet, opened " The Times Fund " for supplying the sick and wounded with comforts. The same day The Times published another despatch from Russell. " The manner in which the sick and wounded are treated is worthy only of the savages of Dahomey. . . . The worn out pensioners who were brought as an ambulance corps are totally useless . . . there are no dressers or nurses to carry out the surgeons' directions, and to attend on the sick during the intervals between his visits. Here the French are greatly our superiors. Their medical arrangements are extremely good, their surgeons more numerous and they have also the help of the Sisters of Charity . . . these devoted women are excellent nurses."

The country seethed with rage. Russell's statement that our arrangements compared unfavourably with those of the French was intolerable, and the next day a letter in *The Times* demanded angrily, " Why have we no Sisters of Charity ? "

It was read by Sidney Herbert, who in December 1852 had been appointed Secretary at War, and was now responsible for the treatment of the sick and wounded. The administration of the British Army was then divided between two Ministers, the Secretary for War and the Secretary at War. The Secretary at War was responsible for the financial administration of the army, and since the cheese-paring, the callous economies, the criminally inadequate arrangements had been executed in his name, the blame must lie at the door of Sidney Herbert. His situation was painful. It was not only that one of the main objects of his life was to improve conditions for the British private soldier—he had inherited his concern for the troops from his father, who had fought as a volunteer in the disastrous Flanders campaign of 1793-4 and written a diary in which he recorded the terrible and unnecessary sufferings of the troops ; but his political position was now extremely delicate. His mother had been Russian, daughter of the Russian Ambassador, and the famous Woronzoff road which was to be of such overwhelming importance to the British Army in the Crimea led to the Woronzoff palace at Yalta which belonged to his uncle. Suspicion was inevitable ; and a storm of national fury burst on his head. The military authorities, enraged by the interference of *The Times*, refused to admit that anything was wrong. The departments hastened to justify themselves : ample stores had been sent out, were just arriving, the evacuation of Varna had caused delay, by now there must be superfluity. Sidney Herbert was not convinced and acted on his own responsibility. He wrote to the British Ambassador at Constantinople, Lord Stratford de Redcliffe, giving him *carte blanche* to purchase anything he considered necessary for the hospitals, and on October 15th he wrote to Miss Nightingale inviting her to go to Scutari in command of a party of nurses, with the Government's sanction and at the Government's expense.

She had already acted on her own account and, without consulting the Herberts, had arranged to sail for Constantinople with a party of nurses in three days' time. She had hesitated to approach them, embarrassed by the attacks being made on Sidney Herbert; but when her plans were completed, she called at 49 Belgrave Square on the morning of Saturday, October 14th. The Herberts had gone to Bournemouth for the week-end.

Her party of nurses had been organised with the assistance of Lady Maria Forester, a widow of strong Evangelical views devoted to philanthropic works. Lady Maria herself was useless because she was untrained, but on October 11th she offered £200 to pay the expenses of three nurses if Miss Nightingale would take them to Scutari. The offer was accepted, and Miss Nightingale decided to take at her own expense Mrs. Clark, the elderly housekeeper from Harley Street. On the 12th she saw Lord Palmerston, who approved the scheme and asked Lord Clarendon, the Foreign Secretary, to write to Lord Stratford de Redcliffe. Next day she saw Dr. Andrew Smith, Director of the Army Medical Service, who gave her a letter of introduction to the Chief Medical Officer at Scutari, Dr. Menzies. Arrangements were made for the party to leave London on October 17th and to catch the boat from Marseilles to Constantinople; and Uncle Sam went down to Embley to break the news to the Nightingales.

On Saturday afternoon Miss Nightingale wrote to Liz Herbert: "My dearest, I went to Belgrave Square this morning for the chance of catching you, or Mr. Herbert even, had he been in Town. A small private expedition of nurses has been organised for Scutari and I have been asked to command it. I take myself out and one nurse. . . . I do not mean that I believe the *Times* accounts, but I do believe we may be of use to the poor wounded wretches." She asked Liz to negotiate her release from her engagement with the Harley Street committee—unless the committee thoroughly approved she could not honourably break her engagement; and, would Sidney approve? "What does Mr. Herbert say to the scheme itself? Does he think it would be objected to by the authorities? Would he give us any advice or letters of recommendation? And are there any stores for the Hospital he would advise us to take out. Dr. Smith says nothing is needed." Finally, would Liz write to the Ambassadress, Lady Stratford de Redcliffe, and say: " This is not a Lady but a real Hospital Nurse . . . and she has had experience ".

This letter crossed one written by Sidney Herbert at Bournemouth on the Sunday, in which he formally asked her to take charge of an official scheme for introducing female nurses into the hospitals of the British Army:

DEAR MISS NIGHTINGALE,

You will have seen in the papers that there is a great deficiency of nurses at the Hospital at Scutari.

The other alleged deficiencies, namely of medical men, lint, sheets, etc., must, if they have really ever existed, have been remedied ere this, as the number of medical officers with the Army amounted to one to every 95 men in the whole force, being nearly double what we have ever had before, and 30 more surgeons went out 3 weeks ago, and would by this time, therefore, be at Constantinople. A further supply went on Thursday, and a fresh batch sail next week.

As to medical stores, they have been sent out in profusion; lint by the *ton* weight, 15,000 pairs of sheets, medicine, wine, arrowroot in the same proportion; and the only way of accounting for the deficiency at Scutari, if it exists, is that the mass of stores went to Varna, and was not sent back when the Army left for the Crimea; but four days would have remedied this. In the meanwhile fresh stores are arriving.

But the deficiency of female nurses is undoubted, none but male nurses having ever been admitted to military hospitals.

It would be impossible to carry about a large staff of female nurses with the Army in the field. But at Scutari, having now a fixed hospital, no military reason exists against their introduction, and I am confident they might be introduced with great benefit, for hospital orderlies must be very rough hands, and most of them, on such an occasion as this, very inexperienced ones.

I receive numbers of offers from ladies to go out, but they are ladies who have no conception of what an hospital is, nor of the nature of its duties; and they would, when the time came, either recoil from the work or be entirely useless, and consequently— what is worse—entirely in the way. Nor would these ladies probably ever understand the necessity, especially in a military hospital, of strict obedience to rule. . . .

There is but one person in England that I know of who would

be capable of organising and superintending such a scheme; and I have been several times on the point of asking you hypothetically if, supposing the attempt were made, you would undertake to direct it.

The selection of the rank and file of nurses will be very difficult: no one knows it better than yourself. The difficulty of finding women equal to a task, after all, full of horrors, and requiring, besides knowledge and goodwill, great energy and great courage, will be great. The task of ruling them and introducing system among them, great; and not the least will be the difficulty of making the whole work smoothly with the medical and military authorities out there. This it is which makes it so important that the experiment should be carried out by one with a capacity for administration and experience. A number of sentimental enthusiastic ladies turned loose into the Hospital at Scutari would probably, after a few days, be *mises à la porte* by those whose business they would interrupt, and whose authority they would dispute.

My question simply is, Would you listen to the request to go and superintend the whole thing? You would of course have plenary authority over all the nurses, and I think I could secure you the fullest assistance and co-operation from the medical staff, and you would also have an unlimited power of drawing on the Government for whatever you thought requisite for the success of your mission. On this part of the subject the details are too many for a letter, and I reserve it for our meeting; for whatever decision you take, I know you will give me every assistance and advice.

I do not say one word to press you. You are the only person who can judge for yourself which of conflicting or incompatible duties is the first, or the highest; but I must not conceal from you that I think upon your decision will depend the ultimate success or failure of the plan. Your own personal qualities, your knowledge and your power of administration, and among greater things your rank and position in Society give you advantages in such a work which no other person possesses.

If this succeeds, an enormous amount of good will be done now, and to persons deserving everything at our hands; and a prejudice will have been broken through, and a precedent established, which will multiply the good to all time.

I hardly like to be sanguine as to your answer. If it were " yes ", I am certain the Bracebridges would go with you and give you all the comfort you would require, and which their society and sympathy only could give you. I have written very long, for the subject is very near to my heart. Liz is writing to Mrs. Bracebridge to tell her what I am doing. I go back to town tomorrow morning. Shall I come to you between 3 and 5? Will you let me have a line at the War Office to let me know?

There is one point which I have hardly a right to touch upon, but I know you will pardon me. If you were inclined to undertake this great work, would Mr. and Mrs. Nightingale give their consent? The work would be so national, and the request made to you proceeding from the Government who represent the nation comes at such a moment, that I do not despair of their consent. Deriving your authority from the Government, your position would secure the respect and consideration of every one, especially in a service where official rank carries so much weight. This would secure to you every attention and comfort on your way and there, together with a complete submission to your orders. I know these things are a matter of indifference to you except so far as they may further the great objects you have in view; but they are of importance in themselves, and of every importance to those who have a right to take an interest in your personal position and comfort.

I know you will come to a wise decision. God grant it may be in accordance with my hopes!

Believe me, dear Miss Nightingale,

ever yours,

SIDNEY HERBERT.

The terms of this letter were accepted by Miss Nightingale and considered by her to be her charter. They make it clear that from the inception of her mission she was to be an administrator.

It was not as an angel of mercy that she was asked to go to Scutari—relieving the sufferings of the troops was scarcely mentioned. The consideration of overwhelming importance was the opportunity offered to advance the cause of nursing. Were nurses capable of being employed with success to nurse men under such conditions? The eyes of the nation were fixed on Scutari. If the nurses acquitted themselves creditably, never again would they be despised. " If this succeeds ", Sidney Herbert had written, " an enormous amount of good will have been done now . . . a prejudice will have been broken through and a precedent established which will multiply the good to all time."

Before she had time to write a reply he had received her

letter, and on the Monday afternoon he called on her at Harley Street, bringing a letter from Liz: " My own dearest noblest Flo. I *knew* you would do it. . . . God be thanked. Sid longed to go to you last week . . . I will write a ' cut and dry ' letter to the committee in Harley Street and bear all the blame if any can possibly attach itself to such a work ! Go then at once, and God prosper it and you. Your own loving E. H. Would that I could come to town to you at once. But my nurse is ill and away and I cannot leave my children. . . ."

Sidney Herbert warned Miss Nightingale that he was by no means satisfied with the assurances he was receiving from the army authorities, and that he was sending out immediately a " Commission of Enquiry into the State of the Hospitals and the Condition of the Sick and Wounded ". The Commission had three members, a well-known barrister, Mr. Benson Maxwell, and two doctors, Dr. Cumming and Dr. Spence. Its purpose was to establish the facts, but it was not empowered to take action and could not alter existing arrangements. She was to work with the Hospitals Commission, send in official reports and in addition write privately to him telling him confidentially what she could not write officially.

The number of nurses in the party was fixed at forty. She was doubtful of her ability to control more than twenty, but Sidney Herbert insisted that twenty would not be a sufficiently large number to make the experiment impressive. He would have preferred an even larger number than forty. On Wednesday, October 18th, Sidney Herbert, supported by the Duke of Newcastle, placed Miss Nightingale's appointment before the Cabinet, the Duke of Newcastle, who knew her personally, writing: " We felt that anything she undertook would be successful ". The appointment was unanimously approved, and next day she received a formal confirmation written and signed by Sidney Herbert as Secretary at War. She was appointed " Superintendent of the Female Nursing Establishment of the English General Hospitals in Turkey ", and her authority was defined: " Everything relating to the distribution of the nurses, the hours of their attendance, their allotment to particular duties is placed in your hands, subject of course to the sanction and approval of the chief medical officer; but the selection of the nurses in the first instance is placed solely under your control." Precise as these instructions appeared, they contained a flaw. The words "Superintendent of the Female Nursing Establishment of the English General Military Hospitals in *Turkey*" were subsequently contended to limit her authority to Turkey, and to exclude her from the Crimea.

The Cabinet sent an intimation of her appointment and a copy of her instructions to Lord Raglan, the Commander-in-Chief, to the Principal Medical Officer in the Crimea, Dr. Hall, and to the Purveyor-in-Chief, together with a letter instructing them to "use every endeavour to assist Miss Nightingale in the performance of the arduous duties she has undertaken". A sum of £1000 was handed to her for the expenses of the journey out, and she was instructed to draw freely on the Commissariat at her discretion on her arrival at Scutari.

Her appointment caused a sensation. The story of the Cabinet meeting, the official instructions, the letter to the Commander-in-Chief flew from mouth to mouth. No woman had ever been so distinguished before, and Fanny and Parthe were ecstatic. Uncle Sam had experienced some difficulty in obtaining their consent when Miss Nightingale proposed to go as a private volunteer. Now they raised no objection. Forgetting they had brought her to the verge of insanity by their opposition, they congratulated themselves on the scope of the experience which qualified her for her mission. "It is a great and noble work", wrote Parthe to a favourite cousin. "One cannot but believe she was intended for it. None of her previous life has been wasted, her experience all tells, all the gathered stores of so many years, her Kaiserswerth, her sympathy with the R. Catholic system of work, her travels, her search into the hospital question, her knowledge of so many different minds and classes. . . ."

Parthe and Fanny hastened from Embley to London to share in the excitement, and, in the haste of packing, the owl Athena was left shut in an attic, where she was found later dead; she required constant attention and was subject to fits. When the lifeless body was put into Miss Nightingale's hands she burst into tears. "Poor little beastie," she said, "it was odd how much I loved you." It was the only sign of emotion

141

she showed on the eve of departure. Otherwise she was, wrote Parthe, " as calm and composed as if she was going for a walk ".

Most of her time was spent in her rooms at Pall Mall steadily and methodically winding up her affairs. Everything was left in perfect order, all her obligations were fulfilled. Even a set of Sunday school lessons on the life of Christ, which she had promised for the village school near Embley, was completed before she left.

She had made up her mind to start on Saturday, October 21st, four clear days only after she had received Sidney Herbert's letter. Nurses had to be engaged, she was determined they should wear uniform, which must be made, tickets and berths must be reserved. Σ and her husband had agreed to accompany her, and Mr. Bracebridge took over the finances of the expedition and made the travelling arrangements, adding to the prevailing excitement by hiring one of the new fast hansom cabs and driving about London at ten miles an hour.

The headquarters of the expedition were at the Herberts' London house, 49 Belgrave Square. Mary Stanley, Mrs. Bracebridge, Lady Canning and Lady Cranworth sat all day in the dining-room prepared to receive a rush of applicants— but few came. Kinglake, the historian of the Crimean Campaign, called them " the Angel Band ". It had been intended to engage forty, but in the end only thirty-eight women who could conceivably be considered suitable presented themselves. " I wish people who may hereafter complain of the women selected could have seen the set we had to choose from ", wrote Mary Stanley to Liz Herbert in October 1854. " All London was scoured for them. . . . We felt ashamed to have in the house such women as came. One alone expressed a wish to go from a good motive. Money was the only inducement." " As to that stuff about the ' enthusiasm ' of the nursing in the Crimean campaign—that is all bosh ", wrote Miss Nightingale to Sir John McNeill in 1867 ; " we had, unfortunately for us, scarcely one woman sent out who was even up to the level of a head nurse." The nurses were to receive 12s. to 14s. a week with board lodging and uniform. After three months' good conduct they received 16s. to 18s., and after a year's good conduct 18s. to 20s. The average wage of a nurse in a London hospital was 7s. to 10s. Each nurse signed an agreement submitting herself absolutely to Miss Nightingale's orders. Misconduct with the troops was to be punished by instant dismissal. A nurse invalided home was to have her expenses paid first class, but one sent home for misconduct must travel third class on salt rations. No young women were accepted, the majority being stout elderly old bodies. Miss Nightingale wrote later from Scutari that in future " fat drunken old dames of fourteen stone and over must be barred, the provision of bedsteads is not strong enough ". A uniform dress was provided, but each nurse brought with her underclothing, four cotton night-caps, one cotton umbrella and a carpet-bag. No coloured ribbons or flowers were allowed. No nurse in any circumstances was to go out alone or with only one other nurse. She must either be with the housekeeper from Harley Street, Mrs. Clark, or with three other nurses. In no circumstances was any nurse to go out without leave. Strong liquor was permitted in moderate quantities. At dinner each nurse was to be allowed one pint of porter or one pint of ale, at supper half a pint of porter, or half a pint of ale, or one glass of Marsala or one ounce of brandy.

Lady Canning and Lady Cranworth kept a " large and melancholy " book in which they recorded the particulars of each applicant. Candidates came from the humblest class— " Maid-of-all work ", " Very poor ", " Has been for a few days in St. George's Hospital ". Subordinate clerks in Government service signed testimonials recklessly. " Many ", wrote Miss Nightingale, " were (undisguisedly) sent out as paupers to be provided for, who could not otherwise gain their living."

Fourteen professional nurses who had experience of serving in hospitals were engaged; the remaining twenty-four were all members of religious institutions. The party was non-sectarian; nurses, insisted Miss Nightingale, were to be selected " with a view to fitness and without any reference to religious creed whether Roman Catholic nuns, Dissenting Deaconesses, Protestant Hospital nurses or Anglican sisters ".

With the assistance of Manning it was arranged that ten Roman Catholic nuns, five from a convent in Bermondsey and five from an orphanage in Norwood, should join the party, and it was conceded that they should be completely under Miss Nightingale's control. If she were to weld this hetero-genous, undisciplined collection of women into an efficient instrument she must have absolute and unquestioned authority; her word must be law; a nun or a sister nursing for Miss Nightingale must take her nursing orders from Miss Nightin-gale and not from her mother superior; and the mother superior must take her nursing orders from Miss Nightingale and not from the bishop.

It was an extraordinary concession for Manning to have obtained, and, as far as the original nuns were concerned, it worked with perfect smoothness. The five Norwood nuns, though amiable, proved inexperienced, but the five from Bermondsey were very nearly the most valuable members of the party. Their superior, known as Rev. Mother Bermondsey, became one of Miss Nightingale's dearest friends.

Three other religious bodies were approached for nurses. St. John's House, a High Church sisterhood in Blandford Square, Miss Sellon's Anglican sisterhood, known as the Sellonites, in Devonport, and an Evangelical body, the Pro-testant Institution for Nurses, in Devonshire Square.

The Sellonites agreed to accept Miss Nightingale's authority, and sent eight sisters who were especially valuable as they had had experience in nursing cholera in the slums of Plymouth and Devonport during the cholera epidemic of 1853. The authorities of St. John's House demurred, but after being visited first by Sidney Herbert and then by the Chaplain-General of the Forces allowed themselves to be persuaded and sent six sisters. The Protestant Institution flatly refused—their nurses were to be controlled only by their own committee. The refusal was unfortunate. As a result, the party contained a preponderance of Roman Catholics and members of the High Church. Out of the thirty-eight nurses, twenty-four were either professed nuns or Anglican sisters. The remaining fourteen, the hospital nurses, were, as Clarkey observed, of no particular religion unless the worship of Bacchus should be revived.

But religious differences were not the only difficulty. Amongst women who were prepared to devote themselves to the sick, there were two totally different conceptions of the functions of a nurse. The hospital nurse, drunken, promiscuous and troublesome, considered that her function was to tend her patient's sick body and restore him to physical health by carrying out the doctor's orders. The religious orders, sisters and nuns, were neither drunken nor promiscuous, but were apt to be more concerned with the souls of their patients than with their bodies. Since the middle of the eighteenth century the great mediaeval tradition of nursing among religious orders had decayed. Physical and spiritual were thought incompatible; at one point the sisters at St. Vincent de Paul had been forbidden to put diapers on boy babies. Lofty sentiments were encouraged but cleanliness was ignored. "Excellent self devoted women," wrote Miss Nightingale of certain nuns, "fit more for heaven than a hospital, they flit about like angels without hands among the patients and soothe their souls while they leave their bodies dirty and neglected." This conception was not held only by religious orders. It was shared by a number of educated women who spent much of their time among the sick, but described themselves not as nurses but "ladies". In 1854, just before the Crimea, Mary Stanley published a book entitled *Hospitals and Sisterhoods*. The first chapter, headed " Wants of English Hospitals ", refers solely to the shortage of chaplains and the opportunities for spiritual regeneration wasted for want of " lady visitors ". The shortcomings of the wards are totally ignored.

The ancient conception of the paramount claim of suffering humanity, the conception symbolised in the ceremonial washing of beggars' feet by kings, had passed away. The gentlewoman refused to perform menial tasks. She was not a nurse concerned with the body, she was a "lady" concerned with the soul. She smoothed a pillow and said a prayer but would not empty a bed-pan. Miss Nightingale refused to admit " ladies ", as such, into her party. All must be nurses, all must eat the same food, have the same accommodation, wear the same uniform, except the nuns and sisters, who were allowed to wear their habits. And the uniform was extremely ugly. It consisted of a grey tweed dress, called a " wrapper ", a grey worsted jacket, a plain white cap and a short woollen cloak. Over the shoulders was worn a holland scarf described as "frightful", on which was embroidered in red the words "Scutari Hospital". There was no time to fit individual wearers, various sizes were made up and issued as they came in, with unhappy results. Small women got large sizes, tall women got small. That a "lady" could be induced to appear in such a get-up was certainly a triumph of grace over nature, wrote one of the nuns. The uniform had not been designed to make the wearer look attractive. Scutari was a disorderly camp, teeming with drink-shops, prostitutes and idle troops, and a distinguishing dress was necessary for the nurses' protection. A Crimean veteran told Sir Edward Cook that he saw a nurse seized by a soldier in the street of Scutari, but the man's mate recognised the uniform. "Let her alone," he said, "don't you see she's one of Miss Nightingale's women."

Before Miss Nightingale left England she called again on Dr. Andrew Smith. He was jocose. The ladies, he assured her, would undoubtedly be a comfort to the men. Ladies had finer instincts ; they might, for instance, see a spot on a sheet where a mere man might easily overlook it. As for medical duties—well, he did not think Miss Nightingale and her nurses could possibly go wrong in administering a nice soothing drink of capillary syrup to any man who seemed uncomfortable. She contemplated taking a quantity of stores, but he assured her stores were unnecessary. There was now a positive profusion of every kind of medical comfort at Scutari and, in addition—the repetition comes like a chorus—vast quantities of stores were expected daily from Varna.

On Saturday morning, October 21st, 1854, the party left London Bridge to travel via Boulogne to Paris. One night was to be spent in Paris and four nights in Marseilles, where in spite of the assurances of Sidney Herbert and Dr. Andrew Smith Miss Nightingale intended to buy a large quantity of miscellaneous provisions and stores. Uncle Sam was to go as far as Marseilles to assist her. From Marseilles the party were to proceed to Constantinople in a fast mail boat, the *Vectis*.

Among the Nightingale papers is preserved a small oblong black notebook, fastened with an elastic band and covered with American cloth. It contains three letters, the only personal papers Miss Nightingale took with her to Scutari. One from

Fanny bestowed on her the maternal blessing she had so long sought in vain, one from Manning commended her to the Protection, Worship and Imitation of the Sacred Heart, the third was from Richard Monckton Milnes—" So you are going to the East ", he wrote ". . . you can undertake that, when you could not undertake me."

When the party started, the "ladies" did not wish to sit in the same railway carriage as "hired nurses". When "ladies" and nurses were associated, the "ladies" expected to be treated as parlour boarders, be spared all menial work, have the best rooms, eat the best food and have their washing and mending done by the nurses.

The party reached Boulogne at dinner-time and were given an ovation. Many of the fisherwives of Boulogne had sons and brothers in the French Army, and they seized and shouldered the baggage and carried it in triumph to the hotel, refusing to accept payment. The landlord placed his establishment at the disposal of the party, desired them to order what they would for dinner, and refused to be paid.

The ladies would not sit with the nurses at dinner, though the nurses were in difficulty, as they knew no French. Miss Nightingale waited on the nurses and ate with them herself. "We never had so much care taken of our comforts before ", one of them said to her. "It is not people's way with us."

Tickets to Paris had already been bought, but the railway insisted on transporting their baggage free. The party arrived at the Gare du Nord, Paris, at 10 P.M., and was welcomed by an enthusiastic crowd and cheered on the way to the hotel where M. Mohl had arranged rooms and supper. Uncle Sam, writing to Embley, described Florence and Mrs. Bracebridge going from room to room trying to fit the party in, followed by Mr. Bracebridge, who, carrying a large box with all the cash in it under his arm, was highly excited, constantly interrupting Florence with exclamations and irrelevant reminiscences, and reproaching her for being so confoundedly silent. Mr. Bracebridge was followed in turn by M. Mohl, who implored him to come downstairs and eat his supper like a good boy.

Miss Nightingale had hoped to add to her party some Sisters of Charity of British nationality from the convent of St. Vincent de Paul, but permission was refused.

The next day the party left for Marseilles. Clarkey, who saw them off, wrote to Hilary Bonham Carter that the Bacchantes would be a deal more useful because they were not gentle-folky. In Marseilles Miss Nightingale set about purchasing stores. In her bedroom, but NOT, explained Uncle Sam, at bedtime, she received a motley crowd of merchants, shopkeepers, dealers, officials from the French Government and the British Consulate, army officers, *The Times* correspondent and a Queen's Messenger " with the same serenity as in a drawing-room ". She was looking handsomer than ever, he noted, and the impression she created was extraordinary.

On October 27th the party sailed in the *Vectis*. She was a horrible ship, built for carrying fast mails from Marseilles to Malta, infested with huge cockroaches and so notorious for her discomfort that the Government had difficulty in manning her. Miss Nightingale, a wretchedly bad sailor, was prostrated by sea sickness. On the second day out the *Vectis* ran into a gale. The guns with which she was armed had to be jettisoned, the stewards' cabin and the galley were washed overboard. Miss Nightingale suffered so severely that when Malta was reached she was too weak to go ashore.

The rest of the party went sightseeing in the charge of a major of militia. The party was made up partly of Anglican sisters in black serge habits, partly of Roman Catholic nuns in white habits and partly of hospital nurses. The hospital nurses were placed in the middle where they would have no chance to misbehave, and the major marched the party from point to point in military formation. The major would shout, " Forward black sisters ", and the Anglican sisters in their black serge habits got into motion ; but the white nuns would straggle, and there came a shout, " Halt ! Those damned white sisters have gone again." Malta was full of idle troops, and soon the party was followed by a crowd of soldiers. One of the Anglican sisters heard a sergeant remark that he should think " them ancient Amazons we read about took a deal of drilling ".

On November 3rd, still in atrocious weather, the *Vectis*, " blustering, storming, shrieking ", wrote Miss Nightingale, rushed up the Bosphorus, and anchored off Seraglio Point next day. Constantinople, in the pouring rain, looked like a washed-out daguerreotype. On the opposite shore stood the enormous Barrack Hospital. Everyone was on deck eager to see their goal. "Oh, Miss Nightingale", said one of the party, "when we land don't let there be any red tape delays, let us get straight to nursing the poor fellows!" Miss Nightingale, gazing at the gigantic pile, replied: "The strongest will be wanted at the wash tub."

At breakfast-time the *Vectis* anchored, and during the morning Lord Stratford, the British Ambassador at Constantinople, sent across Lord Napier, the Secretary of the Embassy. Lord Napier found Miss Nightingale, exhausted from the effects of prolonged sea sickness, stretched on a sofa. Fourteen years later he recalled their first meeting: ". . . I was sent by Lord Stratford to salute and welcome you on your first arrival at Scutari . . . and found you stretched on the sofa where I believe you never lay down again. I thought *then* that it would be a great happiness to serve you."

The nurses were to go to the hospital at once, for wounded were expected from the battle of Balaclava, fought on October 28th. Painted caïques, the gondola-like boats of the Bosphorus, were procured, the nurses were lowered into them with their carpet-bags and umbrellas, and the party was rowed across to Scutari.

The rain having ceased, a few fitful gleams of sunshine lit up the Asian shore, which, as it grew clearer, lost its beauty. The steep slopes to the Barrack Hospital were a sea of mud littered with refuse; there was no firm road, merely a rutted, neglected track. As the caïques approached a rickety landing-stage the nurses shrank at the sight of the bloated carcase of a large grey horse, washing backwards and forwards on the tide and pursued by a pack of starving dogs, who howled and fought among themselves. A few men, limping and ragged, were helping each other up the steep slope to the hospital, and groups of soldiers stood listlessly watching the dead horse and the starving dogs. A cold wind blew. Some wretched-looking women shivered in tawdry finery.

The nurses disembarked, climbed the slope and passed through the enormous gateway of the Barrack Hospital, that gateway over which Miss Nightingale said should have been

written " Abandon hope all ye who enter here ".   Dr. Menzies
and Major Sillery, the Military Commandant, were waiting to
receive them.   That night Lord Stratford wrote to the Duke
of Newcastle : " Miss Nightingale and her brigade of nurses
are actually established at Scutari under the same roof with
the gallant and suffering objects of their compassion ".

VIII FROM THE EUROPEAN SHORE of the Bosphorus, from the magnificent house where the British Ambassador lived, the great quadrangle of the Turkish Barracks glimmered golden, magnificent as a giant's palace, but at close quarters romance vanished. Vast echoing corridors with floors of broken tiles and walls streaming damp, empty of any kind of furniture, stretched for miles. Miss Nightingale calculated there were four miles of beds. Everything was filthy, everything was dilapidated. The form of the building was a hollow square with towers at each corner. One side had been gutted in a fire, and could not be used. The courtyard in the centre was a sea of mud littered with refuse. Within the vast ramifications of the barracks were a depot for troops, a canteen where spirits were sold and a stable for cavalry horses. Deep in the cellars were dark and noisome dens where more than 200 women, who had been allowed by an oversight to accompany the army, drank, starved, gave birth to infants, carried on their trade as prostitutes and died of cholera. "But it is not a building, it's a town!" exclaimed a new arrival.

To reach the Barrack Hospital meant martyrdom for wounded men. There was no pier, and the rickety landing-stage could only be used by small boats. The men were taken out of the sick transports and lowered into caïques or rowing-boats; after landing they were jolted on stretchers over rough ground up a precipitous slope.

Although so near Constantinople the situation was isolated. The only communication with Constantinople was by boat, and the Bosphorus was swept by sudden storms which cut off all communication for three or four days at a time. At Scutari were the principal cemeteries of Constantinople, but no markets or shops, only a " profusion of tombs, fountains and weeping willows "—and ample opportunities for drunkenness and vice. As soon as the British Army occupied Scutari a horde of Jews, Greeks and Armenians descended. Tents, booths, ramshackle sheds used as drinking-shops and brothels sprang up round the barracks, and spirits of the worst quality were drunk by the troops in enormous quantities. Regiments sent to Scutari rapidly deteriorated, and on one night, out of 2400 troops stationed in the barracks, 1400 were reported drunk.

These were obvious drawbacks, but the vast building hid a more fatal secret. Sanitary defects made it a pest house, and the majority of the men who died there died not of the wounds or sickness with which they arrived but of disease they contracted as a result of being in the hospital.

The catastrophe which destroyed the British Army was a catastrophe of sickness, not of losses in battle. There were two different sicknesses. The troops on the heights before Sebastopol fell sick of diseases resulting from starvation and exposure. When they were brought down to Scutari and entered the Barrack Hospital they died of fevers resulting from the insanitary construction of the Barrack Hospital assisted by insufficient food, filth and overcrowding. The second sickness was the more fatal. When the war was over it was found that the mortality in each regiment depended on the number of men which that regiment had been able to send to Scutari. Men who were kept on the heights before Sebastopol in the hideous discomfort of makeshift regimental hospitals frequently recovered, those who were brought into the Barrack Hospital died. In the months of January and February 1855, when the disaster was at its height, the average number of patients in the hospital at any one time was 2349 and in the same period 2315 men died. This figure was held to be an underestimate. In the confusion which then prevailed a large number of deaths were not recorded.

When Miss Nightingale entered the Barrack Hospital on November 5th, 1854, there were ominous signs of approaching disaster, but the catastrophe had not yet occurred. Food, drugs, medical necessities had already run short, the Barrack Hospital was without equipment, and in the Crimea supply was breaking down. Winter was swiftly advancing, and each week the number of sick sent to Scutari steadily increased.

There were men in the Crimea, there were men in Scutari, there were men at home in England who saw the tragedy approach. They were powerless. The system under which the health of the British Army was administered defeated them. The exactions, the imbecilities of the system killed energy and efficiency, crushed initiative, removed responsibility and were the death of common sense.

Three departments were responsible for maintaining the health of the British Army and for the organisation of its hospitals. The Commissariat, the Purveyor's Department and the Medical Department. They were departments which during forty years of economy had been cut down nearer and still nearer the bone. In 1853 Dr. Andrew Smith, the Director-General of the British Army Medical Service, received £1200 a year and had only twelve clerks to execute the entire administration of his department. The screw, he said, had been applied so tightly that when the order came through to spend money freely he simply did not believe it. The Purveyor's Department had been reduced to a staff of four, and at the outbreak of war it was extremely difficult to find anyone with sufficient experience to send out as a Purveyor-in-Chief. Mr. Ward, "poor old Ward", the Purveyor at Scutari, was over seventy years of age, a veteran not only of the Peninsula but of Walcheren. His staff consisted of two inexperienced clerks and three boys who also acted as messengers. Mr. Filder, the Commissary-General, a Peninsula veteran, complained in 1855 that he was expected to conduct and record the whole business of supplying the British Army in the Crimea with the help of three incompetent clerks.

These departments had no standing. Dr. Andrew Smith told the Roebuck Committee that it would have been considered impertinence on his part to approach the Commander-in-Chief with suggestions as to the health of the army. Lord West remarked that the doctors appeared to him to possess no powers whatever. A commissary officer did not rank as a gentleman, while the purveyor was despised even by the commissary. Ill paid, despised, not highly qualified and painfully anxious for promotion, their fear of their superior officers, especially of the military authorities, was abject. It was something, wrote Miss Nightingale, which no one outside the army had any idea of, it was absolutely Chinese. Men of courage, of determination and of character might have risen above the system, as Dr. Alexander, the ablest man in the medical service rose above it, but such men did not usually choose to become commissariat officers, purveyors or army surgeons.

The method by which the hospitals were supplied was confused. The Commissariat were the caterers, bankers, carriers and store-keepers of the army. They bought and delivered the standard daily rations of the men whether they were on duty or in hospital. The bread and the meat used in the hospitals, the fuel burned there were supplied by the Commissariat. But the Commissariat did not supply food for men too ill to eat their normal rations. At this point the Purveyor stepped in. All invalid foods, known as " medical comforts ", sago, rice, milk, arrowroot, port wine, were supplied by the Purveyor. But though these comforts were supplied to the hospital by the Purveyor, he did not obtain them : all the Purveyor's contracts were made by the Commissariat. The Purveyor never dealt directly with his merchant and had no power over him. If goods were unsatisfactory the Purveyor could only complain to the Commissariat. Though the standard daily rations of the men in hospital were bought and delivered by the Commissariat, it was the Purveyor who cooked and distributed them. Yet he had no authority over their price, suitability or quality, having to accept what the Commissariat sent unless he could claim the consignment was unfit for human consumption. Mr. Filder, the Commissary-General, cross-examined by the Roebuck Committee, said with heat that for his part he never had understood where the duties of the Commissariat ended and the duties of the Purveyor began. Mr. Benson Maxwell, an eminent lawyer and a member of the Hospitals Commission, declared that though he had spent some weeks in the hospitals he was perfectly unable to disentangle the respective duties of Commissariat and Purveyor.

Relations between the doctors and the Purveyor were even more obscure. A doctor might order a man a special diet, but it depended on the Purveyor whether the patient received it or not. Having made a requisition on the Purveyor, the doctor was powerless. Dr. Andrew Smith stated before the Roebuck Committee that he could not say what his position was with regard to the Purveying Department. If he made a complaint the Purveyor told him it was not his province. " Then ", said Dr. Smith, " I must go to the War Office and get them to carry out what I ought to have the power to carry out."

He was asked : " Has this uncertainty with regard to the power of providing necessaries and comforts in the hospitals been in existence ever since you have been at the Medical Board ? " " Yes, and long before that."

Though the system placed executive power in the hands of the Commissariat and the Purveyor, it was only a limited power. Certain goods only might be supplied. Each department had a series of " warrants " naming definite articles. " The Purveyor ", wrote Miss Nightingale, " only gives such amounts of articles as are justifiable under his 'warrants', by which he is governed, and is not responsible for those wants of the soldier in hospital which are in excess of the warrants, whatever may be the evidence before him, either in the requisition of the medical officer or the personal observation which, it would appear, he was bound to make of what was close under his eyes." If any official supplied or ordered articles not named on the warrants he was liable to be held personally and financially responsible by the Government. It was no empty threat. Colonel Alexander Gordon told the McNeill and Tulloch Commission of Enquiry into the Supplies for the British Army in the Crimea that at that moment a lawsuit was pending between the Government and an officer relating to his issue of stores and comforts for the troops during the Caffre War.

The result was the extraordinary shortages. When the sick and wounded came down to Scutari from the Crimea they were in the majority of cases without forks, spoons, knives or shirts. The regulations of the British Army laid down that each soldier should bring his pack into hospital with him, and his pack contained a change of clothing and utensils for eating. These articles were consequently not on the Purveyor's warrant. But most of the men who came down to Scutari had abandoned their packs after Calamita Bay, or on the march from the Alma to Balaclava, at the orders of their officers. Nevertheless, the Purveyor refused to consider any requisitions on him for these articles.

Officials were trained not to make trouble, not to spend money, never to risk responsibility; and at Scutari, grossly overworked as they were, they were placed in a situation which demanded courage and resource. The system, while it discouraged action, was enormously prolific of forms, requisitions, dockets, cross-checks, authorisations and reports. In the hospitals at Scutari every requisition, however trifling, had to be checked and countersigned by two doctors, one of them a senior officer. No medical officer was permitted to use his discretion. The surgeon on duty had to make as many as six different daily records of the " Diet Roll ", the particulars of food and comforts to be consumed by each patient. A senior surgeon was required to inspect every department of the hospital, including kitchen and store-rooms, daily and report in writing in duplicate to the Inspector-General. As soon as a man attained proficiency in his profession and became a first-class surgeon, he spent so much time filling in forms and drawing up reports that the care of the patients was left to inexperienced juniors. Dr. Menzies, Senior Medical Officer at the Barrack Hospital, stated that he was so inundated with office work that he had no time to go into the wards. " It must be admitted ", the Roebuck Committee agreed, " that he had no time left for what should have been his principal duty, the proper superintendence of these hospitals."

The Barrack Hospital was the fatal fruit of the system. When the General Hospital was unexpectedly filled with cholera cases and Dr. Menzies was abruptly notified that the casualties from the Alma and a further large number of cholera cases were on their way, he was instructed to turn the Turkish Barracks into a hospital. The preparation and equipment of a hospital formed no part of his duties, his task being to instruct the Purveyor. He sent for " poor old Ward " and told him to prepare the Turkish Barracks for the reception of wounded. He had then, in accordance with the rules of the service, performed his duty. How Mr. Ward was to conjure hospital equipment at a moment's notice out of the drink-shops, brothels and tombs of Scutari, how he was to collect labour to clean the vast filthy building when no labour existed nearer than Constantinople, was not Dr. Menzies's concern. Mr. Ward also knew the correct procedure. He had no authority to expend sums of money in purchasing goods in the open market, and in any case many of the articles required were not on his warrant. He requisitioned the Commissariat on the proper forms, the Commissariat wrote on the forms

" None in store ", and the matter was closed. The wounded arrived and were placed in the building without food, bedding or medical attention. At a later date Dr. Menzies instructed the Purveyor to issue the men with shirts. This was not done, and the men continued to lie naked. Dr. Menzies was asked by the Roebuck Committee why he had not seen to it that his order was carried out. He replied that it was no part of his duty to see that an order was executed. Having issued the instruction correctly and placed it on record, his duty was done. " Their heads ", wrote Miss Nightingale in 1855, " are so flattened between the boards of Army discipline that they remain old children all their lives."

When furious attacks were made on the Government and the medical administration of the army, doctors, purveyors and commissariat officers were aggrieved. They declared that according to the regulations of the Service their duty had been performed. They also declared that a new standard of comfort was being demanded for the soldier which he had never previously enjoyed and which was wholly unsuitable.

The destruction of the British Army in the Crimean campaign was materially assisted by the attitude of his officer to the private soldier. Savage physical suffering was endured by officers and men alike, and the officers were courageous, stoical, physically tough—Sir George Brown, who commanded the Light Division, had had his arm cut off in the Peninsula and had been thrown on some straw in the bottom of a cart ; Lord Raglan had had his arm amputated without an anaesthetic after Waterloo and had called out : " Here, bring that arm back, there is a ring my wife gave me on the finger." But officers regarded the men they commanded as denizens of a different world.

The private soldier of 1854 did not bear a good character. The young man who was the disgrace of his village, the black sheep of the family, enlisted. The Duke of Wellington described his army, the army which won the victories of the Peninsula and Waterloo, as " the scum of the earth enlisted for drink ". The soldier was a dangerous brute to be kept in subjection only by flogging, punishment, drill and iron discipline. Officers had no feeling of responsibility towards their men. " During the time I have been in the Crimea, that is since the landing . . . no general officer has visited my hospital nor, to my knowledge, in any way interested himself about the sick ", Dr. Brush of the Scots Greys wrote to the Hospitals Commission. " Unless those high in Command do take an interest in their sick soldiers . . . until they do lend a helping hand to their medical officers it will not be possible for the duties of the medical department to be efficiently carried on." " Too marked attention cannot be drawn to the apathy and indifference ", wrote Dr. Marlow of the 28th Regiment from the heights before Sebastopol ; " very tolerable structures have been raised for the occupation of individuals while men labouring under disease are left on the damp ground in a leaky tent ". When it became evident that the army would have to winter before Sebastopol under conditions of appalling severity, a large number of officers threw up their commissions and went home. Many of these, like Lord George Paget, who had taken part in the Charge of the Light Brigade, were men of unquestioned personal courage. They were astounded when they were cut in their clubs. Lord George, in fact, returned, though to a post at headquarters.

Miss Nightingale was told : " You will spoil the brutes " ; she heard the troops described by their officers as " animals ", " blackguards ", " scum ". And the medical authorities were enraged by what they considered unreasonable demands— clean bedding, soup, hospital clothing were " preposterous luxuries ". " Poor old Ward ", cross-examined as to the state of the Barrack Hospital by the Hospitals Commission in December 1854, said : " I served through the whole of the Peninsula War. The patients never were nearly so comfortable as they are here. . . . In general the men were without bedsteads. Even when we returned to our own country from Walcheren and Corunna the comforts they got were by no means equal to what they have here."

The doctors at Scutari received the news of Miss Nightingale's appointment with disgust. They were understaffed, overworked, it was the last straw that a youngish Society lady should be foisted on them with a pack of nurses. Of all Government follies, this was the worst. The Army Medical Department had already declared itself against the introduction of women as nurses for soldiers. It had been tried by employing the men's wives as nurses and it had failed—the women behaved improperly with the men, and both got drunk together. The Army Medical Department had laid down that female nurses in a military hospital were " an unwise indulgence unfavourable to medical discipline and to the recovery of the patients ".

However, now they had no choice but to submit; open opposition would be dangerous, for Miss Nightingale was known to have powerful backing, to be the intimate friend of Sidney Herbert and on friendly terms with half the Cabinet. Opinion was divided as to whether she would turn out a well-meaning, well-bred nuisance or a Government spy. For their part, regimental officers received the news with an indulgent smile. Colonel Anthony Sterling, attached to the Highland Brigade, a friend of Sir Colin Campbell and brother of John Sterling, the friend of Carlyle, wrote in November 1854 : " The ladies seem to be on a new scheme, bless their hearts. . . . I do not wish to see, neither do I approve of, ladies doing the drudgery of nursing."

However, on November 5th Miss Nightingale and her party were welcomed into the Barrack Hospital with every appearance of flattering attention and escorted into the hospital with compliments and expressions of goodwill. When they saw their quarters the picture abruptly changed. Six rooms, one of which was a kitchen and another a closet ten feet square, had been allotted to a party of forty persons. The same space had previously been allotted to three doctors and, in another part of the hospital, was occupied solely by a major. The rooms were damp, filthy and unfurnished except for a couple of beds and a few chairs. There were no tables, there was no food. Miss Nightingale made no comment and the officials withdrew. It was a warning, a caution against placing reliance on the flowery promises, the resounding compliments of Stratford Canning, first Viscount Stratford de Redcliffe.

Lord Stratford had been British Ambassador to Constantinople three times and associated with Turkey since 1807. His influence was immense, he was virtually a dictator; his latest " reign " at Constantinople had lasted, with a two years' intermission, for sixteen years. The Turks called him " the great Elchi ", the great ambassador. Physically he was extremely handsome, and he prided himself on his presence—" the thin rigid lips, the majesty of brow of a Canning ". He lived magnificently and travelled with twenty-five servants and seventy tons of plate.

Before the Roebuck Committee Sidney Herbert stated that Lord Stratford was called in because the Government at home realised that the Commissariat officers, etc., were nervous of spending money and were probably at sea. The Duke of Newcastle added that he felt the fear of responsibility in subordinate officers was so great that it would be impossible to get them to draw money and apply it unless the intervention of Lord Stratford took place. But Lord Stratford never did intervene. Mr. Macdonald, sent out to expend *The Times* fund, was informed by Lord Stratford that he had full authority from the Government to order any supplies he chose from the bazaars at Constantinople, and that the French hospitals had adequately equipped themselves from these bazaars, but, said Mr. Macdonald, "in some extraordinary way these powers were not used ".

Miss Nightingale described Lord Stratford as bad-tempered, heartless, pompous and lazy. He loved to consort with kings and emperors, he loved to write bad poems in majestic rhythms and keep his attachés up until the small hours while he read them aloud. He was jealous of his inferiors. " The Elchi ", wrote Lord Napier, " would never employ anyone on serious work who was at all near himself, so I spent the best years of my life at a momentous crisis doing nothing." He was not the man to interest himself in a hospital for common soldiers. In his magnificent palace on the Bosphorus he lived for two years with, said Miss Nightingale, " the British Army perishing within sight of his windows ", and during those two years he visited the hospitals only once, when she " dragged " him there for a visit of only one and a half hours.

After receiving Sidney Herbert's letter, Lord Stratford informed Dr. Menzies that if anything was required for the hospitals both *The Times* fund and public money were available. Dr. Menzies was thoroughly alarmed ; the suggestion that civilian funds should be used to make good deficiencies in army administration struck him with horror. He refused to admit anything was wrong : as far as present wants extended, the hospitals were satisfactorily supplied, and as for future needs he referred once more to the stores expected from Varna. The Ambassador accepted this assurance. He did not go across and see the hospitals for himself, nor did he send anyone else to inspect them or ask for details. He wrote to Sidney Herbert that there did not appear to be anything required, and passed on to a project very near his heart : the subscriptions to *The Times* fund would be difficult to return, and he pressed that they should be devoted to the building of a Protestant Church in Constantinople. Though he was strongly Protestant in sympathies, the project was by no means a religious one. It would be a diplomatic triumph. To have procured permission from the Sultan to build a church of a rival religion in Constantinople, a Mohammedan city, was a mark of extraordinary favour, and the building of the church would immensely increase British prestige.

That night, as Miss Nightingale was calculating how she could cram her party of forty into five small rooms and a kitchen, Lord Stratford wrote a flowery letter to the Duke of Newcastle complimenting her on the " accomplishments " she brought into the field of charity and venturing to hope that " much comfort may be derived by the sick and wounded from that attractive source ".

Fourteen nurses were to sleep in one room, ten nuns in another, Miss Nightingale and Mrs. Bracebridge shared the closet, Mr. Bracebridge and the courier-interpeter slept in the office, Mrs. Clark, who was to be cook, and her assistant must go to bed in the kitchen. There was one more room upstairs, and the eight Sellonites must sleep there. They went upstairs, and hurried back. The room was still occupied—by the dead body of a Russian general. Mr. Bracebridge fetched two men to remove the corpse while the sisters waited. The room was not cleaned and there was nothing to clean it with ; it was days before they could get a broom, and meanwhile the deceased general's white hairs littered the floor. There was no furniture, no food, no means of cooking food, no beds. Most of the party prepared to sleep on so-called Turkish " divans ", raised wooden platforms running round the rooms on which the Turks placed bedding ; there was, however, no bedding. While the nurses and sisters unpacked, Miss Nightingale went down into the hospital, and managed to procure tin basins of milkless tea. As the party drank it she told them what she had discovered.

The hospital was totally lacking in equipment. It was hopeless to ask for furniture. There was no furniture. There was not even an operating table. There were no medical supplies. There were not even the ordinary necessities of life. For the present the nurses must use their tin basins for everything, washing, eating and drinking.

They must be prepared to go short of water. The allowance was limited to a pint a head a day for washing and drinking, including tea, and it was necessary to line up in one of the corridors where there was a fountain to obtain it. Tomorrow the situation would become worse, a battle at Balaclava had been fought on October 25th, and transports loaded with sick and wounded were expected.

The party had to go to bed in darkness, for the shortage of lamps and candles was acute. Sisters and nurses lying on the hard divans tried to console themselves by thinking how much greater were the sufferings of the wounded in the sick transports. The rooms were alive with fleas, and rats scurried beneath the divans all night long. The spirits of all, wrote Sister Margaret Goodman, one of the Sellonites, sank.

The doctors ignored Miss Nightingale. She was to be frozen out, and only one doctor would use her nurses and her supplies. Though the patients were in desperate need, and she could supply what was wanted from her purchases in Marseilles, her stores were refused. Her nurses were refused though the patients were being attended by hospital orderlies who were hopelessly unsatisfactory. According to the regulations of the army, orderlies were either convalescents, in which case they were recalled to their regiments as soon as they had learned to be of use, or they were " weak, stupid and clumsy fellows " or " skulkers " whom the army found useless. The work of attending the sick was forced on them, they almost invariably disliked it, and their numbers were totally inadequate.

Mr. Macdonald told the Hospitals Commission : " Nurses were offered by Miss Nightingale and not accepted " ; and he experienced similar difficulty himself. He had *The Times* fund to spend, the urgency of the need for supplies was tragically evident, but he had the greatest difficulty in " squeezing out " of the doctors an admission of what was needed. The medical authorities drew together in a close defensive phalanx. Admit failure! Accept help for the army from civilians, from *The Times* under whose attacks the army authorities were smarting! From a high Society miss who happened to be on dining terms with the Cabinet! Their experience of army methods, of confidential reports, told them that the man who consorted with Miss Nightingale or who supplied his wards through *The Times* fund would be a marked man.

She realised that before she could accomplish anything she must win the confidence of the doctors. She determined not to offer her nurses and her stores again, but to wait until the doctors asked her for help. She would demonstrate that she and her party wished neither to interfere nor attract attention, that they were prepared to be completely subservient to the authority of the doctors.

It was a policy which demanded self-control; the party were to stand by, see troops suffer and do nothing until officially instructed. Though Miss Nightingale could accept the hard facts that a few must be sacrificed in order that the army might be saved; and that the experiment on which she was embarked could never succeed against official opposition, yet she inevitably came into conflict with her nurses.

A day passed and some stores arrived. She made them sort old linen, count packages of provisions. The hardships of life continued. They stood in the corridor to get their pint of water. They ate out of the tin bowls, wiped them with paper, washed their faces and hands in them, wiped them again and drank tea from them. Discomfort would have been ignored if the sufferings of the wounded had been relieved, but they were not relieved. The cries of the men were unanswered while old linen was counted and mended—this was not what they had left England to accomplish. They blamed Miss Nightingale. And she was silent. She did not explain. The capacity to explain had gone out of her nature. The nurses, sentimental and emotionally undisciplined, gained an impression that she was indifferent to the sufferings of the wounded.

On Sunday, November 6th, the ships bringing the wounded from Balaclava began to unload at Scutari. As on other occasions the arrangements were inadequate, and the men suffered frightfully; they were brought up to the hospital on stretchers carried by Turks, who rolled their bleeding burdens about, put the stretchers down with a bump when they needed a rest, and on several occasions threw the patient off. Screams of pain were the accompaniment to the unhappy procession, and Sister Margaret Goodman recorded the case of a soldier who died as a result.

Still Miss Nightingale would not allow her nurses to throw themselves into the work of attending on these unhappy victims. She allocated twenty-eight nurses to the Barrack Hospital and ten to the General Hospital a quarter of a mile away. All were to sleep in the Barrack Hospital and all were to wait. No nurse was to enter a ward except at the invitation of a doctor. However piteous the state of the wounded, the doctor must give the order for attention. She sent her nurses to church to sit through an admirable sermon by the chief Chaplain, Mr. Sabin. If the doctors did not choose to employ the nurses, then the nurses must remain idle.

She was also determined to send no nurse into the wards until she knew that nurse could be relied on. The reliability of the nurse was as important to the success of the experiment as the co-operation of the doctors, and for nearly a week the party were kept shut up in their detestable quarters making shirts, pillows, stump-rests and slings and being observed by her penetrating eye. The time, sighed one of the English Sisters of Mercy, seemed extremely long.

In any case, no directions had been issued governing the employment of nurses. They were entirely in the hands of the doctors. " No general order ", wrote Miss Nightingale in 1856, " ever existed defining the duties of the nurses in the various hospitals to which they were respectively attached. . . . The number admitted into each division depended on the medical officer of that Division, who sometimes accepted them, sometimes refused them, sometimes accepted them after they had been refused; while the duties they were permitted to perform varied according to the will of each individual medical officer . . . and according to the estimation in which each individual nurse was held by each individual medical officer."

Whatever the regulations laid down, the nurses must submit. Their role was to acquiesce even in what was absurd. By no other means could the doctors be convinced that the nurses were neither critics nor reformers but obedient instruments in their hands.

Miss Nightingale herself rigidly obeyed regulations. On a later occasion she was sitting by the bedside of a man critically ill and found his feet stone cold. She told an orderly to fetch a hot-water bottle. The man refused, saying he had been told to do nothing for a patient without directions from a medical officer. She accepted the correction, found a doctor and obtained a requisition in proper form. For weeks she stood by in silence while the skill of highly efficient nurses was wasted.

" Our senior medical officer here ", she wrote to Sidney Herbert in January 1855, " volunteered to say that my best nurse, Mrs. Roberts, dressed wounds and fractures more skilfully than any of the dressers or assistant surgeons. But that it was not a question of efficiency, nor of the comfort of the patients, but of the ' regulations of the service '."

She was first able to get a footing in the hospital through the kitchen. A state of starvation existed in the Barrack Hospital. According to regulations a private soldier in hospital was placed on what was known as a whole diet, a half-diet or a spoon diet, the first representing the man's ordinary rations cooked for him by the hospital, the second about half his rations and the third liquid food. In addition he was supposed to receive " extra diet ", wine, milk, butter, arrowroot, jelly, milk puddings, eggs, etc., as prescribed by the surgeon attending him and procured through the Purveyor.

But to cook anything at the Barrack Hospital was practically impossible. The sole provision for cooking was thirteen Turkish coppers each holding about 450 pints. There was only one kitchen. There were no kettles, no saucepans, the only fuel was green wood. The tea was made in the coppers in which the meat had just been boiled, water was short, the coppers were not cleaned and the tea was undrinkable. The meat for each ward was issued to the orderly for the ward, who stood in line to receive it from the Purveyor's Department. The Purveyor was understaffed, and when the hospital had 2500 patients one clerk did all the issues, and the orderlies had to wait an hour or more. When the orderly had the meat he tied it up, put some distinguishing mark on it and dropped it into the pot. Some of the articles used by the orderlies to distinguish their meat included red rags, buttons, old nails, reeking pairs of surgical scissors and odd bits of uniform. The water did not generally boil, the fires smoked abominably. When the cook considered that sufficient time had been taken up in cooking, the orderlies threw buckets of water on the fires to put them out, and the contents of the coppers were distributed, the cook standing by to see that each man got his own joint; the joints which had been dropped in last were sometimes almost raw. The orderly then carried the meat into the ward and divided it up, usually on his bed, and never less than twenty minutes could elapse between taking it out of the pot and serving it. Not only were the dinners always cold, but the meat was issued with bone and gristle weighed in, and some men got portions which were all bone. Those who could eat meat usually tore it with their fingers—there were almost no forks, spoons or knives. Men on a spoon diet got the water in which the meat had been cooked, as soup. There were no vegetables; only, sometimes, dried peas.

Orderlies cooked extras over fires of sticks in the wards and the courtyard. One of them, Edward Jennings, told the Hospitals Commission on December 14th, 1854: "I boil chickens in an old tin in the ward. I also cook the sago and other things as well as I can . . . the doctor does not give me any directions. I cook all the extras and give them to the man at once and he can do what he likes with them. . . . I never did anything in the way of cooking until I became an orderly." The administration of medicines was left to the orderlies, and it was their practice to give the day's medicine in one draught. When wine was ordered the orderlies drank it themselves. They also ate the rations of men who were ill or asleep. One of the Sellonite sisters saw a young orderly eat up eight dinners.

The food was almost uneatable by men in rude health; as a diet for cholera and dysentery cases it produced agonies. The torture endured by the men when the pangs of hunger

166

were superimposed on diarrhoea was frightful. " I have never seen suffering greater," wrote one observer.

The day after Miss Nightingale arrived she began to cook " extras ". She had bought arrowroot, wine and beef essences and portable stoves in Marseilles. On the 6th of November, with the doctors' permission, she provided pails of hot arrowroot and port wine for the Balaclava survivors, and within a week the kitchen belonging to her quarters had become an extra diet kitchen, where food from her own stores was cooked under the direction of Rev. Mother Bermondsey and Mrs. Clark. For five months this kitchen was the only means of supplying invalid food in the Barrack Hospital. She strictly observed official routine, nothing being supplied from the kitchen without a requisition signed by a doctor. No nurse was permitted to give a patient any nourishment without a doctor's written directions.

Again she came into conflict with her nurses. Many of them rebelled against waiting for an official sanction before feeding men who were evidently dying for want of food.

The Purveyor was furiously resentful. In the second week of November the Duke of Cambridge visited the hospital and told Dr. Menzies he was extremely dissatisfied with the dinners supplied to the men. Dr. Menzies complained to the Purveyor, who at once blamed Miss Nightingale. The kitchen was occupied by Miss Nightingale so that the cooks had not the opportunity of cooking the men's dinners properly ; and Miss Nightingale interfered in the kitchen, cooking arrowroot and making jelly, and upsetting all the arrangements. Asked for an explanation by the Hospitals Commission, she said that her nurses never used the hospital kitchen, and that she herself had never set foot in it after her first tour of the hospital. All cooking done by her was done exclusively in her own quarters, with her own apparatus.

Cooking was all she had managed to accomplish when, on November 9th, the situation completely changed. A flood of sick poured into Scutari on such a scale that a crisis of terrible urgency arose and prejudices and resentments were for the moment forgotten.

167

IX IT WAS THE OPENING of the catastrophe. The destruction of the British Army had begun. These were the first of the stream of men suffering from dysentery, from scurvy, from starvation and exposure who were to pour down on Scutari all through the terrible winter. Over in the Crimea on the heights above Sebastopol the army was marooned, as completely as if on a lighthouse. Thousands of men possessed only what they stood up in. After the landing at Calamita Bay and after the battle of the Alma, when the troops were riddled with cholera and the heat was intense, the men had, by their officers' orders, abandoned their packs.

Seven miles below the heights lay Balaclava, the British base. There had been one good road, the Woronzoff road, but the Russians had gained possession of it in the battle of Balaclava on October 25th. There remained a rough track. The weather was still moderately good, but the track was not metalled and put into order before the winter. Men to carry out the work were non-existent. There was no native labour to be hired in this deserted spot. There were no tools. Above all, there was no transport. The army was still without waggons or pack animals.

Balaclava had become a nightmare of filth. Lord Raglan had been attracted by its extraordinary harbour, a land-locked lagoon calm, clear and almost tideless, so deep that a large vessel could anchor close inshore. But Balaclava was a fishing village of only 500 inhabitants, a single street of white vine-wreathed houses clinging to a precipitous ravine. No steps were taken to inspect Balaclava before it was occupied or to keep it in a sanitary condition. The army which marched in was stricken with cholera, and within a few days the narrow street had become a disgusting quagmire. Piles of arms and legs amputated after the battle of Balaclava, with the sleeves and trousers still on them, had been thrown into the harbour and could be seen dimly through the water. Bodies of dead men rose suddenly and horribly out of the mud to the surface. Anchor chains and cables were fouled by limbs and trunks. The surface of the once translucent water was covered with brightly coloured scum, and the whole village smelt of sulphuretted hydrogen.

On November 5th the Russians had attacked at Inkerman, on the heights above Sebastopol. In a grim battle fought in swirling fog the British were victorious. But victory was not reassuring. The British troops were exhausted; their commanders were shaken by the revelation of Russian strength. It was evident that Sebastopol would not fall until the spring.

And now an ominous incident occurred. A Mr. Cattley was attached to the British Army as chief interpreter. Mr. Cattley knew the Crimea well, and he sent in his resignation. He saw a great disaster ahead. The British Army was going to winter on the heights before Sebastopol, and the British Army was not only totally destitute of supplies but without the means of being able to get supplies should they ultimately arrive. Moistened by the dews of autumn, and churned by the wheels of heavy guns, the rough track from Balaclava to the camp had become impassable. Mr. Cattley wrote to Lord Raglan warning him that winter was near, that the climate of the Crimea was subject to sudden and terrifying changes, and tendering his resignation. Lord Raglan made light of the warning and besought Mr. Cattley to withdraw his resignation. He did so and stayed to die in 1855.

The weather changed rapidly, icy winds blew—and the troops on the heights above Sebastopol had no fuel. Every bush, every stunted tree was consumed, and the men clawed roots out of the sodden earth to gain a little warmth. As it grew colder they had to live without shelter, without clothing, drenched by incessant driving rain, to sleep in mud, to eat hard dried peas and raw salt meat. The percentage of sickness rose and rose and the miserable victims began to pour down on Scutari. The authorities were overwhelmed. The first transports were not even expected. Through an oversight, notification that they had sailed was received only half an hour before the sick and wounded began to land. Utter confusion resulted, official barriers were swept away, and everyone was pressed into service. The Hon. and Rev. Sidney Godolphin Osborne, a personal friend of Sidney Herbert, had come out as a volunteer to act as chaplain to the troops in hospital, and had been cold-shouldered by the authorities; now he found himself assisting

at operations. Mr. Augustus Stafford, M.P., who had come
to Scutari to investigate the hospitals privately, and had had
difficulty even in obtaining admission, had a saucepan thrust
into his hand and was asked to go down to the wretched pier
to pour some kind of warm stimulant down the throats of men
writhing in agony.   " Everyone helped ", he told the Roebuck
Committee, " the official people were assisting as much as
possible but the number of official people was too small and the
arrival was so great, a flood of sick came upon them, bursting
in so suddenly that the means of the hospital were not able to
meet it."

It was Miss Nightingale's opportunity—at last the doctors
turned to her. Her nurses dropped their sorting of linen and
began with desperate haste to seam up great bags and stuff
them with straw. These were laid down not only in the wards
but in the corridors, a line of stuffed sacks on each side with
just room to pass between them.

Day after day the sick poured in until the enormous building was entirely filled. The wards were full, the corridors
were lined with men lying on the bare boards because the supply
of bags stuffed with straw had given out. Chaos reigned. The
doctors were unable even to examine each man. Mr. Sabin,
the head Chaplain, was told that men were a fortnight in the
Barrack Hospital without seeing a surgeon. Yet the doctors,
especially the older men, worked " like lions " and were frequently on their feet for twenty-four hours at a time. " We
are lucky in our Medical Heads ", Miss Nightingale wrote to
Dr. Bowman on November 14th. " Two of them are brutes
and four are angels—for this is a work which makes angels or
devils of men. . . . As for the Assistants, they are all cubs and
will, while a man is breathing his last under the knife, lament
the ' annoyance of being called up from their dinners by such
a fresh influx of wounded '. But unlicked cubs grow up into
good old Bears, tho' I don't know how, for certain it is the old
Bears are good."

The filth became indescribable. The men in the corridors
lay on unwashed rotten floors crawling with vermin. As the
Rev. Sidney Godolphin Osborne knelt to take down dying
messages his paper became covered thickly with lice. There
were no pillows, no blankets, the men lay, with their heads on

their boots, wrapped in the blanket or greatcoat stiff with blood and filth which had been their sole covering perhaps for more than a week. There were no screens or operating tables. Amputations had to be performed in the wards in full sight of the patients. Mr. Osborne describes the amputation of a thigh " done upon boards put on two trestles. I assisted . . . during the latter part of the operation the man's position became such from want of a table he was supported by my arm underneath, a surgeon on the other side grasping my wrist." One of Miss Nightingale's first acts was to procure a screen from Constantinople so that men might be spared the sight of the suffering they themselves were doomed to undergo.

She estimated that in the hospital at this time there were more than 1000 men suffering from acute diarrhoea and only twenty chamber pots. The privies in the towers of the Barrack Hospital had been allowed to become useless; the water pipes which flushed them had been stopped up when the Barracks were used for troops, and when the building was converted into a hospital they had never been unstopped. Mr. Augustus Stafford said there was liquid filth which floated over the floor an inch deep and came out of the privy itself into the ante-room. He told the Roebuck Committee: " The majority of the cases at the Barrack Hospital were suffering from diarrhoea, they had no slippers and no shoes, and they had to go into this filth so that gradually they did not trouble to go into the lavatory chamber itself." Huge wooden tubs stood in the wards and corridors for the men to use. The orderlies disliked the unpleasant task of emptying these, and they were left unemptied for twenty-four hours on end. In this filth lay the men's food—Miss Nightingale saw the skinned carcase of a sheep lie in a ward all night. " We have Erysipelas, fever and gangrene ", she wrote ". . . the dysentery cases have died at the rate of one in two . . . the mortality of the operations is frightful. . . . This is only the beginning of things." By the end of the second week in November the atmosphere in the Barrack Hospital was so frightful that it gave Mr. Stafford the prevailing disease of diarrhoea in five minutes. The stench from the hospital could be smelt *outside* the walls.

A change came over the men, said Mr. Macdonald. The

classification between wounded and sick was broken down. The wounded who had been well before began to catch fevers, " gradually all signs of cheerfulness disappeared, they drew their blankets over their heads and were buried in silence ".

Fate had worse in store. On the night of November 14th it was noticed that the sea in the Bosphorus was running abnormally high, and there was a strange thrumming wind. Within a few days news came that the Crimea had been devastated by the worst hurricane within the memory of man. Tents were reduced to shreds, horses blown helplessly for miles, buildings destroyed, trees uprooted. The marquees which formed the regimental field hospitals vanished and men were left half buried in mud without coverings of any kind. Most serious of all, every vessel in Balaclava harbour was destroyed, amongst them a large ship, the *Prince*, which had entered the harbour the previous day loaded with warm winter clothing and stores for the troops.

From the moment of the sinking of the *Prince* no more was heard of the profusion of stores expected from Varna—everything lacking was said to have gone down in the *Prince*.

The hurricane rendered the situation of the army desperate. Such few stores and such little forage as it possessed were destroyed. Winter began in earnest with storms of sleet and winds that cut like a knife as they howled across the bleak plateau. Dysentery, diarrhoea, rheumatic fever increased by leaps and bounds. More and more shiploads of sick inundated Scutari. The men came down starved and in rags. " They were without their shoes and their shirts had been thrown away in utter disgust at their filthiness or torn in shreds . . . they were swarming with vermin ; their trousers were all torn ; their coats ragged . . . sometimes they came down without any coats at all ", said Mr. Macdonald in his evidence before the Roebuck Committee. The men told the nurses to keep away because they were so filthy. " My own mother could not touch me ", said one man to Sister Margaret Goodman.

By the end of November the administration of the hospital had collapsed. The Commissariat Department was the first to break down. No proper accounts had been kept since the first influx of the sick and wounded from Alma, and the disasters of the hurricane and the loss of the *Prince* overwhelmed it. And the Purveyor was rendered helpless by the collapse of the Commissariat. Medical direction of the hospital had almost ceased to exist, assisted by an inexplicable action on the part of the Government. It had been decided that Dr. Menzies was incompetent and should be recalled; the officer chosen to succeed him was Dr. Cumming. But Dr. Cumming was one of the three members of the Hospitals Commission, and when he arrived in Scutari neither he nor Dr. Menzies knew how to proceed correctly. Dr. Menzies stated he was not aware what his duties should be because he had been superseded by Dr. Cumming. Dr. Cumming did not feel he could take control and issue orders in a hospital on which he was supposed to be making a report. Through a further piece of ill-luck Dr. Spence, the second doctor on the Hospitals Commission, was drowned in the *Prince*, and the work of the Commission was held up three weeks. Meanwhile Dr. Menzies and Dr. Cumming each refrained from giving orders, so that the hospital was left without direction.

" In the confusion at Scutari ", Mr. Augustus Stafford told the Roebuck Committee, " I was never able to distinguish where one department began and the other ended. . . . Whenever I had anything to do with the authorities at Scutari, I never met with anything but personal courtesy and a wish to reform the evils . . . but through all the departments there was a kind of paralysis, a fear of incurring any responsibility, and a fear of going beyond their instructions."

For instance, Mr. Stafford determined to get the lavatories cleaned. He approached Dr. Menzies, who said it was none of his business. " If he had got in 12 or 13 men to clean out the lavatories he would immediately have been pounced on by another department and told that it belonged to that department." Mr. Stafford then went to Major Sillery, Military Commandant of the Hospital, who freely admitted the urgent necessary of the work, but asked where the money was to come from. He was " very nervous and anxious, very much distressed and perplexed ". He had no instructions to execute the work, the money would have to be advanced and he had no security for repayment. Mr. Stafford offered to pay himself. Major Sillery was horror-struck; and refused. Mr.

Stafford declared that if the lavatories were not cleaned he would write a letter and have it read aloud in the House of Commons. He then retired to bed with diarrhoea.

In his evidence before the Roebuck Committee Mr. Stafford made it clear that he did not blame Major Sillery. "He was most anxious to do all he could for the improvement and amelioration of the hospitals, but he had no money. He did not consider, neither did I, that he was called on to risk the money which he, as a man deriving his support from his profession would have had to do, if he had advanced this money for the payment of 16 Turks to cleanse the lavatories."

And then in the misery, the confusion, a light began to break. Gradually it dawned on harassed doctors and over-worked officials that there was one person in Scutari who could take action—who had money and the authority to spend it—Miss Nightingale.

She had a very large sum at her disposal derived from various sources and amounting to over £30,000, of which £7000 had been collected by her personally; and Constantinople was one of the great markets of the world. During the first horrors of November, the gathering catastrophe of December, it became known that whatever was wanted, from a milk pudding to a water-bed, the thing to do was to " go to Miss Nightingale ".

She made Mr. Macdonald, Sidney Godolphin Osborne and Mr. Augustus Stafford into her staff. To win their confidence was not easy. Officials at Scutari had been insolent to Mr. Macdonald, and had tried to prevent him from entering the hospitals; he regarded Miss Nightingale as a Government nominee, and was prepared to oppose her. Mr. Osborne and Mr. Stafford, burning with indignation at the sufferings of the troops, were also " on the point of going into opposition ". Through the influence of Henry Reeve, the political writer whose wife had been Miss Nightingale's friend, Delane of *The Times* instructed Mr. Macdonald to call on Miss Nightingale. She won him over and he became her Chief-of-Staff.

Each day she ascertained what comforts were lacking in the Purveyor's Store, what articles supply was short of, what requisitions had been made which had not been met. Mr. Macdonald then went into Constantinople and bought the goods, which were placed in her store and issued by her upon requisition in the official form by a medical officer. Nothing, with the exception of letter-paper and pencils, was ever given out without an official requisition duly signed. Gradually, Mr. Macdonald told the Roebuck Committee, the doctors ceased to be suspicious and their jealousy disappeared.

In one urgent work she met no opposition. Just as it was no one's business to clean the lavatories, so it was no one's business to clean the wards. The first commission Mr. Macdonald executed for Miss Nightingale was the purchase of 200 hard scrubbing-brushes and sacking for washing the floors. She insisted on the huge wooden tubs in the wards being emptied, standing quietly and obstinately by the side of each one, sometimes for an hour at a time, never scolding or raising her voice, until the orderlies gave way and the tub was emptied.

Her next step was to wash the men's clothes. Mr. Macdonald stated that for five weeks after he arrived at Scutari no washing was done at all. The Purveyor had been instructed to make a laundry contract and had done so with a Greek, who was quite unable to fulfil his obligations; he either failed to wash at all or washed in cold water, and shirts came back as filthy as they were sent, still crawling with lice. The men said they preferred their own lice to other people's and refused to part with their shirts, stuffing them, filthy and vermin-ridden, under their blankets. The total amount of washing satisfactorily accomplished for the vast hospital was seven shirts. Miss Nightingale made arrangements to rent a house outside the barracks and have the washing done by soldiers' wives. She consulted Dr. Menzies, telling him she wished to have boilers put in by the Engineers Corps. "Oh, but that is putting you to a great deal of trouble", said Dr. Menzies. "I should think the Purveyor would be able to make arrangements." The boilers were installed and the cost paid out of *The Times* fund.

Within the hospital her principal ally was Dr. McGrigor, first-class Staff Surgeon, a young, energetic man, not, she said, wedded in everything to what had been done in the Peninsula. He accepted her nurses and made full use of them.

For a time she tried to work with Lady Stratford. On November 7th, two days after her arrival, she wrote to Lord Stratford asking for sheets, shirts and portable stoves for cooking

" extras ". He sent her Lady Stratford instead. Lady Stratford would not come across to Scutari (she had been in the Barrack Hospital once and the stench had made her sick), nor did she send linen and stoves, but she offered to get anything that was required in Constantinople. Miss Nightingale asked her to obtain twelve waggons to bring heavy goods up to the Barrack Hospital. Next day she looked out and saw drawn up before her quarters seven glass and gilt coaches and five other vehicles, which she had to pay off out of her own private funds. " This lark of the Ambassadress's ", she wrote, " cost Miss Nightingale 500 piastres." Lady Stratford, "in consequence of want of practical habits of business, with the kindest and most benevolent intentions was nothing but good and bustling and a time waster and an impediment ".

By the end of December Miss Nightingale was in fact purveying the hospital. During a period of two months she supplied, on requisition of Medical Officers, about 6000 shirts, 2000 socks and 500 pairs of drawers. She supplied nightcaps, slippers, plates, tin cups, knives, forks, spoons " in proportion ". She procured trays, tables, forms, clocks, operating tables, scrubbers, towels, soap and screens. She caused an entire regiment which had only tropical clothing to be refitted with warm clothing purchased by Mr. Macdonald in the markets of Constantinople when Supply had declared such clothing unprocurable in the time—Supply was compelled to get all its goods from England. " I am a kind of General Dealer ", she wrote to Sidney Herbert on January 4th, 1855, " in socks, shirts, knives and forks, wooden spoons, tin baths, tables and forms, cabbages and carrots, operating tables, towels and soap, small tooth combs, precipitate for destroying lice, scissors, bed pans and stump pillows."

Before Sebastopol conditions grew steadily worse. The stores lost in the hurricane were not replaced. Men, sick or well, lay in a foot of water in the mud covered only by a single blanket. Every root had been burned, and the men had to eat their food raw : meat stiff with salt and dried peas. Tea was withdrawn and green coffee, needing roasting and pounding, was issued instead, because good results had been obtained from the use of green coffee in the Caffre War. There was no bread. As the percentage of sick climbed and climbed, double turns of duty were thrown on the survivors. Men were in the trenches before Sebastopol for thirty-six hours at a stretch, never dry, never warmed, never fed. The sick were brought down to Balaclava strapped to mule-litters lent by the French—there was no British transport of any kind— naked, emaciated and filthy. They were universally suffering from diarrhoea, and strapped to the mules they could not relieve themselves. After waiting hours without food or shelter in the icy wind or driving sleet at Balaclava, they were piled on to the decks of the sick transports and brought down to Scutari. And yet the catastrophe had not yet reached its height.

At the beginning of December, when the Barrack Hospital was filled to overflowing, a letter from Lord Raglan announced the arrival of a further 500 sick and wounded. It was impossible to cram any additional cases into the existing wards and corridors, and Miss Nightingale, supported by Dr. McGrigor, pressed to have put in order the wing of the hospital which had been damaged by fire before the British occupation; it consisted of two wards and a corridor and would accommodate nearly 1000 extra cases. But the cost would be considerable, and no one in the hospital had the necessary authority to put the work in hand. She had been repeatedly assured by Sidney Herbert that Lord Stratford had *carte blanche*; now she applied to him, and Lady Stratford came across to Scutari escorted by a couple of attachés. Preferring not to come inside the hospital, she held conferences with the Purveyor and Major Sillery in the courtyard, and 125 Turkish workmen were engaged to repair the wards. After a few days a dispute about the rate of wages arose and the Turkish workmen struck. Miss Nightingale wrote to Lord Stratford, who denied the slightest knowledge of the business, Lady Stratford withdrew, worried Major Sillery had neither money nor authority. On this Miss Nightingale took matters into her own hands. She engaged on her own responsibility not 125 but 200 workmen, and paid for them partly out of her own pocket and partly out of *The Times* fund. The wards were repaired and cleaned in time to receive the wounded.

Not only did she repair the wards, she equipped them. The Purveyor could provide nothing. " Orderlies were wanting, utensils were wanting, even water was wanting ", she wrote to Sidney Herbert on December 12th, 1854. " I supplied all the utensils, including knives and forks, spoons, cans, towels, etc. . . . and was able to send on the instant arrowroot in huge milk pails (two bottles of port wine in each) for 500 men." The number of sick and wounded finally received was 800. One of the men described his sensations when he at last got off the filthy sick transport and was received by Miss Nightingale and her nurses with clean bedding and warm food —" we felt we were in heaven ", he said.

The affair caused a sensation. Its fame reached the Crimea and was discussed in Colonel Sterling's mess. He was outraged. " Miss Nightingale coolly draws a cheque. Is this the way to manage the finances of a great nation ? *Vox populi ?* A divine afflatus. Priestess Miss N. Magnetic impetus drawing cash out of my pocket." It was the first important demonstration of what men at Scutari called the " Nightingale power ". Respect for the " Nightingale power " was increased when it became known that her action had been officially approved by the War Department and the money she had spent refunded to her.

But to Miss Nightingale these victories were only incidental, she never for a moment lost sight of the fact that the object of her mission was to prove the value of women as nurses. But, unhappily, no difficulties with doctors or purveyors were as wearing or as discouraging as her difficulties with her nurses.

" I came out, Ma'am, prepared to submit to everything, to be put on in every way. But there are some things, Ma'am, one can't submit to. There is the Caps, Ma'am, that suits one face and some that suits another. And if I'd known, Ma'am, about the caps, great as was my desire to come out to nurse at Scutari, I wouldn't have come, Ma'am." This, Miss Nightingale wrote to Dr. Bowman on November 14th 1854, was a specimen of the kind of question which had to be adjusted in the midst of appalling horror. " We are ", she wrote, "steeped up to our necks in blood." Mrs. Roberts from St. Thomas's was worth her weight in gold, Mrs. Drake from St. John's House was a treasure, but most of the other hospital nurses were not fit to take care of themselves—one had been sent home in disgrace for drunkenness as soon as the *Vectis* arrived and been replaced by a deaconess from the branch of the Kaiserswerth Institution at Constantinople. Nurses had to be forbidden to enter any ward which contained men even moderately well, to be forbidden to be in the wards on any pretext after 8 P.M. The Bermondsey nuns were admirable, so were two of the Sellonite sisters, but the white sisters from Norwood had nursed only in an orphanage, and with the best will in the world were unfitted for hospital work. To convince any of them, nurses or sisters, of the necessity for discipline was almost impossible. Why should a man who desperately needed stimulating food have to go without because the nurse who had the food could not give it to him until she had been authorised by a doctor? It was felt that Miss Nightingale was callous. It was said that she was determined to increase her own power and cared nothing for the sick.

These difficulties came to a head in December in the case of Sister Elizabeth Wheeler, one of the Sellonites. Sister Elizabeth, who was nursing wards of men suffering from diarrhoea and dysentery, saw the men brought in emaciated and in agony from the fearful pangs of hunger superimposed on diarrhoea, and her heart bled for them. She was a nurse of experience, and in her opinion the amount of food given to the men was inadequate: she was not allowed sufficient milk, eggs or port wine. A passionate and emotional woman, she had on several occasions forced her way in to Miss Nightingale and made a scene, demanding larger quantities. Miss Nightingale refused to supply anything except what was ordered by the doctor and written and confirmed on the diet roll. She did, however, apply to Dr. McGrigor for a doctor to go round her wards with Sister Elizabeth, listen to what she had to say, and then make out a new diet roll. Sister Elizabeth was furiously angry. She wrote letters home describing the fearful state of the wards and accusing the doctors of callousness and inhumanity. Unhappily one of her relatives passed on a letter to *The Times*. It was published on December 8th, 1854, as a letter from a heroic Scutari nurse, and was made full use of in the campaign *The Times* was conducting against the Government. Miss Nightingale was horrified, nothing more unfortunate could have occurred. She was trying to convince the doctors of the complete loyalty of her nurses, here was a complete contradiction; she was trying to weld the nurses into a disciplined band by means of her authority, and here her authority was directly attacked. Dr. McGrigor was her principal ally; there were intrigues against him, and she feared Sister Elizabeth had put a weapon in the hands of his enemies. An investigation took place before the Hospitals Commission in December 1854, Miss Nightingale and Sister Elizabeth both giving evidence. Sister Elizabeth's letter was not correct in its facts, for she had represented herself as nursing the wounded, but she had never nursed surgical cases. She had given a very high number of deaths and conveyed the impression that the deaths had occurred in a single ward when in reality they were the deaths for an entire division of the hospital. Her assertions were held to be inaccurate, and she was asked to resign.

Sister Elizabeth's attitude was common to a large number of Miss Nightingale's nurses. Reluctance to accept her authority and obey her instructions was constant from the beginning to the end of her mission, and many of her nurses heartily disliked her.

However, she had managed to establish herself, and now her nurses were fully occupied. She had also acquired two new and loyal workers in Dr. and Lady Alicia Blackwood, who had come out at their own expense after the battle of Inkerman. Dr. Blackwood obtained an appointment as Military Chaplain, Lady Alicia applied to Miss Nightingale to know where she could be most useful. After a few seconds of silence, and with a peculiar expression of countenance, Miss Nightingale said: " Do you mean what you say ? " Lady Alicia was rather surprised. " Yes, certainly, why do you ask me that ? " " Oh! because I have had several such applications before, and when I have suggested work, I found it could not be done, or some excuse was made; it was not exactly the sort of thing that was intended, it required special suitability, etc." " Well, I *am* in earnest," said Lady Alicia. On this Miss Nightingale asked her to be responsible for the wretched women who had been allowed to accompany the army and had been sent down from Varna. More than 260 women and infants were living in dark cellars beneath the Barrack Hospital; soldiers' wives, widows and prostitutes were crowded together, men from the Depot were forced to live with their wives in a room containing fifty or sixty other persons, a soil pipe drained into the corner of one cellar, drinking was incessant and the place was a pandemonium of drunkenness, cursing and swearing. Lady Alicia removed the more respectable among the women, setting them to work in the laundry, and began a lying-in hospital. The children were separated from the adults, and a system of doling out food through Mr. Bracebridge was adopted which, Miss Nightingale said, became the curse of the hospital. Thirty-six women and thirty-six infants under the age of three months howled together daily outside Mr. Bracebridge's door— the Turks called them his thirty-six wives.

On the 14th December she wrote Sidney Herbert a cheerful letter :

What we may be considered as having effected :—

(1) The kitchen for extra diets now in full action.
(2) A great deal more cleaning of wards, mops, scrubbing brushes, brooms and combs given out by ourselves.
(3) 2000 shirts, cotton and flannel, given out and washing organised.
(4) Lying-in hospital begun.
(5) Widows and soldiers' wives relieved and attended to.
(6) A great amount of daily dressing and attention to compound fractures by the most competent of us.
(7) The supervision and stirring-up of the whole machinery generally with the concurrence of the chief medical authority.
(8) The repairing of wards for 800 wounded which would otherwise have been left uninhabitable. (And this I regard as the most important.)

She never wrote quite so cheerfully again. On December 14th she suddenly discovered, through being shown a letter written by Liz Herbert to Mrs. Bracebridge, that a party of nurses numbering no fewer than forty-six had left London under the leadership of Mary Stanley and were actually due to arrive at Scutari the next day.

She had not been consulted or informed, and the despatch of the party was in direct contravention of her agreement with Sidney Herbert. There was an even more serious aspect : at this critical moment, when she was struggling with difficulties caused by Sister Elizabeth and her authority was being questioned, the party was consigned not to her but to Dr. Cumming; she had been publicly passed over. The significance of this action was not lost on either her friends or her enemies at Scutari, and Sidney Godolphin Osborne wrote that he feared the Nightingale ministry seemed to be coming to an end.

She was furiously angry, and on December 15th she wrote Sidney Herbert a scathing letter:

DEAR MR. HERBERT,

When I came out here as your Supt. it was with the distinct understanding (expressed both in your own hand writing and in the printed announcement which you put in the *Morning Chronicle* which is here in everyone's hands) that nurses were to be sent out at my requisition only, which was to be made only with the approbation of the Medical Officers here. You came to me in great distress and told me you were unable for the moment to find any other person for the office and that, if I failed you, the scheme would fail.

I sacrificed my own judgment and went out with forty females, well knowing that half that number would be more efficient and less trouble, and that the difficulty of inducing forty untrained women, in so extraordinary a position as this (turned loose among 3000 men) to observe any order or even any of the directions of the medical men, would be Herculean.

Experience has justified my foreboding. But I have toiled my way into the confidence of the medical men. I have, by incessant vigilance, day and night, introduced something like order into the disorderly operations of these women. And the plan may be said to have succeeded in some measure, *as it stands*. . . .

At this point of affairs arrives at *no one's* requisition, a fresh batch of women, raising our number to eighty-four.

You have sacrificed the cause, so near my heart. You have sacrificed me—a matter of small importance now—you have sacrificed your own written word to a popular cry. . . .

The quartering them *here* is a physical impossibility, the employing them a moral impossibility.

You must feel I ought to resign, where conditions are imposed on me which render the object for which I am employed unattainable—and I only remain at my post until I have provided in some measure for these poor wanderers. You will have to consider where they are to be employed, at Malta, Therapia or elsewhere or whether they are to return to England—and you will appoint a Superintendent in my place until which time I will continue to discharge its duties as well as I can.

Believe me, dear Mr. Herbert,

yours very truly,

FLORENCE NIGHTINGALE.

She had not done with him. She added a stinging post-script.

P.S. Had I had the enormous folly to write at the end of eleven days experience to require more women, would it not seem that you, as a Statesman, should have said " Wait until you can see your way better ". But I made no such request. The pro-portion of Roman Catholics which is already making an outcry you have raised to 25 in 84. Dr. Menzies has declared that he will have two only in the General Hospital—and I cannot place them here in a greater proportion than I have done without exciting the suspicion of the Medical Men and others.

In order that Sidney Herbert should not imagine she had written hastily she completed the letter by a statement at the foot : " Written 15 December. Posted 18 December."

On Sidney Herbert's part there was honest misunderstand-ing. He was harried, in poor health and almost worked to death. In the confused, unbalanced mind of Mary Stanley there was a mixture of religious fervour—she had secretly determined to become a Roman Catholic before she started for Scutari—and jealousy. The third person concerned, Liz Herbert, was prone to act emotionally and incalculably, to be easily swept into indiscretions ; and she, like Mary Stanley, was blinded by religious fervour ; though Liz Herbert did not become a Roman Catholic in her husband's lifetime, she was received into the Roman Church after his death.

Mr. Bracebridge spoke angrily of " Popish plots ", and that, Miss Nightingale said, was ridiculous. Yet behind the unreliable fervours of Mary Stanley and the easily persuaded emotionalism of Mrs. Herbert was the formidable figure of Manning, who wished to focus on the nuns of his church the fame and the glory which surrounded the Scutari nurses. He had no animus against Miss Nightingale ; they remained friends and she said on several occasions that he had treated her fairly ; but the arrival of Mary Stanley's party dealt her mission

183

a blow from which it never completely recovered. Before the arrival of the newcomers on December 15th, she was well on the way to complete success. After it, though she achieved personal triumphs, her authority was not established until her mission was almost ended. Her orders were constantly disobeyed, her right to command questioned, and the original purpose of the undertaking became obscured by a fog of sectarian bickering.

The high percentage of Catholics and High Church Anglicans in her original party had already provoked an outcry. Before she arrived at Scutari a letter published in the *Daily News* on October 28th, signed " Anti-Puseyite ", attacked her for recruiting her nurses from the Sellonites and a "Romanist establishment". Why, "Anti-Puseyite" demanded, had Lady Maria Forester been passed over? And he quoted Sidney Herbert's letter, which he declared to be animated by party spirit. (Parthe and Fanny had indiscreetly passed the letter round among their friends, and it had been copied.) Liz Herbert had written to the *Daily News* saying that Miss Nightingale was a member of the established Church of England, having been originally brought up a Unitarian. But the storm continued.

" Protestant Churchman " and " Bible Reader " wrote to the *Standard* to denounce her as an " Anglican Papist ". Dark references were made to " Anglo-Catholic ladies at the War Office ", " Jesuit conspiracies ", and the activities of " the pervert Manning ". One parson went so far as to caution his parishioners against sending any help to Scutari through a party composed of female ecclesiastics and Romish nuns instead of common-sense nurses.

If Mary Stanley had publicly announced her intention of joining the Roman Catholic Church Sidney Herbert would not have allowed her to go to Scutari. But she kept it a secret and took with her Mother Frances Bridgeman of Kinsale, an Irish nun of ardent and rebellious temperament who openly avowed she intended to execute a spiritual as well as a medical mission.

It was Miss Nightingale's fate to be attacked by both sides, to have to endure what she called the " Protestant Howl " and the " Roman Catholic Storm ". She belonged to a sect which, as the Dean of Elphin phrased it, is unfortunately a very rare one, the sect of the Good Samaritan.

Mary Stanley had been instrumental in collecting the first party, and could not have organised the second in good faith. Its constitution was contrary to Miss Nightingale's rules. The fifteen Irish nuns considered they were under no obligation to obey anyone but their Superior, Mother Bridgeman, and Mother Bridgeman acknowledged only the authority of her Bishop. The fact that the party was consigned to Dr. Cumming proved a clear intention to evade Miss Nightingale's authority. The party consisted of 9 ladies, 15 nuns and 22 nurses, 46 in all. It had been hastily collected. Many of the " hired nurses " were ludicrously without experience, one old woman, Jane Evans, having spent her life looking after pigs and cows. Out of the whole 46 no fewer than 20 had come out with the intention not of nursing but of being " assistant ecclesiastics ". Miss Stanley led the party, which was escorted by Dr. Meyer, a physician, and the Honourable Jocelyn Percy, M.P., described by Kinglake as a young fellow who had conceived a passionate admiration for Miss Nightingale, and left a life of ease and luxury with the object of becoming her fag and her footman. They travelled, like the first party, via Paris and Marseilles, but Mary Stanley had large ideas. A courier went ahead and took rooms for them in the dearest hotel in Paris, and Clarkey was asked to procure a dozen bottles of the best vinegar aromatique in case the nurses and ladies encountered bad smells ; she bought them wholesale and secured a discount.

The journey was discouraging. The " hired nurses " got drunk in the train and horrified the ladies by the vulgar peals of laughter which came from their carriage, one or two were drunk at dinner, several collapsed and revealed they suffered from delicate health, one appeared in an array of rings and brooches. Mary Stanley's spirits sank when she was told by a woman who seemed respectable that the language used was terrible ; most of the women had come out in the hope of getting husbands, and drunkenness was universal. Writing a character of each of her party to Liz Herbert, Mary Stanley admitted that the women chosen were too old ; perhaps a closer enquiry should have been made into their antecedents

and characters. The truth was she disliked and despised
" hired nurses "; the scheme she had come out to put into
operation was the scheme of " religious visitors ".   Among the
few " quiet sensible " women was Miss Polidori, the aunt of
Dante Gabriel Rossetti.   There was an unhappy moment at
Marseilles when the hired nurses protested vehemently at being
given quarters inferior to the rest of the party.   When they
embarked for Constantinople in a French vessel, the *Egypt*,
Mary Stanley hoped that the language might prove a barrier
between the hired nurses and the sailors.

On December 15th, between three and four in the afternoon, the *Egypt* anchored outside Constantinople.   Mr. Bracebridge went on board and advised the party not to disembark.
There literally was not a vacant corner in Scutari : Miss
Nightingale's quarters were already accommodating forty in
space adequate for three, and food, water and fuel were seriously
short ; nurses required the strictest supervision, and Miss
Nightingale could not deal with any more.   She would break
down.   The whole scheme would be ruined.   Dr. Meyer and
Mr. Percy were taken aback, and it was agreed that the nurses
and ladies should remain on the boat while the gentlemen went
to report the arrival of the party to Dr. Cumming.   He rebuffed
them.   Were people at home utterly ignorant of conditions at
Scutari—why had this party been sent out without his consent ?   Dr. Cumming refused to take any responsibility,
declining flatly to employ the nurses and ladies in the hospitals.
He could not, even if he had been willing, find them any
accommodation at Scutari, which was crammed to overflowing.
Lord Stratford had agreed to lend them temporarily a house at
Therapia belonging to the Embassy, and there they must go
until arrangements could be made to send them home.   Next,
Dr. Meyer and Mr. Percy went to Miss Nightingale, who summoned Mr. Bracebridge as a witness.   The interview was sadly
different from anything the romantic Mr. Percy had anticipated.   She was in a cold fury.   She refused to take any
responsibility for the party—she had never asked for them,
they had come without her consent.   Mr. Bracebridge took
down notes of what passed and later called on the two gentlemen with a memorandum of the conversation which they were
requested to sign.

One fact in particular was weighing very heavily on both gentlemen's minds. Owing to the style in which the party had travelled they had spent the whole of the £1500 with which they had started and were penniless.

Off they hurried to see the new Military Commandant, Lord William Paulet—Major Sillery had been recalled that week. The Military Commandant of a hospital was all-powerful, and Lord William was implored to assist them. But he could do nothing. It was a physical impossibility to find accommodation for the party in Scutari, and he certainly could not force nurses on doctors who did not want them. He spoke vaguely of the possibility of finding work for some of the party at a new hospital which was shortly to be opened at Abydos. Meanwhile he recommended them to go to Therapia.

There was nothing for it but to retire. Dr. Meyer and Mr. Percy remained behind in Constantinople trying to find employment and accommodation for the party, Mary Stanley and the other women went to the Embassy house at Therapia, where squabbles immediately broke out between the nurses and ladies. Mary Stanley instructed the " hired nurses " to do the housework : they were to wash, cook and sweep, to do the ladies' mending and to wait on them at table. The nurses rebelled, pointing out that this was not the work they had been brought out to do.

By the end of December the need for money had become urgent. Dr. Meyer and Mr. Percy had failed to make any arrangements for the nurses in Constantinople, and Lord and Lady Stratford, though " kindness itself ", did not advance any money. Dr. Cumming was applied to, but he refused to make any advance except from his own private funds. On the 21st the two gentlemen brought Mary Stanley to interview Miss Nightingale ; Dr. Cumming and Mr. Bracebridge were present, and notes of the conversation were taken down. Mary Stanley explained her plan : ten of the Protestants were to be appropriated as assistants by the chaplains and ten of the nuns by the priests, " not as nurses but as female ecclesiastics ". Miss Nightingale absolutely refused to countenance the scheme ; it was directly contrary to the instructions she had received from the War Office. She denied any responsibility for the party ; it had not been consigned to her and its

187

direction, maintenance and employment were not her affair. It was out of the question for her to finance them from the money entrusted to her, and she read aloud the letter she had written on December 15th and posted on December 18th to Sidney Herbert.

She then offered to lend Mary Stanley £90 from her own private income for the immediate necessities of the party, and it was unwillingly accepted. Later she lent another £300. That evening Mary Stanley wrote to Liz Herbert that it needed " all her love for Flo " not to feel hurt at being treated so *officially* and being made to discuss all arrangements before witnesses. She added that she did not think the Herberts need be anxious about Florence; as far as looks and *power* went she had never seen her in greater force.

And before Sebastopol the catastrophe steadily grew, and more and still more sick poured down. Four thousand were received in seventeen days between December 17th and January 3rd, and the death-rate steadily rose. Mr. Bracebridge wrote to Sidney Herbert on December 14th : " Flo has been working herself to death, never sits down to breakfast or dinner without interruption : often never dines . . . the attempt to do more will kill her . . . today 200 sick landed looking worse than any others yet."

Yet, harassed and distracted as she was, when her first anger was over she saw that it would be disastrous to send the party back. Racial and religious issues were involved, and Lord Napier had gone so far as to say that in his opinion there would be almost a rebellion in Ireland if the Irish nuns under Mother Bridgeman were sent home. A scandal would do the cause she had at heart irreparable harm. She must swallow her grievance.

On December 24th she saw Mary Stanley, Mr. Percy and Dr. Meyer again, and suggested a compromise. Some of the Irish nuns should be taken at once into Barrack Hospital, and to make room for them the white sisters from Norwood, who were not experienced in hospital nursing, should be sent home. She would write to Manning and make it clear that no blame attached to the Norwood nuns. This arrangement

188

would not increase the number of Roman Catholic nuns in the hospital, which was something Dr. Cumming refused to contemplate. The rest of the party must stay at Therapia, since there was not a square inch of room to be had in Scutari, but she would endeavour to get some nurses accepted at the new Convalescent Hospitals which were to open in a few weeks. She refused absolutely to have anything to do with the scheme for religious visiting.

Miss Nightingale was, wrote Mary Stanley to Liz Herbert, " very low. She feels that to employ the women herself is impossible—to send them back to England is to incur universal odium and perhaps mar for ever her future powers of usefulness."

On Christmas Day she wrote to Sidney Herbert: "You have not stood by me but I have stood by you. . . . All that I said in my letter to you I say *still* more strongly. Please do read it. . . . My heart bleeds for you, that you the centre of the Parliamentary row should have to attend to these miseries, tho' you have betrayed me. . . . I believe it may be proved as a logical proposition that it is impossible for me to ride through all these difficulties. My caïque is upset . . . but I am sticking on the bottom still. But there will be a storm will brush me off."

The storm burst immediately. Fine weather was never to return. The Sisters from Norwood, bathed in tears, bitterly resented being sent home and Father Michael Cuffe, the Roman Catholic chaplain, told Miss Nightingale in an angry interview that she was like Herod driving the Blessed Virgin across the desert. " Pray confirm Father Michael Cuffe in his position here ", she wrote to Sidney Herbert; "it is the only agreeable incident that I have had." Mother Bridgeman refused to allow her nuns to enter the Barrack Hospital without her—it would be " uncanonical ". She declared they must have their own Jesuit chaplain and refused the ministrations of Father Michael Cuffe, who was the official Roman Catholic chaplain. Miss Nightingale was on her feet for twenty hours at a time and dressing wounds and sores for eight hours at a stretch; but instead of rest she had arguments with Mary Stanley and Mother Bridgeman. Loud-voiced, assertive, voluble, Mother Bridgeman, christened by Miss Nightingale

" Rev. Brickbat ", was determined to force an entry into the Barrack Hospital with all her fifteen nuns *vi et armis*. Between them, Miss Nightingale wrote to Sidney Herbert on December 27th, they were leading her " the devil of a life ".

If Roman Catholic anger was aroused so was Protestant suspicion. " I grieve to say ", wrote Mrs. Bracebridge to Liz Herbert on December 28th, " that Miss Stanley's *false position* is already working fearful mischief, she is acting a very double part and is in league with the Revd. Mother Bridgeman of Kinsale to *force* Flo, if she can, to give way and appoint them together to the General Hospital where they will work their proselytizing unmolested. Miss Stanley is nothing more or less than a tool in hands of the Roman Catholics and she is put in a position to do enormous harm."

Next a Miss Tebbut at the General Hospital was accused by the Evangelicals of circulating improper books in the wards : she had lent a patient a copy of the *Christian Year*. Miss Nightingale herself was once more denounced by both sides. There had been Father Michael Cuffe's denunciation, and now a Protestant writer, getting information of her close friendship with Rev. Mother Bermondsey, gave the alarm of " Catholic Nuns transferring their allegiance from the Pope to a Protestant Lady ". When the paper containing this article reached Scutari, Sister Mary Gonzaga, a Bermondsey nun and a most efficient nurse, laughingly called Miss Nightingale " Your Holiness " and she in turn called Sister Mary " My Cardinal ". She was heard to say, " I do so want my Cardinal ", and a Protestant scandal ran through the hospital.

Protestants and Catholics not only quarrelled with each other but among themselves. Mother Bridgeman refused to meet the Bermondsey nuns, and her Jesuit Chaplain refused the sacrament to them. A Protestant chaplain wrote to the Secretary of State for War denouncing one of the Protestant nurses as a "Socinian "—a follower of Socinus, who denied the divinity of Christ—and demanded her instant removal. Dr. Blackwood, who had strong Evangelical views, was alleged to have preached against the nuns. One of the Irish nuns converted and re-baptized a soldier on his deathbed, and was promptly sent away by Miss Nightingale. " I do not intend

to let our little society become a hot bed of R.C. intriguettes ",
she wrote to Sidney Herbert.

Charges and counter-charges from clergymen, priests,
private persons, doctors and nurses flew backwards and
forwards between Whitehall and Scutari. Documents were
actually placed before the Secretary of State for War, and *The
Times*, in an article published on January 9th, 1855, commenting on the progress of Miss Nightingale's mission, stated:
" The success of the experiment as a feature of the medical
department of the army cannot be considered as decisively
established until certain religious dissensions which have arisen
are set at rest. . . . There is some danger of the whole undertaking coming to an abrupt conclusion."

The very practice she had stipulated in her interview with
Sidney Herbert as one that must at all costs be avoided—the
selection of nurses for sectarian reasons and not for their
efficiency as nurses—was thrust on her despite herself by the
composition of the second party. Presbyterians now wrote demanding that "some Presbyterian nurses" be sent out, and she
felt she must acquiesce. When the nurses arrived two immediately went out with a pair of orderlies and were brought back
hopelessly intoxicated. She had to send them home, but she
knew there would be a storm not because she was sending home
two nurses but because she was returning two Presbyterians.

" Meanwhile ", she wrote to Lady Canning, ". . . the
second party of Nuns who came out now wander over the
whole Hospital out of nursing hours, not confining themselves
to their own wards, or even to patients but ' instructing ' (it is
their own word) groups of Orderlies and Convalescents in the
corridors, doing the work each of ten chaplains."

However, by January 2nd something had been arranged.
Dr. Cumming had been persuaded to raise the number of
nurses to fifty, "for which", wrote Miss Nightingale, "we owe
him eternal gratitude". Mother Bridgeman still refused to
allow her nuns into the Barrack Hospital, but some of the best
" hired " nurses had been sent for and some of the " ladies "
had gone to the General Hospital, where one of them, Miss
Tebbut, finally became Superintendent. Mr. Percy had
" sneaked home like a commander who has set so many
Robinson Crusoes on a desert island ", and Dr. Meyer had

obtained a post at a convalescent hospital in Smyrna. "Enough of this subject, of which among these realities of life and death I am thoroughly sick", wrote Miss Nightingale to Sidney Herbert.

In the second week of January 1855 she received his answer to her letter of December 18th. He accepted full blame, confirmed her authority, implored her not to resign, left everything to her discretion and, finally, authorised her, if she thought fit, to send the second party home at his personal expense. Liz wrote equally penitent. Miss Nightingale was moved; the letters were " most Generous and I deeply feel it. At the same time I do not regret what I said."

She then ceased recriminations and throughout the misfortunes caused by Mary Stanley's party never again reminded Sidney Herbert that he was responsible for their ever having arrived at all.

After two months of hospital life Mary Stanley found herself utterly disillusioned. She no longer wished to go to the Barrack Hospital—it was filthy, vermin-infested, she had found fleas on her dress; and Florence expected far too much in the way of discipline: " Few English-women of education would submit to the kind of subjection she requires ". She had planned to bring her party out, stay long enough to perform a few heroic deeds, and then go back covered with glory to England. Instead she found herself stranded at Therapia exhausted by squabbles between nurses and ladies; her consolations were the frequent visits she paid Lady Stratford at the Embassy and her intimacy with the Irish nuns and their private chaplain, Father Ronan. Father Ronan had not come out on the *Egypt*: it had been felt that things would be smoother if he travelled out quietly on another boat. Now he was established in Constantinople and was preparing Mary Stanley for reception into the Roman Church; she was actually received some time during the spring, but was advised that she need feel under no obligation to publish the fact. At the end of January it was suggested that the Turkish Cavalry Barracks at Koulali should be turned into a hospital, and Mary Stanley, encouraged by Lady Stratford, determined to take it over with her nuns, nurses and ladies and run it in her own way. At the same time Lord Raglan suggested that eleven nurses should be sent to the General Hospital at Balaclava.

Miss Nightingale did not wish nurses to go, for the Hospitals Commission had reported adversely on the hospital there : it was filthy, inefficient, the orderlies were undisciplined, and Balaclava was even more crammed with troops than Scutari. However, certain nurses, led by a Welshwoman, Elizabeth Davis, from Mary Stanley's party, were determined to escape Miss Nightingale's discipline, and she herself was unwilling to refuse Lord Raglan. She gave way, and eleven volunteers under the control of the Superior of the Sellonite sisters went to Balaclava. Mary Stanley herself, with Mother Bridgeman and ten of her nuns, went off to Koulali, refusing to ask Dr. Cumming's permission and declaring she would arrange the purveying of the hospital herself. Five or six " hired nurses ", who were first class, preferred to stay at Scutari, and the remaining five of Mother Bridgeman's nuns were accepted by the General Hospital at Scutari, whence Miss Nightingale received constant complaints of their religious activities. Thus Mary Stanley's party was dissolved.

But Mary Stanley's own reign at Koulali was short. It was to be run on the lady plan, with Lady Stratford supplying the hospital and making it comfortable without all the difficulties which Miss Nightingale raised. There were to be maids of all work to do the menial tasks. The ladies were not to wear uniform. Liz Herbert sent " white furred coats " and was asked for straw bonnets. Miss Nightingale was understandably annoyed by the Koulali plan. " I have ", she wrote to Sidney Herbert on February 12th, " . . . by strict subordination to the authorities and by avoiding all individual action, introduced a number of arrangements, within the regulations of the service, useful on a large scale but not interesting to individual ladies ; e.g. four extra diet kitchens of which two, which I administer, feed above seven hundred of the worst cases, furniture and clothing, washing, bath-house, lock-up cupboards, etc. etc. This is not so amusing as pottering and messing about with little cookeries of individual beef teas for the poor sufferers personally, and my ladies do not like it. I acknowledge it, at the same time it is obvious that what I have done could not have been done had I not worked with the medical authorities and not in rivalry with them. . . . Cumming and I work hand in hand, and I have carried through him almost all that was possible under these awful difficulties. And he comes to me every evening. I protest emphatically now, before it is too late against the Koulali plan, i.e. the lady plan. It ends in nothing but spiritual flirtation between the ladies and the soldiers. I saw enough of that here ; it pets the particular man, it gets nothing done in the general. . . . The ladies all quarrel among themselves. The medical men laugh at their helplessness, but like to have them about for the sake of a little female society, which is natural but not our object."

Koulali was not ready when Mary Stanley arrived. The second day she was having tea with Lady Stratford, who had come over escorted by Lord Napier, when two steamers suddenly anchored before the hospital and 300 sick were carried in. There were no beds, no food. Sacks were hastily stuffed with straw, ladies made lemonade. That night Mary Stanley went round the wards and discovered her health would not stand the strain. More sick poured in, and she became hysterical. " I cannot stay ", she wrote to Liz Herbert. " I am not strong enough for the work. I have long been forced to give up special ward work." When she applied to Miss Nightingale for more ladies the letter was referred to Dr. Cumming, who visited Koulali and was not pleased. He found that the ladies did little but stroll about with notebooks in their hands, and refused to send any more. The Embassy was outraged, and Lord William Paulet said threateningly that Dr. Cumming had better remember that his was a *Government* appointment. Confusion at Koulali increased. Stores vanished. It was impossible to keep the hospital even decently clean. Mortality steadily rose until Koulali had the highest mortality rate of any hospital, higher even than the Barrack Hospital. Mary Stanley's letters became desperate. " I feel anxious to come home before the strain has quite worn me out. For my mother's sake I dare not do more . . . dear Mrs. Herbert don't be sorry to see me." Alarmed at the predicament into which she had thrust herself, she had even appealed to Miss Nightingale ; in the name of their old affection, she must be allowed to explain. In her reply, just, implacable, chilling, Miss Nightingale ended their friendship. " I have nothing further to say. And for ' explanation ', I refer you to yourself. I have nothing to forgive. For I have never felt anger. I have never known you. There has been no 'difference' between us—except a slight one of opinion as to the distribution of Articles and the manner of doing so to Patients. The pain you have given has not been by differing nor by anything for which forgiveness can be asked, but by not being yourself, or at least what I thought yourself. You say truly how I have loved you. No one will ever love you more.—Florence Nightingale."

In March Lady Stratford sent for the Head Chaplain, Mr. Sabin, and attacked him on the subject of Mary Stanley's grievances. It was monstrous to accuse her of Romanist propaganda; the truth was Miss Nightingale was jealous of Miss Stanley. Mr. Sabin lost his temper and told Lady Stratford that she had been "grossly imposed on": the rumours of Roman Catholic propaganda at Koulali were true, and Mary Stanley was actively assisting Mother Bridgeman. He himself had received trustworthy information from home that Miss Stanley had in fact been received into the Roman Church, and was only waiting to declare herself. Lady Stratford was horrified—her husband's Protestant views were well known. "Don't tell Lord Stratford!" she cried. Immediately afterwards Mary Stanley went home.

Miss Nightingale had known the truth all along, but her sense of honour would not allow her to make use of it. "Now observe, dear Mr. Herbert", she wrote on March 5th 1855, "this bother is none of my making. I have kept strict honour with Lady Stratford and also with Dr. Cumming about Mary Stanley's religious opinions. I could so easily have defeated her representations by 'telling of her' as the children say, and Mrs. Herbert will think that I have. . . . Koulali has excited suspicion without me, or in spite of me. Cumming asked the question one day in my room whether Miss Stanley were not an R.C. and I put it off in order that he might not say he heard it from me."

Mary Stanley had gone, but she had undermined Miss Nightingale's authority, prejudiced her relations with officials, intensified religious animosity and left Mother Bridgeman behind her to cause future difficulties. It was but a minor consolation that Lady Stratford sent in a bill for £8200 for purveying Koulali which the authorities had to pay.

At this difficult juncture Miss Nightingale's position was strengthened by Queen Victoria. On December 6th the Queen wrote to Sidney Herbert: "Would you tell Mrs. Herbert that I beg she would let me see frequently the accounts she receives from Miss Nightingale and Mrs. Bracebridge, as I hear *no details of the wounded* though I see so many from officers etc., about the battlefield and naturally the former must interest *me* more than anyone. Let Mrs. Herbert also know that I wish Miss Nightingale and the ladies would tell these poor noble wounded and sick men that *no-one* takes a warmer interest or feels *more* for their sufferings or admires their courage and heroism *more* than their Queen. Day and night she thinks of her beloved troops. So does the Prince. Beg Mrs. Herbert to communicate these my words to those ladies, as I know that *our* sympathy is valued by these noble fellows."

"The men were touched", wrote Miss Nightingale to Sidney Herbert on December 25th. "'It is a very feeling letter' they said. 'She thinks of us' (said with tears). 'Queen Victoria is a Queen that is very *fond* of her soldiers.'" The message was read aloud by the chaplains in the wards, posted up in the hospitals and published in the newspapers. On December 14th the Queen had sent gifts to the men and a personal message to Miss Nightingale, who was entrusted with the distribution of the gifts. The Queen wished her to "be made aware that your goodness and self devotion in giving yourself up to the soothing attendance upon these wounded and sick soldiers had been observed by the Queen with sentiments of the highest approval and admiration". Would she suggest something the Queen could do "to testify her sense of the courage and endurance so abundantly shown by her sick soldiers?"

Miss Nightingale was already pressing Sidney Herbert to change a regulation affecting the sick soldier's pay; 9d. a day was stopped from the pay of the sick soldier while he was in hospital, even though his sickness was the direct result of active service, while the wounded man was stopped only 4½d. a day. Now she wrote directly to the Queen asking her to have the stoppage made the same for sickness as for wounds provided the sickness was incurred as the result of duty before the enemy. She also asked that a Firman might be requested from the Sultan making over the military cemeteries at Scutari to the British. The Queen acted immediately on both suggestions. On February 1st it was announced that the men's pay would be rectified as from the battle of the Alma, and in the same month Lord Clarendon, the Foreign Secretary, successfully applied to the Sultan for a Firman transferring the ownership of the cemeteries to the British.

Officials engaged in opposing Miss Nightingale were thus reminded that her influence was very great. If the arrival and conduct of Mary Stanley and her party had shaken Miss Nightingale's prestige, Queen Victoria assisted materially to restore it. " It did very much having as our friends the great men ", wrote Miss Nightingale to Mrs. Herbert in 1855.

In January 1855 the sufferings of the British Army before Sebastopol began to reach a fearful climax. William Howard Russell described the wounded arriving at Balaclava, strapped to the mules lent by the French: " They formed one of the most ghastly processions that ever poet imagined. . . . With closed eyes, open mouths and ghastly attenuated faces, they were borne along two by two, the thin steam of breath visible in the frosty air alone showing that they were alive. One figure was a horror, a corpse, stone dead, strapped upright in its seat . . . no doubt the man had died on his way down to the harbour. . . . Another man I saw with raw flesh and skin hanging from his fingers, the raw bones of which protruded into the cold, undressed and uncovered."

Still no stores had reached the army. What had happened to them (the Roebuck Committee demanded later)? Huge quantities of warm clothing, of preserved foods, of medical comforts and surgical supplies had been sent out—where did they all go? It was never discovered. The Roebuck Committee found it impossible not to suspect dishonesty, but Miss Nightingale reached a different conclusion. Large quantities unquestionably vanished in the Turkish Customs House, a " bottomless pit whence nothing ever issues of all that is thrown in", but she declared notwithstanding that stores were available all the time the men were suffering, never reaching them through the " regulations of the service ". She cites a number of instances in her *Notes on Matters affecting the Health, Efficiency and Hospital Administration of the British Army*. In January 1855, when the army before Sebastopol was being ravaged by scurvy, a shipload of cabbages was thrown into the harbour at Balaclava on the ground that it was not consigned to anyone. This happened not once but several times. During November, December and January 1854–55, when green coffee was being issued to the men, there were 173,000 rations of tea in store at Balaclava; 20,000 lb. of lime juice arrived for the troops on December 10th, 1854, but none was issued until February. Why? Because no order existed for the inclusion of tea and lime juice in the daily ration.

Again, at the end of December there were blankets enough in store, says Miss Nightingale, to have given a third one to every man. But the men lay on the muddy ground with nothing under them and nothing over them since their blankets had been lost in battle or destroyed in the hurricane, because the regulations did not entitle them to replacement. At Scutari the Hospitals Commission recorded in January 1855 : " Goods have been refused although they were, to our personal knowledge, lying in abundance in the store of the Purveyor. This was done because they had not been examined by the Board of Survey." Miss Nightingale wrote to Sidney Herbert in March of that year. " The *Eagle* has now been arrived three weeks, and no use whatever has been made of her stores. Cumming says they have not yet been ' sat on '." In February when the men were lying naked in the bitter cold Mr. Wreford, the Purveyor, admitted to the Hospitals Commission that he had received a large quantity of shirts a fortnight ago, but he had done nothing with them, did not even know the quantity as he had not yet had a ' board '." On February 15th Miss Nightingale wrote to Sidney Herbert : " I received a requisition from the Medical Officers at Balaclava for shirts. . . . I went to the Purveyor, as I always do, to give him a chance. The Purveyor answered 1st that he had no shirts. ' Yes,' I said, ' you have received 27,000 landed four days ago.' 2nd that he could not unpack them without a board—to which I answered that on every bale I had seen the number within marked, and he could send one or two bales making a memorandum for the Board—3rd that they were at the General Hospital and he could not get an order in time. It ended by his accepting my offer to send a bale of my shirts which he might replace to me afterwards." Packing was hopelessly inefficient. When the men were lying on the bare floor in the Barrack Hospital a large consignment of cots arrived without legs; close stools were sent without lids; boots arrived in impossibly small sizes. It was notorious that large fortunes were made in England out of Crimean army contracts.

On January 2nd 1200 sick men arrived in one consignment at Scutari. Eighty-five per cent of these, wrote Miss Nightingale, were cases of acute scurvy. For want of lime juice and vegetables the men's teeth were dropping out, in some cases they were losing toes. On January 4th she wrote to Sidney Herbert enclosing copies of requisitions on the Purveyor, "properly signed by a 1st class staff surgeon, Dr. O'Flaherty", for supplies required for Barrack Hospital:

Flannel shirts	Answer	None in store
Socks	,,	None in store
Drawers	,,	None in store

N.B. There are some tea-pots and coffee-pots.

Required for Barrack Hospital

Plates	None in store
Tin drinking cups	None in store
Earthenware urine cups	Metal plenty
Bedpans	Some
Close stools	Plenty but frames missing
Pails for tea	None at present

In January 1855 there were 12,000 men in hospital and only 11,000 in the camp before Sebastopol; and still the ship-loads came pouring down.

It was, Miss Nightingale wrote, "calamity unparalleled in the history of calamity". The British Army was being destroyed, but Lord Stratford, she wrote to Sidney Herbert on January 8th, "absorbed in politics does not know the circumstances. Lord W'm Paulet knows them but partially, Menzies knows them but will not tell them, Wreford knows them and is stupefied. The medical officers, if they were to betray them, would have it reported personally and professionally to their disadvantage. Lord Wm. Paulet and Dr. Forrest the new

Medical Head, I see are *desperate*. Matters are worse than they were two months ago, and will be worse two months hence than they are now."

In this emergency she became supreme. She was the rock to which everyone clung, even the Purveyors. She described "Messrs. Wreford, Ward and Reade, veterans of the Spanish War, coming to me for a moment's solace, trembling under responsibility and afraid of informality". "Nursing", she wrote on January 4th to Sidney Herbert, "is the least of the functions into which I have been forced."

Her calmness, her resource, her power to take action raised her to the position of a goddess. The men adored her. "If she were at our head", they said, "we should be in Sebastopol next week." The doctors came to be absolutely dependent on her, and Colonel Sterling wrote home: "Miss Nightingale now queens it with absolute power".

Sidney Herbert had asked her to write to him privately in addition to her official reports, and during her time in Scutari and the Crimea she wrote him a series of over thirty letters of enormous length, crammed with detailed and practical suggestions for the reform of the present system. It is almost incredible that in addition to the unceasing labour she was performing, when she was living in the foul atmosphere of the Barrack Hospital incessantly harried by disputes, callers, complaints and overwhelmed with official correspondence which had to be written in her own hand, she should have found time and energy to write this long series of vast, carefully thought out letters, many as long as a pamphlet. She never lost sight of the main issue. At the time of the arrival of the Mary Stanley party she wrote: "There is a far greater question to be agitated before the country than that of these eighty-four miserable women—eighty-five including me. This is whether the system or no system which is found adequate in time of peace but wholly inadequate to meet the exigencies of a time of war is to be left as it is—*or* patched up temporarily, as you give a beggar half pence—or made equal to the wants not diminishing but increasing of a time of awful pressure."

On January 8th, at the height of the "calamity unparalleled in the history of calamity", she wrote: "I have written a plan for the systematic organisation of these Hospitals upon a principle of centralisation under which the component parts might be worked in unison. But on consideration deeming so great a change impracticable during the present heavy pressure of calamities here, I refrain from forwarding it, and substitute a sketch of a plan, by which great improvement might be made from within without abandoning the forms under which the service is carried on. . . ." Page after page of practical detailed suggestions follow, dealing with the reorganisation of the Purveyor's department, the establishment of a corps of medical orderlies, the rearrangement and improvement of the cooking and service of the men's food, the establishment of a medical school at Scutari, where at present there was " no operating room, no dissecting room ; post-mortem examinations are seldom made, and then in the dead house (the ablest Staff surgeon here told me that he considered he had killed hundreds of men owing to the absence of these) ". Finally, she made an urgent plea for medical statistics. " No statistics are kept as to between what ages most deaths occur, as to modes of treatment, appearances of the body after death, etc., etc., etc., . . . Our registration is so lamentably defective that often the only record kept is—*a man died* on such and such a day."

In another immense letter of January 28th she elaborated her scheme for reorganising the interior administration of the hospitals. The Purveyor was to be abolished, the hospital to have its own storekeeper, the Commissariat to supply all the food under the direction of a " kind of Hotel-keeper " in the hospital. Each bed in the hospital was to have its own furniture and bedding supplied with it. The hospital was to be an entity in itself, not an appendage produced by the union of several departments.

She asked nothing for herself, nor did she use her influence to make life easier for herself by securing advancement for her friends. The only record of her having solicited promotion was on behalf of Dr. McGrigor. She asked Sidney Herbert to promote him a Deputy Inspector-General two years before the proper time and thus do " a service to humanity at the expense of the Regulations of the Service ". If Dr. McGrigor were not promoted the work he was doing could be stopped by the simple process of the authorities bringing into the hospital someone senior to himself, in which case he would no longer be entitled to give orders. Dr. McGrigor was promoted.

Her facts and figures were freely used by Sidney Herbert and other members of the Cabinet, and important changes made in British Army organisation during the course of the Crimean War were based on her suggestions. On September 20th, 1855, a Royal Warrant was issued authorising the formation of a Medical Staff Corps. This corps did away with the unsatisfactory orderly system, the Warrant being based on the suggestions contained in her letter of January 8th. A Medical School was founded during the campaign, and the suggestions respecting the Purveyor, though not carried out immediately, formed the basis of reforms executed at a later date.

In spite of the improvements in the Barrack Hospital, something was horribly wrong. The wards were cleaner, the lavatories unstopped, the food adequate, but still the mortality climbed. The disaster was about to enter its second phase. The men were dying, not of the diseases with which they entered the hospital but of disease they caught in the hospital. At the end of December an epidemic broke out described variously as " Asiatic cholera " or " famine fever ", similar to cholera brought over by starving Irish immigrants after the Irish potato famine, and by Miss Nightingale simply as " gaol fever ". By the middle of January the epidemic was serious— four surgeons died in three weeks, and three nurses and poor old Ward, the Purveyor, and his wife died. The officers on their rounds began to be afraid to go into the wards ; they could do nothing for the unfortunates perishing within ; they knocked on the door and an orderly shouted " All right, sir " from inside.

The snow ceased and faint warmth came to the bleak plateau before Sebastopol on which the British Army was encamped. The number of men sent down by sick transports stopped rising. The percentage of sick was still disastrously, tragically high, but it was stationary.

But in the Barrack Hospital the mortality figures continued to rise. Sister Margaret Goodman saw an *araba*, a rough Turkish tumbril, heaped with what she took to be the carcases of beasts. They were the naked emaciated bodies of dead English soldiers. A large square hole of no great depth was dug by Turks, the bodies were tossed into this until they came level with the top, then a layer of earth was shovelled over all and the Turks stamped it down. They then drove off. The English were unable to bury their dead. A fatigue party could not be mustered whose strength was equal to the task of digging a pit.

In England fury succeeded fury. A great storm of rage, humiliation and despair had been gathering through the terrible winter of 1854–55. For the first time in history, through reading the despatches of Russell, the public had realised " with what majesty the British soldier fights ". And these heroes were dead. The men who had stormed the heights at Alma, charged with the Light Brigade at Balaclava, fought the grim battle against overwhelming odds in the fog at Inkerman had perished of hunger and neglect. Even the horses which had taken part in the Charge of the Light Brigade had starved to death.

On January 26th Mr. Roebuck, Radical member for Sheffield, brought forward a motion for the appointment of a committee " to inquire into the condition of the Army before Sebastopol and the conduct of those departments of the Government whose duty it has been to minister to the wants of that Army ". It was a vote of censure on the Government, and it was carried in an uproar by a majority of 157. The Government fell and Sidney Herbert went out of office, but Miss Nightingale's position was not weakened. The new Prime Minister was her old friend and supporter, Lord Palmerston. The two offices of Secretary for War and Secretary at War were combined and held by Lord Panmure, who was instructed to show consideration for her wishes and opinions. Her reports were regularly forwarded to the Queen and studied by her. Sidney Herbert wrote to assure her that he had no intention of giving up his work for the army because he was out of office. She was still to write to him, and he would see that her reports and suggestions were forwarded to the proper quarters. He would continue to be, she wrote, " our protector in this terrible great work ".

At the end of February, Lord Panmure sent out a Sanitary Commission to investigate the sanitary state of the buildings used as hospitals and of the camps both at Scutari and in the Crimea. The Commission was formed at the suggestion of Lord Shaftesbury, Palmerston's son-in-law and Miss Nightingale's old friend. Her name did not appear, but the urgency, the clarity, the forcefulness of the instructions are unmistakably hers. "The utmost expedition must be used in starting your journey. . . . On your arrival you will instantly put yourselves into communication with Lord William Paulet. . . . As no time is to be lost, you may reserve your detailed and minute reports and give in the first instance a statement only of the things to be done forthwith. . . . It is important that you be deeply impressed with the necessity of not resting content with an order but that you see instantly, by yourselves or your agents, to the commencement of the work and to its superintendence day by day until it is finished."

This Commission, said Miss Nightingale, " saved the British Army ". It consisted of Dr. John Sutherland, an official of well-known ability and advanced views from the Board of Health, Mr., later Sir, Robert Rawlinson, a civil engineer of eminence, and Dr. Gavin. With the ill luck which seemed to dog all Crimean undertakings, Dr. Gavin was accidentally killed by his brother letting off a pistol shortly after his arrival, and his place was filled by Dr. Milroy. In addition the three Commissioners took with them the Borough Engineer and three sanitary inspectors from Liverpool, where a sanitary act had been in operation longer than anywhere else in the country, and shipped out a large quantity of building material.

They were followed by another Commission, the McNeill and Tulloch Commission of Enquiry into the Supplies for the British Army in the Crimea. This Commission of Enquiry went direct to the Crimea and did not call at Scutari. It consisted of Colonel Alexander Tulloch, R.E., and Sir John McNeill, who had had many years' experience first as a doctor and then as an administrator in India and Persia. He had been Poor Law Commissioner in Scotland, and thanks to his energy and initiative the Highland peasants, though almost as dependent as the Irish on potatoes, had escaped the worst consequences of the failure of the potato crop in 1846–47.

The Sanitary Commission landed at Constantinople at the beginning of March and began work instantly. Their discoveries were hair-raising. They described the sanitary defects of the Barrack Hospital as " murderous ". Beneath the magnificent structure were sewers of the worst possible construction, mere cess-pools, choked, inefficient and grossly over-loaded. The whole vast building stood in a sea of decaying filth. The very walls, constructed of porous plaster, were soaked in it. Every breeze, every puff of air, blew poisonous gas through the pipes of numerous open privies into the corridors and wards where the sick were lying. "It is impossible", Miss Nightingale told the Royal Commission of 1857, "to describe the state of the atmosphere of the Barrack Hospital at night. I have been well acquainted with the dwellings of the worst parts of most of the great cities of Europe, but have never been in any atmosphere which I could compare with it." Nurses had noticed that certain beds were fatal. Every man put in these beds quickly died. They proved to be near the doors of the privies, where the poisonous gases were worst. The water supply was contaminated and totally insufficient. The Commissioners had the channel opened through which the water flowed, and the water supply for the greater part of the hospital was found to be passing through the decaying carcase of a dead horse. The storage of water was in tanks in the courtyard, and these had been built next temporary privies, erected to cope with the needs of men suffering from the prevalent diarrhoea. The privies were open and without any means of flushing or cleaning. The courtyard and precincts of the hospital were filthy. The Commissioners ordered them to be cleared, and during the first fortnight of this work 556 handcarts and large baskets full of rubbish were removed and 24 dead animals and 2 dead horses buried. The Commission began to flush and cleanse the sewers, to lime-wash the walls and free them from vermin, to tear out the wooden shelves known as Turkish divans which ran round the wards and harboured the rats for which the Barrack Hospital was notorious. The effect was instant. At last the rate of mortality began to fall. In the Crimea spring came with a rush, the bleak plateau before Sebastopol was bathed in sunlight and carpeted with crocuses and hyacinths. The road to Balaclava became passable, the men's rations improved, and the survivors of the fearful winter lost their unnatural silence and began once more to curse and swear.

The emergency was passing, and as it passed opposition to Miss Nightingale awoke again.

X MISS NIGHTINGALE'S MISSION falls into two periods. There is first the period of frightful emergency during the winter of 1854–55. In Sidney Godolphin Osborne's opinion, if at that time Miss Nightingale had not been present the hospitals must have collapsed. Every consideration but that of averting utter catastrophe went by the board, opposition died away and she became supreme.

But as soon as things had slightly improved official jealousy re-awoke. In the second period, from the spring of 1855 until her return to England in the summer of 1856, gratitude—except the gratitude of the troops—and admiration disappeared, and she was victimised by petty jealousies, treacheries and misrepresentations. Throughout this second period she was miserably depressed. At the end of it she was obsessed by a sense of failure.

By the spring of 1855 she was physically exhausted. She was a slight woman who had never been robust, was accustomed to luxury and was now living in almost unendurable hardship. When it rained, water poured through the roof of her quarters and dripped through the floor on an officer beneath, who complained that " Miss Nightingale was pouring water on his head ". The food was uneatable, the allowance of water was still one pint a head a day, the building was vermin-infested, the atmosphere in the hospital so foul that to visit the wards produced diarrhoea. She never went out except to hurry over the quarter of a mile of refuse-strewn mud which separated the Barrack from the General Hospital.

When a flood of sick came in she was on her feet for twenty-four hours at a stretch. She was known to pass eight hours on her knees dressing wounds. " She had an utter disregard of contagion ", wrote Sidney Godolphin Osborne. ". . . The more awful to every sense any particular case, especially if it was that of a dying man, the more certainly might her slight form be seen bending over him, administering to his ease by every means in her power and seldom quitting his side until death released him." It was her rule never to let any man who came under her observation die alone. If he were conscious she herself stayed beside him, if he were unconscious she sometimes allowed Mrs. Bracebridge to take her place. She estimated that during that winter she witnessed 2000 deathbeds. The worst cases she nursed herself. " I believe ", wrote Dr. Pincoffs, a civilian doctor who worked in the Barrack Hospital, "that there was never a severe case of any kind that escaped her notice, and sometimes it was wonderful to see her at the bedside of a patient who had been admitted perhaps an hour before, and of whose arrival one would hardly have supposed she could be already cognisant." One of the nurses described accompanying her on her night rounds. " It seemed an endless walk and one not easily forgotten. As we slowly passed along the silence was profound ; very seldom did a moan or cry from those deeply suffering fall on our ears. A dim light burned here and there, Miss Nightingale carried her lantern which she would set down before she bent over any of the patients. I much admired her manner to the men—it was so tender and kind."

Her influence was extraordinary. She could make the men stop drinking, write home to their wives, submit to pain. " She was wonderful ", said a veteran, " at cheering up anyone who was a bit low." " She was full of life and fun when she talked to us ", said another, " especially if a man was a bit down-hearted." The surgeons were amazed at her ability to strengthen men doomed to an operation. " The magic of her power over men was felt ", writes Kinglake, " in the room—the dreaded, the bloodstained room—where operations took place. There perhaps the maimed soldier if not yet resigned to his fate, might be craving death rather than meet the knife of the surgeon, but when such a one looked and saw that the honoured Lady in Chief was patiently standing beside him—and with lips closely set and hands folded—decreeing herself to go through the pain of witnessing pain, he used to fall into the mood of obeying her silent command and—finding strange support in her presence—bring himself to submit and endure."

The troops worshipped her. " What a comfort it was to see her pass even ", wrote a soldier. " She would speak to one, and nod and smile to as many more ; but she could not do it all you know. We lay there by hundreds ; but we could kiss her shadow as it fell and lay our heads on the pillow again content."

For her sake the troops gave up the bad language which has always been the privilege of the British private soldier. "Before she came", ran another letter, "there was cussing and swearing but after that it was as holy as a church."

When the war was over Miss Nightingale wrote: " . . . The tears come into my eyes as I think how, amidst scenes of loathsome disease and death, there rose above it all the innate dignity, gentleness and chivalry of the men (for never surely was chivalry so strikingly exemplified) shining in the midst of what must be considered the lowest sinks of human misery, and preventing instinctively the use of one expression which could distress a gentlewoman."

It was work hard enough to have crushed any ordinary woman, yet, she wrote, it was the least of her functions. The crushing burden was the administrative work. Her quarters were called the Tower of Babel. All day long a stream of callers thronged her stairs, captains of sick transports, officers of Royal Engineers, nurses, merchants, doctors, chaplains, asking for everything from writing-paper to advice on a sick man's diet, demanding shirts, splints, bandages, port wine, stoves and butter.

She slept in the storeroom in a bed behind a screen; in the daytime she saw callers sitting and writing at a little unpainted deal table in front of it. She wore a black woollen dress, white linen collar and cuffs and apron, and a white cap under a black silk handkerchief. Every time there was a pause she snatched her pen and went on writing.

No one in the party was capable of acting as her secretary. The requisitions, the orders, the records, the immense correspondence entailed by the acknowledgment and recording of the "Free Gifts" (the voluntary contributions sent out from home), the reports, the letters, must all be written by herself. Mrs. Bracebridge had superintendence of the "Free Gift Store", otherwise she had no assistance of any kind.

It was terribly cold and she hated cold. There was no satisfactory stove in her quarters—one had been sent out from England but it would not draw and she used it as a table and it was piled with papers. Her breath congealed on the air, the ink froze in the well, rats scampered in the walls and peered out from the wainscoting. Hour after hour she wrote on; the staff of the hospital declared that the light in her room was never put out. She wrote for the men, described their last hours and sent home their dying messages, she told wives of their husband's continued affection, and mothers that their sons had died holding her hand. She wrote for the nurses, many of whom had left children behind. She wrote her enormous letters to Sidney Herbert, she wrote official reports, official letters, she kept lists, filled in innumerable requisitions. Papers were piled round her in heaps, they lay on the floor, on her bed, on the chairs. Often in the morning Mrs. Bracebridge found her still in her clothes on her bed, where she had flung herself down in a stupor of fatigue.

She spared herself nothing—but the joy had gone out of the work. The high spirit, the faith which had sustained her through the first months faded as she learned the power of official intrigue.

" Alas among all the men here ", she wrote to Sidney Herbert in February 1855, " is there one really anxious for the good of these hospitals? One who is not an insincere animal at the bottom, who is not thinking of going in with the winning side whichever that is? I do believe that of all those who have been concerned in the fate of these miserable sick you and I are the only ones who really cared for them." A month later she wrote : " A great deal has been said of our self sacrifice, heroism and so forth. The real humiliation, the real hardship of this place, dear Mr. Herbert, is that we have to do with men who are neither gentlemen nor men of education nor even men of business, nor men of feeling, whose only object is to keep themselves out of blame."

She had crossed the path of such a man, and the great conflict of her mission was about to begin.

Dr. John Hall, Chief of Medical Staff of the British Expeditionary Army, had been kept occupied in the Crimea, but the hospitals of Scutari were under his control and he had no intention of allowing them to get out of hand. He had joined the Army Medical Service in 1815, though he had not qualified as an M.D. until 1845. His name had been associated with an unsavoury case in which a private stationed at Hounslow Barracks had died after receiving a flogging of 150 lashes, and he was known throughout the army as a strict disciplinarian averse to pampering the troops. He did not believe in chloroform, and in his letter of instruction to his officers at the opening of the campaign on August 3rd he warned them against its use. " The smart use of the knife is a powerful stimulant and it is much better to hear a man bawl lustily than to see him sink silently into the grave." He was revengeful, powerful, a master of the confidential report. Lord Cardigan told the Roebuck Committee that he had been struck by the " absolute terror " with which the doctors regarded Dr. Hall. Miss Nightingale wrote to Lady Cranworth that a doctor's promotion depended " upon a trick, a caprice of the Inspector General (i.e. Dr. Hall), and the Director General (i.e. Dr. Andrew Smith), and may be lost for an offensive word reported perhaps by an orderly and of which he never hears and which he may never have said ". In May 1856 she wrote: " In the last two months at this hospital alone, two medical officers have been superseded upon evidence collected in the above manner ".

Dr. Hall entered upon his duties in the Crimea with a sense of injustice. He had been in Bombay, he had been due for promotion, and he thought he deserved a post at home. He had solicited such a post and heard with disgust that he had been appointed Chief of Medical Staff of the British Expeditionary Army. In October 1854 he was sent by Lord Raglan to inspect the hospitals at Scutari. The hospitals were then filthy and destitute. However, Dr. Hall wrote on October 20th to Dr. Andrew Smith stating he had " much satisfaction in being able to inform him that the whole hospital establishment here (i.e. at Scutari), has now been put on a very creditable footing and that nothing is lacking ".

It was a fatal statement. He had committed himself. Henceforward he had to stand by what he had said, and his subordinates had to back him up. Dr. Menzies dared not contradict Dr. Hall's specific statement. He repeated it parrot-like to Lord Stratford, to Dr. Andrew Smith. It was not until Sidney Herbert received Miss Nightingale's first report that the truth was known. In December 1854 he told Lord Raglan: " I cannot help feeling that Dr. Hall resents offers of assistance as being slurs on his preparations ".

In the spring of 1855 Dr. Hall was boiling with rage. He

had never wanted his post, and now it looked as if he were going to be discredited into the bargain. The Hospitals Commission had reported unfavourably on his hospitals and, worse, he had been censured by Lord Raglan.

The most notorious of the sick transport scandals was the case of the *Avon*. The first man had been put on board the *Avon* at Balaclava on November 19th, 1854, the last man on December 3rd. The men were laid on the bare deck without any covering but greatcoat or blanket. One young assistant surgeon was instructed to attend to several hundred men, and so they were left for a fortnight. The state of the ship and the condition of the men was then indescribable. A regimental officer was induced to visit the ship and, horrified by what he saw, galloped at once to Lord Raglan. Though it was midnight Lord Raglan sent at once to Dr. Hall demanding immediate action. An enquiry was held, Dr. Lawson, the Principal Medical Officer at Balaclava, was held responsible and severely censured for " apathy and lack of interest in the welfare of the sick ", and Dr. Hall was recommended to relieve him of his duties. Further, in a General Order of December 13th, 1854, Lord Raglan stated he could not acquit Dr. Hall himself of blame in this matter. Dr. Hall judged the time had come to assert himself. He was by no means beaten. He knew his powers, he had his friends, and within his own department he was invincible. The question whether Dr. Cumming or Dr. Menzies was in command at the Barrack Hospital had been settled by the promotion of Dr. Cumming and the appointment of Dr. Forrest to take Dr. Menzies's place. After a few weeks Dr. Forrest resigned and went home in despair, and Dr. Hall then appointed Dr. Lawson to take his place. The man responsible for the *Avon* was to be Senior Medical Officer at the Barrack Hospital.

Miss Nightingale received the news with horror. " Before destroying our work Dr. Hall begins to caress us with his paws ", she wrote, and she warned Sidney Herbert : " The people here will try the strength of the old system against Government reforms with a strength of purpose and a cohesion of individuals which you are not likely to give them credit for ".

Dr. Lawson was a walking reminder of what the medical department could do. He had been censured and was to be relieved of his duties; he had been relieved of his duties—to assume them in a different place. The Commander-in-Chief, Lord Raglan, had been powerless. Dr. Hall knew how to protect his own, and he knew how to punish the disloyal. Dr. Smith and Dr. Hall were absolute masters of the Army Medical Department and no Nightingale power, no Sidney Herbert could save those unhappy slaves who offended their masters.

A wave of terror swept over the medical staff at Scutari. Miss Nightingale's remarkable achievement in purveying became "playing a game to ruin poor old Wreford" the Purveyor. She was, she told Sidney Herbert at the end of January, informed every day that she was "bent on destroying the poor old man". Lord William Paulet and Dr. Cumming approached her with a new suggestion—she should purvey the Purveyor privately. The stores obtained and paid for by her should pass secretly to him and be distributed by him. She asked them to put their proposal in writing, and the matter dropped.

Dr. Cumming continued to call on her every day, but he became nervous. He had been a member of the Hospitals Commission, but presently he was refusing to carry out his own recommendations. For example, the Hospitals Commission had stressed the urgent necessity of equipping the wards with bedding and utensils, and in March 1855 a large quantity of hospital stores arrived with which Dr. McGrigor had the wards equipped. Dr. Cumming ordered the new equipment to be removed.

Another broken reed was Lord William Paulet, who frankly detested his job. He had been sent out because he had wealth, position and prestige, and Major Sillery had failed because he had none of these. "Lord Wm. Paulet is appalled at the view of evils he has no idea what to do with", wrote Miss Nightingale; ". . . and then he shuts his eyes and hopes when he opens them he shall see something else . . . and sometimes he denies the state of things to relieve his feelings . . . he says himself this place is unmendable, and he is not the person to mend it." He told her he would much rather go up to the front and be shot at. As things became more difficult he withdrew—he put his head, she said, under his wing, spending his time with Lady Stratford picnicking along the picturesque shores of the Bosphorus, accompanied by hampers of the delicacies for which the Embassy chef was famous, ostensibly for the purpose of inspecting possible sites for convalescent hospitals. Nothing was to be expected from Lord William Paulet.

Dr. McGrigor began to succumb to Lawson's influence. He avoided Miss Nightingale, he ceased to be urgent in pressing the fulfilment of the recommendations of the Hospitals Commission. He was, she wrote, " the one of all others who really wished to help—but he was weak ". She felt betrayed, though she still had her triumphs. A whole corridor which the Purveyor had declared himself before witnesses unable to equip was fitted out by her and Mr. Macdonald from Constantinople by nightfall. "What I have done I shall continue doing ", she wrote, ". . . but I am weary of this hopeless work."

Within the hospital the work of the Sanitary Commission was having rapid effect. The fearful mortality rate of February had fallen in the three weeks ending April 7th to $14\frac{1}{2}$ per cent, by April 28th to 10·7 per cent and by May 19th to 5·2 per cent.

Thanks to Miss Nightingale's purveying—the Purveyor's stores were still empty, and the authorities were slipping back into a state of mind when equipment was thought an unnecessary extravagance for a hospital—there were plenty of drugs, surgical instruments, baths, hot-water bottles and medical comforts. Dr. Pincoffs noted that these were present in satisfactory quantities when he joined the hospital in the spring. There were also operating tables, supplied by her for the second time : the first set had been burned as firewood in the great cold of January 1854.

Food had been miraculously improved by Alexis Soyer, the famous chef of the Reform Club, who arrived in March 1855 with full authority from Lord Panmure. Soyer came out at his own expense attended by a " gentleman of colour " as his secretary. In manner and appearance he was a comic opera Frenchman, but Miss Nightingale recognised his genius and became his friend. "Others ", she wrote, "have studied cookery for the purpose of gormandizing, some for show. But none but he for the purpose of cooking large quantities of food in the most nutritive and economical manner for great quantities of people." Though the authorities received him " very coolly ", Soyer was armed with authority and he proceeded to attack the kitchens of the Barrack Hospital which Miss Nightingale never entered. He composed recipes for using the army rations to make excellent soup and stews. He put an end to the frightful system of boiling. He insisted on having permanently allocated to the kitchens soldiers who could be trained as cooks. He invented ovens to bake bread and biscuits and a Scutari teapot which made and kept tea hot for fifty men. As he walked the wards with his tureens of soup the men cheered him with three times three. Finally, he gave a luncheon attended by Lord and Lady Stratford and their suite, at which he served delicious dishes made from army rations.

In one thing Soyer failed. Like Miss Nightingale, he strongly objected to the way the meat was divided ; since weight was the only criterion one man might get all bone ; why should not the meat be boned, and each man receive a boneless portion, with the bones being used for broth ? The answer from Dr. Cumming was that it would need a new Regulation of the Service to bone the meat.

In May 1855 Miss Nightingale wrote to Sidney Herbert to describe " the first really satisfactory reception of sick ". Two hundred men from the *Severn* transport were received, bathed, and their hair cut and cleansed. Their filthy clothes and blankets were taken from them, they were given clean hospital gowns, put into decent beds and given well-cooked nourishing food. In spite of obstacles, disappointments, opposition, she had, to this degree, succeeded.

And now that the Barrack Hospital was reasonably satisfactory she determined to go to the Crimea. There were two large hospitals at Balaclava. One, the General Hospital, had been established at the time of the British occupation in September 1854 and, like the General Hospital at Scutari, had been intended to be the only hospital. This was the hospital in Dr. John Hall's personal charge on which the Hospitals Commission had reported adversely. The enormous numbers of sick had necessitated further accommodation, and a hospital of huts called the Castle Hospital had been erected on the heights above Balaclava harbour. Both had a staff of female nurses, and disquieting news had reached Miss Nightingale of the nurses' conduct, particularly at the General Hospital.

And now the fatal flaw in her instructions appeared, and her authority in the Crimea proved to be by no means established. No official notification had been published setting out her duties, and as early as March 1855 she asked Sidney Herbert to press for a public statement on her position. Precise information as to her standing, her instructions and the assistance to be afforded to her had been sent to Lord Raglan, Lord Stratford and Dr. John Hall. But Lord Raglan was occupied with the problems of a disastrous campaign, Lord Stratford was indifferent, Dr. John Hall was malicious. He asserted that, as her instructions named her " Superintendent of the Female Nursing Establishment in the English Military General Hospitals in *Turkey* ", she had no jurisdiction over the Crimea.

The seriousness of the situation was not appreciated at home. Mr. Augustus Stafford wrote : " The nature of her difficulties is NOT understood and perhaps never will be ". Supported by Dr. Hall, nurses in the Crimea were defying her authority. One of them, Miss Clough, a " lady " of Miss Stanley's party, had broken away and gone to join Sir Colin Campbell's Hospital above Balaclava, inspired by romantic enthusiasm for the Highland Brigade. " She must be a funny fellow, she of the Highland Heights ", commented Miss Nightingale. A constant rebel was Mrs. Elizabeth Davis, the Welshwoman brought out by Mary Stanley. She had begun to dislike Miss Nightingale before she saw her. " I did not like the name of Nightingale. When I first hear a name I am very apt to know by my feelings whether I shall like the person who bears it ", she wrote. She had had experience in nursing, and was selected for the Barrack Hospital. Once there she proved a storm centre. She refused to obey orders or to conform to the system for the distribution of the "Free Gifts". She accused Miss Nightingale of using these for her own comfort and alleged that, while the nurses were fed on filaments of the meat which had been stewed down for the patients' soup, Miss Nightingale had a French cook and three courses served up every day. Finally, she joined the party of eleven volunteers who went, against Miss Nightingale's wishes, to Balaclava in January 1855.

Once there she made an alliance with Dr. John Hall, and another important personage in the Crimea, Mr. David Fitz-Gerald, the Purveyor-in-Chief. Mr. FitzGerald was as angrily opposed to Miss Nightingale as was Dr. Hall, and as equally determined to keep her out of the Crimea.

Elizabeth Davis, an excellent cook, had assumed command of the kitchen in Balaclava General Hospital, which she conducted with rollicking extravagance, rejoicing in feeding up the handsome young officers who were her special pets. It was Miss Nightingale's rule that none of her nurses should attend on or cook for officers except by special arrangement. At one issue Mrs. Davis received " 6 dozen port wine, 6 dozen sherry, 6 dozen brandy, a cask of rice, a cask of arrowroot, a cask of sago and a box of sugar " ; and her requisitions for the General Hospital were filled at once by Mr. FitzGerald without being countersigned by Dr. Hall. The situation became too much for the Superintendent, the Superior of the Sellonites, who, Miss Nightingale said, " lost her head and her health ", collapsed, and went home. In her place another of Mary Stanley's party was appointed, Miss Weare, a fussy, gentle old spinster who swiftly became dominated by Mrs. Davis and Dr. Hall. Miss Weare confided to Dr. Hall how much more *natural* she found it to obey a gentleman. Miss Nightingale was very wonderful, of course, but she could not get used to taking orders from a lady.

With the " Free Gifts " Mrs. Davis and her allies were even more open-handed. In an orgy of distribution ninety bales and boxes were given away without any record of who had received them.

The " Free Gifts "—" these frightful contributions ", Miss Nightingale called them, together with the labour of acknowledging them, storing them in safety and distributing them satisfactorily, were becoming the bane of her life. Ever since November 1854 parcels had been sent from England for the troops. " There is not a small town, not a parish in England from which we have not received contributions," she wrote in May 1855, " not one of these is worth its freight, but the smaller the value, of course, the greater the importance the contributors attach to it. A 'good' parcel contains perhaps 14 lbs. arrowroot and 3 pairs muffettees, old rag, a few flannel bands, 3 dozen comforters and some Welsh wigs. . . . These people think it is a pleasure to me to dispense these things. If you knew the trouble of landing, of unpacking, of acknowledging! The good that has been done here has been done by money, money purchasing articles in Constantinople."

Among the "Free Gifts" were articles of value. Queen Victoria had sent a number of water-beds, there were also provisions, groceries, wine, brandy, soup and clothing. If the nurses had unrestricted access to the "Free Gifts" they took articles out and gave them to their favourite patients or helped themselves. To keep a check was difficult; the store, like every other place in Scutari, was overrun by rats, and the Maltese, Greek and Turkish labourers who worked round the hospital were dishonest almost without exception.

After her arrival on November 5th, 1854, Miss Nightingale kept an exact record of every article received and issued by her. After February 15th, 1855, the distribution was taken over by Mrs. Bracebridge on the understanding that the "Free Gifts" were to be given out to the troops and only on requisition by medical men. When Miss Nightingale went to the Crimea Mrs. Bracebridge was left in sole charge.

On May 2nd, 1855, she sailed from Scutari for Balaclava in the *Robert Lowe*. "Poor old Flo," she wrote to her mother, "steaming up the Bosphorus and across the Black Sea with four nurses, two cooks, and a boy to Crim Tartary . . . in the Robert Lowe or Robert Slow (for an exceedingly slow boat she is), . . . taking back 420 of her patients, a draught of convalescents returning to their regiments to be shot at again. 'A Mother in Israel', Pastor Fliedner called me; a Mother in the Coldstreams, is the more appropriate appellation."

Besides Soyer and a French chef, the party included Soyer's secretary, the "gentleman of colour", Mr. Bracebridge and a boy named Robert Robinson, an invalided drummer from the 68th Light Infantry. He described himself as Miss Nightingale's "man"—Soyer could not resist asking him whether he was twelve years old yet—and was accustomed to explain that he had "forsaken his instruments in order to devote his civil and military career to Miss Nightingale ". He carried her letters and messages, escorted her when she went from the Barrack Hospital to the General Hospital, and had charge of the lamp which she carried at night. Among the Nightingale papers is a manuscript account of his experiences during the campaign, entitled " Robert Robinson's Memoir ". He was, said Soyer, " a regular *enfant de troupe*, full of wit and glee ".

On May 5th, six months after her arrival at Constantinople —" and what the disappointment of those six months have been no one could tell ", she wrote, " but still I am not dead but alive "—the *Robert Lowe* anchored in Balaclava harbour. Balaclava was crammed to overflowing, and she was invited by the Captain to make her quarters on board the ship, which soon, wrote Soyer, resembled a floating drawing-room, as doctors, senior officers and officials, including Sir John McNeill of the Tulloch and McNeill Commission and Dr. Sutherland of the Sanitary Commission, came to pay their respects. In the afternoon, escorted by a number of gentlemen, she went ashore to report herself to Lord Raglan. She appeared, says Soyer, in a " genteel Amazone ", and rode a " very pretty mare which by its gambols and caracoling seemed proud to carry its noble charge ". Lord Raglan being away for the day, she decided to visit the mortar battery outside Sebastopol. The astonishing sight of a lady in Balaclava accompanied by a crowd of gentlemen, many of them in glittering uniforms, produced " an extraordinary effect ". The news spread like wildfire that the lady was Miss Nightingale, and the soldiers rushed from their tents and " cheered her to the echo with three times three ". At the Mortar Battery Soyer requested her to ascend the rampart and seat herself on the centre mortar, " to which she very gracefully acceded ". He then " boldly exclaimed, ' Gentlemen, behold this amiable lady sitting fearlessly upon the terrible instrument of war ! Behold the heroic daughter of England, the soldiers' friend." Three cheers were given by all. Meanwhile five or six of her escort had picked bouquets of the wild lilies and orchids which carpeted the plateau. She was requested to choose the one she liked best and responded by gathering them all in her arms.

The party then cantered home, Miss Nightingale looking strangely exhausted. It was, she said, the unaccustomed fresh air.

The next morning, accompanied by Soyer, she began her inspection. It was a depressing task. The hospitals were dirty and extravagantly run, the nurses inefficient and undisciplined. She was received with hostility and, at the General Hospital, with insolence. " I should have as soon expected to see the Queen here as you," said Mrs. Davis.

She ignored hostility and rudeness. She got out plans with Soyer's assistance for new extra diet kitchens at the General Hospital. She decided Miss Weare must be replaced —the General Hospital was evidently out of hand. She then went up to the Castle Hospital, the new hospital of huts where Mrs. Shaw Stewart (the " Mrs." was a courtesy title), a difficult woman herself, was having a difficult time. Mrs. Shaw Stewart, one of Mary Stanley's party, was one of the few women of social position who had any real experience in nursing. She was the sister of Sir Michael Shaw Stewart, M.P., and had undergone training in Germany and nursed in a London hospital. She was skilful, kind, a magnificent worker, but she would be a martyr. Do what her friends would, conciliate her, defer to her, coax her, she maintained she was being ill-treated. She was, however, together with Mrs. Roberts from St. Thomas's, Mrs. Drake from St. John's and Rev. Mother Bermondsey, regarded by Miss Nightingale as outstanding, a " true heroine ". At the Castle Hospital she had no need to imagine persecution, for Dr. Hall was making her work as difficult as possible. He caused immense inconvenience by insisting that all her requisitions must be sent to him personally. Work which the Sanitary Commission had directed was not even started, her kitchens were inadequate, the Purveyor habitually held up her supplies and, finally, Dr. Hall made a practice of sending her messages of criticism through her staff.

The strength of the old system was very powerful in Balaclava and the army authorities were determined to teach civilian meddlers a lesson. They were also contriving to obstruct the Sanitary Commissioners, refusing to recognise their credentials or to give them facilities for inspection. Miss

Nightingale gathered herself together to do battle, but before anything could be accomplished she collapsed. After seeing Mrs. Shaw Stewart she had admitted great weakness and fatigue, and the next day, while interviewing Miss Weare, she fainted. The Senior Medical Officer from the Balaclava General Hospital was hastily summoned; after he had called two other doctors into consultation a statement was issued that Miss Nightingale was suffering from Crimean fever.

All Balaclava, says Soyer, was in an uproar. It was decided that she must be removed from the ship. The harbour was being cleansed by the Sanitary Commission, and the men working to remove the ghastly debris found the stench so horrible that they constantly fainted and had to receive an official issue of brandy. She must be taken to the pure air of the Castle Hospital on the heights. A solemn cortège transported her from the ship, four soldiers carrying her on a stretcher and Dr. Anderson and Mrs. Roberts walking by her side; Soyer's secretary—Soyer himself was away—held an umbrella over her head, and Robert Robinson walked behind in tears, being, in his own words, " not strong enough to help carry or tall enough to hold the umbrella ". By this time she was delirious and very ill. At Balaclava the troops seemed in mourning, and at Scutari the men when they heard the news, "turned their faces to the wall and cried. All their trust was in her ", a Sergeant wrote home.

For more than two weeks, nursed by Mrs. Roberts, she hovered between life and death. In her delirium she was constantly writing. It was found impossible to keep her quiet unless she wrote, so she was given pen and paper; among the Nightingale papers are sheets covered with feverish notes. She thought her room was full of people demanding supplies, that an engine was inside her head, that a Persian adventurer came and stood beside her bed and told her that Mr. Bracebridge had given him a draft for £300,000, and she wrote to Sir John McNeill asking him to deal with the man because he had been in Persia. In the height of the fever all her hair was cut off. The news went round the camp, and Colonel Sterling wrote that he heard the Bird had had to have her head shaved —would she wear a wig or a helmet !

At home the tidings were received with consternation, and

when it was known that she was recovering strangers passed on
the good news to each other in the streets.

On May 24th a horseman wrapped in a cloak rode up to
her hut and knocked. Mrs. Roberts sprang out—" Hist, hist,
don't make such a horrible noise as that, my man." He asked
if this were Miss Nightingale's hut. Mrs. Roberts said it was
and he tried to walk in. Mrs. Roberts pushed him back.
"And pray who are you?" she asked. " Oh, only a soldier,
but I must see her, I have come a long way, my name is Raglan,
she knows me very well." " Oh, Mrs. Roberts, it is Lord
Raglan," called Miss Nightingale. He came in and, drawing
up a stool to her bedside, talked to her at length. That night
he telegraphed home that Miss Nightingale was out of danger,
and on May 28th Queen Victoria was " truly thankful to learn
that that excellent and valuable person Miss Nightingale is safe".

She was frantic to settle the urgent problems at Balaclava,
but her weakness was so extreme that she could not feed herself
or raise her voice above a whisper. The doctors advised her
to go to England, or failing that to Switzerland. She refused,
and Mrs. Bracebridge, who had hastened from Scutari to look
after her, pointed out that she was such an execrable sailor that
a long sea voyage in her present state might well kill her. It
was arranged that she should be taken to Scutari on a transport
and occupy a house belonging to Mr. Sabin, who had gone
home on sick leave. When she was convalescent she was to
go to the Embassy Villa at Therapia.

A curious incident followed. Dr. Hadley, the Senior
Medical Officer at the Castle Hospital, had attended her,
though she had Dr. Sutherland as her personal physician. Dr.
Hadley was a friend of Dr. John Hall, and the two doctors
selected the transport, the *Jura*, on which she was to go to
Scutari. She was actually on board when Mr. Bracebridge
discovered that the *Jura* was not calling at Scutari but going
direct to England. Miss Nightingale was hurried off the
transport in a fainting condition by Mr. Bracebridge and Lord
Ward, and crossed to Scutari on Lord Ward's steam yacht.
On October 19th, 1855, she wrote to Sidney Herbert: " It
was quite true that Doctors Hall and Hadley sent for a list of
vessels going home, and chose one, the Jura, which was not
going to stop at Scutari *because* it was not going to stop at

Scutari, and put me on board her for England, and Mr. Bracebridge and Lord Ward took me out at the risk of my life to save me from going to England ".

The voyage was rough, the yacht was kept at sea an extra day, and Miss Nightingale was dreadfully ill. At Scutari all the high officials were on the landing-stage to greet her, but her weakness and exhaustion were such that she was unable to speak. She was terribly changed, emaciated, white-faced under the handkerchief tied closely round her head to conceal her shorn hair. Two relays of guardsmen carried her to Mr. Sabin's house on a stretcher, as sick and wounded were always carried. " Just like we men ", a soldier said to Lady Alicia Blackwood. Twelve private soldiers divided the honour of carrying her baggage. The stretcher was followed by a large number of men, absolutely silent and many openly in tears. " I do not remember anything so gratifying to the feelings ", wrote Soyer, " as that simple though grand procession."

Mr. Sabin's house had windows opening on to the Bosphorus—the most famous view in the world which, she said, she had never had time to look at—and a green tree in a garden behind. Here she began slowly to recover.

For the next few weeks she lived in the world of the convalescent, a world filled with small things. Sidney Herbert had sent her a terrier from England, and she had an owl, given her by the troops to take the place of Athena, and a baby. The baby belonged to a Sergeant Brownlow, and while its mother was washing for the hospital used to spend its day in a sort of Turkish wooden pen which she could see from her bed. Its merits, she wrote afterwards, were commemorated in the chapter on " Minding Baby " in *Notes on Nursing*. Parthe composed and illustrated and sent her " The Life and Death of Athena, an Owlet ". Mrs. Bracebridge read it aloud while Miss Nightingale alternately laughed and cried and noticed how the terrier kept fidgeting about and drawing attention to himself, " knowing by instinct we were reading about something we loved very much and being jealous ". By July she was better and had decided she was not going away anywhere. " If I go, all this will go to pieces ", she wrote to Parthe on July 9th. Dr. Sutherland told her the fever had saved her life by forcing her to rest, and implored her to spare herself. She dared not. She had been compelled to leave the Crimea before she had settled anything, and she was receiving reports that the situation was going from bad to worse. Every day her authority was being more flagrantly disregarded. As soon as was humanly possible she must go back to Balaclava and fight it out.

She spent a few days at Therapia with Mrs. Bracebridge, then returned to Mr. Sabin's house and resumed ordinary life. She contrived to give an impression of complete recovery. Lothian Nicholson visited her on his way up to the Crimea and was " quite enthusiastic about her good looks ". Her cropped hair was growing in little curls which gave her a curiously touching and childish appearance. The Bracebridges wrote that her improvement was delightful and wonderful.

But as she recovered the stormclouds gathered. She was about to enter the most difficult and exhausting phase of her mission. During her illness Lord Raglan died and was succeeded by General Simpson, a soldier of many years seniority who had barely seen active service.

General Simpson had originally been sent out to the Crimea by Lord Panmure in February 1855 to report on Lord Raglan's staff, especially the Quartermaster-General, General Airey, and the Adjutant-General, General Estcourt, who were suspected to be largely responsible for the disasters of 1854–55. " The result of my observations since coming here is that we are in a REGULAR FIX ", wrote General Simpson in his first letter to Lord Panmure. His intelligence was not great, his social position inferior, he was against new-fangled notions of pampering the troops, and Miss Nightingale never succeeded in establishing the personal contact she had enjoyed with Lord Raglan. " The man who was Lord FitzRoy Somerset " (Lord Raglan as youngest son of the Duke of Beaufort bore the title of Lord FitzRoy Somerset before being created Baron Raglan in 1852) " would naturally not be above interesting himself in hospital matters and a parcel of women—while the man who was James Simpson would essentially think it infra dig ", she wrote in November 1855. Moreover, for some reason the official instructions as to her position and authority which had been sent by Sidney Herbert when Secretary at War to Lord Raglan were not passed on to General Simpson.

She learnt that in the Crimea the kitchens which she had planned with Soyer had not been built, supplies were still being withheld from Mrs. Shaw Stewart, the conduct of the nurses was still unsatisfactory. In July she sent up a French man-cook, to whom she paid £100 a year out of her own private income, but the authorities refused to employ him. She requested that the ineffectual Miss Weare should be relieved as Superintendent of the General Hospital. Dr. Hall's reply was to appoint Miss Weare Superintendent of the Monastery Hospital, a new hospital for ophthalmic cases and convalescents, and ignore her request.

As she was bracing herself to gather strength and return to the Crimea a fresh blow fell. The Bracebridges wished to go home. They had come to the end of their endurance. For nine months they had shared the fearful sights, the horrible smells, the uneatable food, the insolence, the petty slights and the perpetual rudeness. They had endured, toiled, sacrificed themselves and yet—they had not been a complete success. Their devotion was as strong as ever, Miss Nightingale's affection as grateful. " No one can tell what she has been to me ", she wrote of Selina, but Selina had muddled the " Free Gift " store, and Mr. Bracebridge's relations with the officials were increasingly unhappy.

He was an inveterate partisan, generous, honest, indiscreet, irritable. Miss Nightingale said, " he wished me to liberate my soul, as he calls it, and say as many disagreeable things as I can ". He was elderly and the heat and flies of Scutari affected his health. He had been in charge of the finances of the expedition, and Miss Nightingale, though his integrity was unquestioned, was by no means certain of the good order of his accounts. Though she was barely convalescent she would not hear of delay in the Bracebridges' departure. Everything was made easy. It was given out that they were going home for a few months and would come back in the autumn, but she knew they would never return. As soon as they sailed on July 28th she went back to her quarters at the Barrack Hospital, retaining Mr. Sabin's house and sending her nurses there by turns to have a rest.

The medical authorities did not welcome her. They felt that the state of the hospital was now satisfactory and her help was not needed; there was an unwillingness to consult her and an outbreak of complaints. On July 28th Dr. Davies notified the authorities of extravagance on the part of Miss Nightingale's nurses. " Quart mugs of arrowroot are given to the men at night, the quantity is too great and they cannot drink it." Miss Nightingale in reply notified the authorities that " though quart mugs are used by order the quantity inserted in them is only a pint". Orderlies caught in wrong-doing had only to say Miss Nightingale had given the order to be exonerated. Some of the admirable work of the Sanitary Commission was being undone. The engineering works were not completed and the men began once more to drink water that looked like barley water. Trouble in controlling the nurses was continuous. Two nurses broke out one Saturday night and were brought back dead drunk. "A great disappointment to me", wrote Miss Nightingale, " as they were both good natured hard working women." She let them off with a caution, but one added promiscuousness to her misdoings and had to be dismissed. A passage was arranged and the woman escorted on board ship. As soon as her escort was out of sight she got off the ship, went into Constantinople and was brought back to Miss Nightingale dead drunk once more.

Nurses who did not drink got married. Lady Alicia Blackwood related that one morning six of Miss Nightingale's best nurses came into her room followed by six corporals or sergeants to announce their impending weddings. On one occasion an emissary from a Turkish official called on Miss Nightingale with an offer to purchase a particularly plump nurse for his master's harem.

She lost one of her best nurses on August 9th when Mrs. Drake, from St. John's House, died of cholera at Balaclava. Next she was involved in unpleasantness through the death of Miss Clough, who had got into difficulties on the " Highland Heights ". She disliked living in a hut, could not control the orderlies, was accused of financial irregularities, quarrelled with everyone, fell ill and asked to be sent home. On the boat she became worse and was put ashore at Scutari, where she died. Miss Nightingale had to receive her body, arrange her funeral, communicate news of her death to her relations at home and straighten her affairs. A private soldier of the 42nd

Regiment and his wife had accompanied her as servants, with their wages guaranteed by Dr. Hall. Their wages were owing and had to be paid by Miss Nightingale and Brigadier-General Cameron, of the Highland Division.

Much more serious trouble followed. After Mrs. Bracebridge went home Miss Nightingale appointed a Miss Salisbury to take charge of the " Free Gift " store at a salary. From the moment she took up her post she began writing letters home accusing Miss Nightingale of neglecting the patients, of wasting the " Free Gifts " and of having been concerned in Miss Clough's sudden death. These letters found their way to Mary Stanley, who was now in London.

Miss Salisbury next began thieving from the store on a considerable scale. Food, drink, linen, disappeared at such a rate as to be noticeable. Miss Salisbury accused the nurses, and her explanations were accepted until one of the nurses accused Miss Salisbury herself. A search was ordered not only of Miss Salisbury's room but of the room of two Maltese kitchen-workers whom she had introduced. The results were staggering. The beds of the Maltese were found to be entirely constructed of piles of stolen goods, while in Miss Salisbury's room every box, every package, every crevice and cranny was crammed.

Miss Nightingale summoned the Military Commandant. Lord William Paulet had just gone home and had been replaced by General Storks, a man of first-rate ability and one of her staunch admirers. The wretched Miss Salisbury was now grovelling on the floor, sobbing, screaming and clutching at Miss Nightingale's feet, imploring her not to prosecute, but to send her home, now, at once, immediately. A grave mistake was made. Miss Nightingale wished above all things to avoid a scandal and she and General Storks agreed that the wisest course was to send Miss Salisbury home with as little fuss as possible. She sailed immediately. But after she had gone it was discovered that she had been stealing not only Free Gifts but government stores as well. General Storks suggested that in order to trace the stores and discover her accomplices her desk, which in the flurry of departure she had left behind, should be opened and searched and letters that came for her should be opened and read.

When Miss Salisbury arrived in England she declared she had been ill-treated. The gifts were decaying in the store because Miss Nightingale refused to let them be used, or used them herself, and Miss Salisbury had abstracted them in order to give them to the poor fellows for whom they were intended. Why, she demanded, had not the police been called in if what Miss Nightingale asserted was true? Miss Salisbury was soon in conference with Mary Stanley, and a formal complaint against Miss Nightingale was drawn up based on the points that Miss Salisbury had been shipped off without a chance to clear herself, and that her letters had been illegally opened. Through Mary Stanley's influence the complaint was submitted to the War Office.

Within the War Office there were two parties, a reform party and an anti-reform party. Sending out four Commissions of Enquiry, sending out even Miss Nightingale herself, had not been accomplished without battles. The anti-reform party had been defeated and were ready to use any weapon that came to hand. At their head was Mr. Benjamin Hawes, Permanent Under-Secretary at the War Office.

Miss Salisbury's complaint was submitted to Mr. Hawes and he chose to take it very seriously. An official letter was written to Miss Nightingale and General Storks—who had schemes for the reform of army administration which Mr. Hawes did not find sympathetic—not inviting a report but requesting them to justify their conduct.

Miss Nightingale had now to add to her labours the fearful task of straightening out the " Free Gift " store. Miss Salisbury's accusations and the action of the War Office became known in London, and her family blamed the Bracebridges; W. E. N., wrote Uncle Sam, " *would* give out against good B." Someone must go out to be with Florence. Aunt Mai volunteered, but Miss Nightingale would not take her from her family. Parthe and Fanny suggested Hilary Bonham Carter without success. Aunt Mai then tactfully suggested she should go out for a short time until the Bracebridges returned— ostensibly in the autumn—and Uncle Sam rather unwillingly consented.

On September 16th Aunt Mai arrived at Scutari bringing with her a storekeeper for the " Free Gift " store, an experienced clerk named Willis. She burst into tears at her first sight of Florence, altered by her illness, thin and worn, and with her hair cut short looking curiously like the child of thirty years ago. The web of partisan intrigue, the petty thwartings, irritations and discourtesies in which she was forced to live horrified Aunt Mai. " The public generally imagine her by the soldier's bedside ", she wrote on September 18th, 1855; " . . . how easy, how satisfactory if that were all. The quantity of writing, the quantity of talking is the weary work, the dealing with the mean, the selfish, the incompetent."

The pressure of work was enormous. During her first week Aunt Mai recorded getting up at 6 A.M. and copying until 11 P.M., and next day getting up at 5 A.M. and copying again until 11 P.M.

At the beginning of October Miss Nightingale went back to the Crimea, where a new tempest had blown up, with, in its centre, Rev. Mother Bridgeman—"Mother Brickbat". Miss Nightingale had never succeeded in persuading Mother Bridgeman to acknowledge her authority. Mother Bridgeman had gone with her nuns to Koulali, where they issued " extras ", wine, invalid food and clothing at their own discretion and without a requisition from the doctor in charge. Lord Panmure, on his appointment as Secretary of State for War, had asked Miss Nightingale to relinquish Koulali, and she had consented. But the lavishness there became such a scandal that the Principal Medical Officer insisted that the Scutari system must be adopted. The nuns then resigned, saying their usefulness was destroyed.

At the end of September 1855 Miss Nightingale had learned that Mother Bridgeman and her nuns, without either informing her or asking her permission, had gone to the General Hospital, Balaclava, where Mother Bridgeman was to be Superintendent. She asked Dr. Hall for an explanation and he alleged that he had written her a letter asking for more nurses, but had had no reply and had been forced to take action. No such letter had been received.

Mother Bridgeman then wrote announcing that four of her nuns who were still working at the General Hospital, Scutari, were to proceed to Balaclava. Miss Nightingale pointed out that to remove nurses who were engaged in her service was against all rules. Mother Bridgeman refused to give way and Miss Nightingale appealed to Lord Stratford; it was, she wrote, impossible for her to carry on her work if interference with the control of her nurses was permitted. At the same time, in a private letter, she told him that she was quite ready to arrange for the nuns to go to Balaclava; if any women were to be at the General Hospital, Balaclava, she thought nuns the least undesirable, but arrangements must be made through her and not over her head. Lord Stratford hastened in complimentary terms to assure her of his entire agreement, but informed her that she should approach not himself but General Storks.

When Miss Nightingale considered the situation she came to the conclusion that her personal resentment must be swallowed. Wide implications were involved. The new recruits brought out to replace the army which had perished in the winter of 1854–55 were largely Irish and Catholics, and it was already being said that they were being deprived of spiritual ministrations. " Had we more nuns ", she wrote to Mrs. Herbert in November 1855, " it would be very desirable, to diminish disaffection. But *just not* the Irish ones. The wisest thing the War Office could no now would be to send out a few more of the Bermondsey nuns to join those already at Scutari and counter balance the influence of the *Irish* ones, who hate their soberer sisters with the mortal hatred, which, I believe, only Nuns and Household Servants *can* feel towards each other."

She returned to the Crimea determined, in her favourite phrase, to "arrange things". On September 8th Sebastopol had quietly and ingloriously fallen, evacuated by the enemy, and the end of the war was only a question of time. General Simpson had resigned his command and gone home suffering from Crimean diarrhoea and been succeeded by Sir William Codrington. She was desperately anxious to keep things together, not to come to shipwreck at the eleventh hour. She was ready to conciliate—to conciliate Dr. Hall, conciliate Mother Bridgeman, conciliate Mr. FitzGerald, the Purveyor.

The weather was bad, sailing delayed and the passage finally made in a gale. She was prostrated. Outside Balaclava it proved impossible to make the narrow opening to the harbour or even to bring out a tug. While the transport rose and fell on huge swells a small boat was brought alongside. A sailor took her under the arms and held her over the side of the ship, and as the boat rose dropped her into it.

At first it seemed that she might succeed in " arranging things ". It was an advantage to be without Mr. Bracebridge : " I find much less difficulty in getting on here without him than with him ", she wrote in November 1855. " A woman obtains that from military courtesy (if she does not shock either their habits of business or their caste prejudice), which a man who pitted the civilian against the military element and the female against the doctors, partly from temper, partly from policy, effectually hindered." On the surface she was on friendly terms with Dr. Hall and Mr. FitzGerald. In fact, Mr. Fitz-Gerald went so far as to confess to her he hoped that Mother Bridgeman's nuns would not import extravagant Koulali habits into Balaclava.

And then a copy of *The Times* for October 16th, 1855, arrived at Balaclava, and all her work was undone. It contained a report of a lecture given by Mr. Bracebridge at the Town Hall, Coventry. Everything Mr. Bracebridge had previously said, which she had implored him to refrain from saying publicly, he had now repeated. The lecture was a furious and inaccurate attack on the British Army authorities and the British Army doctors. He described the shocking state of the hospitals when she arrived and asserted that she had reformed them in a few days. He abused Mr. Wreford, the Purveyor-in-Chief, by name. He attacked army surgeons, calling them ignorant and callous and alleging that they refused to employ treatments which the French had proved successful. He gave specific instances of the ill-treatment of troops by doctors, but these were rumour and not fact.

The harm done was incalculable. Other papers reprinted Mr. Bracebridge's allegations, and it was believed that Miss Nightingale had instigated a Press attack on the Army Medical Department. Everything asserted of her by Dr. Hall was felt to be justified.

" When one reads such twaddling nonsense ", wrote Dr. Hall to Dr. Andrew Smith, " as that uttered by Mr. Brace-bridge and which was so much lauded in the ' Times ' because the garrulous old gentleman talked about Miss Nightingale putting hospitals containing three or four thousand patients in order in a couple of days by means of the ' Times ' fund, one cannot suppress a feeling of contempt for the man who indulges in such exaggerations and pity for the ignorant multitude who are deluded by these fairy tales."

Angry as Dr. Hall was, he was no more furious than Miss Nightingale herself. On November 5th she told Mr. Brace-bridge she wished for no " more irresponsibility of opposition ". She objected in the strongest possible manner to his lecture, " *First*, because it is not our business and I have expressly denied being a medical officer . . . *secondly*, because it justifies all the attacks made against us for unwarrantable interference and criticism, and *thirdly*, because I believe it to be utterly un-fair ". Alas, the damage had been done, and it was irremediable. She contemplated the wreckage of her endeavours with despair.

" I have been appointed a twelvemonth today," she wrote to Aunt Mai, " and what a twelvemonth of dirt it has been, of experience which would sadden not a life but eternity. Who has ever had a sadder experience. Christ was betrayed by one, but my cause has been betrayed by everyone—ruined, destroyed, betrayed by everyone alas one may truly say except-ing Mrs. Roberts, Rev. Mother and Mrs. Stewart. All the rest, Weare, Clough, Salisbury, Stanley et id genus omne where are they? And Mrs. Stewart is more than half mad. A cause which is supported by a mad woman and twenty fools must be a falling house. . . . Dr. Hall is dead against me, justly provoked but not by me. He descends to every mean-ness to make my position more difficult."

As if she had not enough to endure she was taken ill again and forced to enter the Castle Hospital with severe sciatica. Minus the pain, which was great, she wrote to Mrs. Brace-bridge that the attack did not seem to have damaged her much. " I have now had all that this climate can give, Crimean fever, Dysentery, Rheumatism and believe myself thoroughly acclimatised and ready to stand out the war with any man."

In a week she was up and working again, ignoring personal humiliations as long as female nursing in military hospitals might emerge as a unified undertaking at the end of the War. No official statement came to establish her authority, and Dr. Hall gave out that she was an adventuress and to be treated as such. " He has been justly provoked by Mr. Bracebridge's lecture from which I utterly dissent ", she wrote. Minor officials treated her with vulgar impertinence. The Purveyor refused to honour her drafts. When she went to the General Hospital she was kept waiting. On November 4th the new diet kitchen was opened at the Castle Hospital, and for twenty-four hours following the new installation it was impossible to make the officers' toast. Dr. Hall at once made an official complaint, alleging that the officers were being neglected by Mrs. Shaw Stewart, although, wrote Miss Nightingale, " from April until November, every egg, every bit of butter, jelly, ale and Eau de Cologne which the sick officers have had has been provided out of my or Mrs. Shaw Stewart's private pockets ". Dr. Hall, she said, would like to broil her slowly on the fires of her own diet kitchen.

She would not be provoked. She persisted in visiting Mother Bridgeman, and when Sister Winifred, a lay sister from Mother Bridgeman's party, died of cholera she went to the funeral and joined in the prayers. " Mother Brickbat's conduct has been neither that of a Christian, a gentlewoman, or even a woman ", Miss Nightingale wrote to Mrs. Herbert. " At the same time I am the best personal friends with the Revd. Brickbat and I have even offered to put up a cross to poor Winifred to which she has deigned no reply. But anything to avoid a woman's quarrel which *can* be done or submitted to on my part *shall* be done—and submitted to."

All she had accomplished by coming to the Crimea, she wrote, was that the extra diet kitchens which should have been erected in May were erected in November. At the end of November she was hastily summoned back to Scutari, where a new cholera epidemic had broken out. Before she left she wrote to Sidney Herbert : " There is not an official who would not burn me like Joan of Arc if he could, but they know the War Office cannot turn me out because the country is with me— that is my position ". The admiration and affection with which the people of England regarded her roused in the Crimean authorities dislike and distrust. But their masters at home, Ministers to whom public opinion was of importance, had a different outlook, and in November, when her prestige in the Crimea had never been so low or her difficulties so great, an astonishing demonstration of public feeling and affection in England placed her in the position of a national heroine whom no one could afford to ignore.

XI   A LEGEND had been growing up in England, the result of the survivors of the British Army coming home and telling up and down the country the story of Miss Nightingale and the Barrack Hospital. The legend was born, and gained strength in cottages, tenements and courts, in beer-houses and gin shops. The rich might grow romantic, and dukes, in the slang of the day, declare themselves " fanatico for the new Joan of Arc ", but the legend of Florence Nightingale belonged to the poor, the illiterate, the helpless, whose sons and lovers she refused to treat as the scum of the earth. " The people love you ", wrote Parthe, " with a kind of passionate tenderness which goes to my heart."

The hacks of Seven Dials, where topical doggerel was produced for the mob, hymned her in innumerable songs. " The Nightingale in the East ",[1] decorated with a wood-cut of, apparently, a lady reposing in a tent bed, and to be sung to the tune of the " Cottage and the Wind Mill ", was still popular at regimental reunions fifty years later. One of its eight verses runs:

> Her heart it means good for no bounty she'll take,
> She'd lay down her life for the poor soldier's sake;
> She prays for the dying, she gives peace to the brave,
> She feels that the soldier has a soul to be saved,
> The wounded they love her as it has been seen,
> She's the soldier's preserver, they call her their Queen.
> May God give her strength, and her heart never fail,
> One of Heaven's best gifts is Miss Nightingale.

Another adapted the popular song " The Pilot that weathered the storm " to " Fair Florence who weathered the storm ". Another entitled " God Bless Miss Nightingale " contained sentiments which, in the circumstances, were ironical:

> God bless Miss Nightingale,
> May she be free from strife;
> These are the prayers
> Of the poor soldier's wife.

[1] Contrary to present custom, Scutari, the Crimea, and even Constantinople, are described by Miss Nightingale and her contemporaries as being " in the East ". She writes of " my time in the East ", the Nightingale Fund Committee speaks of her " services in the Hospitals of the East ", the War Office addresses orders " to the Army in the East ".

Others were " Angels with Sweet Approving Smiles ", " The Star in the East ", " The Shadow on the Pillow ", " The Soldier's Cheer ". The output of songs continued after the war. In 1857 Parthe wrote to Sir John McNeill thanking him for copies of " six pretty new ones ".

Quantities of a biography, printed in Seven Dials, were sold, price one penny. " *The only and unabridged edition of the Life of Miss Nightingale. Detailing her Christian and Heroic Deeds in the Land of Tumult and Death which has. made her Name Deservedly Immortal, not only in England but in all Civilised Parts of the World, winning the Prayers of the Soldier, the Widow and the Orphan.*"

A Staffordshire figure labelled " Miss Nightingale " depicts her not with the famous lamp, but carrying two cups on a small tray and romantically dressed in a long, white flowered skirt, a blue bodice with a pink bow, and wearing red slippers. Her portrait was eagerly demanded, but the family did not dare supply it because she had an objection to having her portrait circulated. The likenesses of her were imaginary; one print shows her as a lady with a Spanish comb in her hair, dark and passionate; another depicts a golden-haired Miss in a bower of roses. Boxes of notepaper were sold with a view of Lea Hurst at the top. Strangers called at Embley and asked to be allowed to see her desk. Shipowners named their ships after her. A life-boat was called the *Florence Nightingale*, one of the crew writing first to make sure the name was " got all correct ". Sir Edward Cook quotes a newspaper cutting which records that " The Forest Plate Handicap was won by Miss Nightingale beating Barbarity and nine others ". A popular tableau at Madame Tussaud's presented " A Grand Exhibition of Miss Florence Nightingale administering to the Sick and Wounded ".

The successive tidings of her illness, her recovery and her determination to stay at her post until the end of the war raised public feeling to boiling-point, and Sidney Herbert felt the authorities might usefully be reminded that she had the country at her feet. A committee was formed of which Richard Monckton Milnes was a member and Sidney Herbert honorary secretary, and on November 29th, 1855, a public meeting was called at Willis's Rooms, in St. James's Street, " to give expression to a general feeling that the services of Miss Nightingale in the Hospitals of the East demand the grateful recognition of the

British people ". The Duke of Cambridge was chairman, and spoke; though his admiration for Miss Nightingale was great, there was a slight doubt as to whether he could "say it in English"; however, he acquitted himself with credit. The Duke of Argyll, Lord Stanley, Sidney Herbert and Richard Monckton Milnes also made speeches, and Sidney Herbert read the letter from Scutari in which a soldier described the men kissing Miss Nightingale's shadow as she passed, which suggested the poem "Santa Filomena" to Longfellow. The meeting was crowded to suffocation and wildly enthusiastic, and similar meetings were held throughout the country. The first intention was to present an article of gold or silver suitably inscribed, "something of the teapot and bracelet variety", wrote Parthe, but so much money came in that it was decided to establish a Nightingale Fund, to enable Miss Nightingale to "establish and control an institute for the training, sustenance and protection of nurses paid and unpaid". The Nightingales did not attend the meeting—Parthe and Fanny were afraid they would be overcome by emotion, W. E. N. that he might be asked to speak. After the meeting Fanny held a reception of "notabilities" in her sitting-room at the Burlington Hotel, and wrote: "This 29th of November. The most interesting day of thy mother's life. It is very late, my child, but I cannot go to bed without telling you that your meeting has been a glorious one . . . the like has never happened before, but will, I trust, from your example gladden the hearts of many future mothers." Miss Nightingale wrote back quietly: "My reputation has not been a boon in my work; but if you have been pleased that is enough ".

The formation of the Nightingale Fund was mentioned in General Orders to the Army in the East, and it was suggested that subscriptions should take the form of contributing a day's pay. Dr. Hall refused, but otherwise the response was good and nearly £9000 was subscribed by the troops.

After the formation of the fund Queen Victoria, to "mark her warm feelings of admiration in a way which should be agreeable", presented a brooch designed by the Prince Consort, a St. George's Cross in red enamel surmounted by a diamond crown; the cross bears the word "Crimea", and is encircled with the words "Blessed are the merciful". On the reverse is the inscription, "To Miss Florence **Nightingale**, as a mark of esteem and gratitude for her devotion towards the Queen's brave soldiers from Victoria R. 1855". In a published message the Queen expressed her desire that Miss Nightingale would wear the brooch, which is now in the Royal United Service Institution in Whitehall, "as a mark of the high approbation of your Sovereign", and stated that it would give her "very great satisfaction when you return at last to these shores to make the acquaintance of one who has set so bright an example to our sex".

Miss Nightingale was not gratified: praise, popularity, prints, jewels left her unmoved. She wrote to Parthe in July: "My own effigies and praises were less welcome. I do not affect indifference towards *real* sympathy, but I have felt painfully, the more painfully since I have had time to hear of it, the éclat which has been given to this adventure of mine. . . . The vanity and frivolity which the éclat thrown upon this affair has called forth, has done us unmitigated harm and brought mischief on perhaps the most promising enterprise that ever set sail from England. Our own old party which began its work in hardship, toil, struggle and obscurity has done better than any other. . . . The small still beginning, the simple hardship, the silent and *gradual* struggle upwards; these are the climate in which an enterprise really thrives and grows. . . ."

In reply to the resolution sent by the committee of the Nightingale Fund she wrote: "Exposed as I am to be misinterpreted and misunderstood, in a field of action in which the work is new, complicated, and distant from many who sit in judgment upon it,—it is indeed an abiding support to have such sympathy and appreciation brought home to me in the midst of labour and difficulties almost over-powering". She could not, however, contemplate undertaking anything in addition to her present work, and would only accept the fund on condition that it was understood that there was great uncertainty as to when she would be able to employ it.

The fact was that the organisation and reform of nursing no longer filled her whole horizon, and there was more behind her refusal to take immediate advantage of the fund than the undoubted truth that she was overwhelmed with work.

Nursing had become subsidiary to the welfare of the British Army. " What the horrors of war are", she wrote in May 1855, " no one can imagine. They are not wounds, and blood, and fever, spotted and low, and dysentery, chronic and acute, and cold and heat and famine. They are intoxication, drunken brutality, demoralisation and disorder on the part of the inferior ; jealousies, meanness, indifference, selfish brutality on the part of the superior."

She set herself a new and gigantic task—she determined to reform the treatment of the British private soldier.

A mystical devotion to the British Army had grown up within her. In the troops she found the qualities which moved her most. They were victims, her deepest instinct was to be the defender of victims, they were courageous, and she instantly responded to courage. Their world was not ruled by money, and she detested materialism. The supreme loyalty which made a man give his life for his comrade, the courage which enabled him to advance steadily under fire, were displayed by men who were paid a shilling a day.

She did not sentimentalise the British private soldier. " What has he done with the £1—drank it up I suppose ", she scribbled at Scutari. " He asks us to find a post for his wife ", runs another note ; " he had better say which wife." Queen Victoria offered to send eau de cologne for the troops, but she said someone had better tell her a little gin would be more popular. She was told one of the wounded wanted company and observed she knew the company he pined for, that of a brandy bottle under his pillow. She was content to accept and love the troops as she accepted and loved children and animals. She called herself the mother of 50,000 children. "No one ", she wrote in a private note, " can feel for the army as I do. People must have seen that long dreadful winter to know what it was. I can never forget."

" I have never ", she wrote to Parthe in March 1856, " been able to join in the popular cry about the recklessness, sensuality, and helplessness of the soldiers. On the contrary I should say (and perhaps few women have ever seen more of the manufacturing and agricultural classes of England than I have before I came out here) that I have never seen so teachable and helpful a class as the Army generally. Give them opportunity promptly and securely to send money home and they will use it. Give them schools and lectures and they will come to them. Give them books and games and amusements and they will leave off drinking. Give them suffering and they will bear it. Give them work and they will do it. I would rather have to do with the Army generally than with any other class I have attempted to serve."

At Scutari—and Scutari was a typical army depot—the troops were given no opportunities but to drink. When a man became convalescent he was discharged to the Depot, and inevitably he drank in the spirit shops and drank liquor so poisonous that men frequently fell down after swallowing only a small quantity. A large proportion of every batch of convalescents was carried back drunk within twenty-four hours. "*Dead* drunk," said Miss Nightingale, "for they die of it and the officers look on with composure." When she was in the Sabins' house she could hear the troops and convalescents "howling" in the shacks of the bazaar.

It became clear to her that she must look after the troops not only when they were ill but when they were well. What she did for them outside the hospital was as important as what she did inside the hospital.

In May 1855, after strenuous opposition, she opened a small reading-room for men able to walk but not to leave the hospital. The authorities feared that the men would get above themselves if they read instead of drinking, and she was accused of "destroying discipline". However, their conduct was excellent. She found that a great many of the men could neither read nor write, and she asked if she might engage a schoolmaster. This was absolutely refused. "You are spoiling the brutes", Lord William Paulet told her.

She discovered the men drank their pay away because they were dissatisfied with the official method of sending money home through the Paymaster. Rightly or wrongly they believed they were defrauded and their ignorance exploited. This was a conviction not confined to the men. "In Scutari I have had thousands of sovereigns at a time in my bedroom", she wrote to Douglas Galton in 1862, "entrusted to me by officers who preferred making me their bankers because of the

239

perpetual source of discord. 'Offend the Commissary or Purveyor and you won't be able to get your money.'"

She made it a practice to sit in her room for one afternoon a week and receive the money of any soldier in the hospital who desired to send it home to his family. The money went to Uncle Sam, who bought postal orders which he dispatched to the various addresses. About £1000 a month was brought in, involving her in a very large amount of extra work, book-keeping, records and correspondence. When the men were discharged from hospital and rejoined their regiments in the Crimea they wished to continue sending money home through the post. She submitted a scheme to the authorities, but it was refused.

In November 1855, in her letter of thanks for Queen Victoria's brooch, she laid before the Queen the causes and remedies of the prevalent drunkenness in the army and the men's difficulties in remitting money home. On December 21st the Queen sent the letter down to a Cabinet meeting. Lord Granville said that Palmerston, the Prime Minister, thought it excellent, and Clarendon, the Foreign Secretary, said it was full of real stuff; but Panmure said it only showed that she knew nothing of the British soldier. The same day he wrote to Sir William Codrington, the Commander-in-Chief in the Crimea: " the great cry now, and Miss Nightingale inflames it, is that the men are too rich; granted, but it is added that they have no means to remit their money home. In vain I point out that this is not true. . . . We have now offered the Post Office to them, but I am sure it will do no good. The soldier is not a remitting animal; all who are inclined to do so, do remit continually, but there are many so selfish and brutish, whose appetite is their God, and every-thing is offered up to gratify its sensual longings. You must change the class of the British soldier if you would have it otherwise."

Lord Panmure proved wrong. Offices where money orders could be obtained were opened at Constantinople, Scutari, Balaclava and the headquarters of the camp outside Sebastopol, and £71,000 was sent home in less than six months. It was, said Miss Nightingale, all money saved from the drink shops.

When Lord William Paulet was replaced by General Storks she found an enthusiastic collaborator; working hand in hand they brought discipline and order to the Barrack Hospital and its neighbourhood. First, the drink shops were closed, the streets of the village and the surrounding neighbourhood were patrolled after dark, and every man found drunk was court martialled "for disgracing the regiment to which he belonged". Next, in September 1855, a large recreation room for the army called the Inkerman Coffee House was opened, with the aid of private funds. A committee of civilians, medical officers and chaplains undertook the management, and the Purveyor was treasurer. Miss Nightingale wrote to England for copybooks, maps, puzzles, chessmen and draughtsmen, pictures and "exciting books". Eugène Sue's *Mysteries of Paris* was a favourite. The Queen sent a print after Winterhalter, "The First of May", depicting the aged Duke of Wellington presenting a casket on the first birthday of his godson Prince Arthur. A second recreation room for patients in the Barrack Hospital was opened in a wooden hut in the courtyard. There were no rules except that women were not allowed. The walls were hung with maps and prints, the room was furnished with armchairs and writing-tables; newspapers and writing materials were paid for by Miss Nightingale. "The men", she wrote, "sat there reading and writing their letters, and the Library of the British Museum could not have presented a more silent or orderly scene." The officers had told her that the men would steal the notepaper and sell it for drink, but this never occurred.

In August 1855 the orderlies were disbanded and replaced by the Medical Staff Corps organised on the lines suggested in her letter to Sidney Herbert of January 8th, 1855. The Medical Staff Corps received training and remained permanently in the hospital.

By the spring of 1856 four schools, conducted by professional schoolmasters, had been opened. "The lectures", she wrote, "were crowded to excess so that the men would take the door off the hut to hear. Singing classes were formed and the members allowed to sing in the Garrison Chapel. The men got up a little theatre for themselves, for which dresses and materials were lent by a private hand, and this theatre was, I believe, always perfectly orderly. Football and other games for the healthy, dominoes and chess for the sick, were in great request. . . . A more orderly population than that of the whole Command of Scutari in 1855–1856, though increased by the whole of the Cavalry being sent down there for winter quarters, it is impossible to conceive."

It was an astonishing achievement, and during the winter of 1855–56 the picture of the British soldier as a drunken intractable brute faded away never to return. " She taught ", said an eye-witness, " officers and officials to treat the soldiers as Christian men."

But the achievement had been accomplished only at the price of unremitting toil. Throughout the summer of 1855, when she was desperately ill, through the autumn when she was alone, weak and crushed by the enormous demands of her official work, she had somehow to accomplish the additional heavy correspondence, the persuading, the interviewing, the accounting and listing involved in her welfare work. She had never completely recovered from her illness in May. She still had sciatica, she was losing weight rapidly and her ears gave trouble.

Lady Hornby, wife of the British Commissioner to Turkey, met her at a Christmas party given by Lady Stratford. " I felt quite dumb ", Lady Hornby wrote, " as I looked at her wasted figure and the short brown hair combed over her forehead like a child's, cut so when her life was despaired of from a fever but a short time ago. Her dress . . . was black, its only ornament being a large enamelled brooch, which looked to me like the colours of a regiment. . . . To hide the close white cap a little, she had tied a white crepe handkerchief over the back of it, only allowing the border of lace to be seen. . . . She was still very weak, and could not join in the games, but she sat on a sofa, and looked on, laughing until the tears came into her eyes."

While she was in her present state of health she could not be left alone, and after Mr. Bracebridge's indiscretion it was out of the question for him to return and relieve Aunt Mai. " I shall lose Mary ", wrote Uncle Sam despairingly. " I cannot look at this state of things patiently . . . after all, though Flo is far more important to the public, she did not and never could form the absolute ingredient in the inner life of her domestic circle that Mary does to us."

At home there was no conception of the situation confronting Miss Nightingale. The welfare work had succeeded but in every other direction she was failing. The good she had done was being undone, the decisions she had formed were being reversed, and she was not only helpless but perpetually tormented by official spite.

The Depot within the Barrack Hospital building had been condemned by the Sanitary Commission and the troops evacuated. Faced with difficulty in procuring recruits to replace the army lost before Sebastopol, the Government raised a German Legion of mercenaries, and, ignoring all protests, the military authorities put the Legion into the Depot. Cholera broke out and spread to the hospital, and one of the first to die was Dr. McGrigor. His successor refused to allow the nurses to administer medicine and restricted their duties to feeding the patients and changing their beds, thus reducing their status once more to that of domestic servants. The hospital at Koulali finally collapsed, and after being requested to relinquish it Miss Nightingale found herself saddled with the unpleasant task of winding-up its affairs. The Superintendent of a hospital for officers at one of the Sultan's Palaces died and she was requested to take the patients into the Barrack Hospital. She agreed, and two scandals ensued. One nurse was accused of ill-treating her patients, another of being too kind to them and receiving visits at midnight. Most sordid, most heart-breaking of all, was the case of Miss Salisbury.

Night after night, when the enormous mass of her daily work had been done, she must sit up wrestling with her statement for the War Office. It was bitterly cold; the stove sent out from England would not draw, and the charcoal brazier made her head ache. " They are killing me ", she told Aunt Mai. When the New Year of 1856 dawned her health had still further deteriorated, she had earache, continual laryngitis and found it difficult to sleep. In the dark icy cold she paced her room obsessed by failure. " The victory is lost already ", she told Aunt Mai. " But it is won on some points," Aunt Mai reminded her, and added, when reporting the conversation to Uncle Sam, "if you could hear what the Hospital was and

243

what it is through her struggles you would say so." It was unbelievable, wrote Aunt Mai again, how she worked; Aunt Mai could never have imagined any labour so unceasing, so unending. "Food, rest, temperature never interfere with her doing her work. You would be surprised at the temperature in which she lives . . . she who suffers so much from cold. . . . She has attained a most wonderful calm. No irritation of temper, no hurry or confusion of manner ever appears for a moment."

But the calm was only on the surface. Aunt Mai wrote confidentially to Mrs. Herbert that after a long, difficult interview Florence often seemed about to faint with exhaustion. After the interviews in connection with the Salisbury case she had collapsed on several occasions. She lay on the sofa unable to speak or eat, and yet if anyone came to see her on business she pulled herself together and appeared normal.

In January 1856 the McNeill and Tulloch Commission into the Supply of the British Army in the Crimea laid its final report before Parliament and confirmed what Miss Nightingale had already told Sidney Herbert. The disaster of the winter of 1854–55 had been unnecessary, a compound of indifference, stupidity, inefficiency and bureaucracy. The report, though restrained and dispassionate, named a number of senior officers as being negligent, indifferent and inefficient. Among them were Lord Cardigan, Lord Lucan and Sir Richard Airey, the Quartermaster-General. The facts in the report had been communicated to the Government six months ago, yet almost all these officers had been promoted or decorated and none had been removed from his position. The publication of the report created a storm, and Lord Panmure directed a Board of General Officers to assemble at Chelsea to " allow the officers adverted to in the report to have an opportunity of defending themselves ". Extensive whitewashing was to be done. Immediately following the establishment of the Board a fresh list of decorations and promotions was published. Benjamin Hawes got a K.C.B. and so did Dr. John Hall. "Knight of the Crimean Burial grounds I suppose ", wrote Miss Nightingale.

It seemed the triumph of all she had been fighting against, the final defeat of justice by power. " I am in a state of chronic rage," she wrote on March 3rd, 1856, "I who saw the men come down through all that long long dreadful winter, without other covering than a dirty blanket and a pair of old regimental trousers, when we knew the stores were bursting with warm clothing, living skeletons devoured by vermin, ulcerated, hopeless, speechless, dying like the Greeks as they wrapped their heads in their blankets and spoke never a word. . . . Can we hear of the promotion of the men who caused this colossal calamity, we who saw it? Would that the men could speak who died in the puddles of Calamita Bay!"

There seemed no end to weariness, disillusion, falseness. Lady Stratford, fêting her on Christmas Day, turned aside to assure a visitor she fully believed Miss Salisbury's story. Mary Stanley busily spreading rumours at home, yet wrote letters breathing devoted affection. Mother Bridgeman was still unsubdued and rebellious in the Crimea, and Miss Nightingale's own position was still officially unsupported. Now a new misery was added. At the beginning of December Mr. FitzGerald, the Chief Purveyor in the Crimea, encouraged by Miss Salisbury's success, wrote a " Confidential Report " on Miss Nightingale and her nurses which was forwarded by Sir John Hall to sympathetic quarters at the War Office. It was not a report but a series of accusations. She herself was accused of insubordination, her nurses were described as dishonest, extravagant, disobedient, inefficient and immoral. Mother Bridgeman and her nuns were warmly commended for zeal, skill, economy and obedience.

It was, said Miss Nightingale, " a tissue of unfounded assertions, wilful perversions, malicious and scandalous libels ", but the readiness with which its malice was received and exploited in official quarters added enormously to her difficulties.

Fact was disregarded. She was accused of unjustly removing Mrs. Shaw Stewart from being Superintendent of the General Hospital, Balaclava, when in fact Mrs. Shaw Stewart, Miss Nightingale's personal friend and staunch supporter, had been urgently requisitioned by the medical authorities to put the newly opened Castle Hospital on its feet. The Castle Hospital contained twice as many patients as the General Hospital and was a promotion.

In May 1855 she had wished to replace Miss Weare as

Superintendent of the General Hospital. Dr. Hall refused, advancing as a reason Miss Weare's successful management of the sick officers. In the Confidential Report it was stated that Miss Nightingale persisted in maintaining Miss Weare at her post in spite of the fact that Dr. Hall had demanded her removal on account of her unsuccessful treatment of sick officers.

So immoral were her nurses, alleged the Confidential Report, that five had been sent home for promiscuous conduct on a single ship. Of the five nurses named, four were her " very best nurses ", honourably invalided home " broken by their exertions ". One had actually been officially commended by Mr. FitzGerald himself. The fifth had not gone home at all but was working at Scutari.

Mother Bridgeman's nuns were commended for their economy and obedience to the medical authorities, though in fact the nuns had left Koulali on account of their enormous expenditure, and Mr. FitzGerald himself had said he hoped they would not bring their system with them to Balaclava.

Miss Nightingale was made aware of the existence of the report through Lady Cranworth, who was a friend of Sir Benjamin Hawes. The report was shown to Lady Cranworth, and it was intimated that Miss Nightingale would be wise to make a reply. She was not allowed to see the report, the substance only of the allegations was conveyed. However, she wrote a full refutation. In reply she was told that her statement "in some cases did not meet the exact point". There was no other comment. Since she had never seen the original document, the result was not surprising.

In February 1856 her difficulties reached a climax. She was asked to send nurses to the Crimea by the Chief Medical Officer of the Land Transport Corps. This much-needed Corps had been raised in the autumn of 1855 and placed under the command of an excellent officer, Colonel McMurdo, but it had been raised too hastily. Some of the corps were weakly lads, some old men, some Asiatics, most were drunkards. Discipline was poor, the camps were filthy, and cholera broke out. But the situation was such that she doubted if she dared send nurses. Mr. FitzGerald, elated by the success of his Confidential Report, was refusing to honour her drafts; she was owed £1500 which she could not get; Mother Bridgeman reigned at Balaclava; the Hall and FitzGerald party were openly declaring they intended to root her out of the Crimea.

She had already written, on January 7th, an official letter to the War Office complaining of Sir John Hall's action in sending Mother Bridgeman to Balaclava over her head, but it had brought no result. Before she went further she wrote to Dr. Sutherland, who was at Balaclava, asking him if he thought it wise for her to bring nurses to the Crimea. On February 4th Dr. Sutherland told her she should make no such attempt. He advised her to " state a case fully to the War Department and ask them to place you on a proper footing with the authorities here ". The position, he said, turned on the employment of the words " in Turkey ", which the Crimean authorities contended did not include the Crimea.

However, there were indications that Sir John Hall was uneasy. He withdrew his support from Mr. FitzGerald: the statements in the Confidential Report, he said, were made on Mr. FitzGerald's personal responsibility. " Mr. FitzGerald is in fact thrown overboard ", wrote Dr. Sutherland. Miss Nightingale scribbled on the margin of the letter, " I am not at all surprised. . . . I always expected it."

On February 20th, 1856, she wrote formally to Sidney Herbert enclosing Dr. Sutherland's letter and asking him to urge the War Department to telegraph a statement of her powers to the military and medical authorities in the Crimea. " It is obvious that my usefulness is destroyed, my work prevented or hindered, and precious time wasted, by the uncertainty of the relations in which I am left with the Crimean authorities."

On the same day she wrote him a private letter. She was very angry. " The War Office gives me tinsel and plenty of praise, which I do not want, and does not give me the real business like efficient standing which I do want. . . . The War Office sent me here. And surely it should not leave me to fight my own battle. . . . If they think I have not done my work well, let them re-call me. But, if otherwise, let them not leave me to shift for myself, in an ever recurring and exhausting struggle for every inch of the ground secured to me by the original agreement." She demanded that he should read the correspondence relating to the Confidential Report which was at Lady Cranworth's house and move for the production of papers in the House of Commons, to include her original instructions and agreement, the Confidential Report and her refutation, and letters written by Sir John Hall. "This is bad treatment. . . . I am assured that the people of England would not suffer this for me."

In reply he assured her that her position was to be cleared up. By some mischance it appeared that the new Commander-in-Chief, Sir William Codrington, like General Simpson, was unaware of her official status. As for moving for papers in the House of Commons, he refused. "I am going to criticise you and scold you", he wrote. "You have been overdone with your long, anxious, harassing work. . . . The Salisbury party, the Stanley party would, of course, take up the Hall and Fitz-Gerald view and press their particular cases and the public, distracted, indolent, weary would settle that it was a pack of women quarrelling among themselves, that it is six of one and half a dozen of the other, and everyone is equally to blame all round. . . . These are misrepresentations and annoyances to which all persons in office, and you are in office, are exposed —a single flower of the sort from which the bed of roses on which Secretaries of State repose is made." She answered on March 6th that she was being asked to do the work of a Secretary of State without the status of a Secretary of State. The War Office was feeble and treacherous, she wrote, and she pictured them saying: "Could we not shelve Miss N? I daresay she does a great deal of good but she quarrels with the authorities and we can't have that."

On March 10th Sir John Hall wrote her a suave and courteous letter inviting her to bring ten nurses to the hospital of the Land Transport Corps. She accepted the invitation, but attached so little importance to his good-will that she took with her everything she and her nurses could need, not only food but stoves.

On the day she left, March 16th, 1856, a despatch, establishing her position in terms far beyond anything of which she had ever dreamed, reached the Crimea.

The despatch had a curious history. In October 1855 a certain Colonel Lefroy, with the title of "Confidential Adviser to the Secretary of War on Scientific Matters", appeared, first in Scutari then in the Crimea. He was, in fact, engaged on a secret mission. He was to observe and report to Lord Panmure the truth about the state of the hospitals. He conceived the greatest admiration for Miss Nightingale, they became intimate friends and he assisted in her welfare work for the troops. Colonel Lefroy reached home at the beginning of February. He possessed, and was said to be the only man who did possess, very great influence over Lord Panmure. He pressed her case with warmth. In an official minute he wrote that the medical men were jealous of her mission—Sir John Hall would gladly upset it tomorrow if he could. She had asked for a telegram defining her position, but Colonel Lefroy went further; he wished her to have the unique distinction of her name in General Orders: the bulletin issued daily by the Commander-in-Chief and posted in every barrack and mess. "A General Order", he wrote, ". . . is due to all she has done and sacrificed. Among other reasons for it, it will put a stop to any spirit of growing independence among those ladies and nurses who are still under her, a spirit encouraged with no friendly intention in more than one quarter."

A battle ensued. Minutes flew backwards and forwards. It was pointed out to Lord Panmure that the despatch as worded amounted to a censure on Sir John Hall, but Panmure refused to alter it. Curious information was reaching him as to the state of the General Hospital, Balaclava, from sources other than Colonel Lefroy. At the end of December Sir William Codrington had written complaining of the amount of liquor consumed by the sick. "Last week's expenditure . . . for the sick there, which cannot number above 3000 in all, was 124 dozen port wine, 116 dozen porter and other things, in all 3244 bottles." The next week was "272 dozen port wine, 86 dozen porter, 8 dozen brandy, 6 dozen ale; in all 4264 bottles." Lord Panmure decided that the despatch was to be issued as it stood. On February 25th the despatch left the War Office and was published by Sir William Codrington in General Orders on March 16th. "The Secretary of State for War has addressed the following despatch to the Commander of the Forces, with a desire that it should be promulgated in General Orders: 'It appears to me that the Medical Authorities of the Army do not correctly comprehend Miss Nightingale's position as it has been officially recognised by me. I therefore think it right to state to you briefly for their guidance, as well as for the information of the Army, what the position of that excellent lady is. Miss Nightingale is recognised by Her Majesty's Government as the General Superintendent of the Female Nursing Establishment of the military hospitals of the Army. No lady, or sister, or nurse, is to be transferred from one hospital to another, or introduced into any hospital without consultation with her. Her instructions, however, require to have the approval of the Principal Medical Officer in the exercise of the responsibility thus vested in her. The Principal Medical Officer will communicate with Miss Nightingale upon all subjects connected with the Female Nursing Establishment, and will give his directions through that lady.' "

It was triumph. It was more than she had ever asked. It was complete defeat for the Hall party, the Stanley party, the Salisbury party. She reached Balaclava on March 24th, in a blinding snowstorm, and was formally welcomed by Sir William Codrington. Next day she took her ten nurses to the Hospital of the Land Transport Corps about a mile and a half from Balaclava.

Her struggle was over and the war was all but over, too. A Peace Conference was meeting in Paris, hostilities had ceased, and a formal declaration of peace was expected at any moment. Once more she strove to compose her differences with Mother Bridgeman. " She used many arguments in vain to convince me I ought again to connect myself and my sisters with her ", Mother Bridgeman wrote. Anything Mother Bridgeman wished Miss Nightingale would do. Once more she failed. Mother Bridgeman refused to submit to Miss Nightingale's control, she refused to be " humbled " or " mortified ", and she insisted on going home at once. " I have piped to her and done the Circe in vain ", Miss Nightingale wrote to Sidney Herbert. On March 28th, with a passage arranged by Sir John Hall and glowing testimonials from him and Mr. Fitz-Gerald in her pocket, Mother Bridgeman sailed for home.

Yet, though defeated, Sir John Hall and Mr. FitzGerald were still able to make themselves unpleasant. Sir John Hall questioned and delayed Miss Nightingale's requisitions, made difficulties about the nurses' duties, raised points that had been settled months ago, even objected to using the extra diet kitchens. Mr. FitzGerald in turn contrived to deprive her party of rations; no refusal was received, but she was sent from department to department, given endless forms to fill up, found this official out and that official engaged, and still no food was forthcoming. She applied to Sir John Hall and was informed that he could entertain no complaints relative to the Purveyor. On April 4th she wrote to Sidney Herbert: "We have now been ten days without rations. . . . I thank God my charge has felt neither cold nor hunger. . . . I have, however, felt both. . . . During these ten days I have fed and warmed these women at my own private expense by my own private exertions. I have never been off my horse until 9 or 10 at night, except when it was too dark to walk home over these crags even with a lantern, when I have gone on foot. During the greater part of the day I have been without food necessarily, except a little brandy and water (you see I am taking to drinking like my comrades of the Army). But the object of my coming has been attained and my women have neither suffered nor starved." She had fed her party on the provisions she had brought from Scutari and cooked on her own stoves.

Two of the hospitals were five miles up the country, the Monastery Hospital was five miles the other way; there were no roads, only rough tracks. Now the weather had become bitterly cold and snowstorms were continuous. Soyer, who accompanied her, wrote: "The extraordinary exertions Miss Nightingale imposed on herself . . . would have been perfectly incredible if not witnessed by many and well ascertained. . . . I have seen that lady stand for hours at the top of a bleak rocky mountain near the hospitals, giving her instructions while the snow was falling heavily." The long hours in the saddle without food proving too much for her weakened health, a mule cart was procured, but one night it overturned on one of the rough tracks. Colonel McMurdo then presented her with a springless, hooded baggage cart, which gave some protection from the weather. This was the Crimean carriage in which she said she henceforward " lived ", and which is still preserved at St. Thomas's Hospital, London.

In 1857 Miss Nightingale related a curious story to Sidney Herbert: " When I was in the East most of the Blue Books pertaining to the War used to be sent out to me—I never read them or the Newspapers or any other paper. Sir John Hall asked me for my copy of Maxwell's Commission (the Hospitals Commission) which I lent him and which he did not return to me for upwards of a year. . . . When he returned it to me several pages were cut out. I, never having read it, knew not what they were. . . . When I returned to England I sent out for another copy and then I found that what Hall had cut out was the whole of *Alexander's* evidence and indeed all the most valuable parts. . . . I know, from Dr. Hall himself, that he believed my copy to be the only one in the Crimea. . . . I have reason to believe that he made use of the mutilated copy with those in Command—and was not detected."

His ingenuity in petty persecution was inexhaustible. On March 28th, Mother Bridgeman and her nurses having left the General Hospital, Miss Nightingale went down to take over and found the nurses' huts locked. Sir John Hall had given the keys to Mr. FitzGerald, who had locked the doors and taken the keys away. A message was sent to Mr. Fitz-Gerald. Could Miss Nightingale have the keys, please—she was outside the huts and would wait there until the keys came. It was late in the afternoon and snowing. She waited, an hour and another hour. Darkness fell. Still she waited with the snow thick on her, and at last the keys came.

The General Hospital was filthy. "The patients were grimed with dirt, infested with vermin, with bed sores like Lazarus (Mother Bridgeman I suppose thought it holy)", wrote Miss Nightingale on April 17th, 1856. The Bermondsey nuns were horrified. After two days had been spent in washing, scrubbing and disinfecting, and three days in cleansing the patients and their bedding—one man was such a mass of bed sores that it took six hours daily to dress him—Sir John Hall paid a visit of inspection and at once wrote an angry letter. He was "disgusted at the state of the hospital and ordered it all to be put back in the admirable order it was in previously", and he desired the Principal Medical Officer in charge of the hospital "not to interfere with the Purveyor Mr. FitzGerald's admirable arrangements".

It was a letter designed for the official file, to stand as a useful piece of evidence if the state of the Balaclava General

Hospital under Mother Bridgeman was ever called in question. Miss Nightingale did not answer it; she was sickened.

The only " diversion " was provided by Miss Weare, who had been sent to the Monastery Hospital. Though over seventy, Miss Weare was causing a scandal. " She spent ", wrote Miss Nightingale, " much of her time cooking good things, eating, drinking and gossiping with an old Medical Officer until the small hours of the morning. I don't think I ever felt in such a ridiculous position in my life, as when I was called upon by the authorities to put a stop to the midnight gossipings as causing ' scandal ' and I had to speak to these two old fogies each of whom was twice as old as myself. Both were over 70."

On April 29th peace was proclaimed to the Allied Armies, but she felt no exultation, she looked forward with a sense of doom. " As I stood on the Heights of Balaclava, and saw our ships in the harbour so gaily dressed with flags while we fired a salute in honour of peace . . . I said to myself, ' More Aireys and more Filders, more Cardigans, more Halls. We are in for them all now and no hope of reform.' Believe me when I say that everything in the Army (in point of routine versus system) is just where it was eighteen months ago. . . . ' *Nous n'avons rien oublié ni rien appris*.' . . . In six months all these sufferings will be forgotten."

English and Russian soldiers were fraternising and getting drunk together. English officers were getting up steeplechases and breaking their necks. Interpreters were in request to arrange for collections of Crimean crocuses and hyacinths to be sent home to English gardens, and Lord Panmure was writing to Sir William Codrington on the importance of bringing the army home without beards.

The authorities were anxious to get the troops home before the hot weather came. On June 3rd, 1856, Lord Panmure told Miss Nightingale, " the period is now fast approaching when your generous and disinterested labours will cease ", and by the end of June the hospitals were almost empty. The nurses began to go home by detachments, and one of the first was Jane Evans, the old farm-worker, "made happy by the possession of a buffalo calf she had reared, to which beast, with herself, a free passage was granted ". Mrs. Shaw Stewart went home, the persistent martyr who had been the prop and mainstay of Crimean nursing. Rev. Mother Bermondsey was invalided from Scutari—" What you have done for the work no one can ever say ", wrote Miss Nightingale. " My love and gratitude will be yours dearest Reverend Mother wherever you go. . . . I do not presume to give you any other tribute." Miss Tebbutt, one of Mary Stanley's " ladies " who had proved an excellent nurse, went to Embley to rest, and Miss Nightingale wrote, " as she has only a mother at home it would give great pleasure if the mother were invited too ". Miss Noble, another of Miss Stanley's " ladies ", went to take up a post Miss Nightingale had procured for her. " She has been one of our best, kindest and most skilful surgical nurses, I feel a real attachment for her ", she wrote to Lady Cranworth. Every nurse was to be provided for. No one was to be " thrown off like an old shoe ". " That they remained with me I consider proof that I considered them, on the whole, useful to the work and worthy of having a part in it ", she wrote. Those she did not feel she could ask the Government to assist she helped out of her private pocket. A nurse who had been drunken, but had pulled herself together and done well was to be met when she arrived in London, given money if she needed it, and have a place found for her. A Miss Laxton had been disgraced for receiving visits from an officer; Miss Nightingale thought she had been too severely treated and asked W. E. N. to meet her and supply her with money. One thing only she implored— that her party should keep out of print. " If I do not conclude our campaign without saving all my ladies and nurses from expressing themselves in print (Oh that mine enemy would write a book!) I shall think myself quite out generalled."

At the end of June she returned to Scutari, where the camp was empty, the Inkerman Café deserted, only a few convalescents lingering where once lines of dying men had lain on the bare floor. Father Michael Cuffe went home, who once had compared her to Herod but now, she wrote, " ate out of her hand ". The Sellonite sisters, the " ancient dames in black serge" who had proved among the best of her nurses, departed in tears.

On May 5th Lord Ellesmere, moving the Address on the conclusion of peace in the House of Lords, paid a tribute to the closing of her mission : " My Lords, the agony of that time has become matter of history. The vegetation of two successive springs has obscured the vestiges of Balaclava and Inkerman. Strong voices now answer to the roll call, and sturdy forms now cluster round the colours. The ranks are full, the hospitals are empty. The angel of mercy still lingers to the last on the scene of her labours ; but her mission is all but accomplished. Those long arcades of Scutari in which dying men sat up to catch the sound of her footsteps or the flutter of her dress, and fell back content to have seen her shadow as it passed, are now comparatively deserted. She may probably be thinking how to escape, as best she may on her return, the demonstrations of a nation's appreciation of the deeds and motives of Florence Nightingale."

On July 16th, 1856, the last patient left the Barrack Hospital and her task was ended.

Once more Fanny and Parthe began to hope. Surely she must be satisfied at last, surely now she would come and live at home, repose on her laurels and enjoy them. Would she accept an official reception, or should they meet her privately at Aix ? They wrote Aunt Mai a great many letters. What were Florence's plans ?

Aunt Mai answered that she mentioned no plans : she seemed in high spirits, in great good looks, but they must make no mistake, her health was seriously shaken. She was painfully thin and, when alone, deeply depressed. She did not enjoy her fame ; she was afraid of it. Her reputation stood so high that whatever she did must disappoint expectations. As to her agreeing to settle down at home, of that Aunt Mai, hastening tactfully to agree that nothing could be more desirable, held out no hopes whatsoever.

The nation passionately desired to honour her. She had emerged from the War with the only great reputation on the British side. The Government offered a man-of-war to take her home in state, and Parthe wrote that " the whole regiments of the Coldstreams, the Grenadiers and the Fusiliers would like to meet her, or failing that they would like to send their bands to play her home wherever she might arrive, by day or night ".

The Mayors of Folkestone and Dover desired Mr. Augustus

Stafford to " find out privately where Miss Nightingale would first touch English ground in order to rouse the whole community ". There was a rumour that she would go to Lea Hurst. Committees met, triumphal arches were planned, there were to be bands, processions, addresses from the parish, and a carriage drawn by the neighbourhood to take her home. She rejected everything. She was bereaved ; a haunted woman. She began to write private notes again : " Oh my poor men, I am a bad mother to come home and leave you in your Crimean graves—73 per cent in 8 regiments in 6 months from disease alone—who thinks of that now ? " At night Aunt Mai heard her pacing endlessly up and down.

On July 28 she embarked at Constantinople for Marseilles, travelling incognito with Aunt Mai as " Mrs. and Miss Smith ". A Queen's Messenger travelled in the same boat to attend to formalities. There preceded her what she called her " Spoils of War " : a one-legged sailor boy, a Russian orphan, a large Crimean puppy and a cat had already arrived at Embley.

From Marseilles she went to Paris, where she left Aunt Mai and walked in unexpectedly at 120 rue du Bac. M. Mohl was at home, but Clarkey was in England. She stayed the night and next day went on alone to England. At eight in the morning she rang the bell at the Convent of the Bermondsey Nuns. It was the first day of their annual retreat, and she spent the morning in prayer and meditation with Rev. Mother. In the afternoon she took the train north, still alone, and in the evening walked up from the station to Lea Hurst.

Parthe, Fanny and W. E. N. were in the drawing-room, but Mrs. Watson, the housekeeper, was sitting in her room in front of the house. She looked up, saw a lady in black walking alone up the drive, looked again, shrieked, burst into tears and ran out to meet her.

Two figures emerged from the Crimea as heroic, the soldier and the nurse. In each case a transformation in public estimation took place, and in each case the transformation was due to Miss Nightingale. Never again was the British soldier to be ranked as a drunken brute, the scum of the earth. He was now a symbol of courage, loyalty and endurance, not a disgrace but a source of pride. "She taught officers and officials to treat the soldiers as Christian men." Never again would the picture of a nurse be a tipsy, promiscuous harridan. Miss Nightingale had stamped the profession of nurse with her own image. Jane Evans and her buffalo calf, Mother Bridgeman and her proselytising, Mary Stanley's ladies and their gentility, the hired nurses and their gin have faded from memory. The nurse who emerged from the Crimea, strong and pitiful, controlled in the face of suffering, unselfseeking, superior to considerations of class or sex, was Miss Nightingale herself. She ended the Crimean War obsessed by a sense of failure. In fact, in the midst of the muddle and the filth, the agony and the defeats, she had brought about a revolution.

XII SHE SAID SHE HAD SEEN HELL, and because she had seen Hell she was set apart. Between her and every normal human pleasure, every normal human enjoyment, must stand the memory of the wards at Scutari. She could never forget. She wrote the words again and again, in private notes, on the margins of letters, on scraps of blotting-paper; whenever her hand lay idle the phrase formed itself—" I can never forget ".

She was a haunted woman, but she was pursued not by ghosts but by facts, the facts of preventable disease. Blood was calling to her from the ground, the blood of the ghastly army of vermin-devoured skeletons who had died before her eyes in the hospitals of Scutari ; but their blood called " not for vengeance but for mercy on the survivors ".

The mortality of the Crimean disaster, 73 per cent in six months from diseases alone, was the ghastly fruit not of war but of the system which controlled the health administration of the British Army. The system was in operation still. Every day, every hour in Chatham, Woolwich, Knightsbridge, York, wherever the British Army had barracks and hospitals, the system was murdering men as surely as it had murdered them in Scutari. The Crimean tragedy cried aloud not for revenge but for reform. She, and she alone it seemed, had discerned this self-evident truth, had realised what that long, long dreadful winter of 1854 implied. " Otherwise there was not one man, gentle or simple, out of all those thousands, officer or private, to say ' This shall not be ' ", she wrote in a private note of August 1856. The summons to save the British private soldier had come to her.

She recoiled. It was too much. Must she pass her life struggling with the forces which had defeated her in the Crimea ? Since girlhood she had found fulfilment in physical tending of the sick ; must she now renounce all human contacts for the aridity of official correspondence, the compiling of statistics, the drafting of regulations, the formality of official interviews ?

There were midnight agonies, tears, prayers. Fanny,

Parthe, W. E. N., hearing her pace her room, thought she was struggling with fearful memories; but she was struggling with herself. She did not find it easy to submit. But the voices of ten thousand of her children spoke to her from their forgotten graves. " I stand at the altar of the murdered men," she wrote in a private note of August 1856, "and while I live I fight their cause." Early in September she wrote a message to the parishioners of East Wellow: " We can do no more for those who have suffered and died in their country's service. They need our help no longer; their spirits are with God who gave them. It remains for us to strive that their sufferings may not have been endured in vain—to endeavour so to learn from experience as to lessen such sufferings in the future by forethought and management."

She obeyed the summons. She a woman, ill, alone, exhausted, a voice, she cried, crying in the wilderness, prepared to undertake the gigantic task of reforming the health administration of the British Army—but she resented her fate. She wept for herself. She grew angry. No one appreciated what she had been forced to renounce for the sake of the work. No one appreciated the enormous urgency of the work itself. The characteristics which had been so marked in her youth, the benevolence, the patience, the quality which Clarkey described as " Flo's extraordinary bonté " faded. Her astonishing mind developed, her penetration, infinite capacity for taking pains, persistence, iron will to work, scrupulous sense of fair play became still more extraordinary, but the woman of her early years gradually ceased to exist.

She confided in no one, explained nothing. Her family and her friends were bewildered, but she would not enlighten them. The time when she had ached for sympathy was past; she revelled now in the consciousness that she had no sympathisers, no one to confide in. She was alone.

The urgency of the situation drove her. Action must be taken now, within the next few months, while the Crimean disaster was still fresh in the nation's mind. The iron was hot and must be struck. How was she to strike it? London was empty. Politicians and administrators were taking their summer holidays. The war was over; it had been discreditable and there was a universal wish to forget it.

Early in August she wrote to Lord Panmure announcing her arrival in England and asking for an official interview in which she might make her report to him as Secretary of State for War. Lord Panmure was in Scotland shooting grouse. He replied through his secretary on August 13th that he could see no necessity for an immediate interview. Later he would be delighted, as always, to hear Miss Nightingale's views. Meanwhile, " it will be more pleasant for you to rest a little while ".

She wrote to Sidney Herbert. He was fishing salmon on his estate in Ireland. She drove herself to write him letter after letter, lying on her sofa sick and exhausted, her fingers hardly able to hold the pen, entreating him, imploring him, commanding him to take action for the army now, at once, before it was too late.

On August 16th he told her candidly that he thought her letters overwrought. She should follow the excellent prescription of his doctor in Carlsbad, " *Ni lire, ni écrire, ni réfléchir* ". Sidney Herbert, above all men, was weary and disgusted with the whole sordid fruitless business of the Crimean War. He had nearly killed himself with overwork, he had been involved in humiliating scandals, he had failed to accomplish what he wished, and he had emerged with his reputation damaged. On August 26th he wrote to Mr. Sam Smith that Florence's state of mind was causing him concern; complete rest was badly needed, but since he realised, having regard to her temperament, that this was almost impossible, he advised her relations to plan a life for her of " some, tho' very limited and moderate, occupation ". When she was fully restored to health she might perhaps take up some " comparatively unexacting " nursing work in a large hospital. He did not suggest a meeting, indeed he avoided her.

She became frantic. Did no one realise that men were being done to death daily, that another catastrophe on a grand scale was inevitable unless something were done quickly? Her whole being cried out for action. " If I could only carry *one* point which would prevent *one* part of the recurrence of the colossal calamity, then I should be true to the brave dead ", she wrote in a private note of August 1856.

What could she do? Sidney Herbert had failed her,

Panmure evaded her. She was so ill it seemed madness to contemplate work. She found difficulty in breathing, suffered from palpitations, and was overcome by nausea at the sight of food. W. E. N., unable to contemplate her condition, left Lea Hurst and retreated to the peace and the shadows of the library at Embley.

If only she would rest: her family, her friends, the whole world in an international chorus implored her to rest. A host of unknown admirers from every country in Europe, from America, from Asia, in letters, newspaper articles, poems, songs, implored her to repose on her laurels and for weeks, months, years to rest. She could not. She was driven by the certainty that delay was fatal. And yet—if delay was fatal a false step was fatal too. On August 25th, in a long letter to Colonel Lefroy, she explained her dilemma.

Special difficulties, she wrote, confronted her. To initiate a scheme of army reform was in any case a task of immense difficulty. For her it was almost insuperably difficult, and for two reasons. The first was that she was a woman—that was very bad; the second, that she was a popular heroine, which was worse. The two together formed a pill which officialdom would never swallow. Any scheme known to emanate from her would instantly be rejected because it came from her. Sir Benjamin Hawes had written inviting her to put forward suggestions for improvements in the Army Medical Department in a form which he could officially submit to the heads of the department. She had reason to believe the invitation was given with the object of creating an opportunity for registering an official rejection of her proposals, and she had refused. Dr. Pincoffs had asked her to be patroness and organiser of a scheme to provide treatment for discharged wounded men, and she had told him that if he used her name the authorities would see to it that the scheme failed, "so great is the detestation with which I am regarded by the officials". Frankly, she continued, she did not know how to proceed. She had even reached the point of wondering if it might not be wiser to put off the idea of introducing any scheme of reform immediately, in spite of the fact that the moment was so propitious, and go to work gradually. She might begin to work in the military hospitals at home as she had worked in Scutari and

gradually reorganise the whole system. The Queen had
written to her and the Queen would certainly grant female
nursing departments in all military hospitals. Again the
difficulty was her position as a national heroine. It was
nothing but an embarrassment. " The buz-fuz about my
name ", she wrote contemptuously, " has done infinite harm."

Suddenly she scribbled a postscript : " If I could only find a
mouthpiece ". She was convinced that she herself would
shortly die—if only she could find someone to carry on the
work ! " If I could leave one man behind me ", she wrote in
a private note ; and she returned to the idea again and again.
" Who is this woman who thinks she can do what our great
men don't do ? But if I could leave one man behind me, if I
fall out on the march, who would work the question of reform
I should be satisfied, because he would do it better than I."
She needed a man who would be acceptable to the official
world, who would carry weight in official circles, but who
would be ready to submit himself to her and be taught by her.
Where could such a man be found ? She did not think of
Sidney Herbert.

After Miss Nightingale's return from the Crimea she never
made a public appearance, never attended a public function,
never issued a public statement. Within a year or two most
people assumed she was dead. She destroyed her fame
deliberately as a matter of policy. The authorities expected
that on her return she would make revelations. She neither
revealed, nor attacked, nor justified herself. She wrote nothing,
she made no speeches, she was not even seen. Instead, with
infinite patience and self-effacement, she set out to win the
authorities over to her side. She was laying aside a powerful
weapon ; at the moment adoration of her had reached an extraordinary pitch. " She may truly be called the voice of the
people of the present ", wrote Dr. Pincoffs to Fanny. In
Sheffield a lady who resembled Miss Nightingale found herself
surrounded by a large but respectful crowd, who pressed round
her asking for permission " just to touch her shawl ". Society
wished to lionise her and she was inundated with invitations.
The Duke of Devonshire, who had formed a collection of Press

cuttings relating to her work, presented her with a model of Athena in silver, and wished to give a reception in her honour at Chatsworth. She refused. She refused interviews, receptions, presentations. She refused to go out to dine. She refused to be painted. " The publicity and talk there have been about this work have injured it more than anything else ", she wrote in a private note of August 1856, " and in no way, I am determined, will I contribute by making a show of myself."

Her post-bag was enormous, but she would barely glance at it. " As to her indifference to praise it is quite extraordinary ", wrote Parthe. Congratulatory letters arrived in " hail storms ". Unknown admirers showered gifts, poems, songs, illuminated addresses and proposals of marriage. Begging letters came " in shoals ". An unknown gentlewoman asked to be provided with a post, " but nothing derogatory because I am an Irish lady of good family " ; one gentleman requested her to get his jewellery out of pawn and another asked for the gift of a donkey ; a young lady wrote : " I have had a passion for soldiers all my life and now wish to get my bread by it." " How would you construe this ? " Miss Nightingale scribbled in the margin.

Parthe wrote the acknowledgments. Miss Nightingale herself wrote no letters, signed no autographs, granted no interviews. The few who did receive a personal reply were humble people— the parishioners of East Wellow, the working-cutlers of Sheffield who presented her with a canteen of cutlery, 1800 working-men of Newcastle-on-Tyne who sent her an address. As far as the rest of the world was concerned Miss Nightingale had disappeared.

At the end of August Sidney Herbert returned from Ireland ; they met briefly at the Bracebridges' house and he was " lukewarm about army reform ". Then he retired to Wilton. She was in despair when suddenly she was given an opportunity of the most dazzling and unexpected nature.

Early in September her old friend Sir James Clark invited her to stay at his house in the Highlands. He wrote at Queen Victoria's desire : the Queen wished to hear the story of Miss Nightingale's experiences with the army, not only officially but privately. Sir James's house, Birk Hall, was only a mile or two from Balmoral. She would be commanded to Balmoral for an official interview, but in addition the Queen intended to have private conversations with her at Birk Hall.

She rose from her sofa and flew to work, determined to do much more than relate the story of her experiences. She would seize the opportunity to convince the Queen and, equally important, the Prince Consort of the urgent necessity for immediate army reform. Her case must be presented in a way to impress the Prince, who took a keen interest in army affairs and whose meticulous accuracy and love of detail were notorious. Since she must be ready with facts and figures, with tables and statistical comparisons, she plunged into correspondence with experts she had known in the Crimea, Sir John McNeill, Colonel Tulloch and Colonel Lefroy.

Her plan was to ask for a Royal Commission to examine the sanitary condition, administration and organisation of barracks and military hospitals and the organisation, education and administration of the Army Medical Department. For the first time in history the living conditions of the private soldier in peace and war, his diet and his treatment in health and sickness would, she hoped, be scientifically investigated. In addition to the Royal Commission she intended, on Colonel Lefroy's advice, to ask permission to address a Confidential Report to Lord Panmure which would be a frank account of her own experiences. " In some form or other we have almost a right to ask at your hands an account of the trials you have gone through ", wrote Colonel Lefroy on August 28th, " the difficulties you have encountered, the evils you have observed . . . no other person ever was, or can be, in such a position to give it."

On September 15th, accompanied by W. E. N., she arrived at Sir John McNeill's house in Edinburgh ; and was joined there by Colonel Tulloch for four days' furious and concentrated work. Her condition was causing grave anxiety, she was weak, emaciated and still experiencing nausea at the sight of food ; nevertheless, she was able to work day and night sorting, digesting and collating the vast mass of figures and facts which had been collected in the course of the McNeill and Tulloch enquiry. Her few free hours were spent in visiting and inspecting barracks, hospitals and institutions.

Sidney Herbert played no part in getting up the case. He

did not even advise. Writing to Miss Nightingale from Wilton on September 9th, he was affectionate but detached. " I hope your Highland foray will do you good. I am sure it will if you find help and encouragement for your plans." It seemed he did not take her seriously.

On September 19th Miss Nightingale left Edinburgh with W. E. N. for Birk Hall; and on September 21st she was commanded to Balmoral for an afternoon's talk with the Queen and the Prince Consort.

The meeting, an informal one, lasted for more than two hours and was a triumphant success. " She put before us ", wrote the Prince in his diary that night, " all the defects of our present military hospital system and the reforms that are needed. We are much pleased with her ; she is extremely modest." " I wish we had her at the War Office ", wrote the Queen to the Duke of Cambridge, the Commander-in-Chief.

She was commanded to Balmoral again and yet again. She conversed with the Prince Consort on metaphysics and religion and went with the royal party to church. On several occasions she dined informally. Most important of all, the Queen, as she had indicated, paid her private visits. One day she appeared suddenly quite alone, driving herself in a little pony carriage, and took Miss Nightingale off for a long walk. Another day she came over alone and unannounced, spent the afternoon, stayed to tea, and there was " great talk ". Parthe reported Lord Clarendon as having said the Queen was " enchanted with her ".

The first step had been successfully taken, but Miss Nightingale was aware that it was only the first step. Under the Constitution the Queen and the Prince had no power to initiate action ; that was exclusively in the hands of the Ministers of the Crown. On September 26th Miss Nightingale wrote to Uncle Sam : " Everything is most satisfactory. Satisfactory that is as far as their *will*, not their *power*, is concerned." Next day, in a letter to Sir John McNeill, she described the " great willingness " of the Queen and the Prince Consort and the Prince's secretary, Sir George Grey, to listen and ask questions. She had seen them all three repeatedly, together and separately. By their good-will and eagerness, she said soberly, her hopes were " somewhat raised ".

Before the warrant for the Royal Commission could be issued, the Queen must be advised to do so by the Secretary of State for War. Lord Panmure must be convinced of the necessity for army reform.

The next week Lord Panmure was to be in attendance at Balmoral, and the Queen, almost too anxious to be of use, insisted that Miss Nightingale come to Balmoral to meet him : " The Queen has wished me to remain to see Lord Panmure here rather than in London ", she wrote to Fanny on September 25th, " because she thinks it more likely something might be done with him here with her to back me. I don't but I am obliged to succumb."

Lord Panmure was a difficult subject whose personal appearance was surprising; he had an enormous head, crowned with thick upstanding tufts of hair, and a habit of swaying it slowly from side to side which had earned him the nickname of " the Bison ". Detail he hated, nor did he appreciate system. His position as Secretary of State for War involved an immense amount of work which, as Sidney Herbert said, he " found easy through the simple process of never attempting to do it ". He detested bothers, and had been infuriated by Sir John McNeill's and Colonel Tulloch's revelations in their Report on the Supplies for the British Army in the Crimea, though he himself had appointed them and given them their instructions. He had gone through their report before its official publication with the avowed object of cutting out anything that seemed unpleasant, and he had desisted only because he found that the only way to render the report innocuous was to rewrite the evidence. He had been heard to say that he wished both Sir John McNeill and Colonel Tulloch at the devil.

The greatest difficulty in dealing with him arose out of his habit of procrastination. He would not take action, for he had discovered that if action is avoided consequences are avoided too.

Yet despite these defects he was a man of character. When he was a boy of fifteen his father had quarrelled with his mother, and he was informed that he must choose between his parents. If he broke completely with his mother he would enjoy all the privileges of an eldest son with a large income and a safe seat in the House of Commons; if he persisted in seeing his mother he would be cut off with £100 a year and a commission in the army. He refused to be separated from his mother and never saw his father again. After twelve years in the 79th Highlanders he retired with the rank of Captain and entered politics, living, in the words of his biographer, " as best he could on a yearly income of £1000 and £10,000 down which he raised on a post-obit from the Jews ". In 1852, after thirty-six years of estrangement, his father died, and at the age of fifty-one he succeeded to vast estates and a large income. Now at Brechin Castle, in Forfarshire, he lived as a feudal chieftain. He was an enthusiastic sportsman, and his deer forests, his salmon rivers and his grouse moors were the best in Scotland; one of his chief interests was the promotion of measures for the protection and improvement of game. Good stories were told of him. When he was introducing the deputation on the Tweed Acts for the protection of salmon the Home Secretary was Sir George Lewis, who was a scholar rather than a sportsman. After listening attentively to the chairman's speech for some minutes Sir George enquired: " Do I understand you to say, sir, that the salmon sometimes visits the sea ? " Panmure brought his stick down on the floor with a loud crash. " Good God ", he burst out, " with how little wisdom is this country governed ? "

In 1855 his favourite nephew, Captain Dowbiggin, was serving before Sebastopol; and to an official telegram to General Simpson, then commanding the British forces, he added this cautious postscript: " I recommend Dowbiggin to your notice, should you have a vacancy and if he is fit ". In those early days of telegraphy operators were accustomed to condense, at their own discretion, messages that seemed verbose, and the postscript reached headquarters in the simple form, " Look after Dowb ".

Panmure was a religious man, keenly interested in the organisation of the Free Church of Scotland and an active member of the assembly. During his life generosity was not considered one of his characteristics; but after his death among his papers was found a long list of persons to whom he had been paying annuities in secret.

To win over Panmure was a formidable task, and the ground

was carefully prepared. The Queen wrote informing him of the proposed meeting—" Lord Panmure will be much gratified and struck with Miss Nightingale—her powerful clear head and simple modest manner ". The Queen also fell in with a stratagem designed to prevent Panmure from evading the main issue. Miss Nightingale wrote her a letter outlining her suggestions for army reform; this the Queen accepted " with great grace ", and a copy of it was then sent to Panmure with the information that the Queen had accepted the original. By this means it was hoped that the main lines of the discussion would be defined.

Sir John McNeill anticipated " considerable advantage from your interview with Lord Panmure . . . he probably has no very accurate, or perhaps a very inaccurate, notion of what sort of person Miss Florence Nightingale is ". Colonel Lefroy wrote that he looked for " great results ". Sidney Herbert was pessimistic. She had written to him before the Queen's invitation asking him to arrange for her to see Panmure. He had, at one point, promised to meet her if he were in London for a " combined attack on the Bison ". But he had evaded her by never being in London. Before her interview with Panmure she wrote from Birk Hall to remind him of this " very important promise ". It had been impossible to refuse the Queen's invitation, but " I would rather have seen Panmure with you. However the one does not preclude the other. And I hope you will (like the Cid) stand up for the cause of the poor Army Hospitals which, I assure you, have not won a step of ground yet by the experience of the war."

His reply was discouraging. There was no harm in her trying to see what she could do with Panmure, but " I am not sanguine, for tho' he has plenty of shrewd sense there is a vis inertiae in his resistance which is very difficult to overcome ".

On October 3rd, 1856, Miss Nightingale went to Balmoral, while W. E. N. " fled ". He was, as he had written of himself, "incapable of practical solution of the wants of others ". The interminable conferences, the endless wrestling with dry masses of figures and facts, the spectacle of Florence already half-dead from exhaustion became unbearable. Birk Hall was chilly, it rained incessantly, and he caught a cold; so once more he retreated to the peace of the library at Embley. Miss Nightingale wrote to Sir John McNeill on October 7th: "My father has, I am sorry to say, turned tail and fled. He was cold in the Highlands, had a cold—and went home."

On October 5th the interview took place, and Miss Nightingale's success exceeded all expectations. Lord Panmure succumbed to the spell which drunken orderlies, recalcitrant nurses and suspicious officials had been powerless to resist. "You may like to know", wrote Mr. John Clark, Sir James's son, "that you fairly overcame Pan. We found him with his mane absolutely silky; and a loving sadness pervading his whole being." On November 2nd Sidney Herbert wrote: "I forget whether I told you that the Bison wrote to me very much pleased with his interview with you. He says that he was very much surprised at your physical appearance, as I think you must have been at his. God bless you."

When she returned to Birk Hall, Panmure, like the Queen, came to see her privately, and it seemed that she had obtained everything. There was to be a Royal Commission and the instructions were to be drawn up in accordance with her suggestions. She was to be invited to make a "Confidential Report"; and the request was to come jointly from Lord Panmure as Secretary of State for War and Lord Palmerston as Prime Minister. Netley, the first general military hospital to be built in the country, was in process of construction: Lord Panmure volunteered to send her the plans and invited her to make observations, declaring himself to be at her service to discuss details as soon as they were both in London at the end of the month. When she left Birk Hall to go south the prospect was rosy. On October 12th an Aberdeen newspaper announced: "Miss Nightingale, that justly celebrated lady, passed through Aberdeen yesterday on her way south. She left by the 10.45 train and although she had taken every precaution to prevent the knowledge of her presence, a considerable number of people were present, anxious to see her and, if opportunity offered, to pay her some mark of the homage due to exalted virtue and philanthropy. She, however, shunned observation and speedily took her place and sat back in the carriage that was to convey her off. The parties who had the satisfaction of seeing her, described her as a very handsome good looking young lady of an evidently retiring disposition."

Some years later Clarkey wrote down what Miss Nightingale had told her of her impressions at Balmoral. "She was struck with the difference between the minds of the Queen and Prince Albert and the fine folk about them and how little the latter were capable of appreciating them. For instance the Duchess of Wellington and Lady Someone did nothing but complain what a dull place it was and how tiresome—they seemed occupied with nothing but trifles, but the Queen and Prince Albert's whole thoughts were about Europe, the Crimea War, etc. etc. etc.—all things of importance. She says that the Queen is a remarkably conscientious person, but so mistrustful of herself, so afraid of not doing her best, that her spirits are lowered by it."

Miss Nightingale spent a few days in Edinburgh with Sir John McNeill; stayed for a fortnight at Lea Hurst establishing contact with " Crimean confederates " ; and on November 1st, accompanied by Fanny, Parthe and W. E. N., went to London to the Burlington Hotel, the " dingy old Burlington ".

She had drawn up a list of names for the Commissioners. Civilians and military men were to be equally balanced. On the civilian side she put forward Sir James Clark, Sir James Martin, Dr. Sutherland and Dr. Farr.

Dr. Farr was of special importance. He was a pioneer in the science of statistics, then in its infancy, and she intended, with his help, to make a statistical comparison of the rate of sickness and death in barracks with the rate in civilian life. It would, she believed, be startling.

Many years later Miss Mary Farr, Dr. Farr's daughter, recalled that as a child she overheard a conversation between Miss Nightingale and her father. Miss Nightingale wore a black *moiré* silk dress and a black lace shawl; and the young Miss Farr was struck by her tall figure, her graceful carriage and her beautifully poised head. She was explaining her scheme for comparing the relative healthiness of life in barracks and out, and Dr. Farr replied : " Well, if you do that you will make yourself enemies ". She drew herself up. " After what I have seen I can fire my own guns," she said.

Dr. John Sutherland was one of the leading sanitary

authorities of the day. He had been one of the original Inspectors appointed under the first Board of Health of 1848, and held a post as Sanitary Adviser to the Board of Health. He had been head of the Sanitary Commission of 1855, had become Miss Nightingale's intimate friend, and was her personal physician. He was an invaluable worker but was prone to a flippancy she found intensely irritating. On November 12th, 1856, he wrote: " I am led to believe there must be a foundation of truth under the old myth about the Amazon women somewhere to the East. All I can say is that if you had been Queen of that respectable body in old days Alexander the Great would have had rather a bad chance. Your project has developed far better than I expected."

On the military side she intended to press for Sir Henry Storks, who had worked " hand in hand " with her in army welfare work at Scutari, Colonel Lefroy, Dr. Balfour, assistant surgeon to the Grenadier Guards and an able statistician, and, most important of all, Dr. Alexander. " Get ALEXANDER ", Dr. Sutherland had written. " Nobody else if you cannot. He is our man."

Sidney Herbert called Alexander " unquestionably the ablest man in the British Medical service ". He had been first-class Staff Surgeon to the Light Division and had spent the Crimean campaign in the fighting line. William Howard Russell described him at Calamita Bay as " a gentle giant of a Scotchman, sitting on the beach with a man's leg in his lap ", and pouring out the vials of his wrath on Sir John Hall for landing the army without medical supplies. Throughout the war he was distinguished by his skill, his powers of organisation and his fearless independence. His achievements did not endear him to his superiors, and at the close of the campaign he was relegated to a second-class appointment in Canada. If he were to be a member of the Commission, it would be necessary for the authorities to reconsider their decision and recall him. It was impossible to put forward the names of Sir John McNeill and Colonel Tulloch owing to their dispute with Lord Panmure.

The stage was set for the play, but the principal player lingered: Sidney Herbert still hesitated. He would not come to London. He remained at Wilton and Miss Nightingale's letters became impatient. "If you come to London during the next fortnight will you have the goodness to let me know you are there", she wrote on October 31st, ". . . I should have much to tell you about my 'Pan', could I only see you." In the first week of November he did come to London and called to see her; and when he left he had agreed to accept the chairmanship of the Commission. The spell cast by her presence coupled with his own sense of duty had been too powerful for him. He was far from well, easily tired, easily depressed—the fact was, he already carried within him the seeds of incurable disease. His term at the War Office during the Crimean campaign had half broken his heart; he viewed the future with gloom.

When Lord Panmure made an appointment to call at the Burlington Hotel on November 16th expectation ran high. "I long to hear what results you obtain from the Bison", wrote Sidney Herbert. During the morning Sir James Clark sent her a note by hand: "I think it would be well, when you see Lord Panmure to make him understand that the enquiry is intended as, and must comprehend, an investigation into the whole Medical Department of the Army and everything regarding the health of the Army". Sir James Clark had opportunities of observing Panmure at Court, and he realised that he had no idea of the revolutionary and explosive ideas which lay concealed under Miss Nightingale's quiet, modest manner. Panmure had come to his first meeting fearing that "with so strong a hold on the feelings of the nation, she is not unlikely to use it for personal ambition". He had found a charming, well-bred woman, completely altruistic, and he acknowledged he had misjudged her. He was destined to discover that her altruism was more troublesome than most women's ambition.

The interview was a very long one. Once more her extraordinary personal charm worked its spell, once more she triumphed. The main point was achieved. The Commission was to go forward and its scope was to be "general and comprehensive, comprising the whole Army Medical Department and the health of the army at home and abroad". As soon as Panmure had left she sat down and scribbled Sidney Herbert a long, gay, disconnected note: "My 'Pan' here for three hours . . . will have Drs balanced. Not fair : two soldiers reckon as against civil element. Whenever I represented it (I did not know old ' Pan ' was so sharp), he offered to take off Colonel Lefroy ! So I had to knock under. Won't bring back Alexander, will have three Army Doctors. So like a sensible General in retreat I named Brown, Surgeon Major Grenadier Guards, therefore not wedded to Dr. Smith, an old Peninsular and Reformer. . . . He [Panmure] had generously struck out Milton." (Mr. Milton had been sent to Scutari to straighten out the purveying, and her verdict had been that he dealt only in " official whitewash ".) " Seeing him in such a ' coming-on disposition ' I was so good as to leave him Dr. Smith the more so as I could not help it.

" Have a tough fight of it : Dr. Balfour as secretary. Pan amazed at my condescension in naming a Military Doctor ; so I concealed the fact of the man being a dangerous animal and obstinate innovator.

" Failed in one point. Unfairly. Pan told Sir J. Clark he was to be on. Won't have him now. Sir J. Clark has become interested. Agreeable to the Queen to have him—just as well to have Her on our side. . . . Besides things Ld. P. finds convenient to forget, has really an inconveniently bad memory as to names, facts, dates and numbers. . . . Does not wish it to be supposed he takes suggestions from me, a crime indeed very unjust to impute to him."

Outside the Commission a point of first-class importance had been won. Dr. Andrew Smith, Director-General of the Army Medical Department, was very shortly due to retire ; and Lord Panmure had pledged his word that Sir John Hall should not be made Director-General as long as he was in office.

She had done a great deal, but the pressure necessary for complete success could not be applied by her. Sidney Herbert must do that. He must be made to understand that everything depended on him ; and she finished her note with these words : " You must drag it through. If not you, no one else."

A few days later an official letter from Panmure invited Sidney Herbert to accept the chairmanship of the Commission. He accepted, subject to certain conditions, chief of which was

Alexander's recall from Canada. Miss Nightingale allowed herself to be optimistic. Further battle over the personnel of the Commission was inevitable, but the main point had been achieved.

And then, inexplicably, nothing further happened. The official announcement of the issue of the Royal Warrant to set up the Commission, which should have been made within the next few weeks, never came. No further arguments took place on personnel. Sidney Herbert's letter asking for Alexander's recall was not discussed. Instead, Sidney Herbert received a friendly note from Lord Panmure regretting he was unable to write as he had gout in both his hands. " Gout is a very *handy* thing; and Lord Panmure always has it in his hands when he is called upon to do anything ", Miss Nightingale wrote to Sir John McNeill on December 15th. " Lord Panmure appears to be more convinced of the necessity for the reform than eager to carry it out ", she told Lord Palmerston. " Perhaps eagerness is not Lord Panmure's characteristic."

Unfortunately at the moment Panmure was being put to the greatest possible trouble by Miss Nightingale's friends, Sir John McNeill and Colonel Tulloch. The storm raised by the inconvenient revelations made in their report was still raging. He had appointed them out of a genuine sense of duty and horrid bothers had resulted. It seemed only too probable that the Commission on the Health of the Army would result in even greater bothers, and there was certainly a strong party against it at the War Office. Miss Nightingale, who was so charming and could be so very persuasive, pushed him one way, but when he left her and returned to the War Office the permanent officials pushed him the other.

The solution was to do nothing, to be friendly and pleasant, because unfriendliness and unpleasantness also led to bothers, but to take no action whatsoever. Without apparent reason the Commission appeared to be fading away.

" Do not allow yourself to be discouraged by delays ", wrote Sir John McNeill on December 19th; but to Miss Nightingale, whose overwrought mind burnt with unearthly brilliance in her sick body, delay was intolerable. She suffered torments of frustration, pouring herself out once more in private notes. " My God, my God why hast thou forsaken me ", she wrote at Christmas 1856. " We are tired of hearing of the Crimean Catastrophe. We don't want to know any more about the trenches cold and damp, the starved and frozen camp, the deficient rations, the stores which might have served the great army of the dead lying unused. . . . Generals who, looking at dead dogs polluting the atmosphere where men lay, said 'You are spoiling the brutes'. G.H.Q. feeding their horses on the biscuits the men could not eat; and saying that anyway they kept the horses fat. . . . Words were given in plenty to the great Crimean Catastrophe, but the real tragedy began when it was over." Hour after hour her pen rushed on, hour after hour she paced her room sleepless, raging against the indifference, the forgetfulness of the world. In letter after letter she incited her fellow workers to action. Her shrewd eye had penetrated the Bison's secret. " My Lord is ", she wrote, " as I have often found the most bullyable of mortals." She entreated that he should be bullied. She besought Sidney Herbert to write threatening to resign the chairmanship publicly unless the Royal Warrant for the Commission was issued forthwith. She vowed, " I will never leave Panmure alone until it is done ". Her personal relations with him remained pleasant. She said and wrote hard things of him : " he has no courage and no conscientiousness ", she wrote in November ; but their correspondence was conducted with arch playfulness. " Here is that bothering woman again ", she wrote on January 22nd, 1857, " just to remind you I am in London awaiting your decision." Panmure jestingly called her " a turbulent fellow " and sent her presents of game.

But he could not evade her entirely. As well as being involved together on the subject of the Royal Commission they were waging what she called a private campaign on the subject of Netley Hospital. When he had volunteered to send her the plans for her observations he had wished to pay her a compliment. Before he could take breath she had fallen upon the opportunity with relentless thoroughness, obtaining leave to " report confidentially " with the assistance of Dr. Sutherland. She inspected, she consulted authorities, she drew up exhaustive reports bristling with statistics derived from sources both at home and in Europe. She prepared additional memoranda, dealing in detail with certain aspects of the case, she drew up

275

alternative suggestions. Finally, she condemned the Netley plans root and branch and sent the whole result to Lord Panmure.

He felt he had accidentally released a genie from a bottle. The accumulated experience of fourteen years was suddenly put at his disposal; the fruit of her researches in France, Germany, Italy, London and Switzerland; of the endless miles she had tramped down the corridors of hospitals, prisons, asylums, orphanages; of the endless questions she had asked; the endless figures she had tabulated. He was taken aback. Moreover, since issuing the invitation a fact which he had failed to take into account had been brought to his notice. Building had progressed so far that radical alterations were impossible. He wrote her a soothing letter. Her objections were no doubt sound but there were " susceptibilities " to be considered. But she was not to be put off; she appealed to the Prime Minister, her old friend Lord Palmerston, and during the Christmas holidays of 1856 went over to his house, Broadlands, to dine and sleep and open his eyes to the truth about Netley.

On January 17th Lord Palmerston wrote Panmure a sharp letter. Miss Nightingale had left on his mind a conviction that the plan was fundamentally wrong; and that it would be better to pull down everything that had been built and start again. " It seems to me ", wrote the Prime Minister, " that at Netley all consideration of what would best tend to the comfort and recovery of the patients has been sacrificed to the vanity of the architect, whose sole object has been to make a building which should cut a dash when looked at from the Southampton river. . . . Pray therefore stop all progress in the work till the matter can be duly considered."

Lord Panmure was aghast. Vistas of bother, of explanations to be made, letters to be written, answers to questions in the House, unrolled themselves before him. There would be " rupture of extensive contracts ", " reflections cast on all concerned in the planning of the designs ". In addition there were 70,000 reasons which were completely unanswerable—it would cost £70,000 to pull down the partially constructed building and start again. The vision of himself attempting to explain away a loss of £70,000 to the House was a nightmare he refused to contemplate. Work at Netley went on.

Lord Palmerston wrote again. He continued to feel very anxious about Netley Hospital, and he would rather pay for throwing it brick by brick into Southampton Water than construct a building which should be a charnel house rather than a hospital.

Still Panmure would not be moved. He offered to incorporate improvements, but reconstruction was impossible. Miss Nightingale refused to give up hope. Were not her criticisms admitted to be justified, her new plans to be infinitely superior to the old? She argued, cajoled, threatened, but she was defeated. The 70,000 reasons conquered; and Netley was constructed on the existing plans.

Time has proved her to be correct. Throughout its history Netley has been a difficult, depressing and unsatisfactory hospital. The design she put forward was the " pavilion " design, separating the building into blocks. " The object sought ", she wrote, " is that the atmosphere of no one pavilion or ward should diffuse itself to any other pavilion or ward, but should escape into the open air as speedily as possible, while its place is supplied by the purest obtainable air from outside." Each pavilion was to form a separate detached hospital with an administration in common. Though the bacteriological nature of infection had not yet been discovered, Miss Nightingale deduced from her own observation the fact that, keeping patients isolated in small groups, decreased the incidence of hospital diseases. The pavilion design is to be seen in the Herbert Hospital at Woolwich and, until it was damaged by air bombardment, in St. Thomas's Hospital, Lambeth, both of which were built under her supervision. Netley, with its large central block, its long corridors, its impressive façade is a typical eighteenth-century hospital built fifty years too late.

Once defeat was a fact she accepted it and laboured with good-will to introduce improvements which should make the original plans tolerable. Her correspondence with Lord Panmure was more than usually playful. Netley was christened " the patient ", and she advised him of the progress made in letters written in the form of bulletins on the patient's condition. Nevertheless, she had been defeated, and by the spring of 1857, with the issue on Netley lost and the Commission still delayed, her spirits were at their lowest. " I am very miserable", she wrote to Mrs. Bracebridge in February. "I think he [Panmure] means to shelve me." There was a slackening in the zeal of her supporters, and Sidney Herbert, who had been unwell all the winter, announced his intention of going abroad for a cure. She alone burned at white heat, perpetually on the edge of physical collapse but never ceasing to bully the Bison, "which", she wrote to Sidney Herbert, "is a petty kind of war-fare very unpleasant ".

Frustration had its inevitable effects : she could not sleep, could not eat, spent the nights pacing her room or writing private notes. " No one ", she wrote in a private note of February 9th, 1857, " can feel for the Army as I do. These people who talk to us have all fed their children on the fat of the land and dressed them in velvet and silk while we have been away. I have had to see my children dressed in a dirty blanket and an old pair of regimental trowsers, and to see them fed on raw salt meat, and nine thousand of my children are lying, from causes which might have been prevented, in their forgotten graves. But I can never forget. People must have seen that long long dreadful winter to know what it was."

Disappointment piled on disappointment. Early in 1857 the exasperating affair of the McNeill and Tulloch Report came to a head. The Report of the Chelsea Board set up with the avowed intention of whitewashing the officers concerned was published, all blame was removed from individuals, and the gigantic misfortunes endured by the army were attributed to the non-arrival of a certain single consignment of pressed hay. Lord Panmure accepted it, disowning the Commissioners he had himself appointed, and the McNeill and Tulloch Report was set aside.

By March 1st Miss Nightingale had reached complete despair. " Lord Panmure has broken all his promises," she wrote to Sir John McNeill, " defeated the Army Reformers at every point, simply by the principle of passive resistance, the most difficult of all resistances to overcome, the easiest of all games to play. I think our cause is lost. . . . Mr. Herbert is ill and going abroad and so ends all chance of a Commission to enquire into the Sanitary State of the Army, of which he was to have been chairman."

In fact the first hopeful signs had already appeared.

On February 18th, after six months' delay, Panmure had written from the War Office with an official request for her Confidential Report. "Your personal experience and observation, during the late War, must have furnished you with much important information relating not only to the medical care and treatment of the sick and wounded, but also to the sanitary requirements of the Army generally. I now have the honour to ask you to favour me with the results of that experience . . . should you do so . . . I shall endeavour to further as far as lies in my power, the large and generous views which you entertain on this important subject."

She was not elated. She had no faith in Panmure's intentions of furthering her "large and generous views". She believed he meant to shelve the Commission and she regarded the report as a sop to her, something to keep her quiet, which in due course would also be shelved. Nevertheless, she at once set to work. If he failed her she had a larger audience. She had put the weapon of publicity aside, but the weapon still lay ready to her hand. At the end of February she wrote to Sidney Herbert: "All that Lord Panmure has hitherto done (and it is just six months since I came home) has been to gain time. . . . He has broken his most solemn promise to Dr. Sutherland, to me and to the Crimea Commission. And three months from this day I publish my experience of the Crimea Campaign and my suggestions for improvement, unless there has been a fair and tangible pledge by that time for reform."

It was a threat which could not fail to make the Bison uneasy, and there were other indications that public opinion was turning in the direction of Army Reform. The whitewashing done by the Chelsea Board had by no means settled the matter of Sir John McNeill and Colonel Tulloch; their report had been set aside, but the nation refused to acquiesce. Meetings of protest had been held in many large towns; addresses of sympathy and support from citizens and municipalities had been presented to them. Feeling in the country became reflected so strongly in the House of Commons that Panmure was forced to act, and he attempted to buy off the Commissioners by offering them each £1000 cash down, on the understanding that the matter was to be considered closed.

They indignantly refused, and Miss Nightingale, who had been agitating behind the scenes as a part of her campaign of bullying the Bison, pressed Sidney Herbert to raise the matter in the House. On March 12th he moved a humble address to the Crown, amid loud applause, praying that Her Majesty might be pleased to confer some signal mark of favour upon Sir John McNeill and Colonel Tulloch. The atmosphere of the House was such that Lord Palmerston accepted the motion without a division. " Victory ! " scribbled Miss Nightingale that night. " Milnes came in to tell us." Colonel Tulloch was created a K.C.B. and Sir John McNeill, already a G.C.B., was created a Privy Councillor. " They have been borne to triumph on the arms of the people ", she wrote.

Slowly and reluctantly the Bison was forced to capitulate. In the spring of 1857 a British Expeditionary Force was sent to China ; and Miss Nightingale was urgent that the supplying of the troops should not repeat the costly mistakes of the Crimea. Through Sir James Clark she approached Dr. Andrew Smith, still Director-General of the Army Medical Department. Finding him surprisingly receptive, she drew up plans for diet, accommodation and medical equipment which were transmitted through Sir James Clark, who reported that Dr. Smith " has attended to almost everything I suggested—the ventilation of the ships, the diet of the troops ; and they are to have fresh meat and vegetables during the whole voyage and while on the station when it is possible. . . .The Duke of Cambridge backed our recommendations."

Unquestionably the tide was setting towards reform ; and once the tide had turned Panmure was not the man to resist.

On April 27th he paid another official call at the Burlington Hotel. So extraordinary was Miss Nightingale's position, so clearly was it recognised that she was the leader of the Reform party, that Panmure brought the official Draft of the Instructions for the Royal Commission to her before submitting it to the Queen. It was a long and difficult interview. The forces of reaction were in retreat, but they were by no means conquered ; and War Office officials had provided Panmure with a list of Commissioners which in Miss Nightingale's opinion would have nullified the enquiry. " Every one of the members of the Commission was carried by force of will against Dr. Andrew Smith ", she wrote to Sidney Herbert that evening.

She won all along the line. The Bison's capitulation was, for the moment, complete. Dr. Alexander was to be recalled from Canada. Colonel Lefroy could not be spared from his work in the War Office, but in his place she secured her old admirer and Crimean confederate, Mr. Augustus Stafford, M.P. Sir Henry Storks was to sit, so was Sir James Clark and Sir James Martin. Dr. Graham Balfour was accepted as secretary, Dr. Sutherland sat as sanitary expert. Sidney Herbert was, of course, chairman. " I could do nothing without him ", she scribbled on the edge of a document. On his suggestion a " good examining lawyer ", Sir Thomas Phillips, was added to assist in taking evidence. Only one member of the old gang was included—Dr. Andrew Smith inevitably sat as Director-General of the Army Medical Department. The Instructions, the official directions indicating the ground the Commission was to cover, were drawn up by Miss Nightingale herself. " She has finished her instructions for the Commission ", wrote Fanny to W. E. N. at the end of April; ". . . we hear from Sutherland etc. that they are quite perfect, that they ' cover all the ground, prompting the questions to be asked to get out all the information she requires '."

The Instructions were accepted without alteration by Panmure. On May 5th the Royal Warrant was issued, and the following week the Commission began to sit.

XIII THE STRAIN ON HER WAS ENORMOUS. Three months before she had been an invalid; now, as well as working night and day on the Commission, she was turning her Confidential Report into an important work covering the whole field of army medical and hospital administration in the recent war, in previous wars and in peace. This work emerged six months later as *Notes on Matters affecting the Health, Efficiency and Hospital Administration of the British Army*, a volume of nearly 1000 closely printed pages, crammed with figures, facts, tables and statistical comparisons. The strain was intensified by the petty irritations, the tensions, the emotional conflicts, inseparable from the Nightingale family life.

In November 1856 Fanny, Parthe and W. E. N. went to the Burlington Hotel. W. E. N. soon fled to the peace and shadows of the library at Embley, but Fanny and Parthe remained to extract the fullest possible enjoyment from their position as the mother and sister of Miss Florence Nightingale. "No one", she wrote in a private note, "has enjoyed my reputation more than my own people." Strangers stopped Fanny and Parthe in the hotel and in the streets to enquire after Miss Nightingale. Letters were written to Fanny. " I hardly know how to express myself about your daughter's delicate health ", an unknown admirer wrote. " She has the sympathy of two continents (one might say of all humanity)." Parthe struck the Crimean note in her conversation, christened Aunt Mai " My Scutari Aunt ", created little mysteries round her sister. " It is the earnest wish of Mrs. and Miss Nightingale (the mother and sister of Miss Florence Nightingale) to have an interview with Sir John McNeill at 30 Old Burlington Street—almost at any hour ", she wrote in December 1856. She assumed the role of the privileged guardian of her sister's shrine. " I cannot conceive of anything more beautiful than her state of mind. She is so calm, so holy ", she told a cousin in the autumn of 1856. " I cannot believe she will live long ", she wrote to Clarkey. " Long or short we bless God and are content that our darling has been permitted and enabled to do so much for Him and for mankind. . . . My heart is full and it is running over."

Fanny and Parthe were profuse in fine phrases and expressions of affection. In practice they behaved with total want of consideration. The only place, besides her bedroom, where Miss Nightingale could work was a little inner drawing-room opening off the outer drawing-room. She sat in the inner room working at a table piled with papers, immersed in figures or talking in low tones to Dr. Sutherland or Dr. Farr, while in the outer drawing-room Fanny and Parthe entertained their friends, interrupting her whenever the fancy took them. A carriage was provided for Fanny and Parthe, but it was not put at her disposal. She used cabs, or, if a cab was not available, travelled in the public omnibus, an unusual proceeding for a woman of her social position in the fifties. Several times she mentions having been stranded, unable to get cab or omnibus and forced to walk in wind and rain. In November 1856 Fanny told W. E. N.: "Yesterday Flo went with Sir John Liddell and her good angel Hilary to Chatham, setting off at 9½ o'clock and not returning until 9½ at night; 30 miles to Chatham by rail, several miles in cabs and, Sir John says, up to 20 miles walking about the 3 hospitals". The next morning she walked about the wards of St. Mary's, Paddington, of which she had been made an Honorary Life Governor, in the afternoon she went down to Bermondsey and walked about the wards of a hospital there, and came back late to the Burlington and sat up until the small hours working with Dr. Sutherland and Dr. Farr. In another letter Fanny described Lord Panmure sending round a messenger to announce his intention of calling for a conference. Though it was early in the morning Miss Nightingale had already gone to Aldershot to inspect barracks and hospitals; meanwhile another urgent message came from Dr. Sutherland—he could not prepare for the committee meeting on the alterations to Netley Hospital to be held next day unless he had her help.

It would have been hard work for a woman in good health; that Miss Nightingale could perform it in her physical condition was unbelievable. Statistical science was in its infancy. Statistics relating to the British Army were almost non-existent. She was doing the work of a pioneer, visiting civil and military institutions, barracks, infirmaries, asylums and prisons. Sir John Liddell, Director-General of the Navy Medical Department, became her friend, and at his invitation she visited naval hospitals at Haslar and Woolwich. She drew up recommendations for improvements in ventilation and diet and prepared a scheme for the introduction of a female nursing staff. After a day of toil she returned, almost fainting with exhaustion, to be scolded by Fanny and Parthe because she would not go to parties.

In the middle of November, when she was preparing for her first important interview with Lord Panmure, Parthe was taken ill. London did not suit her, the Burlington was stuffy and airless. She caught a cold, lost her voice, and became feverish. She insisted on being nursed by her sister. To the burdens of overwork and ill health Miss Nightingale had at this critical moment to add the care of an exacting and unreasonable invalid. Parthe declared Florence was to blame for her illness since she stayed at the Burlington only to be with her.

Again the old painful story dragged itself out. But it was impossible for Miss Nightingale not to perceive that Fanny and Parthe coveted not her companionship and affection but the reflected glory from her celebrity. " I was the same person who went to Harley Street and who went to the Crimea ", she wrote in a private note of November 1856. " Nothing was different except my popularity. Yet the person who went to Harley Street was to be cursed and the other blessed . . . this false popularity has made all the difference in the feelings of my family towards me." " Nothing has been learnt from their former experience," she wrote in another note, " but the *world* thinks of me differently."

After her return from the Crimea she took her furniture out of the rooms she had used at Harley Street. In a pretty little scene before a gathering of admirers and friends Parthe begged to be allowed to keep the blue teacups " as a remembrance ". In a private note Miss Nightingale commented that Parthe might also keep as a remembrance the fact that she never crossed the threshold of Harley Street without having hysterics.

Financial arrangements were a constant source of irritation. Fanny never ceased to resent Miss Nightingale's allowance of £500 a year, and behaved as if £500 a year was immense wealth. She made a practice of sending in accounts for a proportion of the hotel bill, for any expenditure that could possibly be construed as having been incurred for or through her younger daughter. Miss Nightingale was forced to appeal to W. E. N. On January 12th, 1857, she wrote: "In a difficult life (and mine has been more difficult than most) it is always better clearly to decide for oneself

> what grievances one will bear being unavoidable
> what grievances one will escape from
> what grievances one will try to remove

you have mentioned and do mention to me the perpetual grievance it is to you to have such expenses in the female part of your family. . . . London . . . they say they do it on my account. I will just once, say it is *not* so. You say they spent four months in London last year. Did they stay in London on my account while I was in Russia? If they did so it must have been to buy me one bonnet. . . . Everything else was ordered through the post. . . .

"I am sure my dear mother has a dim and vague perception of this viz—that her motherly feeling owes me something more (in the way of facilities to carry out those objects which they approve, now, and which the world approves) than £500 and leave to visit at Embley and Lea Hurst. . . . She tries to smuggle my accounts into hers. She tries in various ways to do me a little contraband good—then when you complain of the confusion and extravagance, also too truly, of her accounts, she forgets this and says 'Oh, it's all Flo's boys' [Miss Nightingale was educating four orphan boys who lived at Embley] or 'It's all Florence's bills.' And she sits down and writes items against me, almost at random, often over charged. . . .

"They have a kind of perception too, that, as they have carriage, house, maid etc. etc., besides the money, and as I have only £500, without carriage, maid etc. etc., therefore they ought to give me a share of the carriage in London, and although I practically never do have it, yet you cannot be surprised at their having some feeling . . . and although it is a *moral* impossibility that they should give up one of their

' homes ', Embley, Lea Hurst or the Burlington to ' mother '
me, yet at the root of what they do is this feeling, viz—that
they ought. . . .

" I assure you upon my honour that I never have asked, nor
shall I ever ask them, to come to London . . . they will always
make me the excuse for coming to London. . . . I assure you
I am quite willing and always intend to keep myself within my
£500 a year . . . the tradesmen should always be told to send
their bills *straight* to me and these not pass through *their* hands
at all. . . . I can safely assert that I believe they have not
made me a single present—they even charged me for the
chocolate and candles they sent out when I was ill. . . ."

The problem was insoluble. The truth was that where
money was concerned Miss Nightingale was Fanny's daughter.
She was high-handed, not squandering money but disregarding
it, and she was incurably generous. Almost every 1st of
January she wrote in a private note, " This year I *must*
retrench ", but she never succeeded in living on £500 a year.

When the Commission began to sit, pressure on her steadily
increased. Fanny and Parthe were with her at the Burlington
Hotel, W. E. N. stayed at Embley. Early in May Fanny
wrote that Florence had spent the morning in Belgrave Square
" coaching up " Sidney Herbert for the sitting of the Commission next day and " the afternoon at Highgate performing
the same office for Dr. Sutherland ", returning to work far
into the night. Next day she set off for Highgate at 9 A.M.,
worked there until after dark, then went on to work with Dr.
Farr and did not get back to the Burlington until very late.
The day after that she started for Highgate at 8.30 A.M.,
worked there until 7.30 P.M., came back to the Burlington to
find a message from Sidney Herbert, went straight off again
to Belgrave Square and did not get back until after 11 P.M.

Meanwhile Fanny and Parthe gave breakfasts and dinners,
drove in the Park, received callers and paid calls. Through
a mistake, one of their bedrooms was let. Fanny and Parthe
stayed in the hotel but Miss Nightingale turned out, sleeping
at an annexe in Albemarle Street and coming into the Burlington to eat and work. By June Parthe and Fanny were weary,
but they would not go home. " I am very tired ", wrote Fanny
to W. E. N., " and if it were not for the absolute necessity for

our being here to enable her to go on with her most important work, I should long ago have been back at Embley with you dearest. This world and its turmoils are too much for me." The season ended. London became, wrote Parthe, " dismal as for a funeral ", but Florence would not go away and, until she went, Fanny and Parthe were determined not to go either.

Alarming reports reached W. E. N. at Embley. He wrote to Aunt Mai and asked her to call at the Burlington and see what could be done—Fanny was unwell, Parthe was unwell and Florence was apparently dying. Aunt Mai hurried to London to find she had stirred up a hornet's nest. She hastily retreated with a burst of apologies : " Dearest Parthe. I am anxious to prevent two things being thought which may APPEAR other than they are. 1, that there was any want of consideration for your dear mother either on F. N.'s part or mine. 2, that I was interfering in any way. When I came to the Burlington on Monday not only did I not know what would be best to do. I only knew that each *wished* to do what was best for all, and that it was very difficult to do what was desirable for each." And so on for five, six, seven pages.

The summer wore on and became a nightmare. The weather was heavy, close, without sun but with great heat. The rooms at the Burlington were dark and airless, the sky perpetually grey. Water-carts sprinkled the streets to lay the dust, but the water they used was putrid and produced a horrible smell. Still Florence had not finished her work, still Fanny and Parthe refused to leave her. " The days draw on and bring each their burden ", wrote Parthe to Aunt Julia on August 17th and signed herself " yours wearily ".

Parthe became resentful. She confessed herself unable to see that this working herself to death for which Florence was so cried up was at all necessary. " The irritable edge o desire for perfection grows on her ", she wrote to W. E. N. in August. " I never saw anything like her ways of doing all herself. She will not even let one write a note if she can help it." Writing to Aunt Julia she acidly described the nervous collapses which overtook Miss Nightingale after a spell of work. She became helpless as a child, the food had absolutely to be put in her mouth or it did not reach her. On the previous evening Parthe had been entertaining a few friends. Florence came in and was so anxious to avoid them that she went straight up to bed without even an egg. " She was quite unable to order an egg for herself so she went to bed without ", wrote Parthe.

Ten years later Miss Nightingale described to Clarkey what she had endured from Fanny and Parthe in the summer of 1857. " The whole occupation of Parthe and Mama was to lie on two sofas and tell one another not to get tired by putting flowers into water. . . . I cannot describe to you the impression it made on me." She was in a fever of fatigue. Every day brought more than could possibly be accomplished in a year. She longed, she wrote, for rest as a man dying of thirst longs for water. In this state she reached the Burlington one evening to be told that the Duke of Newcastle had called to see her. As she passed through the drawing-room Fanny and Parthe were lounging on the sofas. " You lead a very amusing life ", they said to her. " It is a scene worthy of Molière ", she wrote, " where two people in tolerable and even perfect health, lie on the sofa all day, doing absolutely nothing and persuade themselves and others that they are the victims of their self devotion for another who is dying of overwork."

All that was left to her was to struggle on until the report of the Commission appeared and until *Notes on Matters affecting the Health, Efficiency and Hospital Administration of the British Army* was finished so that she could die with a quiet mind. She had condemned herself to death for the sake of the work ; she was immolating herself, she demanded nothing less than immolation from her helpers, and she became a ruthless task-mistress.

Her position was extraordinary. She was, as the men round her delighted to call her, the Commander-in-Chief. She collected the facts, she collated and verified them, she drew the conclusions, she put the conclusions down on paper and, finally, she taught them to the men who were her mouthpieces. As each witness came up for examination she prepared a memorandum on the facts to be elicited from him and coached Sidney Herbert before each sitting of the Commission. " These men seem to make her opinions their law," wrote Fanny to W. E. N. in June 1857.

" By Sidney Herbert's desire ", Miss Nightingale wrote in a reminiscence, " I saw everyone of the witnesses myself and reported to him what each could tell him as a witness in public." " I shall require great assistance from and through you ", he had written to her in November 1856. " I shall like to see all that you are writing as it goes on, if you see no objection. It would probably tell me much and lead me to question and so learn more." Notes from him reached her two or three times a day while the Commission was sitting. " Let me know what you think ", " Give me your notes on this ", " What are we to do? " " What shall we say? " " This is Hebrew to me, will you look it over ", " Your report is excellent ", " I am at a standstill until I see you ".

" Sidney is again in despair for you ", wrote Mrs. Herbert in the summer of 1857. " Can you come? You will say '*Bless* that man, why can't he leave me in peace!' But I am only obeying orders in begging for you."

" She is the mainspring of the work," burst out Dr. Sutherland to Aunt Mai in May 1857. " Nobody who has not worked with her daily could know her, could have an idea of her strength and clearness of mind, her extraordinary powers joined with her benevolence of spirit. She is one of the most gifted creatures God ever made."

The Reformers christened themselves the " band of brothers ", the Burlington Hotel was " the little War Office ", the meals they shared were " our mess ". Within this circle was an inner council of three—Miss Nightingale, Sidney Herbert and Dr. Sutherland. Though Dr. Sutherland had sacrificed his life to Miss Nightingale, he still irritated her. In 1855, when he was appointed to the Sanitary Commission, he was at the opening of a distinguished career. He was Sanitary Adviser to the Government Board of Health and received £1500 a year for part-time duties. He met Miss Nightingale at Scutari, became her slave, and his career was at an end. He worked with her throughout the Sanitary Commission on the Health of the Army without remuneration. She never thanked him and seldom had a good word for him. Once in February 1857, when they were working together on the plans for Netley, she wrote to him : " As for Sanitary matters—Lord help you I'm only a humbug. I know nothing about them except what I have learnt from you. But you would never have found a more practical pupil." It was the only acknowledgment she ever made.

He was untidy. He left his papers scattered over the sofa at the Burlington, and when she came in tired she had to tidy them up. He was unmethodical. He was unpunctual. He put letters in his coat pocket and forgot all about them. He lost documents. He was frivolous. He wanted to join parties of pleasure, he wanted to take holidays, he wanted to stay at home during the week-ends and garden.

He took a great deal of care of his health. " Sutherland once more fancies himself laid up with bronchitis ", she wrote in February 1857. Most exasperating of all, he was deaf. The more annoyed she became, the less he appeared to hear. She threatened to buy him an ear-trumpet, and he sent his wife to explain that his was no ordinary deafness but a peculiar nervous affliction. When she was pleased with him Miss Nightingale laughed at him and called him the " baby ", when she was annoyed she belaboured him with the full force of her invective, and he became " my pet aversion ". Dr. Sutherland described himself to her as " one of your wives ".

Dr. Sutherland made his wife write for him when he feared Miss Nightingale was angry, and during the immense labours of the summer of 1857 she had to write frequently. In one note sent down from Highgate by hand she begged Miss Nightingale to forgive her husband for not keeping an appointment. " The rain is so tremendous that he would be drenched in five minutes so he hopes the Commander-in-Chief will excuse him for this once." He was not excused. First thing in the morning a messenger arrived with an angry letter. " I *hope* you will have seen Dr. Sutherland before the return of your messenger," wrote Mrs. Sutherland. " I am so sorry he could not go to you last night. I am afraid it worried you." " My dear Lady ", wrote Dr. Sutherland on May 22nd, 1857, "do not be unreasonable. . . . I would have been with you yesterday had I been able but alas my will was stronger than my legs." One evening at the Burlington Hotel he was late with an urgent report. After a scene he consented to stay and finish it. When Miss Nightingale read it through she was not satisfied and sent up to Highgate telling him to come back at once and go through it with her again. Dr. Sutherland lost his temper and refused, upon which she collapsed and fell into an " agitated half fainting state ". Aunt Mai hurried up to Highgate and implored Dr. Sutherland to come or he would kill her. He came immediately and expressed "great sorrow and penitence".

Her demands were fantastic, yet once within her orbit it was impossible not to be fascinated. The tremendous vitality, the passion of feeling she poured into her work made the rest of the world colourless. Mrs. Sutherland was devoted to her husband, devoted to her domestic life; Miss Nightingale broke up the Sutherlands' home. Dr. Sutherland was a strict Sabbatarian; she made him work on Sundays. He complained he was ill, he complained he was overworking, she abused him. Yet Mrs. Sutherland adored her. She became " Miss Nightingale's fag ", shopping for her, running errands, buying oranges, pencils, new-laid eggs, dark curtains. She called her " My dear dear friend ", " My dear and ever kind friend ". It was impossible to know Miss Nightingale without recognising that she possessed qualities which allowed her to transcend the ordinary rules governing human behaviour.

She pressed hard on Dr. Sutherland but she pressed even harder on Sidney Herbert. The phrase she had scribbled against his name when the Commission was first set up she repeated again and again, " Without him I can do nothing ". His standing, his prestige, his power with the House of Commons, were the means by which the Commission was raised to first-class importance. His powers were incomparable—if only she could get him to devote them to the work. But he was still hanging back. He complained of his health, he suffered from lassitude, fits of depression and general malaise. They were the first symptoms of mortal disease, but to Miss Nightingale working, as she was convinced, under sentence of death, driving herself on by sheer force of will, fainting from exhaustion, forcing herself to get up and grind on again, Sidney Herbert's complaints were " fancies ". She spoke of them contemptuously as " fancies ". She grumbled about him. Aunt Mai noted that he was " less reliable than the others ". Speaking of a difficult negotiation Miss Nightingale said : " Mr. Herbert and no one else can do it. If I can only bring him up to the scratch." Through the summer of 1857 she was devoured by impatience and forcing herself to be reasonable. " I send you some rough notes of mine, which please return if you have no time to read." "There is no hurry about reading me, it will do any time, I hope you will not be alarmed at the infliction, it is not going to go on." "Please be so good as to return me those notes of mine I troubled you with, as I have no copy. It does not signify about your reading them as I could tell it you all in ½ an hour."

Working together, they were unequalled. Her industry, energy and passion for facts, his incomparable talents as a negotiator, were a combination impossible to resist. "He was a man of the quickest and the most accurate perception I have ever known", she wrote. "Also he was the most sympathetic. His very manner engaged the most sulky and the most recalcitrant witnesses. He never made an enemy or a quarrel in the Commission. He used to say, 'It takes two to make a quarrel and I won't be one.'"

As the Commission proceeded it became evident that the Reformers were succeeding beyond all their hopes. The long hours of close work, the exhausting journeys, the interviews were bearing fruit, and Miss Nightingale's case for reforming the living conditions of the British Army was proving unanswerable. There were moments of discouragement. Dr. Sutherland did not do what she had hoped. "Sutherland does not carry the weight in the Commission which his brains ought to give him", she wrote to Sir John McNeill on June 27th. "He lets very inferior men put him down owing to his want of pith. It vexes me and upsets the conclusions I want to impress on Mr. Herbert." But as witness after witness retired, "bowled over", as the Reformers gleefully put it, by her inexorable facts, the tide set more and more strongly towards reform.

In May Dr. Andrew Smith was examined. He cut a poor figure. "Never was man so shown up as Smith", wrote Dr. Sutherland. He gave no further trouble and allowed himself, wrote Sir John McNeill in June, "to slip quietly into the current of reform".

In the middle of June Sir John Hall gave evidence. Miss Nightingale had endured insolence at Sir John Hall's hands, he had been able to humiliate her, flout her authority and finally defeat her. Now the tables were turned, and she had him at her mercy, but she wrote: "We do not want to badger the old man in his examination, which would do us no good and him harm. But we want to make the best out of him for our case."

In July came the turn of the most important witness of all, Miss Nightingale herself. How much dared she and should she say? Sidney Herbert wished her to make no reference whatever to her Crimean experiences. He did not want her to " make bad blood by reviving controversial issues ". His plan was for her to appear personally before the Commissioners but to be asked only questions on hospital construction. Miss Nightingale disagreed. Sidney Herbert's plan combined the two worst possible policies for her. She would appear in person and provoke the personal attention—the " buz fuz "— which she was convinced did the work harm and yet say nothing of importance to compensate. " I am quite as well aware as he can be ", she wrote to Sir John McNeill on July 7th, 1857, " that it is inexpedient and even unprincipled to bring up past delinquencies, but it would be untrue and un-conscientious for me to give evidence upon an indifferent matter like that of hospital construction, leaving untouched the great matters which affect (and have affected) our sick more than any mere architecture could do. . . . It would be treachery to the memory of my dead. . . . I have no idea what to do. But I see most evil in this plan of examining me so as to make me say nothing." She decided not to give evidence at all. " Let me entreat you to reconsider your determination ", wrote Mr. Augustus Stafford, M.P., on June 11th. " The absence of your name from our list of witnesses will diminish the weight of our Report, and will give rise to unfounded rumours. It will be said either, that we were afraid of your evidence and did not invite you to tender it, or, that you made suggestions the responsibility for which you were reluctant to incur in public." Sir John McNeill wrote that her evidence was vital. " My evidence is only theoretic while yours is all from experience. Yours is so much more valuable than any other that I think it may turn the scale."

A compromise was reached : she did not appear in person ; she submitted written answers to questions, but she did not confine herself to hospital construction. Her evidence was read by the Commissioners " with the greatest eagerness and admiration " and was agreed to be conclusive. " It must ", wrote Sir James Martin, one of the Commissioners, ". . . prove of the most vital importance to the British soldier for ages to come."

Her evidence is of great length, occupying thirty closely printed pages of the report of the Commission, and is a verbatim reproduction of part of that great work which she completed in the same month, *Notes on Matters affecting the Health, Efficiency and Hospital Administration of the British Army.*

The enormous volume of the *Notes* was written by Miss Nightingale in six months at the same time as she was working day and night on the Commission. It is a work on the grand scale. The canvas is immense, great masses of detail, vast quantities of facts and figures are handled with admirable lucidity, yet detail never obscures the main theme. The huge volume written at white-hot speed burns with an urgency which still strikes the reader with a physical shock.

She opens by establishing the connection between the efficiency of the army as a fighting machine and the administration of its health services; historically the administration of the health of the British Army has always been a cause of inefficiency. " Insensibly the question of Army Hospitals and their defects have become part of wider questions, involving the health and efficiency of the Army and the means of preserving them. . . . The Crimean experience has not been solitary but . . . on the contrary in our continental wars like causes have produced like results." She examines in detail the frightful mortality on the ill-fated expedition to Walcheren in 1809 and in the general hospitals during the Peninsular War, drawing the conclusion that general hospitals as at present administered are not sources of healing but main causes of sickness and death. " We shall see how much of the mortality in the Crimean Case was due to the frightful state of the General Hospitals at Scutari; how much it depended on the number which each regiment was unfortunately enabled to send to these pest houses." She then deals in detail with the medical history of the Crimean War, giving her own personal experience, information derived from her contact with the four Crimean Commissions of Enquiry and from interviewing and corresponding with officers, private soldiers, doctors, nurses and engineers. The object of this detailed examination, she explains, is not to focus attention on the Crimean Campaign but to use it as a test case, a gigantic experiment in military hygiene. " It is a complete example (history does not afford its equal) of an army after falling to the lowest ebb of disease and disaster from neglects committed, rising again to the highest state of health and efficiency from remedies applied. It is the whole experiment on a colossal scale . . . we had in the first seven months of the Crimean Campaign, a mortality among the troops at the rate of sixty per cent per annum from disease alone . . . we had, during the last six months of the war, a mortality among our sick little more than among our healthy Guards at home and a mortality among the troops only two-thirds what it is among the troops at home."

In six long and detailed sections she examines the causes, the course and the cure of the Crimean disaster, quoting facts and figures, giving tables, plans, diet sheets, proving conclusively that the hospital was more fatal than the battlefield, that bad food, inadequate clothing, insanitary conditions led inevitably to defeat, while good food, proper clothing, tolerable conditions restored discipline and efficiency.

Let the past, she pleads, be buried, but alter the system so that the soldier is more humanely treated in future. " It would be useless as injudicious to select individual instances or persons as the objects of animadversion. The system which placed them where they were is the point to be considered. . . . Let us try to see whether such a system cannot be invented as men of ordinary calibre can work in, to the preservation and not to the destruction of an Army. It has been said by officers enthusiastic in their profession that there are three causes which make a soldier enlist, viz. being out of work, in a state of intoxication, or, jilted by his sweetheart. Yet the incentives to enlistment, which we desire to multiply, can hardly be put by Englishmen of the nineteenth century in this form, viz. more poverty, more drink, more faithless sweethearts."

The most important part of the book follows, and Miss Nightingale examines the living conditions of the British soldier in time of peace. She wrote as no one had ever written before. For the first time the soldier was considered as a citizen, for the first time it was stated that a decent life makes a better soldier, for the first time it was denied that the fighting man must be outlawed and brutalised to make him fierce enough to fight.

In sections developed in minute detail she deals with practical administration, the organisation of regimental and general hospitals, the necessity for military sanitary officials, the necessity for a military statistical department, the education, employment and promotion of medical officers, soldiers' pay and stoppage, the diet and cooking arrangements of the army, the commissariat, washing and canteens, soldiers' wives, the design and construction of hospitals and barracks.

On these subjects she had collected and digested an enormous mass of facts never before assembled. She had corresponded with sanitary experts, engineers, architects, doctors, army surgeons, statisticians. She reproduced plans of the best hospitals and institutions in Europe. She appended specifications and tables, she was a pioneer in the use of statistical diagrams. For the section on diet she consulted Professor Christison, then the leading authority in Europe, and added recipes, embodying his recommendations, composed for use in regiments and hospitals by Soyer. For the section on hospital and barrack design she consulted Edwin Chadwick, who had been responsible for the first great sanitary report on London of 1844, and Sir John Jebb, the architect of model prisons. Not only is the necessity for reform proved but the remedy is given. " No other person could have written it ", wrote Sir John McNeill in July 1857.

On almost every page was something which provoked furious thought, but one disclosure in particular proved sensational. It was the result of the comparison she had told Dr. Farr in 1856 that she intended to make.

She had collected figures which proved living conditions in the barracks of the British Army in time of peace to be so bad that the rate of mortality in the army was always double, and in some cases more than double, the rate of mortality of the civilian population outside. For instance, in the parish of St. Pancras the civil rate of mortality was 2·2 per 1000. In the barracks of the Life Guards, situated in St. Pancras, the rate was 10·4. In the borough of Kensington the civil rate of mortality was 3·3. In the Knightsbridge barracks, situated in the borough of Kensington, the rate was 17·5. Yet the men in the Army were all young strong men who had been subjected to a medical examination to guarantee their physical fitness, while the civilian population included old people, infants and the physically unfit. " The Army are *picked* lives ", she wrote. " The inferior lives are thrown back into the mass of the population. The civil population has all the loss, the Army has all the gain. Yet, with all this, the Army from which the injured lives are subtracted dies at twice the rate of mortality of the general population. 1500 good soldiers are as certainly killed by these neglects yearly as if they were drawn up on Salisbury Plain and shot." In a phrase which became the battle-cry of the Reformers she declared : " Our soldiers enlist to death in the barracks ".

Here was something very different from the dry bones of administrative reform, very different from jobbing back to old disasters, old grievances in the Crimea. The Crimean disasters had faded from the public mind, but the event which had obscured them, the Indian Mutiny, had focused attention on the army once more. " Our soldiers enlist to death in the barracks " was a challenge no Government could afford to ignore.

There were two channels through which her disclosure could reach the public, through the Commission and through publication of the *Notes*. In July, the month in which she completed the *Notes*, it became evident that, owing to the white-hot speed at which she had driven the Commission, its Report would be written in August. She decided to put the *Notes* on one side—it was a confidential report addressed only to Lord Panmure and easily shelved by him, while facts stated before a Royal Commission and included in its report could not be suppressed. The enormous volume, representing such agonising effort, such almost incredible toil, was sacrificed. Lord Panmure was not presented with *Notes on Matters affecting the Health, Efficiency and Hospital Administration of the British Army* until after he had received the report of the Commission in November 1857. The public never had the opportunity of seeing it at all. It was never published and has remained unread. " It is an old story now ", Miss Nightingale wrote of the *Notes* in December 1858. She had a few copies privately printed at her own expense which from time to time she gave away, and in these alone this monumental work survives.

In July she began to write the report of the first Royal

Sanitary Commission on the Health of the Army. She lists the Report as " one of my works ". Success had been achieved, but at the price of her health. " Most people in her state ", wrote Aunt Mai to W. E. N., " would be in bed not attempting to work but . . . if she can keep up for this time her object will be gained. . . . I felt uneasy to see her but Dr. Sutherland says . . . to get forward the work so that she can be spared is the best way she can be helped." She had set herself a goal : to finish the report. Everything was to be sacrificed, every-thing was to be endured until it was completed. When that was done she would rest.

But one day at the end of July she scribbled a sentence on the margin of a draft : " Reports are not self executive ". She wrote the sentence again and again, in a private note, in a letter, on scraps of paper. " Reports are not self executive." She had realised that her task would end only when the recom-mendations of the report were put into force. Panmure had nearly succeeded in shelving the Commission ; he would cer-tainly try to evade the bothers involved in carrying out its recommendations. Once more the Bison must be bullied.

On August 7th, 1857, Sidney Herbert wrote to Lord Pan-mure and communicated the outstanding points which would emerge from the report. In suave terms he pointed out that the disclosures as to the living conditions of the army were sensational, that public attention would certainly be arrested, that there would be a scandal and the Government would be attacked in the House. He suggested the Government should protect itself by taking measures to remedy the worst of the abuses before the report came before the House. " The simultaneous publication of the recommendations of the Com-mission and of new orders and regulations already intro-duced by the Government to remedy the abuses the Report disclosed, will give the Government the prestige which prompti-tude always carries with it."

He then outlined a plan drawn up by Miss Nightingale which put the reorganisation of the health administration of the army into the Reformers' hands. Four sub-Commissions were to be appointed at once by Lord Panmure and Sidney Herbert was to be chairman of each. The four Commissions would begin to put the recommendations of the report into practical operation at once. Each Commission would have executive powers, and finance would be provided by an interim grant from the Treasury.

The four sub-Commissions would:

(1) put the Barracks in sanitary order;
(2) found a Statistical Department for the Army;
(3) institute an Army Medical School;
(4) completely reconstruct the Army Medical Department, revise the Hospital Regulations and draw up a new Warrant for the Promotion of Medical Officers.

The fourth sub-Commission was christened the "wiping Commission" by Miss Nightingale, because its wide scope enabled the Reformers to wipe the slate clean and start afresh.

On August 9th Sidney Herbert told her that "Panmure writes fairly enough but he has gone to shoot grouse". A week later Panmure was forced to come south on urgent business, was caught "on the wing" at the War Office, and after a long discussion agreed to the four sub-Commissions "in general terms". Sidney Herbert then left for Ireland to fish for a month, writing on August 14th that he went "with a lighter heart after seeing Pan. But I am not easy about you. Here am I going to lead an animal life for a month, get up early, pursue your animal, catch him, eat him and go to sleep. Why can't you who do man's work take man's exercise in some shape?"

Miss Nightingale was still at the Burlington, still toiling in the stuffiness and heat, still plagued by Fanny and Parthe. The report was completed, but the four sub-Commissions must be prepared. It must be decided in what places and from what persons evidence should be taken and what questions should be asked. In addition, she was unexpectedly overwhelmed with work in connection with the Nightingale Fund. On August 11th she had a complete collapse.

"I must be alone, quite alone", she suddenly broke out to Parthe. "I have not been alone for 4 years." She was at her last gasp. She had eaten no solid food for four weeks and had lived on tea. Parthe forgot her grievances and was frightened. "It was very affecting poor dear", she wrote to Aunt Mai. When Miss Nightingale was calmer she told Parthe: "I who required more time alone than anybody, who could not live without silence and solitude, have never had one moment to myself since I went to Harley Street. I don't call writing being alone. It is by far the greatest sacrifice I have made." She refused to go to Embley, she refused to be nursed. She must go away by herself. She admitted she was ill, and consented to take a cure at Malvern, but she must be quite alone. "She took", wrote Fanny to W. E. N., "a sudden resolution to go to Malvern. There was only a place in Johnson's quite at the top. Nothing would induce her to take anyone but George [a footman]. There she has taken her weary limbs. It makes us very unhappy to think of her so forlorn and comfortless."

She was very ill, so ill that it was generally thought she must die, and in London Harriet Martineau brought her obituary notice up to date for the *Daily News*. "In August 1857," wrote Miss Nightingale, "after my work at the Royal Sanitary Commission and after 4 years of anxiety and exertion, I was told that my life was not worth 24 hours purchase—and I knew it too." Dr. Sutherland wrote imploring her to stay on at Malvern, pointing out as her physician that the Burlington Hotel, dark, stuffy and in the centre of London, was the worst possible place for a person in her state of health. "The day you left town," he wrote at the end of August, "it appeared as if all your blood wanted renewing and that cannot be done in a week. You must have new blood or you can't work and new blood can't be made out of tea at least so far as I know. . . ."

Ill as she was, she seized her pen and wrote him an enormous angry letter. Her brain wandered, her sentences were incoherent, her writing straggled over the page but she still had strength to be irritated by him. ". . . Had I lived anywhere but handy would Mr. Herbert have used me? Had I not been ever at hand *could* he have used me? . . . Now had I lost the Report what would the health I should have 'saved' have profited me, or what would the ten years of my life have 'advantaged' me exchanged for the ten weeks this summer? Yes, you say, you might have walked, or driven, or eaten meat. Well . . . let me tell you Doctor, that after any walk or drive I sat up all night with palpitation. And the sight of animal food increased the sickness. . . . Now I have written myself into a palpitation. . . . I have been greatly harassed by seeing my poor owl lately without her head, without her life, without her talons, lying in the cage of your canary . . . and the little villain pecking at her. Now, that's me. I am lying without my head, without my claws and you all peck at me. It is *de rigueur, d'obligation*, like the saying something to one's hat when one goes into church to say to me all that has been said to me 110 times a day during the last 3 months. It is the obbligato on the violin, and the twelve violins all practise it together, like the clocks striking twelve o'clock at night all over London, till I say like Xavier Le Maistre '*Assez, je le sais, je ne le sais que trop*'."

Dr. Sutherland replied on September 7th that she was decidedly wrong in passing herself off for a dead owl. He himself had got all the pecking " and your little beak is of the sharpest ". Nevertheless, he loved her. " You little know what daily anxiety it has caused me to see you dying by inches in doing work fit only for the strongest constitutions. When I think of it all I can hardly bear the sight of a report. . . . One thing is quite clear that women can do what men could not do, and that women will dare suffering knowingly where men would shrink."

His affection and concern only provoked her. Impatience was gaining on her. Everything was to be wiped out of her life but work. Friendship, health, affection, all must go because there was so much to do. So much to do, the words beat in her sick brain. Work loomed always before her, mountains of it, endless labour, endless toil which somehow must be struggled through. Mr. Herbert went away to fish, Dr. Sutherland prated of rest. Did they not understand, could they not understand that the only way anything could be accomplished was by unremitting effort, unceasing toil ? Did they think she had brought herself to the verge of the grave for her own amusement ?

She wrote Dr. Sutherland a cross, snubbing note. He was to cease this nonsense about being afraid of her and this nonsense about her taking a rest. Far from taking a rest she ordered him to come to Malvern on Monday, when she intended to start work again. Everything, figures, facts, plans for the four new sub-Commissions must be ready for Mr. Herbert when he came back to London.

"I have your note Caratina Mia," Dr. Sutherland wrote on September 11th, "and write to say how sorry I am that I should seem to be afraid of your biting me. . . . But what are Mr. Herbert and I to do when you are buried? How is the play to go on without Hamlet? . . . The daughters of Sermiah be too much for me. I'll take the veil. I'll retire from the world. I won't be compared to a warming pan and you need not do that again or I'll do something desperate. . . . There's no help for it then but my coming down on Monday."

He arrived to find her apparently at death's door. For once her iron will was defeated and she was forced to stay in Malvern for over a month. She was too weak to leave her sofa and unable to sleep for more than two hours during the night. Her pulse raced, and she was given two cold-water packs a day to bring it down. In spite of her physical condition she obstinately continued to work.

Fanny and Parthe, both unwell themselves and sobered by the frightening spectacle of her collapse in London, made only half-hearted attempts to join her. W. E. N. came to Malvern and insisted on seeing her for a few minutes. He was horrified. " Her days may be numbered ", he wrote to Fanny. " Her breathing betrays her moments of distress, her power to take food fails her if excited, her nights are sleepless in consequence. . . . 'Tis a sad tale. I'm not able to say more. Adieu, ' W. E. N.' I've said too much ".

Once more Aunt Mai was called in. In the middle of September she left her husband and family and went to Malvern. She was expected to return in a week or two but she did not return. Husband and family were put on one side, and when Miss Nightingale returned to the Burlington at the end of September Aunt Mai went with her.

The collapse of August 1857 was the beginning of Miss Nightingale's retirement as an invalid. For the first year after her return from the Crimea, though she had gone into strict retirement as a public figure, she had led her normal life. She had had strength, she said, to " rush about ". She had gone up to Dr. Sutherland in Highgate and come back to dine with Sidney Herbert in Belgrave Square, she had visited hospitals and inspected barracks, she had gone for " a little walk " almost every day in the Park. Though she had refused to attend functions she had seen her friends. "You should know Lord Stanley . . . come and dine with him here on Sunday", Richard Monckton Milnes had written in February 1857. After August 1857 she had strength only to work. "It is an intolerable life she is leading," wrote Parthe to Clarkey in December 1857, "lying down between whiles to enable her just to go on." She could work only for half an hour at a time. After any prolonged exertion her exhaustion was frightening and she often fainted.

She not only became an invalid, she began to exploit her ill health. From the summer of 1857 she used her illness as a weapon to protect herself from her family. The summer had discouraged Fanny. She had been ill and she announced that her health would not permit her to "attempt the Burlington" in the winter. Parthe, however, wrote that she proposed coming to London. It was impossible. Aunt Mai was told to write and tell Parthe not to come. Parthe was furious. Did Florence think her own sister was not capable of doing what was wanted for her? She insisted on coming.

Miss Nightingale's reply was to have an "attack". Aunt Mai wrote in the greatest agitation. After reading Parthe's letter Florence had been ill all night. Dr. Sutherland had been much alarmed and had said he could not sleep for thinking of her. "It was excessive hurried breathing with pain in the head and the heart." As a result, Parthe did not come to London. W. E. N. then insisted on coming, he must see Florence and discuss her future plans. She had another "attack" and he retreated.

It was evident that in the present state of her health, while her life, as Aunt Mai wrote, "hung by a thread", it was too much for her to see her family. They must keep away from her.

This unpalatable news was conveyed to the Nightingales by Aunt Mai in a series of letters of immense length, every page criss-crossed, every statement wrapped in layer upon layer of explanation, withdrawal and apology.

They were forced to give way. "I cannot delay five minutes to tell you the load your letter has lifted from my mind", wrote Aunt Mai to "all at Embley" in the autumn of 1857. "I was *so* anxious about that letter, for, though I dare not for all your dear sakes unsay a word of it, it seemed so very grievous both to you and to me to say 'do not come to her'. . . . Whatever agitates her, that we must avoid. I see from experience it brings on that difficult breathing."

By January 1858 a point had been reached at which Aunt Mai could suggest that Parthe and Fanny had better give up coming to London at all. "My fear would be", she wrote to "dear friends at Embley", "that if you were staying in London and she trying to think day after day *when* would she see you, thus would be caused the agitation we so dread." In an undated note of 1858 Fanny wrote to Parthe: "My dear—Florence thinks we are staying in town for her sake, so we must go on Friday". Parthe made one further effort. In February 1858 she wrote that she was coming up to London with Fanny for the season and intended to stay at the Burlington. This announcement brought on another " attack ". Parthe and Fanny gave way. They must come to London but they would go to another hotel. Miss Nightingale's condition improved instantly and Aunt Mai wrote to W. E. N.: "Thank God all seems relieved ".

Fortunately a new interest was occupying Parthe's mind. In the previous summer Fanny, writing to W. E. N. from the Burlington, described a visit from Sir Harry Verney, " an old guardsman, very much interested in Flo's work, his wife died last year and left as her earnest request that her daughters should become acquainted with F. but F. had not time for young ladies and she would not see Sir H."

Sir Harry Verney, head of the Verney family and owner of the historic mansion of Claydon House, in Buckinghamshire, was fifty-six years old and one of the handsomest men in England. He was immensely tall, his features were aristocratic and aquiline and he possessed an air of nobility so extraordinary that people turned to look after him in the street as if he were a visitant from another world. He had originally held a commission in the Life Guards and intended to make a career in the army. When he inherited the family estates in Buckinghamshire he was so horrified by the miserable condition of his land and his tenants that he gave up the army and devoted himself to becoming a model landlord. Agriculture and the agricultural labourer, owing to a long depression, were shamefully neglected. Sir Harry became a pioneer in rural housing and administration. He drained and reclaimed land, built model cottages, founded schools and was active in the administration of the poor law. When the cholera broke out in Aylesbury Sir Harry worked among the sick, and subsequently collected funds to build the county hospital at Aylesbury. At the age of thirty he went to Cambridge, where his abilities won him the friendship of the philosopher Whewell. He became Liberal member for Buckinghamshire in 1832 and held the seat for periods amounting to thirty-one years. Members of the Verney family had represented Buckinghamshire, either the shire or the borough, at frequent intervals since the reign of Edward VI. Sir Harry was an intimate friend of Lord Shaftesbury, an Evangelical, an active member of the Bible Society, the Church Missionary Society and the Evangelical Alliance, but he never obtruded his opinions or " lost the tone of good society ". Clarkey, who met him with a strong prejudice because she said she " detested psalm singers ", declared he was " a jewel ".

Before the end of the summer of 1857 Sir Harry was a frequent caller at the Burlington. He fell in love with Miss Nightingale and asked her to marry him, and she refused him.

During the winter he stayed at Embley, and it began to be evident that he was becoming attached to Parthe. The engagement was announced in April and the marriage took place quietly at Embley in June 1858. Sir Harry had a grown-up family of three sons and a daughter. Writing to his eldest son Edmund to announce his engagement, he described Parthe as being " in her fortieth year, with the appearance of a lady but without the beauty of her sister Florence ".

The prospect of becoming Lady Verney occupied Parthe's mind, the business of marrying a daughter delighted and distracted Fanny. Hilary Bonham Carter told Clarkey in May 1858 that she had been seeing Fanny and Parthe in London and spent " some horrible long days fussing and shopping with Aunt Fanny ", but though Fanny and Parthe were staying in a hotel close to Florence " they did not wish to interfere with her in the slightest ". At last she was left alone.

XIV A HUSH FELL OVER HER LIFE. She moved to new rooms in an annexe of the Burlington— three bedrooms and a dressing-room on one floor, a double sitting-room on a floor below. The street was quiet, the house had none of the bustle of the hotel. The atmosphere was heavy with solemnity. Voices were lowered, feet trod lightly as her fellow workers were shown into the drawing-room where she lay prostrate on the sofa. She was convinced, everyone round her was convinced, that she had at most a few months to live. All that was left to her was " to help the work forward as much as possible and then die in peace ", and she was treated as if she were already on her deathbed.

Aunt Mai broke up her family life. She shut up her house, her husband and girls went to stay at Embley, and she came to the Burlington to make Florence's last months on earth easy. Her son-in-law, Arthur Hugh Clough, became Florence's slave. In August 1854 he had seen her off to Scutari, in August 1856 he was with her at Birk Hall, looking up trains, writing letters and acting as her courier. Throughout the winter of 1856 and the spring of 1857 her dependence on him increased, and by the autumn of 1857 his life was hers. He came to the Burlington every day, wrote notes, delivered reports, fetched letters, tied up parcels and was content, she wrote, " to do the work of a cab horse ". The Nightingales, cowed, remained at a distance. Aunt Mai and Clough became the twin guardians of a shrine.

It was a strange, hot-house existence, led under the shadow of impending death. One day Miss Nightingale had a long conversation with Clough in which she arranged all the details of her funeral. She wrote many letters " to be sent when I am dead ". On November 26th, 1857, Sidney Herbert was given as a sacred trust the task of carrying out the reforms recommended in the report of the Commission. He was not to regret the manner of her death. " You have sometimes said you were sorry you employed me. I assure you that it has kept me alive. . . . You have always been . . . the defender of what is weak and ugly and dirty and undefended rather than of what is beautiful and artistic. You are so now more than ever for us. ' Us ' means in my language the troops and me. . . . I hope you will have no chivalrous ideas of what is ' due ' to my ' memory '. The only thing that can be ' due ' to me is what is good for the troops."

On December 11th, 1857, she gave Parthe directions for her burial. Her love for the troops and her association with the men had made her feel what she never expected to feel—a superstition. She had a yearning to be buried in the Crimea, " absurd as I know it to be. For they are not there."

In November 1857 she made a will in which the property she would one day inherit from her father and mother was to be used to erect a model barrack, " with day rooms, separate places to sleep in . . . lavatories, gymnastic places, reading rooms etc., . . . not forgetting the wives but having a kind of Model Lodging House for the married men."

Personal remembrances were to be sent to Mrs. Herbert, Dr. Sutherland and Sir John McNeill, " after I am dead ", and Parthe was instructed to bring them from Embley.

It was an atmosphere in which emotion ran riot and the exalted affection between Miss Nightingale and Aunt Mai burst into strange flower. Wounded by the behaviour of Fanny and Parthe during the summer, she conceived an idea which she called the " Virgin Mother ", to explain the love and sympathy she felt in Aunt Mai, the indifference she felt in Fanny. " Probably there is not a word of truth in the story of the Virgin Mary ", she wrote in a private note of 1857. " But the deepest truth lies in the idea of the Virgin Mother. The real fathers and mothers of the human race are NOT the fathers and mothers according to the flesh. I don't know why it should be so. It ' did not ought to be so '. But it is. Perhaps it had better not be said at all. . . . What is ' Motherhood in the Flesh ' ? A pretty girl meets a man—and they are married. Is there any thought of the children? The children come without their consent even having been asked because it can't be helped. . . . For every one of my 18,000 children, for every one of these poor tiresome Harley Street creatures I have expended more motherly feeling and action in a week than my mother has expended for me in 37 years."

In another note she wrote : " I have had a spiritual mother

without whom I could have done nothing, who has been all along a ' Holy Ghost ' to me and lately has lived the life of a porter's wife for me.   Who left her own people and came out to Scutari to me."

On Aunt Mai's side affection passed into worship.   " My child, my friend, my guide and uplifter, my dearest one on earth or in heaven ", she wrote.   She submitted completely. " Be sure my beloved I have not even a secret wish to remonstrate, to oppose *anything* ", she wrote in September 1857. Recalling this period to Clarkey Miss Nightingale said : " We were like two lovers ".

Her family had agreed not to expect letters from her, her energy must be preserved for work, Aunt Mai was to send reports.   And now, lying on the sofa in the drawing-room, seldom sitting up and almost never going out, she proceeded to toil as she had never toiled before.   In November 1857 Aunt Mai wrote : " Mr. Herbert for 3 hours in the morning, Dr. Sutherland for 4 hours in the afternoon.   Dr. Balfour, Dr. Farr, Dr. Alexander interspersed."   A little later : " Flo is working double tides, labouring day after day until she is almost fainting ".   The task differed from the task of a year ago when the material for the Commission was being collected. " There is now the most important work of all to be done namely to gain the fruit of the Report in working the Reforms which have been its purpose—they have now not only to work but to fight."   Florence, reported Aunt Mai, said never in her life had she toiled as she was toiling now.   Without her knowledge, without her extraordinary powers of perception, her unrivalled talents for handling vast masses of material, success would have been impossible.   " Dr. Sutherland quite admits ", wrote Aunt Mai, " that . . . completion depends on her.   She alone can give facts which no one else hardly possesses . . . she alone has both the smallest details at her finger ends and the great general view of the whole.   He has been saying all this while at his luncheon, now he is at his work, and I only hope he won't too soon say ' Will you tell her I am at a standstill until I see her ', for she is now resting, and I am always afraid to hear those words which don't at all the less come because he begins by saying, ' I don't want her at all, I only want her to rest '."

Lord Panmure was behaving over the four sub-Commissions exactly as he had behaved over the Commission itself. He had been frightened by Sidney Herbert into agreement but, under pressure from within the War Office, he lost his nerve and once more retreated to the Highlands where he shot grouse, left letters unanswered and refused to come to London.

" Pan is *still* shooting ", wrote Sidney Herbert on September 28th. " In future you must defend the Bison, for I won't." Miss Nightingale sent letters to Brechin Castle, she got wind of a flying visit Panmure was secretly paying to London and sent him round a note by hand. She declared in a letter to Sir John McNeill on October 10th : " I shall not leave P. alone till this is done ". Her personal relations with Panmure continued playful. Grim determination was masked by compliments and jokes. She wrote him humorous notes, he sent her grouse. In private she raged against his " unmanly and brutal indifference ". " I have been three years serving in the War Department ", she wrote to Sidney Herbert in November 1857. " When I began there was incapacity but not indifference. Now there is incapacity and indifference."

Lord Panmure was being rent apart. The Reformers were powerful, they had public opinion with them, and public opinion was to be dreaded, but the reactionary party within the War Office were powerful and to be dreaded as well. On the administrative side Sir Benjamin Hawes was capable of causing infinite trouble, while Dr. Andrew Smith was fighting furiously against the " wiping " sub-Commission, which wiped the slate clean for the complete reorganisation of the Army Medical Department. In November 1857 pressure from the War Office was so great that Panmure revoked the " wiping " sub-Commission. The Reformers were appalled, Sidney Herbert forced Panmure to see him, and after a long and stormy interview this sub-Commission was reinstated.

It became clear to Miss Nightingale that the issue turned on the ability of each side to frighten Panmure. Whichever side could frighten him most thoroughly would be victorious.

She devised a new idea. Public opinion was the Reformers' strongest weapon. She would instruct public opinion and at the same time put pressure on Panmure through a Press campaign which should tell the nation the truth about conditions in the army.

In 1857 great influence was exercised by the "heavies"— the quarterlies and the reviews. She planned to get articles published in the heavies with the help of Sidney Herbert. He would contribute the prestige of his name and position while she supplied facts. On March 12th, 1858, she sent him a list of possible contributors, suggested channels through which they could be approached, described the style of their previous writings and added outlines of suitable articles and a list of editors to whom the articles should be sent. The outlines, the facts, even the headings for all articles were supplied to contributors by her. " I enclose a sketch, add to it, take away from it, alter it ", she wrote to Edwin Chadwick in August 1858. Lord Stanley, Sidney Herbert, Edwin Chadwick, who had sat on the first Poor Law Commission of 1834 and instigated the first Sanitary Commission of 1839, wrote for her, and Henry Reeve, the powerful editor of the *Edinburgh Review* and her old friend, accepted one of the articles, though she complained that he " mangled it in the ministerial interest ". She refused to sign anything herself. Her contribution was an unsigned pamphlet, *Mortality in the British Army*, which was one of the earliest, if not the earliest, instance of the presentation of statistical facts by means of pictorial charts—Miss Nightingale believed she invented this method. The facts that the majority of deaths in the Crimean mortality were due not to war but to preventable disease, and that mortality in barracks was double the mortality in civil life, were driven home at a glance by means of coloured circles and wedges. The text was an explanation of the diagrams based on the Reformers' battle-cry, " Our soldiers enlist to death in the barracks ". Sidney Herbert printed the charts and the memorandum as an appendix to the report of the Commission, and the pamphlet was published as " Re-printed from the Report of the Royal Commission ". Miss Nightingale had 2000 copies printed at her own expense, and sent them to the Queen, the Commander-in-Chief, Members of both Houses, Commanding Officers and doctors, with a personal letter designed to provoke the recipient's curiosity. " It is always more gratifying to people to have a thing which

they think other people have not got ", she wrote to Sidney
Herbert on Christmas Day 1857. One letter runs: " It is
confidential and *I* have no right to give away copies ". " This
is for your own reading ", she writes in another. And, " Please
do not leave this about ". Three copies of the charts were
handsomely framed and sent to the War Office, the Horse
Guards and the Army Medical Department. She never discovered if they were hung.

By the end of 1857 Panmure had given way. Pressure in
the Press and in the House was gaining strength, and the
publication of the report of the Royal Sanitary Commission
on the Health of the Army could not be deferred. The four
sub-Commissions were granted and set up in December.
" With such ample instructions as you may guess them to be,
when I tell you they were written by me ", wrote Miss Nightingale to Sir John McNeill.

She did not go to Embley for Christmas, but stayed in
London at the Burlington with Aunt Mai and Clough. The
year 1858 dawned brightly for the Reformers, and as the
summer came they gained success after success; even though
in February 1858 Lord Palmerston's government fell, Lord
Panmure went out of office, and for a moment it appeared
as if his exit might be fatal. Dr. Andrew Smith had at last
retired, and the next man in order of seniority was Sir John
Hall. Lord Panmure had pledged his word that as long as
he held office Sir John Hall should never be Director-General,
but at this crucial moment Panmure was succeeded by General
Peel. Miss Nightingale was in an agony. The appointment
hung in the balance, and she raged at the fate which had
decreed the Bison's disappearance at the one moment when he
could be of use. However, Sidney Herbert, with his matchless
talent for negotiation, approached General Peel. On February
27th Peel promised he would make no appointment until he
had conferred with Sidney Herbert, but would not commit
himself further. Sidney Herbert continued to put himself in
Peel's way, not speaking directly on the appointment but
" throwing in a little praise of Alexander when talking or
writing on other subjects ". His persuasiveness was effectual.
On May 25th he wrote that he had won the day. Sir John
Hall was passed over and Alexander was appointed Director-

General of the Medical Department of the British Army and officially gazetted on June 11th.

A citadel had fallen. Alexander was a man of first-class intelligence and Miss Nightingale's intimate friend. Co-operation would replace obstruction from within the Medical Department at the War Office. " Smith is really gone ", wrote Sidney Herbert. " It is no use trying to realise the enormous importance of such a fact." Yet another victory followed. On May 11th in the House of Commons Lord Ebrington moved a series of resolutions on the health of the army founded on the report of the Royal Sanitary Commission. He called attention to the figures published in the report revealing the high mortality in barracks compared to the mortality in civil life. " Improvements ", he concluded, are imperatively called for not less by good policy and true economy than by justice and humanity." There were deafening cheers. After reading the account of this debate Sir John McNeill wrote to Miss Nightingale on May 13th : " To you more than to any other man or woman alive will henceforth be due the welfare and efficiency of the British Army. I thank God that I have lived to see your success."

Throughout the summer of 1858 she was at the Burlington, going out of London only twice for a week's cure of "fresh air and water packs " at Malvern. She travelled by railway in an invalid carriage attended by Aunt Mai as " dragon " and Clough as courier. Bystanders were struck with awe. She was carried in a chair, and usually her bearers were old soldiers, who carried her as if she were a divinity. A space was cleared on the platform, curious onlookers were pushed back, voices were hushed and the station-master and his staff stood bareheaded as she was carried into the carriage. She was already becoming a legend.

Though she cut herself off from the world her rooms at the Burlington, the " little War Office ", were a hive of industry, and she laid herself out to make working with her as convenient as possible. She lived at the " dingy old Burlington " because it was central, but she had made her rooms cheerful with new carpets and curtains at her own expense. Lady Ashburton, who before her marriage had been Miss Louisa Stewart Mackenzie, "beloved Zöe ", sent flowers and plants from

Melchett Court every week, Fanny supplemented the catering of the Burlington with game, hot-house fruit, eggs and cream. Miss Nightingale was very ready to provide her fellow workers with breakfasts, luncheons and dinners. " If you will come and talk ought it not to be with dinner ? " she wrote to Dr. Farr in 1859. " Please come here you shall have dinner at 7 ", she wrote to Dr. Balfour in 1859. She offered the delegates to the Statistical Congress of 1860 " a room, breakfast, dinner and a place to work at any time—a better dinner with notice ". She used the opportunity of a friendly meal to exert a little pressure. " The D.G. is coming to breakfast tomorrow ", she wrote in 1860. " I always think it worth while to keep him ' *straight* '." She seldom joined these parties herself, but from her couch she kept a hand on detail. " Take care of your cream for the breakfast—it is quite turned." " Put Dr. Balfour's big book back where he can see it while drinking his tea ", she told Aunt Mai.

She visited no one, but very eminent visitors came to her. The Queen of Holland, the Crown Princess of Prussia, the Duke of Cambridge called on her regularly. Kinglake consulted her when he was writing his *Invasion of the Crimea*. She was not impressed. " I found him exceedingly courteous and agreeable," she wrote to Edwin Chadwick, " looking upon the war as a work of art and emotion—and upon me as one of the figures in the picture . . . upon figures (arithmetical) as worthless--upon assertion as proof. He was utterly and *self sufficiently* in the dark as to all the real causes of Crimean Mortality." " Though I have no doubt he is a good counsel he strikes me as a very bad historian ", she wrote to Sir John McNeill on May 3rd, 1857. She was anxious to convince Kinglake of the accuracy of the McNeill and Tulloch Report and told Sir John McNeill that she " took the reports of the Chelsea Board and your own and pasted out for him on sheets of large foolscap the parallel, or rather contradictory, passages. I mean the passages of the Chelsea Board Report as completely refuted by yours. The Duke of Cambridge was present at our conversation. At that time Mr. Kinglake professed himself convinced." However, when in 1880 the sixth volume of Kinglake's history which dealt with the controversy was published she found that he had supported and approved the Chelsea Board's findings. She never forgave him. She called him " that master of juggle and stage deception . . . that pantomime manager ". Kinglake's well-known description of herself and her work she dismissed shortly : " He meant it to be kind, but it was fulsome ".

Manning visited her and she wrote to him in February 1860 as " one of those whom I *know* to be friendly to me ". She told Sidney Herbert that Manning had always treated her fairly ; he advised her on the special needs of the Catholic regiments of the army.

In the spring of 1858 she had begun an important friendship. Captain Douglas Galton, a brilliant young Royal Engineer, was the army's leading expert on barrack construction, ventilation, heating, water supply and drainage. He held an important War Office appointment, had been appointed referee for the consideration of plans for the drainage of London, and was a member of the Barrack sub-Commission. He was, wrote Hilary Bonham Carter, " in every way a recommendable specimen, very clever, very gentlemanly, very scientific . . . his father is a rich man with a fine house in Worcestershire ". He was also a family connection, for in 1851 he had married the beautiful Marianne Nicholson. In 1857 Marianne and the Nightingales were reconciled, and Clarkey was asked to meet her at a breakfast given by Fanny and Parthe at the Burlington. " In comes Marianne by invitation ", wrote Clarkey to Mrs. Bonham Carter on July 18th ; " we are all loving, she is always as pretty and much improved in character, she takes an interest in amendments and don't never flirt no more. Let people talk against matrimony ! "

After the Barrack Commission was set up Miss Nightingale and Douglas Galton met and corresponded almost daily. She absorbed him. She was too busy to see Marianne but she wrote her kind letters and was godmother to one of the Galton children. Otherwise Marianne's name was not mentioned. Once at the foot of a long letter dealing with the construction of a hospital at Woolwich he scribbled in pencil : " Marianne had a boy this morning ".

The support of Douglas Galton, the appointment of Alexander as Director-General of the Army Medical Department, the appointment of Dr. Balfour to establish a statistical department within the War Office strengthened Miss Nightingale's hand, and in the autumn of 1858 she judged the time was ripe for another Press campaign. The only way to influence Ministers, she wrote, was through the public.

Notes on Matters affecting the Health, Efficiency and Hospital Administration of the British Army was lying unused. Copies were sent to the Queen, the Commander-in-Chief, Members of the Cabinet, War Office officials and well-known public figures with the same type of covering letter as before. " This is an advance copy of a Confidential Report ", she wrote. " May I ask you not to mention to anyone that you have this Report." Her plan was to make the second campaign more popular than the first and to include the daily newspapers as well as the " heavies ". A copy was sent to Harriet Martineau with a letter calculated to provoke her interest by warning her, " this Report is in no sense public property ".

Harriet Martineau was a leader-writer of the *Daily News*. The daughter of an unsuccessful sugar-refiner, deaf, sickly, physically unattractive and born without the senses of taste or smell—she said she had only once in her life been able to taste a leg of mutton and found it delicious—she had become a political power through her writings. She had hit on the idea of conveying knowledge in the form of fiction, and in an enormously successful series of tales had illustrated the facts of political economy, taxation and the poor law. Her prestige was very great, she dined out every day except Sunday, Cabinet Ministers asked her advice, she had been offered and had refused a Government pension, and Richard Monckton Milnes, Kingsley, Gladstone, Bulwer Lytton, Sydney Smith, Carlyle and Lord Brougham were her friends.

Like Miss Nightingale, she suffered from bad health, and her character was, she wrote, gloomy, jealous and morbid. In 1839 she was pronounced to be suffering from an incurable disease, and had spent five years in bed. She recovered, cured by mesmerism. In 1855 she was announced to be dying of heart disease, but in fact she did not die until twenty years later.

She was a passionate supporter of the movement for " Women's Rights ", unlike Miss Nightingale who, though she did more to open new worlds to women than perhaps any other woman, was not a feminist. Miss Nightingale dedicated herself to the cause of the unfortunate, the weak, the suffering and the defenceless, and it was a matter of indifference to her whether they happened to be women or men.

She forbade Harriet Martineau to use the *Notes* as the text for a sermon on pioneer women. " I have a great horror of its being made use of after my death by ' *Women's Mission-aries* ' and those kinds of people. I am brutally indifferent to the wrongs or the rights of my sex ", she wrote on November 30th, 1858. Miss Martineau used information from the *Notes* for a series of articles on the army which were published in the *Daily News* and successfully reprinted in 1859 in book form under the title *England and her Soldiers.*

In December 1858 Miss Nightingale herself wrote a short popular version of the facts contained in the *Notes* and in the report of the Royal Commission; it was published anony-mously under the title, *A Contribution to the Sanitary History of the late War with Russia,* and Sir John McNeill described it as " complete and unanswerable ".

It was a hopeful period. The four sub-Commissions, in spite of official opposition, were accomplishing a great deal. Barracks were being inspected and plans laid for rebuilding and reconditioning. Alexander was hard at work on the new regulations which were to transform the Army Medical Depart-ment. For the future, developments of the greatest importance were taking shape.

In the summer of 1857 the Indian Mutiny had broken out. Miss Nightingale longed to leave her desk and go out to the troops, but Sidney Herbert prevented her. " I may tell you in confidence ", she wrote to Dr. Pattinson Walker in 1865, " that in 1857, that dreadful year for India, I offered to go out to India in the same way as to the Crimea. But Sidney Herbert . . . put a stop to it. He said that I had undertaken this work, caused him to undertake it and that I must stay and help him." She consoled herself with the reflection that by her work for the army in England she was saving more lives than by going to India. " What are the murders committed by these miserable Bengalese compared to the murders com-mitted by the insouciance of educated cultivated Englishmen? " she wrote to Sidney Herbert in September 1857. As a result of the Mutiny India passed from the government of the East India Company to the government of the Crown, and the welfare of the troops in India became the responsibility of the British Government. In the course of the Royal Commission appalling reports were received of sanitary conditions in India, and for six months Miss Nightingale had been asking for a second Royal Sanitary Commission to deal with the health of the army in India. Now she seemed likely to succeed. The first Secretary of State for India to be appointed after the passage of the Control of India Bill in 1858 was Lord Stanley, her admirer and friend, and there was every probability that the Commission would be set up in the near future.

All too soon the sky darkened. In August 1858 Alexis Soyer died. At the time of his death he was collaborating with her on the Barracks' Commission, and one of his last acts was to open, on July 28th, his model kitchen at the Wellington Barracks. On August 28th she wrote to Douglas Galton : " Soyer's death is a great disaster. My only comfort is that you were imbued before his death with his notions."

But the disaster of Soyer's death was as nothing compared with the next disaster that threatened—the breakdown of Sidney Herbert's health. He had never been robust. After his term of office during the Crimea his health had broken down and he had gone abroad for a cure, and during the Royal Commission he had broken down again. In June 1857 Aunt Mai had written : " Mr. Herbert not at all well, which I am afraid weighs heavily on Flo's mind. He is going for a week's change into the country." A week's change was not enough ; he returned still exhausted and wished to take a cure abroad, but Miss Nightingale refused to consent. Two months of fishing in Ireland, and riding and shooting at Wilton during the long vacation, partially restored him, but when he had returned to London in the autumn of 1857 he had to grapple with the enormous tasks of obtaining and setting up the four sub-Commissions and then of administering them, since he was chairman of each of the four.

The work was crushing, physically. Inspection of barracks meant constant travelling, there was opposition, commanding officers were insolent ; facilities for inspection were refused and the Commissioners were kept waiting on barrack squares in cold and wind. " The Big-Wigs were surly ", he wrote after a visit to Aldershot in March 1858. Physical exertions were succeeded by the close and gruelling labour of drafting and revising regulations, for three of the sub-Commissions dealt with administration. (Miss Nightingale's rough agenda for one week's work ran : " Draft Instructions and Regulations defining the duties of etc. etc., and revising the Queen's Q.M.Gs, Barrack and Hospital Regulations, a new Constitution for the Army Medical Board and a Warrant for Promotion ".) The strain was too great. From the beginning of 1858 a marked deterioration in his health began.

In January of that year he was suffering from acute neuralgia and tic in the temples. Miss Nightingale recommended " saturating a small piece of cotton with chloroform and camphor, putting it up the nose and inhaling strongly ". He followed this prescription, did it too frequently and made himself sick. At the end of the month he wrote : " My head is very shaky in the neuralgic way ". On February 2nd he was apologising for missing a conference—" I am fairly broken down, but will be up again directly ". He got up but felt so ill that he had to go back to bed. Three days later he wrote that he was suffering tortures from headache and was unable to work. " Had Orsini [1] my head to throw under the carriage it must infallibly have blown the whole dynasty to atoms." Early in March he was poorly. " The east wind and snow bring back my shaky head." On the 15th March he was in bed again—" Here I am idling away my time in bed. I have been heartily ashamed of myself these last few days." Three days later he was still in bed, though he explained : " I am really not ill, only washy and weak which I always recover wonderfully ".

Never did a man receive less sympathy. Miss Nightingale working, as she believed on her deathbed, had small consideration for lesser ailments. What was a headache, a feeling of wretchedness compared with what she was enduring ? It was

[1] Felice Orsini, Italian revolutionary, attempted to assassinate Napoleon III, whom he regarded as the principal obstacle to Italian freedom. On the evening of January 14th, 1858, Orsini and his accomplices threw three bombs at the Imperial carriage, when the Emperor and Empress were on their way to the theatre. The Emperor and Empress escaped but several other persons were killed and many wounded. Orsini was executed on March 13th, 1858.

no new thing for her to complain of him. They had differed
when she was in the Crimea. He had evaded her on the subject of Army Reform when she came home. " Ten years have
I been endeavouring to obtain an expression of opinion from
him and have never succeeded yet ", she wrote to Sir John
McNeill in November 1857. She was accustomed, she wrote
in the same letter, to tell him that his " honour " was at
stake; Sidney Herbert was " the most sensitive of men on
the subject of his personal obligations ", and " this gives
me a hold over him ". Nevertheless, she finished the letter
with the phrase she used so often, " without him I could do
nothing ".

She drove him. That was her function. He did not
shrink from her white-hot energy, her implacability—he
needed its vitalising warmth. The fundamental differences
between their two characters balanced each of them and gave
their collaboration its immense value. But because they were
so different complications ensued. They irritated each other.
Miss Nightingale, so prone to hero-worship, lavished no
admiration on Sidney Herbert while he was alive ; her eulogies
were written after his death. She was impatient with him,
she hunted him, she grumbled at him ; and Sidney Herbert,
renowned for his urbanity and gentleness, scolded her. He
told her she was irritable, exacting, impatient, that she
exaggerated and was too fond of justifying herself. He never
broke into the panegyrics commonly indulged in by her fellow
workers. Only the words used by him at the end of every
note he wrote her, at every interview they had together, " God
bless you ", spoke of the affection between them. The tie
which united them was so strong that it did not need support.
" We were identified ", she wrote to Clarkey in 1861. " No
other acknowledgment was needed."

She was not alone in thinking Sidney Herbert took his ailments too seriously. " How can a man like you get ill? " wrote
Delane, editor of *The Times*, on February 6th, 1858. " If I
could lead your life I would live 1000 years, and never have a
headache."

While on one hand Miss Nightingale drove him, on the
other he was urged on no less relentlessly by his wife. Far
from resenting his work with Miss Nightingale, Liz encouraged

it ; work with Florence was the part of her husband's life which she most thoroughly shared.

Before his marriage Sidney Herbert had been the close friend of the beautiful and unhappy Caroline Norton, the original of George Meredith's *Diana of the Crossways*, and one of three lovely sisters nicknamed the Three Graces. The granddaughters of Sheridan, they had inherited his wit and captivating charm. One sister became Lady Dufferin, one became Duchess of Somerset, and Caroline herself married the Hon. George Chappel Norton, younger brother of Lord Grantley. It was an unhappy match; George Norton, an unsuccessful barrister, had a violent temper, and the Nortons were incessantly in financial difficulties. Caroline, who had written poetry and novels since she was in her teens, became a professional author and achieved considerable success. She had wit and brilliant beauty, and the parties she gave in her little drawing-room in Storeys Gate became famous. One of her most intimate friends was Lord Melbourne. George Norton, though insanely jealous, was willing to profit from his wife's friendships, and in 1831 he was made a Metropolitan Police Magistrate by Lord Melbourne. Five years later he brought proceedings charging Lord Melbourne with committing adultery with Caroline. The case caused a sensation, and rumour said that George Norton had been bribed to bring the action to discredit Lord Melbourne in the eyes of the young Princess Victoria. But though the action failed—the jury dismissed the case without even calling upon the defence— Caroline's reputation had been irretrievably damaged.

After the action the Nortons separated and the tragedy of Caroline's life began. As a woman living apart from her husband she had no rights either over her income or her children. Her children, whom she adored, were removed and George Norton not only refused to make her an allowance but brought an action demanding the money she made from her books. She did not think her children were well treated ; her youngest boy, after being taken away, died at the age of nine as the result of a fall from a pony. The miseries she endured she expressed in a privately printed pamphlet on the right of mothers to the custody of their children, *English Laws for Women in the Nineteenth Century*, and a *Letter to the Queen*, on

Lord Cranworth's Divorce Bill, published in 1855. Her pamphlets and her story were instrumental in bringing about an improvement in the laws relating to women.

In the early forties Sidney Herbert, " beautiful as an angel ", chivalrous, brilliantly clever, immensely rich, was always to be seen at Caroline Norton's house. Caroline was not only beautiful, she was powerful. Motley the historian described her face as " most dangerous, terrible, beautiful ", hair " violet black . . . eyes very large with dark lashes, and black as death; the nose straight; the mouth flexible and changing; with teeth which in themselves would make the fortune of any ordinary face ". She had force and she had altruistic passion. In 1836 she had written *A Voice from the Factories*, a plea for the sweated worker. Her attachment to Sidney Herbert was well known, and Percy Dacier, the hero of *Diana of the Crossways*, was said to have been drawn from him.

Sidney Herbert was now first in the succession to Wilton. His father's eldest son by his first marriage had, in 1814, contracted a disastrous marriage with a Sicilian pseudo-countess, which the family had tried in vain to annul, and in 1827 had succeeded to the title as the twelfth Earl of Pembroke. It was evident that his health was hopelessly impaired, and, as he had no children, it had become increasingly desirable that Sidney Herbert should marry. In 1846 he married Miss Elizabeth à Court, who had been devoted to him since childhood, who was beautiful, well born and devoutly religious; they had been married for eighteen months when Miss Nightingale met them in Rome. Caroline Norton disappeared from his life. In 1847 Fanny Allen met one of Sidney Herbert's "intimates" who "detailed the course of his [Sidney Herbert's] marriage and the loosening of the tie between him and Mrs. Norton, who behaved very well on the occasion and assured him when he married she would never cross his path ".

Liz Herbert's devotion to her husband was possessive. Miss Nightingale, meeting her in Rome, had noticed her almost unbalanced affection for Sidney, her eagerness to be everything to him, to share his every thought. She was insecure. " You know all I have to bear more than anyone else ", she wrote to Miss Nightingale after Sidney's death. " It is strange but I think his whole family believe *he did not love me*." Far from remonstrating with Florence for driving Sidney too hard, Liz supported her. She acted as Sidney's secretary, not because she was jealous but because she craved to be near her husband, to share his life. Miss Nightingale, though she had no opinion of Liz's capacities, appreciated her sincerity. " Sidney Herbert's wife just did the Secretary's work for her husband . . . out of pure sympathy ", she wrote to Clarkey. " She had no depth, she was frivolous, she did not understand his policy . . . but she could write his letters for him ' like a man '." Liz clung to Florence—she had clung to her from the first moment they met in Rome in 1849, because through her she drew nearer to Sidney.

Thus urged, goaded, driven, Sidney Herbert struggled through 1858, and immeasurably greater demands were made on him the next year. Early in 1859 it became evident that what Miss Nightingale described to Harriet Martineau as " eight months importunate widowing of Lord Stanley " was to be successful. A Royal Sanitary Commission was to be set up to do for the army in India what the Royal Sanitary Commission of 1857 had done for the army at home, and Sidney Herbert was invited to be chairman. It was a hideously laborious prospect. The work would be gigantic, the state of India was inextricably confused, the opposition obstinate, the distance from which data must be collected was an enormous complication. His health was steadily deteriorating, and he still had to devote long hours to the four sub-Commissions. Nevertheless, he felt himself bound to accept, and the Queen issued the warrant setting up the Commission in May 1859. A month later an even greater task was thrust on him. The Government had fallen in March, and in the general election which followed Lord Palmerston was returned to power. He invited Sidney Herbert to become Secretary of State for War, the office held by Lord Panmure and latterly by General Peel. It was, on the face of it, a triumph. What could not Sidney Herbert do for Army Reform in the place of Panmure ? But his first sensation was one of despair. He must accept, he had no choice, his duty lay clear before him—but he knew he was not equal to the task. On June 13th he wrote to Miss Nightingale : " I must write you a line to tell you I have undertaken the Ministry of War. I have undertaken it because I believe that in certain branches of administration I can be of use, but I do not disguise from myself the severity of the task, nor the probability of my proving unequal to it. But I know you will be pleased at my being there. I hope the first sensations on accepting are not to be taken as true indications of the satisfaction which the change of life is to give. The prospect of hard and difficult work with an imperfect machinery in the office and a desperate battle to be fought in Parliament against a numerous and keen enemy in front, with a discontented and doubtful support at one's back, is not exhilarating. I will try and ride down to you tomorrow afternoon. God bless you."

She received the news soberly. "Dearest I hardly can congratulate you," she wrote to Liz on June 14th, " but you know what I think about it. I don't expect even him to turn apes into wise men and lions into Unas. I am afraid he has inefficient servants, a disorganised department and a silly C-in-C to deal with. But for all that, (and all the more because of all that), it is a great national benefit his undertaking it. And certainly he is the only man who could do it. . . . I don't believe there exists a more disorganised office than the War Office."

The Reformers seemed now to be in a strong position. Sidney Herbert was Secretary of State for War, Alexander was Director-General of the Army Medical Department. The Royal Sanitary Commission on the Health of the Army of 1857 was being put into operation and a new Commission on the Health of the Army in India was being set up. It seemed there was every reason for optimism; but there was no optimism. Instead there was depression. The Reformers felt that the future was dark.

Only now, when so much progress had been made, did the almost insuperable difficulties confronting them emerge. The basic difficulty was the administrative system of the War Office itself. The War Office, Colonel Lefroy had written in 1856, was like " a rickety clumsy machine, with a pin loose here and a tooth broken there and a make-shift somewhere else, in which the forces of Hercules may be exhausted in a needless friction before the hands are got to move, so is our Executive, with the Treasury, the Horse Guards, the War Department, the Medical

Department, all out of gear, but required to move together before a result can be attained ". In 1858 Sidney Herbert had complained of the infuriating manner in which General Peel was obstructed by his subordinates. General Peel possessed " the best intentions possible ", but he was unable to put his intentions into practice. The War Office subordinate officials had been able to frustrate him, " spoiling, interfering and delaying ". The favourite method was " excessive minuting ". Matters were held up for months while papers relating to them went the rounds with a minute attached. " These War Office subs are intolerable ", wrote Sidney Herbert, ". . . half a dozen fellows sitting down to compose minutes, just for the fun of the thing, on a subject which they cannot possibly know anything about." Papers were mislaid, misdirected, unnecessary queries were raised. One large set of papers dealt with the diet of the War Office cat. " There are rats in the W.O.—also a cat ", wrote Miss Nightingale to Sidney Herbert in 1860. " There are 17 months minutes to apply for 6d a week for her. 40 minutes say that she ought to live on rats. Other minutes that she ought to have milk—but that 6d a week is too much. Others again ask what she is to live on in the meantime. I am very anxious to know what is your decision. Whether you have given any as yet—whether you think fivepence three farthings would be too much ? I incline to fivepence halfpenny."

Principals were subjected to the criticism of their subordinates. " To put a set of subordinates to report upon the doings of their immediate chiefs seems to be the method of doing business in this department ", wrote Miss Nightingale to Sidney Herbert on December 24th, 1858. " Thus Mr. Herbert, Dr. R. Airey, Mr. Alexander, Dr. Sutherland, Dr. Croomes are appointed to draw up the regulations. Belfield, Beatson, Milton and Robertson, subordinates in the same office are appointed to report upon said regulations." New departments had been created within other departments and the new always subjected to the old, so that the final decision on the work of doctors and scientists rested with clerks. " A good illustration of the system is this ", she wrote to Sidney Herbert on August 16th, 1860. " Hawes being now absent leaves the whole of the business to Dewry [a clerk] to settle—

so that Dewry has to control the duties of all the Scientific Officers." In November 1859 she summed up her experience. " The War Office is a very slow office, an enormously expensive office, and one in which the Minister's intentions can be entirely negatived by all his sub-departments and those of each of the sub-departments by every other."

Sidney Herbert had just had a demonstration of War Office power in the matter of the Army Medical School. Miss Nightingale had set out the necessity for an Army Medical School in *Notes on Matters affecting the Health, Efficiency and Hospital Administration of the British Army*. " Young men were formerly sent to attend sick and wounded soldiers who *perhaps* had never dressed a serious wound . . . who certainly had never been instructed in the most ordinary sanitary knowledge, although one of their most important functions was hereafter to be the prevention of disease in climates and under circumstances where *prevention* is everything." The school was designed to provide training in military hygiene and military surgery. Miss Nightingale drew up the regulations in consultation with Sir James Clark, and the nomination of its professors was left entirely in her hands. The third of the four sub-Commissions which Sidney Herbert extracted from Lord Panmure was concerned solely with it.

The nominations were made in 1857. Dr. Parkes, the great military sanitarian, was to be Professor of Hygiene and Dr. William Aitken, later Sir William Aitken, to be in charge. Panmure could not be got to the point of making the appointments; he would not actually appoint anyone " even if the Angel Gabriel had offered himself, St. Michael and all angels to fill the different chairs ", wrote Sidney Herbert. Panmure went out of office and General Peel succeeded him, but still nothing was done. Then General Peel was succeeded by Sidney Herbert, who wrote that something should be done about the Army Medical School " at last ". He converted nominations into appointments, but delay continued; the officials in the War Office were not yet defeated. Premises were selected at Fort Pitt, Chatham, yet work on them did not begin; the professors were appointed, but their salaries were not paid; requisitions were sent in for instruments and equipment, but they were not filled. Month added itself to month, it was a year, it was two years, it was nearly three years since the original authority for the establishment of the school had been given, and still nothing had been accomplished. In 1860 Sidney Herbert insisted on fixing a date for the opening of the school. Three letters sent by Miss Nightingale to Douglas Galton, in August of that year, relate what occurred. The first from Dr. Aitken, marked " Wail no 1 ", states : " No work even begun ". The second also from Dr. Aitken, marked " Wail no. 2 ", states : " No money for instruments ". The third from Miss Nightingale herself, dated September 3rd, 1860, marked " Wail no. 3 ", relates the " disaster of the opening day ". " On Saturday I had a letter from the Professors of the Medical School quite desperate . . . the authority for the instruments and the money had not yet come. Ten of the students arrived. They stared at the bare walls and in the absence of all arrangements for their work concluded the school was a hoax."

It was one of a hundred petty triumphs scored by a jealous and strongly entrenched bureaucracy. A new issue had become clear. Progress was impossible with the existing machinery. Before reforms could be carried through the War Office itself must be reformed.

Sidney Herbert must nerve himself to yet another gigantic task. The amount of work exacted by the office of Secretary of State for War was in itself enormous ; General Peel had been " overpowered " by it, Panmure had surmounted it " by the simple process of never attempting to do it ". Sidney Herbert was attempting far more than either of his predecessors. He nominally resigned in June 1859 the chairmanship of the Commission on the Health of the Army in India, but he continued to be chairman of the four sub-Commissions. And the Chancellor of the Exchequer was Mr. Gladstone, whose two ruling passions were national economy and anti-militarism. Sidney Herbert came into conflict with both. Mr. Gladstone's passion for economy produced interminable wrangles on the Army Estimates and the Estimates for Defence ; his anti-militarism made him unwilling to provide amenities for the British soldier. Liz sent Miss Nightingale a riddle : " Why is Gladstone like a lobster ? Because he is so good but he disagrees with everybody ! "

Yet Sidney Herbert felt once again he had no choice. War Office reform must be begun and he had been called to do it. He formed a departmental committee to report on War Office reorganisation under the chairmanship of Lord de Grey, Under-Secretary for War, and in consultation with Miss Nightingale a scheme was prepared. Its objects, she wrote, were " to simplify procedure, to abolish divided responsibility, to define clearly the duties of each head of a department and of each class of office ; to hold heads responsible for their respective departments with direct communication with the Secretary of State ".

She approached this new task with a determination so grim that it was almost despair. The enthusiasm, the exhilaration with which she had approached the first Royal Commission of 1857 were gone for ever. She was being crushed, as Sidney Herbert was being crushed, by the weight of her labours. " I am being worked on the tread-mill ", she wrote.

Miss Nightingale had no secretary. The compilation of statistics, the noting down of columns of figures, the laborious comparisons were done by herself. The innumerable letters, the immensely long reports were written by her own hand. The physical effort of writing down the enormous number of words she produced each day was staggering. The only method of duplicating was to have the text set by a printer and copies struck off. She had this done at her own expense, recording that from 1857–60 she spent £700 out of her own private income on printing.

As she toiled her sense of resentment grew fiercer. The men she worked with only wanted the work that could be got out of her, they were indifferent to her happiness. She had condemned herself to loneliness and solitude for the sake of the work. She never went out, she hardly saw a friend. Clarkey had been in London and she had not been able to spare time to see even Clarkey. Who among her fellow workers would do the same? Was ever suffering like mine? Was ever self-sacrifice like mine? she constantly asked herself. Sidney Herbert with his health, Dr. Sutherland with his desire for holidays, Dr. Alexander, even Aunt Mai, even Clough, all aggravated her, all were inadequate.

A thousand petty difficulties irritated her. Since she had

no strength to go out she wished for larger and airier rooms. The only suitable suite was occupied by a Mrs. Ellison. Aunt Mai wrote to Mrs. Ellison, called on her, explained the circumstances. Mrs. Ellison cherished an admiration for Miss Nightingale and agreed to move. But on the very day the move was to have taken place Mrs. Ellison was taken ill, and meanwhile Miss Nightingale's rooms had been let and the new tenant clamoured to get into them. Her nerves were on edge, and even a minor disaster drove her into a frenzy; at night the slightest noise woke her and once awake she could not sleep again. It was suggested that she should take a house, and Aunt Mai went down to see W. E. N. and persuaded him to agree to the extra expense. But her requirements for a house were exacting, it must be central, airy, convenient, quiet. Aunt Mai " panted from agent to agent " but could find nothing.

At the end of the summer of 1859 she had another collapse, with the familiar symptoms of fainting, breathlessness, weakness and inability to digest food. It was impossible for her to leave London, impossible for her to pass another summer at the Burlington. She compromised by taking rooms at Hampstead, a custom she continued for many years. Dr. Sutherland and Clough came daily and stayed all day. Aunt Mai took the opportunity of going home to see her family, and Hilary Bonham Carter took her place as " dragon ". Sidney Herbert, also kept in London by his work, rode out nearly every evening from Belgrave Square.

For a short interval she was quiet. Hilary, writing a bulletin to Embley, described her " lying on her couch, wrapt up in her delicate blanket, her little head resting on the pillow peeping from the blanket gives her quite an infantine appearance ". In September Fanny came to Hampstead—she had not seen Florence for nearly six months. " I drove to Hampstead on Friday ", she told Parthe, now Lady Verney; " I found Hilary drawing from a model, a live woman . . . who soon took me up to our dear F. lying in bed with a fire and the window open. She received me as if we had only just been parted, very affectionately, but her manner was nervous as if she feared to touch upon exciting subjects. . . . She would have made a beautiful sketch, lying there reclining upon

328

pillows in a blue drifting gown, her hair so picturesquely arranged, her expression most trusting, hardly harmonising with the trenchant things she sometimes says, her sweet little hands lying there ready for action. . . . I did not stay long. She said she should send for me again, and did. Hilary brought the message ' tell dear Mother she must come again '. However I thought it best not to go." There were, Fanny noticed, " several pussy cats " in the room ; one was lying on Florence's shoulder. She had always had " a passion for almost any kind of creature "—the society of animals soothed her nerves and cats were becoming her favourite companions. M. Mohl's genuine Persian cat, in spite of being called La Grande Mademoiselle, was the ancestress of her pets. She always had four or five cats in the room, they lay on her pillow, curled themselves round her neck, upset her ink and left paw marks on her papers.

She was now in bed or on her couch continuously. She never walked, she seldom went out. Fanny noticed that her face was flushed, her hands hot, and that talking seemed an effort.

Nevertheless, ill though she might be, the attitude of her circle towards her physical condition was changing. Time had passed. She still spoke as if she were on her deathbed, her life was still described as hanging by a thread, but—it had been hanging by a thread for two years.

In June 1859 Aunt Mai wrote to Embley that she did not now have the " daily fears " she had at one time. Dr. Sutherland told Fanny in September that he did not now think Miss Nightingale's life would be shortened, as she herself expected it would be. There was even a family unpleasantness over her invalidism. The Verneys came to London and she said she was not well enough to see Parthe. Meanwhile her maid told Sir Harry that she was fairly well. Sir Harry was offended, which brought on one of her " attacks " of " agitated breathing ". Aunt Mai explained in a long apologetic letter that " it is now not her life but her getting *worse* which hangs upon a thread ".

Aunt Mai's family became impatient. Two years had passed since Aunt Mai, who was greatly beloved at home, had gone to the Burlington. A serious sacrifice had been made. She was, Miss Nightingale said, " an organiser in practical things and has so much tenderness ". Uncle Sam had written that she " formed the absolute ingredient in the inner life of her domestic circle " and the circle was a wide one, including husband, children, grandchildren and a large family house.

In the early summer of 1859 Uncle Sam came up to London to see Aunt Mai, and was uneasy about her. She was not a young woman, she suffered from rheumatism and she confessed to feeling unwell. He wrote to Fanny complaining, not to Florence ; she had established herself in a position where none of the family dared write to her direct. Aunt Mai hastened to assure Fanny she was really quite well and " should be so very sorry if Florence heard a word of it. Really and truly I am quite well now. You know Sam writes impulsively and nervously." Uncle Sam continued aggrieved. She had already been away two years, she might be away for twenty. His grievance did not stop at Aunt Mai—there was Clough. His daughter Blanche's life had been broken up by Florence's absorption of Clough. For the past year Blanche had been living with her children in her father's house, while Clough stayed in London. Clough was delicate, his health was causing grave anxiety, and it was felt Florence asked too much of him.

At the end of September 1859, when Miss Nightingale left Hampstead and went back to the Burlington, Uncle Sam did his best to persuade Aunt Mai to leave her. Miss Nightingale was very angry. To her, Aunt Mai's problem was not a personal problem. Aunt Mai's presence in London was essential to the work. Since she was the instrument chosen to do the work, if she suffered the work must suffer. She insisted that Aunt Mai must return.

In October, back in the Burlington once more, she had Aunt Mai and Clough to slave for her and cherish her, the familiar round of conferences and interviews, the inevitable burden of crushing work. But though outwardly everything was the same, inwardly nothing was the same. Difficulties were piling up. She was anxious over Clough's health and Aunt Mai's troubles with her family. The task of War Office reform became daily more complicated, more hopelessly involved, more infinitely laborious. Above all, there was the constant menace of Sidney Herbert's failing health. Everywhere she turned she saw threats of disaster.

XV TO CONTEMPLATE THE WORK which Miss Nightingale performed for the army produces a sensation of weariness. It is too much. No one person should have driven herself to accomplish all this. What must not these mountains of paper, these innumerable reports and memoranda, these countless letters, have cost in fatigue, in strain, in endless hours of application, in the sacrifice of every pleasure? And yet by 1859 work for the army was only a part of her labours. From military hospitals and military nursing she had passed to civilian hospitals and civilian nursing, from working for the army she had passed to working for the nation and the world.

She returned from the Crimea with the intention of devoting her life to the British Army. It was impossible. Her knowledge, her genius and her experience were such that she could not be allowed to limit herself to military affairs.

In her evidence before the Royal Sanitary Commission of 1857 she was asked: " Have you devoted attention to the organisation of civil and military hospitals?" She replied: " Yes, for thirteen years I have visited all the hospitals in London, Dublin and Edinburgh, many county hospitals, some of the Naval and Military hospitals in England; all the hospitals in Paris and studied with the ' Sœurs de Charité'; the Institution of Protestant Deaconesses at Kaiserswerth on the Rhine, where I was twice in training as a nurse, the hospitals at Berlin and many others in Germany, at Lyons, Rome, Alexandria, Constantinople, Brussels; also the War Hospitals of the French and the Sardinians."

The Commissioners were startled. It was an experience such as no other person in Europe possessed; and it was impossible that its benefits should be restricted to the British Army.

In a letter to Dr. Farr, written during the autumn of 1859, Miss Nightingale described her feelings when she became aware of the deplorable state of civil hospitals. She came back from the Crimea, she said, suffering from a delusion. She knew military hospitals were in administrative confusion, but she imagined civil hospitals to be much better; and her state of mind when she discovered civil hospitals to be "just as bad or worse" was "indescribable".

Administrative confusion was universal. New wine was being poured into old bottles. The confusion of Scutari, the confusion of the War Office, the confusion of the great London hospitals, were symptoms of a general confusion. Enormous expansions of population had taken place, but administrative machinery had not expanded. The seething masses of the nineteenth century were being dealt with by the restricted methods of the eighteenth and, as Miss Nightingale pointed out, a system which answers admirably for 100 people breaks down when called upon to cope with 1000. A great deal of her work for hospitals was connected with the installation of improved methods of administration and organisation, improved methods of design and construction, improved articles of equipment. It is work which has long since been superseded and for which she won little sympathy.

During the long, losing fight over the construction of Netley Hospital she learnt that abysmal ignorance of the first principles of hospital construction existed even among educated and liberal-minded people. She suffered a notable defeat because no single person concerned had had the faintest idea that any special importance ought to be attached to the way in which a hospital was designed. Steps must be taken to educate public opinion, and through Netley she entered the field of public health. In October 1858 Lord Shaftesbury arranged that two papers written by her on Hospital Construction should be read at the annual meeting of the Social Science Congress. They were received "with enthusiasm", and she expanded them into a book which was published in 1859 under the title *Notes on Hospitals*.

Notes on Hospitals was successful, a second edition was published in 1860, and a third, rewritten and with additions, in 1863. Sir James Paget described it as "the most valuable contribution to sanitary science in application to medical institutions that I have ever read". It has suffered the common fate of practical works that break new ground and its novel and revolutionary contentions have become commonplaces, but it remains readable. Miss Nightingale's writings may lack form, she put no construction into them, and she chose titles which warned the reader of want of plan—*Notes on Matters affecting the Health, Efficiency and Hospital Administration of the British Army, Notes on Hospitals, Notes on Nursing, Suggestions for Thought*; but the informality of her method produces a vivid and personal approach. The opening paragraph of *Notes on Hospitals* rivets attention:

> It may seem a strange principle to enunciate as the very first requirement in a Hospital that it should do the sick no harm. It is quite necessary nevertheless to lay down such a principle, because the actual mortality in hospitals, especially those of large crowded cities, is very much higher than any calculation founded on the mortality of the same class of patient treated *out* of hospital would lead us to expect.

It was her revolutionary thesis that the high rate of mortality, then invariable in large hospitals, was preventable and unnecessary. Hospitals showed their appallingly high death-rate because they flouted the elementary principles of sanitary science. The answer to hospital mortality was neither prayer nor self-sacrifice, but better ventilation, a higher standard of cleanliness, better drainage and better food. Floors and walls and bedsteads which could be scrubbed, windows and corridors placed to carry away foul air, proper heating and a larger cubic allowance of air per patient would bring the rate of mortality down. *Notes on Hospitals* draws an alarming picture of contemporary hospital conditions; walls streaming with damp and often covered with fungus, dirty floors, dirty beds, overcrowded wards, insufficient food and inadequate nursing turned the hospital from a place of healing into a pest house. What were known as " hospital diseases " flourished perpetually in the wards, hospital gangrene, hospital fever, hospital pyaemia and hospital erysipelas. In Winchester Infirmary there had recently been an epidemic of hospital erysipelas in which sixteen patients died in one week.

Following the success of *Notes on Hospitals* she was constantly asked for advice on Hospital Construction. The plans for the Birkenhead Hospital, the Edinburgh Infirmary, the Chorlton Infirmary, the Coventry Hospital, the Infirmary at Leeds, the Royal Hospital for Incurables at Putney, the Staffordshire Infirmary, and the Swansea Infirmary were submitted to her. The county of Buckinghamshire rebuilt its Infirmary at Aylesbury " in accordance with the requirements specified in Miss Nightingale's *Notes on Hospitals* ". At her instigation a pitched battle was fought in Winchester, which resulted in a new county hospital being built on a new site instead of the old hospital in the city, where the erysipelas epidemic had raged, being patched up. The Government of India officially consulted her on the plans for the new General Hospital at Madras. The Crown Princess of Prussia requested a personal interview in which she submitted plans for a new hospital in Berlin. The Queen of Holland submitted hospital plans. The King of Portugal asked her to design a hospital in Lisbon. She did so, the plans were accepted, and she then learned that the hospital was intended not for adults, but for children; the King of Portugal waved aside her protests—it did not matter, the children would have all the more room. In the course of his duties Douglas Galton went to Cherbourg to view the works which were turning it into a great naval base. She wrote: " I hope you have brought me back Cherbourg as a small token from France ". He had, in fact, been instructed to request her advice; and the plans for the French naval hospital there were inspected and passed by Miss Nightingale.

She had to deal with an enormous mass of practical detail. The organisation and equipment of hospital kitchens, hospital laundries and hospital wash-houses involved the choice of baths, taps, sinks and basins. The piping of water was novel, and each choice was in some degree an experiment. She wrote hundreds of letters to ironmongers, engineers, builders and architects. Huge bundles of these survive, though notes attached to the bundles state " Many destroyed ". An immense series of letters was written to Douglas Galton, dealing with such subjects as the superiority of plate-glass for windows, the proper person to carve in the kitchen, the necessity for bathrooms to be securely locked when not in use, the preference of sick men for washing at a table with a basin in a slab (white enamel showing dirt, it is therefore in this case preferable to slate, which does not), the construction of shutes for soiled linen, the best variety of saucepans, the popularity of maps in recreation rooms. She did not like the dark-green

334

walls which were becoming popular in hospitals and wished to have "the palest possible pink". She forwarded one long report with the title "A treatise on sinks".

Every set of plans was examined with infinite pains and treated in precise detail. "I am always afraid of laying down anything like a universal plan", she told Edwin Chadwick in 1860. A letter on the design of the new hospital at Woolwich dealt with the operating theatre: "The door of the operating theatre opens into a passage only 4 feet wide. The door of the operating ward had better be nearly opposite that of the operating theatre, not some distance away as in the plan, owing to the difficulty of turning a patient on a stretcher. Or the passage must be much wider." On problems such as the distribution of clean linen, the keeping of patients' food hot, the proper distance between beds in wards she corresponded with doctors, matrons and hospital superintendents all over the world.

Every department of hospital administration showed urgent need for reform. In 1859 each hospital followed its own method of naming and classifying diseases. Miss Nightingale embarked on a campaign for uniform hospital statistics. With the help of Sir James Paget and Sir James Clark she drew up a standard list of diseases and drafted model hospital statistical forms which would, she wrote, "enable us to ascertain the relative mortality of different hospitals, as well as of different diseases and injuries at the same and at different ages, the relative frequency of different diseases and injuries among the classes which enter hospitals in different countries, and in different districts of the same countries".

In 1858 she had been elected a member of the newly formed Statistical Society, and at the Statistical Congress of 1860 the principal subject for discussion was "Miss Nightingale's Scheme for Uniform Hospital Statistics". She broke her rule of social isolation and gave a series of breakfast parties at the Burlington during the conference. Hilary Bonham Carter acted as hostess, and the guests were taken in one by one to talk to her as she lay on her couch. The model statistical forms were well received. St. Mary's Hospital, Paddington, St. Thomas's, St. Bartholomew's and University College Hospital agreed to use them at once. A year later representatives of

Guy's, St. Bartholomew's, the London Hospital, St Thomas's, King's College Hospital, the Middlesex and St. Mary's, Paddington, met and passed a resolution that they would adopt a uniform system of registration of patients and publish their statistics annually, "using as far as possible Miss Florence Nightingale's Model Forms".

She found statistics " more enlivening than a novel " and loved to " bite on a hard fact ". Dr. Farr wrote in January 1860 : " I have a New Year's Gift for you. It is in the shape of Tables." " I am exceedingly anxious to see your charming Gift ", she replied, " especially those returns showing the Deaths, Admissions, Diseases." Hilary Bonham Carter wrote that however exhausted Florence might be the sight of long columns of figures was " perfectly reviving " to her.

In the spring of 1859 St. Thomas's Hospital found itself in a dilemma. The South Eastern railway was about to build a line from London Bridge to Charing Cross, and St. Thomas's, then situated in the Borough, lay directly in the path proposed for the new line. The railway company were seeking to acquire the site on which the hospital was built, and the Governors of the Hospital were unable to agree on the policy to be pursued. Some wished the railway company to acquire the whole site and move the hospital to a new district ; others wished for only a part of the site to be sold so that the work of the hospital could continue in the Borough. A deadlock was reached, and in February 1859 Mr. Whitfield, the Resident Medical Officer, called on Miss Nightingale and asked her to help. In his opinion the whole site should be sold and the hospital rebuilt in another district. Would she influence the Prince Consort, who was a Governor, to adopt this point of view ?

She was already interested in St. Thomas's. Her nurse in the Crimea, the celebrated Mrs. Roberts, had been a St. Thomas's sister, and the matron, Mrs. Wardroper, a woman of outstanding character and a pioneer of nursing reform, was her friend. But she would not allow herself to be easily convinced. She went into the matter thoroughly, studied figures, interviewed railway and hospital officials and came to the conclusion that Mr. Whitfield was correct. She then sent a memorandum to the Prince Consort. On December 23rd,

1859, Colonel Phipps, the Prince Consort's Private Secretary, wrote acknowledging the memorandum, " which has received the immediate attention any communication from you would be sure to command ". It was, he wrote, " a subject of the greatest pride to me to be permitted to assist in any work of yours ", and, on behalf of himself and the Prince, he enquired as to her health—" there is *no* Englishman to whom it must not be a source of deep interest ". Three days later he wrote again, enclosing a copy of a letter the Prince Consort had addressed to the Governors; the Prince had read her memorandum and been converted. " In the Prince's letter to the Governors you will find your own arguments and sometimes even your own words embodied ", wrote Colonel Phipps. The letter was read at the next Governors' meeting and, wrote Mr. Whitfield, " wrought wonders ".

However, the battle was not yet won, for a new point was raised. Financially it might be preferable to sell the whole site and rebuild elsewhere, but there was surely an ethical consideration. Ought the hospital to leave its ancient position among the people it had served for centuries? Again an appeal was made to Miss Nightingale. She responded by collecting statistics of patients treated in the hospital, and analysed them to discover whether the majority of patients did in fact come from the surrounding neighbourhood. On August 14th, 1860, she wrote to Dr. Farr that " St. Thomas' appears to keep its statistics for the purpose of checking obstreperous patients, which is an object certainly, but not a scientific one ". She was, however, able to obtain sufficient evidence to prove that the largest number of patients treated at the hospital did not come from the immediate neighbourhood but from districts further away ; and that, by moving the hospital, only a small percentage of patients would be affected. A memorandum containing this evidence was drawn up by her and submitted to the Governors and the Prince Consort, and as a result it was agreed that the whole site should be sold and the hospital moved.

Yet another crisis followed. The Governors, becoming greedy, decided to ask the railway company the then very large sum of £750,000. Miss Nightingale, called in once more, pointed out that, if the demand was persisted in, the company

337

would go to arbitration; and the sum awarded would almost certainly be smaller than the present offer. Her advice prevailed; the entire site in the Borough was sold by agreement and the hospital moved to its present position in Lambeth.

These negotiations produced a close association. Mr. Whitfield became devoted to her, and Mrs. Wardroper the matron was already a close friend. She became identified with St. Thomas's and in time held a position in the hospital which was almost that of patron saint.

Her interest in nursing and nursing reform had never diminished, though her work for the army had pushed it into second place. She had the Nightingale Fund of £45,000 at her disposal to found a Training School for Nurses, but there had been great difficulty in finding suitable connections for the school. In 1859, when she became concerned with the affairs of St. Thomas's, she began work on a scheme to establish the school there.

While she worked on this scheme for training the professional nurse she wrote a little book on nursing for the use of the ordinary woman, and it became the most popular of her works. *Notes on Nursing* was intended to make the millions of women who had charge of the health of their children and their households " think how to nurse ". " It was ", she wrote, " by no means intended . . . as a manual to teach nurses to nurse." It is a book of great charm, sympathetic, sensible, intimate, full of witty and pungent sayings, and possessing a remarkable freshness. " It is as fresh as if nobody had ever before spoken of nursing ", wrote Harriet Martineau, and Sidney Herbert wrote in January 1860 that it was " more interesting than a novel ". Neither its good sense nor its wit has dated, and *Notes on Nursing* can be read today with enjoyment.

When the book was published in December 1859 it caused a mild sensation. Habits of hygiene now taken for granted were then startling innovations. Mothers of families were shocked when Miss Nightingale attacked the education of the mid-Victorian girl, to whom " the cox combries of education " were taught, while she was left in ignorance of the physical laws which governed her own body. Harriet Martineau, on June 11th, 1860, described a friend and her daughter Fan paying a round of visits and finding *Notes on Nursing* on every table. " But Fan was ashamed wherever she went to hear the women talk. Such conceit, such ignorance, such insensibility she could not have conceived—the stuff they talked was perfectly amazing. One young lady : ' That about the skin and washing and hot water. I don't believe a word of it.' ' Try.' ' Ho-Ho I shan't try. I'm quite satisfied with my skin and don't want it better than it is.' "

The book was not cheap—the price was 5s.—but 15,000 copies were sold within a month ; and Miss Nightingale recorded, in March 1860, that Harrison's, who printed the original edition, had offered her 500 guineas for the copyright. The book was reprinted at 2s. and later at 7d. Thousands of copies were distributed in factories, villages and schools, and it was translated into French, German and Italian. " There is not one word in it written for the sake of writing but only forced out of me by much experience in human suffering ", she wrote to Sir John McNeill on July 29th.

It is impossible to doubt, after reading it, that Miss Nightingale was a gentle and sympathetic nurse. She understood that the sick suffer almost as much mental as bodily pain. " Apprehension, uncertainty, waiting, expectation, fear of surprise, do a patient more harm than any exertion. Remember he is face to face with his enemy all the time, internally wrestling with him, having long imaginary conversations with him." " Do not cheer the sick by making light of their danger." " Do not forget that patients are shy of asking." " It is commonly supposed a nurse is there to save physical exertion. She ought to be there to save (the patient) taking thought."

She spoke of the " acute suffering " caused a sick person by being so placed that it is impossible to see out of the window ; of the " rapture " brought to an invalid by a bunch of brightly coloured flowers ; of the intense irritation caused to an invalid by a noise such as the constant rustling of a nurse's dress. She understood the relief afforded a sick person by being taken out of himself. " A small pet animal is an excellent companion for the sick. A pet bird in a cage is sometimes the only pleasure of an invalid confined to the same room for years." She loved babies and recommended visits from the very young. " No better society than babies and sick people for each other."

339

It will be recalled that when she was convalescing in Mr. Sabin's house at Scutari she had become fond of a certain Sergeant Brownlow's baby; and when the 7d. edition of *Notes on Nursing* was published she added a chapter on " Minding Baby " inspired by this child. " And now girls I have a word for you ", the chapter opens. " You and I have all had a great deal to do with ' minding baby ', though ' Baby ' was not our own baby. And we would all of us do a great deal for baby which we would not do for ourselves." Jowett of Balliol said that a world of morality was contained in the parenthesis " though ' baby ' was not our own baby ". She received letters telling her that this chapter was most fruitful in results. Unhappily, Sergeant Brownlow's baby died shortly after the return of the troops to England from the Crimea, owing, she said, to the insanitary condition of the barracks in which the father's regiment was quartered.

She attacked " invalid food ". As a result of invalid diet thousands of patients are annually starved, she declared. " Give 100 spoonfuls of jelly and you have given one spoonful of gelatine which has no nutritive power whatever. Give a pint of beef tea and you have given barely a teaspoonful of nourishment. Bulk is not nourishment." Milk, in her opinion, was the best of all invalid foods, and she urged also that people who are ill should not be deprived of vegetables. Tea " admittedly has no nourishing qualities but there is nothing yet discovered which is a substitute to the English patient for his cup of tea ". Invalid food must be carefully served : Do not give too much, do not leave any food by the patient's bed. " Take care nothing is spilt in the saucer."

In a series of pungent paragraphs she cut to pieces the current idea of a nurse. " No *man*, not even a doctor, ever gives any other definition of what a nurse should be than this— ' devoted and obedient '. This definition would do just as well for a porter. It might even do for a horse. It would not do for a policeman." " It seems a commonly received idea among men, and even among women themselves, that it requires nothing but a disappointment in love, or incapacity in other things, to turn a woman into a good nurse." " Lord Melbourne said ' I would rather have men about me when I am ill; I think it requires very good health to put up with women.' I am quite of his opinion."

Though she denounced the education of the Victorian girl, and advocated the training of women, *Notes on Nursing* ends with a vigorous attack on the " jargon about the rights of women ". " Keep clear of both the jargons now current everywhere", she wrote; " . . . of the jargon, namely about the ' rights ' of women, which urges women to do all that men do including the medical and other professions, merely because men do it, and without regard to whether this *is* the best that women can do; and of the jargon which urges women to do nothing men do, merely because they are women, and should be ' re-called to a sense of their duty as women ' and because ' this is women's work ' and ' that is men's ' and ' these are things which women should not do ' which is all assertion and nothing more. . . . You do not want the effect of your good things to be ' How wonderful for a *woman*!'; nor would you be deterred from good things by hearing it said ' Yes, but she ought not to have done this, because it is not suitable for a woman.' But you want to do the thing that is good whether it is suitable for a woman or not." To praise women for doing what men did habitually and easily, she wrote, was to reduce them to the status of Dr. Howe's idiots whom, after two years of ceaseless labour, he succeeded in teaching to eat with a knife and fork.

Six months after the publication of *Notes on Nursing*, the scheme for establishing a Training School for Nurses, endowed with the proceeds of the Nightingale Fund, was at last carried through. For the past three years she had been " continuously deluged " with suggestions for spending it. On January 31st, 1856, while still at Scutari, she had written that she must decline considering any scheme for the present; she was too much overwhelmed with work to plan, and she was afraid of failure. " People's expectations are highly wrought ", she wrote. " They think some great thing will be accomplished in six months, although experience shows that it is essentially the labour of centuries—they will be disappointed to see no apparent change, and at the end of a twelve-month will feel as flat about it as people do on a wedding day at 3 o'clock when breakfast is over."

But she was powerless to curb public interest. The sum subscribed had been large, the publicity great. In March 1856, she wrote : " The first fruits of a long series (as I expect) of the brick and mortar plans of needy or philanthropic adventurers who wish to get hold of the ' Nightingale Fund ' have already come in upon me. . . . I take at random those which first present themselves. One is a magnificent elevation with my statue on the top to be called the ' Nightingale Hospital ' . . . another is a Home for Nurses with no hospital at all. One advises me to admit none but gratuitous services. This includes a threat if the obnoxious word ' Sister ' is allowed, and a terrible warning as to the ' cut of our aprons ' which are to be ' Large and White ', and a caution as to ' Celibacy ', which I was not aware before came into the question. We are also solemnly assured that the ' Apostles received a salary ' (How much was it ?) and that the Nurses must lead an ' *ordinary* life '. I thought the object was they should not be ordinary nurses. One offers me a clergyman and his sons and insists upon a service every day in the week, probably a son for each day and the Father on Sunday. Another insists on no Clergyman at all and a strictly secular education. One desires to confine my operations to the Work Houses, another to the Hospitals and a third recommends the training of nurses for private families only. One wishes for an ' Order ', another for an ' Asylum ' for old age, and a third for high wages which will enable each to save for herself."

She saw before her a fresh succession of the religious intrigues which had so nearly wrecked the nursing in the Crimea, and she refused to move. " If I do *anything* at present I shall be smothered in the dust raised by these religious hoofs ", she wrote.

In March 1858 she wrote to Sidney Herbert asking to be released from the responsibility of conducting the Fund. She was struggling with the enormous amount of work produced by the Royal Sanitary Commission, and she asked that the Council of the Fund should select an object to which the Fund could be applied and that she herself should retire. " I have been for some time hesitating as to the course I ought to take with regard to the large Fund which is called by my name ", she wrote on March 23rd, 1858. " I find my health so much impaired and I am consequently so unequal to begin a work which to be properly performed will require great exertion and unceasing attention, that I feel it incumbent upon me, and due to the Contributors, to beg you to communicate to the Trustees and Council my inability to undertake the task." Sidney Herbert dissuaded her. The money was well invested and could accumulate; there was no need for immediate action. The subscribers expected that she personally would "animate the work"; and he did not see how she could with propriety dissociate herself from it.

She unwillingly agreed, but continued to feel that the Nightingale Fund was a millstone round her neck. She was afraid of private charities. She had been driven nearly frantic by the necessity of finally clearing up the frightful matter of the Free Gifts. In 1857, at her most over-driven, she had been forced to produce sixty-eight pages of *Statements exhibiting the Voluntary Contributions received by Miss Nightingale for the use of the British War Hospitals in the East with the Mode of the Distribution in 1854, 1855, 1856.* Her fingers had been burnt by private charities and she was unwilling to involve herself again. Moreover, she had been annoyed by an attempt by the Council of the Nightingale Fund to dictate to her what her activities should be. It was proposed that she should be asked for a pledge that she would work in civil hospitals and not in Military hospitals. "I might go to the Opera and Races," she wrote to Sidney Herbert on October 31st, 1856, "no pledge against amusing myself existing, but I might not take Government employment being pledged to work for Civil Hospitals by the Fund. . . . I never can cease while I live, doing whatever falls in my way in the work I have mentioned above, viz. the Military Hospitals, which God and you have so singularly put into my hands."

By 1859, however, it was evident that some action must be taken. She was now an invalid, it was most unlikely that she would ever be sufficiently recovered to become the active superintendent of a large institution; and in any case her achievements were so great that as the superintendent of an institution she would be wasted. The scheme of founding a training school for nurses was revived. She was to be the patroness and organiser; and a sub-committee of the Nightin-

343

gale Fund Council, including Sidney Herbert, Sir John McNeill, Sir James Clark, Dr. Bowman—her old friend from Harley Street—and Clough, was appointed to hurry the scheme forward.

She hoped to work with Dr. Elizabeth Blackwell, but the plan failed. "During March and April in town", Miss Nightingale wrote to Sidney Herbert on May 24th, 1859, "I saw and corresponded with pretty nearly all the hospital authorities and female superintendents in esse or in posse that could be applied to the Fund. I will not tell you in writing (tho' I could any day viva voce) all the pros and cons and the different plans I have successively tried to initiate. The most promising, that of the 'London' qua hospital and of Miss Blackwell qua superintendent, has fallen through. And I am bound to say that the Hospital showed itself far more accommodating than the lady. (She is going back to America.) Miss Erskine, who was Superintendent of the Naval Hospital at Therapia, I have wooed in every way. She will not be won to leave her own family again. It is vain to try her any more.

"Those grapes are green—So I will not deplore these two and sundry other schemes—one of which was to tack ourselves on to St. John's House at King's College Hospital. For various reasons that will not do. I have talked over the matter at great length with Sir John McNeill. For some months past I have also discussed it with some of the authorities at St. Thomas's Hospital. The Matron of that Hospital is the only one of *any existing* Hospital I would recommend to form a 'school of instruction' for Nurses. It is not the *best conceivable* way of beginning. But it seems to me to be the *best possible*. It will be beginning in a very humble way. But at all events it will not be beginning with a failure, i.e. the possibility of upsetting a large Hospital—for she is a *tried* Matron."

Mrs. Wardroper, matron of St. Thomas's Hospital, a gentlewoman by birth, had been left a widow with young children at the age of forty-two, and had taken up nursing. Training was unknown—she entered the wards of a hospital and learned what she could from experience. Miss Nightingale wrote, "her force of character was extraordinary, and she seemed to learn from intuition". She was appointed matron of St. Thomas's in 1853, a remarkable achievement

MISS NIGHTINGALE AND MR. BRACEBRIDGE SURVEYING SEBASTOPOL FROM CATHCART'S HEIGHTS, MAY 1855

After a drawing by Parthenope Lady Verney.

SIR HARRY VERNEY, BART., AND MISS NIGHTINGALE ON THE LAWN
OF CLAYDON HOUSE, 1889

for a woman of her upbringing and class. In 1854 Miss Nightingale had applied to Mrs. Wardroper for nurses to go to the Crimea, and through her obtained her best nurse, Mrs. Roberts. Mrs. Wardroper's personal appearance was striking: she was tall, dark and possessed a personal magnetism which enabled her to impose discipline on the most refractory nurses and patients; she had great powers of administration, was a tireless worker and an ardent reformer. When Miss Nightingale revisited St. Thomas's after her two years in the East she found Mrs. Wardroper had achieved astonishing results. "She had already made her mark; she had weeded out the inefficient, morally and technically; she had obtained better women as nurses; she had put her finger on some of the most flagrant blots, such as night nursing . . . but no training had yet been thought of." Mrs. Wardroper held the post of superintendent of the Nightingale Training School for twenty-seven years, and a great part of the success of the school was due to her energy and determination.

The scheme for a training school for nurses was not universally welcomed. A strong party in the medical world thought that nurses did very well as they were, and that training would merely result in their trespassing on the province of the doctors. Both Mrs. Wardroper and Mr. Whitfield, the Resident Medical Officer at St. Thomas's, showed courage in committing their hospital to the scheme; and in May 1860 Mrs. Wardroper wrote warning Miss Nightingale that they must be prepared for " rather harsh criticism ".

Strong opposition came from within St. Thomas's itself, led by the Senior Consulting Surgeon, Mr. J. F. South. In 1857, when the scheme of a training school was first discussed, Mr. South published a little book, *Facts relating to Hospital Nurses. Also Observations on Training Establishments for Hospitals.* He was at the top of his profession, President of the College of Surgeons and Hunterian Orator, besides being senior consulting surgeon at St. Thomas's, and " not at all disposed to allow that the nursing establishments of our hospitals are inefficient or that they are likely to be improved by any special Institution for Training ". He argued that the sisters learned by experience and could only learn by experience, that the nurses were subordinates " in the position of house-maids " and needed only the simplest instruction, such as how to make a poultice. He asserted that the nursing at St. Thomas's hospital was already on a very high level. " That this proposed hospital nurse training scheme has not met with the approbation or support of the medical profession is beyond doubt ", wrote Mr. South. "The very small number of medical men whose names appear in the enormous list of subscribers to the (Nightingale) Fund cannot have passed unnoticed. Only three physicians and one surgeon from one London Hospital and one physician from a second are found among the supporters." The Nightingale Training School was launched in an atmosphere of criticism. Its way was not to be made easy and the probationers would be watched by unfriendly eyes.

The object of the school was to produce nurses capable of training others. The Nightingale nurses were not to undertake private nursing, they were to take posts in hospitals and public institutions and establish a higher standard. They were to be missionaries, and as such they must be above suspicion. If scandal centred upon a Nightingale nurse, an active opposition was eagerly waiting to fasten on it. One piece of indiscretion, one false step and hopes of reforming the nursing profession and elevating its status might be set back for years. The future of nursing depended on how these young women behaved themselves. As a result, candidates to become Nightingale probationers were subjected to minute examination and there was great difficulty in finding young women of suitable character.

In May 1860 advertisements appeared inviting applications for admission. The response was discouraging. However, fifteen candidates were chosen and on July 9th, 1860, the Nightingale School opened. No pupil was admitted without a certificate of good character, and the training was to last for one year—so long a period was hitherto unheard of. The Nightingale probationers lived in a nurses " Home " ; this was a novel idea originated by Miss Nightingale, and it was received with disapproval by the opposition. An upper-floor of a wing of St. Thomas's was fitted up so that each probationer had a bedroom to herself, there was a common sitting-room, and the sister in charge had a bedroom and sitting-room of her own. Books, maps, prints and a supply of flowers

346

from Embley were sent by Miss Nightingale, though Mrs. Wardroper feared that flowers came dangerously near over-indulgence. The Nightingale probationers wore a brown uniform with a white apron and cap. Board, lodging, washing and uniform were provided by the Fund. Each probationer was given £10 for her personal expenses during training. At the end of the year's course the nurses who had satisfied the examiners were placed on the hospital register as " Certificated Nurses ". A first-class cash gratuity of £5 and a second-class cash gratuity of £3 were offered to nurses who were certified to have worked efficiently in a hospital for one year after completing their training.

It was a standard of life which nurses had never been offered before, and the opposition sneered at Miss Nightingale's " lady nurses ". She did not believe nurses should be housemaids. " The Nurses ", she wrote, " should not scour; it is waste of power." The Nightingale probationers worked hard, attending daily lectures from the medical staff and sisters of St. Thomas's Hospital and bi-weekly addresses from the chaplain. They were required to take notes, to be ready to submit their notebooks at any time for inspection and to pass examinations both written and oral; they acted as assistant nurses in the wards and received practical instruction from surgeons and sisters. What was required of them in work, however, was as nothing compared to what was required in behaviour. Every month a report entitled " Personal Character and Acquire-ments " was filled in by Mrs. Wardroper, who exercised the closest possible supervision over every probationer. The details of the report, planned by Miss Nightingale, were minutely comprehensive. Two main heads, " Moral Record " and " Technical Record ", were further subdivided; " Moral Record " had six subdivisions—punctuality, quietness, trust-worthiness, personal neatness, cleanliness, ward manage-ment and order. " Technical Record " had fourteen sub-divisions which were again subdivided, in some cases a dozen times. Mrs. Wardroper wrote against each head " excellent ", " good ", " moderate ", " imperfect " or " o ". In addition she wrote confidential personal reports on each probationer.

Even this information was felt by Miss Nightingale to be

347

insufficient. She was obsessed by the importance of these young women. The future of nursing hung on their behaviour. Their natures, their thoughts, might wreck or make the work. If only she could get inside their minds. She originated a new scheme by which each probationer was required to keep a daily diary which was read by her at the end of the month. " I am sure ", wrote Mrs. Wardroper, " that your approbation will stimulate them to increased perseverance." Miss Nightingale noticed that some of the probationers were weak in spelling and arranged for them to have spelling drill.

Flirtation was punished by instant dismissal—the girls selected and trained to redeem nursing must not allow themselves to be women ; their mission was to prove that the woman can be sunk in the nurse. No Nightingale probationer was permitted to leave the Home alone, two must always go out together. " Of course we always parted as soon as we got to the corner ", wrote one of the original probationers in a reminiscence.

The character and behaviour of each probationer was discussed by Miss Nightingale and Mrs. Wardroper in anxious conferences and long letters. One set of letters considered in detail whether a certain young woman ought to be dismissed because she " made eyes ". She was a competent nurse and her moral character was " said to be unexceptionable ", but she seemed unable to refrain from " using her eyes unpleasantly ". Before she was dismissed, however, ought they not to consider whether she might not grow out of this objectionable habit as she became older ?

Strictness was necessary. The Nightingale nurse must establish her character in a profession proverbial for immorality. Neat, lady-like, vestal, above suspicion, she must be the incarnate denial that a hospital nurse need be drunken, ignorant and promiscuous. It soon became evident that the school was succeeding. Within a few months a flood of applications was being received to bespeak the services of Nightingale probationers as soon as their period of training was completed.

A second experiment, financed out of the Nightingale Fund at the end of 1861, was the establishment of a Training School for Midwives. With the co-operation of the authorities of King's College a maternity ward was equipped, and the physician accoucheurs of the hospital agreed to assist in giving a six months' training; it was a scheme which Miss Nightingale had had at heart since her Harley Street days. On September 24th, 1861, she wrote to Harriet Martineau: "In nearly every country but our own there is a Government School for Midwives. I trust that our school may lead the way towards supplying a long felt want in England."

The school trained midwives, not only to work in hospitals, but to deliver women in their own homes. During their training at the hospital the candidates paid for board and lodging, but received instruction free. A promising beginning was made, and a number of owners of large estates sent women at their own expense to be trained as village midwives. Unfortunately, after more than two years of success, an outbreak of puerperal sepsis brought the scheme to an abrupt end, but Miss Nightingale's interest in rural problems of health continued, and she was constantly consulted on the selection and training of village nurses.

Through these years of unremitting toil her sole recreation was theological and metaphysical speculation. She never went out, she seldom rose from her couch. She had separated herself from her family, she had cut herself off from her friends. Aunt Mai and Clough shared her passion for metaphysical discussion, and the speculation the three shared gave their affection a transcendental quality.

In the summer of 1858 she turned again to the philosophical manuscript she had written in 1851 designed to provide a new religion for intelligent artisans. She sent it to Dr. Sutherland, who wrote on July 7th to Aunt Mai that he "disagreed entirely and vehemently" with her theory, but "I have preferred sending this to you because poor Florence is very unwell and in our own work we have enough of difference of opinion to make it desirable not to have more". In spite of this discouragement Miss Nightingale, assisted by Aunt Mai and Clough, did a considerable amount of work on the manuscript during the following year, and at the end of 1859 had it privately printed under the title *Suggestions for Thought*.

She had a strong affection for the book, she believed it to be an important work, and she determined to obtain unbiased opinions. She sent out a number of copies anonymously,

349

with a letter asking if, in the opinion of the recipient, the book should be offered to the general public. A copy was sent to Richard Monckton Milnes, who identified the author and wrote to her on January 21st, 1860: " I do not think the theory of omnipotent and implacable *Law* is any more satisfactory to the disturbed and distracted mind than that of a beneficent and benevolent Deity ". As to its suitability for the " Artizans of England " he could not express an opinion as he had " a morbid horror of touching on these subjects with what people call the ' lower classes ' ". The book, he added, should be revised. The letter ended on a wistful note : " My two little women are well and happy. I am as much of both as I believe is good for me."

From John Stuart Mill she obtained unqualified approval. *Suggestions for Thought* was not sent to him anonymously—a copy was brought to him by Edwin Chadwick, who first sent him a copy of *Notes on Nursing*. " I do not need it ", wrote Mill, " to enable me to share the admiration which is felt towards Miss Nightingale more universally, I should imagine, than towards any other living person." He read *Suggestions for Thought* with care, annotating the copy in the margin ; and he wrote on September 23rd, 1860, giving his verdict in favour of publication. He was " strongly in the affirmative . . . there is very much of it with which I am in entire agreement and strong sympathy ".

An anonymous copy was sent to Benjamin Jowett by Clough. Jowett, at this time a tutor of Balliol, was Clough's close friend. He wrote one letter of criticism to Clough " for your friend " ; the second, written on July 22nd, was addressed directly to Miss Nightingale. His verdict was unfavourable : he had " received the impress of a new mind ", but the book must be rewritten. " It is absolutely necessary that it should have some regular plan." He thought that " here and there I traced some degree of irritation in the tone, the book appears to me full of antagonisms—perhaps these could be softened ".

She also sent a copy anonymously to Sir John McNeill, who also identified the author ; and he, too, told her the book must be rewritten and replanned. She wrote that she had not time or energy to undertake it, and regretfully laid the book aside, sending the manuscript to Richard Monckton Milnes for safe keeping. Yet she was not entirely convinced. More than ten years later she sent the manuscript to the historian, Froude. Once more the verdict was unfavourable, and this time she resigned herself. She wrote to him in July 1873: "What you say about its 'want of focus', want of 'form', of its 'bleating propensities', is of course felt by me more than anyone. I would re-write every word—if I could."

Suggestions for Thought was a failure, but it had brought her friendship with Benjamin Jowett. "I do so like Mr. Jowett", she scribbled on the margin of one of Jowett's first letters. In 1860 he was already a celebrated Oxford character. He was a fellow and tutor of Balliol and Regius Professor of Greek, and his personal appearance, wit and eccentricities were University legends. In appearance he was short, cherubic and strikingly handsome on a miniature scale; undergraduates nicknamed him the "downy owl". He spoke in a small piercing voice, "that small sweet voice once heard never to be forgotten".

Jowett, who had no private means, had been educated at St. Paul's, and he had made his career by force of his attainments. In a University which was traditionally the stronghold of conservatism he represented a new order, and he had to endure opposition and disappointment. In 1854 he had failed to be made Master of Balliol; in 1855 he was made Regius Professor of Greek, but his opponents contrived that the appointment should be financially worthless. Four chairs, of which the Regius Professorship of Greek was one, had been founded by Henry VIII; the emoluments attached to the other three chairs were increased—but that held by Jowett was excluded. Until 1865 he received only £40 a year as Regius Professor of Greek. His enemies declared that his ambitions were more social than scholarly, and that he was fonder of the dinner-party than the library. Unquestionably he was worldly wise. It was said that he was entertaining a young cousin to dinner, and the youth was describing to Jowett how he made his way in the world. "When a man insults me I always ask him to dinner," he said. Jowett burst into delighted laughter, and rubbing his hands together exclaimed: "You'll do, dear boy, you'll do."

As Regius Professor Jowett did not confine himself to editing dictionaries and commentaries, but lectured on Plato and encouraged undergraduates to bring him Greek verses and Greek prose: an innovation which scandalised the conservative party in the University. He succeeded in having Plato read in public schools which had previously confined themselves to Aristotle and rhetoric. He was intensely interested in young people, saw his pupils constantly, advised them, and received their confidences. " He wished ", wrote Miss Nightingale, "to bring together the University life and the life of the world, so that the University life should be a direct preparation for the life of the world." He had, she said, " a genius for friendship ". He identified himself with his friends, forming friendships with their friends and relations and entering into their business. When a friend obtained a secretaryship in the Educational Department, the office of the Privy Council became of " sustained interest " to Jowett. He loved children ; he could be, he wrote, "almost mad with fun", delighted in playing the fairy godfather and being " patron in general to all poor devils ". When he became Master of Balliol in 1870 he gave entertainments so wildly assorted that his dinner-parties were known in the University as " Jowett's Jumbles ". The butler was once heard to repress a groan as he took off a guest's coat. "I hope you have no cause for anxiety at home", enquired the guest. " No, sir, it's nothing," replied the butler, " only the Master invited twelve to dinner tonight and you are the eighteenth who has come."

Between Jowett and Miss Nightingale acquaintance quickly became intimacy. Like all the men who were fond of her, Jowett scolded her—she was not to exaggerate, not to fuss, not be so hard on people ; she was to try to be more cheerful, to look back on what she had accomplished and be proud of herself. Affection became devotion, and it was known to their friends that Jowett was pressing her to marry him. She refused, but their friendship was unaltered. They corresponded constantly, and she leaned on his devotion and advice. " My darling Jowett ", she called him.

She needed friendship, for as 1860 drew to its close the structure for which she had sacrificed everything in life crashed round her ears in ruin—Sidney Herbert's health finally collapsed.

XVI   IT WAS THE WORST POSSIBLE MOMENT for him to break down. Everything depended on War Office reorganisation, and War Office reorganisation could be pushed through by Sidney Herbert alone. " One fight more, the last and the best ", wrote Miss Nightingale; let him nerve himself to this final task and he should be released. He should be allowed to resign his office. He should go away where he would, abroad, or to Wilton, or to Ireland. He should shoot, fish, hunt and never be worked on the treadmill again. But he must not fail now. It was a possibility she refused to contemplate. Resentment against life, against fate, against Providence, blinded her. Why should not Sidney Herbert do as she had done ? She had been declared to be at death's door and had driven herself to work day and night. She had proved that serious illness need not interfere with work ; he must do the same. He could not be excused. The work was greater than the man. He must go on, he must be compelled to go on.

She had the habit of disregarding his complaints, and she shut her eyes to his physical condition now. Indeed, his health varied. In November 1859 he insisted on going down to Wilton, spent the week hunting and wrote : " I have been drenched to the skin every day and enjoyed myself very much ". Surely if he could hunt five days a week he could find enough strength to carry through War Office reform. She admitted his health had deteriorated, but so had her own. In February she wrote to Manning : " I am so much weaker that I do not sit up at all now ".

Sidney Herbert's health was not to be the sole catastrophe ; from the beginning of 1860 blow after blow rained on her as if Fate was determined to discover how much she could be made to bear.

In February Dr. Alexander suddenly died of a cerebral haemorrhage. Behind his death lay a history of obstruction and petty intrigue. The departmental machine had been strong enough to break him. Men he had trusted, who had been placed in their positions through his recommendation, had

353

betrayed him. Disillusioned, snubbed, frustrated, he had laboured through the immense amount of work entailed by the Sanitary Commission, and he was engaged in drafting the new Army Medical Regulations when he died. " The honestest man I ever knew ", wrote Sidney Herbert. In a Memorial Letter published by the *Lancet*, Miss Nightingale wrote : " I have never seen his like for directness of purpose, unflinching moral courage and honesty. . . . He died of over-work." His loss was irretrievable ; there was no one to replace him. " His loss undoes a great part of the work I have done ", Miss Nightingale wrote to Sir John McNeill in March 1860. " I wish I had not lived to see it. . . . Mr. Herbert asks who is to be his successor and it seems as if there was not one man in the Department whom one wished to see Director General."

By an unkind fate the next man in seniority was a Dr. Linton, who had opposed her at Scutari and who was the close friend of Sir John Hall and Sir Benjamin Hawes.

While she was still distracted by the loss of Alexander, another blow fell. Aunt Mai returned to her family. Since the previous autumn Aunt Mai's position had been intolerable. Uncle Sam refused to visit her when she was with Florence—he said he would be " de trop ". Her second daughter was to be married that summer and she implored her mother to come home. Aunt Mai had been away from her family over two and a half years, and it was undeniable that Florence, who had taken her from them because she was dying in 1857, was still alive. In the early summer of 1860 she decided it was her duty to return.

Her decision provoked intense bitterness. Miss Nightingale refused to see her or speak to her. Aunt Mai wrote to Embley that she could not send her usual report on Florence's health because she had not seen her for over a week. " I am afraid Florence has no confidence in me any more." Miss Nightingale's bitterness was for the work—not herself. Aunt Mai had dealt the work a fatal blow by depriving her at this critical juncture of the sympathy of the one nearest and dearest to her. " For that was what she was ", Miss Nightingale wrote. Most heartbreaking of all, she had gone back to sacrifice herself to the Moloch of family life, to devour her children and be devoured by them. " There was a time when my

Aunt Mai thought as we do ", wrote Miss Nightingale to Clarkey in 1865. " But she is gone back, just as Republicans become always the worst Jesuits, to the very worst Fetish she could find."

She did not forgive Aunt Mai for nearly twenty years; they never met and the correspondence between them ceased. Uncle Sam was forgiven. She had shared no ideals with him and felt no sense of betrayal. She continued to consult him in her financial affairs and to write him friendly letters.

She could not be left alone. Parthe was married, Fanny far from well; and in June 1860 Hilary Bonham Carter came to the Burlington to take Aunt Mai's place. Clough remained faithful, calling daily and devoting every moment he could snatch from his office to the work, but his health, too, was causing anxiety, and on December 7th, 1860, Miss Nightingale wrote a depressed letter about him to Uncle Sam: " I have always felt that I have been a great drag on Arthur's health and spirits, a much greater one than I should have chosen to be, if I had not promised him to die sooner ".

Alexander was dead, Sidney Herbert fatally handicapped by ill health, and the burden on her increased. It was out of the question for her to leave London, and in August she went to Hampstead once more. She was very feeble, lying all day in bed by an open window in her rooms in South Hill Park, finding solace in the society of her cats and of children. She had Clough's children to stay with her, and on September 1st, 1860, she wrote to Clough's wife describing a visit from the baby. " ' It ' came in its flannel coat to see me. No one had ever prepared me for its Royalty. It sat quite upright, but would not say a word, good or bad. The cats jumped up upon it. It put out its hand with a kind of gracious dignity and caressed them, as if they were presenting Addresses, and they responded in a humble grateful way, quite cowed by infant majesty. Then it put out its little bare cold feet for me to warm, which when I did, it smiled. In about twenty minutes, it waved its hand to go away, still without speaking a word."

Sidney Herbert rode out to see her every day. Forced to stay in London for the second summer in succession, he was weary, feverish and dispirited. The amount of work for ever piling up round him was frightening. He felt " a total inability to deal with business ". " He shrank ", Miss Nightingale wrote to Sir John McNeill in July 1861, " from the Herculean task of cleansing the Augean stable."

Through July, August and September he complained of biliousness, lassitude and headaches. In September Liz asked Florence not to come back to the Burlington because the daily ride out to Hampstead did Sidney so much good ; and she stayed in Hampstead with Hilary Bonham Carter through the autumn.

Sidney Herbert was enduring a martyrdom, while the two women closest to him shut their eyes and drove him on. More than a year before he had told his wife : " Every day I keep the War Office with the House of Commons is *one day taken off my life*". Since then, with Miss Nightingale urging him on one side and Liz on the other, he had forced himself to continue with both. Now he was nearly at the end of his powers. In October and November 1860 his health suddenly grew worse. Perhaps, wrote Florence, it was the London air. She conferred with Liz. He was so much better out of London— perhaps the solution was not to stay in Belgrave Square but to take a house in Hampstead. Liz agreed, and Mrs. Sutherland was sent round the house agents. It was too late. No change of air could save Sidney Herbert now. Early in December he collapsed.

He was pronounced to be suffering from kidney disease, incurable and at an advanced stage : the amount of work he was doing must be cut down drastically and at once. It was practically a death warrant. On December 5th he rode out to Hampstead to see Miss Nightingale. " He was not low, but awe struck ", she wrote to Uncle Sam on December 6th ; " I shall always respect the man for having seen him so."

He remained with her for several hours, his intention being to consider what his future course of action should be. In fact it had already been settled for him. Liz had been to see Florence earlier, before Sidney was well enough to ride out, and they had agreed between themselves what he was to be persuaded to do. Three courses were open to him. He could retire altogether ; he could give up the War Office, and keep his seat in the House of Commons ; he could go to the

356

House of Lords, give up the House of Commons and keep the War Office. For his own sake the first was the best. The doctors had enjoined complete and absolute rest as his only chance. He was worn out and he longed for the peace and quiet of Wilton.

But that choice neither Miss Nightingale nor his wife would allow him to contemplate, nor indeed did he contemplate it himself. Work was his fate. He recognised that and inclined towards the second course. He would give up the War Office and keep his seat in the House of Commons. He was a House of Commons man, he had sat in the House for twenty-eight years and had been brilliantly successful there. He could " do with the House what no one else could ". He was an orator and a matchless negotiator. The work of the War Office he frankly detested. It did not suit him. His talents were wasted. He had never had, as Miss Nightingale frequently told him, any genius for administration. He could not, drive himself as he would, master the enormous mass of intricate detail which War Office reorganisation involved. His mind recoiled from it.

But Miss Nightingale's task was to persuade him to keep the War Office. For the sake of the work, for the sake of War Office reorganisation, he must be persuaded to resign his seat in the Commons, keep the War Office, and go to the House of Lords.

The interview was long, very long, but she succeeded. For the sake of the work the War Office should be kept. " A thousand thanks", wrote Liz, "for all you have said and done." She had forced him to sign his death warrant.

She still refused to admit how fatally ill he was. How else could she justify what she had done? The shock of the doctors' verdict had been great, but presently she began to minimise it: doctors were often wrong; people with so-called fatal diseases often lived for years. " I hope you will not judge too hardly of yourself from these doctors' opinions ", she wrote on December 8th, ". . . it is *not* true that you cannot (sometimes) absolutely mend a damaged organ, almost always keep it comfortably going for many years, by giving Nature fair play. The presence of a large amount of albumen is not proof, in itself, of anything but that Nature is getting rid of something which ought not to be there. Help her by not trying to make any more. I know a very active intellectual London man, now 65, whose albuminous symptoms were accompanied by one, the most advanced of all, which you have never had, but who by sleeping in the country etc., has given himself 15 years good life and may have 15 more. . . . I am not going to bore you with a medical lecture. But I do hope you won't have any vain ideas that you can be spared out of the W.O. You said yourself that there was no one to take your place—and you must know *that* as well as everybody else. It is quite absurd to think Lord de Grey can do it. . . . You cannot be the only person who does not know that you are necessary to the re-organising of the W.O. It is more important to originate good measures than to defend them in the H. of C. . . . I don't believe there is anything in your constitution which makes it evident that disease is getting the upper hand. On the contrary."

He tried to follow her directions. He went down to Wilton and wrote cheerfully on the 12th: " I went out hunting, had a lovely bright day and a good run, and I slept like a top for the first time for some days ".

Early in January he was created a baron with the title of Lord Herbert of Lea, and took his seat in the House of Lords. A friend asked him if he found addressing the Lords difficult. " Difficult ? " he said. " It was like addressing sheeted tombstones by moonlight."

Miss Nightingale showed him no softness, and it almost seemed as if she regarded bad health as her personal monopoly ; what was he called on to bear more than she had borne ? " To him retaining office and giving up the H. of C. is like what it was to me giving up men and taking to regulations ", she wrote to Harriet Martineau on January 1st, 1861. Only once did she permit herself a quick horrified glance at the truth, when, on January 13th, she wrote to Harriet Martineau : " I see death written in the man's face. And, when I think of the possibility of my surviving him, I am glad to feel myself declining so fast." She hid herself behind impatience, harshness ; she blamed him. It was a relief to blame him and to close her eyes to the grim certainty advancing inexorably upon her.

His illness was generally regarded with suspicion. In

358

January 1861 the *Daily News* attacked him in articles said to have been inspired by Benjamin Hawes. He was represented as running away to the House of Lords in pique after having taken on more than he could manage. As late as June 1861 Sir John McNeill declared " the change [to the House of Lords] was almost avowedly an admission of weakness, perhaps mainly physical, but still weakness ".

Liz began to drag her husband on an anxious, melancholy round, consulting doctor after doctor, starting with eminent specialists, descending to fashionable quacks, trying treatment after treatment, each started in expectation of a miraculous cure, each only too soon discarded.

Throughout these months Miss Nightingale was plagued by domestic difficulties and disasters. The management of the Burlington she considered inefficient. She had advanced ideas on fresh air and open windows which she tried in vain to put into operation. On August 16th, 1860, she drew up an agreement : " If for one fortnight from this time I find all the doors shut and all the windows open, including those of the two water closets, which also must have their seats shut, I will give the servants a doctor's fee, viz—one guinea ", signed " F. Nightingale ". To this agreement a slip is pinned, " On going downstairs today I found every door open and every window shut ".

During this summer she suffered intense irritation from noise made by a water cistern immediately over her bedroom. Shortly afterwards the Burlington changed hands, and she refused to return unless the whole " water apparatus " was removed from over her head ; the new landlord gave his word of honour that it should be done. In the autumn Dr. Sutherland and Hilary Bonham Carter went to inspect her rooms and reported that under the new proprietor there was " a great improvement in house keeping and cleanliness ". But on January 21st, 1861, with a " loud bang ", the cistern emptied itself on her head. Writing to Hilary Bonham Carter next day she described " the ceiling saturated, water dripping at every pore into a wilderness of pots and pans, paper ruined and new carpets wrenched up ". She herself caught a severe chill. Sir Harry Verney, W. E. N. and Uncle Sam were summoned and the landlord was called in. After putting forward various excuses he was driven into a corner by Miss Nightingale and forced to admit that the cistern had never been removed at all. On a fragment of paper she dashed off an angry private note— she considered her male supporters had been ineffectual. " I have had a larger responsibility of human life than ever man or woman had before. And I attribute my success to this. I NEVER GAVE OR TOOK AN EXCUSE.

" Yes, I do see the difference between me and other men. When a disaster happens, I act—and they make excuses."

She had now been at the Burlington for two years, and it was both uncomfortable and expensive. Fanny and Parthe talked of buying a house, but W. E. N. was unwilling to sink a large sum of money in purchasing a house for Florence in her present state of health. However, the difficulty and expense of housing her steadily increased. For months she had two sets of accommodation, the rooms in Hampstead and in the Burlington. She slept at Hampstead and was driven in every day to the Burlington to work, sleeping odd nights at the hotel at her convenience.

In April 1861, Colonel Phipps, Private Secretary to the Prince Consort, wrote to W. E. N. offering Miss Nightingale, on behalf of the Queen, an apartment in Kensington Palace. On April 20th she wrote to W. E. N. sharply declining : " I have to see a great many people on a great variety of subjects and *no residence* would be any use to me which was not near enough the business centre of London to allow me to see these people *at a moment's notice* ". W. E. N. pressed her to reconsider her decision, and a few days later she wrote again with extreme irritation She had discovered that, without her knowledge, the Board of Trade had been approached to find an apartment for her in one of the royal residences. " Sir Harry Verney consulted by Phipps asks Parthe, who advises Kensington. . . . They might as well dispose of me in marriage. What does Parthe know about my work ? Where should I be now if I had taken Parthe's advice ? . . . I cannot see how Sir Harry having been Col. Phipps' school-fellow makes him competent as an adviser."

Miss Nightingale was not easy to live with. In a letter to Uncle Sam on June 2nd, 1861, she described her mental state. " It is the morbid mind of a person who has *no* variety, *no* amusement, *no* gratification or change of any kind . . . no one ever understands . . . the morbid *conscience* of anybody whose nervous system has been overtasked. I am always thinking I might do more or I had better not have done what I did do." Her physical condition was distressing. " *Every day*, from 5 or 6 P.M. to 8 or 9 the next morning, I am totally disqualified from *anything*, even reading an amusing book by that ' grasping' action of the heart . . . like being hung. . . . In addition to this on an average of two days in every week I am totally unable to do anything. . . . I can only lie quietly in bed . . . if I tempt myself by getting up I am entirely laid aside for 3 or 4 hours by the exertion of dressing." Trifles assumed immense importance; finding a servant a new situation and writing a character for her destroyed her peace of mind, she said, for fourteen hours.

When Hilary Bonham Carter joined her a new difficulty arose. Since 1859 Hilary had been devoting an increasing amount of time to her, and Hilary's family complained, first, that Hilary was being victimised, as Aunt Mai had been, and, secondly, that Florence was taking up all Hilary's time and preventing her from working at her drawing.

Miss Nightingale blamed herself. Hilary must devote a certain number of hours each day to work, and to encourage her she agreed to sit for a statuette. It was an important concession, for she had a moral objection to having her likeness taken in any form. " I do not wish to be remembered when I am gone," she said. She had only twice consented to have her photograph taken, once at the direct request of Queen Victoria; in 1864 Watts tried to paint her, but she would see him only twice, and the portrait never progressed beyond a half-finished sketch. The artist asked Mrs. Nightingale to send him photographs and portraits that he might work from, but there were none to send. " Who *can* have persuaded her to sit to him ? " Fanny wrote to Aunt Mai.

For the bust by Steell, now in the Royal United Service Institution, she gave only two sittings ; and then only because it was to be paid for out of the proceeds of a fund raised by small subscriptions from the non-commissioned officers and men of the British Army. On April 9th, 1859, Hilary Bonham Carter wrote to M. Mohl : " I should tell you (tho' it is at present a secret thing) that the bust of the soldiers with their penny subscription has been done . . . please do not mention it to anyone, she begged that we should not do so, and I've seen what useless requests to sit etc. etc. may be brought upon her. . . . She could not sit regularly, nor could she have had a stranger at all, nor could a stranger have done it. Fortunately she had known in Edinboro' more than two years ago a sculptor of much talent, whom she liked too, so much that she said she would sit to him if ever she sat to anyone. (Her friends entreated her much to do so at the time but she always disliked the operation and had always so much to do that it is not wonderful she postponed it—and *sine die*.) So the sculptor was telegraphed for. He had thought and dreamed about making this bust, and I don't think it could have been better. Under the circumstances it is astonishingly good—for she could only give two sittings and not long ones, they wearied her so."

Hilary had been given a unique opportunity. She began the statuette and at first progressed well. Clarkey wrote to Fanny : "I thought it very like, the face was a little too flat and thin and we talked a great deal about it, but it is the only thing that will represent her (Flo) pretty much as she was ". But she did not finish it. Months went by, Hilary stayed with one sister while her husband was away, nursed another sister's children through measles ; but she did not complete the statuette.

" Hi ! It is now the seventh month since you told me that little horrid thing would be done ' Next Monday '—since then 30 Mondays have elapsed ", Miss Nightingale wrote to her in July 1860. Hilary had become uncertain, she altered, doubted, despaired. "What is the state of Hilary's idol ? " wrote Fanny to Parthe. "Like all idolatry I fear it will wreck her fair fame—so much finishing and delaying cannot answer." At the end of August Miss Nightingale refused to leave the Burlington for Hampstead until the statuette was done. Hilary was forced to finish it, but she was dissatisfied and began another. " Really I hope in 5 or 6 weeks you may have the *right* one and really this is so much more like ", she wrote to Parthe.

The second statuette was not satisfactory. Hilary took

advice from everyone and was "almost ill of trying to alter and improve to meet everyone's views and strictures". The head of the first was united with the body of the second. The face was worked over again and again. Finally, she lost heart altogether. "Of the shortcomings and errors of the thing itself, also I don't *think* there is one unknown to me. . . . I am not at present equal to setting to work again—If I am up to it I hope one day to make another ' *last* ' edition but I don't yet know when it will be . . .", she wrote to Parthe in 1861.

The statuette was not finished until the spring of the next year. The sculptor Thomas Woolner was called in to give technical advice on the final version, and it was exhibited at the Royal Academy of 1862. Miss Nightingale's family did not like it. "I have seen our F. in the Royal Academy", wrote Fanny to Parthe, "and am shocked at the poor little finnikin minnikin they call Florence." Nevertheless, and in spite of the fact that it is slight and amateurish, a sketch rather than a finished portrait, the statuette is one of the best likenesses of Miss Nightingale. In 1866 Mrs. Sutherland wrote: "There are photographs of the statuette which (though it seems odd to say so) are more characteristic than the actual portraits, none of which . . . give a real idea of what you were ten years ago".

Unwillingly Miss Nightingale realised that with all her talent, all her charm, all her intelligence, Hilary was frittering her life away. She sat up half the night writing letters which Miss Nightingale did not want written. She exhausted herself over the housekeeping. She got up before seven when she might just as well have stayed in bed. She came home with a cold and would go out again to buy flowers. In January 1861 she was ill and continued to ail through February; in March she went to do a cure at Malvern, and while she was there Miss Nightingale wrote telling her not to come back. "Dearest. I hope that you will have guessed that long before last year had ended, I had quite come to the conclusion that it would not be right for me any more to absorb your life in letter writing and house-keeping. For this I gave you my reasons in five big conversations. . . . If I could, if we were on that kind of terms together, I would go down on my knees and ask you to forgive me for having made such a use of your life. Few things, I believe I may say nothing, weigh now so much on my mind as that I should have authorised, i.e. by its being done in my service, an expenditure of life to avoid which *I* left home. . . . If you like to come back on the terms about the Atelier and the hours which we discussed by letter— as my guest and friend—oh my very best and dearest friend— but not as my letter-writer and housekeeper—let us now discuss what those hours shall be, you settling them before you come back. . . . I have been long convinced that for chronic invalids the best plan is not to have a friend with them to live, unless that friend has a profession of her own and it is a convenience *to her* to live with them.

" That is why a man friend is, I do believe the best, *while* women are what they are now—forlorn as it is to be without a woman friend. And short, and above all definite, stays are better than long undefined stays—the former to be renewed, if desired, by both sides. Now dearest you have my say. I feel I ought to have said and acted upon it all long ago. You will say that I ought not to have said it now. Because you have never felt what I felt about the matter of your life. I hope you will not think that this is said on impulse, or founded on any misunderstanding. It was my conviction two years ago and has been growing ever since. Ever dearest yours gratefully and lovingly. F."

Hilary did not return, and sending her away, Miss Nightingale told Clarkey, was like amputating her own limb.

A month later a fresh blow fell. Clough's health gave way completely. He was told his only chance of survival was complete rest in a warm climate, and in April 1861 he and his wife went abroad to Greece.

She was left entirely alone. In a year she had lost Alexander, Aunt Mai, Hilary and Clough. Only Dr. Sutherland, whom she did not love, was left. She had suffered intense emotional and nervous strain and she was in no condition to face the enormous burden of work involved in War Office reform combined with racking suspense over Sidney Herbert's health.

In January 1861 the scheme for War Office reorganisation was launched. There was to be a pitched battle between the forces of reform and the forces of bureaucracy. Sidney Herbert on the one hand, Benjamin Hawes on the other. Every department was to be reorganised, each official's duties defined and his sphere of responsibility stated and limited. Benjamin Hawes would be stripped of the greater part of his present power, and it was thought he would probably be forced to resign. But Miss Nightingale was not confident. Sidney Herbert was the pivot, Sidney Herbert was the essential, Sidney Herbert alone could carry the scheme through—and she feared Sidney Herbert was weakening. " Our scheme of reorganisation is at last launched at the War Office," she wrote to Sir John McNeill on January 17th, " but I fear Hawes may make it fail. There is no strong hand over him."

Again she hid fear behind impatience. She wrote to Douglas Galton in January that Sidney Herbert was the weak spot in the War Office reorganisation scheme. " No one appreciates as I do Mr. H's great qualities. But no one feels more the defect in him of all administrative capacity in details." Next month she complained of the difficulty in getting him to take action. She told Douglas Galton she had had a long conference with Sidney Herbert on War Office reform: " I don't attach too much value to this. We have had such talks any time this three years and he has never done anything." She accused him of failing to carry out his own intentions. By March she was frantic, declaring that Sidney Herbert was inefficient. She warned Douglas Galton, " though he says he will set about your committee as soon as ever you like, make haste, for he is like the son who said ' I go and goeth not ' ". She railed at his delays, she complained of " the difficulty of bringing him up to scratch ", the impossibility of getting a decision from him, his " total incapacity for attending to an administrative question for a single hour ". She obstinately refused to recognise that he was a dying man. " He is a great deal better of that there is no doubt ", she wrote to Liz in March, and added, " he is a bad patient ". On May 14th she wrote: " I am sure the Cid thinks ' *Oh she does not know how weak I feel* and how much worse in general health ' . . . but I do. I see it every time I see him and sorrowfully perceive that he *is* weaker and thinner—and yet I don't think him worse in general health, not materially worse. He has not one cardinal symptom of confirmed disease." On May 31st she wrote : " You are always in the clouds or in the slough of despond about him. There is no proof that he has organic disease, other than incipient." The opinion of the doctors was against her, but she dismissed their opinion. " Almost all London physicians are quacks."

She spared him nothing; she stood behind him insisting that his sick mind should flog itself on, his weary spirit brace itself for fresh struggle. No one intervened on his behalf, Liz seconded her demands, and he bore it all with " angelic temper ", frequently expressing his admiration for poor Florence who though so gravely ill still worked on. By the end of May it was useless for her to rail at him—what she demanded he no longer had the power to attempt. Disease was advancing with horrible swiftness. He spent the mornings on a sofa in Belgrave Square drinking gulps of brandy until he had the strength to crawl down to the War Office, where he arrived too exhausted to work. In fact, he was dying on his feet ; an examination, made after his death two months later, showed disease so far advanced that it was a miracle he had been able to work at all for the past year.

The end came in June. In the first week in June he collapsed, and on June 7th he wrote to Miss Nightingale telling her he could struggle no longer. He must resign the War Office and retire. It was the letter of a beaten man. " As to organisation I am at my wits end. The real truth is that I do not understand it." He suggested that he should remain in office for a few weeks longer so that he could carry through, as a last gesture, certain points of internal organisa-tion and military hospital reform.

On June 8th she replied, bitterly, contemptuously and cruelly. He had failed her. She refused to accept his health as an excuse. " I believe you have many years of usefulness before you. I have repeated so often my view of your case— and I never felt more sure of any physical fact in my life—that I will not trouble you with writing my letters all over again." She told him what his failure meant. Their work was ruined. War Office reorganisation was a general wreck. The reform of military hospitals was a general wreck. The suggestion that he should stay on in office just long enough to carry through

366

certain essential reforms she contemptuously rejected. " *No* reform had better be done by anyone about to leave office. . . . How perfectly ineffective is a reform unless the reformer remains long enough at the head TO MAKE IT WORK." For herself personally there was nothing he could do, but on Douglas Galton's behalf she asked him to establish and define Galton's position at the War Office, where his authority had been questioned. " I consider your letter as quite final about the reorganisation of the W.O. And I promise never to speak of it again. Many women will not trouble you by breaking their hearts about the organisation of an office—that's one comfort. . . . *Hawes has won.* If you will not think me profane I will say ' Hell hath gotten the victory.' "

She cut herself off from him. He was still at the War Office preparing to hand over to his successor. She would not see him or write to him. Uncle Sam remonstrated with her and was told, " there is no uneasiness between me and Lord H. I am sure he does not at all realise what I feel about his failure, but thinks I do not see him or write to him because of my own health." He did realise and he could not bear it. Her anger he had always been able to bear, but he could not endure her unhappiness. " Poor Florence "—he used the phrase so often. She gave up so much and she was doomed to fail. He had always seen that she must fail, that the sacrifice must be in vain ; from the beginning he had known that the task she insisted on undertaking was too difficult. But she had almost made him believe that faith could move mountains. Poor Florence.

It was not in his nature to leave her to eat her heart out ; he had always said, "It takes two to make a quarrel and I won't be one ". Ill and harried as he was, he went to face her. She was in the old familiar rooms at the Burlington. Here, where so much had been endured, so much had been hoped, so much had been sacrificed, a terrible interview took place. In September 1861 in a letter to Harriet Martineau she described what passed between them. She was a woman possessed, she was consumed with grief and rage, she would not see that she had before her a dying man. By failing to endure —and who could be asked to endure more than she had endured ?—he was dooming the British Army. She felt no more pity for him than if he had in fact been an inanimate tool breaking at the crucial moment in her hand, and she lashed him with her tongue. " A Sidney Herbert beaten by a Ben Hawes is a greater humiliation than the disaster of Scutari," she told him implacably. " No man in my day has thrown away so noble a game with all the winning cards in his hands." She said that he bore it all. He did not justify himself. " And his angelic temper with me I shall never forget."

Did she break his heart, or had he already passed beyond her power to wound? The end had almost come. He had intended when he resigned to remain at the War Office clearing up his work for some weeks, but within a fortnight he had another and even more serious collapse. He was ordered to give up work at once, and to go to Spa for a cure. On July 9th he came to the Burlington to say good-bye to her. They were not alone. He could no longer walk easily, and he was brought in a carriage and assisted up the stairs. She never saw him again.

He managed to reach Spa, but his condition was hopeless. He wished to be at Wilton, and on the 25th he came home. It was evident that he was dying. He reached Wilton, saw again the place where he loved every spot as if it was a living person, and early in the morning of August 2nd, 1861, he died. Liz kept notes of his last hours and his last words for Florence. His last coherent thought, she wrote, was of Douglas Galton's position in the War Office which Florence had asked him to establish, his last murmur " Poor Florence . . . poor Florence, our joint work unfinished." " And these words he repeated twice."

Miss Nightingale was in Hampstead when she heard the news. She was overwhelmed. Anguish, despair rushed in on her like the bursting of a dam. She hurried down to the Burlington where she collapsed, and she was seriously ill for nearly four weeks. Uncle Sam took charge of her affairs, informing all correspondents by her orders that " a great and overwhelming affliction entirely precludes Miss Nightingale from attending to any business ".

The structure of her existence had been destroyed at a single blow. " He takes my life with him ", she told W. E. N.

" My work, the object of my life, the means to do it, all in one depart with him. . . . Now not one man remains (that I can call a man) of all whom I began work with five years ago. And I alone of all men ' most deject and wretched ' survive them all. I am sure I meant to have died." Successive frenzies of grief, of longing, of rebellion swept over her; the blow was too cruel, too undeserved, too hideous in the utter wreckage it involved. She found it difficult not to blame God, who possessed, after all, absolute power, for letting Sidney Herbert die. Sidney Herbert's death "involved the misfortune moral and physical of five hundred thousand men", and it would have been "but to set aside a few trifling physical laws to save him ".

There was no doubt of her agony and yet—it was not quite what might have been expected. She felt grief, longing, the hopeless regret which follows bereavement, but she did not feel remorse. She felt she was justified. She knew that Sidney Herbert had found the burden of life almost too heavy to bear, that he had been overworked, harried and subjected to unjust criticism, and she regretted it had been necessary for her to add to his burdens. But the necessity had existed, it had been her duty to act as she did; and she had nothing with which to reproach herself. In the letter to Harriet Martineau of September 9th she wrote : " I too was hard on him ". It was the only admission she ever made that she had anything to regret. In the same letter in which she told Harriet Martineau of the " angelic temper " with which he bore the hard things she said to him, she added implacably, " at the same time he knew that what I said was true ".

He died with a broken heart, but she never admitted she had done anything towards breaking it. That had come about through a combination of the world's cruelty and his own weakness. She never felt she was to blame.

Yet now he was dead an extraordinary change took place in her. Did she feel she wanted to make up to him for something? While Sidney Herbert was alive she had been the teacher, he the pupil, she had been the hand, he the instrument. Now he was dead she called him her " Master ". It was the name by which she always referred to him. She who had criticised him never uttered now a word that was not

369

praise, she who had lashed him with her tongue, now abased herself before him. She spoke of herself as his adoring disciple. " I loved and served him as no one else ", she wrote to Sir John McNeill.

She developed an intense possessiveness about him. No other claim must equal hers; no knowledge of him could be compared with her knowledge. " I understood him as no one else ", she wrote. It was the old story. What she felt, what she endured, must be unique. No illness was to be compared with her illness, no self-sacrifice was to be compared with her self-sacrifice, no grief could rival her grief. She would not even admit a wife could be more bereaved. " How happy widows are," she wrote to Uncle Sam on August 14th, 1861, " because people don't write them harassing letters in the first week of their widowhood and yet I know of no widow more desolate than I."

Hand in hand with intense jealous emotion came resentment. The world did not understand, friends did not understand, they had wrong ideas, miserable misapprehensions.

In fact, the world was doing Sidney Herbert less than justice. His obituary notices were cold. The disasters in the Crimea were remembered, but it seemed that no one was aware of the benefits which had since been conferred on the British Army through him. His friends thought that something should be written which did justice to his achievements ; and Miss Nightingale was approached by Gladstone to write a short memoir. On August 21st, in a turmoil of grief, irritation and misery, she wrote a vast letter to Sir John McNeill saying she knew nothing about what had appeared in newspapers. As far as she was concerned, she had stopped all newspapers from the day of Sidney Herbert's death because she could not bear to read one line about him. But " before he was cold in his grave his wife, Mr. Gladstone and the War Office have done nothing but harass me. . . . Twice in the *first week* after his death I was written to for materials for his life. Mr. Gladstone was one of these as you will guess. And he enclosed me a sketch written by *her*. There was not one word of truth in it from beginning to end ! ! ! She represented him as having triumphed (and quoted words *of his* to this effect) in having effected the reorganisation of the War Office, which he died of regret for not having done. I told Mr. Gladstone a little of the real truth and wrote at his request a slight sketch of what he had done. (And the week was not out before *she* wrote to me for another.) . . . This is just what I most dreaded and least asked. In fact I really would hide myself in the East of London not to do it."

Grief, resentment, irritation, despair, discharged themselves in the floods of words, which were her safety valve. But when irritation and resentment were discharged, as in all the crises of her life, justice and generosity remained behind ; and when fury at Liz's obtuseness had run its course, there emerged recognition of her qualities and rights, and Miss Nightingale became the support and consolation of Sidney Herbert's widow.

During the first fortnight after her husband's death, Liz wrote to her five times. "You will say the children ought to be a comfort to me," she wrote on August 14th, 1861, "but I suppose I am not naturally fond of children—at any rate I have never been used to be much with them. He was *my all*. He is gone." "I am coming to town at the end of the month and do so long to see you", she wrote on September 9th, 1861. "I would not do you the harm I did once. There is nothing left for me to hope or fear." "You know all I have to bear more than anyone else ", she wrote in November 1861.

She continued to include Miss Nightingale in her family life after Sidney Herbert's death. "I cannot help repeating that there is a great 'fond' of justice and magnanimity in her ", Miss Nightingale wrote to W. E. N. in May 1862. "I am always first with her because I was first with him. My claim to be consulted, to be informed is always recognised."

But she could not leave Sidney Herbert's reputation to the uninformed panegyrics of his wife or to the faint praises of men like General Sir John Burgoyne, who said at a memorial meeting : "Lord Herbert's hobby was to promote the health and comfort of the soldier and his pet was Miss Nightingale who followed the same pursuit." She reconsidered her decision and went to the Burlington, where she shut herself up for a fortnight, writing an account of Sidney Herbert's work for the army which she sent to Mr. Gladstone. He did not use it. On November 8th, 1861, she wrote to Dr. Graham

Balfour: " Mr. Gladstone called upon me and, as I was not able to see him, wrote to me to furnish a short memoir of what my dear master and I had done during the five years that he and I worked together. . . . I believed this was for a newspaper article. But Mr. Gladstone, after he had received it, wrote to me and said it was 'too important' for that and it was to be worked up into something ' longer and better '. I have heard nothing more, nor am I anxious to hear."

On August 21st she had told Sir John McNeill that she had asked Gladstone to assume Sidney Herbert's mantle. " I took advantage of my opportunity and told Mr. Gladstone a little of what he [Sidney Herbert] had *not* done, asking him whether I should tell him the rest, and *asking* him whether I should *ask* him to help in it for S. Herbert's sake. The reply was truly Gladstonian—cautious, cold, complimentary yet eloquent—but evidently intending to do nothing."

Her memoir was privately printed in 1861 and privately circulated under the title, *Private and Confidential. Sidney Herbert—on his Services to the Army.* In 1862 the memoir was enlarged, read as a paper at the London meeting of the Congrès de Bienfaisance in June and subsequently published as a pamphlet under the title, *Army Sanitary Administration and its Reform under the late Lord Herbert.*

Sidney Herbert has left little impression. His term of office was a period of great and promising beginnings fated to come to almost nothing. Many years were to pass before the reforms for which he and Miss Nightingale laboured became realities. Much of what he did was undone by his successors; many improvements have necessarily been superseded and forgotten.

None the less, his term of office is marked by the first improvements in the health administration and living conditions of the British Army. When the Barrack and Hospital Commission began to inspect the barracks and hospitals of the British Army in 1857 it was found the troops were living in slum conditions. Barracks were frequently undrained and without water supply. Rooms were unlighted except by farthing dips —the allowance was two to a large room, and the resulting illumination was so dim that it was impossible to see to read. Cooking facilities were totally inadequate, and boiling was almost invariably the only method of cooking. Married couples lived, ate and slept together in low, dark, unventilated rooms where privacy was unknown. As many as thirty couples were quartered in one room, separated from each other only by blankets hung from the ceiling. Barrack rooms had no means of heating. The men had no facilities for keeping clean. One jack-towel, one piece of soap and one basin was the ordinary allowance for fifty men. There was no means of drying wet clothes. The men had no place where they could read or write. As in Scutari, the only facilities the authorities provided were facilities for drinking. Overcrowding, insufficient ventilation, defective drainage, in conjunction with bad food badly cooked, resulted in the prevalence of the " pulmonary and zymotic complaints " which were responsible for raising the death-rate in barracks to double the figure of the death-rate in civil life. Conditions in military hospitals were equally deplorable.

Under Sidney Herbert a start was made on demolishing buildings condemned by the Commissioners and on reconditioning others. Barrack rooms and hospital wards were warmed and ventilated. Farthing dips were replaced by gas. Water was laid on. Kitchens were provided with ovens for roasting and baking. A training school for army cooks was established on lines laid down by Soyer. After his death much of this work was abandoned or shelved, with the result that thirty years later the nation was shocked by a series of barrack scandals. Nevertheless, what had been done was of importance. General principles laid down in the Barrack Commission's Report had actually been put into practice, and the British Army owes Sidney Herbert the first substantial improvements in its barracks and hospital accommodation.

On June 8th, 1861, Miss Nightingale had written to him: " The whole Army world is beginning to acknowledge the essential importance of ' Regimental Statistics '. Col. Greathed, really a first rate man, says that, however kind, anxious and efficient comm. officers (himself included) are about their men, *not one* has the least idea how many he took out, how many he brought back, why he lost them or how etc. etc."

Under Sidney Herbert the Statistical Branch of the Army Medical Department was established and the first Annual Report on the Health of the Army issued in 1861.

In face of strong opposition he succeeded in founding the Army Medical School. The school weathered its early misfortunes at Chatham and was subsequently moved to Netley, where it remained until it became the nucleus of the Royal Army Medical College of today.

Most difficult of all, the Army Medical Department was reorganised. A new warrant for Army Medical Officers and new regulations for the Army Medical Department were drawn up in 1858 and 1859 and forced through during Sidney Herbert's term of office, but they have long since vanished in subsequent reorganisations and reforms. What Sidney Herbert and Miss Nightingale succeeded in achieving, through years of thankless toil and heartbreaking disappointment, can best be conveyed in general terms. They succeeded in establishing the principle that the soldier's *health* must be looked after as well as his sickness. They succeeded in introducing the idea of sanitation into army administration by means of a Sanitary Code which constituted the regimental medical officer the sanitary adviser of his commanding officer and placed joint responsibility on both doctor and commanding officer for the health of the troops under their care. The regulations they drew up for the administration of regimental and general hospitals in peace and in war were based not merely on disciplinary but on sanitary requirements. The supplying of hospitals was reformed by a new Purveyors' Warrant which " defined with precision the duties of each class of Purveying Officers together with their relation to the Army Medical Department ". A Corps of Hospital Orderlies was instituted to replace the stupid and drunken louts who had caused so much suffering to the sick in the Crimea. The commanding officer and the medical officer were to act in consultation. The good health of his men was to be as much the business of their commanding officer as their proficiency in drill.

In forcing the importance of the soldier's health on his officers, they did not stop short at physical health. They included his moral and mental well-being. To officers who, a short time ago, had been accustomed to have their troops habitually billeted in common alehouses, they declared that the barracks must be made the soldier's home. A committee was appointed, including Colonel Lefroy, Douglas Galton and Dr. Sutherland, to plan the establishment of soldiers' clubs, reading-rooms and recreation rooms in every barracks and to supply the troops with opportunities to play out-door games and attend concerts, lectures and courses of training in work-shops as an alternative to "the demoralising dram shop". The committee was set up at Miss Nightingale's request as a result of her army welfare work at Scutari. Its official report was not published until August 24th, 1861, after Sidney Herbert's death, but meanwhile clubs and reading-rooms with opportunities for "rational recreation" had been established with "great success" at Chatham, Gibraltar and Montreal. A large part of the expense was met by Miss Nightingale and Mr. Herbert from their private purses and from funds contributed by their friends.

At the end of her paper on Sidney Herbert's services to the army Miss Nightingale gave some striking figures. In the three years during which Sidney Herbert was Secretary of State for War only one-half of the men who entered the army died per annum (on home stations) as had previously died. The total mortality on home stations from all diseases was less than the former mortality from chest diseases and consumption alone. Such was the immediate and startling result of better food, more warmth, more sanitation and more fresh air. Sidney Herbert, she wrote, should be remembered "as the first War Minister who ever seriously set himself to the task of saving life".

It was his personal tragedy that fate called on him to expend his genius on a subject for which he was temperamentally unsuited. But he did not sacrifice himself in vain. The British Army was fortunate in finding such a champion. Without his influence, the prestige deriving from his high standing, and his altruism, the cause of the British soldier might well have languished for another half-century. He died before his work was done and no outstanding reform is associated with his name, but he succeeded in making the health of the British soldier an issue of first-class importance, which no subsequent administration could ignore. The Royal Sanitary Commission to enquire into the Health of the Army of 1857 may not have done all that was anticipated in the first flush of hope. But that it should have sat at all was a triumph and marked the dawn of a new age.

When Miss Nightingale had finished writing her memoir she left the Burlington for ever. It was haunted, she could never bring herself to go back there. She could see Sidney Herbert in the street. " I could not bear to look down Burlington Street where I had seen him so often." And Sidney Herbert was not the only ghost. She could see Alexander; Clough, now desperately ill; Aunt Mai who had deserted her; Hilary, the limb she had been forced to cut off. " I have quite decided not to return to the Burlington where one by one my fellow workers whom I had so laboriously got together have been removed from me ", she wrote to W. E. N. on September 9th, 1861. She retired to Hampstead, where she isolated herself completely. She would see no one, fellow workers, family or friends. To overwhelming grief was added blank despair as report after report reached her of Sidney Herbert's work being undone. During the first week after his death three important decisions he had taken were reversed by the Duke of Cambridge, the Commander-in-Chief, " who absolutely cringed to him when alive ", she wrote to Sir John McNeill on August 21st. " On one of these occasions Lord de Grey, who *happened* to be in G. Lewis' room (everything happens —is not done—at that miserable place) said, ' Sir, it is impossible; Ld Herbert decided it—and the Ho of Commons voted it ' and walked out of the room. It was less wise than honest. But it had its effect for the time. G. Lewis was awed and the C-in-Chief silenced. *But only for the time.*"

On September 24th she wrote to Harriet Martineau : " The Commander in Chief rides over the weak and learned Secretary of State (Sir G. Lewis) as if he were straw. Day rooms, Barrack Inspections, Hospitals, all the Sanitary Improvements, it is the same. Not one will they leave untouched." " As for me ", she wrote to Sir John McNeill on August 21st, " I feel like the Wandering Jew—as if I *could not* die."

XVII SHE WAS CONVINCED that her life work was ended. The death of Sidney Herbert had closed the door through which she entered the official world. Great as her influence had been, intimately as she had been concerned in army administration, all had depended upon him. She had never had any official status, she could not force the War Office to use her. She had been inside because he was inside. Now he was gone she would be shut out.

It was the general opinion. In a letter written by one of Aunt Mai's daughters in September 1861, Fanny asked Edwin Chadwick to suggest some new field of work for Florence, "her own being now closed against her". He agreed that her army work was ended, but foresaw for her a long, useful life of labour for others in some different sphere. In the furnished rooms in Hampstead she was wretchedly ill. All the familiar symptoms of her collapses reappeared, fainting, extreme weakness, nausea at the sight of food. In addition, she suffered from nervous twitchings. She insisted on remaining alone.

In 1863 Miss Nightingale wrote of the widowed Queen Victoria: "she always reminds me of the woman in the Greek chorus, with her hands clasped above her head, wailing out her inexpressible despair". It is an apt description of her own behaviour after the death of Sidney Herbert. Shut away in the rooms in Hampstead she wrote letter after letter wailing out ruin. " My poor Master has been dead two months today," she wrote to Dr. Farr on October 2nd, 1861, " too long a time for him not to be forgotten. . . . The dogs have trampled on his dead body. Alas! seven years ago this month I have fought the good fight with the War Office. AND LOST IT." " Every day his decisions . . . his judgments are over-thrown. . . . We have lost the battle. Now all is over ", she wrote to Harriet Martineau in September. " Would I could hide myself underground not to see what I do see ", she told Lady Herbert on August 17th. The overwhelming nature of her loss was recognised and treated with respect. " My heart and

377

hand misgive me", wrote W. E. N. in August 1861, "at the thought of approaching even within the shadow of such grief as yours."

But as the weeks went by sympathy became tempered with irritation. As far as her fellow workers were concerned she might as usefully have been underground as shut away in Hampstead wailing out despair. At the end of September Douglas Galton wrote to her sharply : " Notwithstanding what you say, Sidney Herbert *did* do a great deal, doubtless he left something still to be done. The Medical Department is in itself a great achievement. But perhaps your motto is ' Nihil actum, si quid agendum ' " (Nothing has been accomplished if there is still something to be done). Army reform had not utterly perished with Sidney Herbert. The edifice had collapsed, but there were workers still among the ruins. Douglas Galton was temporary assistant Inspector-General of Fortifications and supervised the erection and maintenance of barracks and hospitals. Lord de Grey, a convinced reformer and a disciple of Sidney Herbert, had been appointed Under-Secretary of State for War. Sir George Lewis, Sidney Herbert's successor, was not unfriendly. On October 21st, 1861, Richard Monckton Milnes wrote, encouraging her to return to work : " I should like you to know how you will find Lord de Grey willing to do all in his power to further your great and wise designs. I say ' in his power ' for that, as you know, is extremely limited. You won't like Sir G. Lewis, but somewhere or other you ought to do so ; for in his sincere way of looking at things and in his critical and curious spirit he is by no means unlike yourself. He makes up his mind, no doubt, no doubt far better to the damnabilities of the work than you would do. . . . I write this about de Grey because I was staying with him not long ago and he expressed himself on the subject with much earnestness."

Even in the dark weeks immediately following Sidney Herbert's death a few points had been gained. In September 1861 the scope of Douglas Galton's appointment as temporary assistant Inspector-General of Fortifications, which had been disputed, was defined and his authority acknowledged over all new barracks and hospital construction works. At the same time the scope of the Barrack and Hospital Commission, on which

Dr. Sutherland was the most influential and active member was enlarged to take in the Mediterranean stations.

A considerable victory was won over the proposed construction of a new General Military Hospital at Woolwich. The Duke of Cambridge, the Commander-in-Chief, had steadily opposed the building of this hospital, and as soon as Sidney Herbert was dead he pressed for cancellation of the scheme. This was the occasion when Lord de Grey " happened " to be in Sir George Lewis's room and said, with more honesty than wisdom : " Sir, it is impossible. Lord Herbert decided it and the House of Commons voted it." The building went forward and eventually, at Miss Nightingale's suggestion, was called the Herbert Hospital.

It was true something might still be done, but how woefully little ! A point here, a point there, might with infinite labour be carried, but all high hopes, all grand schemes had perished. " It is really melancholy ", wrote Douglas Galton after Sidney Herbert had been dead a fortnight, " to see the attempts made on all hands to pull down all that Sidney Herbert laboured to build up."

Victory was no longer a possibility, but every inch of ground must be contested in retreat, to preserve something in the midst of disaster.

Miss Nightingale was drawn back, but the work was bitter to her now. She had dreamed of great achievements ; there were to be no great achievements. All that was left was " desperate guerilla warfare ". Heart-broken and weary, she revolted. " It cannot last. I am worn out and cannot go on long ", she wrote to Harriet Martineau on September 14th, 1861.

Seclusion proved impossible. As soon as she finished her paper on Sidney Herbert's services to the army she went back to Hampstead to shut herself up again, but fresh demands came flooding in. Difficulties were arising in the disposition of the Sidney Herbert Memorial Fund. She was anxious that part of the sum raised should be devoted to the endowment of a Prize Medal at the new Army Medical School. But the success of the school was still dubious, and if she was to succeed in obtaining part of the Memorial Fund she must exert personal influence on the committee. She must come back to London.

At this point she received an appeal which it was impossible to ignore. In April 1861 civil war had been declared between the Northern and Southern States of America. In October an appeal from the Secretary at War in Washington reached Miss Nightingale through the agency of Harriet Martineau, who had a channel of communication with the Northern States through her publisher in New York. She was asked for help in organising hospitals and the care of the sick and wounded. On October 8th she told Dr. Farr she had sent to Washington " all our War Office Forms and Reports, Statistical and other. . . . It appears that they, the Northern States, are quite puzzled by their lack of any Army Organisation ". She also sent Miss Dix, the Superintendent of Nurses at Washington, her evidence before the Commission of 1857, and Harriet Martineau reported that Miss Nightingale's writings were " quoted largely and incessantly in medical journals as a guide to military management in the Northern States ". No channel of communication with the Southern States was available, though Miss Nightingale wrote that she was " horrified at the reports of the sufferings of their wounded ". It was being made evident, had she been willing to be encouraged, how far public opinion had been educated in the importance of health administration to an army in the field. The Secretary of War was petitioned to appoint a Sanitary Commission, plans were drawn up for the inspection of camps, for the introduction of female nurses into hospitals, and for the improvement and supervision of hospital diet and cooking. What she herself had done in the Crimea was reproduced. Though circumstances prevented much of this work being successful, the attempt showed a great change had taken place.

She became involved in a very large correspondence, advising charitable committees, organisations for sick and wounded relief, and religious bodies and women's associations who were working for army welfare. In 1865, when the war was over, the Secretary of the United States Christian Union wrote to her : " Your influence and our indebtedness to you can never be known ".

To remain in Hampstead was impossible, and early in November 1861 she was persuaded to accept Sir Harry Verney's repeated offer of the loan of his London house, and moved to 32 South Street. She was still very feeble, but she persisted in being alone.

She had only been in London a few days when she received another shattering blow: Arthur Hugh Clough died in Florence on November 12th, 1861. Her grief for him was second only to her grief for Sidney Herbert. "Oh Jonathan, my brother Jonathan, my love for thee was very great, passing the love of women", she wrote to Sir John McNeill on November 18th. Clough had united with intellect and wit an extraordinary ability to inspire affection. "I do not know that I have ever cared so much for any man of whom I had seen so little as I did for Clough", Sir John McNeill wrote on November 19th. Miss Nightingale was blamed for misusing his talents, for hastening his end by driving him too hard, and Clough's family did not refrain from expressing their resentment. A fragment of a letter written to her by Jowett in December 1861—the remainder of the letter has been cut away—advises her to "disregard this attack arising from common misery at the death of our dear friend".

It was her nature to be exacting, but she had been both affectionate and generous to Clough. In 1858 she had insisted on making him and his wife a present of £500. "And I had rather they should not say thank you", she wrote. "As for Clough being shy, if I could give him £10,000 a year, it would be a poor acknowledgement of what he has done for us." She helped when he went abroad, especially when he went on his final journey in 1861, and she was devoted to his children, who stayed with her for weeks at a time; her papers contain frequent notes of presents of game, fruit, flowers and concert tickets sent to his house. She had introduced him to his wife, and at her weakest and most harassed she never forgot to send Blanche flowers on the anniversary of her wedding day.

Clough had complemented her as Sidney Herbert had complemented her; he gave her affection and sympathy, his brilliance and grace brought charm into her life. She gave him the energy, the conviction, the certainty which he had somehow fatally lost. His death inflicted a mortal wound. Coming only three months after the death of Sidney Herbert, when she was struggling to recover herself, the effect was crushing. She was totally unnerved. On November 18th she wrote to Douglas Galton, " now hardly a man remains (that I can call a man) of all those I have worked with these five years. I survive them all. I am sure I did not mean to."

" Hardly a man (that I can call a man)." She had used that phrase before when Sidney Herbert died and she was speaking of the most faithful, the most devoted, possibly the most able of them all, of Dr. Sutherland. He alone had done what she demanded, he alone had given up his whole life to the work, yet she had never loved him, never could love him. To love was essential to her; and with Clough lost, Alexander lost, Sidney Herbert lost, she felt herself horribly alone.

On November 19th Hilary Bonham Carter went to see her; she had collapsed and been very ill. " She wept very much ", wrote Hilary to Clarkey on November 20th. " She thinks she may perhaps withdraw her hand from Government matters entirely."

But she was not to be allowed to withdraw her hand. She could not be spared. A fortnight after Clough's death she received an urgent appeal from the War Office. England now seemed on the brink of war with the Northern States of America: two agents of the Southern States had been taken by force from the neutral British steamship *Trent* and carried prisoner to a Northern port. It was an outrage on the British flag, war seemed inevitable, and the Government decided to send reinforcements at once to Canada. On December 3rd Lord de Grey wrote asking if he might call and be advised by her " as to sanitary arrangements generally " for the expedition, including transport, hospitals, the clothing and feeding of the troops and comforts for the sick.

Ill, shattered, sunk in grief though she was, she summoned energy to work night and day. She did far more than advise. She redrafted the proposed instructions to officers in charge of the expedition, and on December 10th Lord de Grey wrote to tell her that every one of her alterations had been adopted. She ascertained the average speed of transport by sledge and calculated the time required to transport the sick over the immense distances of Canada. She drew up schemes for relays of transport and for the setting up of depots containing necessary stores. She investigated the question of clothing and recommended that buffalo robes should be issued to the troops in place of blankets. Her astonishing capacity for detail was unimpaired. On December 19th she wrote to Douglas Galton : " Your draft does not define with sufficient precision the manner in which the meat is to get from the Commissariat into the soldiers' kettle ; and the clothing from the Q.M.G.'s store on to the soldier's back. You must define all this. Otherwise you will have men, as you did in the Crimea, shirking responsibility."

The Canadian Expedition was a successful piece of work. " I have been working just as I did in the time of Sidney Herbert ", she wrote to Clarkey on December 13th, 1861. " We have been shipping off the Expedition to Canada as fast as we can. . . . The War Office were so terrified at the idea of the national indignation if they lost another army, that they have consented to everything."

Through the intervention of the Prince Consort war was avoided. Though mortally ill, he roused himself from his deathbed to insert, with his own hand, modifications in the British despatch which made it possible for the Northern States to withdraw without humiliation. It was his last public act, and a fortnight later he died. Miss Nightingale felt his death was a great national disaster of which the nation was oblivious. " He was ", she wrote to Clarkey, " really a minister. This very few knew. He neither liked nor was liked, but what he has done for this country no one knows."

The Canadian Expedition was a turning-point. She was back in harness, work came rushing in, retirement was impossible. Weary, heartbroken, grief-stricken though she might be, her private feelings must be laid aside and she must force herself to work once more. In a letter to Clarkey, written in December 1861, she compared herself to the widowed Queen. " The Queen has really behaved like a hero. That nervous, anxious, fidgety woman, whose love for him was quite abject in its devotion, has buckled to business at once. . . . She is the only woman in these realms, except perhaps myself, who has a MUST in her life—who must set aside her private griefs and attend to the *respublica*."

Jowett once said Miss Nightingale was the only person he had ever met in whom public feelings were stronger than private feelings. But that did not mean that her private feelings were weak; on the contrary, they were almost over-whelmingly strong, and in 1861, though her sense of duty forced her to dedicate herself to the *respublica*, she was unrecon-ciled to her lot. She resented more than ever the sacrifice demanded of her, she fell even more frequently into frenzies of grief, rage and disgust with the world.

She was horribly lonely. She had no friend, she had no helper. She was entering a period of great toil, relentless self-sacrifice, discouragement, and she had no single soul to give her support.

She looked round the world and what did she see? Women everywhere. The world was full of women and not one of them would help. Rage seized her. What had she not endured from the pretensions, the foolishness, the frivolity, the selfishness of women! All her grief, her pain, concen-trated itself into a passion of contempt and dislike for her own sex. On December 13th she began to pour out to Clarkey, who had just written a book on Madame Récamier, an enor-mous, disconnected diatribe on women : ". . . you say 'women are more sympathetic than men '. Now if I were to write a book out of my experience, I should begin, *Women have no sympathy*. Yours is the tradition—mine is the conviction of experience. I have never found one woman who has altered her life by one iota for me or my opinions. Now look at my experience of men.

" A Statesman, past middle age, absorbed in politics for a quarter of a century, out of *sympathy* with me, remodels his whole life and policy—learns a science, the driest, the most technical, the most difficult, that of administration as far as it concerns the lives of men,—not, as I learned it, in the field from the living experience, but by writing dry regulations in a London room, by my sofa, with me.

" This is what I call real sympathy.

" Another (Alexander whom I made Director General) does very nearly the same thing. He is dead too.

" Clough, a poet born if there ever was one, takes to nursing administration in the same way, for me.

" I only mention three, whose whole lives were re-modelled by sympathy for me. But I could mention very many others—

Farr, McNeill, Tulloch, Storks, Martin, who in a lesser degree have altered their work by my opinions. And, most wonderful of all—a man born without a soul, like Undine—Sutherland. All these elderly men.

" Now just look at the degree in which women have sympathy—as far as my experience is concerned. And my experience of women is almost as large as Europe. And it is so intimate too. I have lived and slept in the same bed with English Countesses and Prussian Bauerinnen, with a closeness of intimacy no one ever had before. No Roman Catholic Supérieure has ever had the charge of women of the most different creeds that I have had. No women has excited ' passions ' among women more than I have.

" Yet I leave no school behind me. My doctrines have taken no hold among women. Not one of my Crimean following learnt anything from me—or gave herself for one moment, after she came home, to carry out the lesson of that war, or of those hospitals. I have lived with a sister 30 years, with an aunt four or five, with a cousin two or three. Not one has altered one hour of her existence for me. Not one has read one of my books so as to be able to save me the trouble of writing or telling it all over again.

" Hilary is the type of want of sympathy. Because she is the most unselfish, and because she has a ' passion ' for me. Yet have I not influenced her by one inch. Nay rather all these women have influenced me, much more than I have them. Parthe always told me, as a reproach, that I was ' more like a man '. Indeed I began to think it was true.

" No woman that I know has ever *appris à apprendre*. And I attribute this to want of sympathy. . . .

" It makes me mad the ' Woman's Rights ' talk about the ' want of a field ' for them—when I know that I would gladly give £500 a year for a Woman Secretary. And two English Superintendents have told me the same. And we can't get *one*.

" As for my own family, their want of the commonest knowledge of contemporary history makes them quite useless as secretaries. They don't know the names of the Cabinet Ministers. They don't know the offices at the Horse Guards. They don't know who of the men of today is dead and who is alive. They don't know which of the Churches has Bishops and which not.

" Now I'm sure I did not know these things. When I went to the Crimea I did not know a Colonel from a Corporal. But there are such things as Army Lists and Almanacs. Yet I never knew a woman who, out of sympathy, would consult one—for my work.

". . . A woman once told me my character would be more sympathised with by men than by women. In one sense, I don't choose to have that said. Sidney Herbert and I were together exactly like two men—exactly like him and Gladstone. And as for Clough, oh Jonathan, my brother Jonathan, my love for thee was very great, PASSING THE LOVE OF WOMEN.

" In another sense I do believe it is true. I do believe I am 'like a man', as Parthe says. But how? *In having sympathy*. I am sure I have nothing else. I am sure I have no genius. I am sure that my contemporaries, Parthe, Hilary, Marianne, Lady Dunsany, were all cleverer than I was, and several of them more unselfish. But not one had a bit of sympathy.

". . . Women crave *for being loved*, not for loving. They scream at you for sympathy all day long, they are incapable of giving *any* in return, for they cannot remember your affairs long enough to do so. . . . They cannot state a fact accurately to another, nor can that other attend to it accurately enough for it to become information. Now is not all this the result of want of sympathy? If you knew what it has been to me, having my aunt instead of S. Herbert, Hilary instead of Clough, etc. etc. etc.—not because the man had power the women none. But simply from what I say of want of attention. I'm sure I don't think what falls from my lips pearls and diamonds. Only, if they are not going to listen, I had so much rather not say it. I'm none too fond of talking. . . .

" People often say to me, you don't know what a wife and mother feels. No, I say, I don't and I'm very glad I don't. And *they* don't know what *I feel*. Why, dear soul, Blanche went away and left her husband for a year ! I am the only person who made any effort to save his life and gave him £500 to go abroad, my hard earned savings. And they are living on that now, his wife and sisters, at Florence. . . .

" I am sick with indignation at what wives and mothers will do of the most egregious selfishness. And people call it all maternal or conjugal affection, and think it pretty to say so. No, no, let each person tell the truth from his own experience.

" Ezekiel went running about naked, 'for a sign'. I can't run about naked because it is not the custom of the country. But I would mount three widows' caps on my head, ' for a sign '. And I would cry. This is for Sidney Herbert, I am his real widow. This is for Arthur Clough, I am his true widow (and I don't find it a comfort that I had two legs to cut off, whereas other people have but one). And this, the biggest widow's cap of all, is for the loss of all sympathy on the part of my nearest and dearest. (For that my aunt was. We were like two lovers.)

". . . This is the shortest day, would it were the last. Adieu dear friend. I am worse. I have had two consultations and they say that all this worry has brought on congestion of the spine, which leads straight to Paralysis. And they say I must not write letters. Whereupon I do it all the more."

Her health was approaching a new crisis. She had already collapsed twice within the last six months, once when Sidney Herbert died in August and again when the news of Clough's death reached her in November. She was alone, devoured by grief, remorse and resentment, unable to rise from her bed, unable to eat. In this condition she had forced herself to work day and night on the Canadian Expedition. On Christmas Eve 1861 she collapsed and was dangerously ill, more dangerously ill than she had been since her collapse in the summer of 1857.

For some weeks she was expected to die. She longed to die but her iron constitution triumphed, and by the middle of January she was able to sit up in bed. But a further stage had been reached in the decline of her health. After this last illness she became bed-ridden and did not leave her room for six years. She moved from house to house but could not walk—she had to be carried. She never saw the outside world, to exchange one set of four walls for another was the only variation in her outlook.

By the end of January 1862 she was convalescent, and she

insisted that the Verneys should come back to their house in time for the spring season. Once more she had to find somewhere to live. In her present state of health a hotel was out of the question and W. E. N. offered to pay the expense of taking a furnished house. A suitable one was found in Chesterfield Street, Mayfair. She spent £100 on new carpets and curtains, and in this house, " a fashionable old maid's house in a fashionable quarter ", through the spring of 1862 she slowly struggled back to sufficient health to enable her to work.

She was gloomy and despairing now beyond description; hope had left her; she was like a man brought back to health so that he might be able to walk to the gallows. " I have lost all ", she wrote to Fanny on March 7th, 1862. " All the others have children or some high and inspiring interest to live for—while I have lost husband and children and all. And am left to the dreary hopeless struggle. . . . It is this desperate guerilla warfare ending in so little which makes me impatient of life. I, who could once do so much . . . I think what I have felt most during my last 3 months of extreme weakness is the not having one single person to give one inspiring word, or even one correct fact. I am glad to end a day which never can come back, gladder to end a night, gladder still to end a month."

The task which lay before her was indeed daunting. The reformers had been appalled at Sidney Herbert's death, but even so they had not fully realised his value. On June 6th, 1862, Miss Nightingale admitted to Douglas Galton: " One did not appreciate the power of Sidney Herbert's hand at the War Office while he was alive ". Her close intimacy with Sidney Herbert could not be repeated, but it was a malign stroke of fate which replaced Sidney Herbert by Sir George Lewis— no two people could have honestly found each other more difficult to understand than Sir George Lewis and Miss Nightingale. His virtues were of a kind which she was unable to appreciate. He was one of the best classical scholars in Europe, extremely industrious, and of unimpeachable integrity, but he lacked warmth. Greville said he was as cold-blooded as a fish. He had written several books in a restrained and polished style on classical and political subjects and had considerable wit. One of his sayings, " the indiscretion of biographers adds a new terror to death ", was often quoted by Miss Nightingale. In his position as Secretary of State for War he deserved sympathy; he had been unwilling to take office, and had accepted only out of public spirit. He felt himself to be temperamentally unfitted for his duties, and was aware that he was ignorant of army administration. He had held his most congenial office when Chancellor of the Exchequer. " I can fancy no fish more out of water than Lewis amidst Armstrong guns and General Officers ", Sidney Herbert had written on July 16th, 1861, adding that he was a gentleman and an honest man. But the nature of his breeding and integrity belonged to the eighteenth rather than the nineteenth century. He was no philanthropist, no reformer. He was able, as Richard Monckton Milnes said, to make up his mind to the " damnabilities of the work ".

By an unhappy accident he had already crossed swords with Miss Nightingale. In 1860, when he was Home Secretary, plans were being prepared for taking a Census in 1861, and Miss Nightingale had wanted " a column on the enumeration paper in which should be entered the number of sick people in each house, with the Diseases. In this way we should have a return of the whole Sick and Diseases in the United Kingdom for one spring day, which would give a good average idea of the Sanitary State of all classes of the population." She also wished to include a House Enquiry which would furnish statistics of the number of occupants in each house, and the number of cellar and basement dwellings and back-to-back houses; and prepared a memorandum which was submitted to Sir George Lewis. She received a snub: both her points, she was informed, had already been considered before the Census Bill was introduced, and it had been decided that the question of health or sickness was " too indeterminate " and that the enumeration and description of houses was not a proper subject to be included in a census of population. She refused to accept defeat, had a question asked in the House, and received a further snub. Sir George Lewis replied that he did not see that the information, even if it could be obtained, would be particularly instructive. She was extremely angry. " It is mere child's play to tell us that what every man of the millions who belong to Friendly Societies does every day of his life, as to registering himself sick or well, cannot be done in the Census ", she wrote on May 10th, 1860, to Mr. Robert Lowe. " It is mere childishness to tell us that it is not important to know what houses the people live in. . . . The connection between the *health* and the dwellings of the population is one of the most important that exists." She refused to let the matter drop, enlisted the sympathy of Lord Shaftesbury and Lord de Grey, and put up a fight in the House of Lords. Again she was defeated, and she attributed it to the fact that Sir George Lewis would not give himself the trouble of forcing the departments to redraft their questions. Henceforward she disliked him. She referred to him as the Muff, she called him cowardly and lazy, she said he was weak.

On his side Sir George Lewis was friendly. In the spring of 1862 he suggested he should call, but she refused on the grounds of her recent illness. Knowing her to be a classical scholar, he sent her one of the classical *jeux d'esprit* in which he excelled, the nursery rhyme " Hey Diddle Diddle " translated into Latin verse. She was not flattered, but enraged, and wrote to Douglas Galton that Sir George Lewis would do far better to keep his mind on the War Office. Meanwhile Sir George followed up " Hey Diddle Diddle " in Latin with " Humpty Dumpty " in Greek.

She never would meet him. The spell which she had cast over Panmure she never would attempt to cast over him. They corresponded politely, but there was never any approach to friendship and he remained one of the few people for whom she refused to say a good word.

However, owing to Sir George Lewis's lack of experience in army administration, Lord de Grey was becoming of increasing importance, and since the Canadian Expedition he had become her friend. Lord de Grey had been born to great position and great wealth. His father, Lord Ripon, was Prime Minister at the time of his birth, and his birthplace was 10 Downing Street. He united an instinctively aristocratic outlook with radical and even revolutionary views. When a young man he had been a member of the Christian socialist movement, and had written a pamphlet which was suppressed. Much of his life was spent in secret spiritual struggles and, at a later date, he astonished his friends by temporarily retiring from public life and entering the Roman Catholic Church. His integrity was beyond question, his capacity for work great, and his sense of public duty very high.

When Miss Nightingale re-entered the War Office after the Canadian Expedition she had Lord de Grey behind her and influence within the departments through Douglas Galton and Dr. Sutherland. Outside the War Office she had a powerful friend and protector in Lord Palmerston, who had become Prime Minister again in 1859.

Almost immediately a crisis arose. On May 15th, 1862, Sir Benjamin Hawes, Permanent Under-Secretary for War, unexpectedly died. Both the man and his office had been major obstacles in the path of reform. The Permanent Under-Secretary for War stood in an administrative bottle-neck. All recommendations and all decisions from all departments of the War Office came to him and were dealt with by him. The departments had contact solely with him; they had no contact with the Minister, the Secretary of State for War. In the course of years his power had become absolute. He could block what schemes he chose, keep back recommendations, fail to pass on decisions; he could frustrate the intentions of the Minister, who was almost helpless in his hands. "He was", wrote Miss Nightingale, "a dictator, an autocrat, irresponsible to Parliament, quite unassailable from any quarter, immovable in the middle of a (so-called) Constitutional Government and under a Secretary of State who *is* responsible to Parliament." One of the fundamental principles of her scheme of War Office reorganisation had been the abolition of the office of Permanent Under-Secretary.

The office had been attacked and the attack had failed. Benjamin Hawes had beaten Sidney Herbert. Now Fate had intervened and he was dead. Supported by Lord de Grey, she pressed urgently for reform. The office of Permanent Under-Secretary should be abolished, the work divided into two parts and performed by two Under-Secretaries, each directly responsible to the Secretary of State for War. The purely military work was to be done by the Military Under-Secretary, a post, already in existence, which had been created by Sidney Herbert, and the health and sanitary administration of the army should be done by a civilian with the title of

Assistant Under-Secretary. She made the bold suggestion that Douglas Galton should be allowed to resign his commission and be appointed to this post as a civilian.

A pitched battle ensued. Objections to splitting the office of the Permanent Under-Secretary into two were strengthened by the name of Sir Charles Trevelyan being put forward as Benjamin Hawes's successor. Sir Charles was an able man and an admirable administrator whom Miss Nightingale liked and respected. But she was not to be turned from her determination. The system was wrong; and " there could be no more fatal mistake than to attempt to offset the evil of a system by introducing into it individuals of merit ". As Permanent Under-Secretary under the present system, Sir Charles Trevelyan would still be " an absolute despot though a wise one ", she wrote to W. E. N. on May 24th, 1862 ; and, " inasmuch as Trevelyan is a better and abler man than Hawes, it would have been *worse* for my reform of principle ".

She succeeded. It was agreed that the work of the office should be divided ; its importance was halved and it became no longer worthy of Sir Charles Trevelyan's consideration.

The next step was to secure the appointment of Douglas Galton as Assistant Under-Secretary. Official opposition was determined, and Miss Nightingale appealed directly to the Prime Minister, Lord Palmerston. Unprecedented as the proposal might be, no other person possessed the necessary qualifications. Lord Palmerston spoke to the Commander-in-Chief, who told him that the appointment was " simply impossible ". Lord Palmerston refused to be deterred. Miss Nightingale had convinced him, as six years ago she had convinced him in the matter of the plans for Netley Hospital. He had been thwarted then, he did not intend to be thwarted now. He ignored the Commander-in-Chief, and directed Sir George Lewis to make the appointment, which he obediently did. Miss Nightingale, who despised Sir George Lewis's powers of administration, said he did not understand what he was doing. On May 24th Douglas Galton was appointed.

She had won a notable victory. With Douglas Galton in charge of the health and sanitary administration of the army, with Lord de Grey as Parliamentary Under-Secretary, with Sir George Lewis acquiescent, she saw War Office reorganisa-

tion as a certainty in the near future; and she allowed herself
to rejoice. On May 24th, 1862, heading her letter " The
poor Queen's Birthday ", she wrote to W. E. N. : " I must tell
you the first joy I have had since poor Sidney Herbert's death.
Lord Palmerston has forced Sir G. Lewis to carry out Mr.
Herbert's and my plan for the re-organisation of the War
Office *in some measure*. Hawes' place is not to be filled up.
Galton is to do his work as Assistant Under-Secretary. . . .
Lord de Grey says he can re-organise the War Office with
Captain Galton, because Sir G. Lewis will know nothing
about it and never inquires. Sir G. Lewis wrote it (innocently)
to the Queen yesterday and Douglas Galton was appointed
today, resigning the Army of course. . . . It has come too
late to give any happiness to Galton, as it has come too late for
me. He seems more depressed than pleased. And I do
believe, if he feels any pleasure, it is that now he can carry out
Sidney Herbert's plans in some measure. And it may seem
some compensation to you for the enormous expense I cause
you, that, if I had not been here, it would not have been done.
Would that Sidney Herbert could have lived to do it himself! "

Her jubilation was short-lived, for no radical change took
place in the War Office. She had hoped too much both from
the reform and the reformers. The reconstitution of the office
of Permanent Under-Secretary was ignored by the departments; Douglas Galton and Lord de Grey, sincere, talented
and hard-working, did not possess the genius, the driving force
which alone could have accomplished what she had called
" the fearful task of cleansing the Augean stable ". Where
Sidney Herbert had failed it was not surprising that Douglas
Galton and Lord de Grey did not succeed.

She was forced to realise that War Office reorganisation as
she and Sidney Herbert had planned it, the wholesale reconstruction of the War Office from top to bottom, was never to
be. She took it quietly; there were no recriminations. In
Sidney Herbert's time she had believed up to the end that success
was possible—if he would only exert himself. She knew that
Douglas Galton and Lord de Grey, with the best intentions,
had not the ability to succeed. On August 8th, 1862, she wrote
to Sir John McNeill : " Lord de Grey and Douglas Galton
miscalculated their powers and their intelligence when they

promised to re-organise the W.O. The administrative work they do well."

It was final defeat and she accepted it. She continued to press Douglas Galton and Lord de Grey in season and out of season for departmental efficiency, but the grand project of complete War Office reorganisation was relinquished for ever.

It was not revived even when, on April 13th, 1863, the situation was changed once more by the sudden death of Sir George Lewis. Three men were possible candidates for the office of Secretary of State for War—Lord Panmure, Mr. Cardwell and Lord de Grey. The prospect of having the Bison once more at the War Office was distasteful, but even more distasteful was the prospect of Mr. Cardwell. Edward Cardwell, who ten years later carried through the most important army reforms of the century, was a man to whom Miss Nightingale failed to do justice. He had been a scholar of Winchester and Balliol, he was conscientious, industrious, eminently discreet, kind-hearted and an excellent public servant. But he lacked charm. Nor did he commend himself to her by being the devoted disciple of Gladstone. They had already met in 1857, while she was working on the first Royal Sanitary Commission, and they had not been attracted to each other.

She plunged into a campaign to secure the appointment of Lord de Grey, but in spite of his experience of army administration there were obstacles. Mr. Gladstone, who was Chancellor of the Exchequer, considered that the Minister in charge of an office representing as much public expenditure as the War Office should sit in the House of Commons rather than in the Lords. It was also known that the Queen was doubtful of the advisability of appointing a Secretary of State for War who had never been in the Cabinet. Miss Nightingale's anxiety was intense.

While Lord de Grey worked under the acquiescent Sir George Lewis it had been possible to carry out Sidney Herbert's plans to some extent, but with Panmure or Cardwell in Sir George Lewis's place the Sidney Herbert régime would end for ever.

Lord Palmerston had been the friend and admirer of Sidney Herbert, and she appealed to him, speaking not with her own voice but with the voice of Sidney Herbert. On April 15th Sir Harry Verney was sent down to read Lord Palmerston a letter she had written, and to read it slowly, so that the contents should not fail to register. On the afternoon of April 15th he wrote describing the interview. " Lord Palmerston was so good as to admit me. I said I had seen you this morning, and that by your desire I requested him to allow me to read a letter to him from you. He said ' Certainly '; and I read it to him rather slowly. Having read it, I said that you had mentioned this morning that within a fortnight of Lord Herbert's death, he had said to you more than once that he hoped Lord de Grey would be his successor. I then added ' I have not to request any reply or any observations on Miss Nightingale's letter. I have only to thank you for your kindness in allowing me to read it.' He took the letter and put it in his pocket. He then asked how you were and where, and I told him. There is a Cabinet at 5.30 this afternoon." A copy of the letter was also sent to Mr. Gladstone before the Cabinet meeting.

At the same time Miss Nightingale appealed urgently to Harriet Martineau for newspaper support. A draft of a telegram, written in her own hand and sent on April 16th, 1863, runs : " From Florence Nightingale to Harriet Martineau— Agitate, agitate, for Lord de Grey to succeed Sir George Lewis ". On the following day the *Daily News* published a leading article pressing for his appointment.

In fact the matter was already decided. Lord Palmerston had once more been convinced. On April 16th, the day after the Cabinet meeting, he went down to Windsor and read Miss Nightingale's letter to the Queen. The appointment of Lord de Grey was then settled ; it was announced as officially approved on April 22nd, 1863.

The appointment ensured that Miss Nightingale's influence in army affairs continued, but her position was not the position she had held when Sidney Herbert was alive. She had then been closely concerned in the internal affairs of the War Office. She had done the work of an administrator. In 1863, not only was her friendship with Lord de Grey very different from her close intimacy with Sidney Herbert, but there was no urgent task, such as the Royal Sanitary Commission of 1857 had been, to bring her directly into War Office affairs. She herself wrote in 1862 that she had done the work of a Secretary of State at the War Office for five years but she was doing that work no longer. She had passed from being an administrator to being an adviser.

As an adviser her position was extraordinary: " I interfering with Government affairs; and the captain of my ship without whom I should never have done it, dying and leaving me, a woman, in charge", she wrote to M. Mohl on January 1st, 1864. "What nonsense people do talk to be sure, about people finding themselves in congenial positions and looking out for congenial work! I am sure if anybody in the world is most unsuited for writing and official work it is I. And yet I have done nothing else for seven years but write Regulations."

For the next four years every problem affecting the health and sanitary administration of the British Army was referred to Miss Nightingale, though she was not only a woman but an invalid who never left her house and for months on end did not leave her bed. She was one of the first experts in Europe on sanitary questions, her vast, detailed and personal knowledge was matchless, and she had infinite wisdom in the ways of Government departments. She had not been writing regulations for seven years in vain. The busy Minister, the harassed Under-Secretary who requested information from Miss Nightingale received it in a form he could immediately use. She was an adept at the carpentry of drafting: " Send me the two versions and I will dove-tail them in ", she wrote in 1862. She had enormous knowledge of the history of the departments, she knew the course of every transaction for years past, she knew where to go for information, she knew where papers were to be found. Secretaries borrowed copies of documents from her which were inexplicably missing from War Office files. She saved trouble to busy men. Once there was work to be done she asked neither for credit nor consideration, only to be allowed to do it. Ministers, Under-Secretaries, Assistant Secretaries wrote to her daily asking her as an expert for expert assistance. It was as if she were indeed a retired Secretary of State with vast experience, willing to devote his life to anonymous and unpaid work. She drafted hundreds of minutes, she drew up warrants and regulations, she wrote official memoranda, letters and summaries for the Ministers' use, she composed instructions.

Her genius for financial administration was extraordinary. She devised a cost-accounting system for the Army Medical Services which was put into operation between 1860 and 1865 and, eighty years later, was still in use. In 1947 the Select Committee on Estimates reported favourably on it, commented that it worked admirably, though in other departments systems installed within the last twenty years had been discarded, and enquired with whom it had originated. They were told—Miss Nightingale.

Her discretion was absolute. In October 1861, in the darkest hours after Sidney Herbert's death, Harriet Martineau proposed that she should supply facts for a series of articles attacking the Commander-in-Chief, the Duke of Cambridge, who was eagerly destroying everything Sidney Herbert had achieved. Harriet Martineau assured Miss Nightingale that she would " shame the Horse Guards ". She refused. There was no prospect at present of getting the Duke of Cambridge removed. Until he could be got rid of he must be endured and, if possible, made use of. She had not achieved her present position through attacks and sensational revelations. In her old phrase, she had " toiled her way into the confidence of the officials ". She was employed not because she was feared but because she made herself useful.

War Office Abstracts list the questions on which she was engaged during one year as a new *Warrant for Apothecaries, Proposals for Equipment of Military Hospitals,* a scheme for the *Organisation of Hospitals for Soldiers' Wives, Proposals for the revision of Army Rations, Warrant and Instructions for Staff Surgeons, Instructions for treatment of yellow fever, Proposals for revision of Purveying and Commissariat in the Colonies, Revised diet sheets for Troop-Ships, Proposals for appointments at Netley and Chatham, Instructions for Treatment of Cholera.* And these were sidelines ; her main work for the Army was still concerned with the improvement of barrack and hospital accommodation and the reform and reconstruction of the Army Medical Department, the two contributions Sidney Herbert had succeeded in making which she carried forward as a sacred trust.

In 1862 the Barrack and Hospital Commission became a standing commission, with Dr. Sutherland as a perpetual member. At the same time the authority and importance of the Commission were increased by taking it out of the control of the Army Medical Department and making it responsible directly to the Secretary of State for War. The new instructions for the reorganised Commission were written by Miss Nightingale, and on June 25th Douglas Galton told her: "Lord de Grey said he had adopted exactly your Minute about the Instructions to the Commission". In 1865 the scope of the Barrack and Hospital Commission was further enlarged and its name changed to the Army Sanitary Committee. In this form it remained in existence for more than thirty years.

She exercised authority over plans for building and reconstructing barracks and hospitals. Douglas Galton had all construction works under his control and submitted almost all plans to her. He leaned, as Sidney Herbert had leaned, not only on her judgment but on her remarkable ability to tear the essentials out of great masses of detail, and her astonishing, unwearying thoroughness. A specimen memorandum on the plans for the new general military hospital at Malta covers more than two dozen foolscap pages.

It was the toughest and driest work, only occasionally enlivened by a gleam of humour. In 1863 Douglas Galton sent her plans for model cavalry barracks; she returned them with the request that the horses should be provided with windows to look out of. "I do not speak from hearsay but from actual personal acquaintance with horses of the most intimate kind", she wrote on June 4th, 1863. "And I assure you they tell me it is of the utmost consequence to their health and spirits when in the loose box to have a window to look out of. A small bulls eye will do. I have told Dr. Sutherland but he has no feeling." On this letter Dr. Sutherland scribbled: "We *have* provided such a window and every horse can see out if he chooses to stand on his hind legs with his fore feet against the wall. It is the least exertion he can put himself to."

The weight of her authority on questions of sanitary construction was recognised outside the War Office. In 1865 the Colonial Office decided to issue a Report on Colonial Prisons, and a Mr. Wright was appointed to prepare it. Asking if he might submit his conclusions for Miss Nightingale's criticism he wrote : " Supposing them to be approved by you, it will be a great advantage if I may state that you approve them ".

The task of reconstructing and reforming the Army Medical Service was the most difficult of all her tasks. Sidney Herbert had succeeded in forcing through new regulations, and as a result new duties and increased responsibilities had been given to medical officers, but almost nothing had been done to improve the conditions of the Service so that men of superior calibre might be attracted into it. " You MUST do something for these doctors," Miss Nightingale wrote to Douglas Galton on December 24th, 1863, " or they will do for you—simply by not coming to you." She urged better training, increased pay, more privileges—but without success. Military expenditure was being cut to the bone and the pay of army doctors was an easy target. On April 6th, 1864, she wrote to Sir James Clark : " I have written threatening letters both to Lord de Grey and to Captain Galton. . . . I have shown how, when we are expecting duties from the Medical Officer, such as sanitary recommendations to his Commanding Officer, which essentially require him to have the standing of a gentleman with his Commanding Officer—we are doing things such as dismounting him at parade, depriving him of presidency at Boards, etc., which, in military life, to a degree which we have no idea of in civil life, deprive him of the weight of a gentleman among gentlemen." The cost of sickness and invaliding to the army was fantastically in excess of any paltry sums spent on the remuneration of doctors. Why would the officials ignore self-evident truths ? She beat herself against their indifference and their stupidity. She became very angry. Week after week, month after month, year after year, through 1862, 1863, 1864, she kept pounding away, writing letters almost daily, in one of the most persistent of her campaigns. " I wrote *for the tenth time* a statement of eight pages with permission to make any use of it they pleased, with my signature as to Lord Herbert's intentions ", she told Sir James Clark on April 9th, 1864, pressing for an increase of pay for medical officers. " You may think I am not wise in being so angry ", she wrote again on April 15th. " But I assure you, when I write civilly I have a civil answer—*and nothing is done.*

When I write furiously, I have a rude letter—*and something is done* (not even then always, *but only then*)."

Bitter opposition came from within the Medical Department itself: the senior members had scores to settle dating back to the Crimea. Opposition blazed up into fury when, in 1862, Miss Nightingale and the Medical Department found themselves on different sides in the controversy over the Contagious Diseases, i.e. Venereal Diseases, Act.

The proportion of men in the British Army invalided with syphilis was disconcertingly high, and since 1861 the War Office had been debating measures to reduce it. The Medical Department recommended that the continental system, by which prostitutes were licensed, inspected and, if necessary, forced to submit to medical treatment, should be adopted. To this system Miss Nightingale was passionately opposed. She considered the continental system morally disgusting, unworkable in practice and unsuccessful in results.

In the hospitals and barracks of Scutari and Balaclava, in the crowded slums of London, she had come into close contact with prostitution. The quality of her mind, her common sense, her humanity freed her from contemporary prejudice. In 1862 she wrote to Edwin Chadwick that the causes of vice in the Army were not " moral but physical ". " They are ", she wrote, " 1. Filthy crowded dwellings. 2. Drunkenness. 3. Ignorance and want of occupation." The way to improve the soldiers' morals was to improve his living conditions. " In civil life you don't expect that *every* workman who does not marry before he is 30 will become diseased ", she wrote to Douglas Galton in June 1861. " In military life you do. Why? Because a workman may have occupation and amusement and consort with honest women. People always say a woman can't know anything about it. It is because I know more about the actual workings of the thing than most men that I cannot hold my tongue. . . . Every time you provide a hospital for sick wives and children, means for making marriage respectable, for making the soldier's life comfortable you are doing something towards it [prevention]. I wish my life were beginning. I think I could do something to inoculate the country with this view of preventing instead of ' cure '." She advanced her views with such force that in 1862 she was officially invited to submit a paper, giving her first-hand experience in barracks and hospitals. With the help of Dr. Sutherland and Dr. Graham Balfour, head of the Army Statistical Department, she compiled statistics proving that the licensing and inspection of prostitutes did not result in a decrease in venereal disease. She had copies of her paper privately circulated among members of the Government, accompanied by a letter in which she urged that the only way to decrease venereal disease was to give the soldier more chances for respectable marriage, better housing, opportunity to learn a trade and places of recreation besides the public-house. Lord de Grey told Douglas Galton that he was shaken by her figures, but Mr. Gladstone, though he said he should approach the question with circumspection, " doubted the possibility of making a standing army a moral institution ".

She had made sufficient impression for the Government to proceed cautiously. In 1863 a committee was set up by the War Office to investigate the results of police inspection of prostitutes in what were termed " protected " armies. The instructions for the committee were drawn up by Miss Nightingale and she was invited to submit a list of suitable members.

Meanwhile the Army Medical Department was becoming more and more infuriated. Though Miss Nightingale's name did not appear, it was an open secret that she was the moving spirit. In July 1863 one of the few scurrilous attacks ever made on her came from a member of the Department, who wrote her anonymously a letter of " vulgar and indecent abuse ", daring her, she told Harriet Martineau on July 25th, to continue with her opposition.

Her reply was to reprint the paper she had written at the official invitation of the War Office and send it to twenty persons likely to influence public opinion ; using the title *Note on the supposed Protection afforded against Venereal Disease by recognising Prostitution and placing it under Police Regulation.* She also supplied Harriet Martineau with figures for a series of articles in the *Daily News.*

The suggestions put forward by the Army Medical Department were of incredible naïveté. One doctor told Dr. Sutherland, " quite gravely, that the only way would be to attach a certain number of these women to each regiment and place them under religious instruction ". Miss Nightingale re-marked, "the prostitutes who survive five years of this life should have good service pensions ". She had great faith in the effect of the enquiry made by the War Office Committee. In January 1864, when a bill enforcing police regulation had actually been drafted and was about to come before the Commons, she wrote to Sir Harry Verney, "wait until the W.O. Committee has published THE FACTS as to the amount of venereal disease in the (so-called) protected armies ". She was wrong. In spite of the War Office enquiry, public opinion was not converted, the House of Commons was overwhelmingly in favour of police regulation and inspection; and in 1864 the Contagious Diseases Act became law. Miss Nightingale said that the War Office deserved the V.C. for their cool intrepidity in the face of facts. The Contagious Diseases Act remained in force until 1883, when it was repealed through the efforts of Mrs. Josephine Butler and Sir James Stansfeld.

The passage of the Act left her depressed. Was she succeeding to any degree, was she accomplishing anything at all? Ill, lonely, grief-stricken, toiling incessantly, living without the slightest relaxation, she was haunted by a settled conviction of failure. Any compromise was defeat. Everything was to be measured against perfection; if it fell short of perfection there was no good in it; and yet, if she would only see it, she was repeatedly presented with solid evidence of how much she had achieved.

In the spring of 1864 she was asked to supply information for a speech to be made in the House of Commons. Lord Hartington, who was Under-Secretary for War, was to defend the increase in the cost of the hospital and medical services for the Army, which had risen from £97,000 in 1853 to no less than £295,000 in 1864. Surely here was cause for congratulation, here was proof of extraordinary progress? She refused to be cheered. She sent Lord Hartington a detailed memorandum, setting out what the nation got for its money, which he used with success. She experienced no gratification and pronounced the speech to be very dull.

In the spring of the following year she had even more remarkable proof of progress. Lord Panmure, now sitting

in the House of Lords as Lord Dalhousie, made an attack on
sanitary principles in general and sanitarians in particular; he
attacked the Herbert Hospital as being " all glass and glare "
and providing only a fraction of the accommodation of his
hospital at Netley; he attacked the wasteful system which
Lord Herbert had inaugurated by paying attention to sanitarians; and, finally, he made a personal attack on Miss
Nightingale herself. He " could not help thinking that all
these unnecessary knick-knacks in hospitals were introduced
partly from the habit, which prevailed at the War Office, of
consulting hygienists not connected with the Army ".

She had prepared Lord de Grey with a reply, and with
customary fair-mindedness had reminded him that Lord
Dalhousie had genuine grievances; he had never received
credit for the measures he took to save the army in the Crimea
or for advising the Queen to issue the warrant for the Royal
Sanitary Commission of 1857. She recommended that his services to the army should be handsomely admitted; in her opinion
the defence of I ~rd Herbert and the sanitarians would then be
more telling. But defence was not necessary—the speech fell
flat. Lord Dalhousie's attack on sanitary science was out of
fashion. In eleven years so great a change had taken place
that his voice seemed to come from a past age.

" Do not fear ", Lord Stanley wrote to Miss Nightingale
on July 10th, 1863, " that Lord Herbert's work will be left
unfinished : sanitary ideas have taken root in the public mind,
and they cannot be treated as visionary. . . . The ground
that has been gained cannot be lost."

If she felt any satisfaction she did not record it. War Office
affairs had become of secondary importance; memoranda, the
drafting of minutes, warrants and instructions, the never-
ending toil involved in the scrutiny of plans for barracks and
hospitals had become sidelines. Another vast undertaking
had come into her life which was overwhelming her and crushing her as no other previous labour had done—the Royal
Sanitary Commission on the Health of the Army in India.

XVIII ONCE MORE, as Miss Nightingale approaches this enormous task, one is overcome by a feeling of hopelessness. It is too much to attempt, the labour is too gigantic, the questions involved too vast and too intricate, the difficulties of distance, language, communication must prove insuperable. She herself is now a bed-ridden invalid of over forty, shattered in health and overwhelmed with other work. Nevertheless, in 1862 and 1863 she reached the peak of her working life; her will conquered her physical disabilities; she drove herself to work as she had never worked before, and as, after this period, she was never able to work again.

The warrant setting up the Royal Sanitary Commission on the Health of the Army in India was issued on May 19th, 1859. Sidney Herbert was then chairman, but he resigned when he became Secretary of State for War in June 1859, and was succeeded by Lord Stanley. However, he continued to be the moving spirit of the Commission and received daily reports from Miss Nightingale. The personnel of the Commission consisted of three sanitary experts, including Dr. Alexander and Dr. Sutherland, a statistician, Dr. Farr and two members of the India Council. Unfortunately Dr. Alexander died before the real work of the Commission began. After his death Miss Nightingale, although on friendly terms with all the members of the Commission, worked almost exclusively with Dr. Sutherland and Dr. Farr.

The Commission did not go to India but sat in London. The taking of evidence should have begun in November 1859, but owing to the great distances from which facts had to be collected the assembling of the preliminary data took more than a year, and the Commission did not begin to sit until the autumn of 1861. Sidney Herbert was then dead and the burden of the work fell on Miss Nightingale.

Sidney Herbert had left her a frightful legacy in the Indian Sanitary Commission. Without him, she repeatedly said, she would never have contemplated it. Lord Stanley, " that noble and industrious lord ", was not altogether satisfactory

404

to her. They were friends, but he was cool, "singularly cool", one of his contemporaries called him, cautious and critical. Every hour he could snatch from Government business was spent in Lancashire managing his large estates. He was intellectual, he read widely, he possessed a fine library, and at Cambridge he had been a member of the distinguished society called the Apostles. A Liberal in sympathies, he supported the rights of nonconformists, was interested in administrative reform, and admired John Stuart Mill. After the Greek revolution in 1862–63 he was offered and refused the throne of Greece. His coolness, slowness to take action, refusal to be driven, threw Miss Nightingale into frenzies of irritation. She did not realise his value. The fact that the movement to improve Indian sanitation had behind it a man of Lord Stanley's known stability was in reality of the greatest assistance to her.

The whole undertaking bristled with difficulties. The situation in India was not favourable. In the daily life of India the passage of the Control of India Bill had made only a small upheaval. The power of the East India Company had long been a shadow; its Governor-General had become merely the agent through which the British Government found it convenient to rule. But in the administrative departments there was confusion. The final transfer of authority from the Great House, the headquarters of the East India Company, to the India Office was not accomplished without friction. The policy of the British Government of converting and absorbing the surviving administrative machinery of the East India Company resulted in the preservation of much that was inefficient and out of date. " The state of the India Office is inconceivable ", wrote Miss Nightingale to Douglas Galton in 1862; "just the routine of the old G.I.C. (General India Council) has survived the wreck—the worst part—they are just waddling on doing nothing."

Difficulties were increased by the fact that the transfer was not yet complete. Many records were still at the Great House, and the representatives of the defunct Company were not always inclined to be co-operative. To compile satisfactory statistics as to the health and sickness of the troops it was necessary to obtain figures from two different sources—for the

Queen's troops and the Company's troops; and each source was resentful of the other. Early in May 1859, before the warrant for the Commission was issued, she had discovered that no satisfactory figures and records, on which she and Dr. Farr could work, existed either at the Great House or the War Office, and that to obtain even ordinary documents relating to India in London was a hopeless task. She approached the Great House in June 1859 with a request for copies of the Indian Medical Service Regulations, and received the reply that they only possessed one copy which they dared not part with, and she had better write to India. She decided to obtain all her information at first hand, and, in consultation with Sir John McNeill and Sir Charles Trevelyan, at this time Governor of Madras, she drafted a *Circular of Enquiry* which was to be sent to every military station in India. She also wrote to 200 larger stations asking for copies of all regulations, including local Regulations, relating to the health and sanitary administration of the army. Finally, she wrote individually to all military and medical officers of high rank in India with whom she was acquainted, or to whom she could obtain introductions, asking for their good-will and co-operation.

The *Circular of Enquiry* was planned to yield great masses of facts from which would emerge a history of the health of the troops in every Indian station for the past ten years. " We must, of course, have the most minute statistics—both for soldiers and officers in the Queen's, Company's and Native troops," Miss Nightingale wrote to Dr. Farr on June 2nd, 1859, " and these we should get by this method for 10 years." Minutely detailed questions were designed to yield figures of sickness mortality and invaliding and the age and length of service of each man at the time of death or invaliding, also facts as to hospital and barrack accommodation and the situation and other amenities of each station. The Circular was to be filled up and signed by the Commanding Officer, the Medical Officer and the Engineering Officer. Officers of high rank had already been approached. Now, through the good offices of such friends as Sir Charles Trevelyan, officers on each station were written to personally, asked to help by filling up the Circular, and to send any additional information in their possession.

As the reports returned from India they were sent to Miss Nightingale, who analysed them, assisted by Dr. Sutherland and Dr. Farr. The task was colossal. Literally tons of paper were involved. When she took a house the reports required a whole room to house them. When she moved they filled two vans. She wrote in 1863 that they cost her £4 : 10s. to transport every time she changed house.

Eventually the Station Reports filled the second volume of the Indian Sanitary Commission's Report, a folio volume of nearly 1000 pages in small type. They are documentary evidence of immense value, providing a detailed picture, which is recorded nowhere else, of military life in India, both British and native, in the years immediately preceding and following the Mutiny. No official survey of India was undertaken until 1872.

As the analysis proceeded it became clear that facts of such overwhelming importance were being disclosed that they must constitute the basis of the Commission's Report. Yet Miss Nightingale, who had originated the scheme and executed it, from the drafting of the questions to the analysis of the replies, was not a member of the Commission nor did she qualify as a witness. How was her work to be included? The solution proved the extraordinary place she had earned in official estimation. She was officially invited, in October 1861, to submit in due course " Remarks " on the Station Reports, which should be signed by her and incorporated under her name into the report of the Commission. By August 1862 the analysis was complete and she had written her remarks under the title *Observations by Miss Nightingale*.

After *Notes on Nursing, Observations* is the most readable of her writings. Ill, exhausted and bereaved, she had never written anything with fiercer vitality. She intended *Observations* to be provocative. True, what had officially been requested—and was expected—was a convenient summary, but she perceived that the official request gave her a heaven-sent opportunity. The extreme difficulty of arousing public opinion on Indian sanitation was due first to blank ignorance, second to complete want of any source of information. *Observations* was designed first to startle and then to inform. To make the text more interesting she introduced woodcuts, executed by Hilary Bonham Carter from sketches sent from

India. Illustrations had never been used in a Blue Book before, and the Treasury was taken aback. An agreement was reached by which Miss Nightingale paid, not only for the drawings and the blocks, but for the extra expense involved in printing them.

She did not intend to allow *Observations* to be shelved until the publication of the Commission's report. She had a large number of copies privately printed, and during the autumn of 1862 sent them out, to the Queen—" she may look at it because it has pictures "—to Harriet Martineau, to Cabinet Ministers and to the members of the India Council. The result was all she had hoped. " Miss Nightingale's Paper is a masterpiece in her best style," Dr. Farr told Dr. Sutherland on December 1st, 1862, " and will rile the enemy very considerable—all for his good, poor creature." She told a frightful story with accuracy. " The picture is terrible but it is all true ", wrote Sir John McNeill on August 9th, 1862. " There is no one statement from beginning to end which I feel disposed to question, and there are many which my own observation and experience enable me to confirm."

Statistics showed that for years the death-rate of the British Army in India had been 69 per 1000. " It is at that expense ", wrote Miss Nightingale, " that we have held dominion there for a century ; a company out of every regiment has been sacrificed every twenty months." This enormously high death-rate was not the inevitable result of the climate. The diseases from which troops died like flies were not specifically tropical diseases, they were the diseases which had produced the mortality in the Barrack Hospital, the result of overcrowding, lack of drainage, bad water, in fact, camp diseases rendered a hundred times more deadly in India by climate and the proximity of native populations living in conditions of appalling filth. At Agra, in the native city, the streets were impassable owing to heaps of refuse of the most disgusting nature, no latrines or privies existed—" the population resort to the fields " and corpses were buried within the compounds of houses. Native settlements had been allowed to spring up actually within British cantonments. At Bangalore there was a native population of over 100,000 within cantonments, at Kamptee of over 70,000, destitute of any means of sanitation without latrines or privies " flinging all filth into the streets ". The bazaars were "simply in the first savage state of social life " ; they were allowed to spring up near barracks, and the stench from the bazaars affected the health of the troops.

Barracks were primitive in construction, built of lath and plaster with floors of earth varnished over with cow dung " like Mahomet and the dung hill, if men won't go to the dung hill, the dung hill it appears comes to them ". The water supply was deplorable. Only two stations supplied a chemical analysis, one of which read " like an intricate prescription ", other stations contented themselves by describing their water as " smells good " or " smells bad ". At Hyderabad, in Scinde, the water " visibly swarmed with animal life ". It was almost universal to use the same tank for drinking and bathing. At Bangalore the tank used for drinking was known to be the outlet for the whole drainage of a filthy bazaar of 125,000 inhabitants. The Commander-in-Chief wrote : " The disgustingly filthy nature of the source from which the water used at Bangalore is taken has been brought to notice scores of times by me during the last $4\frac{1}{2}$ years but as usual nothing has been done ".

No drainage whatever existed " in any sense in which we understand drainage. The reports speak of cess pits as if they were dressing rooms ", wrote Miss Nightingale. The Indian authorities were like the London woman who, when asked to point out the drains, said : " No, thank God, Sir, we have none of them foul stinking things here ". Means of washing were practically nil, stations were either without lavatories or, if lavatories existed, they had no fittings. One station washed in " earthenware pie dishes on a wooden form ". " If the facilities for washing were as great as those for drink, our Indian army would be the cleanest body of men in the world ", commented Miss Nightingale. Drunkenness was universal and universally accepted. True, the sale of spirits to troops in the bazaars was strictly forbidden but licences to sell spirits in bazaars were disposed of officially. " The Govt sells licence to sell drink in the bazaar and orders men not to profit by it. The present law is like lighting a fire and then charging it not to burn anything." A station was described as " temperate " in which one man out of every three admitted to hospital was suffering directly from the effects of drink. No effort was made to prevent the soldier from drinking, the only question which appeared to interest the authorities was how he had better get drunk. He was encouraged to kill himself on spirits bought at the canteen rather than on spirits bought in the bazaar. "May there not be some middle course whereby the men may be killed by neither?"

The diet of the army was "absurd". The soldier received a standard diet at all stations irrespective of climate, altitude or season. Means of cooking were inferior to the culinary amenities of Scutari, and the favourite situation for the kitchen was next door to the cess-pit.

Barracks were crammed with troops. One report stated that "300 men per room were generally accommodated without inconvenient overcrowding". "What is *convenient* overcrowding?" enquired Miss Nightingale. Married quarters were criminally inadequate. "At Dum Dum 554 women and 770 children", wrote Miss Nightingale, "were crowded together while their husbands were fighting and as many died as in the Cawnpore massacre in the Mutiny." The Principal of the Lawrence Asylums for children said that "the children of British soldiers in the plains die so early that only one in five is found surviving the fifth year of residence there".

Troops had no occupation, no means of recreation and no opportunities for exercise. In the hot weather they were customarily confined to barracks from 8 A.M. to 5 P.M. At Cawnpore in the hot weather they were compulsorily confined to barracks for 10½ hours a day. They had nothing to do, nothing to read, nowhere to go; out of 24 hours they lay on their beds for 18.

Hospitals were inferior in construction and comfort even to barracks. Often they were merely sheds supported on poles. There was no system of hospital orderlies. Patients were washed and nursed by a ward coolie hired at 4 rupees a month who was not a soldier and, in a cholera epidemic, usually ran away. When a man was dangerously ill one of his comrades was sent for and then, in Miss Nightingale's words, "The Regimental Comrade not knowing the language, nurses the Patient by beating the Coolie".

The allowance of tubs and basins was 1 per 100 men. Washing was done by pouring water over the patients from a tin pot. There was no day room for men well enough to get up. Convalescents spent 24 hours a day in bed. Privies were highly offensive and gangrene and erysipelas widespread. Troops would conceal their illness rather than go into hospital. " You might say of them as of the Pasha's new fort on the Dardanelles. He would be much safer outside it than inside it ", wrote Miss Nightingale.

But bad as these conditions were they paled before what was endured by native troops. The native troops received no rations and had no barracks, no lavatories, no baths, no kitchens, no sanitary supervision of any kind. They lived in huts, used the ground round them as privies without hindrance, and left cleansing to the rains. The squalor of their huts was indescribable, bodies of animals and of human beings were left unburied for days; the water they drank was stinking and they starved themselves of food to hoard their pay for their families. Consequently, though temperate, they were decimated by disease.

To rectify these conditions involved a new problem. The position of the army in India differed entirely from the position of the army at home. The standard of living conditions in the army in England had been below that of the towns in which troops were stationed. The aim of the Commission of 1857 had been to raise the living conditions of the soldier to the same level as the living conditions of the ordinary citizen. In India the army was surrounded by an immense native population. Of what use to improve and sanitate its barracks and hospitals when next door lay the bazaar and native city in all their filth? To improve conditions for the troops the whole sanitary level of the country must be raised. " The salvation of the Indian Army must be brought about by sanitary measures everywhere ", Miss Nightingale wrote. The health of the army and the people of India went hand in hand.

Another great mission had come to her. Work in military hospitals had inevitably led her to civil hospitals; sanitary work for troops in India led her to work for the health of the peoples of India. By the time she had finished the report she was as much concerned with the one as the other. " This is the dawn of a new day for India in sanitary things, not only as regards our Army but as regards the native population ", she wrote to Harriet Martineau on May 19th, 1863.

In the autumn of 1862 the Commission expected to issue its report within a few months, and the *Observations* were intended to whet public appetite for the fuller information contained in it. Miss Nightingale had completed her vast and laborious work. She had, with Dr. Sutherland's assistance, made an abstract of the Station Reports, condensing and analysing the evidence and grouping it for easier reference under the Presidencies, Bombay, Bengal, Madras, and at Lord Stanley's request she had, assisted by Dr. Sutherland, drafted the report, and the Commission had accepted her draft almost verbatim. "I have done and shall do all in my power ", wrote Lord Stanley on July 10th, 1863, " to make it public that to Dr. Sutherland and you we mainly owe that the Report has assumed its present shape." By August 1862 her work was actually in type, and she told Sir John McNeill that Lord Stanley had pledged himself to carry the report through the Commission in September. Delay followed. Dr. Farr had not completed the statistical sections and it was Christmas before they were complete. The amount of material involved was colossal—" The bulk of the Report ", wrote Henry Reeve, " is truly appalling "—the two enormous volumes comprised no less than 2028 closely printed pages, and the task of getting them into shape was difficult and slow. In December Miss Nightingale was threatening to " go and live over the Stationery Office until the Indian Report is through and drive thereby McCulloch into a lunatic asylum and force him to resign. His intellects never could stand me ! " The final stage of the great work was not reached until May 1863.

Once more, and even more clearly than in the case of the Sanitary Commission of 1857, she realised that the report would not be self-executive. India could not be left to carry out her own sanitary work alone. Native doctors and officials had been " dreadfully kept down " but at the same time were infuriatingly complacent. European officials behaved with " incurable ignorance or incurable frivolity ". On September 9th, 1863, she wrote to Harriet Martineau : " I gave a copy of the full Report to Colonel Wilberforce Greathed of the siege of

Delhi, a most gallant soldier and capable man, Asst. Military Secretary at the Horse Guards and a very important man to us, brother of the Colonel Greathed who has put his name to our report. His only answer is 'that he hoped it was not true'. Is not this disheartening? He is one of the best men in the Service."

There was no conviction of the necessity for sanitation in India, and there was no experience. There must be direction, there must be constant supervision, from England. She proposed that a Sanitary Department should be established at the India Office to draw up and enforce a sanitary code for all India. She fought passionately and obstinately, but she did not succeed. The Sanitary Commission on the Health of the Army in India was a military commission, instructed to concern itself with military affairs. Between the civil and military administration in India there was friction; no suggestions for changes in civilian administration would be entertained which emanated from a military Commission, and the establishment of a Sanitary Department for all India necessarily involved such changes. She had to give way. She did, however, succeed in establishing some sanitary control at home. Two Indian representatives were added to the Barrack and Hospital Commission and its powers were extended to include India; as a result all sanitary works for the Army in India would pass through Dr. Sutherland's hands. Miss Nightingale was reasonably satisfied. The working Commission, she told Harriet Martineau, was " not quite in the original form proposed, but in what may prove to be a better working form because grafted on what exists ". Lord de Grey was now Secretary of State for War and at the War Office the report would be received sympathetically. The sky seemed to be clearing and Miss Nightingale, relieved from the enormous burden under which she had staggered for two years, allowed herself a moment of elation. On May 19th, 1863, she wrote to Harriet Martineau: " I cannot help telling you in the joy of my heart that the final meeting of the Indian Sanitary Commission was held today—that the Report was signed and that, after a very tough fight, lasting over three days to convince these people that a report was not self executive, our working commission was carried ".

The next step was to prepare for the publication of the report. India was in the public mind, and Miss Nightingale had no difficulty in arranging the most comprehensive Press campaign she had yet achieved. She obtained a note from Lord Stanley authorising her to receive a number of copies as part-author of the report, and she persuaded the printer to let her have advance copies. These she sent to influential journalists with a personal letter briefly outlining the contents, and emphasising that the recipient was being given early and exclusive information. By the time the report was officially issued, leader-writers had had time to acquaint themselves with the essence of the two enormous volumes. Indeed, the remarkable amount of information that Miss Martineau, for instance, had managed to acquire in a day or two caused so much surprise that the secret leaked out. Miss Nightingale was told that the Clerk to the Commission took three days to recover from the shock when he discovered what she had done.

She was confident that the report would be read, not only by Members of Parliament, but by the public. So many copies of the Army Sanitary Report of 1857 had been sold that the Government had made a profit, and she anticipated that the sales of the Indian Report would be larger still.

But disaster followed. Either a genuine mistake occurred or, as she believed, she was the victim of a deliberate plot. It appeared that an attempt was made, if not to suppress the whole report, then at least to suppress the disclosures most unpalatable to the Government.

The Government was experiencing immense difficulties in India and being subjected to a great deal of criticism. Unquestionably the disclosures in the report would have added to their difficulties. Moreover, many of the abuses exposed had grown up under the East India Company, and so recent was the transfer of authority that there had not yet been time to rectify what would, officials assured each other, in due course be rectified. A strong body of opinion in official circles both in India and London thought the report exaggerated and the statistics incorrect. In August 1863 Lord Stanley was warned that an official attempt was to be made to " impugn " its statistics by officers in India. At the War Office and the India

Office Miss Nightingale's share in it was well known and strongly resented.

Unknown to her the Clerk to the Commission prepared a new and shorter edition : shorter because it left out the facts on which the report was based—the Station Reports, her abstract of the Station Reports and her Observations. The ground was covered by giving a *Précis of the Evidence*, executed with so little competence that reference was repeatedly made to passages in the sections which had been eliminated. This edition was to be the only one on sale to the public and was to be the edition presented to both Houses of Parliament. A thousand copies only had been printed of the original report, the type for the two enormous volumes having already been broken up. Even these copies were not obtainable. They were " reserved " by the Government.

On July 20th Miss Nightingale wrote to Sir James Clark : " There has been a perfect outcry (and I think a legitimate one) because the two folio book is not to be sold, not to be had, not to be published, not to be presented to Parliament, and that the 8vo makes references passim to a work which is not to be had. Officers—of all men those one most wants to interest— will not look at the 8vo copy and say the Government is keeping something back. And officials say we don't want opinion (in the Report) we want facts (in the Blue Book)." She refused to believe that the affair was an unfortunate mistake. The Report contained too many inconvenient revelations. On August 11th she wrote to Harriet Martineau, " the Govern- ment wished to suppress the sale ".

She could do nothing ; it was impossible to set up and reprint the two enormous books. The position must be ac- cepted and she must set to work to see what could be salvaged from yet another wreck.

She discovered that the 1000 " reserved " copies were to be had " on application " by Members of Parliament. By an irony of Fate the address to which applicants were directed was the Burial Board, where the Clerk to the Commission happened to hold a post. She wrote to Members with whom she was acquainted begging them to apply and heard that for the first time in history there was a run on a Blue Book.

Next she published the *Observations*. Though she was

vexed that the publisher issued it at what seemed to her the high price of 2s. 6d. (she said she had given him for nothing the blocks for the illustrations which had cost her £54), the book had an excellent sale and was widely reviewed. Copies went out to India and were read by officials first with anger, then with conviction. Many years later Sir Bartle Frere was asked what had started the movement for sanitary reform in India. It was not the Blue Book, he said, which no one read, but a certain little red book " which made some of us very savage at the time but did us all immense good ".

Finally, she persuaded Lord de Grey to allow her to rewrite the abridged edition. It was manifestly not only unjust but absurd that the only form of the report available should omit the evidence she had worked for years to obtain at the instruction of the Government. Might she not be allowed to prepare a new edition, with a *Précis of Evidence* accurately done, which could be circulated among army officers and officials; it was absolutely essential that these men should be correctly informed of the facts. Lord de Grey was doubtful—he was Secretary of State for War and did not wish to appear to be acting over the head of the India Office; but she persisted. " Surely ", she wrote in August 1863, " Sir Charles Wood [Secretary of State for India] will be very grateful to you for remedying his *mistake*." The inevitable objection that the Treasury would not authorise the expense she met by offering to pay the cost herself; and at the end of August she was instructed to proceed. A year later the new edition was finished, and it was given additional weight by an official preface, written by Lord de Grey, recommending it to the attention of commanding, medical and engineering officers.

With the issue of the revised edition all she could do on the report itself was finished. Its possibilities had been enormous and it had been a crushing disappointment.

She began to work on setting up the administrative machinery which should put its recommendations into practice.

She had to serve not two masters but three. Before any sanitary measures could be taken for the welfare of the army in India, the War Office, the India Office and the Government of India itself must all agree to act. All recommendations emanating from the Commission were suspect because it was a War Office Commission, yet as a final complication the strongest opposition of all came from within the War Office itself, and from the military officials in the Government of India.

There was no obligation for the War Office or the India Office to act on the recommendations of the report: they must be persuaded, worried, threatened, cajoled into action. And it must be done now while the report was still fresh. She " baited " Lord Stanley; but he was not Sidney Herbert, nor was the problem as simple as it had been in 1857. She could not infect him with a sense of urgency. " The first step ", he wrote to her on July 10th, 1863, " is to ask what the War and India Departments will do. If on consideration they consent to the appointment of the commissions recommended with, or without, modification of our plan, the thing is fairly started. But we must give them time to read the report. . . . I quite agree in what you say as to its being a duty to help the ministry of the day in working out their plans. . . . But such help cannot be offered by an outsider—it must be asked by those who are responsible. If Sir C. Wood desires assistance in giving effect to the sanitary projects, I will not refuse it. There is ample time to consider all this."

She became angry. Lord Stanley was cool; behind his back she called him indifferent. He disliked unconsidered action; behind his back she called him lazy. But she persisted, inducing Lord de Grey to go to see Sir Charles Wood to persuade him to consult Lord Stanley. Once procedure was correctly followed, Lord Stanley was willing to do his best. On July 24th he wrote: " I have had several conversations with Sir C. Wood and from the language he now holds I consider it settled that the report of the Commissioners will be acted upon. . . . I hope therefore that we may look on our work as done for the present. . . . So far, all has gone well."

For the moment all did go well, an official despatch was sent to India recommending the formation of sanitary commissions in each Presidency; the two additional members to represent India were added to the Barrack and Hospital Improvement Commission and she was asked to prepare a list of suggestions for sanitary improvements which might be sent to India and be the foundation of a sanitary code.

An outcry followed, furious opposition coming from officials in the India Office, in the War Office, in India itself. The report was once more attacked: it was incorrect, it was out of date, the picture it gave was totally false. So powerful were the protests that action ceased. It became evident that sanitary reform would only be carried out in the teeth of resistance from every authority concerned, and Miss Nightingale was driven from rage to despair. Her health had never been so bad. All her work was done in bed and she dragged herself to a couch only to receive important visitors. All through the summer she stayed in London, ill, miserable and alone. Lord Stanley had gone to the country and would not be persuaded to return. The work of the Indian Sanitary Commission was at a standstill. All her gigantic labours seemed once more to be dissolving into thin air.

Suddenly, however, the scene changed. In October 1863 Lord Elgin, the Viceroy, was taken seriously ill. It was known that he could live only a few weeks, and among his possible successors was Sir John Lawrence. New hope irradiated Miss Nightingale. She knew and passionately admired Sir John Lawrence. Sir Charles Wood asked Lord Stanley's advice, and Lord Stanley requested her views. She implored him to press for Sir John Lawrence's appointment. The fact that he was in the Indian Civil Service told against him, because it was not customary to appoint a civilian; but he had displayed military genius in the Mutiny, and at this particular moment a war seemed imminent on the North-West Frontier. On November 20th Lord Elgin died and on November 30th Sir John Lawrence was appointed.

His appointment as Viceroy of India opened a new period in her life. He was the first of a series of Indian officials of the highest rank who became her intimate friends, and through whose affection and admiration she gained an inside influence in Indian affairs approximating to some extent to the influence she had exercised at the War Office while Sidney Herbert was alive and in office.

Her position in Indian affairs was even more extraordinary than her position at the War Office. She had never been to India, she never did go to India, and yet she was considered an expert on India and consulted on its affairs by men who had lived there all their working lives. This knowledge was the reward of her enormous labours on the Station Reports. To her bedroom had come a return from almost every military station in India, not from one Presidency or one district but the entire Peninsula. Year after year she had toiled, examining, classifying, grouping. She possessed prodigious powers of absorbing, retaining and marshalling masses of facts, and when she had completed her task the whole vast teeming country lay before her mind's eye like a map.

Sir John Lawrence had first called on her when she was in the midst of her work on the Station Reports in 1861. Both felt an instant attraction. He had striking personal beauty, his height, curling golden hair and flashing blue eyes evoking admiration and awe and in part accounting for his power over native races. He was fearless, chivalrous, incorruptible and deeply religious. Lord Stanley, who possessed a talent for happy phrases, described his quality by saying that he had " a certain Homeric simplicity ". His brother, Sir Henry Lawrence, also an Indian administrator of great ability, had conducted the famous defence of the Residency at Lucknow during the Indian Mutiny and been killed there on July 4th, 1857. Miss Nightingale wrote that in the great mass of the Station Reports she could see improvement in the fearful state of cities and bazaars wherever the hand of the Lawrences could be traced.

The Lawrences came of an Ulster Prebsyterian family, and John Lawrence was one of twelve children, all above the average in beauty and ability. His father had commanded the 19th Regiment of Foot, and he passionately desired to be a soldier. It was a crushing disappointment when he found he was to be taken into the East India Company's service with a civil and not a military appointment. " A soldier I am and a soldier I will be," he exclaimed, and he conducted his life with a soldier's fearlessness, directness, discipline and austerity. Fate brought him the opportunity to display military genius. When the Mutiny broke out he was Governor of the Punjab. His swift action and personal courage, his bold disposition of the troops in his province, and above all his popularity and influence with the native population, prevented upper India from rising. From the Punjab he was able to send troops who turned the tide of war and saved Delhi. In recognition of these services he was created a baronet, sworn of the Privy Council, given the freedom of the City of London and voted an annuity of £2000 a year by the East India Company, one of its last acts before being taken over by the Crown.

In spite of a fiery temper—he had been seen hurrying out of church to belabour a disobedient servant—he was one of the band of Indian administrators who possessed deep sympathy with the native races. He was disgusted by the mass executions which followed the suppression of the Mutiny, and he repeatedly protested against the severities of certain military authorities. Miss Nightingale wrote to M. Mohl on January 1st, 1864 : " His love of and trust in the native races—his fear and distrust of the British Military authorities are sad and remarkable because so true—at least I can vouch for cause for the latter. With great simplicity he implies that the natives are much more capable of civilisation—even of sanitary civilisation—than our Army authorities in India. He looks upon our occupation as a conquest and we as camped out all over India, having hitherto attempted little but Martial Law over the conquered country. You must not betray him. For I received a hint from Head Quarters to tell him to be more conciliatory with our Army." He was devoted to his wife, who accompanied him everywhere ; it was said he was uneasy if she were out of the room even for a moment. In 1859 he was threatened with blindness as a result of consistent over-work—" I have not had a day's rest for sixteen years ", he wrote ; and he resigned the governorship of the Punjab and came home. In 1860 he was offered the governorship of Bombay, which he refused. He was then elected a member of the newly established India Council.

He was just the man to captivate Miss Nightingale : she called him a Bayard, a knight of a better era. " What would Homer have been ", she wrote to Harriet Martineau in 1865, " if he had had such heroes as the Lawrences to sing." When his appointment as Viceroy was announced her delight knew no bounds. " There is no more fervent joy, there are no stronger good wishes than those of one of the humblest of your servants ", she wrote.

It seemed that a golden age must be about to dawn, and even Lord Stanley allowed himself to be optimistic. " Sir J.

Lawrence's appointment is a great step gained ", he wrote to Miss Nightingale on December 1st, 1863. " I believe now there will be little difficulty in India."

He went on to make a remarkable suggestion, the more remarkable coming from a man with his regard for official etiquette. The new Viceroy must be instructed in the Indian sanitary question ; he wished him to learn, not from any official, but from Miss Nightingale. With a lifetime spent in India behind him, the Viceroy was to come to be taught by an invalid lady who had never been to India in her life. " But why should he not see you ? " wrote Lord Stanley. " The plans are, in the main, yours ; no one can explain them better ; you have been in frequent correspondence with him. . . . Your position in respect of this whole subject is so peculiar that advice from you will come with greater weight than from anyone else."

Sir John Lawrence had only a week before he sailed, but he called on December 4th, 1863. The interview, wrote Miss Nightingale, was one never to be forgotten. The Viceroy remained with her for several hours, the Indian Sanitary Report was discussed in detail, and he declared himself " heart and soul for Sanitary Reform ". On December 10th she wrote to Dr. Farr that Sir John Lawrence had instructed her " to do what I had almost lost the hope of being allowed to do, viz—of sending out full statements and schemes of what we want the Presidency Commissions to do. I should be glad to submit to you copies of papers of mine which he [Sir John Lawrence] desired me to write, and which he took out with him, as to the Constitution of the Presidency Commissions." The machinery for putting the recommendations of the report into practice was to be set up at once : and *Sanitary Suggestions* were to be issued for the Government of India to work on immediately. The attack on the veracity and accuracy of the Indian Sanitary Report was dismissed as nonsense. " Sir John Lawrence so far from considering our Report exaggerated, considers it under the mark ", she wrote triumphantly on December 10th.

At last it seemed that the mountain that was India was being moved. Following the appointment of Sir John Lawrence, Lord de Grey asked her to draft an official document from the War Office to the India Office formally enquiring what steps the India Office proposed to take to carry out the recommendations of the Indian Sanitary Commission. In December 1863 the letter was drafted and delivered.

In January 1864, assisted by Dr. Sutherland, Dr. Farr and the celebrated civil engineer, Sir Robert Rawlinson, Miss Nightingale completed her *Suggestions in regard to Sanitary Works required for the Improvement of Indian Stations.* It laid down a schedule of essential works relating to drainage, sanitation, water supply, barrack and hospital construction which each station should either possess or ought immediately to undertake. It was the first sanitary code for India, the starting-point from which, she hoped, great new projects, bringing health and prosperity to millions, would be developed.

Once more hope faded. The *Suggestions* were sent to the War Office, but nothing happened. Sir John Lawrence wrote repeatedly asking what had become of them, and Miss Nightingale could only reply that they had been finished and delivered in January. " Poor man ! " she wrote to Lord de Grey on March 10th, 1864, "he really expects dispatch. He thinks we can write a letter in three months ! He must be more fit for a Lunatic Asylum than a Governor Generalship."

The Barrack and Hospital Improvement Commission inexplicably came to a standstill on Indian work. The two Indian representatives had been duly elected, but the India Office neither made any application to the Commission nor issued any instructions.

In April Miss Nightingale discovered the truth : the War Office and the India Office had fallen out. The India Office had been offended by the letter, sent by the War Office in December 1863, enquiring what action was proposed on the recommendations of the Indian Sanitary Commission. The India office, in short, did not intend to have action proposed to it by the War Office. Lord de Grey told Miss Nightingale that as he had been " snubbed " by Sir Charles Wood he had not forwarded the *Suggestions.* They were still in a pigeon-hole at the War Office.

Nearly a year ago, in July 1863, Lord Stanley had written to Miss Nightingale that difficulties would inevitably arise " out of the conflicting claims of the Indian and home authorities ".

In January 1864 she wrote to Sir John McNeill: "No impression in my life was ever borne in on me more strongly than this, that the Ministers have never considered the respective jurisdictions of the W.O. [War Office] and the I.O. [India Office], and that I.O., W.O., Horse Guards at home, Commander-in-Chief in India, Governor General in India are as little defined as to their respective powers and duties as if India were the Sandwich Islands". But it was a misfortune that a crisis should have arisen now. Official approval and dispatch of the *Suggestions* to India was a matter of the greatest urgency. The Viceroy was eager—he had actually set up the Presidency Sanitary Commissions—but they could do nothing until they received the Government's instructions for action contained in the *Suggestions*.

At this stage Lord Stanley became annoyed. It was seven months since the Commission, of which he was chairman, had reported, and nothing had been done. He considered that a reflection had been cast on his work. His political influence was very great, he was in opposition, and he wrote to Miss Nightingale offering to attack the Government in the House of Commons, or to put pressure on either Lord de Grey or Sir Charles Wood, whichever she thought best. She herself had approached the War Office privately without satisfaction. "The Horse Guards say that they were quite aware of Sir John Lawrence's application and of the delay," she wrote to Douglas Galton in June 1864, "but that 'it is Sir John Lawrence's one and only object of interest, while it is *one of a thousand* of the War Office '. . . . I have told Sir J. Lawrence of the opinion of these dining out *freluquets* as to his hard work."

Lord Stanley went to see Sir Charles Wood and promised to support him in case of any criticism in the House. Sir Charles Wood then accepted the *Suggestions* and submitted them to the Barrack and Hospital Improvement Commission, who adopted them almost in their entirety. The conflict in dignity between the War Office and the India Office was solved by a phrase on the title-page; though the Indian Sanitary Commission had been a War Office Commission, the title-page stated that the *Suggestions* had been "prepared by the said Commission in accordance with letters from the Secretary of State for India in Council ".

As soon as the *Suggestions* were officially approved Miss Nightingale had copies printed at her own expense, which she sent out to Sir John Lawrence. Delay continued in the official issue. The War Office and the India Office fell into an argument as to the number of copies to be printed; and a further two months passed before the official edition was ready. By this time Sir John Lawrence was having Miss Nightingale's advance text reprinted in India, and she wrote to Douglas Galton: "It might be as well to hurry your copies for the India Office who will otherwise receive them first from India."

Once more she was the mainspring of the work. No toil was so wearisome that she shrank from it, no detail too small to receive her attention. Across two continents her burning zeal infused Sir John Lawrence with new strength. Sir Bartle Frere, at this time Governor of Bombay, told her, " men used to say that they always knew when the Viceroy had received a letter from Florence Nightingale; it was like the ringing of a bell to call for Sanitary progress ". Her hand was everywhere. She had drawn up the instructions to the Presidency Commissions and widened their scope, so that they were not only to " supervise the gradual introduction of sanitary improvements in Barracks, Hospitals and Stations " but also to improve the sanitary condition of " Towns in proximity to Stations ". The *Suggestions*, the code by which the Commissions worked, were written by her; the report of the Commission itself was her work. Lying in her bed in London, she held the threads of a network which covered all India.

Sanitary work in the army itself rapidly advanced through the help of the Commander-in-Chief, Sir Hugh Rose. This brilliant and humane General had known Miss Nightingale in the Crimea. Under his command, during the Mutiny, the Central India Field Force performed an historic march, marching across India, a distance of over 1000 miles, in the hot weather, fighting continuously. The fort of Kalpi was stormed by British troops with the temperature standing at 110° F. in the shade. Since June 1860 he had been Commander-in-Chief in India, engaged in the difficult task of amalgamating the East India Company's troops and the Queen's troops into one army. He had issued a general order announcing that in future appointments would be conferred,

not by interest, but solely by merit. He held frequent inspections at which he himself examined officers in their regimental
duties. Officers were made responsible for the welfare of
their troops; and two brigadier-generals were removed from
their commands for failing to visit hospitals during a cholera
epidemic.

Miss Nightingale asked Lord de Grey to send a letter to Sir
Hugh through the proper channels drawing his attention to
those recommendations in the Indian Sanitary Report which
affected regiments. He replied personally, warmly agreeing
with the report, and took immediate action. Regimental
recreation rooms and workshops were opened, regimental
gardens laid out to provide troops with vegetables; libraries,
savings banks, lectures and courses of instruction in trades
started. The regulation two drams of spirits a day was
reduced to one; an Act of the Legislature made any un-
authorised sale of spirits near barracks or cantonments an
offence punishable by a heavy fine. In July 1864 he wrote to
the War Office describing what had been done, and the
despatch was forwarded to Miss Nightingale. On August 11th
she wrote to Douglas Galton: " It is quite worth while, all
that has been suffered, to have this letter from Sir Hugh Rose.
And I forgive everybody everything."

In October 1863 she wrote a paper, read at the Social
Science Congress in Edinburgh, and entitled "How People
May Live and Not Die in India ", which was a short and
popular version of the facts revealed in the *Observations*. It
was immensely successful; the meeting broke up with " Three
cheers for Florence Nightingale ", and the *Scotsman* took the
unusual step of reproducing the paper almost verbatim. In
August of the following year she published the paper as a
pamphlet, with a preface in which she described what had
been done under Sir John Lawrence to remedy the abuses and
set forth the very great improvements which had taken place
in the army.

Once more hope ran high. " I sing for joy every day ",
she wrote in June 1864, " at Sir John Lawrence's Government ", and before Sir John himself she prostrated herself in
an ecstasy of hero-worship. She signed her letters to him
" Yours devotedly ". In October 1864 in the full flood of

optimism she wrote to him: " I feel it a kind of presumption in me to write to you—and a kind of wonder at your permitting it. I always feel you are the greatest figure in history and yours the greatest work in history in modern times. . . . You are conquering India anew by civilisation, taking possession of the Empire for the first time by knowledge instead of the sword."

It was a lyric rapture which, alas, bore little relation to reality. While the machinery of the Sanitary Commissions was being set up all went well; President, Secretary and Commissioners were appointed and coached in their duties, information was collected and schemes formulated on paper. And then—nothing happened. Sir Hugh Rose achieved a great deal for the army, all other plans seemed hopelessly bogged. The machinery was there—but it did not operate.

The truth was that Sir John Lawrence was not altogether successful in the office of Viceroy, which he had accepted solely from a sense of public duty. He was a hero, a born leader of men, just, fearless, simple, beautiful as a god. But the personal courage and military genius which had saved the Punjab were not qualities which shone in the committee room. He had a violent temper, a rough manner, strong prejudices, a want of tact. The difficulties which faced him were appalling. Financially and administratively India was in fearful disorder. The year 1859-60 had shown a deficit of over forty million pounds sterling. The enormous increase in military expenditure, due to the Mutiny, seemed likely to increase and become an intolerable burden, since the extreme antagonism between Europeans and Indians prevented retrenchment.

The structure of government in India prevented the development of the country. The native merchant and trading classes, who alone could bring India prosperity, were depressed. The members of the Viceroy's Council and the Government officials in the Presidencies were almost without exception European officials. The tone of the Government was a military domination tempered by philanthropy. Interdepartmental jealousy was intense: the India Office hotly resented being given orders by the War Office, the viceroy's Council in India resented being given orders by the India Office at home.

Sir John Lawrence landed in January 1864 ; six months later Miss Nightingale told Sir John McNeill that he was " discouraged by difficulties he could scarcely understand or anticipate ". It became known that he was on bad terms with his Council. The native population was distrustful. In June 1864 he described the feeling of hopelessness which overcame him when an attempt to improve the sanitation of Calcutta was construed by the Bengalis as an attack on the Hindoo religion. Miss Nightingale herself found the Indian mentality difficult to deal with. " Nothing can give you any idea ", she wrote to Harriet Martineau in 1862, " of the horrors of the disclosures as to the state of the stations which these Indians make themselves while declaring themselves to be 100 years before England."

Delay succeeded delay; 1864 passed into 1865 and still nothing substantial had been done in India. Once more she was in despair. It was the old weary story of guerilla warfare, the odd point here, the odd point there, snatched from the India Office or the War Office at the cost of infinite toil. But where was the plan? The plan, the constructive campaign, had once more faded away.

XIX WERE THE DISAPPOINTMENTS, the reverses she endured, the common lot of the reformer? She refused to admit it. She was convinced that she was singled out by a malignant fate. She herself, her work, everything she touched, was cursed. She beat herself against the callousness and indifference of the world, she exhausted herself in storms of resentment and despair. Such was the power of her extraordinary nature that in middle age the intensity of her emotion was unabated and she continued to feel as violently, as blindly, as if she were a girl.

It was the old story, repeated now for more than twenty years. She must attain perfection or she had failed. She must have everything or she declared she had nothing. She refused to consider what had been done, only what had not.

Yet how much she had achieved was becoming plainer every day. Lord Stanley's coolness was notorious, but on July 25th, 1864, he wrote to her: "Every day convinces me more of two things; first, the vast influence on the public mind of the Sanitary Commissions of the last few years . . . and next, that all this has been due to you and to you almost alone". Jowett wrote on September 8th, 1865: "Considering what Ministers are, instead of wondering at their not doing all you want, I wonder at their listening to a word you say. A poor sick lady, sitting in a room by herself and they have only not to go near her and not to read her letters and there is an end of her. And yet you seem to draw them."

She would not be comforted; she would allow no gleam of light to penetrate the darkness. Her physical condition was piteous—she could not move without assistance. "I am so weak", she wrote in a private note of 1864. "Oh how weak I am!" Yet she drove herself mercilessly, and the demands of the work were becoming daily more enormous. She headed letter after letter, "Written before it is light". She wrote that she was like the washerwoman who said Heaven would be to have an hour a day with nothing to do. Among the Nightingale papers is a sheet on which she has drawn a large

428

" O ! " and signed it " F. Nightingale. Lonely and weak. March 10 1866."

More than health had been lost in these last years of incessant toil. Sometimes now she doubted. She had been able to be ruthless, she had been able to be without mercy, because she had been sustained by an unshakable conviction that what she did was right. Now she was not sure. A new note crept into her letters. Writing to Clarkey in May 1865 she said she felt like a vampire who had sucked Sidney Herbert's and Clough's blood. Writing to Jowett in July she was humble and confused! " You are quite right in what you say of me. . . . I will try and take your advice. I have tried but it is too late. I lost my serenity some years ago, then I lost clearness of perception, so that sometimes I did not know whether I was doing right or wrong for two minutes together—the horrible loneliness—but I don't mean to waste your time."

Once she had felt proud to be alone, now she dreaded the prospect of perpetual solitude. Her life was closing in. Every hour must be given up to work. Friends, affection, sympathy, all must be sacrificed. How easy it would have been for just one person to come forward—" anyone could have helped me who knew how to read and write and what o'clock it is ", she wrote to Clarkey in 1865. But no one had come and, unwilling though she was, she must bear the enormous burden alone. In the summer of 1865 Clarkey came over to London. She was Miss Nightingale's most intimate friend, and since Sidney Herbert's death they had drawn still closer. " What I lost in Sidney Herbert you only (who lost M. Fauriel) can tell ", she wrote to her in 1862. Yet she could not spare time to see Clarkey. She offered lunch and dinner every day and the use of a sitting-room in her house, but see her and talk to her she could not. " Clarkey Mohl darling," she wrote on June 23rd, 1865, " how I should like to be able to see you, but it is quite quite impossible. I am sure no one ever gave up so much to live who longed so much to die as I do. It is the only credit I claim. I will live if I can, I shall be so glad if I can't."

Clarkey protested against " Flo's solitary confinement system ". She would be a great deal better in health if she were not so strict with herself and allowed herself " a little talk and fun ". Miss Nightingale would not give way, but she sent down by hand—Clarkey was in the house waiting to see her —an explanation of the reasons which forced her present way of life on her. " Darling . . . if you think that my living the Robinson Crusoe life I do is the effect of Stoicism, there never was a greater mistake. It is entirely the effect of calculation. I cannot live to work unless I give up all that makes life pleasant. People say ' Oh see the doctors have said these 8 years she could not live 6 months—therefore it is all a mistake'. They *never* say : she has lived 8 years when the doctors said she could not live 6 months by adopting this kind of life, of sacrificing everything else in order to work. . . . But I have ceased to try to make anybody understand this. I do hope I am getting wiser in this respect—not *explaining*. . . . I NEVER said it was ' best for me '. All I said was, it was best for the work—or rather it is the only way in which the work could be done."

Since her serious illness of Christmas 1861 she could not bear anyone in the room with her : another person's movements or voice irritated her unendurably. The effort of talking, even to an intimate friend, was succeeded by nervous prostration. On October 4th, 1865, she wrote again to Clarkey: " No one ever did give up so much to live who longed so much to die. *Venez me consoler de n'être pas morte.* . . . Yesterday because I saw Dr. Sutherland in the afternoon after the morning's work and my good friend Mrs. Sutherland for a few minutes after him, I was with a spasm of the heart until 7 o'clock this morning, and nearly unfit for work all day. I should not mind it but that I *mustn't* be unfit for work. I *cannot* afford the time."

The distinguished visitors who had called at the Burlington were no longer received. The Queen of Holland wished to call—" I really feel it a great honour ", wrote Miss Nightingale in June 1865, " she is a Queen of Queens. But it is quite quite impossible." She would see no one who was not directly connected with her work. She made, however, one exception. In 1864 Garibaldi came to London ; she admired him intensely, she had never forgotten her girlhood's passion for Italian freedom, and she had regularly sent money to his funds. Now she consented to receive him if he came incognito.

On April 27th he came, using Sir Harry Verney's carriage to avoid notice. She was disillusioned. "Alas, alas, what a pity that utter impracticability", she wrote to Harriet Martineau on April 28th. He was noble and heroic, but he was vague. He had, she wrote, no " administrative capacity ". He "raved" for a Government like the English, but " he knows no more what it is than his King Bomba did ". She could not get him to talk of practical problems of administration—his talk was of Utopia, of the " ideal " good and the " ideal " bad. He would not be brought to discuss theories of government: he said he cared only for " the right ". She noticed that he looked flushed and very ill, worn and depressed —not excited. " One year of such a life as I have led for ten years ", she told Harriet Martineau, " would tell him more of how one has to give and take with a ' representative Government ' than all his ' Utopias ' and his ' ideal '."

Her consolation in her solitude was friendship with Jowett. By 1864 her intimacy with him was closer than her intimacy with any other human being, with the exception of Clarkey. They did not meet frequently, though he occasionally spent an afternoon with her when he was in London, but they exchanged many hundreds of letters. Nearly all Miss Nightingale's personal letters to Jowett, with the exception of a few rough drafts preserved among her papers, have been destroyed, but she kept most of his letters to her. Intense concern for her welfare, intense affection breathe from every line. He was devoted to her and because he was devoted to her she would accept advice and even criticism from him. Jowett alone could tell her not to exaggerate, " as you always do "; Jowett alone could tell her to be calmer " and don't try and move the world by main force"; Jowett alone could tell her not to despise people and, worse still, to let them see that she despised them ; Jowett alone could scold her and she would accept and almost enjoy the scolding. He had entered her life when she was crushed by the death of Sidney Herbert, and his remarkable powers of sympathy and understanding were offered her at a time when she was desperately in need of them. " Mine has been such horrible loneliness ", she wrote to him on July 12th, 1865. " But how many women, maids of all work and poor governesses, have been lonelier than I—and have done

431

much better than I. I think if I had had one friend—such a friend as you have been to me for the past six months. . . ."

Jowett made himself intimate with her family and her friends, staying frequently at Embley, where his learning and wit made him a " plum " for W. E. N.; Fanny called him " that great and good man Mr. Jowett ". He became a friend of Sir Harry Verney and of Clarkey and M. Mohl. In 1863 he celebrated Communion in Miss Nightingale's bedroom and tried to pave the way for a reconciliation with Aunt Mai by suggesting that she should be asked to be present. When Miss Nightingale began the Indian Sanitary Commission he wrote asking to be informed; he had a reason, he told her, for being interested in Indian sanitary reform, since he had had two brothers who had died in India. She consulted him, sent him drafts of her papers for criticism and used his influence. He interested himself in Indian education and became one of the examiners on the first Board of Examiners for the reformed Indian Civil Service. In her work outside India he also made a place for himself. He read and criticised almost everything she wrote, he advised her on policy and wrote papers at her suggestion. She entered into his work with equal sympathy. " You are the only person ", he wrote in 1865, " who encourages me about my work at Oxford. I cannot be too grateful for your words." " I am delighted ", he wrote in 1866, " to have a friend who cares two straws whether I succeeded or not in a matter at Oxford." He counselled her to moderation and enjoyment, " do tell me that you are happier "; she stirred him on to action. She made him promise to take holidays, to cut down reading at night, to take Sundays off from work.

Friendship with Jowett took the only form in which friendship could have been fitted into her life. There was infinite solicitude but there were no demands, there was constant and intimate communication but the communication was by letter and brought no interruption to the routine of work. The friendship was eminently successful, as her friendship with Clarkey was eminently successful. Jowett was in Oxford, Clarkey was in Paris, she was in London. The problem of interference did not arise.

But even though Miss Nightingale had resigned herself to a

Robinson Crusoe way of life she still had to find a place to live. Already her wanderings had been extensive. She had left 9 Chesterfield Street, the " fashionable old maid's house ", in the autumn of 1862, faced with a large claim for dilapidations which W. E. N. had eventually to be asked to settle. She then went back to the Verney's town house, 32 South Street. In January 1863 she wrote to Sir Harry Verney thanking him for " a so comfortable three months in your beautiful house ". The view down Park Street, where the houses had stripes of yellow ochre and grass-green shutters, reminded her of a French town, and even the public-house at the corner was, she said, " a vestal for purity ". But the Verneys wanted to come back to their house every year for the London season, and she had to turn out, with all her papers and impedimenta—to occupy the same house as Parthe was impossible. For a time she had a floor in a hotel in Dover Street, but this proved expensive and unsatisfactory, and in the spring of 1863 she took a furnished house in Cleveland Row, St. James's. In the summer she took furnished rooms or furnished houses in Hampstead and Highgate with varying success. She was an invalid, living alone without anyone to supervise her household, and servants were a difficulty. Her life was unusual, her ideas of cleanliness and hygiene strange to her contemporaries, and her standard exacting. " Florence ", wrote Fanny in 1864, " has strange ideas about maids."

Finding a house became a recurrent nightmare. Year after year Fanny, Parthe, Beatrice Smith, Aunt Mai's daughter who, since Parthe's marriage, had been living with Fanny, and the devoted Mrs. Sutherland " panted " from agent to agent trying to find a house that would satisfy her. She must be central, she must be quiet, she had a morbid dread of being overlooked. In 1865 Mrs. Sutherland sent a list of houses on which Miss Nightingale scribbled comments. A house in Bolton Row which she knew "looks as if it had been built for someone to do something wrong in ". Park Street did not suit her—" I stayed there once and was perfectly sleepless ". Norfolk Street was " too near Park Lane and the grinding of luggage vans. Beautiful and noisy." Every year the problem arose, every year there was a house to be found, servants to be engaged, arrangements to be made for moving in ; every year when she moved out there were dilapidations to be settled, invariably with a dispute, because she spent her life upstairs and did not know what her servants did downstairs. For some time Fanny had been trying to persuade W. E. N. that the only solution was to buy a house, but he was unwilling. Fanny was extravagant, Embley and Lea Hurst were expensive to keep up, he was irritated to find himself continually short of money. Yet Florence's accommodation cost more every year—the possibility that she could live on an annual income of £500 was never mentioned now. At last W. E. N. was forced to the conclusion that a permanent house might be an economy. In July 1865 she had taken 34 South Street furnished from Lady Clarges at a rental of £500 a year, and a furnished house in Hampstead, in which she proposed to stay for three months, from Lord Digby at £11 a week. On July 4th W. E. N. wrote to Fanny: " Saturday she goes to Ld Digby's big house at Hampstead £11 a week. 34 South Street, £500 the year, Hampstead if she stays there three months £120. Parthe urges me to offer £7000 for 35 South Street, you are in the same vein. There is nothing for it but to say I will give £5000, you adding your money. Of course I shall consider the money sunk from the time I produce it and shall hope NEVER TO HEAR ANY MORE OF IT. Is it not of course too that the £7000 will not be accepted? "

The £7000 was accepted, and since Miss Nightingale had already taken No. 34 she found herself with two houses on her hands. On October 2nd, 1865, Fanny wrote to Parthe asking her to find a tenant for 34. " Florence writes my dear, that she thinks she had best keep No. 35 for herself, if she should be able to let 34, i.e. if Lady Clarges will let her underlet. She has no one to occupy 34 (or 35) whichever should be left vacant at the end of the month." She tried to persuade the Sutherlands to take 34 but they refused. Eventually a tenant was found, and at the end of October, " with everyone's united efforts ", wrote Fanny, Miss Nightingale moved into No. 35 South Street, which henceforward became her home. The house suited her admirably; it was central, manageable and backed on to the gardens of Dorchester House. She was able to enjoy fresh air, sunlight and trees, and to observe birds, of whom she was passionately fond.

A few years later the street was renumbered : No. 35 became No..10, and at No. 10 South Street she continued to live until her death.

No further attempt was made to provide her with a companion. She moved into her new house to live alone. And, as she moved in, the spectre of desolate solitude, which had crept into her life as one by one her friends were taken from her, stalked nearer. The sword which seemed to hang over all those she loved fell again, and she sustained another great grief.

Of the friends of her youth she had loved none more than Hilary Bonham Carter. Soft, loving, a pleasure to look at and highly gifted, Hilary possessed a remarkable power of inspiring affection. " I was so attached to her ", wrote M. Mohl on September 9th, 1865. " I have never known anyone so made up of kindness." Hilary loved Florence more than anyone else in the world ; she had loved her since they were babies together building houses for their dolls under the trees at Fair Oaks. But Florence disapproved of Hilary, and in 1862 she had sent her away. Clarkey had implored her to take Hilary back—already a suspicion had crossed Clarkey's mind that Hilary's uncertainties, her ineffectualness had a foundation in disease. " My dearest," she wrote on February 5th, 1862, " if she is as useful to you as a limb, why should you amputate her ? . . . She loves you better than anyone else, and it would be balm to her poor worn out spirit if she thought she was useful to you. I say worn out because she is so. I can't think why—I can't understand it . . . the thing she likes best in the world is being with you and being useful to you . . . the last year she spent faddling at Aunt Mai's, at Uncle Nicholson's, at Mrs. Martin's and now I am not sure that this is not necessary to her happiness, this faddling after other people. Now to faddle after folk, who don't want you, is madness . . . but to faddle after those that do is very good employment. Now if she is a limb to you, you are the very person for her, for she dotes on you, it is a pleasure to her and an honour. I agree with you, she ought to do for herself, but I am not sure her nature can bear it. I give it to you as a problem, think on it."

To make Hilary happy by giving way to her was criminal to Miss Nightingale. Clarkey could write, " I can't alter

435

Hilly, I can only give her a little enjoyment"; but Miss Nightingale despised such enjoyment and considered it a betrayal of all she loved in Hilary. She refused to have her back, and Hilary continued to be maid-of-all-work to her family. In the late spring of 1862 her health took a sharp turn for the worse, and Clarkey, who saw her in the summer after an interval of nearly six months, noticed a great loss of power in her. She no longer made any attempt to paint or draw. She was in her sister-in-law's house. She had got up before six, to give her brother breakfast before he went to Scotland, though the house was full of servants; she came in worn out during the afternoon, and instead of resting insisted on going out to buy flowers and arrange them before dinner. "Hilly is devoured by little black relations just like Fleas", Clarkey wrote on August 19th.

The break with Miss Nightingale was complete. "I see nothing of Hilary", Miss Nightingale wrote to Clarkey on February 14th, 1863. "I believe the fact is she *cannot* see me without an appointment and to her everything is possible but keeping an appointment." In March she wrote, "about Hilary. I have only seen her once these six months. She appears to me to be perfectly incapable of making, or keeping, an appointment or of doing anything whatever. I believe she is far from well. But how can it be otherwise? . . . I am never easy about her one moment except when she is with you. I never ask about her. I know what I should hear." In April 1865 Hilary broke down, was examined by a specialist, and said to have a tumour. On May 3rd Miss Nightingale wrote to Clarkey in Paris, "she is seriously ill". Clarkey wished to come and stay in rooms in London to be near her but was persuaded that the complications with Hilary's family would only add to Hilary's distress. Jowett called constantly on Miss Nightingale's behalf and Hilary became devoted to him. On her good days he was able to distract her, and she was fond of making plans to go and stay with him at Balliol when she was better.

In fact she was dying of cancer. On May 16th, 1865, Jowett wrote to Miss Nightingale: "She seemed to be at peace, but she had suffered greatly—poor thing—she said that she had mental trial in past times and that, she found, had been alleviated by trusting in God, but she did not find that physical suffering could be similarly alleviated." In June Miss Nightingale told Dr. Farr, who had become Hilary's friend during the Statistical Congress of 1860, " our dear friend Hilary is less suffering, more quiescent in the disease, more prospect of its being prolonged—no hope of recovery ". In September Hilary became rapidly worse, and on September 2nd Miss Nightingale wrote to Dr. Farr, " our dear friend Hilary is dying painfully—the only wonder is how she lives through each twenty-four hours ". On September 6th she died. " Hilary was released this morning at half past eight. . .", Miss Nightingale told Clarkey, " Oh dearest how she had suffered ! "

Throughout the summer, while she was in London, solitary and overworked, Hilary's terrible illness had been preying on Miss Nightingale's mind. On Hilary's death she broke into frenzy. Rage seized her, made up of resentment, anger and despair—despair at Hilary's wasted talents, at Hilary's wasted life, at the stupidity and indifference of Hilary's family, at the system of family life which permitted such things to be. On September 8th she wrote Clarkey an immense, furious letter : ". . . There is *not a single person*, except yourself, who does not think that Hilary's family were quite right in this most monstrous of slow murders—and all for what ? There is something grand and touching in the Iphigenia sacrifice and Jephthah's daughter. But, if Jephthah had made his vow to sacrifice his daughter to feed his pigs it would only be very dirty and disgusting. And I say, the Fetichism to which Hilary has been sacrificed is very dirty and disgusting. . . . Hilary's really seemed to me to partake of the character of a delusion. Because no one could say stronger things than she has to me, not only against her mother, but to the effect that she was quite aware she was positively a bad influence in her mother's way. And so she was. It was perfectly true. And that she should have been sacrificed to that ! . . . I shall never cease to think as long as I live of you and M. Mohl as of Hilary's *only* friends. The golden bowl is broken—and it was the purest gold—*and the most unworked gold*—I have ever known. I shall never speak of her more, I have done. . . . How I hate well meaning people."

437

Frantic and distraught, she refused to be comforted. Jowett tried to reason with her and in two letters written consecutively on September 7th and 8th besought her to be calm—" don't look upon her life as wasted . . . we cannot quite tell what is lost or wasted in this world. Very few persons can ever be expected to carry on their lives on a systematic plan and persons who have great gifts least of all. (Poor thing, she must have passed through a real fire). . . . I am very much grieved to hear you have been, during the last two months, much worse. . . . I am afraid you have been ' agonised ' by poor Miss Carter's state. . . . I think there are very few such people in the world, so mild and good and with so much intelligence. Do you think they really did suck the marrow out of her life ? . . . I thought she had always a look of physical exhaustion."

Hilary's death had opened old wounds. Miss Nightingale brooded over her relations with her family and the injuries she had received from them. Solitary, feverish, miserable, she revived old unhappinesses and felt them as keenly, as implacably, as if nearly twenty years had not elapsed. She recalled to Clarkey how her family divided her asunder, " soul from spirit, bones from marrow ". They had always been indifferent to her feelings ; no member of her family had enquired after Sidney Herbert all the time he was ill, or after Clough all the time he was ill though they knew she was distracted with anxiety. Even her cat, she told Clarkey on September 17th, 1865, " seemed to know something was wrong the day Hilary died and sat with his arms round my neck. Whereas Parthe, e.g. has never said one word but of hardness to me in all my trial years—my 4 years." Clarkey remonstrated. " Do not dearest dwell on the failings of your poor people ", she wrote in September; ". . . you let their want of comprehension corrode and eat into you. If you would but consider that it is not in the power of people to understand more than they can . . . do dearest be indulgent. I don't care so much about Parthe, tho' I am always charmed to be with her, but your father and mother are so fond of you, it is not their fault if they have not understood you."

She would not be placated. To Clarkey and to Jowett she poured out letter after letter in which Hilary's death, her own

438

past sufferings at the hands of her family, and Parthe's present behaviour united into one furious resentment. She complained that Parthe got people to write letters to her "saying the hardest things", that when she and Parthe met everything she said was "distorted", that Parthe made trouble for her with Sir Harry Verney.

Hilary's death was succeeded by another blow, the death of Lord Palmerston on October 18th. Miss Nightingale regretted him deeply. In a letter to Mrs. Cowper, wife of his stepson, she spoke with feeling of Palmerston's kindness. "In the last overloaded three weeks of the season of 1861, he found time to write every day pleasant letters of political news to Sidney Herbert who was dying. . . . Sidney Herbert used to speak of his kindness with tears in his eyes." In reply Mrs. Cowper gave her intimate details of Lord Palmerston's last illness and affectionate messages from other members of the family. But personal regret was secondary to the serious loss she sustained in no longer having Palmerston to help her in her work. On October 18th she wrote to Dr. Walker, the Secretary of the Bengal Sanitary Commission: "He may be passing away even at this moment. He will be a great loss to us. Tho' he made a joke when asked to do the right thing, he always did it. No one else will be able to carry the things thro' the Cabinet as he did. I shall lose a powerful protector. . . . He was so much more in earnest than he appeared. He did not do himself justice." On October 19th she wrote to Dr. Farr: "I have lost a powerful friend in Lord Palmerston. I rarely asked him to do anything in the Cabinet, as you may suppose. But if ever I did, he made a joke, but he did it."

Through the winter of 1865, her first winter in her own house, she was miserably ill and miserably unhappy. Death and failure, failure in India, her loss of power at the War Office combined to crush her. "I just keep my place on at the War Office by doing all their dirty work for them, i.e. what they are too cowardly to do for themselves—*les lâches*", she wrote to Clarkey in March 1865. She had been bed-ridden for four years, and she began to have severe pains in her back, described as "rheumatism of the spine". She was ordered to have a "rubber", a masseuse, three times a week, but the state of her nerves made treatment difficult. The "rubber" was forbidden to speak. She must come in noiselessly, do her work and withdraw without speaking to Miss Nightingale on any pretext. The treatment had little effect, and she passed the winter and spring in constant pain. "Nothing did me any good", she wrote to M. Mohl in July 1866, "but a curious little new fangled operation of putting opium under the skin which relieves one for twentyfour hours—but does not improve the vivacity or serenity of one's intellect." Yet for the first time for many years her horizons were widening to include something beyond her work. During the long winter nights, lonely, sleepless and in pain she had once more begun to read.

Jowett had borrowed from Tennyson a book by "a poor man, a singular man" who had translated some Persian verses into English. The book was Edward FitzGerald's translation of *The Rubáiyát* of Omar Khayyám. Jowett sent it to Miss Nightingale and she sent it to M. Mohl, who was a leading authority on Persian poetry, asking him to let her have it back because the owner set a fanciful value on the book. "I daresay", she wrote, "you will hardly care to look at it." In another letter she told M. Mohl: "the way it interests me is theologically. Otherwise he seems to me to be a poor mixture of a Mahomet and a Mephistopheles." M. Mohl returned the book with a French translation of Omar Khayyám by Nicholas, which, through Jowett, was sent to FitzGerald. On February 16th, 1868, Miss Nightingale wrote to M. Mohl: "First:— let me tell you that the Nicholas translation of Omar Khayyám was very successful with that strange odd Englishman Mr. FitzGerald (who once translated a part of it into English). . . . I don't know him nor does he know me—nor that I got him the book. He is a rich eccentric Irishman with a yacht and some story attached to him which I forget about a wife to whom he was passionately attached who was unfaithful—I hope I am not taking away the poor woman's character—and he took to yachting and to Persian as a balm for grief. . . . He says that his English version . . . goes off at a steady sale— of about 2 a year—that he is now, encouraged by Nicholas, going to rub up his little Persian upon old Omar again and publish some more (to ' go off ' at the same rate) and this he is actually doing."

Jowett also sent her a new work by his young protégé, Swinburne, *Atalanta in Calydon*. ". . . Do read, if you have not read, Swinburne's 'Atalanta in Calydon'", she wrote to Clarkey on October 8th, 1865. "Forgive its being an imitation of a Greek play. That is its worst fault. . . . But read it. The Atalanta herself, though she is only a sort of Ginn and not a woman at all, has more reality, more character, more individuality (to use a bad word) than all the *jeunes premières* in all the novelists I ever have read—Walter Scott, Bulwer Lytton and all of them." Encouraged by Jowett she once more began to read Greek. She began to resign herself to the fact that the ideal companionship, the ideal sympathy, for which she so passionately longed, were never to be hers, and to make the best of such materials as life offered her.

Her emotions found an outlet in affection for her cats. Their soft silent movements never shocked her nerves, and she felt they gave her sympathy. "Dumb beasts observe you so much more than human beings and know so much better what you are thinking of", she had written to Fanny in 1862 when her grief for Sidney Herbert and for Clough was still fresh.

However busy and over-driven she might be, even during the gruelling hard work on the Indian Sanitary Report, she found time to write long letters, to Clarkey and M. Mohl, about her cats. One was a tom-cat named Thomas. "I do not like to give Thomas away", she wrote to Clarkey in 1861. "He is stupid, ignorant, thievish and dirty. I don't think anyone would keep him and be kind to him as we are. He is so handsome that people in this country come from afar to see him. It was a shock to find he was not to be contented with one wife (*et soror et conjux*). Pussy had four kits more beautiful than herself, of which Thomas killed one and then hit his eldest daughter a tremendous whack on the side of the head, which she survives however. . . . The only reason which makes the servants bear Thomas is that they think Pussy would pine without him." Thomas was sent away and Miss Nightingale told Clarkey: "He did nothing but disgrace himself. He got up the chimney, had to be put in the wash tub and when sent out into the garden at night was not favoured by the Phoenician Venus." She had to have him back.

She mated her cats carefully and gave kittens away as a

mark of special favour to carefully selected homes. In February 1868 she wrote to M. Mohl: "These cats are so capricious. The little cat wanted to get married. So I presented to her the two greatest partis in England, Messrs. Bismarck and Benedek. She would have neither of them. Now she wants me to invite a hideous low cat out of the street— I won't. But I said she might go out if she liked. But she is too shy."

Miss Nightingale worked with a cat " tied in a knot round her neck ". As many as six cats wandered at will about her room and made " unseemly blurs " on her papers. On many of her letters and drafts is still to be seen the print of a cat's paw. On a scrap of paper she wrote: " Special cat you can't mew and have done with it. You've mewed very nicely. Now mew again, in a different key." She amused herself by playing with them and described to Clarkey her efforts to teach one of her kittens to wash itself; and the kitten saying " what an awkward great cat that is ".

The winter of 1865 passed. It was two years since the Report of the Indian Sanitary Commission had been issued, and nothing had been accomplished. The work of pushing on without result, of enormous labours which perpetually came to nothing, was infinitely dreary, infinitely exacting; and the strain on her was increased by the irritation of her relations with Dr. Sutherland.

As they worked together year after year she became more and more dependent on him and found him more intolerably provoking. She admired the ability, but she disliked the man. " I know he is your pet aversion as he is mine ", she wrote to Clarkey in 1862. " Don't believe what Sutherland tells me he told you . . . he only does it to annoy me ", she wrote to Douglas Galton in 1862, " You know how queer he is." As she grew more exacting Dr. Sutherland became more elusive. He lived at Finchley, which Miss Nightingale thought sufficiently distant, but in 1865 he moved even further away to Norwood. At Finchley he had been fond of gardening, at Norwood he had a garden of considerable size which absorbed a great deal of his time. " I find—I don't know whether you find—it more and more difficult to rouse Dr. Sutherland to do the work we *have* to do ", she wrote to Douglas Galton in 1866.

" He has always some *pond* to dig in his garden. Confound
that Norwood." Through the years of crushing labour on the
Indian Sanitary Report she railed at him with increasing
bitterness. She complained of his " incredible looseness of
thought and recklessness of action ". She told Douglas Galton
she was writing down points she wished him to discuss with
Dr. Sutherland, " as he, I am sure, will forget them on the way
down to you ". She scolded him for losing papers—" it is as
I thought, Sutherland took my copy of the Army Medical
Schools Report and now he can't find it ". Sometimes he
would not work, and she was infuriated. " I could not get
Sutherland to do a thing yesterday ", she wrote to Douglas
Galton in 1866. " He was just like one possessed."

She had always been irritated by his deafness. He was
becoming more deaf as he grew older and always found it
totally impossible to hear anything if he were scolded. As her
health deteriorated, speaking loud enough for Dr. Sutherland
to hear exhausted her. From 1864 onwards she developed a
system of communicating with him by scribbling on any piece of
paper which happened to be handy; literally hundreds of such
scribbles are preserved, written on odd scraps of paper of all
descriptions, from the margins of letters to pieces of blotting-
paper. " What *have* you done? " she wrote. " You said you
were going to lay it before your Committee, you had much
better lay it before *me*! " " Well I don't suppose the man
will hurt you." " My dear soul! It's rather late for this."
" There's fish for you at one." " You know they *could* only
have let you out because you were incurable." " Write that
DOWN." " Why did you tell me that tremendous BANGER."
" Which means nothing but that you're too lazy to look at
it." " You've looked at it? For five minutes on Wednesday." " What has become of the 8 copies of the Indian
Report? Where is Barbadoes? Where are the three Registrar
General papers." " As soon as the Indian Report is done *I
go out of town*. I have been so ill for the last 5 or 6 weeks, and
that is the only thing you will do without being driven, which
I am totally unable for." " My son, I could repeat it word
for word from beginning to end." " Oh don't tell me about
it, I'm scarcely alive." " My dear soul—really Sir Bartle
Frere could not have known the fatal the exhausting labour

he has put you to. . . . He is an ogre." On one occasion Dr. Sutherland tried to be reconciled with her and she wrote, " I *won't* shake hands until the Abstract is done ".

Irritated by him as she was, their intimacy was very close. No other person was part of her daily life as he was part. She saw him, however ill she might be, and he acted as host in her house. Many notes refer to visitors. " These two people have come. Will you see them for me? I have explained who you are." " Was the luncheon good? " " Did he eat? " " Did he walk? " " Then he's a liar, he told me he couldn't move."

In the autumn of 1865 there was a serious quarrel. When in 1861 the scope of the Barrack and Hospital Commission had been enlarged to include the Mediterranean stations she was delighted—she did not realise the consequences. In the autumn of 1865 she was told by Douglas Galton that it was extremely probable that Dr. Sutherland would be invited, as representative of the Barrack and Hospital Commission, to go to Algiers, Malta and Gibraltar to investigate recent cholera epidemics. She became frantic. She was ill, overwhelmed with work, and though she might rail at Dr. Sutherland he was indispensable. " For God's sake," she wrote to Douglas Galton on December 15th, 1865, " if you can, prevent Dr. Sutherland going, he is so childish that if he heard of this Gibraltar and Malta business he would instantly declare there was nothing to keep him in England." She had pledged her word to have the Indian reports and abstracts ready before Parliament met after the Christmas vacation—" a thing I should never have done if I thought Dr. Sutherland was to be sent abroad." Dr. Sutherland was offered the appointment and in spite of all her entreaties he went, taking with him the President of the Madras Sanitary Commission and another Indian official who had been sent by the Government to study sanitary works in Europe. She was furious. On January 19th, 1866, she wrote to Dr. Farr: " Dr. Sutherland has been sent to Algiers with my Indians (they might just as well have been sent to stare at Astley's) and I have all his business besides mine to do. If it *could be done* I should not mind. I had just as soon wear out in two months as in two years, so the work be done. But it can't. It is just like two men going

444

into business with a million each. The one suddenly withdraws. The other may wear himself to the bone but he can't meet the engagements which he made with two. Add to this, I have been so ill since the beginning of the year as to be often unable to have my position moved from pain for 48 hours at a time. . . . But bless your heart Dr. S. thinks the world moves round himself, and that all business stops naturally until he comes back, both in India and in England. He makes no arrangements for it while he is away." On January 26th she wrote to Douglas Galton : " I have heard from Algiers. Wombwell's menagerie (including 3 ladies her Majesties Commissioners and the two ladies maids) were after a column in the interior in a cart. H.M.'s Commissioners very sea sick in the cart." Dr. Sutherland was aware he was in disgrace. " I have been thinking," he wrote to her from Algiers on January 28th; " will she be glad to hear from me ? Or will she swear ? " In spite of Miss Nightingale's anger he continued during 1866 to leave London for weeks at a time on visits of inspection to Algiers, Malta and Gibraltar. His visits were by no means comparable to visiting Astley's Circus. He made a *Report on the French Sanitary Service in Algiers* which was very highly thought of by Douglas Galton, and his observations on sanitary works and conditions at the Mediterranean stations had a direct bearing on work in India. However, owing to his absence in the Mediterranean Miss Nightingale was without him during an important crisis in Indian affairs in the spring of 1866. If Dr. Sutherland had been in London she was convinced the outcome would have been very different.

At the beginning of 1866 the Indian outlook brightened— it seemed that the main cause of obstruction in India was to be removed. Delay in carrying out the recommendations of the Commission was due to the fact that the Sanitary Commissions set up in the Presidencies were subordinate to their local Governments. Miss Nightingale had been urging that the Sanitary Commissions should be transformed into a public health service of first-rate importance, standing on its own feet, responsible directly to the Viceroy and the Viceroy's Council, and kept active by a complementing department of experts at the India Office in London. It was the original scheme which she had failed to persuade the Commission to recommend at the time of the signing of the report in May 1863. During the winter of 1865 she made an important ally. Mr. Ellis, a personal friend of Sir John Lawrence and the President of the Madras Sanitary Commission, came home to study sanitary works. She put rooms in her house at his disposal, arranged for Dr. Sutherland to accompany him to barracks, hospitals and institutions, and talked to him at length on the necessity for a public health service in India. He was converted, and in November forwarded to Sir John Lawrence proposals which Miss Nightingale had drafted for the establishment of the service, adding his own strong recommendation. On January 19th Sir John Lawrence wrote that he agreed to the necessity for reconstructing the sanitary organisation and had written a despatch to the Secretary of State for India dealing with Miss Nightingale's draft and requesting certain changes. He did not send her a copy of the despatch as he assumed she would see it. A week earlier Sir Charles Wood, Secretary of State for India, had resigned and been succeeded by Lord de Grey. The situation could hardly have been more favourable; with Lord de Grey at the India Office it seemed that the establishment of an efficient sanitary administration in India was certain. She asked Lord de Grey to send her a copy of Sir John Lawrence's despatch so that she might start work at once, but he replied that he had received no despatch; it would come in by the next mail, no doubt. Several mails came in but no despatch appeared. Meanwhile it became evident that the Government was on its last legs. Within the next few months, even within the next few weeks, it would fall and Lord de Grey would be Secretary of State for India no longer. She became frantic. Mr. Ellis went down to the India Office and investigated. " They swear by all their gods they have no such despatch ", he told her. March went by, April went by. The Government tottered nearer its fall, and still no despatch appeared. Miss Nightingale scolded, implored, threatened, but without result. As a final resort Lord de Grey made a personal search and the despatch was discovered. " At last the Sanitary Minute has been found," he wrote on May 5th, " it was attached to some papers connected with the Finance Department and so escaped notice."

She was ill and Dr. Sutherland away, but by May 7th she

had managed to submit a memorandum to Lord de Grey detailing the scheme for a public health service and incorporating the alterations requested by the Viceroy. The Government was now on the verge of disaster and Lord de Grey harassed and distracted by party business. It was not until June 11th that she was able to extract instructions from him to proceed further. He then requested her to draft a letter which he would submit to the India Council as his official reply to Sir John Lawrence's despatch. The letter was to be a document of outstanding importance. First, it would place before the India Council the scheme for the sanitary administration of India under a public health service, second, it would put on record a complete sanitary picture of India, surveying the problems to be solved and presenting their solution. It was a formidable task, but by dint of further desperate efforts she completed it and sent it to Lord de Grey on June 19th.

She was twenty-four hours too late. On the previous day the Government had been defeated and had fallen.

The blow was crushing. " I am furious to that degree ", she wrote to Douglas Galton on June 23rd, " at having lost Lord de Grey's five months at the India Office that I am fit to blow you all to pieces with an infernal machine of my own invention." In a letter to M. Mohl on July 12th she said she had come to the end of her endurance. She had lost the opportunity of establishing a public-health service in India " by twenty four hours!! I am well nigh done for. Life is too hard for me."

The Tories were now in power, and Miss Nightingale was pushed further outside Government matters. In spite of the position her expert knowledge had won for her at the War Office, in spite of her official work on the Indian Sanitary Commission, she had never regained her former influence. On March 20th she wrote to Clarkey : " While Sidney Herbert was alive I made most of the appointments. This is no bray. . . . *Now* if you can fancy a position where a person can do *nothing* directly, nothing but by frightening, intriguing, ' soaping ' or going on all fours, that position is mine." A letter she wrote to Douglas Galton on June 27th, 1866, showed how conscious she was of being outside Government circles : ". . . now do write to an agitated female F. N. about who is to come

447

WHERE. Does Gen. Peel come to the War Office? If so, will he annihilate our Civil Sanitary element? Is Sutherland to go all the same to Malta and Gibraltar this autumn? Will Genl Peel imperil the Army Sanitary Committee? I MUST know—ye infernal powers! Is Mr. Lowe to come into the India Office? It is all unmitigated disaster to me. For, as Lord Stanley is to be Foreign Office (the only place where he can be of NO use to us), I shall not have a friend in the world. If I were to say more I should fall to swearing. I am so indignant—ever yours furiously. F. N."

For a short time the situation seemed favourable. Lord Stanley went out of his way to be of use; Lord de Grey was succeeded by Lord Cranborne, and Lord Cranborne was Lord Stanley's personal friend. On July 6th Lord Stanley wrote to Miss Nightingale that he intended to see Lord Cranborne and tell him "the whole sanitary story . . . also say that I have advised you to write to him as you have always done to me to my great advantage". Lord Cranborne wrote that he was "very willing to be instructed", and Miss Nightingale impressed on him the extreme importance of Lord Lawrence's despatch on the Sanitary Administration of India, still lying unanswered in the India Office. On July 17th he wrote: "I have made enquiries as to the despatch you mention and find that it is in the office awaiting decision. No confirmation of it shall take place until I have communicated with you on the subject."

Once more delay followed. Before sanitary questions could be considered certain urgent questions relating to the pay and status of Indian officers must be dealt with. Meanwhile Parliament rose and everyone of importance left London. Nothing could be done until the autumn, and again Miss Nightingale must resign herself to inactivity.

Jowett begged her to visit her parents. She had not been home for nine years. Fanny was seventy-eight, she had been ill in the spring, it was feared that her eyesight was failing, and she had recently been in a carriage accident which had left her bruised and suffering from shock. In August, when the Nightingales invariably went north to Lea Hurst, she was not well enough to travel. It was essential that W. E. N. should go to Lea Hurst, and Miss Nightingale agreed to go home to be with her mother.

Fanny in her old age was to be pitied. Parthe had been her companion, but Parthe was now immersed in her own life. She was mistress of the historic mansion of Claydon and of a house in London. Sir Harry Verney, who was in Parliament, took an active part in public affairs, and Parthe had become " very much the fine lady ". She was achieving success as a hostess and she was writing novels, one of which was published in 1865 in the *Cornhill*. The admiring cousins and maiden aunts she had once patronised complained she had dropped them, and she did not often go to Embley. Fanny had Beatrice Smith, one of Aunt Mai's daughters, as a companion, Fanny's eyesight was now so bad that she needed constant help, and she was paid long visits by her sister, Julia Smith. Aunt Julia, like Hilary Bonham Carter, had never married and had spent her life looking after other people's families, but while Hilary was soft and soothing Julia was temperamental. Miss Nightingale as a girl had christened her " the stormy Ju ". In her old age Aunt Julia found herself homeless and unwanted and was subject to fits of hysterical depression during which she wept for hours on end.

Elaborate arrangements were made to receive Miss Nightingale. She travelled in an invalid carriage, and at Embley six rooms on two floors were given up to her. Her rooms and her way of life were to be sacred. She worked incessantly, saw no one, and never left her room except to visit her mother. In September W. E. N. came back from Lea Hurst, in October Dr. Sutherland came to stay and to work; and Miss Nightingale did not return to London until the end of November. While she was at Embley she made an enquiry into the sanitary condition of the towns of Romsey and Winchester, investigated their mortality figures, and addressed a memorandum to their municipalities advising them to improve their drainage systems at once.

The first reunion with Fanny was affectionate, but even now she would not give way to her mother. Fanny might be seventy-eight and almost blind, but she was not to be indulged. Miss Nightingale still implacably disapproved of the way in which Fanny frittered away her life. On August 21st, 1866, immediately after her arrival, she wrote a long letter to Clarkey. She began tenderly enough: " I don't think my dear mother was ever more touching and interesting to me than she is now in her state of dilapidation. She is so much gentler, calmer, more thoughtful. . . ." But as she proceeded irritation and disapproval crept in, and at the end of the letter she wrote sharply, " I can't think Mama much altered except her memory . . . and her habits which have become worse, till now she is seldom up until 5 or 6 P.M. and then goes out in the carriage ".

Miss Nightingale was not an easy visitor. She required a great deal and was critical of the way in which her requirements were met. To argue with her was forbidden. Aunt Mai, writing to Parthe during the summer, repeated a letter from her daughter Beatrice: " In *confidence*. Beatrice finds her concerns with Flo extremely difficult. Beatrice does her best but it is very difficult to explain anything to Flo because of her health. Her heart . . . may *snap* at any extra effort or excitement. Her feeling for Beatrice partakes of the displeasure so often felt when something is done which she thinks might be better done." Aunt Julia, who was spending the summer at Embley, wrote acidly to Parthe: " Her father goes into Flo's room every day, she never leaves it except to visit her mother's room and seems to be so busy that she cannot want any company but theirs. But *I* only speak from report. . . ." In a second letter she complained that she had still not seen Florence and was expected to send messages to her through her maid: " I wish F would take a good long sleep for a fortnight or so, then a good quiet time for thinking with only those about her who will be content to see her and not to make her talk—and after that you would see her, I hope, rise refreshed to a new life."

Only children were allowed to break into Miss Nightingale's solitude. Fanny kept up her custom of having children to stay through the summer months. During August Fanny wrote to Parthe: " I thought our poor F. both excited and exhausted on Sunday, but to-day she has accepted our beautiful baby, who marched into her room, all alone with a flower in each hand, and played upon her bed for 3/4 of an hour ".

When she returned to London affairs in India could hardly have been more discouraging. Sir John Lawrence's despatch on sanitary organisation still lay unanswered at the India

Office, and in India what amounted to the abolition of the Sanitary Commissions was being proposed. Their personnel had already been reduced to two members only; now their place was to be taken by a single " Sanitary Officer " in each Presidency, who was also to be Inspector of Prisons; the Inspector-General of Prisons was to become " Sanitary Commissioner to the Government of India ". It was difficult to see how, after professing to be convinced of the necessity for a public health service on the lines laid down by Miss Nightingale, Sir John Lawrence could have allowed a scheme to be put forward which made sanitary administration a sub-department of the prison department. She was bitterly disappointed—very far away were the days when she had sung for joy at Sir John Lawrence's government. Dr. Sutherland frankly said Sir John Lawrence was hopeless. " He is our worst enemy ", he wrote in 1866; and he advised her before she attempted to do anything further to wait until Sir John Lawrence's term of office ended in the following year. One disappointment followed another. Lord Cranborne, with whom she had made a promising beginning, resigned the India Office in March 1867, and was succeeded by Sir Stafford Northcote. She did not know Sir Stafford Northcote. Jowett, who knew him well, offered her an introduction but she hoped the Government would fall on the issue of Parliamentary Reform. However, through the spring of 1867, though daily expected to resign, it remained in power. Presently a year had passed since Sir John Lawrence had written the despatch on sanitary organisation, a year since the establishment of a public health service in India had seemed a certainty. Miss Nightingale determined to wait no longer. On May 28th she wrote to Douglas Galton : " Our Indian affairs are getting as drunk as they can be and I am resolved to put them straight ". The battle for an Indian public-health service must be resumed. In addition to her previous scheme she intended to press for publication of an annual sanitary report recording work done during the year. It would ensure that " the wholesome light of publicity " illuminated the doings of the public-health service and prevent it from becoming a " secret society ". She asked Douglas Galton whether she should now approach Sir Stafford Northcote, and he advised her to approach not

451

only Sir Stafford but also Sir Bartle Frere, a well-known Indian administrator, who had just been appointed to a seat on the India Council after being Governor of Bombay. Sir Bartle Frere was equally anxious to see Miss Nightingale, and before she had time to write he had asked permission to call. On June 16th she wrote to Douglas Galton : " I have seen Sir Bartle Frere. He came on Friday by his own appointment. And we had a great talk. He impressed me wonderfully— more than any Indian I have seen except Sir John Lawrence ; and I seemed to learn more in an hour from him upon Indian administration and the way it is going than I did from Ellis in six months, or from Strachey in two days, or from Indian Councils (Secretaries of State and Commissions and all) in six years. I hope Sir B. Frere may be of use to us." The friendship became one of the closest of her life. Like so many men of marked ability, he fell under her spell and regarded her with affection, respect and something which approached wonder.

In 1867 Sir Bartle Frere was fifty-two. He had been in the service of the Indian Government since 1834 and, like the Lawrences, possessed deep sympathy with the Indian character. His outstanding achievement was his administration of the province of Scinde which, in eight years, by the exercise of a benevolent justice, he brought from a state of rebellion, backwardness and ignorance to prosperity, security and loyalty. The revenues were practically doubled, 6000 miles of road were built, the construction of railways was begun, the first postage stamps ever used in India were issued and so loyal was the province that he was able, when the Mutiny broke out, to hold Scinde with only 178 European soldiers. When in 1859 he left Scinde to become a member of the Viceroy's Council his departure was mourned as a national disaster. On the Council he pressed for reform, especially for the employment of qualified Indians in administrative posts. In 1862 he was appointed Governor of Bombay. Here he demolished insanitary buildings, introduced scavenging services, established a town council, founded a school for the education of the daughters of Indian gentlemen and substantially reduced the death-rate. While he was Governor of Bombay, Government House was as freely open to Indian gentlemen and their wives as to Europeans. The end of his term of office was clouded by the disastrous failure of the Bombay Bank, but on his return to England in 1867 he was created a member of the India Council.

For the next two months Miss Nightingale and Sir Bartle Frere met almost daily. " I need not tell you how entirely my services are at your disposal ", he wrote after their first interview, and her notes mention his name repeatedly. " Sir Bartle Frere was here 2 hrs." " Sir B. F. here again." " Sir Bartle Frere called at 2.30." It was a connection of great assistance to her. The India Council were notoriously jealous of the Sanitary Commission, which had been initiated not by themselves but by the War Office, and Sir Bartle Frere was a powerful friend. Unlike Sir John Lawrence, he united firmness of purpose with conciliatory manners. He had a mildness of disposition which, it was said, " invited co-operation ".

Once more she began to hope. With Sir Bartle Frere, so sympathetic, so able, so enlightened, surely something might be achieved. What he had done in Bombay was a pattern for what she wished to do for the whole of India. On July 24th she wrote to Douglas Galton: " If only we could get a Public Health Department in the India Office to ourselves with Sir B. Frere at the head of it, our fortunes would be made ". She did not go to Embley in the summer of 1867. There was fresh hope of progress, and she stayed in London.

Sir John Lawrence's term of office was petering out in disappointment as far as sanitary matters were concerned. It seemed that, like Sidney Herbert, he was incapable of grasping an administrative issue. He had acquiesced in the suggestion that the Public Health Service of India should be made a subdepartment under the Inspector of Prisons without apparently understanding what that implied. Now in the summer of 1867 he threw another project into confusion. Three years ago he had asked Miss Nightingale to draw up a scheme for the employment of nurses in hospitals by the Bengal Sanitary Commission. The difficulties were enormous, largely owing to the very poor level of the Indian Medical Service. Miss Nightingale made notes of an interview on the scheme with a doctor whom she considered a typical Indian Medical Officer, holding the high rank of Deputy Inspector-General in Madras.

453

" He came intent on proving to me that no matron was wanted. The Dr. ought to be Matron and wretched coolie women under the Dr. nurses. But, luckily for me, he was drunk. And before he went (he was here $2\frac{1}{2}$ hours) he had admitted everything. He described his lying-in hospital where 'the pupils deliver all the ordinary cases, without a midwife, and without a doctor. The Dr. comes in for the extraordinary cases.' . . . I said ' They are by to see the extraordinary cases delivered ? ' Here he got so drunk that he spent at least half an hour explaining to me that there was nothing to be seen ' that everything was under the bed clothes '. The lying-in patients were all fed by friends from outside and were always naked in bed—except the Europeans. There were 80 leper beds at the General Hospital, always full. He says ' It all answers very well ! ! ' " She wrote to Douglas Galton that after seven years' experience of the Indian Medical Service and of the numerous doctors who had been sent to see her and corresponded with her, she would prefer to rely on Temperance, her maid.

The attempt to employ female nurses must be made with the greatest caution, and she submitted a scheme for employing nurses in a single hospital and observing the result before embarking on any large undertaking. Sir John Lawrence turned the scheme over to the medical service, who blew it up into a grandiose plan for introducing female nursing on a large scale into seven hospitals simultaneously at great expense. This scheme, not Miss Nightingale's, was submitted to the Government of India, who, she said very properly, rejected it. She was angry. It seemed that Dr. Sutherland was right and that Sir John Lawrence was her worst enemy. Sir John McNeill, who had assisted her in preparing her plan, was equally annoyed. " You must wait for a new Governor General ", he wrote in September 1867, " Sir John Lawrence has disappointed me. It would be mere waste of time . . . to argue with men who flounder about in such a hopeless slough of unreason."

She turned her full attention on the task of enlisting Sir Stafford Northcote, who had indicated that he was prepared to hear from her.

By July 25th, 1867, she had completed a memorandum

setting out the urgency of the case for the establishment of an Indian public-health service, reciting what had occurred with regard to the lost despatch and entreating Sir Stafford to perform the noble service of bestowing on India efficient means of attaining and preserving public health.

The memorandum was submitted to Sir Bartle Frere, who approved it enthusiastically. " Nothing could be better than your memo ", he wrote, and he himself took it to Sir Stafford Northcote. On July 30th Sir Stafford wrote Miss Nightingale a friendly and flattering letter. The matter should be attended to at once, and he added that he " attached great weight to any suggestions from one who is so well qualified to speak with authority as yourself ". He accepted several further letters amplifying the scheme; and on August 19th, while she was debating whether the time was ripe to suggest a meeting, he wrote suggesting that he should call on her at South Street " for a little conversation ".

It was an important but nerve-racking opportunity. The Minister was well disposed and he was making the first move but, as she had written to Douglas Galton, he was a " last hope ", and those who knew both Sir Stafford and Miss Nightingale were by no means confident that they would find themselves in sympathy. The tone of his mind was cold, his temperament was cautious. She was nervous. " Hope was green and the donkey ate it (that's me) ", she wrote to Douglas Galton on July 16th. Nevertheless she determined to be bold. If she made an impression on Sir Stafford Northcote she would ask, then and there, for the establishment of a department at the India Office with Sir Bartle Frere at the head of it to control the sanitary administration of India.

On August 20th Jowett wrote her a cautionary letter. " I am delighted to hear you are casting your toils about Sir Stafford Northcote. Do you know that he was elected a fellow of Balliol with A. H. Clough? I think that you may do him, as well as the cause, immense service. May I talk to you as I would to one of our undergraduates? Take care not to exaggerate to him."

The interview had already taken place. Sir Stafford had called at South Street on the day Jowett wrote, and the meeting had been a triumphant success. Dissimilar as Miss Nightingale and Sir Stafford might be, each was completely unself-seeking. Stafford Northcote was, Gladstone said, " a man in whom it was a fixed habit of mind to put himself wholly out of view when he had before him the attainment of great public objects ". He was incapable of prejudice or of resentment. Though his mind was cold, his integrity was unmistakable. When Sir Stafford had gone Miss Nightingale scribbled a note for Dr. Sutherland. " Well—I've won this. We are to have a department in the I.O. for Sanitary business. B. Frere. Anderson. I don't know if he saw how afraid I was of him. For he kept his eyes tight shut all the time. And I kept mine wide open. . . . He was *very* confidential. And we must *worry* him." On the 22nd she wrote to Douglas Galton : " I saw Sir Stafford Northcote on Tuesday. He came of his own accord. The result is (if he does what he says) that there will be a controlling Committee at the I.O. for sanitary things. . . . I wish I could choose the members as I did in Sidney Herbert's time. But I have the greatest faith in Sir B. Frere and he asked me to let him bring Sir H. Anderson here so we shall have the chairman and secretary on our side. I *liked* Sir Stafford Northcote."

Once more the establishment of a public-health service for India seemed just round the corner. " We will make 35 South Street the India Office till this is done ", wrote Sir Bartle Frere.

The phrase touched a chord. Ten years ago when Sidney Herbert was alive the Burlington Hotel had been called the little War Office, and Miss Nightingale scribbled on Sir Bartle Frere's letter " I miss him so ". The wound had never healed. She passed each anniversary of his death, " that dreadful day ", in meditation and prayer. On August 2nd she dated her private letters " 6 years ago ", " 7 years ago ". On this August 2nd, 1867, she wrote in a private note : " I feel myself not only a shattered wreck of what I was but a phantom among phantoms. . . . We do not know until the crash we are so many phantoms." Her grief was tenacious ; she refused to be resigned, as she refused to accept compromise. To be resigned, to compromise was to accept the second best. That she would never do and she kept grief with her. Grief was waiting for her when she turned from her work, grief with grief's companions—frustration, resentment and remorse. And yet—if she had ceased to feel she would have slackened. As great waves of resentment and grief surged up in her she worked harder, vowed more furiously that she would never give way, never succumb to the low standards, the inefficiency and the indifference of the world.

In the autumn of 1867 she did some of the hardest work of her life. In October Sir Stafford Northcote wrote that he had " cleared the decks " and was now ready to give full attention to sanitary matters. On October 23rd he came to see her again. " He comes ", she wrote in a note to Dr. Sutherland, " to be coached in the best way to announce the Sanitary Committee to the War Office. Now you're going to be good aren't you, for I *am* tired and feverish." The second interview was even more successful than the first. The names of the members of the Indian Sanitary Committee were agreed, and Sir Stafford consented to establish the authority of the Sanitary Committee as supreme in India. The War Office Sanitary Committee was in future to act in India in a consultative capacity only. This decision put an end to part at least of the constant friction between the India Office and War Office. Sir Stafford asked her to draft an answer to a despatch just received from the Government of India relating to the appointment and pay of medical officers of health; more important, he asked her to prepare a digest of the progress of the whole Indian Sanitary question from the setting up of the Sanitary Commission in 1859 to 1867.

" I really believe ", she wrote to Dr. Sutherland, " that he will carry out what he consents to do." She plunged into work at once. By the beginning of December she had completed the instructions for the Sanitary Committee, the draft despatch on Medical Officers of Health and the Digest of the Indian Sanitary question. To the digest she had added a Memorandum of Suggestions and Advice. In addition, on her own initiative, she had drafted a suggestion for an important despatch to be sent to the Government of India by Sir Stafford Northcote which would revive the sanitary question in an urgent form. A report on sanitary progress was requested, with particular reference to the *Suggestions in regard to Sanitary Works required for the Improvement of Indian Stations* which had been sent to guide the Indian authorities as long ago as 1864. What had happened, the Secretary of State for India wished to know? What was the present position, what results had been achieved? She submitted her draft with temerity—she was fully aware, she wrote, that Sir Stafford might disapprove the whole scheme. Sir Stafford accepted the suggestion almost in its entirety. The despatch was sent; and the reports received from the Presidencies as a result were printed as a Blue Book in 1868 under the title of the India Office Sanitary Annual, together with Miss Nightingale's digest of the Indian sanitary question, her memorandum on it and a copy of the despatch itself. In future reports were to be sent in by the Presidencies and published every year.

At last she had accomplished something. She had secured a Sanitary Department in the India Office with supreme authority in India, she had secured publication of annual reports which would prevent authorities in India from going to sleep. On February 16th, 1868, she was able to write to M. Mohl in triumph: "By dint of remaining here for 13 months to dog the Minister I have got a little (not tart) but Department all to myself, called 'Of Public Health Civil and Military for India' with Sir B. Frere at the head of it. And I had the immense satisfaction 3 or 4 months ago of seeing 'Printed Despatch No. 1' of said Department. (I never in all my life before, saw any Despatch, Paper or Minute under at least No. 77,981.)"

Again she had paid a heavy price for her success. The thirteen months during which she had shut herself up in South Street working day and night had further impaired her health. She was slowing down. "I do the work in 3 hours I used to do in one", she told Clarkey in July 1867. She would not spare herself on that account. If she were slower, the only consequence was that she must drive herself harder. Once more the limit of what she could inflict on herself was reached, and in December 1867, after the autumn of gruelling work for Sir Stafford Northcote, she collapsed completely. "I broke up all at once," she told M. Mohl in February 1868, "and fled to Malvern on December 26th with a little cat."

For nine days she stayed at Malvern, leaving her address only with Dr. Sutherland, seeing no one and reading nothing.

" It was like living in a cave ", she wrote.

Urgent work called her back—not Indian work; for the moment there was a lull in Indian affairs. She had other calls on her as exacting as India. While she had been working on the Indian Sanitary Commission, gigantic as her labours had been, they were not her only occupation. Her work for public health in England, for hospitals and the reorganisation of nursing, had rapidly expanded and assumed enormous proportions.

XX   IN 1861 Miss Nightingale received a letter from a Mr. William Rathbone of Liverpool, who was the eldest son of a dynasty of Liverpool merchants and shipowners, and the sixth William Rathbone in succession to be senior partner in the family firm. He inherited a tradition of philanthropy and liberalism. His grandfather had been a prominent Abolitionist and his father, though the Rathbones were originally Quakers, had taken a leading part in the struggle for Catholic emancipation. As a young man he was an honorary visitor for the District Provident Society in one of the poorest quarters in Liverpool, and there he witnessed the miseries endured by the poor who were ill in their own homes. In 1859 he founded district nursing, starting in his own district with one trained nurse. Since one nurse proved ludicrously inadequate, he decided to establish, at his own expense, a body of trained nurses to nurse the sick poor in their own homes. Finding that trained nurses of the type he required—responsible, trustworthy and experienced—did not exist, he wrote to Miss Nightingale asking her advice.

Her experiences as a girl in the cottages of Lea Hurst had taught her how urgent was the need for district nursing, and though she was overwhelmed with work on the Indian Sanitary Commission she gave William Rathbone's scheme " as much consideration ", he wrote, " as if she herself were going to be the Superintendent ". She came to the conclusion that the only satisfactory solution was to train nurses specially, and suggested that the Royal Liverpool Infirmary should be approached to co-operate in opening a training school for nurses, with the guarantee that a fixed percentage of the nurses trained at the school should be reserved for the Royal Infirmary. In the following year, at William Rathbone's expense, a Training School and Home for Nurses was opened in connection with the Royal Infirmary, and proved an unqualified success.

William Rathbone, austere in spite of great wealth, unselfish, tender-hearted, devoid of sentimentality to the point of dryness, was a man Miss Nightingale could appreciate, and they became intimate friends. His admiration and affection for her were unbounded; he wrote that he was " proud to be one of her journeymen workers", and when she moved into South Street he presented her with a stand filled with flowering plants, which he kept renewed weekly until his death.

While following up cases from his district he visited workhouse infirmaries and found that, though the sick in the slums were miserable, the paupers in the workhouse infirmaries were more miserable still. The Liverpool Workhouse Infirmary was, on the whole, well administered, but the condition of the sick was wretched beyond description. Twelve hundred sick paupers were accommodated. As in all workhouse infirmaries, such nursing as existed was done by able-bodied female paupers, and owing to the fact that Liverpool was a seaport and the city had large harbour slums, many of the women were drunken prostitutes. These women, wrote Miss Eleanor Rathbone in a memoir of her father, " were superintended by a very small number of paid, but untrained, parish officers, who were in the habit, it was said, of wearing kid gloves in the wards to protect their hands. All night a policeman patrolled some of the wards to keep order, while others, in which the inhabitants were too sick or infirm to make disturbance, were locked up and left unvisited all night."

On January 31st, 1864, William Rathbone made the first move to reform workhouse nursing. He wrote to Miss Nightingale and suggested that a staff of trained nurses and a matron should be sent to the Liverpool Workhouse Infirmary; it was not possible to send nurses from the training school, as the full number trained there was already bespoken by the Royal Infirmary and the District Nursing scheme. If she could find nurses and a matron he offered to guarantee the cost for whatever term of years she thought advisable. It would not be easy to obtain permission to introduce the nurses, and he asked her to draft a letter which he could send to the Vestry who controlled the Workhouse Infirmary, asking for their co-operation.

A long battle ensued. " There has been as much diplomacy and as many treaties and as much of people working against each other, as if we had been going to occupy a Kingdom instead of a Workhouse ", Miss Nightingale wrote to Rev. Mother Bermondsey in September 1864. Permission was not granted until March 1865, and by then she had also become involved in the reform of workhouse nursing in London.

In December 1864 a pauper named Timothy Daly died in the Holborn Workhouse. There was an inquest and it was found that death had resulted from filthiness caused by gross neglect; the newspapers took the case up and there was a public scandal. Miss Nightingale seized the opportunity to write a tactful letter to Mr. Charles Villiers, the President of the Poor Law Board. She ventured to write, she said, because Timothy Daly's case proved the overwhelming necessity for the improvement of nursing in workhouse infirmaries. She reminded him that she had some practical experience of nursing and was responsible for the training of nurses. He might perhaps be interested to hear what was going to be done in the Liverpool Workhouse Infirmary with a staff of trained nurses and a matron from the Nightingale Training School.

Mr. Villiers was ready to listen; he was a friend of Lord Palmerston who, when offering him the post of President of the Board of Trade, had added the distinction of a seat in the Cabinet; he was a friend also of Miss Nightingale's ally, Sir Robert Rawlinson the engineer. A champion of the people's rights, Charles Villiers had devoted many years of his life to the repeal of the Corn Laws to reduce the price of bread. His appearance was romantically handsome, his manner was charming, and his powers of conversation were considered unequalled.

He replied immediately, and at the end of January came to see her. " He called on me last week by his own appointment about a scheme for nursing workhouses ", Miss Nightingale told Harriet Martineau on February 2nd, 1865.

By the end of the interview they were firm friends. He charmed her, while her powers inspired him with intense admiration. Sir Edward Cook describes him bursting out to a friend after he had received one of her memoranda: " I delight to read the Nightingale's song about it all. If any one of them had a tenth part of her vigour of mind we might expect something."

Even at their first meeting more than the reform of workhouse nursing was discussed. She had realised that it was virtually impossible to reform workhouse nursing without reforming workhouse administration, and she urged Mr. Villiers to make use of the death of Timothy Daly to initiate an investigation into the whole question of the treatment of the sick poor.

" They are much more frightened by the death from the Holborn Union than they 'let on'", she wrote to Sir John McNeill on February 7th. " I was so much obliged to that poor man for dying. It was want of cleanliness. Mr. Villiers says that he shall never hear the last of it in the H. of C." Early in February 1865 Mr. Villiers sent his principal assistant, Mr. H. B. Farnall, to see her. Mr. Farnall was Poor Law Inspector for the Metropolitan District, and a man of liberal views. He had been working for Poor Law Reform all his life and knew the almost insuperable difficulties lying ahead, but she inspired him with an astonishing confidence. " From the first," he wrote in December 1866, " I had a sort of fixed faith that Florence Nightingale could do anything."

It was decided to start the investigation in London, and with Mr. Farnall's assistance Miss Nightingale drew up a " Form of Enquiry " to be circulated to every workhouse infirmary and workhouse sick ward in the Metropolitan district. Mr. Villiers approved, and the forms were sent out in February 1865.

In March permission was at last given for the Nightingale nurses to enter the Liverpool Workhouse Infirmary. On May 5th Mr. Villiers told the House of Commons that he was hopeful of great and immediate improvements in workhouse nursing, "in consequence of communications lately received at the Poor Law Board from Miss Nightingale who was now taking much interest in the matter ". On May 16th twelve nurses and a matron, Miss Agnes Jones, arrived at the Liverpool Workhouse Infirmary. " Mr. Rathbone puts down £1200 ", wrote Miss Nightingale. The experiment was at first to be confined to the male wards only.

Once more she was desperately anxious. Once more everything hung on the endurance, the good behaviour and the good sense of a band of young women. She had convinced Mr. Villiers of the possibility of employing trained nurses in workhouse infirmaries, but what if the nurses failed? The task which lay before them was fearful enough to daunt the boldest. Fortunately the matron was a young woman of remarkable character and qualifications who had already been selected by Miss Nightingale as the only woman capable of becoming her successor. Agnes Jones was the daughter of Colonel Jones of Londonderry and the niece of Sir John Lawrence. She was " pretty and young and rich and witty, ideal in her beauty as a Louis XIV shepherdess ", Miss Nightingale wrote to Clarkey. But beneath the prettiness was the soul of a martyr—she had inherited the passionate altruism and uncompromising moral rectitude of the Lawrence family as well as their good looks. Miss Nightingale's work in the Crimea had inspired her to become a nurse and, following in her footsteps, she persuaded her family to allow her to go to Kaiserswerth in 1860. After two years there she wrote to Miss Nightingale, who advised her to complete her training by a year at the Nightingale School at St. Thomas's. She entered in 1863 and was the best probationer Mrs. Wardroper had ever had and Miss Nightingale's " best and dearest pupil ". On completing her training she went to the Great Northern Hospital and was working there as a sister when she was offered the post of Matron of the Liverpool Workhouse Infirmary in August 1864.

She knew how fearful would be the task, and she refused ; but her conscience would not let her rest. Had she not received a call from God ? After days spent in agony and prayer she wrote again and accepted.

In 1868 Miss Nightingale wrote an account of Agnes Jones's work in *Good Words* under the title " Una and the Lion ". The Lion symbolised the paupers Agnes Jones had to nurse, "far more untameable than any lion ". She had nursed in great London hospitals but, she said, until she came to Liverpool Workhouse Infirmary she did not know what sin and wickedness were. The wards were an inferno, the hordes of pauper patients more degraded than animals. Vicious habits, ignorance, idiocy, met her on every side. Drunkenness was universal—thirty-five of the pauper nurses had to be dismissed for drunkenness in the first month. Immorality was universal. Filth was universal. The patients wore the same shirts for seven weeks, bedding was only changed and washed once a month, food was at starvation level, spirits entered the infirmary freely. The number of patients was very large, 1350, rising at times to 1500. There were administrative difficulties; her position and powers were not properly defined; the supply of food to the Workhouse Infirmary was done by contract, and the doctors had no control over it; the task of training the pauper nurses was hopeless. "It is like Scutari over again", Miss Nightingale told her. In February 1868 Miss Nightingale wrote to Clarkey: "What makes Workhouse nursing such an awful strain on all one's faculties is what made the War Hospital nursing so. It is not the hardship and the misery, but it is the struggle with all the authorities for justice —and the struggle with corrupt officials and the old Masters who are all more or less in the power of the Paupers who know of their malpractices."

At first it seemed that the experiment was failing. The governor of the Infirmary had supported the scheme, but Agnes Jones quarrelled with him. She objected to his "want of refinement" and he thought her too strict and unpractical— she was a stiff-necked Presbyterian Irishwoman from Ulster with a hot Irish temper, and had not the tact which enabled Miss Nightingale to manage officials. There were several serious disagreements, described by Dr. Sutherland as "Hibernian Rows". Miss Nightingale intervened, smoothed things over, talked each side round. When affairs in Liverpool reached a deadlock William Rathbone made a flying trip to London to consult her. She was adept at coaxing: Dr. Sutherland, drafting a letter to the governor of the Infirmary, left a blank "for you to fill in with soft sawder".

Gradually the scene changed. Agnes Jones, under Miss Nightingale's influence, became less rigid and her genius as a nurse and as an administrator made itself felt. Old women visiting their husbands reported "wonderful changes in the House" since the London nurses came. Ladies who acted as charitable visitors began to sing her praises, the medical staff asked for more nurses. The results Miss Jones was achieving were so good that they intended to propose she should take over the female as well as the male wards. Most important of all, the cost of maintaining the sick in the Workhouse Infirmary under her régime was less, not more, than before. Agnes Jones, wrote Miss Nightingale, converted the Vestry to the conviction of the economy as well as the humanity of nursing pauper sick by trained nurses.

With this success behind her Miss Nightingale pressed for legislation. It was impossible to correct the abuses which existed in workhouses and workhouse infirmaries until they were put on a new financial and administrative basis. To make the changes required there must be an Act of Parliament.

She did not try to establish a position for herself within the Poor Law Board as she had done with the War Office and the India Office. Mr. Villiers was over sixty, and, much as she liked him, she was forced to realise that he no longer possessed the energy to be her mouthpiece. He could be overruled and had recently been overruled on a vital point. She had persuaded him to add a most important clause to the Poor Law Board Continuation Bill which gave the Poor Law Board powers to compel guardians to improve their workhouses; at present the Board had powers of recommendation only, and their recommendations were frequently ignored. He had not been strong enough to carry the clause through, and in July 1865 it was struck out.

She decided that the Poor Law Board would never produce the necessary legislation—she must go over its head and approach Lord Palmerston. Once more she succeeded. He promised that if she would draft a Bill he would use his influence to get it through the Cabinet. Full of hope, she began work with Mr. Farnall, but another blow fell. It was the moment when Lord Palmerston was taken ill, and on October 18th he died; her hopes of influence in the Cabinet were at an end. " This very next session was to have seen a bill about London poor rates and London Workhouses upon which I had set my heart and which they think will not now get through the Cabinet without Ld Palmerston ", she wrote to Lord Palmerston's stepdaughter-in-law on October 18th.

Though she must depend again on Mr. Villiers she was not left without hope. The answers to the " Form of Enquiry " sent out to London workhouses and workhouse infirmaries revealed facts so shameful that they could not be ignored.

Through the autumn of 1865 she worked on a long memorandum for Mr. Villiers which dealt in detail with workhouse nursing, workhouse schools and requirements of administration and finance in workhouse infirmaries. She put forward a scheme for the Metropolitan area which was intended to be extended later to other areas. The first necessity was to change the mental attitude which made the miseries of the hideous system possible. " So long ", she wrote, " as a sick man, woman or child is considered administratively to be a pauper to be repressed and not a fellow creature to be nursed into health, so long will these shameful disclosures have to be made. The sick, infirm or mad pauper ceases to be a pauper when so afflicted." It was the conception on which she based her attitude towards the human race. Suffering lifts its victim above normal values. While suffering endures there is neither good nor bad, valuable nor invaluable, enemy nor friend. The victim has passed to a region beyond human classification or moral judgments and his suffering is a sufficient claim.

Administratively her scheme for reform was based on three essentials which she termed the A B C of workhouse reform.

(*A*) The sick, insane, incurable and children must be dealt with separately in proper institutions and not mixed up together in infirmaries and sick wards as at present. " The care and government of the *sick* poor is a thing totally different from the government of paupers. Why do we have Hospitals in order to cure, and Workhouse Infirmaries in order *not* to cure ? Taken solely from the point of view of preventing pauperism what a stupidity and anomaly this is ! . . . You must have two kinds of administration, one for sick, for infirm, aged and imbeciles and above all for children and another for paupers. Once acknowledge this principle and you must have suitable establishments for the cure of the sick and infirm."

(*B*) There must be a single central administration. " The entire Medical Relief of London should be under one central management which would know where vacant beds were to be found, and be able so to distribute the Sick etc., as to use all the establishments in the most economical way."

(*C*) " For the purpose of providing suitable establishments for the care and treatment of the Sick, Insane etc., Consolidation and a General Rate are essential." This point was vital ; the future of workhouse nursing and administration turned on it. As long as the workhouses and infirmaries were paid for out of the parochial rates, and staff appointments were made by local authorities with absolute power, there would inevitably be jobbery. Moreover, " to provide suitable treatment in each Workhouse would involve an expenditure which even London could not bear ". At the moment to be a sick or insane pauper in a poor parish was to be horribly penalised.

The memorandum reached Mr. Villiers in December. Her case was unanswerable, and he agreed to press at once for a new London Poor Law Bill. On December 11th Mr. Farnall went to see him and returned full of hope. Great reforms were ahead, he told Miss Nightingale, and the struggle was more than half won. From day to day the situation improved. The *Lancet* sent a special commissioner to enquire into the state of London workhouse infirmaries, and, as a result, the " Association for the Improvement of the Infirmaries of London Workhouses " was formed. In April 1866 the Association sent a deputation to the Poor Law Board pressing for immediate improvement, and Mr. Villiers gave an assurance that legislation might be expected almost immediately. Meanwhile he appointed Mr. Farnall and a doctor to inspect and report on all London workhouse infirmaries and sick wards at once, following the lines of the unofficial investigation already carried out by Miss Nightingale. Newspaper articles began to appear. Delane, editor of *The Times*, called to see Mr. Villiers, and journalists, including Edwin Chadwick, applied to Miss Nightingale for facts. In April the Metropolitan Workhouse Infirmary Bill seemed almost a certainty.

Yet once more everything vanished into thin air. It was the spring of 1866 and the Whig Government was tottering. Workhouse infirmary reform was a controversial subject, and as Lord de Grey delayed on the Indian Public Health Service so Mr. Villiers delayed on the Metropolitan Workhouse Infirmary Bill. " He was afraid ", wrote Miss Nightingale to Harriet Martineau, on May 2nd, " of losing the Government one vote." On June 18th the Government fell, Mr. Villiers went out of office, and the Metropolitan Workhouse Infirmary Bill was lost. " It was a cruel disappointment to me ", wrote Miss Nightingale to M. Mohl on July 12th, 1866, " to see the Bill go just as I had it in my grasp. . . . Alas! There is a pathetic story of Balzac's in which a poor woman who had

468

followed the Russian campaign was never able to articulate any word except 'Adieu, Adieu, Adieu!' I am afraid of going mad like her and not being able to articulate any word but Alas! alas! alas!"

Though all the summer she was very ill, she would not accept defeat. Surely in some direction something could be done. "I had hopes for a time from a Committee of the House of Commons (on which serves John Stuart Mill) on the special Local Government of the Metropolis", she wrote to M. Mohl on July 12th. She sent John Stuart Mill a copy of her memorandum, she approached Edwin Chadwick, who had been asked to advise by John Stuart Mill, offering "to express my conclusions more in detail in answer to written questions (as I have done to 2 Royal Commissions) should the Committee of the House of Commons think it worth while". At first she seemed to be making an impression and the Committee asked her for "a long letter" which she wrote at once, then hope faded as the whole question was postponed. "Because it is July and they are rather hot they give it up for this year", she wrote.

Early in July she had written to Mr. Gathorne Hardy, Mr. Villiers' successor, and on July 25th he replied in a complimentary and discouraging letter. She must not apologise for writing to him, she had "earned no common title to advise and suggest upon anything which affects the treatment of the sick". Indeed, her letter had arrived at the very moment "when a gentleman was urging me to lay before you questions relating to Workhouse Infirmaries". Sufficient compliments having been paid, he made it clear that he had no intention of becoming involved with her. He had "not advanced very far from want of time"; he was "necessarily very much occupied with other business" and anxious "to remedy if possible present and urgent grievances before embarking on legislation for the future". In conclusion, he hastened to assure her he would "bear in mind the offer you have made and in all probability avail myself of it to the full".

He did not invite her to write to him again, he did not suggest calling on her. On the heels of the letter came further discouraging news. Mr. Gathorne Hardy removed Mr. Farnall from his post at Whitehall as Poor Law Inspector of the Metropolitan District, and sent him to Yorkshire. There could be no plainer proof that Mr. Gathorne Hardy did not intend to be on the side of reform. Miss Nightingale was forced to admit she could do nothing further, and went to Embley.

The removal of Mr. Farnall deprived her of her principal source of information at the Poor Law Board, and though Mr. Villiers was her friend, he felt, having so recently resigned office, that it would be improper to do anything to interfere with his successor.

But in October Mr. Gathorne Hardy made Mr. Villiers "frantically angry". On October 31st Miss Nightingale wrote to Douglas Galton that "Mr. Hardy told him, Mr. Villiers, *twice*, in the Ho: of C, that had he only known how to use, with dexterity and wisdom, the weapon of the law, he would have found it a very sufficient weapon". Fresh legislation, Mr. Hardy asserted, was quite unnecessary, provided the existing Acts were properly understood and applied. Since Mr. Villiers had devoted his term of office to framing new legislation, he took this as an attack on himself. He began to write to Miss Nightingale again, expressing his determination " not to sit down under this kind of thing "; he intended to " catch Mr. Gathorne Hardy out " and show him that something more was needed to solve the problem of Poor Law Administration than " a touch of Mr. Gathorne Hardy's magic wand ". On October 28th Miss Nightingale wrote to Edwin Chadwick: " I have had a great deal of clandestine correspondence with my old loves at the Poor Law Board this last two months. The belief among the old loves is that the new master is bent on—doing nothing. There is only one thing of which I am quite sure. And that is that Mr. Villiers will lead Mr. Gathorne Hardy no easy life next February."

In October Mr. Gathorne Hardy appointed a committee of sanitary and medical experts to report " upon the requisite amount of space and other matters in relation to Workhouses and Workhouse Infirmaries ". Among the other matters was included nursing. He did not consult Miss Nightingale, but she put her pride in her pocket and asked to be allowed to contribute. Douglas Galton was on the Committee, and on October 31st she wrote pressing him to put her name forward.

" Tell them Barkis is willin'—more than willin'—to give them a piece of her mind." The committee invited her to submit a paper on nursing; this opening gave her the chance to put forward her scheme of workhouse reform, basing her argument on the obvious truth that the organisation, construction and administration of workhouse and workhouse infirmaries were of vital importance to the nursing system. In 1865 M. Husson, Director of the Assistance Publique of Paris, accompanied by Dr. Sutherland, had inspected London workhouses and work-house infirmaries. She made capital out of his impressions. " No great stretch of the imagination is required to conceive what they think of the system, or no system, reigning here. I allude to the heaping up aged, infirm, sick, able-bodied and sometimes children in the same building, instead of having, as in every other Christian country, your asylum for aged, your hospital for sick, your lunatic asylum, your union school etc. etc. etc. each under its proper administration, and your able-bodied quite apart from any of these categories." She had her paper printed and sent a copy to Mr. Gathorne Hardy with a long, urgent letter. She was writing repeatedly to him, but with no effect. He neither consulted her nor informed her what he intended to do. It was a complete surprise when on February 8th he introduced a Bill which became law in the following month under the title of the Metropolitan Poor Act.

The Reformers had no hand in the Bill, it was extremely unsatisfactory to them, and Miss Nightingale and her fellow workers felt they had been exploited. On February 11th William Rathbone wrote: " I think Hardy's use of our experiment and of your name atrocious ". On a draft copy Miss Nightingale scribbled angrily " Humbug ", " No prin-ciples ", " Beastly ". She was especially angry that no direct provision was made for the improvement of workhouse nursing. For this, however, she herself was to blame. She had written a letter to Mr. Gathorne Hardy reporting the victory of the Liverpool Workhouse Infirmary nursing in which she gave a dramatic description of the opposition and difficulties en-countered at the beginning. He took fright; either he was genuinely alarmed, or he was not sorry to find an excuse for postponing nursing reform; in any case, he publicly gave her letter as a reason for shelving the question for the present.

In fact, resentful though the Reformers might be, the Bill was a great advance. Miss Nightingale campaigned furiously in the hope of getting it amended, securing Sir Harry Verney, Mr. Villiers and John Stuart Mill to criticise the Bill in the House of Commons, but its merits were undeniable and Mr. Gathorne Hardy was both conciliatory and skilful. He put forward the Bill modestly as " only a beginning ", freely admitting that many of the criticisms were justified but emphasising he was doing everything that could be done at present. One by one her supporters became lukewarm. Mr. Villiers, who had begun by calling the Bill a seven months' child born in the Whitehall Workhouse, admitted that it would " set the ball rolling ". John Stuart Mill changed his mind sufficiently to say he " had no doubt the Bill would effect a vast improvement ". Miss Nightingale herself did not suffer her usual torments of despair. After the Bill was passed, in March 1867, she wrote to Rev. Mother Bermondsey almost with cheerfulness: " We have obtained some things, the removal of 2000 lunatics, 80 fever and smallpox cases and all the remaining children out of the Workhouses—(and the providing for them out of a common fund in order to relieve the rates) the paying of all salaries of Medical Officers, Matrons, Nurses etc., out of a Metropolitan (not parochial) rate. . . . Also;—the removing all other sick into separate buildings which are to be improved—and constituting fresh Boards of Guardians for these sick with nominees from the Poor Law Board. This is a beginning, we shall get more in time." The Act provided for forming the whole of the unions and parishes of London into one district for the administration of insanity, fever and smallpox cases hitherto dealt with in the local work-house; it also provided for the establishment of a fund called the " Metropolitan Common Poor Fund ", to which the maintenance of asylums for the aged and insane, the cost of medicines and the maintenance of children in pauper schools were to be charged. The two basic principles for which she had contended were established : in the workhouses the sick, aged, incurable, insane and children were to be separated from the able-bodied, and medical relief was to be a common not a parochial charge. The passage of the Act is generally accepted as marking the beginning of modern medical relief, and in fact Miss Nightingale was largely responsible for its existence. Her influence is clearly to be seen in its provisions, and the change in public opinion which made legislation possible was admitted to be due to her efforts. In the House of Commons Mr. Villiers, speaking on the Bill, mentioned her by name, and in the House of Lords the Earl of Devon, moving the second reading, said : " It would be improper on such an occasion to omit reference to the improved feeling on the subject which had resulted from the admiration the country must feel for the exertions of that excellent and gifted woman, Miss Nightingale."

Another battle was over, but the pause which succeeded it brought her no rest. During the summer of 1867 she was forced to stay in London working desperately on Indian sanitary affairs. She was conscious of driving herself too hard ; if Sidney Herbert or Clough had been alive, she wrote to Clarkey, one of them would have made her stop. But now there was no one to stop her. Indeed, far from being able to spare herself she was forced, in June 1867, to undertake a new and laborious work.

Part of the money raised by the Nightingale Fund had been devoted to establishing a training school for midwives in King's College Hospital. The school flourished, and was considered by Miss Nightingale to be one of her most satisfactory achievements, when it was overtaken by disaster. Puerperal sepsis broke out in the lying-in wards following the delivery of a woman suffering from erysipelas and developed into an epidemic which closed the school. An investigation followed, in the course of which she discovered that no reliable statistics of mortality in childbirth existed. " There appears ", wrote Miss Nightingale, " to have been no uniform system of record of deaths, or of the causes of death, in many institutions, and no common agreement as to the period after delivery during which deaths should be counted as due to the puerperal condition . . . the first step is to enquire, what is the real normal death rate of lying-in women ? Compare the rate with the rates in establishments into which parturition cases are received in numbers. Clarify the causes of death and see if any particular cause predominates in lying-in institutions ; and if so, why so ? And, since the attendance on lying-in women is

473

the widest practice in the world, and these attendants should be trained ; . . . decide this great question as to whether a training school for midwifery nurses can safely be conducted in any building receiving a number of parturition cases." Ill, harassed and over-driven as she was, she set to work with Dr. Sutherland's assistance to collect facts and figures on which statistics could be based. It was a difficult task. Doctors were suspicious of interference and surprisingly ignorant—one doctor told her that ergot was a specific against puerperal sepsis. Institutions were unwilling to disclose their figures. However, working through hospitals and doctors to whom she was personally known she collected preliminary facts which pointed to a startling conclusion. It seemed that in lying-in institutions and hospital wards the rate of mortality was much higher than when patients were delivered at home, however poor and unhygienic those homes might be. She determined that a great mass of further facts must be collected, and began to correspond with doctors, matrons, sanitary experts and engineers throughout the world.

The work involved was enormous. The analysing and tabulating was done by her, and the majority of letters were written in her own hand. The enquiry took three years to complete, years during which the pressure of other work was crushing. At the end of the enquiry she had accumulated a mass of information but had neither time nor energy to put it into shape. A book was planned, but Dr. Sutherland had to put it together, and it was not until 1871 that a small volume was published under the rather apologetic title of *Introductory Notes on Lying-in Institutions*.

It is one of the most interesting of Miss Nightingale's works. She reached the conclusion that the use of small separate rooms was the answer to the high rate of mortality in maternity cases. The same conclusion was reached, independently, by Sir James Simpson, the pioneer of the use of chloroform in childbirth, with whom she corresponded. When she wrote, the great discoveries of bacteriology were still ten years ahead ; Lister had only just made public his first experiments with carbolic acid and the nature of infection was not understood. Miss Nightingale herself regarded " the fear of entering a cab in which a case of fever or small pox has been for half an hour " as " morbid " and wrote of " the myth of scarlet fever being carried in a bedside carpet ". But she did establish, independently, the fact that, whenever a number of maternity cases were collected together, and whenever maternity cases were under the same roof as medical and surgical cases, the mortality rose. The lower mortality in cases delivered at home was due to the fact that " however grand, or however humble, a home may be in which the birth of a child takes place, there is only one delivery in the home at one time ". In London workhouses the death-rate depended on the number of deliveries. Thirteen infirmaries which had no deaths at all in five years, had under sixteen deliveries per annum. "When Waterford Institution had 8 beds in 1 room the mortality was 8 per 1000. When the wards were moved and the number of beds reduced to 4, the mortality fell to 3·4 per 1000." In La Charité in Paris maternity cases were under the same roof as medical and surgical cases, and the mortality in 1861 was 193·7 per 1000, of which over 80 per cent were due to puerperal fever. In the Military Female Hospital at Shorncliffe, an old wooden hut, but close to the sea with sea breezes blowing through it, and in a makeshift wooden hut used as a hospital at Colchester there had never been a death from puerperal fever. " In both these hospitals beds are seldom, or never, occupied all at one time. They have their own attendant and seldom is more than one bed occupied." " Not a single lying-in woman ", wrote Miss Nightingale, " should ever pass the doors of a general hospital. Is not any risk which can be incurred infinitely smaller ? "

She passed on to press for properly trained midwives. The establishment of training-schools for midwives and the improvement of the status and character of women entering the profession was, she wrote, something women owed to themselves to see properly done. She pressed for midwifery as a career for educated women. In 1871 there was an agitation for women to be admitted to the medical profession, an ambition with which she had little sympathy : the crying need was for nurses and midwives. There were plenty of excellent doctors already who were men, why should women want to be doctors ? She added a letter to her book : " Dear Sisters," she wrote, " there is a better thing for women to be than ' medical men ', that is

475

'medical women'." "It is a good thing you are at Lea Hurst," wrote Dr. Sutherland in July 1871, "or your 'dear sisters' would infallibly break your head. They will probably break your windows. However you are clearly right and let them scream and stamp." The book, wrote Miss Nightingale, was "only a beginning, but quite worth the amount of trouble it cost".

The spring of 1867 brought final victory in Liverpool. District nursing was rapidly developing. The city had been divided into eighteen districts, each provided with trained nurses, and each under the general superintendence of a philanthropic lady who assumed the cost. In the Liverpool Workhouse Infirmary the success of the trained nurses was firmly established. First, the cost of the scheme which William Rathbone had borne was officially assumed by the Vestry; next, in March 1867, all the wards in the Infirmary, male and female, were placed under the authority of Agnes Jones. It was triumph, but triumph was short-lived. The winter of 1867 was a time of unemployment and distress, Agnes Jones was already cruelly overworked, and the work entailed by the additional wards was more than any human being could accomplish. "All the winter", wrote Miss Nightingale to M. Mohl in February 1868, "she has had 1350 patients and to fight for every necessary of life for them. She has never been in bed until 1.30 A.M. and always up at 5.30 A.M." The Workhouse Infirmary was overcrowded and the building unsatisfactory. An epidemic of typhus broke out and Agnes Jones caught the infection. She was worn out; she had no power of resistance and sank rapidly. On February 19th, 1868, she died. The last words she spoke to Miss Nightingale were: "You have no idea how I am overworked".

Her death was a catastrophe. There was no one to take her place. Personal loss Miss Nightingale could bear; on the third anniversary of Sidney Herbert's death she had written that the mere personal craving after a beloved presence she felt as nothing, a few years and it would be over—her bitter grief was for the work. After so much had been sacrificed, so much had been achieved, it seemed that the reform of nursing in workhouse infirmaries would collapse for want of someone to carry it on. Miss Nightingale spent, she said, four hours a day writing letters trying to find someone capable of succeeding Agnes Jones. She became frantic. Her bitterness against women, her distrust of women, her resentment of their pretensions flared up again. " I don't think ", she wrote to Clarkey in April 1868, " anything in the course of my long life ever struck me so much as the deadlock we have been placed in by the death of one pupil, combined you know, with the enormous Jaw, the infinite female ink which England pours forth on 'Woman's Work'." It was the most difficult, the most unexpected of all her problems. The work was there, the crying need was there, but the women did not come forward.

" The more chattering and noise there is about Woman's Mission the less of efficient women can we find ", she wrote to Sir John McNeill on February 7th, 1865. " It makes me mad to hear people talk about unemployed women. If they are unemployed it is because they won't work. The highest salaries given to women at all we can secure to women trained by us. But we can't find the women. They won't come." Those who did come gave enormous trouble, and there were moments when it seemed that everything she had achieved by her work in the Crimea would be lost through their unreasonableness and stupidity. " It is not money we want," she wrote to Harriet Martineau in February 1865, " it is workers. . . . We don't aspire, altho' they are needed by the hundred and the thousand, to sending out nurses by the hundred and the thousand. What we want to do is to send a small staff of trained nurses and a *trained training* Matron, wherever we are asked. But the material, especially in the latter (the Matron) does not come to us. We have 23 nurses now in training at St. Thomas's, our largest number. 18 is the number we can entirely support at St. Thomas's but this is no difficulty at all, even at the moment some of our 23 are supported by others. We should never lack the money, but we want the workers. . . . *Applications* have no superfluity at all from any description or class of persons rushing to be trained. We can scarcely make up our number of the right sort. . . . We never have rejected one of the right sort for want of room. But really not many of *any* sort come to be rejected. . . . We have always 10 times as many situations offered as trained persons to fill

477

them. Indeed I am sorry to say that nurses of ours have been made superintendents who were totally unfit for it, and whom we earnestly remonstrated with, as well as with their employers, to prevent them being made Superintendents but in vain—such is the lack of proper persons."

In 1861 it was decided that the new General Hospital in course of construction at Woolwich should be staffed with female nurses under a superintendent. It was a step forward of great importance, intended to be preliminary to an official scheme of military hospital female nursing, but the difficulty of finding a suitable superintendent was so great that it seemed the scheme would have to be abandoned. The only possible candidate was Mrs. Shaw Stewart, who had been one of Miss Nightingale's best nurses in the Crimea but who was difficult to the point of eccentricity.

On being offered the post she refused absolutely to undertake the responsibility of being superintendent. She chose to regard the offer as a conspiracy to keep her out of the hospital, declared she was determined to work in the hospital as a "mere nurse", and demanded that Miss Nightingale should make her a full explanation at a personal interview. When Miss Nightingale declined she became extremely angry and wrote abusive letters; one alone covered sixteen pages closely written on both sides; it attacked Miss Nightingale's policy, conduct and character in the past and present. "She writes because she is precluded from the pleasure of abusing me in person", Miss Nightingale wrote to Clough, who was acting as her secretary, in April 1861. Mrs. Shaw Stewart also wrote at length to Clough offering him her sympathy—"those acting for her have as *I* know a difficult task". On April 9th, 1861, Miss Nightingale wrote in despair: "And this is the woman who has to begin the Military Hospital Nursing Scheme. If she is mad what may she not do, if she is not mad how much worse must we think of her?" There was no choice. Either Mrs. Shaw Stewart must accept or the whole scheme must be abandoned. She was able, a magnificent nurse, and in spite of her difficult temper had worked wonders in the hospitals at Balaclava. In July she announced that she had changed her mind and would accept the post of superintendent after all. "As I expected saving her consistency by a long letter of abuse

478

of me to Lord Herbert ", wrote Miss Nightingale to Clough on July 16th. " She stipulates as a great point that all the nurses shall be Church of England. As the Superintendent has absolute power in this respect she might have had Mahomedans if she had liked."

In 1862 Mrs. Shaw Stewart took up her post, but she did not get on with the governor of the Hospital, Colonel Wilbraham. " Mrs. Shaw Stewart and Colonel Wilbraham are quarrelling ", wrote Miss Nightingale to Douglas Galton in September 1863. " She gets into rages, he is interfering. If some of the things related had happened to me, F. N., instead of to Mrs. S. S., I should have felt the same. Only my feeling would have been expressed by a laugh—hers by a rage." Squabble after squabble was patched up, only for trouble to break out again. There were irritations outside work. Mrs. Shaw Stewart was well connected ; her brother, Sir Michael Shaw Stewart, was a Member of Parliament with considerable influence, and socially she held herself aloof. " Colonel W's mind has been rankling on certain refusals of Mrs. S. S. to come to tea ", wrote Miss Nightingale to Douglas Galton in 1866. After four years of squabbling matters came to a head. Colonel Wilbraham alleged that Mrs. Shaw Stewart treated her nurses " abominably " and struck them repeatedly. He was supported by some of the doctors in the hospital. Mrs. Shaw Stewart, after a violent scene, rushed up to London and asked her brother to intervene on her behalf. In this summer, 1866, Miss Nightingale scribbled a note to Dr. Sutherland— " Well ? It's not at all well." " Did you see a small heap of ashes in the street ? That's me. Mrs. Shaw Stewart has been up to town—she has been here, to her brother and to the W.O. This is a most serious matter. And it's all that fool of a brother."

The result was an official War Office enquiry held in 1868. Miss Nightingale was most unwilling that it should take place. Douglas Galton was involved, and on May 1st of that year she wrote imploring him to treat the matter lightly : " Order Mrs. S. S. to bed for a week, order Colonel Wilbraham and the Drs to bed for a week. Then order them to kiss and shake hands all round." Mrs. Shaw Stewart and her brother would not be dissuaded, and the enquiry was held in June.

Miss Nightingale wrote to Clarkey on June 13th that she did not think she would be able to " drag Mrs. S. S. through. She is right on every point of administration, wrong on every point of temper." Dr. Sutherland attended the enquiry and sent a depressing report—" after six years there is not a single ward nurse in H.M.'s service. All are probationers of short service. Mrs. S. S. admitted to having struck her nurses. I do not remember that there is even a whisper in the evidence against the main result of her nursing." Miss Nightingale, forwarding Dr. Sutherland's report to Douglas Galton, commented : " They all say the same—the nursing is perfect. Do they mean the cooking is perfect in spite of the cook ? " That was precisely what was meant. Although Mrs. Shaw Stewart was severely censured and eventually resigned, the military hospital female nursing scheme was extended to include Netley, where the nursing was taken over by a superintendent and a party of twelve nurses from the Nightingale School in 1869. Mrs. Shaw Stewart blamed Miss Nightingale for her misfortunes and took to appearing without warning at South Street. " I cannot tell you the absolute terror she inspires me with ", Miss Nightingale wrote to Dr. Sutherland on October 7th, 1869. " I feel myself in the power of a mad woman who may make her appearance any day as she did twice before—and will certainly send her replies as fast as they can be got to me (if I write) and telegraph besides. I have had as many as *three* large packets in a day from her."

Mrs. Shaw Stewart had one recommendation, her moral conduct was above reproach—the charge generally made against nurses was their improper behaviour with male patients. " Oh how I wish there were no men ! " wrote Miss Nightingale on the margin of a complaint from a hospital. The Nightingale nurses were setting a very different standard, but they were only a tiny fraction of the whole. The ordinary nurse was still rough, uneducated and usually promiscuous. In 1862 Miss Nightingale wrote to Douglas Galton that she had unhappily proved that " even the most desirably ugly nurses cannot be left without a superintendent ".

Unfortunately the trustworthy superintendent was as rare as the trustworthy nurse. Many first-class nurses were prevented by lack of education from being able to attempt administrative work. Miss Nightingale considered that Mrs. Roberts, who had been her head nurse in the Crimea, was the best nurse she had ever met, but in 1857 she wrote: "She might be a first-class physician and surgeon, learnt by 23 years experience, but not by reading. She *can't* read! not literally." Too often the woman with some education who took up nursing did so only because she had proved herself too unreliable for other work. In 1871 visitors to the Poplar Sick Asylum found the matron in a "low dress with short sleeves, being merry"; she confided to them that she had successfully brought two actions for breach of promise. In military hospitals the difficulty was even greater. In July 1871 Miss Nightingale gave Henry Bonham Carter, Hilary's brother, an account of an interview with the superintendent of a military hospital who had been reported for improper conduct. "She had nursed a Pole and he had left her all his money. Alternatively he had only given one small present to her little girl. Then she began raving about her social position, her poor husband, her character, her age. Who might not take presents if she might not she screamed—she must have been heard all over Lord Lucan's next door—to frighten me. She began by declaring that she would not keep her superintendency a day, she would resign at once. Then it flashed, even over her, that her resignation might be accepted.

"And she shouted—

"that she didn't care for the W.O.—not a fig—she snapped her fingers at them. She would stay where she was and nobody should turn her out, that if the W.O. asked her to resign she would defy them and they should find her a match for them and she should not resign. (Do you know I have the strong impression that there is a great deal to know which we do not know.) She told me she was a saint, she screamed this at least 40 times. She repeated (I am sure 50 times) that she had made the nurses a cake 'with her own hands' as proof of her being 'a mother to them'. She screamed 'You have made me miserable, miserable, miserable' (30 or 40 times). But she was quite evidently trying to practise on me. (I have no doubt she has tried this practice on many, especially her husband.) And the cruelty of her eyes in saying this was frightful to see."

481

The obvious solution was for educated women of a good type to become nurses, but this path too was strewn with difficulties. The " ladies " and " nurses " controversy which had caused so much heart-burning in the Crimea was still raging. On September 13th, 1866, Miss Nightingale wrote Dr. Farr a long letter protesting against statements made by a Dr. Stewart and a Miss Garret, who asserted that she had been " compelled to give up employing lady nurses, had been forced to abandon the introduction of educated women into the profession of nursing " and had " declared that educated women were unable to undergo the training necessary for the purpose ". It was just possible, said Dr. Stewart and Miss Garret, that a middle-class woman might become a nurse but quite impossible for an upper-class lady.

The truth, wrote Miss Nightingale, was exactly opposite. " Be it known to Dr. Stewart who draws a painfully invidious distinction between ' upper ' and ' middle class ', that the *fact* is exactly the contrary from what he represents it. It is far more difficult to induce a ' middle-class ' woman than an ' upper class ' one to go through as Head Nurse the incidental drudgery which must fall to the province of the Head Nurse— or be neglected.

" 1. *No* nurses should do the work of ' scrubbers '— that therefore the Nurse whether she be upper, middle or lower class is equally able to go through the training of a nurse.

" 2. No Lady Superintendent—be she upper, middle or lower class—is qualified to govern or to train nurses, if she has not herself gone through the training of a nurse.

" 3. I don't exactly know what Dr. Stewart and Miss Garret mean by the ' upper ' class. . . . Therefore I will wait to know before I mention many who have gone through the training of a nurse . . . are equally qualified to be Nurses, Head Nurses, to attend an operation or to be Supts—and yet are of what is usually called the ' upper ' class."

Dr. Stewart and Miss Garret also asserted that no nurse should work for pay. Where ladies were concerned it was derogatory for a lady to hire herself out for money ; where nurses of other classes were concerned nursing must be regarded as a vocation and payment must not be the consideration.

Indeed, the first proof of suitability in a nurse was her willingness to serve without any payment at all.

Dr. Stewart and Miss Garret voiced views widely held by Miss Nightingale's contemporaries. The figure of the self-immolating sister of charity was fixed in the public mind, and few people could visualise the professional woman, trained, efficient and highly paid whom she wished to call into existence. " To make the power of serving without pay a qualification is, I think, absurd ", she wrote to Dr. Farr on September 13th, 1866. " I WOULD FAR RATHER THAN ESTABLISH A RELIGIOUS ORDER, OPEN A CAREER HIGHLY PAID. My principle has always been—that we should give the best training we could to any woman, of any class, of any sect, ' paid ' or unpaid, who had the requisite qualifications, moral, intellectual and physical, for the vocation of a Nurse. Unquestionably the educated will be more likely to rise to the post of Superintendent, but *not* because they are ladies but because they are *educated*."

Class was one difficulty, religion was another. " Any woman, of any class, of any sect ", Miss Nightingale wrote again and again. " *Any* woman, from *any* class, of *any* church. I have said that if an R.C. nun come and will submit to our regulations to be trained, take her." At the same time she noted that she had just heard one of her young cousins say that no Roman Catholic should be allowed in a Christian house.

When the right type of woman had been secured and there were no religious objections, difficulties remained. The Nightingale nurses, carefully selected, trained under Miss Nightingale's own eye, were efficient, professional, educated, but they suffered from a feeling of their superiority. " Intolerable conceit is one of our nurses' chief defects", she wrote in 1871. One of the Nightingale probationers—" a good girl," wrote Miss Nightingale, " but using the lowest kind of High Church slang "—refused to sit at meals with an old-style sister from St. Thomas's on the ground that the sister was " low ". When Nightingale nurses were sent to work under matrons who were not Nightingale-trained they were patronising. On one or two occasions Miss Nightingale was asked to recall her nurses because they were too difficult to manage. In December 1871 she described herself as " transfixed with horror " to receive a complaint, forwarded by one of the medical staff, of the behaviour of a Nightingale nurse to the patients at the Highgate Infirmary. " Sir. Is an assistant nurse to be allowed to incur the guilt of being insubordinate to the Patients ? Is she to tell the Patients that the food is good enough for Paupers ? Is it to be endured that she should say that they require a great deal of waiting on ? " She commented in the margin, " very fairly written and signed by two men patients ".

There were difficulties inherent in the very fervour which inspired the new nurse. The woman who was neither frivolous nor in financial difficulties, who was prepared to undergo a rigorous training and subsequently endure the conditions of work in the wards of a hospital or infirmary of the period, was likely to be animated with a fanatic's spirit. Miss Nightingale did not want fanatics, she did not want warfare, especially holy warfare. No one knew better that almost everything was wrong with the conditions and technique of contemporary nursing. But the way to improvement did not lie through rebellion ; she had never been a rebel and she did not mean to send out parties of rebel nurses. Authority must not be flouted but converted. Regulations must be observed because regulations were essential to organisation. If regulations were bad they must certainly be changed, but until they were changed they must be observed. In a private note of 1866 she wrote : " Women are unable to see that it requires wisdom as well as self denial to establish a new work ".

It was a difficult lesson to teach. Women who had trained as nurses inspired by a spirit of devotion found themselves sent to posts where their good intentions were frustrated and their skill wasted. Unhappy and rebellious, they appealed to Miss Nightingale and when she preached patience, yielding, moderation, their disappointment was great. Many lost faith in her, and she frequently mentions having received letters of abuse from unhappy and disappointed nurses. But she would not change her policy. " Do you think ", she wrote to a rebellious nurse on April 22nd, 1869, " I should have succeeded in doing anything if I had kicked and resisted and resented ? . . . I have been shut out of hospitals into which I had been ordered by the Commander-in-Chief, obliged to stand outside the door in the snow until night, have been refused rations for as much as 10 days at a time for the nurses I had brought by superior command. And I have been as good friends the day after with the officials who did these things—have resolutely ignored these things FOR THE SAKE OF THE WORK."

The want of women to train as nurses, the difficulties perpetually arising from their unreasonableness and instability affected Miss Nightingale's attitude towards the feminist question. The movement for the higher education and emancipation of women was gathering strength, and between 1860 and 1870 the first organised efforts were made to enable women to enter the learned professions and to give them the vote. In September 1860 John Stuart Mill asked Miss Nightingale to support the movement to enable women to qualify as doctors on the same terms as men. But she was unsympathetic; her difficulties had left her with the conviction that women already had more opportunities than, at the moment, they were capable of using. She was impatient with "female missionaries", with the "enormous Jaw about Woman's Work". She was convinced that her attitude was based on hard facts derived from her experience, but in fact the truth lay in her own nature.

Her outlook was aristocratic. Equality meant little to her, equality of the sexes, the goal of the early pioneers of feminism, least of all. She had never felt handicapped by her sex or wished to be a man. In all the long history of frustration recorded in her private notes, she never suggests she was frustrated by men because she was a woman. Stupidity frustrated her, not sex. She had been made aware that in the world of affairs suggestions from a woman were accepted less readily than suggestions from a man, but by using the right tactics she had been able to overcome that drawback. Statesmen, Cabinet ministers, public servants had willingly sat at her feet, and she assumed that any woman who chose to take the trouble could achieve the same position. In spite of the extraordinary power of her mind, she was a woman of intensely feminine nature whom men admired and spoiled. She preferred men to women, and sex antagonism, sex rivalry were foreign to her. Nothing exasperated her more than a desire on the part of women to imitate and emulate men.

" To do things just because men do them ! ", she wrote contemptuously. The exaggerated praise lavished on female
achievement infuriated her—why should what was normal for
a man be considered exceptional for a woman ? Why should
it be hailed as remarkable when a woman qualified as a doctor
—not because she qualified brilliantly but because she succeeded
merely in qualifying ?

Dr. Elizabeth Blackwell was the first woman to qualify as
a doctor. She had studied in Paris and qualified in America,
and was now a celebrity. On January 19th, 1862, Miss
Nightingale wrote that she would be " inferior as a 3rd rate
apothecary of 30 years ago ". " Female M.D.'s have taken
up the worst part of a male M.D. ship of 50 years ago ", she
wrote to John Stuart Mill on September 12th, 1860. " The
women have made no improvement, they have only tried to
be ' men ' and they have succeeded only in being third rate
men. Let all women try . . . these women have in my
opinion failed . . . but this is no prior conclusion against the
reasoning."

On September 23rd John Stuart Mill replied, pointing
out the limitations of her argument. " When we consider
how rare first rate minds are, was it to be expected on the
doctrine of chances that the first two or three women who
take up medicine should be more than you say these are—
third rate. It is to be expected that they will be pupils at
first, not masters. . . . Neither does the moral right of women
of admission into the profession depend at all upon the likelihood
of their being the first to reform it."

She remained unconvinced. The moral right did not
interest her. The all-important consideration was the work
waiting to be done in the world. Women made third-rate
doctors and first-rate nurses : there were plenty of first-rate
doctors, there was a shortage of first-rate nurses ; what could
be plainer than the conclusion that women ought to become
nurses, not doctors ? Let women do the work which came to
them and cease to trouble themselves whether or not they
equalled men. In July 1867 John Stuart Mill asked her to
become a member of the first committee of the London
National Society for Women's Suffrage. " A Society has been
formed for the purpose of obtaining the Suffrage for Women.

The honour of your name as a member of the General Committee is earnestly requested." She refused. Again, the moral right of women to have a voice in the government of the country meant little to her. Her objections were practical —" that women should have the suffrage ", she wrote on August 11th, 1867, " I think no one can be more deeply convinced than I. It is so important for a woman to be a ' person ' as you say. . . . But it will be years before you obtain the suffrage for women. And in the meantime there are evils which press much more hardly on women than the want of the suffrage. . . . Could not the existing disabilities as to property and influence of women be swept away by the legislature as it stands at present ? . . . Till a married woman can be in possession of her own property there can be no love or justice. But there are many other evils, as I need not tell you. Is it possible that, if woman suffrage is agitated as a means of removing these evils, the effect may be to prolong their existence ? Is it not the case that at present there is no opposition between the two elements of the nation, but that, if both had equal political power, there is a possibility that the social reforms required might become matter of political partizanship and the weaker go to the wall ? I can scarcely expect that you will have time to answer my humble questions ? " John Stuart Mill answered that he deplored on moral grounds the " indirect influence " to which women were restricted owing to their want of political power. But Miss Nightingale, whose immense influence was all indirect, was devoid of moral qualms and influenced only by practical considerations. " I have thought I could work better, even for other women, off the stage than on it ", she wrote simply.

She declined to believe in the vote as a universal panacea for the wrongs of women. " If women were to get the vote immediately Mr. Mill would be disappointed with the result ", she wrote in a rough draft of a letter to Jowett. The greater part of female misery was due to economics—not to the economic situation of women specifically but the economic situation of the whole nation. She instanced the " frightful burden of pauperism, the overflowing workhouses . . . The wives and daughters of all these people are starving, does Mr. Mill really believe that the giving of any woman a vote will lead to the removal of even the least of these evils?" In a sentence which she used again in writing to John Stuart Mill she spoke of her own position. "In the 11 years I have passed in Government offices I have never felt the want of a vote, because, if I had been a Borough returning two members to Parliament, I should have had less administrative influence". Her arrogance was unconscious, her modesty was genuine. She insisted that the only difference between herself and other women was that she worked and they did not. She never could be brought to admit there was anything else.

Miss Nightingale never was to take any active part in the feminist movement. In 1867 she excused herself not only from becoming a member of the first committee but from joining the London National Society for Woman's Suffrage at all. "I have no time", she told John Stuart Mill at the end of her letter of August 11th. "It is 14 years to this very day that I entered upon work which has never left me ten minutes leisure, not even to be ill. And I am obliged not to give my name where I cannot give my work." In 1868, however, she did become a member, and in 1871 her name was added to the general committee. In 1877 she retracted her opinion of women doctors sufficiently to sign a memorial urging the admission of women to medical degrees at the University of London, but she was never stirred by the cause of the emancipation of women, nor did she place it on the same level as the cause of public health in India and England, of reform of the health administration of the army or of Poor Law reform.

In later life she was conscious she had been unsympathetic, and in 1896 she wrote to Sir William Wedderburn asking him to tell her what the vote would do for the ordinary woman. "I am afraid I have been too much enraged by vociferous ladies talking on things they know nothing at all about to think of the rank and file."

Miss Nightingale was now forty-eight, and she thought of herself as old. Writing to Clarkey in 1868 she spoke of "the course of my long life". Jowett implored her to change her way of living. It was inconceivable that she could intend to spend the rest of her days shut up in one room in London. Early in 1868 fate intervened. Another change of Government destroyed much of her remaining influence in official departments. In March the Tories went out, the Liberals came in, and Mr. Gladstone became Prime Minister.

XXI THE ACCESSION OF MR. GLADSTONE to power was a severe blow to Miss Nightingale. They had never been in sympathy; administration did not interest Mr. Gladstone. The reforms which attracted his powerful and philosophic mind related to political and ecclesiastical regeneration. He disliked soldiers, regarded an army as an undesirable and unchristian institution which, as the world progressed, every civilised nation would discard, and consistently opposed increased expenditure on the welfare of the British soldier. A standing army, he had said, can never be turned into a moral institution.

In Miss Nightingale's opinion the effect of Mr. Gladstone was disastrous. " The administrative state of things here is to me unimaginable ", she wrote to M. Mohl on June 10th, 1869. " They are absorbed in the Irish Church. And meanwhile everything of administration at home is going to the dogs. . . . The War Office is drifting back to what it was before the Crimean War. Pauperism which concerns hundreds of thousands is just let alone. . . . One must be as *miserably* behind the scenes as I am to know how *miserably* our affairs go on." " What would Jesus have done ", she wrote in a private note, " if He had had to work through Pontius Pilate ? "

The tide had turned against her. Very far off were the days when she wrote " Alexander whom I made Director General ". There were no longer men in the departments who spoke the words she put into their mouths and were instruments in her hand. In the War Office her influence was almost at an end ; in 1869 Douglas Galton, her last remaining friend, resigned and took an appointment at the Office of Works, retaining out of his War Office appointments only his seat on the Army Sanitary Committee.

India alone was left. In Indian affairs, in spite of disappointments and unrealised hopes, she had achieved a personal position of very great authority. Sir Bartle Frere consulted her almost daily, and it became an established practice for all papers dealing with Indian Sanitary questions to be sent to her for her comments. The annual report of the

Sanitary Department, the *Indian Sanitary Annual,* was produced under her direction. As local reports of progress from each Presidency came in they went direct to her, and the remarkable knowledge of conditions and progress in remote stations with which she astonished Viceroys, Sanitary Commissioners and Commanders-in-Chief was the result. She drafted the " Introductory Memorandum " to the *Sanitary Annual* commenting on the year's progress. In 1869 the official editors at the India Office wrote : " Sir Bartle Frere hesitates a little as to the omission of all terms of praise ".

The Secretaries of each Presidential Sanitary Commission corresponded with her, and officials of influence, Dr. Hathaway, private secretary to the Viceroy, Dr. Hewlett, sanitary officer for Bombay, Dr. Cunningham, sanitary adviser to the Government of India, " quite unprejudiced, very candid, brimming with information but—about 7 feet 2 in height ", became her friends, and hundreds of letters passed between them. Mr. Ellis, President of the Madras Sanitary Commission, Dr. Walker, sent out to report on the sanitary condition of jails, Mr. John Strachey, first President of the Bengal Sanitary Commission and later Lieutenant-Governor of the North-West Provinces—all three called on her and wrote to her. Miss Carpenter, the founder of schools for Indian girls, wrote to enlist her help in the cause of Indian female education. They corresponded, though Miss Nightingale was critical of work exclusively for women, and refused to take any interest in what she described, in a letter to Lord Napier of Magdala in 1869, as " the curious good work of Mrs. Johnson who took little brown girls, daughters of Sepoys, from dancing naked on the sea shore and taught them to illuminate ".

She refused to view India as a conquest : the enormous responsibility of India had been placed by Providence in the hands of the British people as a sacred trust, and the object of the British official should be to work for the time when the country could be handed back to the people of India endowed with the greatest blessing of Western civilisation—health.

She received numbers of Indian officials and literary men and wrote in 1868 that she had been " quite beset by Parsees ". Among them was the lawyer, educationalist and poet, Manochjee Cursetjee, whom she called the Byron of the East.

He wished to promote a midwifery scheme for Bombay, but she complained, " he *would* talk philosophy while my head was full of midwifery ".   In 1870 she was elected an honorary member of the Bengal Social Science Association, which was largely composed of native gentlemen.   In collaboration with Sir Bartle Frere she wrote a paper addressed to the Village Elder on Indian sanitation which was read at their proceedings.   The Association had it translated into Bengali and distributed widely.   It was subsequently translated into other Indian dialects and distributed through Bombay and Madras.

The manners and customs of the *ryot*, the Indian peasant, and the life of the Indian village fascinated her, and she entered into local problems.   She was, said Sir John Lawrence, the only human being who had ever mastered the Bengal land-purchase system.

Her prestige was partly due to the influence she was known to possess.   She carried weight in high places, and it happened that the number of men holding important offices in India who were her intimate friends steadily increased.

At the end of 1865 her old admirer, Lord Napier, was appointed Governor of Madras, and he wrote asking her to receive him, assuring her that he was " at your orders for any day or hour ", and reminding her that he had had " the happiness and honour of having seen you at the greatest moment of your life, in the little parlour of the hospital at Scutari ".   She was ill, but " managed to scramble up to see him " on January 1st, 1866, and made not only an enthusiast for the cause of sanitation in India but a personal friend.   He signed his letters " ever your faithful grateful and devoted servant " ; he told her " I think I am attached to you irrespective of sanitation " ; he promised her " *You* shall have the little labour that is left in me ".   In Madras his governorship was marked by solid achievements.   Roads and schools were built, drainage and irrigation undertaken, wells sunk, jails remodelled and hospitals reconstructed.   Under the direction of Lady Napier the experimental scheme for gradually introducing female nurses into Indian hospitals, which had been mishandled and subsequently abandoned by Sir John Lawrence, was put into practice in Madras.   Miss Nightingale wrote that Lady Napier was one of the most efficient women she had ever met, and she was not content with visiting the Madras hospitals " as a grande dame ". Lady Napier overhauled the administration, went into the kitchens, tasted the food, and finally sat down with the clerks and went into the accounts; she managed to get the hospitals out of debt by insisting that all supplies were bought through co-operative stores, such as the Army and Navy Stores founded in 1871, instead of dishonest native traders.

In 1868 Sir John Lawrence's term of office as Viceroy ended. On November 23rd, a few days before he sailed, he wrote to Miss Nightingale : " I think we have done all we can do at present in furtherance of Sanitary Improvement and that the best thing is to leave the Local Governments themselves to work out their own arrangements. If we take this course we shall keep them in a good humour." Far from having done all that could be done, she considered that almost nothing had been accomplished ; and as for the local governments being in a good humour, he forwarded by the same mail an official memorandum from Mr. John Strachey sharply criticising the Sanitary Department at the India Office. The instructions they sent out, he asserted, were written from an English point of view, old discussions were " hashed up ", no credit was given the Government for the fact that £2 million a year was being spent on sanitary works, and the department's latest scheme for " a system of sanitary experts sending in reports " was " politically foolish, and indeed absolutely dangerous . . . the existence of a humble but active administrative class is assumed which exists in England but not in India ". The memorandum was, Miss Nightingale scribbled to Dr. Sutherland, " the nastiest pill we have swallowed yet ". However, she restrained her irritation and wrote Sir John Lawrence a final letter " to bless and not to curse ".

And yet when, in April 1869, he called on her with a present of " a small shawl of the fine hair of the Thibetan goat " she succumbed once more to his personal beauty and charm. " When I see that man again ", she wrote to M. Mohl on June 10th, 1869, " all the statesmen of the moment in England whether ' in ' or ' out ' seem to me like rats and weazels. He is very like Rameses II of glorious memory in Egypt." Nevertheless, her heart never quite ran away with her head, and she added, " but when I see him I understand he will not do much in England ".

She had already established her influence over Sir John Lawrence's successor, Lord Mayo. On the morning of October 28th, 1868, Dr. Sutherland, arriving at South Street after a day's holiday, sent up a message that he hoped " there was nothing much on to-day ". " There is a ' something ' which most people would think a very big ' Thing ' indeed ", she replied. " And that is seeing the Viceroy or Sacred animal of India. I made him go to Shoeburyness yesterday and come to me this afternoon because I *could not* see him until you give me some kind of general idea what to state. Thank the Lord I never consorted with them low Irish."

Lord Mayo came and stayed the whole afternoon. Though she liked him personally, his attitude towards the responsibility he had undertaken provoked her wrath. " It is another instance of our incurable frivolity with regard to India ", she wrote to M. Mohl on October 31st, 1868. Lord Mayo was simply a " big Irish child ". He said " quite calmly " that he had not been able to free himself from his previous office as Irish Secretary until October 6th, he was not going to be able to see Sir Stafford Northcote, the Secretary of State for India, at all because Sir Stafford would be busy first electioneering and then staying with the Queen, and he was proposing to go out to India as Viceroy on November 6th " completely uninstructed ". " He came to me to be coached and with Sir Bartle Frere I gave him his Indian education." Jowett wrote that she had earned a new title, " Governess of the Governor of India ", but Miss Nightingale replied that her correct title was " Maid of all (Dirty) Work ".

Lord Mayo was, however, a willing pupil. " He asked me ", she wrote to Dr. Sutherland immediately after the interview, " (over and over again) that we should now, at once before he goes, write down something (he said) that would ' guide me upon the Sanitary Administration as soon as I arrive '. And ' especially (he said) about the Executive '. He asked most sagacious questions about all the men." He was, she scribbled, " not insensible but essentially Irish ".

In Lord Mayo's guide to sanitary administration, " this most noble and complete paper ", Sir Bartle Frere called it,

Miss Nightingale showed a new purpose. Once more she took a step forward and passed from advocating engineering works to laying down an economic policy. Nothing could be done in India until India was fed ; before sanitation must come irrigation—" famine is the constant condition of the people ". Health was impossible, justice was impossible, organisation was impossible, as long as the great mass of the people of India was vitiated and corrupted by being semi-starved from birth to death. Agricultural development, which implied irrigation, must come first of all. Before education, before any of the blessings of Western civilisation were offered to them, the people of India must be fed, and henceforward irrigation works became Miss Nightingale's first aim for India.

She said good-bye to Lord Mayo not, she said, without hope. He might do as a practical man ; his intentions were excellent, he was willing to be instructed and, she wrote in a private note, she liked his character. He was frank and open, the most open man, with the exception of Sidney Herbert, she had ever met. He himself believed that his experience in Ireland, not only in office but on his own estates, would prove useful in dealing with " a subject race ". He was certainly, he told her, the only Viceroy who had ever sold his own cattle in the open market.

A year later she added the Commander-in-Chief to her circle. In December 1869 she received a note from Lord Napier of Magdala asking if he might call. He came on the afternoon of December 14th and was instantly elected to a leading position in her gallery of heroes. " Ah there *is* a man ", she wrote to M. Mohl on April 1st, 1870. " We were like a brace of lovers on our Indian objects."

Robert Cornelis Napier, Lord Napier of Magdala, was a man of exceptional ability and character. In 1868 he had carried out a brilliant campaign in Abyssinia ; his force marched over 400 miles across barren mountains, supplies had to be carried from the coast, communications had to be established and maintained in hostile, trackless country, water had to be produced by the use of steam condensers at the base and carried up to the troops. Yet sickness was almost nil and casualties low. The force landed in January ; by the middle of June the fortress of Magdala had been stormed and

495

the last man withdrawn in perfect order. For this brilliant feat of generalship he received the thanks of both Houses of Parliament, was voted a pension, created Baron Napier of Magdala and made a G.C.S.I. and G.C.B.

Lord Napier of Magdala was tall, extremely handsome and possessed a speaking voice of unforgettable sweetness. Sir Bartle Frere called him " one of the few men fit for the Round Table ". He had begun his career in the Bengal Engineers of the East India Company and risen to be head of the Public Works Department of the Punjab. One of his achievements was the construction of the Bari-Doab canal, 250 miles long, said to have turned a desert into a garden. His genius as a military commander was equal to his talent as an engineer. At the time of the Mutiny he was second in command to Sir Hugh Rose. He was humane, based his discipline on confidence not fear, and devoted himself to the welfare of his troops. His recreations were botany, geology, painting, poetry and the society of children. " For practical ability, for statesmanlike perception of where the truth lies and what is to be done and how to do it, for high aim, for noble disinterestedness there is not a minister in England fit to tie his shoes ", wrote Miss Nightingale in a private note of December 1869.

In January 1870 his appointment as Commander-in-Chief in India was announced, and before he sailed he came for a final conference. " Make no ceremony with me, as an old Père de famille and do not think of getting up and thus fatiguing yourself ", he wrote to Miss Nightingale on March 18th.

" He actually spent his last morning in England with me, starting from this house ", she told M. Mohl on April 1st, 1870. "And I sent away the C.I.C. to India without anything to eat ! He said he had too much to talk about to waste his time in eating." Between them they put on paper a complete scheme of Indian Army reform to be begun at once, ranging from barrack and hospital reorganisation to the provision of education and physical training. Lord Napier asked her to write to Lord Mayo to prepare his mind for the proposals— " a letter from you would have great weight as it was you who raised public opinion in England on these subjects ", he told her.

She allowed herself to hope once more. Surely between Lord Mayo, who had shown himself so ready to be instructed, and Lord Napier of Magdala, who was a master of detail, something would be done. " Lord Napier was the man ", she wrote in a reminiscence; " he would inspect the men's meat, then he would go and inspect the live beasts, then the slaughter house."

It was not Miss Nightingale's nature to console herself, yet some progress had been made in the ten years since the Indian Sanitary Commission began its work. In 1869 Sir Bartle Frere sent her this story. He had heard that in Bombay it was now difficult for Europeans to get a house at the seaside. This was the reason. " Two boy Parsees go to the Grant Medical College. ' Sir, we read there Miss Nightingale's works and other works on air, construction, etc.' The Mamma and Grandmamma in Parsee families are the tyrants. The poor Papa had begged in vain to be allowed to live in his house by the sea. They *would* live in the bad parts of the town. But when the boy came home and found a sick child at home, he would say ' Grandmamma you are killing that child. Miss Nightingale says so.' And Grandmamma listened to the boy, tho' she would not listen to papa. And Grandmamma became a sanitary reformer in spite of herself. And they moved to the new house, out of the narrow street with no windows. To the seaside house."

On November 21st, 1869, in a letter to M. Mohl, Miss Nightingale recorded that she had been " making up Returns in a popular form for one of the Cabinet ministers ". The Municipal Commissioner of Bombay wrote that the " huddled native masses clamorously invoke the aid of the Health Department if but one death from cholera or small pox occurs; whereas formerly half of them might be swept away and the other half think it all right. Now they attribute these deaths to dirty foul water and the like, and openly declare them to be preventable."

In 1872 the engineer to the municipality of Calcutta came to see her with an introduction from her old friend Sir Robert Rawlinson. The growing and overcrowded city of Calcutta was in urgent need of a drainage scheme and a pure water supply; plans had been drawn but difficulties had arisen—

could she exercise any influence? After examining the plans she wrote a detailed memorandum to Sir George Campbell, Lieutenant Governor of Bengal. The difficulties were overcome and the authorisation for the work went through. Few inhabitants of Calcutta, she said, would ever realise the surprising fact that they owed their water supply to her. Her enormous energy, her extraordinary history, her capacity to inspire boundless faith, admiration and affection were producing astonishing results. Mr. John Strachey criticised her sharply more than once, but he told Sir Bartle Frere: " Of the sanitary improvements in India three-fourths are due to Miss Nightingale ". Her fellow workers regarded her as exercising an almost supernatural influence. " I have often known a scrap of paper on which you had written a few words—or even your words printed—work miraculously ", wrote Sir Bartle Frere in 1868.

Man after man who came to see her in the bright austere drawing-room in South Street fell under her spell. Many began with concealed hostility: she was a thorn in the side of bureaucracy, an interfering aggressive woman to be visited only because it was good policy. Few were not converted. Her sincerity, her disinterestedness, her astounding knowledge were irresistible. Honest men, able men, men who had the good of India and its peoples at heart, became her friends.

But her record was not one of uninterrupted success. She had never been to India, her knowledge was a paper knowledge and her persistence had its drawbacks. She owed her success to her ability to persist in the face of opposition. Again and again she proved to be right. When she proved to be wrong she paid the penalty. In 1867 she came to the conclusion that the barracks and hospitals of the army in India were not adequately ventilated. In the hot weather, when infection and disease were most rife, it was the invariable custom to keep the windows shut and only open the doors.[1] In the Crimea, in the hospitals of London, she had proved the supreme importance of fresh air. In the Crimea she had been told that if the windows of the men's huts were opened during

[1] It had long been established in India that it was only by keeping the windows and shutters closed as far as possible during the hours when the sun was up, that the lower temperature of the night could be partly retained to make the day endurable.

the winter the huts would become so cold that the men would die of pneumonia. She had forced the windows to be opened, and the men had not died. Their health had improved and they had contracted less pneumonia. Therefore, when she wrote a memorandum to the Government of India advising that the windows of barracks and hospitals should be kept open through the hot weather and was told the men would be made ill with heat, she would not be convinced. She persisted in pressing for a general order to open the windows, writing to doctors, to the secretaries of the Presidential Sanitary Commissions, to Commanding Officers, to the Viceroy himself, until Sir John Lawrence told her bluntly that nothing on earth, even a direct order from the Government at home, would induce him to issue instructions for windows to be kept open in hot weather.

A laugh went up throughout the length and breadth of India. Her supporters were forced to realise that she might be betrayed into ludicrous mistakes, and even today Miss Nightingale's attempt to open windows in the hot weather is not forgotten.

A more serious failure followed. The report of the Indian Sanitary Commission had urgently recommended improvement in barrack accommodation, and during 1864 an enormous amount of work was done by Miss Nightingale and Douglas Galton on a model barrack plan. She was aware from the beginning that no single standard plan could be laid down and applied throughout India. The country was too vast, climatic conditions too diverse. Her object was to define the essential features which every barrack must possess and to leave the local authorities to adapt them to local conditions.

In March 1864 she wrote to Dr. Hathaway, Sanitary Adviser to the Viceroy. "The Barrack and Hospital plans we are preparing for you are nearly complete. . . . We want to make them as complete as possible. Then it will be left to you to apply the principles as you best can." The scheme was approved by the Government of India and the War Office, and in 1865 she wrote that she had got a grant of seven millions for "my Indian barracks". Work began at once and the plans were passed to the Royal Engineers.

Presently disturbing news reached her. The Royal

Engineers were acting "in a high handed manner". They were determined to erect barracks for the army without civilian interference or advice. Instead of fitting the essential features into designs adapted to different local conditions, they were producing standard plans of their own which they were insisting should be used all over India. The plans were expensive, the War Office had become uneasy, and the reformers were being blamed for "senseless and sentimental extravagance". Though the plans were in fact the precise opposite of what the reformers had laid down, military secrecy was such that they were not only powerless to act but ignorant of what was being done. By the end of 1869 it was evident that the scheme had gone fatally wrong. On December 4th Miss Nightingale wrote to Sir Bartle Frere: "We begged and prayed to be allowed to put up in Poona and the Deccan where the winds are terrific and the ground rocky, one storied barracks—we were *ordered* to wait. Sir Robert Napier [Lord Napier of Magdala, the Commander-in-Chief] was *ordered* to wait until a 3rd class engineer colonel, an ordinary man such as you can find anywhere, sent us 'standard plans', which we were to use and no other and which were extravagantly expensive." At the War Office Dr. Sutherland was helpless. "The part which afflicts me most", he wrote to Miss Nightingale in December, "is the cost of the barracks. . . . Fine costly architecture is no part of sanitary construction and the costly nature of the elevations has been again and again commented on by the W.O.C. [War Office Committee]. You want plain walls, water tight roofs and the deepest verandahs and staircases."

She was in despair. Not a single one of the new barracks, she wrote to Sir John McNeill in 1869, was erected in accordance with the recommendations. Everything had been sacrificed for the sake of an imposing façade of European design totally unsuited to the climate. Good water, drainage, shade, space, all had been neglected.

The troops moved in, and disaster followed. Cholera broke out at several stations, and early in 1870 there was an outcry in *The Times* against the senseless extravagance of erecting palatial buildings in which the troops died.

In February 1870 Dr. Cunningham, Sanitary Commissioner to the Government of India, came home on leave and brought a melancholy account. Miss Nightingale scribbled a note of his remarks for Dr. Sutherland. " The immense block of masonry strikes one at once as quite incongruous and improper. Men cannot drag their cots downstairs out of doors. No pent house roof to keep the rooms shaded. A great palace without any kind of shelter from the sun. Government will provide punkahs and tatties only on one floor. Recreation rooms are there unused with nothing but tables and forms in them. The men lie on their beds for 18 hours a day and think of Cholera. Cholera has broken out in the new barracks at Allahabad, Lucknow, Morar, and typhoid as well at Jullundur."

After Dr. Cunningham, Lord Napier of Magdala called. From reports he had received he feared the position with regard to the barracks was even worse than she supposed. " Instead of the old sunburnt brick which was cool, they had to build the barracks of solid masonry and red brick in order to support the upper storey. The upper part is *never* cool. The slated roofs of the barracks made them intolerable, they scorched the tops of the men's heads. Commanding officers were abandoning the upper storey and even moving their men back into the old barracks, as at Jullundur. Water had not been laid on and there was no drainage. Land inside the canton-ments had been sold to civilians at a high price because inside cantonments they were not subject to rates, but they also were not subject to Army Sanitary rules, and the vicinity of the barracks was filthy. Dirty coolies of the lowest class with their families had been allowed to live in the barracks before the troops moved in, and the barracks were consequently infected and filthy before the troops arrived."

The cause of sanitary reform had received a serious set-back. The money had been forthcoming, the work had been promptly done and the result was complete failure. That the reformers were in no way responsible, that what had been done was a complete contradiction of every essential laid down, was impossible to explain. Military secrecy, military etiquette veiled the issue in hopeless obscurity and not only the public but officials within the War Office who had been in favour of sanitary improvements now associated them with sentimental extravagance.

In January 1870 Lord Mayo wrote to Miss Nightingale

that " the failure of the new Barracks I am sorry to say is now at least generally admitted . . . we have spent enormous sums on these new palaces . . . we have passed through a time of fever and general sickness, some of our Regiments are in a lamentable state from weakness and exhaustion, almost the worst is the 58th, which has, for six months, been occupying the new barracks at Allahabad. . . . I can only say with regard to the barracks that if they turn out to be failures . . . we have bought our experience at a very high figure."

Twenty years later Miss Nightingale noted that most of the barracks had been abandoned, and those which were occupied had been reconstructed.

She was losing ground on all sides. She was already shut out of the War Office and the Poor Law Board, and in India the barrack failure must weaken her hold on Lord Mayo. Yet she hardly rebelled. In the last two years she had changed. " I assure you I don't let these things corrode into me now ", she told Clarkey in 1868. She had worn herself out. Her last collapse, in December 1867, had weakened her not only in body but in mind. She found it difficult to concentrate, and some of her energy, some of her power of fierce feeling had gone. " I am becoming quite a tame beast—fit for a lady to ride or drive—as horse dealers say of their most vicious brutes ", she wrote to M. Mohl in September 1868.

In the summer of that year she went to Lea Hurst for three months. She had not been there since 1856, and the visit marked a change in her way of life. In 1869 she spent three months with her parents at Embley, in 1870 and 1871 a month at Embley and three months at Lea Hurst, in 1872 eight months at Embley.

While she was at Lea Hurst she read the novels of Jane Austen, who, she told Clarkey in September 1868, in her opinion, " ranked second to Shakespeare in the English language for dramatic power ", and the plays of Shakespeare—" I don't know whether Hamlet was mad, he would certainly have driven me mad ". Baron Bunsen, the friend of her girlhood, had died in 1860, and his wife sent her memoir of him to Miss Nightingale. She wrote that it was " bosh ". " Memoirs published so soon after death can't be otherwise. If they are true they are offensive, if they are not offensive they are twaddle."

Jowett spent a week at Lea Hurst, Parthe stayed away: Miss Nightingale had refused to go there unless " Parthe and her governessing are excluded ". She had long talks with W. E. N. on metaphysics. Her mother, she wrote, was " more cheerful, more gentle than I *ever* remember her tho' of course she is much aged. Her memory is nearly gone but to me she is far dearer, far more *respectable* than ever before." Fanny was now eighty, W. E. N. seventy-four.

By the end of September she was bored. She wrote on September 27th imploring M. Mohl to stay on at South Street " until I come which will be, please God, on Friday or Saturday ". Family life, books, friends were not sufficient, she needed an outlet. For some time Jowett had been urging her to write. He was anxious for her to give up a life which was " dependent on temples of friendships and the good will of the Minister ", and in the summer of 1868 she made a resolution to devote an hour a day to writing. At Jowett's suggestion she began a " Treatise on the Reform of the Poor Law ". Her loss of power was at once apparent. Jowett had to send her a draft before she could start and even then she found composition an intolerable strain. The treatise was shortened to an article, but even so she could not complete it.

She asked advice from Sir Harry Verney, who was an authority on the Poor Law, from Parthe, who had had two novels published, and from Dr. Sutherland. In the autumn she wrote in despair to Dr. Sutherland : " I have adopted *all* your corrections and *all* Parthe's and *all* Sir Harry's : and they have taken out all my *bon mots* and left unfinished sentences on every page ; and this *kind* of work really takes a year's strength out of me ; and now you MUST help me ". The article was put into shape by Dr. Sutherland and sent to Froude, who published it in *Fraser's Magazine* for March 1869 under the title " A Note on Pauperism ". It attracted considerable attention, and Sir Robert Rawlinson told Miss Nightingale on March 11th that Carlyle had praised it. She used the arguments of her earlier papers and memoranda on Poor Law reform and added a suggested scheme for large-scale State-subsidised emigration " to bring the landless man to the manless lands ".

In September 1869 she wrote a letter to Dr. Sutherland

enclosing a large mass of notes on the subject, asking him to expand them into a book after her death, and to do the same for *Notes on Lying-In Institutions*. But she herself, though she worked on for more than twenty years, never touched either again. The days of her great achievements, when she had written the huge volume of *Notes on Matters affecting the Health, Efficiency and Hospital Administration of the British Army* with her own hand in six months, were over. She was no longer capable of the sustained effort necessary to write a book.

The energy with which she had once sprung on opportunity like a tiger had also left her. Her suggestion of a State-subsidised emigration scheme attracted the attention of Mr. Goschen, President of the Poor Law Board, and he came to see her, stayed for several hours, and discussed Poor Law matters. In a note of the interview for Dr. Sutherland she wrote: "He does not impress me. I don't think he will ever do much. He is a man of considerable mind, great power of getting up statistical information and Pol. Econ. but with no practical insight. It is an awkward mind—like a pudding in lumps. He is like a man who has been Senior Wrangler and never anything afterwards. But he was extremely communicative." She did nothing further. Five years earlier she would have seized upon Mr. Goschen's communicativeness to create an opening for introducing herself into Poor Law affairs again.

Her life was growing calmer. It had been, she wrote to Jowett in 1865, "a fever and not a fitful one. Neck or nothing has been all my public life. . . . Could I help in the two Royal Commissions I have served, in the 9 years I have served in the W.O. [War Office] exclusive of the Crimea my whole life being in a hurry? If the thing were not done to the day, it were not done at all."

Not only were the demands of the work less frenzied, but she herself was working in a less frenzied atmosphere. A new influence for reasonableness had come into her life. Clough had been succeeded as secretary of the Nightingale Fund by Hilary Bonham Carter's brother, Henry. Henry Bonham Carter was devoted to Miss Nightingale, he gave up more than forty years of his life to her service, but he would not become a slave. When it was getting late, says Sir Edward Cook, he used to say, "Now I must go home to dinner"; he was an excellent man of business and invaluable to Miss Nightingale, but his soul remained his own.

In 1870 some of the urgency of old days returned. War was declared between Germany and France in June, and in July the " National Society for Aid to the Sick and Wounded ", subsequently called the " British Red Cross Aid Society ", was founded at a public meeting in London.

Miss Nightingale was pressed to give up all other work and take control. The need was very great, heartrending reports of the sufferings of the troops on both sides were being received, and excitement ran high. Parthe in particular implored her to devote her talents and her prestige to the cause of the wounded soldier once more. But she refused; she had chosen the realism of organisation, not the romanticism of self-sacrifice, and she would not look back. Her Indian work was more important than anything she could accomplish in the war hospitals of Germany and France. One laborious memorandum on sanitation in India affected the lives of millions on whom, even if her health allowed, she could never turn her back to become the Lady with the Lamp once more.

However, it was not possible to be Florence Nightingale and hold aloof from war : all over the world it was taken for granted that where the horrors of war were, there she would be ; she received an enormous number of letters assuming she was in Europe nursing in a Red Cross hospital. She wrote an appeal for funds which was read at the first meeting of the National Society, and the contributions which poured in addressed to her personally demonstrated how strong was her hold on the heart of the people. Though sixteen years had passed since they learned what she had done at Scutari, they loved her still. In February 1871 she wrote to Harriet Martineau telling her how the contributions came—" from poor congregations of all kinds, from Negroes in the West Indies, from Ragged Schools, National Schools, Factories—not the rich and comfortable but the whole mass of hard working honest frugal stupid people—who have contributed every penny they could so ill spare . . . not to those of their own way of thinking at all but to those who *suffered* most ".

Though she had declined to be in charge of the National Society, its activities were under her direction. Sir Harry

Verney, Douglas Galton and Miss Emily Verney, Sir Harry's daughter by his first wife, were on the executive committee. Henry Bonham Carter and Dr. Sutherland were sent by the Society to visit both the French and German hospitals during the war, and after it the report on the Society's work was written by Dr. Sutherland under her supervision.

She advised the executive committee on organisation and administration. " Those who undertake the work of aiding the sick and wounded must not be sentimental enthusiasts but downright lovers of hard work . . . attending to and managing the thousand and one hard practical details which never the less plainly determine the question as to whether your sick and wounded shall live or die ", she wrote on August 2nd, 1870. It was nine years to the day, she noted, since Sidney Herbert died. " Why does not the Society advertise itself more ", she wrote to Douglas Galton a few days later. " If it had been hiding from its Creditors instead of being an Aid Society it could not have had a more complete success ; if it had been Sick and Wounded itself it could not have done less." The Society eventually collected over £250,000. She advised on practical matters from the administration of field ambulances to the pattern of hospital suits and cooking utensils. She wrote to workers at the seat of war, she interviewed volunteers for service, she directed and supervised the purchase and despatch of supplies. She collected money from her friends which was used chiefly for the relief of prisoners of war and recorded sending out £5000 in one week. Once again in scenes of horror and confusion it was found that the quickest way to get things done was to go to Miss Nightingale. The amount of correspondence involved was a strain. " Every man and woman in the world seems to have come into it with the express purpose of writing to me ", she told Madame Mohl in 1870. " Would I could go to the seat of War instead of all this writing, writing, writing."

She assisted and advised both sides, and after the war received both the bronze Cross of the French Société de Secours aux Blessés and the Prussian Cross of Merit from the German Emperor. Both French and German nurses and workers wrote to her for advice and addressed her as "beloved mistress", " queen and dearest of friends ".

At first her sympathies were with Germany. She considered Napoleon III a tyrant and disliked and despised the Empress Eugénie, whom she described as " the Empress who was born to be a dressmaker ". Germany was the home of liberal thinking, music and philosophy. M. Mohl, whom she loved dearly, was a German, she herself had been trained at Kaiserswerth on the Rhine, the Crown Princess of Prussia was her friend and pupil, Prince Albert, for whom she had a profound admiration, had been a German. Germany stood for music, folk-songs, simplicity and thought. She had to discover that since her girlhood a startling change had taken place, and that in place of Germany had risen Prussia.

At the beginning of the war the German wounded suffered terribly. Hospital organisation had been neglected and broke down. She was, she wrote, " very much behind the scenes " in German hospital work. For the past two years she had been on terms of friendship with the Crown Princess of Prussia Victoria, the Princess Royal, eldest daughter of Queen Victoria. " I have a fresh neophyte ", she had written to Sir John McNeill on Christmas Day 1868, " in the person of the Crown Princess of Prussia, quick intelligence and is cultivating herself in knowledge of sanitary (and female) administration for her future great career. She comes alone like a girl, pulls off her hat and jacket like a five year old, drags about a great portfolio of plans and kneels by my bedside correcting them." The Crown Princess enthusiastically studied *Notes on Nursing*, sent Miss Nightingale plans of hospitals to criticise, and regularly corresponded with her. Among philanthropic and influential German women she had many friends. " Tell Miss Nightingale ", wrote the Grand Duchess of Baden in 1870, " that I have endeavoured to follow implicitly everything she has recommended and that I love and respect her more than anyone in the world."

At the outbreak of war, at the request of the Crown Princess of Prussia, she sent a Nightingale-trained matron of exceptional ability, Miss Lees, to organise the nursing at three large German war hospitals. Another Englishwoman, Mrs. Cox, wife of an officer who had known Miss Nightingale in the Crimea, was also officially employed by the German authorities, and both Mrs. Cox and Miss Lees sent her regular reports.

What was endured by the German wounded at the beginning of the war equalled in horror and far exceeded in scale
anything in the Crimea.   In the autumn of 1870 Miss Nightingale wrote a "Summary of German Hospitals", based on reports
she had received from eye-witnesses.   "No bed sores appear
ever to have been looked at—no black typhus mouths ever
cleansed—no patients ever washed—no bedding ever cleansed—
no windows ever opened—no sick kitchens ever established—
no fresh water ever drunk. . . . Compare this with the
beautiful French hospitals."   But as the tide of war rolled on
the French cracked.   As early as August 17th she wrote to
Clarkey that the French War Office was breaking down.
"Stores, ammunition, clothing, guns, *everything* falling short.
False muster rolls of battalions—men returned at 900 strong
who never were more than 500."   On November 17th she
wrote to M. Mohl: "They are performing operations with
common butchers knives and without chloroform near Orleans
since the 8th and 9th".   The Mohls now left Paris and came
to England.   On December 20th, 1870, she wrote to M. Mohl:
"I think that if the conduct of the French for the last three
months had been shown by any other nation, it would have
been called *as it is* sublime. . . . The Army of the Loire
fighting seven days out of nine, bare foot, cold and frozen yet
unsubdued is worthy of Henry V and Agincourt."

As she discovered that the French were gallant, she discovered that the Germans were suspicious, brutal and surly.
Through her influence a War Office ambulance had been
equipped and sent out to the German Army with the double
purpose of assisting the German wounded and of observing
and noting the treatment and requirements of wounded in a
large-scale modern war.   The Germans would not allow it
to be used.   In November 1870 she wrote to Douglas
Galton that she had heard that the War Office ambulance was
"cold shouldered" by the Prussians, and asked him to find
out the facts.   On December 12th he wrote: "Every
foreign ambulance has a Prussian N.C.O. in it.   Ours is
the only exception because it has only one patient in it—a
casual."

On November 4th, 1870, she wrote to M. Mohl: "Is it not
quite unknown in history that a philosophical, a deep thinking,

the most highly and widely educated and in some respects the most civilised nation of Europe—the Germans, should plunge head foremost into this abyss called Military Despotism? That they should not *see* that that (*soi-disant*) German Unity means only Prussian aggrandisement." The alacrity with which German philosophy and culture hastened to prostrate themselves before the Prussian war machine left her bewildered. " Prussia has placed herself as a god on the altar for Germany to adore ", she wrote in a fragmentary private note. " Now if you take all the greatest names in science, in literature, or metaphysical and religious philosophy, in art, of the last 70 or 80 years in all Germany, will you tell me how many of these came out of Berlin. Yet the higher civilisation is to be subjected to the lower." " The free translation of German nationality is Prussian military supremacy." Anti-British feeling in Germany was being fostered by Bismarck, and in 1871 she drafted a protest to the Crown Princess of Prussia. " It cannot be denied that England is deeply hurt at the conduct of Germany towards her. While, even to the poorest, the English have been straining every nerve to help Germany . . . Germany has requited her by bringing accusations. When the German soldiery find arms in the hands of the French prisoners or wounded or dead with such letters as N.Y., U.S.A. and the names Remington, Colt, etc., they triumphantly allege that these are English arms supplied to France. . . . The officers know perfectly well what the names and letters stand for, but encourage the soldiers to believe that these are English. And this is part of a plan."

German behaviour after the defeat of the French finally alienated her. " After the fighting ", she wrote to M. Mohl in February 1871, " come the miseries of the poor people. Correspondents known and unknown write to me by every post." She wrote of Bismarck's " rapaciousness ", his " want of delicacy or of any nobility ". She had loved the German language, the German mind and the German way of life. All that had perished. There had been a death, but the death was of Germany, not France. Worst of all, she realised that a new age had dawned for Europe. " Prussia ", she wrote in a private note of 1871, " openly says she does these things because the first Napoleon did them 64 years ago. And

France will say, long before 64 years hence, she will do them because the Corporal Emperor King did them so many years ago. Horrible as is the account of wounds and grief and starving people, it is as nothing compared with the principles which this War has put forth and brought to life."

In 1872 Jean Henri Dunant, a Swiss banker, paid a visit to London. He had succeeded in turning what the world assured him was a Utopian dream into hard fact—he had brought about the Geneva Convention. At the age of thirty-one he had been present at the battle of Solferino in 1859 and had witnessed the fearful sufferings of the wounded after the action. The experience changed his life; he devoted himself first to the establishment of the Geneva Convention, which treated all wounded as neutrals, and this led to the formation at Geneva of the International Committee of the Red Cross as an auxiliary to the Medical Services of armies in time of war. In 1872, after the Franco-Prussian war, Dunant visited London and read a paper on the work of the Society. His first words were these: "Though I am known as the founder of the Red Cross and the originator of the Convention of Geneva, it is to an Englishwoman that all the honour of that Convention is due. What inspired me to go to Italy during the war of 1859 was the work of Miss Florence Nightingale in the Crimea."

She had legendary prestige and enormous popular appeal, and while she had these she could not be without power. She had proof that, in spite of all she had lost, she was not without power. At the end of 1868 she heard that as a measure of economy Mr. Gladstone intended to abolish the Army Sanitary Committee, the old Barrack and Hospital Improvement Commission, which was engaged in carrying out the reforms recommended by the Royal Army Sanitary Commission of 1857. It was a legacy from Sidney Herbert and therefore sacred, and it was her sole remaining channel of influence in the War Office. Both Douglas Galton and Dr. Sutherland were members. She wrote a strong protest to Lord de Grey, citing the valuable work done by the Committee and beseeching him to use his influence to save it. Lord de Grey asked her to supply a memorandum, which he sent to Mr. Cardwell, Gladstone's Secretary of State for War, and to Mr. Gladstone himself. The Army Sanitary Committee and also the Army Medical School, which had been threatened, were saved.

Throughout 1870 and 1871 Miss Nightingale debated the possibility that she might " seek office " again. If she pursued Ministers she might make her way into the departments once more. But such a course was contrary to the policy of her life. She had succeeded because she had made herself an instrument in the hands of Ministers, because she had been sought out, not seeking. Mr. Gladstone's Government had no place for her. She despised his Ministers, she called them contemptuously " Gladstone's secretaries ", and though they treated her with deference she felt they were antagonistic. " Here is a note from Mr. Cardwell ", she wrote to Sir Bartle Frere in 1870, " which seems to me, I don't know why, a nasty one." Her powers of working and concentrating had declined, and she had come to depend entirely on Dr. Sutherland. " The only way I can work now ", she wrote to him in 1870, " is by receiving written notes from you, and working them up into my own language, then printing and showing you the work." Among her papers are hundreds upon hundreds of drafts in Dr. Sutherland's hand covering every subject from Indian sanitation to family letters. She had lost faith in herself and leant on his judgment. " I have been through them all," he wrote of the Indian Sanitary reports, " and you may safely say they are very well done."

Her declining influence in Indian affairs finally decided her. Her moderate hopes of Lord Mayo were not being fulfilled. " Lord Mayo ", she wrote to M. Mohl on April 1st, 1870, " is most anxious and disinterested, or it may be ambitious. He is always consulting us. He sent a man home (the Sanitary Commissioner with the Govt. of India) on purpose to consult us just now. He writes and writes—and we write and write—and our letters are masterly. And nothing is done."

Certain solid undertakings pressed on him by Miss Nightingale and Sir Bartle Frere had been put in hand. Preparations were being made to take the first Census Survey of the whole of India. A " Special Cholera Enquiry " into the incidence and possible causes of cholera throughout India was ordered in April 1869. The instructions drawn up by Miss Nightingale and Dr. Sutherland, in the teeth of determined opposition from Indian medical officers, included investigation into water, food, housing and drainage in districts where cholera occurred.

It was not that Lord Mayo wished to do too little, but that he wished to do too much. He had become entangled in grandiose schemes. " Six months after he landed ", Lord Napier of Magdala told Miss Nightingale in 1870, " he was a changed man." " He got ", wrote Sir Bartle Frere in 1874, " into the hands of men who were like the Fisherman's Wife who never would make the best of what the Enchanted Fish gave her but always wanted something better." With Sir Bartle Frere's help Miss Nightingale had preached irrigation to him. To her dismay in 1871 he sent home what Sir Bartle Frere described as a " wild and visionary project " for providing every *ryot* in India with water at once. When it was pointed out that the money to pay for the enormous works involved could not be raised by tax until after the water had been provided Lord Mayo " sulked ".

Miss Nightingale was profoundly discouraged. She had lost Lord Mayo and with him her influence in the Government of India ; under the present Government her influence in the War Office and at the Poor Law Board was at an end ; she was wretchedly ill and overwhelmed with other and vitally important work. She decided she would struggle no more with Government departments. As 1871 passed into 1872 she wrote on a sheet of paper : " 1872. This year I go out of office."

Almost immediately she had proof that her term of office had already ended. In February Lord Mayo, while inspecting a penal settlement, was assassinated by a convict. He was succeeded by Lord Northbrook. She knew Lord Northbrook personally, he had been a friend of Sidney Herbert, but he did not consult her or call to see her before he sailed.

She was deeply wounded. " Why should you be troubled at the Governor General not coming to see you (as he most certainly ought to have done) ", wrote Jowett on April 3rd, 1872. " Put not your trust in Princes, or Princesses or in the War Office or in the India Office ; all that kind of thing necessarily rests on a sandy foundation. I wonder that you have been able to carry on so long with them."

It was sixteen years since she had returned from the Crimea

to instigate the Royal Army Sanitary Commission of 1857. For sixteen years she had laboured in Government departments, sacrificing health, pleasure, friends. She had done the work of a Secretary of State, she had " made the appointments ". Now all that was over. Henceforward she must lead a new life. What kind of life should it be ?

XXII　HER FIRST THOUGHT was to live again for hospitals. One of the most painful sacrifices of her life had been the renunciation of hospital work for administration after her return from the Crimea. She had declared repeatedly that of all people she was least suited to the writing of regulations, that pen-and-ink employment drove her mad, that she starved without human contacts. " My life now is as unlike my Hospital life when I was concerned with the souls and bodies of men as reading a cookery book is unlike a good dinner ", she wrote to Rev. Mother Bermondsey in 1864.

She had already arranged that, when she could work no more, she should be taken to a hospital. In January 1864 she wrote to Mrs. Bracebridge : " You know that I always believed it to be God's will for me that I should live and die in Hospitals. When this call He has made upon me for other work stops, and I am no longer able to work, I should wish to be taken to St. Thomas's Hospital and to be placed *in a general ward* (which is what I should have desired had I come to my end as a Hospital Matron). And I beg you to be so very good as to see that this my wish is accomplished whenever the time comes, if you will take the trouble as a true friend, which you always have been, are and will be."

She was not prepared for her present situation. She had assumed that only death would release her from the obligation laid on her by God to do administrative work. She had assumed that she would leave the work—instead the work had left her. She was " out of office ", but she was not dying. Indeed, though she was fifty-two and an invalid, her expectation of death was more remote than it had been for sixteen years ; she determined, however, to apply to St. Thomas's to enter a general ward as an ordinary patient ; the cost of her establishment at 10 South Street was large and W. E. N.'s financial affairs were not prosperous. While she was " in office ", while she was toiling at the work God had called her to do, the expense had been justified ; now she was out of office the expense should end.

514

She determined to leave the world. She, the most famous woman in two continents, the friend of queens, the adviser of governments and ministers, would end her days lying side by side with poor working women subject to the discipline and the rigours of a hospital general ward. It was a scheme which appealed to her sense of drama, but when she confided it to Jowett he was alarmed. " Something which you said to me on Sunday has rather disquieted me," he wrote on June 22nd, 1872, " and I hope that you will allow me to remonstrate with you about it. You said that you were going to ask admission as a patient to St. Thomas's Hospital. Do not do this. (1) Because it is eccentric and we cannot strengthen our lives by eccentricity. (2) Because you will not be a patient but a kind of Directress to the Institution, viewed with great alarm by the doctors. (3) When a person is engaged in a great work I do not think the expense of living is much to be considered; the only thing is that you should live in such a way that you can do your work best. (4) I would not oppose you living at less expense if you wish, though I think it a matter of no moment; but I would live independently. (5) Do you really mean to live as a patient? It will kill you. I do not add the annoyance to your father of a step which he can never be made to understand; I look at the matter solely from the point of view of your own work. I have cared about you for many years; and though I have little hope of prevailing with you, I would ask you not to set aside these reasons without consideration."

She yielded. Her affection for Jowett triumphed, and she told him she would set aside duty and conscience for his sake and abandon her plan of entering St. Thomas's. On July 11th he wrote that he was flattered he had prevailed and now would she not allow herself a little happiness? A new period in her life was beginning—" will you try to hope and be at peace? " He urged her to be calm, to tranquillise herself, to achieve a philosophical attitude.

But it was impossible, for a great gap yawned in her life. She was out of office, the press of departmental work no longer made every day a fever—and how was she to occupy herself? In a private note of 1872 she wrote: " Never has God let me feel weariness of active life, but only anxiety to get on. Now in old age I never wish to be relieved from new work, but only to have it to do."

Though she had planned to live a life of austerity, poverty and discipline in a general ward at St. Thomas's, she had never intended to retire from participation in the affairs of the hospital, and a new chapter in its history had just opened. In 1871 it moved from its temporary quarters in Surrey Gardens to the new buildings in Lambeth with which she had been closely concerned. The plans embodied her ideas, and every detail of equipment had received her meticulous attention. On the subject of hospital floors alone she had exchanged almost a hundred letters with Dr. Sutherland, Douglas Galton, manufacturers, matrons, doctors, architects. Should they be of pine? Should they be of oak? Of polished cement? Should they be varnished or polished? If polished, should the work be done by a *frotteur* or a housemaid? Sinks and baths were the subject of another enormous correspondence. Manufacturers approached her with their goods. " The Directors will be so influenced by your statements that they will not hesitate in issuing orders for Baths and Sinks of my manufacture ", wrote Mr. Finch, manufacturer of porcelain baths and sinks, in June 1870.

The Nightingale Training School had also reached a crisis. Throughout the previous ten years, in spite of failures and disappointments, the demand for trained nurses had rapidly grown. There were now Nightingale nurses at Netley as well as Woolwich, in the model infirmary at Highgate, to which a training school was attached, at Haslar, and at many London hospitals; and Nightingale-trained superintendents in charge of parties of nurses had gone to Australia, New Zealand and Canada. Miss Nightingale's attention had been distracted from the school by the demands of Poor Law reform and India. Now she turned her attention to it again and found that it had fallen away from its original standards. The aim of the school was to " train more Agnes Joneses ", but, to meet the overwhelming demand, nurses and matrons had been sent out who fell short not only in lofty ideals but in technical skill.

In the spring of 1872 she began an investigation into the teaching and organisation of the Nightingale School. In the new St. Thomas's the school had larger quarters and would train more probationers. She went through the curriculum, she questioned probationers and nurses, she examined candidates' notes, she interviewed doctors. Finding an urgent need for reorganisation and reform, she made a new plan for herself: she would live near St. Thomas's and devote her life to the training school and the hospital. Mrs. Sutherland was set to work to find suitable lodgings in Kennington.

But in the summer of 1872 a drastic change took place in her life and she was forced to return home. For the past three or four years Fanny and W. E. N. had been an increasing anxiety. They were old and ailing; in 1872 W. E. N. was seventy-seven and Fanny eighty-three, and the management of their property and their two establishments at Embley and Lea Hurst had become unsatisfactory. The position was peculiarly difficult. Since W. E. N. had no son, by his uncle's will the properties of Embley and Lea Hurst passed on his death to Aunt Mai and next to her son, Shore. Uncle Sam had become an exacting invalid, and the close ties of blood (in addition to Aunt Mai being W. E. N.'s sister, Uncle Sam was Fanny's brother) made criticism easy and businesslike arrangements difficult.

As soon as Miss Nightingale visited her family again she found herself drawn into family difficulties. She was, she wrote, elected into being the man of business of the family, though most unwilling to accept the position. " People who have carriages and butlers and housekeepers and time they don't know what to do with, and who drive out every day for their pleasure and dress and go out every day, ask me, who have none of these things and am always in bed and have always more to do than if I were an Undersecretary—and am chained to the oar—ask ME to pay their bills and do their business ", she wrote to Clarkey in the summer of 1868: the gibes were at Parthe. Parthe, she wrote, " prided herself on being ' entirely princess' ", Parthe behaved " as if money, carriages, butlers and housekeepers grew on blackberry bushes ", Parthe was " always, as she always has been, the spoilt child ", Parthe fussed over her health and if she had an aching foot " made a tohu-bohu and would not put it to the ground ".

In fact her sister was suffering from the first symptoms of

the arthritis which in a few years turned her into a helpless cripple.

It was not possible for Miss Nightingale to see things go wrong without trying to put them right, and against her will she was forced into assuming responsibility. By the autumn of 1871 her parents' affairs were interfering with her work. On October 3rd she wrote to Jowett from Lea Hurst: " I was due in London to-day—but have been kept here for the last 6 weeks and shall be for a few days more by doing some most harassing and painful business (looking into things which had gone *very* wrong) for my father and mother (which has taken more out of me than two years of real Crimean work). Do not mention this please."

In the summer of 1872 she was forced to leave London and spend eight months with her parents at Embley. In June Fanny's old housekeeper, Mrs. Watson, died: she had been in the Nightingales' service for twenty-five years and had been the first person to welcome Miss Nightingale on her return from the Crimea. Her death was followed by confusion. It was extremely difficult to find anyone whom Fanny and W. E. N. would accept in her place, and during the last years of Mrs. Watson's life the discipline of the household had become slack. The servants, wrote Miss Nightingale, did what they liked, not one of them was doing his or her proper work. To put the household of Embley into order was as difficult as organising the Barrack Hospital at Scutari. Housekeeper succeeded housekeeper with rapidity; W. E. N. complained of the cooking, Aunt Ju had hysterics, Fanny, who was becoming childish and easily upset, was more than usually difficult. In July 1872 Miss Nightingale told Clarkey that Fanny had to have her luncheon carried into three different rooms before she could be persuaded to eat it.

Month followed month, and it was impossible for Miss Nightingale to leave Embley. Life was filled with the misdeeds and complaints of housemaids, kitchen maids, footmen, cooks and with unwelcome discoveries in household and estate accounts. " I am so stifled by dirty anxious cares and sordid *defensive* business ", she wrote in a private note of August 1872. " Like the maid of all work who has to wipe her dirty hands on her dirtier apron before she can touch clean people."

She was imprisoned again, caught in the old unhappiness, the old frustration. Her father and mother clung to her; they were old and helpless and they had no one else : Parthe was useless, Aunt's Mai's daughter Beatrice, who had lived with Fanny, had married, the old servants who loved them were dead, her heart forbade her to abandon them. Miss Nightingale was fifty-two, but she had lost none of her capacity to suffer. " Oh to be turned back to this petty stagnant stifling life at Embley," she wrote in a private note of the late summer 1872, " which has done to death so many of the best with whom I began life. I should hate myself (I *do* hate myself) but I should LOATHE myself, oh my God, if I could *like* it, find ' rest ' in it. Fortunately there is no rest in it, but ever increasing anxieties. Il faut que la victime soit mise en pièces. Oh my God ! "

Her life was tossed to and fro at the mercy of obligations over which she had no control. " There is no longer any consecutive path growing out of my own acts ", she wrote in 1872, " only a succession of disjointed lives and disconnected events." The change in her circumstances was startling enough to try the strongest nerves. In place of a life in which every hour was filled with matters of vital interest and national importance, she found herself in an isolated country house alone with two aged semi-invalids, spending her days in satisfying their exactions, smoothing over their difficulties with their servants and straightening their finances.

Fanny and W. E. N. could not be left alone together. Fanny, childish, almost blind, her memory gone, was a responsibility that W. E. N., seventy-nine and failing, could not undertake. The thought of work piling up in London, of the reform and reorganisation of the Nightingale School crying out to be done, while she was delayed at Embley was agony to Miss Nightingale. All through the winter of 1872 she chafed. In the spring of 1873 she could bear it no longer. She must be in London ; Parthe was ill and could not help—Fanny must come to London. The drawing-room floor at South Street was fitted up as a bedroom and sitting-room, and Fanny came to London in the spring of 1873. W. E. N. agreed to stay at Embley with Aunt Ju to look after him, and wrote frequent letters complaining that he found Aunt Ju interfering and unpunctual and that the cook would send him up rich dishes, which gave him indigestion. " I tell her she must make her kitchen maid cook my plain joint again ", he wrote, ". . . I am in trouble with the over attention—personal—of Butler, Footman, they *will* keep in the room."

In London Miss Nightingale threw herself with desperate haste into the reconstruction of the Nightingale School. The first task was to tighten up the technical side of the training. Soon after she arrived back, her friend Mr. Whitfield, the Resident Medical Officer of St. Thomas's, who had supervised the medical training of the Nightingale probationers since the foundation of the school, gave up the post owing to the extra work involved in the new, enlarged hospital. His place was taken by Mr. Croft, one of the honorary surgeons. In April and May Miss Nightingale and Mr. Croft drew up a new plan of instruction. Members of the honorary staff, in addition to Mr. Croft, agreed to give lectures, the standard of examination was raised and examinations made more frequent, probationers were required to undertake a course of reading planned by Mr. Croft and Miss Nightingale and were also at intervals to submit their notebooks for her inspection. Within a few months he reported that the work was improving and "the answers collectively are much better than they have been for years".

Miss Nightingale held that the training and education of a nurse, or indeed any education or training, was made up of two aspects of equal importance. First, the acquisition of knowledge which was properly tested by the passing of an examination ; second, the development of character which could not be tested by the passing of an examination.

To improve the training of character she created a new post. Mrs. Wardroper, the matron of St. Thomas's, who had originally supervised the probationers, now found, like Mr. Whitfield, that the new hospital made greater demands on her time. An Assistant Superintendent was appointed with the title of Home Sister ; the Home Sister was to hold classes for the discussion and explanation of the medical lectures, but the main purpose of her mission was to exercise moral, spiritual and cultural influence. She was to make herself the girls' friend, she was to encourage them to read poetry, to listen to music, to go regularly to church. She was to inculcate a standard which would keep the Nightingale nurses " above the mere scramble for a remunerative place ".

All influences, however, were secondary to the influence of Miss Nightingale herself. She dominated the school. From 1872 onwards she determined to make herself personally acquainted with every probationer, and as soon as a girl had completed a trial period she was interviewed by Miss Nightingale, who wrote a character sketch which formed the first item in a dossier composed of examination results, notes of further interviews, letters and comments. Miss Nightingale invited the probationers' criticisms and comments on the treatment they received from the sisters and the value of their medical lectures ; she invited comments from the sisters on the character and conduct of the probationers. When she received a complaint or a suggestion which seemed to her to be worthy of notice she wrote a memorandum to the persons concerned.

It was work with human beings again, the work for which she had longed. After the long dry years of toiling at administration her life was rich once more. " I am overwhelmed ", she wrote to M. Mohl on June 21st, 1873, " in a torrent of my Trained Matrons and Nurses, going and coming, to and fro, Edinburgh and Dublin, to and from Watering Places for their health, dining, tea-ing, sleeping—sleeping by day as well as by night."

Her stay in London had to be cut short when Fanny's maid and her maid quarrelled ; Fanny became unwell and had to be taken back to Embley. Just before they left Miss Nightingale was upset by the loss of her favourite cat Mr. Muff, who had been left behind at Embley and allowed to wander in the woods, where he was presumably shot by a keeper ; she was broken-hearted—" I have no one now to say like Ruth ' Intreat me not to leave thee' ", she wrote to M. Mohl in June. " Poor Mr. Muff said it, if ever Ruth did." By the end of June she was back at Embley chafing at being separated from her work, miserable, frustrated.

The solution, Jowett told her, was to resign herself to dropping active work and to concentrate on writing. " The way of influencing mankind by ideas is the more excellent way ", he had told her in 1870. Since duty forced her to be away from London, he urged her once more to make writing the main interest in her life. He greatly admired the powers of her mind, he was convinced she had a message to give the world, and he believed she could spread her message more widely with more happiness to herself if she expressed herself by writing.

In October 1872 he suggested that she should write some essays for the reviews on the Idea of God. " During the ten years and more that I have known you," he wrote, " you have repeated to me the expression ' Character of God ' about 1000 times, but I can't say I have any clear idea what you mean." The suggestion attracted her—all her life, in periods of unhappiness, she had found relief in exercising her mind on philosophical ideas. In January 1873 she wrote to M. Mohl : " Latterly I have been so broken up and broken down. Nothing solaces me so much as to write upon the Laws of the Moral World ; especially as exemplifying if possible, *the character of a Perfect God, in bringing us to perfection through them in eternity. . . .*" She wrote three essays on the Laws of the Moral World which repeated the ideas she had earlier treated at length in *Suggestions for Thought*. Two of the essays were published by Froude in *Fraser's Magazine* for May and July 1873 under the titles " A Note of Interrogation " and " A Sub-Note of Interrogation : What will our Religion be in 1999 ? "

While she worked on these essays she exchanged letters of immense length with Jowett on philosophical and religious subjects—" The Laws of Physical Improvement ", " The Character of God ", " The Nature of Friendship ". He invited her to help him in revising his translations of the Dialogues of Plato—she still had considerable facility in Greek—and he placed a high value on her interpretations. " You are the best critic I ever had ", he told her in 1872. He used her suggestions in his introduction to the *Republic* and wrote, " I am always stealing from you ". In July 1873 she sent him a letter on the *Phaedrus* and he told her that he had " put in most of what you suggested ". She also drafted his sermons and special prayers for use at Balliol.

At the end of 1872 he asked her to make a selection of Bible stories for a Children's Bible. Enclosing her selection she wrote: "The story of Achilles and his horses is far more fit for children than that of Balaam and his ass, which is only fit to be told to asses. The stories of Samson and of Jephthah are only fit to be told to bull dogs; and the story of Bathsheba to be told to Bathshebas. Yet we give all these stories to children as 'Holy Writ'. There are some things in Homer we might better call 'Holy Writ'—many, many in Sophocles and Aeschylus. The stories about Andromache and Antigone are worth all the women in the Old Testament put together, nay, almost all the women in the Bible." She summarised the book of Samuel and the books of Kings as "Witches. Harlots. Talking Asses. Asses Talking. Young Gentlemen caught by the Hair. Savage Tricks. Priests' Tales". Jowett was delighted, and on February 10th, 1873, told her that she would find her suggestions had been adopted almost entirely and that he blessed her every time he took up the book.

And now she discovered there was a message she wished to convey to the world. Its nature was surprising. It had nothing to do with sanitary reform. She had turned away from practical affairs to the life of the soul.

Miss Nightingale was a mystic. She was not a contemplative. Like St. Elizabeth of Hungary, she was an administrator, and like St. Elizabeth she led side by side with her busy active life a secret life of mystical experience. Mysticism involves the use of a formula by following which the soul can train herself to achieve a condition in which union with God becomes possible. The language of the mystic is definite, the mystical way to God is composed not of aspirations but of rules. "Of this process", wrote Miss Nightingale in 1873, "they describe the steps, and assign periods of months and years, during which the steps they say are commonly made by those who make them at all." During her life she had come under two important mystical influences. The first was during her stay in Rome in 1848, when she was deeply impressed by the Madre Santa Colomba and made a retreat at the Convent of Trinità de' Monti. Since then she had regularly read the Catholic mystics, especially St. John of the Cross and St. Theresa. The second occurred during the Crimea when she became an intimate friend of the Superior of the Convent in

Bermondsey which sent her a party of her best nurses. Rev. Mother Bermondsey, who was a woman of remarkable character, an able organiser and administrator, at the same time led an intense mystical life. With her, Miss Nightingale studied the works of the mediaeval mystics, St. Angela of Foligno, Mother Julian of Norwich and the writings of Madame de Chatel and Father Rigoleuc, and, even during the crushing years of the Indian Sanitary Report, wrote her letters of immense length on mystical subjects. The fact that the writers they studied were Catholics was unimportant; dogma does not enter into mysticism, and the journey of the mind to God is taken along the same road whether by St. Bernard or Plotinus.

Miss Nightingale had progressed far in mystical experience. She writes in a private note of " the incalculable benefit of this occasional but frequent intercourse with the Perfect ". Among her papers is a very large number of " spiritual meditations ", written over a number of years in the language of mysticism: " Where shall I find God? In myself. That is the true Mystical Doctrine. But then I myself must be in a state for Him to come and dwell in me. This is the whole aim of the Mystical Life; and all Mystical Rules in all times and countries have been laid down for putting the soul into such a state. . . . That the soul herself should be heaven, that our father which is in heaven should dwell in her . . . that God enlarges the ' palace of our soul ' by degrees so as to enable her to receive Himself, that thus He gives her liberty but that the soul must give herself absolutely to Him for Him to do this . . . this is the conclusion and sum of the whole matter."

The frustration of her life after 1872 made the " incalculable benefits of this occasional but frequent intercourse with the Perfect " even more important. Her letters became increasingly concerned with the lessons to be learned from the mediaeval mystics, and she sent extracts to Jowett. He was dubious, he was temperamentally unsympathetic to mysticism and the mystical rule of life—but gradually she converted him. She pointed out to him the universality of mysticism and the close resemblance between the teachings of the mediaeval mystics and of Plato. The prayer in the *Phaedrus*, " ' give me beauty in the inward soul and may the inward and outward man be at one', expressed in seventeen words the whole, or at least half, the doctrine of St. John of the Cross", she wrote in October 1872.

Her mysticism was not passive. She never deviated from her principle that the purpose of every experience must be increased action. "Religion is not devotion but work and suffering for the love of God", she wrote. When the soul had progressed through the educative stages of the mystical process and was able to achieve the state when union with God could be experienced, "when all our actions, all our words, all our thoughts, the food on which they are to live and have their being, is the indwelling presence of God, the union with God", then the soul was in a fit state to go forth and work. "The way to live with God is to live with Ideas—not merely to think about Ideas but to do and suffer for them." The union of a busy and active life with the practice of mysticism was normal, for many of the mediaeval mystics had been organisers and administrators, and Rev. Mother Bermondsey and the Madre Santa Colomba were women of practical ability, engaged in the administration of hospitals and orphanages. Yet mysticism had come to be regarded as apart from ordinary life, a practice confined to saints enclosed in convents and hermits in their cells. "The 'mystical' state is the essence of common sense", Miss Nightingale wrote, ". . . the ecstatic state is unreal, and should not be at all . . . we *can* only act and speak and think through Him; and what we need is to discover such laws of His as will enable us to be always acting and thinking in *conscious* concert with Him. . . . There will be no Heaven unless we make it. And it is a very poor Theodike which teaches us that we are not to 'prepare' for *this* world—but only to 'prepare' for another. Must we not 'possess' God here, if we want to 'possess' Him hereafter? . . . Desire for personal salvation is not religion." In the autumn of 1872 Jowett suggested she should compile a book of extracts from the mediaeval mystics translated by herself showing the application of mysticism to present-day life. "You will do a good work", he wrote on October 3rd, "if you point out the kind of mysticism which is needed at the present day. . . . The passion of the reason, the fusion of faith and reason—if you can only describe these you will teach people a new lesson."

She began to work on a book and drew up a title-page, " Notes from Devotional Authors of the Middle Ages. Collected, Chosen and freely translated by Florence Nightingale."

As she worked she sent her extracts to Jowett, who became interested in her comments. On April 18th, 1873, he wrote suggesting that she should add a preface to the book, formulating her conception of mysticism and giving guidance as to how mystical books should be used. " I think it is clear ", he wrote, " that this mystic state ought to be an occasional and not a permanent feeling—a taste of heaven in daily life. Do you think it would be possible to write a mystical book which would also be the essence of Common Sense ? "

Through the summer and autumn of 1873 work on the book and the preface was her chief solace. She needed a " taste of heaven in daily life ", her own had become a round of coaxing servants, humouring her parents, struggling to persuade them to allow her to straighten their neglected affairs. By December she wrote to M. Mohl that she was " completely broken ".

Worse, however, was to follow. In January 1874 she escaped for a few weeks : Parthe was a little better, and as she and Sir Harry Verney were able to come to Embley Miss Nightingale hurried to London. On January 10th she heard that her father was dead. He had gone upstairs before breakfast to fetch his watch, slipped on the stairs, and died instantly.

The affection between them had been very deep. " His reverent love for you ", wrote Richard Monckton Milnes on January 13th, 1874, " was inexpressibly touching." But grief only too soon took second place as she became overwhelmed by the painful anxieties, the innumerable difficulties which arose out of his death.

Embley and Lea Hurst were now the property of Aunt Mai. It was not easy to turn out, it was melancholy to see Fanny, eighty-six and childish, weeping because she could not understand why she was being sent away from her home. Unhappiness and friction were inevitable, and the family temperament intensified them. " We Smiths ", Fanny had once said, " all exaggerate " ; they were tenacious, voluble, determined and easily offended. " We are a great many too strong characters," wrote Miss Nightingale to Clarkey in

1874, " and very different; all pulling different ways. And we are so dreadfully *au sérieux*."

Miss Nightingale went down to Embley to be with her mother. All the painful wearing business, she wrote, was left to her, and in a few weeks she was reduced to misery. She asked Aunt Mai to offer Fanny a home at Embley, but Aunt Mai refused—she was seventy-six, was crippled with arthritis, and had the responsibility of an invalid husband. In February Miss Nightingale wrote to M. Mohl: " My father has scarce been dead a month and every imaginable bitterness has heaped up . . . everyone acting independently of every other, tho' in one another's name and at once in total contradiction of each other ". In a long confused letter to Clarkey she complained of the family's treatment of Fanny. Parthe proposed that Fanny should be removed at once from Embley and installed in a house in London with a companion to look after her, though she knew that Fanny was miserable in London and it was difficult in her mental state to find a suitable and trustworthy companion for her. The present companion Miss Nightingale disliked and called her " that cock's egg ". The truth was that everyone was afraid of Parthe; they would say anything behind her back but they cringed to her face. Aunt Mai and her husband, " owing to things and persons being what they are ", would not give Fanny " a home at her old home with their party ". It was unthinkable to force Fanny to go to London; if she must be turned out of Embley the only solution was for Miss Nightingale to give up her work and take her mother to Lea Hurst, which the Smiths did not require and after which Fanny " craved and longed ". " I am utterly exhausted ", Miss Nightingale wrote. " Not a day passes without the most acute anxiety and care. Oh the cruel waste of time, of all real work. If our family could neither read nor write, if they had only a limited number of Serb words at their disposal and if postage were 5/- an ounce, how happy life would be. How happy it was in the Crimea on account of these things; that *was* living in spite of misery." Her sole comfort was the consideration and good sense of Aunt Mai's son, the heir to the property, Shore Smith, " my boy Shore ". The affection she had lavished on him was, she wrote, a thousandfold repaid.

Once more there was no escape. Old, feeble and un-wanted, Fanny had a claim which to Miss Nightingale was impossible to reject. The weary business of clearing up at Embley dragged on. "Everything has gone from my life except pain", she told Clarkey on June 8th, 1874. "Oh God," she wrote in a private note, "let me not sink in these perplexities but give me a great cause to do and die for." In July Embley was given up and she took Fanny to Lea Hurst. "You see I have brought my poor mother down here after all", she scribbled in one of her notes to Dr. Sutherland. "This is all very sorrowful," he scribbled in reply, "but I suppose the dear lady does not know the difference."

Fanny's mind had almost failed and she was blind. Sur-rounded by familiar objects, though she could not see them, hearing familiar voices, though she did not recognise them, she was at peace. But when she was taken to strange places, heard strange voices, she became agitated and unhappy, and wept. In her lucid moments she returned to the past. "Where is Flo?" she asked one day. "Is she still in her hospital?" Then she gave a sigh, "I suppose she will never marry now", she said. So very dim were her apprehensions that Parthe and Clarkey thought Miss Nightingale was making an unnecessary sacrifice: but she could not leave her mother to strangers. The tenderness which helplessness and suffering evoked in her were on Fanny's side now.

Many times in her life she was desperately unhappy, but never unhappier than during the summer and autumn of 1874 at Lea Hurst. It was, she wrote, "utter ship wreck". Writ-ing had been a solace, now writing was impossible and her book on the mystics was laid aside never to be resumed. Every minute which could be snatched from struggling with domestic problems was devoted to trying to preserve some part of her work. She habitually rose before dawn—her letters are headed " 5 A.M.", " 6 A.M. ", " 4-8 A.M. ", " Before it is light ". An enormous amount of writing was required. "Because I am not in London I have to write 100 letters to get one thing done", she wrote. Weariness grew on her. She implored Dr. Sutherland not to crease her drafts "because I have no strength to re-write ". "I have not one oz of strength left ", she wrote. She doubted herself—"I am afraid I am dread-

fully prolix ". " I have put in far too much detail ", she told
him in 1874.

One night, she recorded in a private note, as she started
from an uneasy sleep, the shadow cast by the night-light on the
wall reminded her of Scutari. " Am I she who once stood on
that Crimean height? ' The Lady with a Lamp shall stand.'
The lamp shows me only my utter ship wreck."

Failure haunted her, failure in India, failure in the Nightingale Training School, mistakes, disasters everywhere. In
February 1874 Quetelet, originator of the science of statistics,
died. How much he had accomplished compared to herself.
" What makes the difference between man and woman? "
she wrote. " Quetelet did his work and I am so disturbed by
my family that I can't do mine."

Despair alternated with passionate self-reproach. She
reminded herself that if failure were God's will then to rebel
was the worst failure of all. In spiritual meditations scribbled
during sleepless nights she struggled to accept her fate. " Oh
Father I submit, I resign myself. . . . Deal with me as Thou
seest meet. Oh how vain it is, the vanity of vanities to live in
men's thoughts instead of Gods." Had she not struggled to
lead her life with God? " O my Creator, Thou knowest that
through all these 20 horrible years I have been supported by
the belief (I must believe it still or I am sure I could not work)
that I was working with Thee who wert bringing everyone,
even our poor nurses, to perfection."

Ill, sleepless, unable to eat, she felt herself approaching the
edge of a precipice. She must submit. For the sake of her
mental balance she must force herself to believe that her
present sufferings were not useless but part of God's scheme
for the world. " I *must* believe in the plan of Almighty Perfection to make us all perfect." She must not snatch the
management of the world out of God's hands. In practical
details she found herself apt to give the Divine Will directions.
" I MUST remember God is not my private secretary ", she
wrote on an odd scrap of paper.

It had never been her habit to live in the past, but now
circumstances forced her thoughts backwards. A succession
of deaths removed figure after figure who had played an important part in her early life, and as she pined at Lea Hurst not

only her present but her past seemed slowly dying. " My friends drop off one by one ", she wrote to M. Mohl in May 1873. " Every individual who formed my committee in 1857, many of them hardly older than myself, is dead. And I hang on." In August 1872 Mr. Bracebridge died. A host of memories rushed in on her. Her stay in Rome—" I never enjoyed any time in my life so much as my time at Rome "— his sympathy in her early struggles, his work for her at Scutari, " the only man in all England who would have lived with willingness such a ' pigging ' life ". After the Crimea they had drifted apart, but he was, she wrote in a private note, " the kindest of friends and the best and noblest of men. All his life he was fighting battles against cruelty and oppression." When he died she was at Embley and miserably unhappy. Mrs. Bracebridge's overwhelming grief provoked her to bitterness. In a private note she wrote : " Sometimes I think that I am glad that when I go there will be no such heart rending grief felt for me as when two are parted, who had lived for nearly half a century with each other and for each other—or as I felt when Sidney Herbert died and feel every day more and more. On Friday he will have been dead 11 years." She added, " there are things worse than death ".

In September 1872 Sir Harry Verney's younger daughter by his first marriage, Emily Verney, died ; she was a beautiful girl who had loved Miss Nightingale and gone to Kaiserswerth in imitation of her ; when her health failed she was working with Octavia Hill. On September 10th Miss Nightingale wrote to Dr. Balfour : " The grave has not yet closed over the mortal form of one who was almost as dear to me as my own child— one who would have done a great work for God had she lived. Emily Verney—Sir Harry Verney's only daughter, so lovely, so loving, so loved and with something heroic about her."

In May 1873 John Stuart Mill died suddenly at Avignon. His death, she told M. Mohl, was a great shock to her. On January 31st, 1874, a week or two after W. E. N., Mrs. Bracebridge (Σ), died after a long and painful illness. " A dreary end for her who had been all warmth and radiance ", Miss Nightingale wrote. During Σ's last illness she had sent for news of her every day. " She was more than mother to me, oh that I cannot be a daughter to her now." Mrs. Bracebridge had been Sidney Herbert's close friend and for years had spent the anniversary of his death with Miss Nightingale. " This is to me like the last parting with my past ", she wrote in a private note. ". . . What should I have been without her? . . . To one living with her as I did once she was totally unlike anyone I have ever known ; as unlike as a picture of a sunny scene is to sunshine with its light and warmth ; or as this February lamp we call the sun is to her own sun of the East in Palestine." She cherished relics of Selina after her death, a blue seal ring from Egypt, a blue snake ring and a lock of her hair, " beautiful even in old age ".

In July 1874 another familiar figure vanished—Panmure, afterwards Lord Dalhousie. " I felt the death of Panmure, my old *enemy*, tho' I was always *friends* with him ", wrote Miss Nightingale to M. Mohl on August 11th, 1874, ". . . it was the last breaking up of old associations, of strife and struggle for noble aims and objects ; the last ghost disappearing of my Sidney Herbert life. . . . He used to call me ' a turbulent fellow '."

Chapter after chapter was closing, figure after figure left the stage. She alone survived—but for what?

Shore Smith and his wife Louisa tried to help her, Shore suggesting that he and his wife should have Fanny at their house in London for some months between October and July when it was most urgent for Miss Nightingale to be in London for her work. Parthe could do nothing—her health was worse, and it was evident that she was seriously ill. In addition to Shore Miss Nightingale had a new helper, Miss Paulina Irby.

Paulina Irby had cherished a passionate admiration for Miss Nightingale since girlhood, and, inspired by her example, had gone to Kaiserswerth to be trained as a nurse. She was a Greek scholar and a woman of great nobility of character who had devoted her life to the relief of the sufferings of the Christian populations of Bosnia and Herzegovina, struggling to emancipate themselves from Turkish rule. Fanny, who had taken a fancy to Paulina, invited her to Embley in 1869 to meet Miss Nightingale ; she stayed constantly at Embley before W. E. N.'s death, and, after his death, at Lea Hurst. She looked after Fanny and took some of the domestic burden off Miss Nightingale's shoulders.

It seemed that here were arrangements by which she might have been relieved, but they did not work smoothly. In the summer of 1875 Fanny went to stay with Shore and his wife, but became so ill and unhappy that she had to be taken away. South Street was deserted at a critical juncture, and Miss Nightingale found herself in a villa at Norwood. On June 18th she wrote to Clarkey : " I am ' out of humanity's reach ' in a red villa, like a Monster Lobster in charge of my mother by doctor's orders, as her only chance of recovering strength enough to see her old home (Lea Hurst) after which she cruelly craved. Here she is happy ; happy at least compared to her miserable unhappiness in London. Stranger vicissitudes than mine in life few men have had ; vicissitudes from slavery to power and from power to slavery again—it does not seem like a ' vicissitude ', a villa at Norwood ; yet it is the strangest I yet have had. It is the only time for 22 years that my work has not been the first reason for deciding where I should live and how I should live. Here it is the *last*. It is the caricature of a life."

Miss Nightingale's conscience deprived her of Paulina Irby's help. Paulina was becoming absorbed by the Nightingale family troubles, but she was in England to collect funds for her work in Bosnia, not to look after Fanny. In a private note written in the summer of 1875 Miss Nightingale sternly reminded herself that, however great the temptation to keep Paulina, the decision to send her away must be right. The world, as she had so often told Hilary Bonham Carter, was divided into devourers and the devoured. Was she, F. N., now to become a devourer and allow Paulina to sacrifice herself and her work to " my poor mother's state and the family affairs ? "

At the beginning of 1876 Paulina most unwillingly left England. " I beg you by all the kindness you have shown to me and by the undying love I bear you to send me one or two words or at least a message ", she wrote when she arrived in Bosnia. She left her affairs in charge of Miss Nightingale and Shore, and gave an immense amount of trouble. She was poetic, picturesque, eloquent, she had goodness, nobility, but she had no feeling for facts. " How like she is to Coriolanus ", Miss Nightingale had written on their first meeting.

Paulina had collected money to be expended on orphans. In February 1876 Miss Nightingale told Shore that the money was being spent not on orphans but " on children complete with mothers, on the mothers themselves and on fugitive patriots hiding in the mountains ". Paulina then sent home a circular for Miss Nightingale and Shore to distribute appealing for more funds, stating that they were to be used specifically for the benefit of orphans, but at the same time sending a letter describing how she intended to spend the money, when it was raised, on starving adult refugees. The circular was improperly drawn up, the name and address of the secretary of the fund were not given, there were no accounts of money already expended. " I don't know that I ever was more aggravated by receiving a foolish letter . . . there is *not one fact*", wrote Miss Nightingale to Shore in March 1876. " It is impossible to go on advertising with common honesty in the absence of all facts from her and yet more impossible to issue the circular when the *only* fact she gives me is that she is *not* going to do anything she proposes in the Circular."

Nevertheless, Paulina Irby accomplished a remarkable work, and at one time was keeping 12,000 refugees alive in Bosnia. Miss Nightingale's irritation did not interrupt their friendship. They corresponded and met regularly for another twenty years.

By the end of July 1875 Fanny had recovered sufficiently to be able to travel to Lea Hurst, where Shore had already sent his children. No sooner had she arrived than a domestic upheaval took place : most of the servants left and Miss Nightingale told Clarkey on August 4th that she found herself in charge of the house, of Fanny, and of Shore's children without housekeeper, nurse or governess. Summer turned to autumn and fresh difficulties sprang up on every hand. Parthe's health was very much worse, Fanny missed Paulina, to find a companion for her seemed impossible, and there were financial complications over the settlement of W. E. N.'s estate. In January 1876 Miss Nightingale sustained a great bereavement—M. Mohl died of " a peritonitis ". She was heartbroken : she had cared deeply for M. Mohl and he had been devotedly attached to her. No shadow had fallen on their friendship for nearly forty years. " It seems ", she wrote,

" as if a great light had gone out of the world." Clarkey was tortured by regret. She accused herself of forcing M. Mohl to lead her life, of making him sacrifice his tastes to hers. Miss Nightingale consoled her : " I think you need not, indeed I am sure, torture yourself with thinking you did not appreciate life with him ", she wrote in March 1876. " I have heard you say 100 times that, where the ' central affection ' was what it was in your happy life, all was right. You made him, a melancholy man by temperament, happy, thrice happy too." " Ah me ! " she wrote in April, " why do you torment yourself by thinking ' you did not value ' him. You were the light of his life, the brightness of his firmament. But for you he would have been a melancholy man."

The death of M. Mohl was followed in March 1876 by the death of Dr. Parkes, who had been her supporter ever since they first met at Scutari. He was a great benefactor to the British private soldier ; owing to his efforts the old style knapsack, which constricted the soldier's chest and numbed his arm, causing such pain that men fainted on the march, was replaced by the valise. One of his last acts, on March 9th, 1876, was to dictate a letter to Miss Nightingale. " Your letter reached me on what must be, I believe, my death bed. Perhaps before you receive this I shall be summoned to my account. . . . And now thank and bless you for all the support you have always given me." A few days later he died, and his death precipitated a crisis. He had great influence at the War Office, and was one of the main supports of the Army Medical School, which had never been popular. A party in the War Office had consistently opposed raising the standard of training and personnel in the Army Medical service as an unnecessary extravagance, and at the moment of Dr. Parkes's death it was proposed to abolish the school on the ground of economy. " They could not get the number of candidates to fill the ranks, and to enable this to be done they increased the pay, now to save this they propose to abolish the school ", wrote Dr. Sutherland to Miss Nightingale on April 4th, 1876. She attached great importance to the Army Medical School ; it was essential to the efficiency of the Army Medical Service and it was one of her last remaining legacies from Sidney Herbert. Distracted as she was, she flew to action. With the help of Dr. Sutherland she drew up a long memorandum, which Sir Harry Verney took down and read to the Secretary of State for War. The school was, in fact, without honour only in its own country: Germany had opened schools admittedly in imitation of it and France had adopted the same system, but kept her doctors in training twice as long. Sir Harry Verney reported that the Secretary of State for War listened with close attention; and in May Miss Nightingale was informed not only that the school would continue but that certain reforms she had recommended would be made immediately.

This incident was almost her only ground for satisfaction as her life, during the next few years, steadily darkened. The household at Lea Hurst, with its two invalids, would have been difficult to manage in any case, but the difficulty was increased by the fact that Lea Hurst belonged to Aunt Mai. There was a permanent staff which was engaged by her, and extra servants were brought in for the summer by Miss Nightingale. By the autumn of 1876 she was worn out with domestic difficulties. On November 28th she wrote to Clarkey from Lea Hurst: " The good Shores have taken my mother back. But I am so worn out—not having had one day's nor one hour's rest since my Father's death 3 years ago come January, that I am staying on here for a few days silence. An eternity of silence seems too short to rest me." Difficult as 1876 had been, 1877 was more difficult still. " O my darling ", she wrote to Clarkey in June 1877, " how impatient you are when your sister does but propose to you a companion—think of me—not proposed but obliged—and this is the fourth year and such companions— obliged to take charge of poor Mother, companion and a pack of new and strange servants." In July she told Douglas Galton: " I don't know when I shall be able to work again ". The summer of 1877 was disastrous. One of the servants developed smallpox, there was a scandal and defamatory articles appeared in the local paper. This unpleasant business forced her to stay on in the country, and in October she wrote to Douglas Galton that there was no chance what- ever of her being able to do anything in London during the autumn.

In her opinion the property at Lea Hurst was not well administered, and she set herself to do some of the work which she considered it was the Smiths' duty to do. Family relations were strained further, and she added the innumerable small unpleasantnesses and disappointments inseparable from local affairs to her burden. In June 1878 she wrote to Lord Napier of Magdala that she was "ground to powder in the country by family affairs. I have not had one day's rest since my father's death 4½ years ago. . . . There is no one to do anything for the place or the people."

And yet she managed to keep control of the Nightingale School. When she could get to London she saw her nurses and probationers constantly, every girl who trained at the school was still personally known to her; and, above all, she wrote: to probationers, to nurses, to matrons, to those who were still in the school and those who had left it. Once a girl had become a Nightingale nurse she did not slip out of Miss Nightingale's hands when her training was completed. Miss Nightingale did not approve of her nurses taking posts which had not been arranged by her. A nurse who had trained under her close supervision went to a post arranged and approved by her, and continued to receive letters of advice. When Miss Torrance was appointed matron of the Highgate Infirmary Miss Nightingale sent her more than 100 letters in the first year, and had about the same number of replies. "It takes a great deal out of me", Miss Nightingale wrote to Clarkey in 1875. "I have never been used to influence people except by leading in WORK; and to have to influence them by talking and writing is hard. A more dreadful thing than being cut short by death is being cut short by life in a paralysed state."

Miss Nightingale insisted that her school should perform the dual function which was her conception of education: it must not only teach the mind but it must form the character. "It must be", she wrote in August 1875, "a Home—a place of moral religious and practical training—a place of training of character, habits and intelligence, as well as of acquiring knowledge." In this conception she held the place, if not of a mother, then certainly of a favourite aunt. She was Fanny's daughter in hospitality and generosity, in the pleasure she took in seeing people comfortable and well fed. Fruit, game, jellies, creams, country eggs and butter flowed from her to the Nightingale Home; she had sheaves of flowers sent up from Claydon for the Home and the hospital wards. When a nurse went to a new post Miss Nightingale sent flowers to welcome her. Nurses who were ill had special dishes cooked for them by her cook. Nurses who were travelling found her manservant waiting at the train with a luncheon basket. Nurses who were run down were fed up at her expense. " Get the things out of my money ", she wrote enclosing a detailed diet sheet. If a nurse were prescribed a change or a rest she came forward. Sometimes the nurse would be sent to the seaside at her expense, sometimes asked to stay at Lea Hurst or Claydon. When Miss Nightingale was in London she invited hard-worked nurses for what she called " a Saturday to Monday in bed " at South Street. To be poor, to be in trouble was a certain way to her heart. When she had a probationer to tea at South Street she always presented the girl with a cake on leaving, and if a girl did not seem very well dressed the cake was apt to be larger and richer: this fact became well known and she presently discovered that the girls put on their shabbiest coats to come to tea. Her girls were encouraged to feel that she was always behind them. " Should there be anything in which I can be of the least use, here I am ", was a favourite ending to her letters. To be of use included the practical and the spiritual. She never ceased in countless letters, in numberless interviews, to hold up before her nurses' eyes the spiritual nature of their vocation, to instil into them not only the high standard of efficiency on which she was adamant but a sense of the presence of God.

She was repaid. Her nurses constantly sought her advice. From all over the world they wrote to her, addressing her as " Dear Mistress ", " Beloved Chief ", " Dearest Friend ". She bound them together and she held the threads which bound them. In spite of her exile she made the Nightingale School as much an expression of her own personality as if she had presided over it in the flesh.

She found great pleasure in the company of young women. She liked young people and young people liked her. The spectre of a solitary old age, of " horrible loneliness ", haunted her, and in the " torrent of nurses ", dining, sleeping, tea-ing, coming to her for advice, confiding their difficulties to her, young, enthusiastic, affectionate, she enjoyed the human warmth of which she had been starved.

She was isolated, frustrated by domestic difficulties, and her relationships with her young nurses and probationers became of overwhelming importance. She consulted Jowett about them, and he replied with details of his own experiences with undergraduates. They called the young people in whom they were interested by nicknames and discussed their motives and conduct at enormous length. All her life she had expressed personal feelings in terms of hyperbole; exaggeration was the custom of the age and set in which she had been brought up. Her old friend Lady Ashburton wrote of " the deep joy of communion with my beloved " after spending a day with Miss Nightingale when she was nearly sixty, and repeatedly addressed her as " Guiding Star of my life ".

Miss Nightingale wrote and talked to the young women to whom she became attached in these terms, and her attachments, like all her emotions, verged on the inordinate. Two young women in particular won her affection. Miss Pringle, whom she christened " the Pearl ", and Miss Rachel Williams, called the " Goddess Baby ". Both were excellent nurses, both became matrons of important hospitals, and both were extremely good looking. Rachel Williams in particular was strikingly beautiful. ". . . It was quite a pleasure to my bodily eyes to look at her ", Miss Nightingale wrote when Rachel paid her first visit as a Nightingale probationer. " She is like a queen; and all her postures are so beautiful without being in the least theatrical." The letters she wrote to Rachel Williams and to Miss Pringle were highly coloured. The ups and downs of hospital life, the minor crises inseparable from taking a new post or deciding to go for a holiday, became dramas. In January 1874 Miss Nightingale wrote: ". . . I am well aware that my dear Goddess-baby has—well a baby side, I shall not be surprised at any outburst, though I know full well that in the dear Pearl's terrible distress you will do everything and more than everything possible to drag her through. . . . Only don't break yourself down dear child. . . . I would not have written this much unless urged by seeing my dear Goddess-Baby suffering from delusions." In May 1874, after receiving a delayed letter from Rachel, she wrote : " I have this moment received your charming letter which is just like yourself. And I *must* write and thank you for it at once. It has taken a load off my heart. It is a pure joy to me. . . . And life has not many joys for me my darling." In December 1874 she urged Rachel to come and see her in London. ". . . Telegraph to me any day and come up by the next express. . . . And I will turn out India, my Mother and all the Queen's horses and all the Queen's men, together with one sixth of the human race and lay my energies (not many left) at the Goddess's feet."

Miss Pringle, the Pearl, was addressed as " Dearest little Sister ", " Extraordinary little Villainess ", " Dearest ever Dearest ". Miss Nightingale reproached her tenderly for not having eaten her dinner, and sent it after her in a cab. She implored her to take a much needed holiday—" Dearest very dearest. Very precious to me is your note. Make up your mind to a long holiday ; that's what you have to do now. God bless you. We shall have time to talk." When Rachel Williams or Miss Pringle lunched or dined she took pains to tempt them. " Dishes for Miss Williams ", runs a note to her cook in 1879 : " Rissoles, or fillets of sole à la Maître d'hôtel, or oyster patties, or omelette aux fines herbes, or chicken à la mayonnaise with aspic jelly, or cutlets à la Béchamelle ". Another note runs : " For Miss Williams. Best end of neck of lamb, very delicate. Or minced veal. Or Spring chicken." She delighted in beauty and charm, and the friendship of these lovely and intelligent girls filled an important place in her life. The friendship had also its practical side. The work was furthered, they were the ablest young women she had ever trained.

With enormous effort the Nightingale School could be controlled by correspondence, but there was other nursing work which could not, and in 1874 Miss Nightingale had to turn her back on an important opportunity. She was fully alive to the importance of district nursing. In 1866 she had written that she was " resolved to give herself to District Nursing ". Work for Poor Law Reform, for India, for hospital nursing intervened, and when in 1874 William Rathbone asked her to help him in organising a district-nursing scheme for London she had to refuse—family difficulties prevented her from undertaking anything which required her to be in London. She could not personally organise, but she did everything that could be done from a distance. In 1874 she wrote a pamphlet, *Suggestions for Improving the Nursing Service for the Sick Poor*, and, in accordance with her suggestions, William Rathbone founded the Metropolitan Nursing Association. In April 1876 she wrote and signed a letter to *The Times* which was reprinted as a pamphlet under the title *Metropolitan and National Association for providing Nurses for the Sick Poor. On trained nursing for the Sick Poor, by Florence Nightingale.* It went into two editions. Finally, the first Superintendent of the District Nursing Scheme for London, appointed in 1876, was Miss Florence Lees, one of her ablest nurses, who had served with distinction during the War of 1870.

It was frightful to Miss Nightingale to turn her back on work, frightful not to attempt to do something which ought to be done—and she did not turn her back often enough. In her nursing work she had the Nightingale School to give her direction, but in her Indian work she became confused.

She had fully intended to go out of office in India as well as in England, but she received appeals she could not ignore.

In 1874 she was urgently asked by her old friend Lord Napier of Magdala to use her influence on behalf of the army : barrack improvements promised as long ago as 1864 were still being delayed. She wrote to Lord Cranborne, who had succeeded to the title of Marquis of Salisbury and was Secretary of State for India. He invited her, in terms of the utmost cordiality, to amplify, and forwarded her letters to Lord Northbrook, who replied at once in a long letter, written in his own hand, which Dr. Sutherland described as " capital ". In January 1875 Sir Bartle Frere wrote, " that Caesar should at once sit down and write 6 sheets of 4to paper to show he is taking care of his legions is satisfactory ".

When she could still do so much, when there was so much urgently requiring to be done, she found help impossible to refuse. Lord Salisbury's cordiality, Lord Napier of Magdala's appeal were her undoing, and her determination to stay outside Indian administration faded.

Unfortunately her position had deteriorated. Sir Bartle Frere was no longer in charge of sanitary administration at the India Office. In 1872 he left the India Office to go to Zanzibar to treat with the Sultan regarding the suppression of the Slave Trade, and in 1875 accompanied the Prince of Wales on his tour of India. He was succeeded by Colonel Yule, the celebrated Oriental scholar, who was also an authority on irrigation. Miss Nightingale was on excellent terms with him and later they became close friends, but for the moment Sir Bartle Frere was a serious loss.

She had also, with some indiscretion, associated herself with reformers who were regarded in Government circles as visionary and extreme. Retired officials frequented her house who had been malcontents when they were employed and were firebrands now they were not. They were men haunted by fixed ideas, most of them perfectly correct but frowned on by the India Office. The balance, the irreproachable discretion which had characterised Miss Nightingale, temporarily disappeared. She even transgressed one of her cardinal principles and attempted to put pressure on Government departments by publishing newspaper articles written and signed by herself.

The state of India was sufficient to produce frenzy. There was so much to be done, the problems were so enormous, so urgent, so innumerable. As soon as investigation was made in any direction, fresh abuses emerged which demanded remedy at once. In her mental state she was incapable of crying halt. At this period a letter from her was described at the India Office as " another shriek from Miss Nightingale ". Irrigation was a major issue, irrigation led her to the land question, to rights of tenure, to usury, to taxation, to education, to communication. She became involved in each one. Her correspondence increased, she toiled not at one issue but at twenty.

"The real difficulty is money ", Lord Salisbury wrote to her in 1877. In spite of a reactionary element there was no want of good intentions in the administration of India, and there was no want of talent, but there was complete want of money. " We absolutely do not know where to turn in order to obtain any great increase of revenue ", he told her in 1874. " However great the value of the improvements we cannot afford to be bankrupt. . . . I want you to believe that financial considerations are of some importance."

Every project for improvement came to shipwreck for want of funds. In the great cities of India drainage and good water were crying needs. In Madras the death-rate was rising. In Bombay, thanks to the energy of Dr. Hewlett, the sanitary officer, disease was to some extent controlled, but no less than £72,000 a year was spent on cleansing and consuming rubbish because capital could not be found to instal a proper drainage and sewage system. An immense amount of work was done by Miss Nightingale on plans for municipal drainage and sewage in Madras in collaboration with Mr. Clark, who had already planned the drainage and water supply of Calcutta. In numerous letters to Lord Salisbury and to successive governors of Madras she urged action. She did not succeed. " We must not let it be said or even suspected that sanitary improvement means reckless finance ", Lord Salisbury told her in 1874. She persisted for four years, only to be told, finally, that the Madras Government could find money " only for imperious necessities ". She raged. It was absurd that money could not be found by municipalities for drainage, absurd that, in the frightful condition of Madras, public health was not considered an imperious necessity.

In 1874 she met Sir Arthur Cotton, the great master of irrigation. His record was impressive. He had irrigated Trichinopoly and South Arcot in Southern India by building, with immense success, two dams across the river Coleroon. There was not an individual in the province, it was said, who did not consider the damming of the Coleroon the greatest blessing that had ever been conferred on it. The financial returns were respectively 69 and 100 per cent. He had dammed the Godavery river and irrigated the Godavery district. The Godavery district was in a desperate state after a severe famine, and the district was almost depopulated. After the irrigation works were completed the district became one of the most prosperous in India, and the population doubled. When famine came to Southern India in 1877 four millions perished. In the irrigated districts none perished, and sufficient food was exported to feed three millions who would otherwise have died. Was it not clear that the answer to the problem of India was irrigation? But Sir Arthur Cotton failed to persuade the Government to undertake large-scale irrigation works, and it was a favourite catchphrase to say that he had water on the brain.

Irrigation was admittedly a costly undertaking, but to wait in the hope that the Indian peasant would ever be able to pay for irrigation himself was hopeless. Why did not the Government of India borrow the money for the irrigation works which, as had been proved again and again, doubled the value of the land, brought prosperity and prevented fearful periodic losses of life in famines?

Miss Nightingale sent Lord Salisbury schemes prepared by Sir Arthur Cotton, she demanded a commission on irrigation, she asked that the Government should collect statistics on the cost of irrigation works and their return.

She made little impression. India, with its immense distances, its insoluble problems, its helpless millions, bred despondency. After contact with its vastness and confusion the stoutest heart began to doubt, the clearest mind to waver. Would it be safe, Lord Salisbury pondered, to risk spending the gigantic sums necessary for irrigation works, could it be certain they would succeed, how frightful would be the consequences of failure if the future of the Indian peasant were mortgaged in vain? " Twenty years ago—even ten years ago—the world was much more sanguine, in all things than it is now ", Lord Salisbury wrote in 1875. Miss Nightingale scribbled in the margin, " But is this an argument against irrigation? " Worst of all, the experts differed amongst themselves. One school wished to combine navigation and irrigation—the irrigation canals were to be navigable. Lord Napier wrote to her from Madras, discouraged and out of heart. " Navigation means fullness, irrigation means depletion, to combine the two means suspending irrigation for half the year." Yet if the canals were not made navigable how was the produce to be transported? The expense of road-making was prohibitive. Another school declared the whole project of irrigation to be undesirable. There was only a certain amount of productive power in the soil. With irrigation it would be exhausted in a few years and disaster would follow; irrigation could not create fertility. Sir Arthur Cotton alone stood firm. Money in huge sums must be borrowed and navigable canals made: but as Lord Napier told

Miss Nightingale, Sir Arthur Cotton was considered "a splendid madman".

In 1877 famine ravaged the Presidencies of Bombay and Madras, four million people perished, and irrigation became a burning issue. In 1878 a committee of the House of Commons was appointed to enquire into the possibility and desirability of preventing such famines in future by constructing public works, especially irrigation works, with money raised on loan. Sir Arthur Cotton was summoned to give evidence. Losses in the famine had been enormous, but the districts irrigated under Sir Arthur Cotton's schemes had not suffered. Nevertheless, the committee was hostile to Sir Arthur Cotton, and the recommendations contained in its report were in contradiction of his views.

It was a major defeat, and it brought Miss Nightingale into conflict with the India Office, which did not wish to admit the seriousness of the famine. The official estimate of deaths was a million and a quarter. Her estimate was five to six millions. In the following year the official estimate was revised and raised to more than four million. She had already given offence by her writings, especially by reissuing in 1874 her pamphlet, *Life and Death in India*, with an addition entitled *Life and Death by Irrigation*. It was felt that she made use of information obtained through official sources for journalism. When early in 1878 she applied for figures relating to the famine, she received a snub. On February 7th an official minute was addressed to her: " The Revenue Committee is of opinion that an intimation should be made to Miss Nightingale to the following effect. The various objects of high interest to which she refers are engaging the earnest attention of the Govt. of India and its most experienced officers. This may be taken as a general fact, but in addition to this a special enquiry is about to be made by a carefully selected Commission on the subject of Famines. . . . While then the Secretary of State would on public grounds deprecate the researches which Miss Nightingale wishes to make, as possibly interfering with and embarrassing the comprehensive enquiry of a Commission appointed by the Govt. of India under the orders of H.M. Government, he would as a matter of official propriety, point out to Miss Nightingale, whose active and intelligent philanthropy is universally recognised, that to open the Records of a Public Office to the free inspection of a private individual, however distinguished for character and ability, would constitute a very inconvenient precedent."

She was in disgrace. Nor would she make any attempt at conciliation. She did everything possible to call attention to the disaster of the famine, writing letters to the papers and illustrated weeklies, supplying material for lectures, publishing and signing an article on the "People of India" which was prominently featured in the *Nineteenth Century* for October 1878. She had written it to shock, to tear aside the veil which hid the truth about the Indian famine and the wretched condition of the Indian people. Officials, she was told, described it, as they had described her letters, as a shriek.

And, while she became unpopular at the India Office, at the same time she lost more of her influence in India itself. Lord Northbrook was succeeded by Lord Lytton. She did not know Lord Lytton, he did not call on her and they never corresponded. She disapproved of his policy, which was chiefly directed towards establishing British military supremacy in Afghanistan. In April 1878 Lord Salisbury left the India Office for the Foreign Office and was succeeded by Lord Cranbrook. She had come into contact with Lord Cranbrook when, as Mr. Gathorne Hardy, he was President of the Poor Law Board, and she had never been able to make any impression on him. In August 1878 she made another effort. She sent him "very meekly" the article she had written in the *Nineteenth Century*. "I hope", she wrote, "if you read it you will not call it a shriek. (I am astonished at my own moderation.)" She signed herself, "with some wonder at my own audacity, ever your faithful and grateful servant. Florence Nightingale." Lord Cranbrook replied with a polite and formal note. He had already read her article with interest but thought she generalised too much from one locality.

"Oh that I could do something for India!" she wrote in a private note of 1878. Everywhere she turned she saw huge and vital issues. She tried to enlist the help of Mr. Gladstone in making public the fearful, recurrent losses in Indian famines. She did an immense amount of work on the infinitely complicated and wearisome problems of the Bengal land-tenure system, and engaged in an enormous correspondence with Sir George Campbell, the ex-governor of Bengal, in an effort to work out a system which would check the usury which was the ruin of the Bengal peasant. She did another huge amount of work without result on a book entitled *The Zemindar, the Sun and the Watering Pot*, which aimed at combining an exposure of the land-tenure system with a plea for irrigation. The zemindars, native landlords who held their land direct from the Government and let it out to smaller tenants, were preventing their tenants from deriving benefits from irrigation. " Where Government has charged one rupee, or half a rupee, for water, the zemindar has added three rupees to the rent." She had written the book earlier and some copies had been privately printed in 1874, but Jowett told her she must rewrite it. " You must avoid faults of taste and exaggeration ", he had written in August 1874. " The more moderate a statement is, the stronger it is. . . . You must be careful of the least indiscretion." In 1878 she took up the book again, but the task of rewriting it was beyond her, and she abandoned it.

By 1879 she had reached a depth of despair : progress in India was at a standstill ; out of the effort and sacrifice of twenty years nothing had been achieved. In June 1879 John Lawrence died. His policy was being reversed, improvement of native races, reform of education and administration were being thrown overboard for a " forward " policy in Afghanistan. No commission had been set up on irrigation, sanitary works recommended more than fifteen years ago had not even been begun. Reform in India had failed.

Seldom had Miss Nightingale sunk lower in misery than now. Her life with Fanny continued to present difficulty after difficulty, and in the summer of 1879 the estate at Lea Hurst was involved in a serious scandal. For years she had been pointing out that the water supply and drainage of the village were dangerously defective—" abomination of pigs percolating into the drinking water supply, overflow from the cesspool allowed to lie or to percolate poisoning air and water, contaminated ' Holy Well ' which gives its name to the village ", she had written in a private note of 1878. When in the summer of 1879 a typhoid epidemic broke out she was fiercely attacked on all sides. Those who had suffered held her responsible for the conditions which produced the epidemic, those who had not suffered abused her with equal violence for having now to spend money on rectifying their sanitation. An official enquiry was held; there were articles in the local paper, endless letters. The miserable business dragged on through the summer, the improvements which she considered necessary were not done, and she decided she must spend the autumn at Lea Hurst.

Clarkey begged her to come back to London. Fanny was completely childish, it was very doubtful if she realised where she was, why did Flo persist in burying herself in " that absurd place Lea Hurst? " " Why do you abuse me for being here? " wrote Miss Nightingale on September 13th, 1879. " Do you think I am here for my own pleasure? Do you think any part of my life is *as I please*? Do you know what have been the hardest years of my life? Not the Crimean War. Not the 5 years with Sidney Herbert at the War Office when I sometimes worked 22 hours a day. But the last 5 years and three quarters since my father's death." The autumn dragged on. She had never in her life done anything she did not feel was morally justified, and she did not feel morally justified in leaving her mother now. In private notes she passed once more from preaching resignation to herself to heaping bitter reproaches on her own head. She was rebellious. She had failed in love towards Fanny. She had failed to straighten out the family affairs—" how ill I have fulfilled the responsibilities laid on me? " In her sixtieth year her agony had lost none of its keenness. But release was near. On February 2nd, 1880, Fanny died peacefully at the age of ninety-two, after regaining consciousness for a few hours, during which she listened to her favourite hymns.

XXIII THE CONFLICT which had embittered Miss Nightingale's life for more than forty years was over. At sixty years of age she was free. Not because Fanny was dead, but because she had become reconciled with Fanny and with Parthe as well. All her life resentment against Fanny and Parthe had been a poison working within her. During these last difficult years, before Fanny's childishness, helplessness and blindness, before Parthe's suffering, resentment had melted away.

A change came over her, and the *bonté*, the pervading benevolence, which had been her chief characteristic as a young woman, returned. She became gentler, calmer, even tolerant. In 1881 Uncle Sam died; she became reconciled to Aunt Mai and they began to correspond affectionately again. She wrote to Mr. Gladstone in connection with Paulina Irþy's work and found herself able to be sympathetic to him. With Parthe, for the first time since their childhood, she became intimate. She began to visit Claydon, where a room was set aside for her and called " Miss Nightingale's room ". As Parthe's illness increased, Sir Harry leaned on her; she entered into the lives of his sons and their wives and took an active part in the management of his property and his affairs. " You are our Family Solicitor ", Sir Harry wrote to her in January 1881, " to whom we all turn when we get into a scrape."

Failure began to weigh less heavily on her. Had she achieved nothing, need she reproach herself quite so desperately? On New Year's Eve, 1879, Jowett had written to her : " There was a great deal of romantic feeling about you 23 years ago when you came home from the Crimea (I really believe that you might have been a Duchess if you had played your cards better !) And now you work on in silence, and nobody knows how many lives are saved by your nurses in hospitals (you have introduced a new era in nursing): how many thousand soldiers who would have fallen victims to bad air, bad drainage and ventilation, are now alive owing to your forethought and diligence; how many natives of India (they might be counted probably by hundreds of thousands) in this

548

generation and in generations to come have been preserved
from famine, oppression and the load of debt by the energy of
a sick lady who can scarcely rise from her bed. The world
does not know all this, or think about it. But I know it and
often think about it, and I want you to, so that in the later
years of your course you may see (with a side of sorrow) what
a blessed life yours is and has been. . . . I think that the
romance too . . . did a great deal of good. Like Dr. Pusey
you are a Myth in your own lifetime. Do you know that there
are thousands of girls about the ages of 18 to 23 named after
you? Everyone has heard of you and has a sweet association
with your name."

Could Jowett be right? Ordinary happiness she had never
wanted—" miserable as I am ", she had written in 1867, " I
had rather be as I am than as I see the mass of London Ladies ".
In 1872 when on her way to Embley she had caught a glimpse
of Lord Stanley, now happily married and absorbed in his
country estates, his wife and his library. " I saw them both
at the station," she wrote to Clarkey, " they did not see me.
(They were going to see the Queen) I did not want to speak to
him. I wanted to observe him. I saw it all at a glance. I
should not have known him, so complacent, so obese, so happy
—so bustling. All the great visions dropt away. (I was glad
I had not to speak to him.) All quite forgotten, what once he
was, or might have been. O happiness—like the Bread Fruit
Tree, what a corrupter of human nature thou art ! "

She could look back without regret and now she found she
could do more—she could look forward. In her old age
she was beginning to hope. On June 30th, 1881, she wrote to
Clarkey : " I cannot remember the time when I have not
longed for death. After Sidney Herbert's death and Clough's
death in 1861, 20 years ago, for years and years I used to
watch for death as no sick man ever watched for the morning.
It is strange that now I am bereft of all, I crave for it less. I
want to do a little work, a little better, before I die."

Opportunity was on its way. At the moment she became
free, opportunities for work for India, for nursing, even for the
army, presented themselves once more.

For a short time after Fanny's death she collapsed. She
had to leave London, and went first to Ramsgate, then to a

house lent her by Lady Ashburton at Seaton, in Devonshire. She was ordered a year's complete rest, but the arrears of Indian work and the claims of the Nightingale Training School weighed too heavily upon her, and strongly against her doctor's advice she returned to London at the end of April.

The political scene had just been transformed by the unexpected triumph of the Liberals in the General Election of April 1880. Miss Nightingale was by temperament and upbringing a Whig, but in 1880 the Whigs no longer existed, and partly through her connection with the Verneys—Sir Harry at seventy-eight was standing as Liberal candidate for Buckingham—and partly through her new-found sympathy with Mr. Gladstone, she became an enthusiastic Liberal. The Liberals swept the country, Sir Harry was elected, Mr. Gladstone became Prime Minister, and when Lord Lytton's term of office ended in May her old friend and close ally, Lord de Grey, now Lord Ripon, was appointed Viceroy of India.

Once more official doors were thrown open to her. Of Lord Ripon himself she had the highest hopes; he was an old friend, his advanced and liberal views were well known, he was an able administrator, he had prestige, influence, experience. She did not see him before he sailed, but as soon as he landed they began to correspond, and as his Indian policy unfolded she was enthusiastic.

Two main measures of reform were proposed by Lord Ripon, both highly controversial. The first, introduced by Sir Courtenay Ilbert, the judiciary member of the Viceroy's Council and called the " Ilbert " Bill, gave increased powers to native magistrates. The second aimed at protecting the peasant in Bengal and Oudh by a series of land-reform bills.

In India and at home Lord Ripon's proposals were fanatically opposed. The storm centre was the Ilbert Bill, which gave Indian magistrates, under certain conditions, power to try and sentence Europeans. In July 1883 Miss Nightingale wrote to Queen Victoria: " The so-called ' Ilbert ' Bill is intended to give limited powers to try Europeans, outside the Presidency towns, to Native Magistrates and Judges, who, after long trial of their judicial qualifications, in corresponding positions, have shown themselves worthy to be entrusted with this duty and have risen to that grade where, for their official responsibility, such powers are required ". An absurd situation had arisen. Since 1858 Indians had been allowed to enter the Civil Service and, in spite of the fact that promotion was by no means made easy, certain of them reached the rank of District Magistrate, yet because Englishmen could be tried only by English magistrates an Indian District Magistrate could find himself without authority to try cases which were within the authority of his subordinates.

Hostility to the Ilbert Bill, in fact a carefully guarded and by no means revolutionary measure, was based on racial grounds. Hysteria swept the country. Englishwomen wrote that it was an insult to subject English womanhood to native judges, atrocities committed during the Mutiny were recalled, Indian papers joined in with violence, insults and recriminations were freely exchanged, and India blazed from end to end with hatred.

Almost equally detestable, not only to Europeans but also to a large number of commercially successful Indians, were the proposals for land reform in Bengal and Oudh which endeavoured to protect the *ryot*, the Indian peasant, from oppression and exploitation by placing authority and responsibility in the hands of the head man of each village, thus laying the first foundations of a degree of local government.

Behind the frantic opposition to Lord Ripon's reforms was the grim shadow of the Mutiny. The Mutiny had done irreparable damage. The atrocities committed by Indians on Europeans on lonely stations, the equal atrocities committed by Europeans on Indians as, against the advice of such men as John Lawrence and Lord Napier of Magdala, the European victors avenged themselves in rivers of blood, left a wound which has never yet healed. In 1882 the wound was fresh. The difficulties of an enlightened administrator were increased by the fact that as yet no national consciousness had developed in India, and the reactionary element in the British Government was abetted by a large class of Indians who opposed any measure likely to deprive them of opportunities of exploiting their fellow countrymen.

Miss Nightingale had received her Indian education in a different school. The great Indian administrators who taught her—John Lawrence, Bartle Frere, Lord Napier of Magdala—

were men to whom racial hatred was unknown, whose views of India, formed before the Mutiny, were unwarped by its horrors. They knew and loved India, spent their holidays among the beauties of the country by choice, spoke its languages, studied its literature, opened their houses freely to Indian friends. It had been their creed that the future of India must lie in giving ever-increasing authority to Indians. In this spirit the Queen's Proclamation of 1858 had been drawn up, in which the Crown, assuming the government of India, declared it to be the Sovereign's intention that ". . . our subjects of whatever race or creed be impartially admitted to our service, the duties of which they may be qualified by their education, ability and integrity, duly to discharge ".

Through Lord Ripon, Miss Nightingale believed, light was coming to India at last. After the interminable delays, the endless disappointments—it was twenty years since she had written the " Sanitary Suggestions " for John Lawrence—a new age was dawning. " At last ", she wrote to Lord Ripon in June 1883, " we have a government of India which steadfastly sets its face to carry out the instructions of successive Secretaries of State and successive Parliaments in the spirit of the Queen's Proclamation." In private notes she called Lord Ripon " the saviour of India ". She described his term of office as the beginning of a golden age. " It is the Millennium ! " She signed her letters to him " the most faithful and devoted of your servants ". In July 1883 she forwarded some figures "with deepest reverence and highest hopes for all the great measures by which the Viceroy is bringing peace to the people of India and fulfilling England's pledges. And the love and blessing of India's people be upon him."

She acted as a reference library for Lord Ripon ; he used her encyclopaedic knowledge of Indian affairs, reaching back for over twenty-five years, her close contact with successive administrations, to guide him through the tangled jungle of Indian affairs. Her familiarity not only with facts but with persons was of immense assistance to him in a situation where opposition came not only from without but within. " How well you know the subject of Indian sanitation ", he wrote in July 1883. " If only there were a modicum of your intelligent sympathy to be found in the India Council ! "

For the next four years she was absorbed in crusading for Lord Ripon's reforms. " We shall want all the help you can give at home ", Lord Ripon wrote in 1882. She interviewed every official with whom she could get into touch, she saw native gentlemen, English Members of Parliament, journalists, missionaries. She no longer regularly wrote accounts of interviews, as she had done twenty years ago, but among her papers are notes of visits from Lord Roberts, who called to see her before going out as Commander-in-Chief Madras in 1881; from Sir Courtenay Ilbert, the introducer of the Ilbert Bill; Sir Mountstuart Grant Duff, Governor of Madras ; Mrs. Scharlieb, the celebrated doctor, who practised medicine among the women of India ; Lord Reay, Governor of Bombay ; Mr. W. R. Robertson, Principal of the Agricultural College in Madras. Their visits were not visits of compliment. Again and again, as in the case of Lord Roberts, Mrs. Scharlieb, Sir Mountstuart, Mr. Robertson, she put against the name " he desired me to write notes for him ". She wrote an explanation of the Ilbert Bill for Queen Victoria, she described Lord Ripon's land-reform proposals in a paper entitled *The Ryot, the Zemindar and the Government*, which was read aloud by Mr. Frederick Verney, one of Sir Harry's sons, at a meeting of the East India Association in June 1883.

She exercised influence on Indian administrators from the start of their careers. Jowett was on the Board of Examiners for the Indian Civil Service, and, when candidates were given the opportunity of spending a year at Oxford before going out to India, Arnold Toynbee was selected to lecture on economics to them. Arnold Toynbee was Jowett's friend and became Miss Nightingale's. They corresponded, she made suggestions for lectures which were incorporated in the syllabus, and from time to time persuaded such authorities as Sir George Campbell, Lieutenant-Governor of Bengal, to come to Oxford to deliver special courses.

She was drawn back into army work through a friendship with General Gordon. In April 1880, when Miss Nightingale returned to London after Fanny's death, she received a letter from him asking her to see his cousin Mrs. Hawthorn, wife of a colonel in the Royal Engineers, who wanted help in putting before the War Office facts concerning the neglect and ill-treatment of patients in military hospitals by orderlies. Miss Nightingale took the case up and wrote a memorandum which was submitted to the Secretary for War through Sir Harry Verney. She was not successful. In his reply the Secretary for War stated that he "failed to be convinced". "I have seen such answers in the Crimean War time", she wrote to Douglas Galton in August 1880. "The patient died of neglect and want of proper attendance; but by regulations should not have died, therefore the allegation that he is dead is disposed of." Out of the failure, however, came friendship with General Gordon.

She was instinctively in sympathy with him. His intense Evangelical religiousness did not grate on her; she cared only for saintliness, nothing for the form in which it was expressed, and his attitude towards his soldiers and the people of India exactly corresponded with her own. "I gained the hearts of my soldiers (who would do anything for me) not by my justice, etc., but by looking after them when sick and continually visiting the Hospitals", he wrote to her on April 22nd, 1880. He came to see her repeatedly and they discussed religious experiences. Both were aiming at the same end—a life of union with God producing practical good works. The bond became closer when in May he was appointed private secretary to Lord Ripon, an appointment greeted by universal astonishment. Before he sailed he presented Miss Nightingale with one of his religious writings which he described as "little books of comfort". On his way out he wrote to her, on May 30th: "On board this vessel nothing but discontent with their lot from Indian officers. . . . The element of all government is absent, i.e. the putting of the governors into the skin of the governed. The old Indian was obliged to do so, he was bound in some way to consider the sympathies of the native."

Gordon's understanding of Oriental races was indisputable. He had already a brilliant record of success both in India and China, but a large section of the official world detested him, and he was evidently unsuited to the post of private secretary to the Viceroy, involving official contacts and requiring the tact and social dexterity he lacked. As soon as he reached India he resigned, and after successfully executing a short mission in China he came home.

A period of vacillation followed, but his want of direction did not irritate Miss Nightingale. His difficulty was to find an employment which would satisfy his conscience. The fact that he felt he must exercise his own moral judgment, that he could not undertake to carry out any order he felt to be unethical, closed almost all avenues of official employment to him. As an additional difficulty he had no money on which to live. He spoke of going to work among the sick poor in Syria because Syria was cheap. She entreated him to go to India where there was so much to be done. But India was closed to him. " I would have gone to the Cape, I would have gone to India as you suggest," he wrote in January 1881, "but I would never do so if I had to accept the shibboleth of the Indian or Colonial middle classes. To me they are utterly wrong in the government of the subject races, they know nothing of the hearts of these people, and oil and water would as soon mix as the two races. Men may argue as they like, our tenure of India is very little greater than it was 100 years ago. The people's interests not having been involved or interested in our prosperity or disasters are equally indifferent to either, in fact they hope more from our disaster than from our prosperity." The Government would not allow him to enter India. " I consider my life's work done, that I can never aspire to, or seek employment where one's voice must be stilled to one particular note—therefore I say *it is done*. . . . I cannot visit the sick in London; it is too expensive. I can do so in Syria and where the sick are there is our Lord. My dear Miss Nightingale what am I to do? My life truly is to me a straw, but I must live. I would do anything I could for India but I am sure my advent there would not be allowed. The door is shut."

Eventually, to assist a friend, he accepted an appointment in Mauritius, and from Mauritius he was called to Basutoland to negotiate with a rebellious chief. In spite of another success the Cape Government refused to renew his appointment, and he found himself back in England in November 1882 once more unemployed. After wandering in Palestine for a year he accepted a mission to the Belgian Congo at the request of the King of the Belgians, and went to Brussels, but the Belgian Government refused to sanction his employment. While in

Brussels he received a telegram on January 15th, 1884, from the British War Office. The victories of the Mahdi in the Sudan made instant action necessary, and Gordon was asked to go out as Governor-General. On January 18th he went to the War Office and so great was the urgency that he left for Egypt the same night. He was not able to see Miss Nightingale, but he wrote to Sir Harry Verney, on January 17th, 1884, " I daily come and see you in spirit, you and Miss Nightingale ". A year later, on Monday, January 26th, 1885, Khartoum, which Gordon had defended brilliantly against overwhelming odds for 317 days, fell and he was murdered.

A tremendous outburst of indignation against the British Government followed. Miss Nightingale did not share it. Whether Gordon had succeeded in his mission or not, whether he had been betrayed by the British Government or not, was unimportant. On February 7th, in a letter to Mrs. Hawthorn, she spoke of the creed which she and Gordon shared. Suffering, disappointment, lack of success are the tribute which it is the soul's greatest privilege to present to God. In Gordon's death he had shown " the triumph of failure, the triumph of the Cross ". " With him ", she wrote, " all is well."

She took an active interest in the Gordon Home for Destitute Boys, founded in his memory. In 1887, sending the yearly report to a friend, she scribbled : " Ask them to tea. The *roughest* boys first."

Mrs. Hawthorn's allegations of abuses in military hospitals had been substantiated by independent evidence. In spite of her initial failure, Miss Nightingale persisted, and a Committee of Enquiry was set up in January 1882 under the chairmanship of her old Crimean acquaintance, Sir Evelyn Wood. The first results were disappointing, the committee merely reporting that " improvements in the system of nursing are both practical and desirable ". A member of the committee commented to Miss Nightingale : " This seems rather a mild opinion considering that all the independent evidence went to show that the orderlies were often drunk and riotous, that they ate the rations of the sick and left the nursing of the patients to the convalescents ". Before the report could be issued the Egyptian campaign of 1882 had begun under the command of Lord Wolseley, and much more serious defects became apparent. Supplies were not available to the troops in the right place; hospital equipment was totally insufficient and unsuited to the climate; medical supplies of drugs, dressings, and instruments ran out; cooking arrangements broke down. Miss Nightingale was asked for nurses, and a party of twenty-four, under the charge of a Nightingale-trained matron, went out. Reading their reports she exclaimed : " It is the Crimea over again ! " The proportion of sick was unduly high, and only the small number of troops involved and the short duration of the campaign prevented disaster. The reports of her nurses were supported by independent evidence, and in October 1882 the Committee of Enquiry was reconstituted under the chairmanship of Lord Morley with instructions to enquire into the organisation of the Army Hospital Corps and army hospital, supply, organisation and efficiency in the field generally, including nursing.

The fact was that the reorganisation ordered in Sidney Herbert's time had never been properly carried out. True, the Purveyor's Department had been reorganised, but it had not been transformed into a system designed for efficiency in time of war : the sole aim had been economy in time of peace. Indeed, as Miss Nightingale wrote to Douglas Galton in 1882, the War Office seemed to be as little concerned with war as if it had been a company concerned with coal-mining.

She played a leading part in the second Committee of Enquiry, suggested witnesses, sent briefs for their examination and outlined the facts to be elicited. Each day she was sent minutes of the evidence, and, when the time came for writing the report, she sent to Lord Morley drafts of suggested paragraphs which were submitted through a friend on the committee, Lord Wantage. " I am bound to say most of the best suggestions come from you ", wrote Lord Wantage in May 1883. In June he wrote : " If the Secretary of State carries out the Report some of the most useful improvements will have originated with you ".

As a result of this work she regained some influence at the War Office and became close friends with the Director-General of the Medical Department, Dr. Crawford. " We have not had a man of such unflagging energy since Alexander ", she wrote to Douglas Galton on November 1883. He constantly consulted her, lunched and dined frequently at her house, and became greatly attached to her. She also became intimate with Surgeon-Major Evatt, who had served with distinction in India and now held an appointment at Wool-wich. In collaboration with him she drafted a scheme for extending the recommendations of the Committee of Enquiry to cover military Hospitals in India; it was forwarded to Lord Ripon and approved by him. Meanwhile, Queen Victoria interested herself in the recommendations of the Committee. An article on the Army Medical Service, written by Miss Nightingale and signed by Douglas Galton, had appeared in the *Fortnightly Review* for October 1883, and the Queen wrote expressing herself in complete agreement with the views set forth in it. When the report of the Committee was presented to the Secretary of State for War he agreed that the recom-mendations should be carried out. A year later Miss Nightin-gale was told by Dr. Crawford that every one of the changes recommended had been made—on paper.

She was working in administration again, she had influence at the War Office again, but how strange was the road by which she had returned! Nursing had brought her back to the War Office. The sacrifice of her personal life, the long, bitter years of administrative toil, the thankless labour, the perpetual struggle with exhaustion had come to nothing. "How little is left of all the good work of 1856 and that five years until 1861 for the Army", she wrote to Sir John McNeill in February 1881. But out of the forty unsatisfactory tiresome creatures she had landed at Scutari, out of the drunkenness, the scandals, the back-biting had grown an immense work.

In 1883 Lord Wolseley, the Commander-in-Chief, told the Committee of Enquiry: "I think it would be desirable to call attention in the Queen's Regulations to the great advantage of procuring lady nurses at all stations, both in peace and war". The presence of lady nurses was the surest way to efficiency, they had been of the greatest assistance in his cam-paign in Egypt in 1882, the difference they made to the wards was almost unbelievable. "I am sure that the patients in wards where there was a lady nurse would always receive the wine, food, etc., ordered them by the doctor, and the irregu-larities of orderlies . . . could not take place."

In 1884, when the Gordon Relief Expedition was sent to Egypt, female nurses were officially requested by the Government. Miss Nightingale selected and engaged the party which was put under the superintendence of Miss Rachel Williams, the Goddess-Baby. She also sat on a committee of the National Aid Society (the British Red Cross Society) which sent out a second party at the society's expense. She had Rachel Williams's party to breakfast before they sailed, and inspected their uniforms and sent to each nurse's cabin a bouquet of flowers. Some of those who had gone out with the first Egyptian expedition of 1882 were now sent up the Nile to Wady Halfa. In 1850, during her Egyptian travels, Miss Nightingale had been at Wady Halfa, miserably unhappy. " How little could I ever have thought there would be trained nurses there now ! " she wrote to Miss Pringle, the Pearl, on October 11th, 1884. The nurses proved unquestionably successful. There were difficulties with orderlies, there was a shortage of medical supplies, there was a shortage of experienced sisters, but there was good-will on the part of the authorities. " Government are now doing all they can ", Miss Nightingale wrote to Rachel Williams in the autumn of 1884. " In my day they were hopeless." Reports on her nurses from army doctors were " extremely satisfactory ". She was annoyed to read a frivolous newspaper paragraph referring to the popularity of "afternoon tea in the nurses' tent", but the nurses proved to be not Nightingale nurses.

Her health improved. She visited Claydon, she stayed in a hotel at Seaford during the spring of 1881, she made a habit in fine weather of taking drives in the London parks with Sir Harry Verney. In 1882 she made her first personal visit to the Nightingale Training School ; in November she went with Sir Harry Verney to Victoria station to see the return of the Guards from the first Egyptian campaign ; a few days later she attended a review, sitting on the platform next Mrs. Gladstone ; and on December 4th she was present at the opening of the Law Courts, where Queen Victoria spoke to her and expressed herself pleased to note that Miss Nightingale was looking well.

But the structure of her life was still rigorously laid out for work, and she still refused to see anyone without an appointment. Clarkey came to London unexpectedly, wished to see her, and was refused. " It is now 20 years since I have been able to make an appointment for the same day—or even for the same week ", Miss Nightingale wrote on June 30th, 1880. In 1884 Mr. Gladstone called without an appointment and she would not see him. She still wrote into the small hours, still sent letters dated " Before it is light ", still attempted more than any human being could accomplish. " I am perpetually on the edge of a nervous fever ", she wrote in April 1882. She continued to speak of herself as being on the verge of the grave ; yet one by one the figures who had filled her life were steadily disappearing, and she remained, helpless, almost bedridden, but still alive.

Clarkey began to fail, and her indomitable gaiety—at the age of eighty-six she had been seen dancing to a German band—faded. Through the winter of 1882 she became feebler, and in May 1883 she died. The enormous series of letters in which Miss Nightingale had poured out her inmost thoughts and feelings for more than forty years ceased, and a curtain fell on her private life.

In 1882 her very old friend Dr. Farr, the statistician, died. In 1883 Sir John McNeill died, her constant friend and counsellor, " always so kind and fatherly ", Aunt Mai had written in 1858. In 1884 Sir Bartle Frere died, and in 1885 Richard Monckton Milnes, now Lord Houghton, the man she had once adored.

But in her old age she no longer raged, she no longer resented what had not been accomplished ; now she looked forward. On Christmas Day, 1885, when she was sixty-five, she wrote : " Today, Oh Lord, let me dedicate this crumbling old woman to Thee ". *Nihil actum si quid agendum* was no longer her motto. How much she had changed was proved when, during the next few years, the tide turned against her again.

The storm over the Ilbert Bill was solved by compromise. Lord Ripon agreed to accept certain amendments, of which the most important provided that a European tried before a native judge should have the right to demand a jury, and the Bill was passed in January 1884. Advanced liberals declared Lord Ripon had surrendered, but Miss Nightingale wished him to give way. He had achieved something and paved the way for more complete advances in the future. The situation in India gave her reasonable grounds for hope. The Land Tenure Bills seemed likely to be passed, an agricultural department had been established, and certain self-government measures and a number of educational improvements had been carried out in Bengal.

Unexpectedly Lord Ripon resigned. His term of office had not expired, but so great was the personal animosity against him that he considered his best course was to secure a suitable successor and go home. Lord Dufferin was appointed. He had been brilliantly successful as Governor-General of Canada, he was famous for his tact and personal charm, and he had recently become interested in land questions. On November 6th, at Lord Ripon's request, he called on Miss Nightingale, the fifth Viceroy of India to receive his Indian education at her hands. The interview was successful. ". . . One of the pleasantest sweets of office I have yet tasted ", Lord Dufferin wrote to her on November 13th, " has been the privilege I acquired of coming to pay you that little visit." She reported to Dr. Sutherland: ". . . About Sanitary things he says he is perfectly ignorant, especially of Indian sanitary things. But he says ' Give me your instructions and I will study them on my way out. Send me what you think. Supply the powder and I will fire the shot.' "

Through the early months of 1885 she worked her hardest to ensure that Lord Dufferin should carry on Lord Ripon's work. She wrote a detailed report to Lord Ripon explaining the particulars in which Lord Dufferin needed instruction and encouragement; and she sent Mr. Gladstone two long letters on Indian policy. In an attempt to secure publicity for Indian affairs she organised a Press campaign of welcome to Lord Ripon when he came back to England.

She failed. The Government was tottering. Khartoum had fallen, Gordon had been murdered, and in the storm of indignation which swept the country India was forgotten. A series of what she described as " political earthquakes " followed. Lord Salisbury's Government was defeated in the general election of December 1885. Mr. Gladstone came into power, only to be defeated on the Home Rule Bill. Another general election took place in 1886 and Lord Salisbury returned to power once more. In the excitements of these

561

changes it was hopeless to expect any general interest in Indian reform. She wrote that it was "excruciating" but she resigned herself.

In 1886 she was introduced by Lord Salisbury to Mr. W. H. Smith, Secretary of State for War. He wished to begin a programme of welfare work for the troops and asked for her assistance. A scheme was drawn up, and its accomplishment seemed certain when once more Fate stepped in.

Lord Randolph Churchill, who had been Chancellor of the Exchequer, unexpectedly resigned. The Government was hastily reconstructed, Cabinet offices were redistributed, Mr. W. H. Smith left the War Office and went to the Treasury, and the Army Welfare scheme was shelved. "We *are* unlucky", she wrote to Douglas Galton on December 23rd, 1886.

In 1887 Queen Victoria celebrated her Jubilee, and Miss Nightingale, too, considered 1887 her Jubilee year: her "voices" had called her first in February, 1837, and she had now completed fifty years of service. Retrospection was universal, and Miss Nightingale retraced her own long and eventful past.

On August 5th, 1887, she wrote to Aunt Mai, now completely crippled with arthritis: "Dearest Aunt Mai—Thinking of you always, grieved for your sufferings, hoping you have still to enjoy. In this month 34 years ago you lodged me in Harley Street (Aug. 12) and in this Month 31 years ago you returned me to England from Scutari (Aug. 7th). And in this month 30 years ago the first Royal Commission was finished (Aug. 7). And since then 30 years of work often cut to pieces but never destroyed, God bless you ! In this month 26 years ago Sidney Herbert died, after five years of work for us (Aug. 2). And in this month 24 years ago the work of the second Royal Commission (India) was finished. And in this month, this year, my powers seem all to have failed and old age set in."

Old age had come and she accepted it. The storms had passed and tolerance had replaced the uncompromising desire for perfection. She was entering on her last period of active work and she enjoyed an Indian summer. Her health had improved, her mind was at rest and her work in all directions bore a late harvest.

In India Lord Dufferin proved a faithful pupil, passing with some amendments Lord Ripon's Land Tenure Bills and pressing for irrigation. Lady Dufferin, who had also received an " Indian education " from Miss Nightingale, founded a " National Association for supplying Medical Aid to the Women of India ", and regularly inspected hospitals. With the co-operation of Lord Roberts she obtained official sanction for the employment of female nurses in the military hospitals of India, and the scheme Miss Nightingale had drafted for John Lawrence twenty-two years before was put into operation at the two military centres of Umballa and Rawalpindi. Lord Roberts was accomplishing what Lord Napier of Magdala had wished to see done : he established either a soldiers' club or a regimental institute in every station in India, opened coffee-rooms, and founded an Army Temperance Association.

After a crisis in which they were in grave danger of being abolished, the work of the Presidential Sanitary Commissions was extended and their authority increased. When Burma was annexed in 1887 the Government of India had to find money immediately to pay for the administration of the country, and a Finance Committee was set up to effect economies which would produce the necessary funds. The first victims proposed were the Sanitary Commissions. The funds at their disposal were so small and their authority so restricted that they had accomplished very little. Miss Nightingale, thoroughly alarmed, drew up a strong memorandum, not merely making a case for preserving the Sanitary Commissions in their present form but pressing for their further development. The memorandum was sent to Lord Dufferin, who submitted it to the Finance Committee. As a result the Sanitary Commissions were re-established, their scope and authority enlarged, and they were allocated additional funds. In 1888 the Government of India set up a Sanitary Board in every province which possessed independent and executive authority. It was partial fulfilment at last of the scheme for an independent public-health service which she had so urgently pressed on John Lawrence twenty-four years before.

In the following year another crisis was averted. For some time Dr. Sutherland had been threatening to retire. He was eighty years of age, he was able to act only in an advisory

563

capacity, his hearing was worse, and he suffered increasingly from bronchitis; nevertheless, on the Army Sanitary Committee he was of the greatest importance, for his prestige was immense and his experience unequalled, and he commanded universal deference. His retirement did not only involve the problem of finding an adequate successor : the War Office would not guarantee that any fresh appointment of a paid sanitary expert would be made at all. At the end of 1887 he told Miss Nightingale that he had made up his mind to resign in the following year. She then heard from Mr. W. H. Smith that, as a result of the representations he had made when Secretary for War, the Government intended to spend four millions on barrack improvements. But Dr. Sutherland refused to postpone his resignation, which duly occurred in 1888. For a time the committee was in grave danger. However, when Mr. W. H. Smith left the War Office he had introduced Miss Nightingale to his successor, Mr. Stanhope, who had already called on her ; now she asked him to come again, put the case for the Sanitary Committee before him and succeeded in convincing him. In June 1890 the Army Sanitary Committee was reconstructed, Douglas Galton remained ; a well-known sanitary expert, Dr. Marston, was appointed paid member in Dr. Sutherland's place; and the Indian member was Miss Nightingale's old friend, Dr. Cunningham, late sanitary adviser to the Government of India. The personnel of the committee was satisfactory. Possessing funds and the authority to use them, it carried on the work begun by Sidney Herbert on a scale and with an efficiency for which she had struggled in vain more than thirty years before.

Scheme after scheme came, if not to perfection, at least to partial fulfilment. The drainage of the great Indian cities, especially Madras on which she had been defeated in 1879, progressed at last. The drainage of Black Town, the worst quarter of Madras, was begun in 1882 and the work extended in 1887. In Calcutta she had a new ally, for a niece of Sir Harry Verney married Sir Henry Cunningham, a judge of the High Court of Calcutta and an enthusiastic sanitarian. In 1887, in collaboration with Sir Henry, she drew up a scheme for improved sanitary administration in Calcutta which was forwarded to Lord Dufferin and utilised in connection

564

with the setting up of the independent sanitary boards in 1888.

For twenty years she had been preaching the importance of the Indian village, with its traditional community life, as the unit through which any educative scheme must be developed. In 1889 her efforts were to some extent rewarded by the Bombay Village Sanitation Act. She was closely concerned with the drafting of the Bill, which aimed at educating each village as a self-contained community, the channel of communication being the head man. Lord Reay, the Governor of Bombay, came to see her in London before he sailed, asked her to write notes for him, and remained in regular correspondence with her. Through her efforts all villages in the Presidency, and not only the larger villages, were included in the Act.

In 1891 she managed to focus attention on the progress of Indian Sanitation by arranging, through Douglas Galton, that the International Congress of Hygiene and Demography, to be held in London, should include an Indian section. Indian gentlemen were sent as delegates by the National Indian Association and the Native Association of the Bombay Presidency; they read papers and were entertained at Claydon. " Sir Harry Verney renews his invitations to Claydon to the native Indian delegates ' three or four at a time ' ", she wrote to Douglas Galton on August 1st, 1891. ". . . I may hope to see them one by one if I am able to be there. . . . Do you remember it is thirty years tomorrow since Sidney Herbert died ? "

Lord Dufferin's term of office came to an end. On board ship on his way home he wrote to Miss Nightingale: " Among the first persons whose hands I hope to come and kiss will be yours ". He was succeeded by Lord Lansdowne, a close friend of Jowett. Lord Lansdowne came to see her to receive his Indian education before he sailed, and he corresponded regularly with her. " He did much for us in every way ", she wrote.

She was over seventy-one when she embarked on a complicated undertaking which proved her final crusade for the people of India. The Bombay Village Sanitation Act was not producing results—the authority to improve was provided by the

Act but the funds were not. The perennial, insoluble problem of Indian administration once more raised its head. The people were poor because they were unhealthy; while they lacked drainage and a water supply they could never be anything but unhealthy; but how could they out of their dire and crushing poverty support additional taxation to pay for the necessary works?

She came forward with a scheme to make urgent sanitation a first charge on taxation. The method of taxation was complicated. Very broadly, a certain amount of taxation was fixed while another amount, known as " cesses ", varied from time to time and was devoted to various purposes. She proposed that when a village lacked a pure water supply, lacked drainage, lacked any means of disposing of its refuse, and when it was suffering from cholera or typhoid, its cesses should be applied to remedying these conditions before being applied to any other purpose. Through the winter of 1891 and the early spring of 1892 she prepared a memorandum setting out the case in detail; it was signed by Douglas Galton and other sanitary experts and sent to the Secretary of State for India, who in April 1892 forwarded it to the Viceroy, Lord Lansdowne.

Lord Lansdowne circulated it among the local governments, inviting them to report on it. The familiar history of delay followed. There was a party which thought the cesses should first of all be applied to the making of roads : sanitary works were important, but increased means of communication were the right way to create the prosperity which would enable sanitary works to be paid for. Another party, while agreeing that a pure water supply and " simple latrine arrangements " were more than desirable, considered they should be made a charge on the revenues of the provincial government. Years passed by. Miss Nightingale argued, urged, reminded, interviewed. An enormous quantity of correspondence accumulated. Not until 1894 did she receive an official answer. The Government of India could not see its way to accept her suggestion, but would press the claim of sanitation upon local governments and administrations as opportunity offered.

It was her last campaign. She was still to do an immense amount of work for India, but in an advisory capacity; her

566

vast knowledge, her long experience and the weight of her prestige were called on again and again, but controversy was at an end.

In 1887, the year of Miss Nightingale's jubilee, the following hospitals, institutions and organisations had matrons or superintendents who had been trained at the Nightingale School: the Westminster Hospital, St. Mary's, Paddington, the Marylebone Infirmary, the Highgate Infirmary, the Metropolitan and National Nursing Association, the North London District Association, the Cumberland Infirmary, the Edinburgh Royal Infirmary, the Huntingdon County Hospital, the Leeds Infirmary, the Lincoln County Hospital, the Royal Infirmary, Liverpool, the Workhouse Infirmary, Liverpool, and the Southern Infirmary, Liverpool, the Royal Victoria Hospital at Netley, the Royal Hospital for Incurables, Putney, and the Salisbury Infirmary. Parties of nurses under a Nightingale-trained superintendent had also gone to Sydney, Montreal, India, Ceylon, Germany, Sweden and the United States of America. Training schools modelled on the Nightingale Training School and supervised and directed by Nightingale superintendents had been established at Edinburgh, at the Westminster Hospital, at the Marylebone Infirmary, at St. Mary's, Paddington. The school in connection with the Edinburgh Royal Infirmary was under the direction of Miss Pringle, and that at St. Mary's, Paddington, of Rachel Williams.

Though she had expressed regret that she could not give herself to district nursing, Miss Nightingale held the threads of the movement in her hands. William Rathbone consulted her on every point. " In any matter of nursing Miss Nightingale is my Pope and I believe in her infallibility ", he wrote. During the years following 1880 she formed the movement. Somehow, " by hook or by crook ", she managed to meet nearly all the trained nurses who took up district nursing and to keep up a correspondence with them. The function of the district nurse was established and defined by her. The district nurse must be a sanitary missionary, not an almsgiver, and to be a sanitary missionary she must be trained. There were district nurses

567

who became merely clothes-givers, soup-givers, beef-givers—
" everything ", wrote Miss Nightingale in 1888, " but teaching
cleanliness and *nursing* ".   There were nurses who set themselves up as doctors : in 1882 she discovered that the district
nurses at the Holloway, the village adjoining Lea Hurst,
instead of doing their work were taking in paying patients.
" The district nurse ", wrote Miss Nightingale in 1884, " must
be trained.   She must do the nursing work under Doctor's
orders. . . . But next to this she must ' nurse the room '—i.e.
put it into nursing order so that it shall not hinder the patient's
recovery. . . . She should be the friend not the law giver of
the family. . . . For this purpose she must never e.g. say ' I
hope when I come again all this rubbish will be cleared out
from under the bed ' (where probably there will be old boots,
dirty linen, potatoes etc.)   If she does they will wish her never
to ' come again '.   But she must just do many things herself,
such as clean a disorderly grate, dirty windows, etc., and so
show them how to do it.   She must also know—about nuisances
which she cannot remedy herself—what is in the province of
the Sanitary authorities and give notice at their office.   She
must know if meat, brandy, etc., is required, where to apply for
it (whether Poor Law or Charity) also where, in a very poor
place, for blankets."

Finance was a constant difficulty.   In 1884 Miss Nightingale wrote to Sir Harry's daughter-in-law, Margaret Verney,
that ladies were ready enough to give money to pauperise the
patients but not so ready to give money to train and pay
nurses.   The nurses were kept paupers in order that the
patients might be pauperised.   In 1887 Queen Victoria
decided to devote the major part of the money which had been
presented by the women of England as the " Women's Jubilee
Gift " to the cause of " nursing the sick poor in their own
homes by means of trained nurses ".   Sir James Paget, Miss
Nightingale's old friend, was appointed a trustee.   Consultations took place during which Miss Nightingale convinced him
of the pre-eminent importance of training nurses specially
for district work, and the Jubilee Institute for Nurses was
founded.

Results were beginning to exceed her highest hopes.   In
private notes during 1887 and 1888 she recalled the first

568

beginnings of the work, her attempt in 1845 to train at Salisbury when her parents behaved as if she had wished to be a kitchenmaid, the difficulty of finding nurses to go to the Crimea, and Agnes Jones's experiences in the old infirmaries, when the police were regularly called in to establish order in the wards.

The work had reached a point when nothing could stop its progress; no human failure, no temporary set-back could arrest its irresistible advance. Nevertheless, disappointments still occurred, and in 1887, in the midst of the fulfilment and tranquillity of her Jubilee year, she sustained a serious disappointment: Mrs. Wardroper retired from the matronship of St. Thomas's Hospital. Miss Nightingale felt her loss deeply—Jowett told her she felt it unreasonably. The blow was softened when, in place of Mrs. Wardroper, the Pearl, Miss Pringle, was appointed. Miss Nightingale rejoiced. Her influence at St. Thomas's and her control of the Nightingale School turned on her relationship with the matron; and Miss Pringle was a favourite pupil, an intimate friend, almost a second self. But in 1888 Miss Pringle became converted to the Roman Catholic Church and felt that she could not continue in her post. Miss Nightingale poured out immense letters remonstrating with her in vain; she wrote page upon page of rough notes, drafts of emotional appeals, theological arguments; she jotted down almost indecipherable scribbles— "Put her on her honour", "Doctors' orders", "Is she clinging to be commanded", "Ask Henry B. C. and the Treasurer if they would decline to receive any communication from her for a year", "Get Jowett", "I feel as if I were in a dream. Would to God we could both wake. I who was called at sixteen, I am now a whited sepulchre full of dead men's bones." Miss Pringle had been ill—she had always, in spite of her efficiency, been over-conscientious, fanciful. "Are you really going to find light in a pilgrimage to your grandmother's village?" Miss Nightingale wrote. "A grandmother whom, I understand from you, you have never seen?"

Sir Harry Verney suggested that Canon Scott Holland should be "introduced unexpectedly" to Miss Pringle to confound her with theological arguments, but Miss Nightingale would not consent. "I will not either have the Canon sprung on her, or ask her to see him ", she wrote in June 1889. " I have no faith in the C. of E. *versus* the Church of Rome."

The loss of Miss Pringle, she wrote, was " one of the deep griefs of my life " ; in due course the resignation took effect, and Miss Pringle was received into the Church of Rome. Her place at St. Thomas's was taken by an old Nightingale pupil, Miss Gordon, who in fact worked in close touch with Miss Nightingale and was one of the most outstanding of the remarkable women who have been matrons of St. Thomas's. Miss Nightingale cherished no resentment against Miss Pringle and their friendship continued.

Though Miss Nightingale's influence in nursing was dominant there was opposition to her. It was never contested that her results were not superior, but it was held that the form of training she demanded, the close supervision and the exactions of her school, could not produce nurses in the numbers which were now necessary.

In 1886 a proposal was made which aimed at giving the trained nurse official recognition and at placing her qualifications on a standard basis. A committee of the Hospitals' Association proposed that an independent body of examiners, not connected with the training schools, should be created. This body would set an examination, and when a nurse had passed it she would be entitled to have her name placed on a register of nurses. Thus a standard of technical excellence in nursing would be established and the public would be protected against employing nurses who were incompetent or disreputable.

It was the beginning of a battle which split the nursing world in two. Miss Nightingale opposed the proposal for two reasons. First, she did not think the time was ripe for the step. In forty years' time, she wrote, the nursing profession might be ready, but at the moment nursing was still too young, still too unorganised, and contained divergences too great for a single standard to be applied. This was, in fact, the view which the Hospitals' Association committee had taken. A curious situation had arisen : the committee had violently disagreed—so violently that it broke up ; the majority resigned, and it was a minority who recommended that a register should be established and finally founded the British Nurses' Association, whose object was to press for the register.

The second ground on which Miss Nightingale opposed the scheme was of greater importance. The scheme as put forward was a contradiction of what she believed the training of a nurse should be. She was not necessarily against registration, but she was passionately opposed to the kind of registration proposed. The qualifying of a nurse by examination only took no account of the character training which she held to be as important as the acquisition of technical skill. A nurse, she said repeatedly, could not be tested by public examination as if she were an engineer. Nursing was a vocation as well as a profession, and the two must be united. When a nurse received a certificate from her training school the matron was able to guarantee by personal knowledge that her pupil possessed the qualities of character as well as the degree of technical skill which were essential to the calling of a nurse. In an outside examination conducted by strangers those who came off best would probably be glib and forward girls, not those who would ultimately make the best nurses. Devotion, gentleness, sympathy, qualities of overwhelming importance in a nurse, could never be ascertained by public examination. " Nursing has to nurse living bodies and spirits. It cannot be tested by public examination, though it may be tested by current supervision ", she wrote.

In thirty years she had, she said, " raised nursing from the sink " by training character. She had caused training schools for nurses to be called " Homes " to emphasise the fact that they were places in which character was to be developed, general culture acquired and a moral standard learnt. Now the object of the training school was to be made not the training of character but the granting of a certificate. " You cannot select the good from the inferior by any test or system of examination ", she wrote in 1890. ". . . Most of all and first of all must the moral qualifications be made to stand pre-eminent in estimation."

The British Nurses' Association continued to agitate, and in 1888 a new committee was set up to conduct an enquiry among the training schools and the medical profession on their opinion of a nurses' register. It at once became apparent that opinion was divided and that feeling was running high. Miss Nightingale feared disaster. The nursing world would be divided into two camps. Political differences would become all-important and the work would take second place. She recalled the division of opinion over the Reform Bill when she was a child : those who were for the Bill would refuse to sit at dinner with those who were against it. At that moment in Ireland a doctor applying for a medical appointment was asked whether he was a Unionist or a Home Ruler before he was asked for his medical qualifications.

In 1889 the situation crystallised. The British Nurses' Association published their policy. Their main object was to provide for the registration of qualified British nurses, and to accomplish this they intended to apply for a Royal Charter incorporating the Association and authorising the formation of a register. Nurses were to be deemed to be qualified who were certified by an outside Board as having attained a certain standard of proficiency, and it was suggested that a preliminary qualification should be three years' training in a hospital. The manifesto made a considerable impression, and Princess Christian, Queen Victoria's daughter, accepted the Presidency of the Association.

Miss Nightingale had received a set-back. When the time came to petition for the Royal Charter, Princess Christian would approach Queen Victoria. Moreover, Princess Christian had great influence and was much beloved for philanthropic work. " This makes things awkward for us ", wrote William Rathbone.

Through Sir Harry Verney, Miss Nightingale made overtures to Princess Christian. It was not possible, she found, to compromise, because Princess Christian felt that she was in honour bound to support the policy of the Association of which she was President, and Miss Nightingale settled down to fight.

For the next four years the battle absorbed her. She was seventy and the work was exhausting. Her friends regretted her absorption, for the point at issue seemed unimportant. " It is a comparative trifle ", wrote Jowett in May 1892, " among all the work you have done."

Miss Nightingale, however, was convinced she faced a major crisis : the principle which had governed her work for nursing was at stake. Nor in her opinion would the register as proposed protect the public. The fact that a nurse's name was on it would only mean that at a certain date she had satisfied the examiners in certain tests; it would tell nothing of her subsequent record. If a register were to be useful it should be kept up to date, and include a description of each nurse's character and a recent recommendation from a surgeon or physician.

In 1889 the British Nurses' Association announced that they were applying for a Charter. Miss Nightingale, supported by the matron of the London Hospital and the matron of St. Thomas's and most of the training schools, declared her intention of opposing the application. Two years of controversy followed, and a large number of pamphlets were issued on both sides. Then in 1891 the British Nurses' Association applied to the Board of Trade to be registered as a public company without the addition of the word "Limited", the object of the company being to form a register of nurses and to lay down what should be the qualifications necessary for registration. Miss Nightingale presented to the President of the Board of Trade a case opposing the application, and registration was refused. In the same year a committee of the House of Lords reported on the condition and organisation of London hospitals. William Rathbone was called to give evidence as to the desirability of the proposed register of nurses; he gave evidence against the proposal, and the committee in their report did not recommend the formation of a register of nurses.

But the British Nurses' Association was not yet defeated. Later in the year they obtained permission from the Queen, through Princess Christian, to use the title "Royal", and they then petitioned the Queen herself for a Royal Charter. The petition, in accordance with precedent, was referred to a special committee of the Privy Council and was heard in November 1892.

On both sides this was felt to be the decisive moment, and Miss Nightingale rallied all her forces. A campaign fund was raised and two counter-petitions opposing the grant of a Royal Charter presented, one being signed by the Council of the Nightingale Fund, admittedly the pioneers of the training of nurses, and the other by many thousands of matrons, lady superintendents and principal assistants, doctors and nursing sisters, as well as by superintendents and principals of training schools. The list was headed by the signature of Miss Nightingale. In addition, a letter from her was read to the Committee of the Privy Council by William Rathbone. Eminent barristers appeared on both sides, and two Law Lords sat on the committee. The trial, she wrote, cost £700 at least.

The hearing took a week and was completed by the end of November, the decision was not announced until six months later—in May 1893. The result was victory for no one. True, the Royal British Nurses' Association was granted a Royal Charter, but not in the terms they had sought. The word " register " was removed and the Charter conferred only the right to the " maintenance of a list of persons who may have applied to have their names entered thereon as nurses ".

The battle was over and Miss Nightingale put it behind her. In 1894 she talked and corresponded with Princess Christian regarding a scheme for the formation of a war reserve of nurses by the Royal British Nurses' Association. "We should, I think ", she wrote, " be earnestly anxious to do what we can for Princess Christian as she holds out the flag of truce, in order to put an end, as far as we can, to all this bickering which does such harm to the cause." In 1893 she dedicated a lecture on Sick Nursing and Health Nursing, which was read at the Chicago Exhibition of Women's Work, to Princess Christian.

It was a tranquil end to her last great battle. She was an old lady now, and though her mind was still keen and her energy still remarkable, another change was taking place. Her horizons were narrowing, the world was receding ; for the first time personal relationships were becoming of paramount importance in her life.

XXIV IF LIFE HAD USED HER HARDLY she was compensated now. Few human beings have enjoyed a fuller, happier old age. She was treated with an almost religious deference—ministers, kings, princesses, statesmen waited at her door, and her utterances were paid the respect due to an oracle. To millions of women all over the world she was the symbol of a new hope, the sign of a new age. Nor was she separated from the common joys of life. Though she had never married, she enjoyed the pleasures of matriarchy. In the lives of a large circle of young people, Shore's two daughters and his sons, Clough's son and daughters and Parthe's stepchildren, she held the place of a powerful, generous and respected grandmother.

In old age an extraordinary atmosphere of peace flowed from her. She was formidable still, she preserved her rule of seeing only one person at a time and bent her whole attention on her visitor, making you feel, it was said, like a sucked orange, but she was animated now by the purest benevolence. To confide in her was irresistible. She delighted to concern herself with the small crises of daily life. Clough's son brought her his love affairs, Shore's daughters their examination papers. No detail was too small to command her interest—the character of a servant, the quality of a joint of meat, the treatment of a cold. She delighted to write birthday letters, to send gifts of jellies, fruit, creams, special soups to invalids, to make presents. Sir Harry Verney, suffering from eye trouble, was sent a special lamp-shade, a girl cousin working too hard received concert tickets, Margaret Verney, going on a night journey by train, was sent sandwiches, coffee and a special cushion for her head.

Her sympathy extended itself beyond her family. Her butcher, the policemen on duty at the Park gates near her house, everyone who served her, came within the circle of her benevolence. Their family affairs received her earnest consideration, their health was the object of her solicitude.

To enter her house was to receive an instant impression of whiteness, order and light. "You have such a beautifully tidy house", wrote a schoolgirl cousin. Her bedroom at the back of the house had French windows opening on to a balcony; there were no curtains only blinds, the walls were painted white, and the room was bathed in light.

A stand of flowering plants stood in the window, kept filled throughout the year by William Rathbone, and more flower-boxes stood on the balcony. The house backed on to the gardens of Dorchester House, and outside the windows were trees, flowers and lawns. Birds twittered, and in summer the sunlight filtered through green leaves. Miss Nightingale's bed stood with the windows on her right; behind it was a shelf of books. She had a table beside her bed on which stood a reading-lamp with a green silk shade and a vase of fresh flowers—a large box of cut flowers was sent weekly by Lady Ashburton from Melchett Court. The furniture was unpretentious. There were an armchair, a bureau, a bookcase, another larger table. On the walls were a photograph of John Lawrence's portrait, a lithograph of the ground about Sebastopol, and a few water-colours. The room conveyed an exquisite and fastidious freshness. Flowers were never faded, vases sparkled like crystal, the pillows and sheets of Miss Nightingale's bed were spotless and without a crease.

On her good days she got up after luncheon and received visitors in the drawing-room below, lying on a couch wearing a black silk dress with a shawl over her feet, and a scarf either of delicate white net or fine quality lace round her head. " No gentlewoman ever wears anything but real lace ", she told one of Shore's daughters; she was fond of the Buckinghamshire lace which Sir Harry Verney had made for her. The decoration of the drawing-room was severe, relieved by a profusion of flowers. The windows were curtained in plain blue serge, the walls were white. Round the room were hung the engravings of Michelangelo's ceiling in the Sistine chapel which she had bought in Rome, and there were several bookcases full of books. When young relatives waited in the drawing-room before going up to see Aunt Florence they found the books consisted solely of Blue Books, with one exception, a copy of *The Ring and the Book*.

Visitors, even when staying in the house, never saw Miss Nightingale except by appointment. She never took a meal with anyone, but she did her own housekeeping and took immense pains over her household. " Florence's maids and little dinners perfect ", W. E. N. had written in 1867. Her staff consisted of five maids, her own personal maid, and a man known as " Miss Nightingale's messenger ", who was an old soldier and a member of the Corps of Commissionaires.

The household was highly organised. The proper duties to be performed in the house and in the kitchen at every hour through the day were marked on a chart. The food was ordered by Miss Nightingale and she was particular as to quality. In March 1889 she wrote to a new butcher for " a fore quarter of your best small mutton. I prefer four year old mutton." The following week she wrote, " the neck ' ate ' better than the shoulder tho' off the same piece ", and ordered " a neck of mutton well hung and a leg well hung. Please tell your man to wait, as I always pay weekly." The neck proved " very good but the leg not so good ", and she ordered " 13 to 14 pounds of good sirloin of beef to try ". Meanwhile the butcher's wife had fallen ill. Miss Nightingale was all sympathy, gave advice, sent lemon jelly and when, unhappily, the woman died, wrote : " God be with you and with your children is the earnest prayer of Florence Nightingale ". In March 1892 she telegraphed : " Your neck of mutton tender and excellent please let us have leg mutton as good for tomorrow Wednesday, Nightingale ".

Her taste in food was fastidious. Each day's menu was submitted to her and she made suggestions and criticised the previous day's dishes. " Remember I am a small but *delicate* eater ", she wrote. A couple of oyster patties, or a little broth, and a fried sole was a favourite order. " Why was the glue pot used ? " she wrote against " stewed cutlets ", and against minced veal, " the meat hard and remember mincing only makes hard meat harder ". " Minced beef for my dinner " was the heading of another note. " The beef must be from the under-cut of the sirloin ; mince the beef over a plate which must catch the juices which fall. The meat must be uncooked." " Sauces and gravies are not to be thickened with flour. The bones of the meat are simmered down with vegetables to make the stock, which is then reduced to make the sauces. Use plenty of herbs for flavouring." " Minced veal must be dished up with potato or rice ", but " the potato or rice must not come higher than the veal; there must not be a hole with the veal in it. It must be garnished with small thin pieces of fried rolled bacon round. The little bits of veal are not *mashed* but separate tender bits with sauce poured over—really a very delicate dish." Turnips were to be served by "squeezing out all water, putting through a hair sieve and adding a gill of cream ". " Brisket of beef must be cooked with herbs, onions, carrots, celery in a light broth on the hot plates from 10 A.M. to 9 P.M. *Never* too fast." " Roast pheasant must be hung not too near a good fire and basted every minute or two with good butter for an hour. Roast chicken must be larded *all over*. Roast neck of mutton must be very small, never above 6½ lbs.—not too thin. Streaky fat in the lean makes good mutton. Half the battle is in trimming the fat. The fat *near the bone* should be left to soak down into the meat. A nice brisk fire and 1½ hrs doing. Not too near at first. Keep on basting *every minute or two* in the tasty way, a little salt, flour, butter."

Occasionally she descended into the kitchen herself. On the 23rd of September 1887 she wrote to Margaret Verney: " I found Nelly (the kitchen maid) on a cool day popping everything into the refrigerator as if it were a larder ". She frequently criticised her cook, Mrs. Nield. She was not careful, she was unpunctual, she could not control the younger servants, she muddled her accounts. In October 1889 Miss Nightingale wrote her a note : " Instead of having spent £12. 11. 10½ you have spent £27. 1. 10. And there is due to you £7. 14. 10. instead of your being in hand £6. 15. 1½." Then she reproached herself for her impatience. " Let me remember that as Mrs. Nield to me, so I to God ", she wrote in a private note. Exacting though she was, Miss Nightingale was a good mistress, and Mrs. Nield stayed with her for many years and produced excellent food. " Tell Miss Nightingale the luncheon was a work of art ", said the Crown Princess of Prussia. When, in 1890, Mrs. Nield retired, the household, wrote Miss Nightingale, consisted of " 4 nice girls (besides the cook) 2 of whom, though they look so young, have been with me for 6 years. The Commissionaire for 11 years." Mrs. Nield was succeeded by a cook whom Sir Harry Verney arranged to have sent into the kitchen of the Travellers' Club for training under the chef.

Miss Nightingale's account of an interview in 1886 demonstrates how little she now inspired awe, how readily she felt sympathy. The interview was with a girl who wished to be a nurse. "She showed", wrote Miss Nightingale, "a natural, unconscious, unrestrained interest in interesting things" which "I liked very much." Three remarks struck her favourably. "Oh I do so want to go inside the House of Commons some day just to hear Mr. Gladstone speak once. I know it is difficult and I know the House of Commons is not sitting *now*." "May I just look round the books to see if there is a Tennyson?" "Oh, I'm not a bit tired now."

It was even possible to disagree with her without disturbing her good humour. In 1895 she received a letter upbraiding her for opposing the registration of nurses. She scribbled a note on the margin for Henry Bonham Carter: "Shall I royally disregard it—or shall I give them a BUSTER".

As her character blossomed into benevolence, her physical appearance changed. The slight, tall, willowy girl whose elegance had struck everyone who saw her, whose small head had been set on her neck with the grace of a stag, who had loved to dance and been light as thistledown on her feet, the thin, emaciated, mature woman with lines of suffering deeply engraved on her face, underwent a surprising metamorphosis. She became a dignified stout old lady with rather a large good-humoured face. The shape of her head seemed to change; the face became wider, the neck shorter, the brow much more prominent. Surgeon-Major Evatt, who knew her in her old age, said she resembled Mr. Gladstone, and a relative, introduced to her as a boy, retained as his recollection that she looked "so jolly".

Much of her life centred upon Shore and his wife and daughters and the children of Blanche and Clough; she followed them through their various stages of development, sent eggs and Egyptian lentils when one became a vegetarian, read pamphlets when another became an ardent advocate of co-operation, helped on several occasions with cheques for foreign tours. But her closest association was with the Verney family—to the Verneys she was indispensable.

Each year Parthe became more crippled with arthritis, and in 1883 she had a serious illness. She suffered a great deal and no nurse could control her. Her household fell into confusion, and Sir Harry, now eighty-two, was distracted; so Miss Nightingale went down to Claydon and took command.

To deal with Parthe required endless patience. She was witty and gay, she could write with charm, she was responsible for rescuing and editing the famous Verney Papers which for centuries had been lying neglected in the attics at Claydon, but her good qualities became obscured by her physical condition. She created difficulties about money, she became jealous of her eldest stepson, Sir Harry's heir. She made undesirable favourites among the servants, she wrote painful letters. No one but Florence could soothe her. After 1883 she was completely crippled, and Miss Nightingale became an essential part of the Verney's family life. In addition to her old and deep affection for Sir Harry she was greatly attached to Sir Harry's son, Frederick Verney, who had been ordained a deacon and did social work in London. She corresponded with him and on several occasions he read her papers to scientific and political meetings.

She also became intimate with the wife of Sir Harry Verney's eldest son—Margaret Verney. In 1869, after their first meeting, Miss Nightingale described her as " a sort of heavenly young woman. She is really delicate . . . but looks as if *mentally* she had not turned a hair. As people say of high couraged coursers—a racer. . . . I do not know that I ever saw anyone exactly like her. Only that she is witty and makes jokes she would be exactly like the Virgins and Saints of Fra Angelico. As they might be if they went through contested elections—and attended amputations." Margaret Verney— Miss Nightingale's name for her was " Blessed Margaret "—in addition to saintliness and beauty had capability. She had, wrote Miss Nightingale to Frederick Verney in 1896, " administrative power, that power of detail which makes works succeed and is called capacity for business". She also had a talent for writing, was well read, and in later years edited a second and superior edition of the Verney Papers.

The burden of Parthe's illness had fallen on Margaret Verney, and Miss Nightingale alone could help her. When Parthe wrote Margaret a letter " so outrageously discourteous " that she " destroyed it as if it were a viper . . . I have no wish in the world but to be a daughter but there are some things Mama *must* not say to me ", Miss Nightingale persuaded Parthe to apologise; when she had been at Claydon Parthe was much easier to manage. " I write with a very thankful heart to-night for Mama has been so kind and gentle," wrote Margaret on September 8th, 1887, " and I feel as if the echoes of your loving words and thoughts and prayers still linger here and have an influence for peace . . . the blue room looks to me so chaotic. I wish I could have been here to hang up pictures (they all loll about on chairs at Claydon) and to put a little order into things before you had the room."

The intimacy grew swiftly. " Dearest Miss Nightingale " became " Dearest Aunt Florence " and innumerable letters passed between them breathing affection and solicitude. " We owe you so much ", Margaret Verney wrote. " It must be such a comfort to Papa to have you to refer to in his difficulties." In 1888 she called Miss Nightingale, " the presence which to all of us brings such balm of sympathy and peace ". In 1889 she wrote, " I long so much to see you. Thank you so much for all you have been to us." A month later she wrote, " to see you would be a feast." In 1894 : " Have you been able to sleep ? You cannot think how I *long* to be able to do something for you. . . . If you could invent some wood to hew or water to carry, you would make me so very happy." She signed her letters, " your loving and grateful Margaret ", " your very loving and very grateful Margaret ". In 1892, when Miss Nightingale wrote to ask if a certain date would be convenient for her to come to Claydon, Margaret replied " there never could be found in any almanac any day when it was not convenient and delightful that you should come here ".

In May 1890 Parthe died. It had become her custom to spend Sunday at 10 South Street when she was in London. On Sunday, May 4th, she was carried into the drawing-room, evidently very ill ; she spent that day with her sister, and the next day went down to Claydon. A week later, on May 12th, she died. Their reconciliation had been complete. For seven years Parthe had been a difficult invalid, but Miss Nightingale's patience had never failed and she had never written a word of reproach. " You contributed more than anyone to what enjoyment of life was hers ", wrote Sir Harry on May 15th, 1890. ". . . You and I were the objects of her tender love and her love for you was intense. It was delightful to me to hear her speak of you and to see her face, perhaps distorted with pain, look happy when she thought of you."

Parthe's death brought Miss Nightingale even closer to the Verney family. She went down to Claydon at once and stayed with Sir Harry until the autumn. She devoted herself to him. He became the principal object of her life. He visited her every day, and if she went to London she wrote to him daily; when they were both in London he called on her every morning. He was now nearly ninety, still mentally alert and still magnificently handsome, and she was seventy. One of the few photographs she ever allowed to be taken shows them sitting together on a garden seat at Claydon, smiling at each other. Her health had so far improved that occasionally she was able to take a short stroll leaning on his arm. Claydon was her second home. She invited whom she liked, parties of her nurses were entertained, Indian gentlemen came to lunch, Jowett was a frequent visitor.

It was inevitable that she should interest herself in the management of the estate and inevitable that, having investigated accounts, condition of cottages, health of neighbouring villages, water supply and sanitation, she should find much that needed improvement. It was uphill work. Sir Harry was old, Parthe had been extravagant and careless. Even the treasures in the house itself had been neglected—Margaret found one of the historic family portraits used as a partition to separate stored apples. An immense amount of work was done by Miss Nightingale and Margaret to straighten out the confusion. In the house a degree of order was established, and the drains attended to. " You know ", wrote Margaret in January 1892, " how one goes through phases of discouragement at Claydon. You have established two definite steps forward which we never could have done without you."

In the villages Miss Nightingale embarked on a new scheme. She wished to support the work of the District Nurse with Lady Health Missioners, women who were to be trained to teach village mothers the elementary principles of health in the home. County Councils, which had been established in 1888, had power to spend a certain amount of money on " technical education ". Frederick Verney was chairman of the Technical Education Committee for North Bucks, and through his influence the training of Lady Health Missioners was classed as technical education and a sum of money devoted to establishing a course. The Medical Officer of Health gave a series of lectures, after which the students worked under his direction in villages. The next step was an examination, and those who passed, after a further period of practical work, were engaged as Health Missioners by the Technical Education Committee. Miss Nightingale was convinced that the best way to develop sanitary education, in England as in India, was to use the village as a unit. And, she insisted, " the work *must* be personal "; the Health Missioners were "not to lecture the village women but to work *with* them ".

The scheme was begun in 1892, and though she had Margaret's help she found herself involved in a great deal of work. " Lady *Lecturers* on health are more rife than influenza," she wrote to Margaret in December 1892. " It is a perfect pest. They send their programmes to me ! at Claydon ! ! which is adding insult to injury as the parrot said when they brought him from his native shores to the British Isles and then made him learn English. The Lady *Lecturers* pursue me as fleas do in Italy. . . . I have carefully read with mingled fury and pleasure your excellent summary."

It was a curious reproduction of the work she had done in her best days in India, a reproduction in miniature with Buckinghamshire in place of India, the Aylesbury district in place of Bengal. Even the conclusion repeated itself. Progress was impossible without water. Village sanitation in England, as in India, turned on water supply. " Prizes to cottagers for cleanliness are not desirable ", she wrote to the Medical Officer of Health in November 1891. " The prizes ought to be for handy water supply—to the authorities. . . . It is very pretty in a picture the group at the well of mother and children. It is not pretty in practice. The first possibility of rural cleanliness lies in *water supply*."

Year succeeded year and it seemed that Time had decided to pass Miss Nightingale by, that her Indian summer would last for ever while round her familiar faces were disappearing.

In 1889 Aunt Mai died at the age of ninety-one. In December of the same year Colonel Yule, Sir Bartle Frere's successor at the India Office, died. " I praise God for the privilege of having known you ", he wrote to Miss Nightingale a few days before his death. In July 1891 Dr. Sutherland died. His last articulate words were for her—" give her my love and blessing ", he told his wife.

In 1893 a great grief awaited her : she lost Jowett. During the past few years they had drawn even closer. " The truer, the safer, the better years of life are the later ones ", he had written to her in 1887. " We must find new ways of using them, doing not so much but in a better way." They discussed at length the possibility of founding a professorship or lecture-ship in applied statistics at Oxford. " What we want ", she wrote in 1891, ". . . is to teach the men who are to govern the country the use of statistical facts. . . . What, for instance, is the result of twenty years of compulsory education ? What proportion of children forget all they learn at school ? What is the effect of life in towns on number of children in family and their health ? What do the several classes (in social position and residence) contribute in numbers to the popula-tion ? " The scheme did not materialise ; there was difficulty in establishing a professorship not attached to an examination school, and Miss Nightingale's Trustees were unwilling to allow her to raise her share of the money. But there were long sympathetic discussions of the kind she most enjoyed at South Street and Claydon. In October 1890 Jowett had a heart attack and was expected to die. " I am always thankful for having known you ", he wrote in a farewell letter on October 16th. He recovered, and in November 1890 she went over to Balliol from Claydon to see him, and stayed the night. In May 1892 he had another attack which greatly weakened him, but he still managed to visit her. " I want to hold fast to you dear friend as I go down the hill ", he wrote. In August 1893 he was seen to be sinking—he became too weak to hold a pen ; and on September 18th he dictated his last letter to her : " Fare you well . . . How large a part has your life been of my life. There is only time I think for a few words." On October 1st he died.

Four months later she had to bear another great grief : in

February 1894 Sir Harry Verney died at the age of ninety-three. Six months later, in August 1894, Mr. Shore Nightingale, " My boy Shore ", died, whose kindness, she was never tired of saying, had been one of the great recompenses of her life. " I have lost the three nearest to me in twelve months ", she wrote. But there was no bitterness, none of the resentful anguish which had torn her apart thirty years ago. She was seventy-four, and as she drew nearer to the dividing line between life and death the bodily veil grew thin. It was not loss she faced now, but a temporary separation. And as she looked back over the long years she felt, as she had never felt in the days of her youth, that the sum total of life was good. " There is so much to live for ", she wrote on May 12th, 1895. " I have lost much in failures and disappointments, as well as in grief but, do you know, life is more precious to me now in my old age."

Claydon continued to be her second home, but after Sir Harry's death her visits became less frequent. The affection, the welcome was there. " We already say ' We shall do so and so when Aunt Florence comes'. We long to have you ", wrote Ellin Verney, Margaret Verney's daughter, in September 1895. " We are crazy with joy that you give us so blessed a hope of seeing you in November ", wrote Margaret Verney in October. But the renewal of physical vigour which had been so extraordinary a part of her Indian summer was beginning to fail. The drives were given up, visitors were no longer received in the drawing-room, the journey to Claydon was felt to be too tiring. After 1895 she did not go to Claydon. She never went back to Lea Hurst after Fanny's death, though she maintained a considerable correspondence relating to the property and the tenants. In 1896 Embley was sold, and she said she was sad to have been turned out of Hampshire. Gradually her life closed in; after 1896 she never left South Street, and she spent thereafter the whole of her life in her bedroom.

But it was only her body which had failed, for her mind and spirit remained as vigorous as ever. Indeed, she seemed to gain, as if in compensation, added confidence and hope. " Yes, one does feel the passing away of so many who seemed essential to the world. I have no one now to whom I could speak of those who are gone. But all the more I am eager to

585

see successors ", she wrote in a private note dated " All Saints. All Souls. November 2nd, 1896." She was still actively occupied. " I am *soaked* in work ", she wrote to Douglas Galton in January 1897. The War Office consulted her and she had influence there. Lord Lansdowne, her friend and Jowett's, was Secretary of State for War. During 1896 she was consulted with regard to rations, equipments and medical stores for troops going to Africa, with regard to the condition of barracks at Aldershot and Newcastle-on-Tyne, and even with regard to schemes of internal War Office reorganisation contemplated by Lord Lansdowne. " Not that I am in that line of business now ", she wrote. In 1896 she intervened successfully on behalf of troops in Hong Kong. The garrison had just experienced an outbreak of bubonic plague and the regimental doctor appealed to her. The outbreak was due to the insanitary condition of the barracks—could she help? She prepared a report which was forwarded through Douglas Galton to the Colonial Secretary, and the troops were moved and new barracks built.

In 1897 a Departmental Committee of the War Office was set up to report on the effect of the Contagious Diseases Act of 1864. She had bitterly opposed regulation of prostitution and the registration and medical inspection of prostitutes, but now she changed her mind. The Report disclosed an alarming increase in venereal disease, especially in India, and, though she still held that the only real solution was to improve the living conditions of the troops and provide facilities for education, she was converted to the necessity of taking immediate action to check the disease. She signed a memorial promoted by Princess Christian urging that stringent precautionary measures should be taken at once. To many social reformers her action was tantamount to an apostasy, and she was reproached. At seventy-seven she had lost none of her incisiveness—" she doesn't want to hear facts she wants to be enthusiastic ", she commented after reading a reproachful letter.

She maintained connections with India, corresponding with the Viceroy, Lord Elgin, continuing to receive from the India Office all papers on Indian sanitary matters, and entertaining a large number of Indian gentlemen, educationalists, doctors and administrators. In 1898 she received the Aga Khan.

" He was ", she wrote in a private note, " a most interesting man, but you could never teach him sanitation. . . . I told him as well as I could all the differences, both in town and country, during my life. ' Do you think you are improving ? ' he asked. By improving he meant believing more in God."

In a private note, written when she was seventy-seven, she said : " I thank God for having given me work, constant work. Work with Sidney Herbert, work with Lord Lawrence and never out of work still."

Year by year her legend steadily grew. The world had taken her figure to its heart, but in an extraordinary, an unprecedented, way. No crowd of admirers waited outside her house in South Street ; indeed, the greater part of the world supposed she was dead, had supposed she was dead for the past forty years. Even the survivors of the men she had nursed did not know what had become of her. " I should have communicated with you sooner ", wrote the organiser of an annual banquet of Inkerman survivors in 1895, " but I did not know your address." But whether she was dead or alive was unimportant : the image of her lived with vivid life. Not only in England but in Turkey, Japan, in the United States of America, in Brazil, her name had a magic possessed by no other.

She herself regarded her own legend with impatience. She despised the judgment of the crowd ; she disapproved on moral grounds of personal influence. Shortly before his death Sir Harry Verney succeeded in persuading her to be photographed ; he introduced the photographer unexpectedly during his morning visit to her room at Claydon and she gave way. On July 27th, 1895, she wrote to Margaret Verney : " Mr. Payne —is that the name ?—of Aylesbury, who did the photograph of me for Sir Harry, has written to ask me to give my consent to his publishing and selling my photograph. . . . *I really cannot* ; there is a perfect fury this year of writing to me for my photograph, autograph and a ' few lines '. And a very large number of these are from America—as many as 17 by one mail. The greatest number I throw away hardly reading and never answering. But if I have someone I *must* answer I can only say I have *no* photograph of myself and I don't know where to buy one."

The year of Queen Victoria's Diamond Jubilee, 1897, added

enormously to the Florence Nightingale legend. The Victorian Era Exhibition included a section representing the progress of trained nursing, and it was planned round Miss Nightingale; she was asked for Crimean relics, for pictures of Scutari, for her portrait, for the loan of her bust by Steell. She refused. "Oh the absurdity of people and their vulgarity!" she wrote. "The relics, the representations of the Crimean War! What are they? They are first the tremendous lessons we have had to learn from its tremendous blunders and ignorances. And next they are Trained Nurses and the progress of Hygiene. These are the 'representations' of the Crimean War. And I will not give my foolish portrait (which I have not got) or anything else as 'relics' of the Crimea. It is too ridiculous. . . ."

However, one of the organisers of the exhibition was Lady Wantage, wife of Lord Wantage, who had worked with Miss Nightingale in 1883, and Lady Wantage was exceptionally pretty and charming. She called, and Miss Nightingale, always susceptible to charm, gave way. She wished to substitute a few hard facts about the work of the Royal Sanitary Commissions for Crimean relics, but Lady Wantage, wrote Miss Nightingale, "would not take [them] . . . she stuck to her point and she is *so* charming". Miss Nightingale lent the bust by Steell and tracked down her Crimean carriage. "O my dear Harry," she wrote to Henry Bonham Carter in March 1897, "that wretched Russian car with wretched but active boy and pony, all dismantled, *hangs* round my *neck*. . . . It was discovered all to pieces in an Embley farmhouse when Embley was sold. I never cared *what* became of it."

The exhibition was the scene of extraordinary demonstrations. Her relics were treated by the crowds as holy. Flowers were laid daily before the bust by an unknown hand, old soldiers, it was said, had been seen to come forward and kiss the carriage. It was canonisation, but of an unwilling saint. She was disgusted. In October 1897, when the exhibition was closing, she wrote to Louis Shore Nightingale, Shore's son : "Now I must ask you about my bust. (Here I stop to utter a great many bad words not fit to put on paper. I also utter a pious wish that the bust may be smashed.) I should not have remembered it but that I am told somebody came every day to bedeck it with fresh flowers. I utter a pious wish that that person may be—saved. . . . What *is* to be done about the bust ? "

Her life had turned to a golden evening, and it seemed the golden evening might last for ever. Year after year slid by and still she faced life with relish, still the vigour of her mind was unimpaired. Then the darkest of shadows fell across the tranquil radiance as she began slowly to go blind.

Since 1867 she had had occasional pain in her eyes especially after working at night. After 1884 her sight began to trouble her seriously. " Please remember I have *no* eyes," she wrote to Dr. Sutherland in 1885, " or rather I *have* eyes but they are neuralgic. You must not please tell me to look in the book but mark the passages for me." In 1888 she told Douglas Galton, " my eyes are so bad now. I can hardly see by candle light ". In February 1889 she had become " too blind to read newspapers ". In October she asked Douglas Galton to have a copy of a lecture he was sending her printed large " so that blind eyes can read it ". Three months later she asked him to take over the writing of an article she had been invited to contribute to *Chambers's Encyclopaedia* " because I have no longer eyes to write ".

Her spirit remained undimmed. " No, no a thousand times no. I am not growing apathetic ", she wrote to Sir Robert Rawlinson in 1889. As late as 1898 she re-read Shakespeare and made copious notes. In her letters her phrases were as vigorous as ever. " Do you know the taste of your heart in your mouth ? " she asked Margaret Verney in 1891. She received a present, in 1893, " with a loud purr of gratitude such as the best fish elicits from the cat ". She commented on Macaulay, " he was a most disagreeable companion to my fancy. . . . His conversation was a procession of one." She said of Lord Shaftesbury, " he would have been in a lunatic asylum if he had not devoted himself to reforming lunatic asylums ". She wrote to Margaret Verney in 1896 : " You are not going to let your present house are you ? I shall hate the people who take it with a mortal and undying hatred and pursue them to the confines of eternity."

She was fully conscious, however, of disquieting symptoms. As her sight grew worse she wrote fewer private notes, but in

1895 she wrote " Want of memory ", and in 1896 " How to preserve my sight ! " It was the only mention of her growing blindness she ever made. If fear clutched at her, she concealed it. In earlier life she had talked a great deal about her health, in old age she never mentioned it, but she must have remembered that Fanny had become childish and blind.

Slowly, inexorably, the curtain descended. She had always written with astonishing legibility and firmness (every line of her enormous letters is as easy to read as if it were print), but now the indelible pencil she took to using began to waver, the lines ran across the page, the letters were formed with difficulty. Still her vitality, her gaiety were unquenched. Margaret Verney's daughter, Ellin, married and in 1899 had her first child, a girl. In a spirited correspondence Miss Nightingale did her utmost to have the child named Balaclava, one of the most beautiful names, she declared, in the world. As late as 1900 she wrote to one of Margaret Verney's younger daughters : " I am sorry to see the tide leaving Italian for German. There are as many divine things in one page of Dante as in the whole of Goethe—Faust I can't abide and Margaret ' tumbled down bump ' as Babs would say much too soon to be respectable. Still it is no use, as Canute said, to kick against the tide. . . . As for riding, no ' hockey ', no games will equal it for improving the circulation all over and exercising the muscles and animal courage. A live horse and the sympathy of ' the horse and its rider ' is worth all the bats and (deaf and dumb) balls put together. So ' drat ' hockey and long live the horse ! Them's my sentiments."

Year by year in a steady procession her old friends left the mortal stage. In 1898 Sir Robert Rawlinson died—he had been a Sanitary Commissioner in the Crimean War and had remained her close friend ever since. In 1899 she lost Sir Douglas Galton. In 1902 William Rathbone ; " one of God's best and greatest sons ", she wrote on his funeral wreath. Still her optimism remained undiminished ; still she looked forward with an undaunted spirit. Lady Stephen, one of Shore's two daughters, was sitting, when a girl, with Miss Nightingale, who was lying back on her pillows, and they were speaking of one of the friends she had lost. Lady Stephen said that after a busy life he was at rest. Miss Nightingale at once sat bolt upright. "Oh *no*", she said with conviction, " I am sure it is an *immense* activity."

In 1901 darkness closed in on her. Her sight failed completely and, except with the greatest difficulty, she could no longer read or write. At the same time her mind began to fail; she was not always aware of her surroundings and lay for hours in a state of coma. In 1902 it became evident that someone must assume the direction of her household, but tact was necessary, for she still had periods in which she was her normal self and strongly objected to any encroachment on her authority. A lady named Miss Cochrane was installed with the title of companion secretary and with full authority to use her discretion. In 1904 Miss Cochrane left to be married and was succeeded by Miss Elizabeth Bosanquet, to whom Miss Nightingale became greatly attached and who remained with her until her death.

She fought to keep her grip on life. Her memory was failing but she concealed it. Before she had an important visitor she would have herself coached up to make a good impression. In 1903, before Lord Kitchener called on her, Miss Nightingale sent her companion to look up all the facts about Lord Kitchener's latest policy and memorised them just before the interview. Lord Kitchener remarked on leaving that it was astonishing how Miss Nightingale in her old age followed what was going on.

Every day she had *The Times* read to her. She also enjoyed biographies and articles from reviews which recorded action. One of her favourite books was Theodore Roosevelt's *Strenuous Life*. No longer able to act herself, she enjoyed hearing of action by others. She saw matrons and nurses, and Paulina Irby and Miss Pringle, the " Pearl ", were regular visitors. Sometimes instead of being read to she would recite poetry to herself, passages from Shakespeare, Milton, Shelley and the Italian poets; sometimes she would sing airs from the operas she had loved in her youth in a voice still surprisingly full and sweet.

A time came when there was no more reading, no more reciting or singing. In 1906 it was necessary to tell the India Office that it was useless to send papers on sanitary matters any longer to Miss Nightingale; the power of apprehension had almost left her, she was quite blind and her memory had failed. She saw very few people and she no longer recognised visitors : she took them for friends of her youth, and asked for Sir Harry Verney, who had been dead for twelve years. Hour after hour she lay inert, unconscious, her hands, still pretty in old age, folded peacefully outside the bedclothes. Words no longer reached her, although when her young relatives sang hymns she seemed to recognise familiar tunes and be pleased.

And now when she had passed beyond the power of the world to please or pain a shower of honours fell on her. In November 1907 the Order of Merit was bestowed on her by King Edward VII, the first time it had ever been given to a woman. Since no ceremony was possible, the Order was left at South Street by the King's representative. It was not even certain that she understood the honour she had received. An explanation was attempted, but she hardly seemed to grasp it. " Too kind, too kind," she murmured. In the following year she received the Freedom of the City of London. The Roll of Honour was brought to her bedside and her hand was guided to sign two wavering initials " F. N.", but it was evident that she did not understand what she was signing.

The legend surrounding her silent inert figure burst into new life. Many people reading the news of these signal honours were taken aback to find that Florence Nightingale was still alive. A flood of congratulations poured in, there were poems, songs, illuminated addresses, flowers. The Mayor of Florence sent official congratulations, the Ladies of the Red Cross Society of Tokio, the Florence Nightingale Society of America sent tributes to " the great and incomparable name of Florence Nightingale ", thousands of women who had been christened Florence in her honour banded together to send a joint message. Crimean veterans assured her that she had never been forgotten.

In June 1907 the International Conference of Red Cross Societies had held a conference in London and sent a message to " Miss Florence Nightingale, the pioneer of the first Red Cross movement, whose heroic efforts on behalf of suffering humanity will be recognised and admired by all ages as long as the world shall last ". Now local branches sent messages, regiments remembered her, the Commander-in-Chief, Lord Roberts, wrote a warm personal message in his own hand ; Queen Alexandra wrote, and the Kaiser sent a bouquet of flowers : " *very* beautiful and *very* large ", wrote Miss Bosanquet to Henry Bonham Carter in December 1907, " lily of the valley and splendid pink carnations with *yards* of pink ribbon to match. Do you think the Emperor will wish the Press Association informed ? " This was the Emperor's wish.

May 1910 was the Jubilee of the founding of the Nightingale Training School, and to mark the occasion a meeting was held in New York in the Carnegie Hall at which the Public Orator, Mr. Choate, delivered an eulogium on the great record and noble life of Miss Florence Nightingale. There were now over one thousand training schools for nurses in the United States alone.

She knew nothing. Slowly, with heartbreaking slowness, death approached. Intervals of consciousness became less and less frequent. After February 1910 she no longer spoke. The iron frame which had endured the cold and fevers of the Crimea, which had been taxed and driven and misused in forty years of gigantic labours, still lived on, deprived of memory, of sensation, of sight, but still alive.

The end came on August 13th, 1910. She fell asleep about noon and did not wake again.

In an immensely long will, which finds a place in collections of legal curiosities, she divided her possessions with meticulous detail, distributing prints, books, furniture and mementoes in hundreds of personal bequests. She expressed a wish " that no memorial whatever should mark the place where lies my Mortal Coil " ; if this proved impossible she wished her body " to be carried to the nearest convenient burial ground accompanied by not more than two persons without trappings ". A simple cross without her name, only with initials, and date of birth and death was to mark the spot. She also directed that her body should be given " for dissection or post-mortem examination for the purposes of Medical Science ".

This was not done. But in deference to her wishes the offer of a national funeral and burial in Westminster Abbey was declined. She was buried in the family grave at East Wellow, and her coffin was carried by six sergeants of the British Army. Her only memorial is two lines on the family tombstone, " F. N. Born 1820. Died 1910." She had lived for ninety years and three months.

SOURCES

(1) MSS.

THE NIGHTINGALE PAPERS
THE VERNEY NIGHTINGALE PAPERS
THE HERBERT PAPERS
THE MOHL NIGHTINGALE CORRESPONDENCE
THE CORRESPONDENCE OF MISS HILARY BONHAM CARTER
THE CORRESPONDENCE OF MR. FREDERICK VERNEY
THE LEIGH SMITH PAPERS

Place of publication : London, unless otherwise stated

(2) GOVERNMENT PUBLICATIONS

REPORT UPON THE STATE OF THE HOSPITALS OF THE BRITISH ARMY IN THE CRIMEA AND SCUTARI, TOGETHER WITH AN APPENDIX. Presented to both Houses of Parliament by command of Her Majesty, 1855. (The Hospitals Commission.)

REPORT TO THE RIGHT HON. LORD PANMURE, G.C.B., ETC., MINISTER AT WAR, OF THE PROCEEDINGS OF THE SANITARY COMMISSION DISPATCHED TO THE SEAT OF WAR IN THE EAST, 1855–56. Presented to both Houses of Parliament by command of Her Majesty, March 1857. (The Sanitary Commission.)

FIRST, SECOND AND THIRD REPORT FROM THE SELECT COMMITTEE ON THE ARMY BEFORE SEBASTOPOL; WITH THE PROCEEDINGS OF THE COMMITTEE. Ordered by the House of Commons to be printed, 1 March 1855. (The Roebuck Committee.)

REPORT OF THE COMMISSION OF INQUIRY INTO THE SUPPLIES OF THE BRITISH ARMY IN THE CRIMEA, WITH THE EVIDENCE ANNEXED. Presented to both Houses of Parliament by Command of Her Majesty, 1856. (The McNeill and Tulloch Commission.)

REPORT OF THE COMMISSIONERS APPOINTED TO INQUIRE INTO THE REGULATIONS AFFECTING THE SANITARY CONDITION OF THE ARMY, THE ORGANISATION OF MILITARY HOSPITALS, AND THE TREATMENT OF THE SICK AND WOUNDED; WITH EVIDENCE AND APPENDIX. Presented to both Houses of Parliament by Command of Her Majesty, 1858. (The Royal Sanitary Commission.)

ROYAL COMMISSION ON THE SANITARY STATE OF THE ARMY IN INDIA. REPORT OF THE COMMISSIONERS. PRÉCIS OF EVIDENCE. MINUTES OF EVIDENCE. ADDENDA, 1863. (The Indian Sanitary Commission.)

SUGGESTIONS IN REGARD TO SANITARY WORKS REQUIRED FOR IMPROVING INDIAN STATIONS. Prepared by the Barrack and Hospital Improvement Commission, 1864.

595

Memorandum of Measures Adopted for Sanitary Improvements in India up to the End of 1867; together with Abstracts of the Sanitary Reports Hitherto Forwarded from Bengal, Madras and Bombay. Printed by order of the Secretary of State for India in Council, 1868. Ditto to the end of June 1869. Ditto to the end of June 1870. Ditto to the end of June 1872.

(3) WRITINGS BY MISS NIGHTINGALE

The Institution of Kaiserswerth on the Rhine for the Practical Training of Deaconesses under the direction of the Rev. Pastor Fliedner, embracing the support and care of a Hospital, Infant and Industrial Schools, and a Female Penitentiary. Printed by the Inmates of the London Ragged Colonial Training School, 1851.

Letters from Egypt. Privately printed, 1854.

Statements Exhibiting the Voluntary Contributions Received by Miss Nightingale for the Use of the British Hospitals in the East, with the Mode of their Distribution, in 1854, 1855, 1856. Harrison and Sons, 1857.

Notes on Matters Affecting the Health, Efficiency, and Hospital Administration of the British Army. Founded Chiefly on the Experience of the Late War. Presented by Request to the Secretary of State for War. Privately printed for Miss Nightingale. Harrison and Sons, 1858.

Subsidiary Notes as to the Introduction of Female Nursing into Military Hospitals in Peace and in War. Presented by Request to the Secretary of State for War. Privately printed for Miss Nightingale. Harrison and Sons, 1858.

A Contribution to the Sanitary History of the British Army during the Late War with Russia. Harrison and Sons, 1859.

Notes on Hospitals. John W. Parker and Son, 1859. 3rd edition, almost completely rewritten, 1863. Longmans, Green and Co.

Suggestions for Thought to the Searchers after Truth among the Artizans of England. Privately printed for Miss Nightingale. 3 vols. Eyre and Spottiswoode, 1860.

Notes on Nursing : What it is, and what it is not. By Florence Nightingale. 2nd edn. Harrison and Sons, 1860.

Army Sanitary Administration and its Reform under the late Lord Herbert. M'Corquodale and Co., 1862.

Observations on the Evidence Contained in the Stational Reports Submitted to the Royal Commission on the Sanitary State of the Army in India. By Florence Nightingale. (Reprinted from the Report of the Royal Commission), Edward Stanford, 1863. (The " Observations ".)

Introductory Notes on Lying-in Institutions. Together with a Proposal for Organising an Institution for Training Midwives and Midwifery Nurses. By Florence Nightingale. Longmans, Green and Co., 1871.

LIFE OR DEATH IN INDIA. A paper read at the meeting of the National Association for the promotion of Social Science, Norwich, 1873. With an Appendix on life or death by irrigation, 1874.

THE ZEMINDAR, THE SUN, AND THE WATERING POT AS AFFECTING LIFE OR DEATH IN INDIA. Unpublished, proof copies among the Nightingale Papers, 1873-76.

ON TRAINED NURSING FOR THE SICK POOR. By Florence Nightingale. The Metropolitan and National Nursing Association, 1876.

MISS FLORENCE NIGHTINGALE'S ADDRESSES TO PROBATIONER-NURSES in the " Nightingale Fund" School at St. Thomas's Hospital and Nurses who were formerly trained there, 1872-1900. Printed for private circulation.

FLORENCE NIGHTINGALE'S INDIAN LETTERS. A glimpse into the agitation for tenancy reform. Bengal, 1878-82. Edited by Priyaranjan Sen. Calcutta, 1937.

(4) AUTHORITIES

THE BRITISH EXPEDITION TO THE CRIMEA, by W. H. Russell, LL.D., *The Times* special correspondent. G. Routledge and Co., 1858.

A MEMOIR OF BARON BUNSEN. Drawn chiefly from family papers by his widow, Frances, Baroness Bunsen. 2 vols. Longmans, Green and Co., 1868.

CONSIDERATIONS ON THE MILITARY ORGANISATION OF THE BRITISH ARMY : Respectfully addressed to General His Royal Highness The Duke of Cambridge, K.G., G.C.B., G.C.M.G., Commander-in-Chief, etc. etc. etc. By General Sir Robert Gardiner, K.C.B., Royal Artillery. Byfield, Hawksworth, and Co., 1858.

CONSTANTINOPLE DURING THE CRIMEAN WAR. By Lady Hornby. Richard Bentley, 1863.

CONVERSATIONS WITH M. THIERS, M. GUIZOT, and other distinguished persons during the SECOND EMPIRE. By the late William Nassau Senior, edited by his daughter, M. C. M. Simpson. 2 vols. Hurst and Blackett, 1878.

THE CRIMEAN COMMISSION AND THE CHELSEA BOARD : being a Review of the Proceedings and Report of the Board, by Colonel Tulloch, late Commissioner in the Crimea. Harrison and Sons, 1857.

EMMA DARWIN. A CENTURY OF FAMILY LETTERS, 1792-1896. Edited by her daughter, Henrietta Litchfield. 2 vols. John Murray, 1915.

THE AUTOBIOGRAPHY OF ELIZABETH DAVIS, a Balaclava Nurse. Edited by Jane Williams. 2 vols. Hurst and Blackett, 1857.

DELANE of " THE TIMES ". By Sir Edward Cook. Constable and Co., Ltd., 1915.

DIARY OF THE CRIMEAN WAR. By Frederick Robinson, M.D., Assistant Surgeon, Scots Fusilier Guards. Richard Bentley, 1856.

EASTERN HOSPITALS AND ENGLISH NURSES : the Narrative of Twelve Months' Experience in the Hospitals of Koulali and Scutari. By a Lady Volunteer. Hurst and Blackett, 1856.

England and Her Soldiers. By Harriet Martineau. Smith, Elder and Co., 1859.

English Note-books. By Nathaniel Hawthorne. Kegan Paul, Trench and Company, 1883.

Experiences of a Civilian in Eastern Military Hospitals. By Peter Pincoffs, M.D., late Civil Physician to the Scutari Hospitals. Williams and Norgate, 1857.

Experiences of an English Sister of Mercy. By Margaret Goodman. Smith, Elder and Co., 1862.

The Life and Correspondence of Sir Bartle Frere. By John Martineau. 2 vols. John Murray, 1895.

Mrs. Gaskell and Her Friends. By Elizabeth Sanderson Haldane. Hodder and Stoughton, 1930.

The Life of William Ewart Gladstone. By John Morley. 3 vols. Macmillan and Co., 1903.

Thomas Grant, First Bishop of Southwark. By Grace Ramsay (K. O'Meara). Smith, Elder and Co., 1874.

The Greville Memoirs, 1814–1860. Edited by Lytton Strachey and Roger Fulford. 8 vols. Macmillan and Co., 1938.

Memoir of Sidney Herbert. Sidney Herbert, Lord Herbert of Lea. A Memoir by Lord Stanmore. John Murray, 1906.

Hospitals and Sisterhoods. John Murray, 1854.

India Called Them. By William Henry Beveridge. George Allen and Unwin, 1947.

The Invasion of the Crimea: Its origin, and an account of its progress down to the death of Lord Raglan. By A. W. Kinglake, in 9 vols. 6th edition. William Blackwood and Sons, 1887.

The Letters of Queen Victoria. A selection of Her Majesty's correspondence between the years 1837 and 1861. Published by authority of His Majesty the King. Edited by Arthur Christopher Benson, M.A., and Viscount Esher. 3 vols. John Murray, 1907. Second series, edited by George Earle Buckle, 1861–85. 3 vols. John Murray, 1926. Third series, edited by George Earle Buckle, 1866–1901. 3 vols. John Murray, 1930.

Life and Death of Athena, an Owlet from the Parthenon. Privately printed, 1855.

The Life of His Royal Highness the Prince Consort. By Sir Theodore Martin, K.C.B. 5 vols. Smith, Elder and Co., 1875–80.

The Life and Letters of Sir John Hall, M.D., K.C.B., F.R.C.S. By S. M. Mitra. Longmans, Green and Co., 1911.

Life and Letters of Benjamin Jowett. By Evelyn Abbott and Lewis Campbell. 2 vols. John Murray, 1897.

The Life of Lord Lawrence. By Reginald Bosworth Smith. Nelson and Sons, 1908.

Lord Lawrence. By Sir Richard Temple. Macmillan and Co., 1890.

The Light Cavalry Brigade in the Crimea. Extracts from the Letters and Journal of the late General Lord George Paget, K.C.B., during the Crimean War. John Murray, 1881.

THE LIFE AND STRUGGLES OF WILLIAM LOVETT in his pursuit of Bread, Knowledge, and Freedom. With some short account of the different associations he belonged to, and of the opinions he entertained. Trübner and Co., 1876.

MEMOIR OF THE RT. HON. SIR JOHN McNEILL, G.C.B., and of his second wife, Elizabeth Wilson. By their Granddaughter. John Murray, 1910.

MEMORIES OF THE CRIMEA. By Sister Mary Aloysius. Burns and Oates, Limited, 1897.

THE LETTERS OF JOHN STUART MILL. Edited by Hugh S. R. Elliot. 2 vols. Longmans, Green and Co., 1910.

RICHARD MONCKTON MILNES. The Life, Letters and Friendships of Richard Monckton Milnes, First Lord Houghton. By T. Wemyss Reid. Cassell and Co. Ltd., 1890.

MADAME MOHL. Her Salon and her Friends. A study of social life in Paris. By K. O'Meara. R. Bentley and Son, 1885.

LETTERS AND RECOLLECTIONS OF JULIUS AND MARY MOHL. By M. C. M. Simpson. Kegan, Paul and Co., 1887.

THE CORRESPONDENCE OF JOHN LOTHROP MOTLEY, D.C.L. Edited by George William Curtis. John Murray, 1889.

A NARRATIVE of Personal Experiences and Impressions during Residence on the BOSPHORUS throughout the CRIMEAN WAR. By Lady Alicia Blackwood. Hatchard, 1881.

THE LIFE OF FLORENCE NIGHTINGALE. By Sir Edward Cook. 2 vols. Macmillan and Co., 1913.

THE LIFE OF FLORENCE NIGHTINGALE. By Sarah A. Tooley. Cassell and Co. Ltd., 1910.

FLORENCE NIGHTINGALE, 1820–1856. I. B. O'Malley. Thornton Butterworth, 1931.

A HISTORY OF NURSING. The Evolution of Nursing Systems from the Earliest Times to the Foundation of the First English and American Training Schools for Nurses. By M. Adelaide Nutting, R.N., and Lavinia L. Dock, R.N. G. P. Putnam's Sons, 1907.

PALMERSTON. By Philip Guedalla. Ernest Benn, 1926.

THE PANMURE PAPERS, being a selection from the correspondence of Fox Maule, second Baron Panmure, afterwards eleventh Earl of Dalhousie, K.T., G.C.B. Edited by Sir George Douglas, Bart., M.A., and Sir George Dalhousie Ramsay, C.B., late of the War Office, with a supplementary chapter by the late Rev. Principal Rainy, D.D. Hodder and Stoughton, 1908.

PIONEER WORK IN OPENING THE MEDICAL PROFESSION TO WOMEN, and AUTOBIOGRAPHICAL SKETCHES. Elizabeth Blackwell, M.D. Longmans, Green and Co., 1895.

HENRY PONSONBY. His Life from his letters, by Arthur Ponsonby. Macmillan and Co., 1943.

REMINISCENCES, Julia Ward Howe, 1819–99. Houghton, Mifflin and Co., Boston and New York, 1900.

SCUTARI AND ITS HOSPITALS. By the Hon. and Rev. Sydney Godolphin Osborne. Dickinson Brothers, 1855.

SEVASTOPOL. OUR TENT IN THE CRIMEA; AND WANDERINGS IN SEVAS-
TOPOL. By Two Brothers. Richard Bentley, 1856.

SEVENTY-ONE YEARS OF A GUARDSMAN'S LIFE. By General Sir George
Higginson, G.C.B., etc. John Murray, 1916.

THE EARL OF SHAFTESBURY, K.G. In Memoriam. October 1-9, 1885.
Ragged School Union.

THE LIFE AND WORK OF THE SEVENTH EARL OF SHAFTESBURY, K.G. By
Edwin Hodder. Cassell and Co., Ltd., 1887.

THE HISTORY OF ST. THOMAS' HOSPITAL. By F. G. Parsons, D.Sc.,
F.R.C.S., F.S.A. 3 vols. Methuen and Co. Ltd., 1932.

SKETCH OF THE HISTORY AND PROGRESS OF DISTRICT NURSING. By William
Rathbone. Macmillan and Co., 1890.

SOYER'S CULINARY CAMPAIGN. Being Historical Reminiscences of the
Late War, with The Plain Art of Cookery for Military and Civil
Institutions, the Army, Navy, Public, etc. etc., by ALEXIS SOYER,
author of "The Modern Housewife", "Shilling Cookery for the
People ", etc. G. Routledge and Co., 1857.

THE STORY OF THE HIGHLAND BRIGADE IN THE CRIMEA. Founded on
letters written during the years 1854, 1855, and 1856, by Lieutenant-
Colonel Anthony Sterling. Remington and Co., Ltd., 1895.

WITH LORD STRATFORD IN THE CRIMEAN WAR. By James Henry Skene.
Richard Bentley and Son, 1883.

LIFE OF STRATFORD DE REDCLIFFE (VISCOUNT CANNING): from his Memoranda and Private and Official Papers, by S. Lane Poole. 2 vols.
Longmans, Green and Co., 1888.

A HISTORY OF THE BRITISH ARMY. By the Hon. J. W. Fortescue. Vol. xiii.
Macmillan and Co., 1930.

INDEX

Herbert, Mrs. Sidney (Lizzie): becomes acquainted with F. N., 69; suggests F. N. as Superintendent of Institution for care of sick gentlewomen, 110; told by F. N. of Scutari project, 136; her letter to Mrs. Bracebridge on Mary Stanley's departure for Scutari, 181-4; possessive devotion to her husband, 321; acts as her husband's secretary, 322; thanks F. N. for persuading Sidney Herbert to stay at War Office, 357; supports F. N.'s demands upon him, 366; grief at his death, 370, 371

Herbert Hospital at Woolwich, 379

Hewlett, Dr., 491, 542

Highgate Infirmary, 536, 567

Holborn Workhouse scandal, 462

Holland, Canon Scott, 569

Holland, Queen of, 313, 334

Holyoake, Jacob, 99

Hong Kong barracks, 586

Hornby, Lady, 242

Hospital statistics, 335

Hospitals, conditions in (1845), 57, 58

Hospitals, F. N.'s work on administrative reforms, 335

Hospitals, London, House of Lords committee on, 573

Hospitals Commission, 162, 166, 180, 198; unfavourable report on Scutari hospitals, 211

Hospitals with Nightingale matrons, 567

Houghton, Lord. *See* Milnes

Howe, Dr. and Julia Ward, 48, 49, 59

Huntington County Hospital, 567

Husson, Monsieur, 471

Ilbert, Sir Courtenay, 550, 553

Ilbert Bill, 550, 551, 560

India, Army, British: death-rate, 408; mortality of soldiers' children, 410; conditions in hospitals, 410; plight of native troops, 411; condition of barracks, 409, 410; Royal Commission on health of army sought by F. N., 317; Commission in being, 404 *et seq.*; report completed, 412; suspected plot to suppress disclosures, 414, 415; action on recommendations held up by departmental quarrels, 423; F. N.'s barracks and hospital plans disregarded, 499-501; Soldiers' Clubs and Institutes, 563

India, Census survey, 511; cholera enquiry, 511; Land Tenure Bills, 563; military hospitals: employment of women nurses, 558, 563; Nightingale nurses in India, 567

India Office, Sanitary Annual, 458; Department of Public Health, Civil and Military, 458

Indian famine, 544, 545

Indian Irrigation, 542

Indian mutiny, 316

Indian Sanitary Commission, 203, 204, 213, 219, 225, 243, 497; personnel reduced to two, 451; proposal that Prison Inspectors became Sanitary Commissioners, 451, 453; instructions for Sanitary Committee completed by F. N., 457; Commission's authority increased, 563; sanitary board set up in every province, 563; army sanitary committee reconstructed, 564; Bombay Village Sanitation Act, 565; public health service proposed, 446; memorandum by F. N., 455; F. N.'s scheme for taxation, 566

Indian women, National Association for supplying medical aid to, 563

Irby, Miss Paulina, 531-3, 591

Jones, Miss Agnes: apprenticeship at Kaiserswerth and training at Nightingale school, 464; F. N.'s "best and dearest pupil", 464; disagreements at Liverpool Infirmary, 465; death, 476

Jowett, Benjamin: letters to F. N., 350, 381, 428, 512, 515, 526, 548, 549, 572; friendship with F. N., 350-2; on F. N.'s "public feelings", 383, 384; persuades F. N. to visit her parents, 448; warns her not to exaggerate to Sir Stafford Northcote, 455; implores her to change her way of living, 488; visit to Lea Hurst, 503; persuades F. N. not to become hospital patient, 515; urges her to make writing her main interest, 521, 522; asks her for Bible stories for children, 523; on mysticism, 526; consulted by F. N. about her relationship with her nurses, 538; letter in praise of F. N., 548, 549; on Board of Examiners for Indian Civil Service, 553; death, 584

Jubilee Institute for Nurses, 568

Kaiserswerth, 63, 73; F. N.'s first visit to, 82; her pamphlet on, 83; life at, 89-91; Miss Agnes Jones at, 464

Mohl, Julius: character, 28, 29; friendship formed with F. N., 30; marriage to Mary Clarke, 65; his "kind paternity" to F. N., 115; death, 533, 534

Mohl, Madame (Mary Clarke): meets the Nightingales, 26; character, 26, 27; falls in love with F. N., 29; friendship with Claude Fauriel, 30; marriage of, 65; efforts to gain F. N. her freedom, 105; F. N. criticises her book on Madame Recamier and compares men with women, 384, 387; unable to see F. N., 429, 430; letters from F. N. on Hilary Bonham Carter's death, 438, 439; F. N.'s outburst on women's inefficiency, 477; F. N. declines to see her, 559; death, 560

Montreal, Nightingale Nurses at, 567
Morley, Lord, 557
Mortality in the British Army, 310
Mysticism, F. N.'s experience in, 523-6

Napier (and Ettrick), Lady, 493
Napier (and Ettrick), Lord, 149, 492, 543
Napier of Magdala, Lord, 491, 495-7, 501, 512, 540
Napoleon III, 24, 25, 64, 507
National Society for Aid to the Sick and Wounded, 505
Netley, Royal Victoria Hospital, 567
Netley Hospital: F. N. invited to inspect plans, 269; her report condemning them, 275, 276; intervention by Lord Palmerston, 276, 277; F. N.'s "Pavilion" design, 277; reason for F. N.'s defeat, 332
Nicholson, Mrs. G. T. (sister of Mrs. Nightingale), 3
Nicholson, Miss Hannah, religious discussions with F. N., 47
Nicholson, Henry (F. N.'s cousin), in love with F. N., 33; presses F. N. to become engaged to him, 46; marriage proposal rejected by F. N., 53; death, 85
Nicholson, Lothian, 113, 223
Nicholson, Marianne (F. N.'s cousin): F. N.'s "passion" for, 33; anger with F. N. for not accepting her brother Henry, 46; breaks friendship with F. N., 52; marriage to Capt. Douglas Galton and reconciliation with the Nightingales, 314
Nicholson, William, 50
Nightingale, Florence: birth at Flor-

ence, 1; character, 6-8, 10, 14, 107, 128, 236, 262, 597; education by her father, 11; early sanctimoniousness, 12; a call from God, 16; her dream world and her voices, 17, 46, 76; her self-criticism, 31, 41, 529, 547; religious tendencies, 98-100; devotion to Aunt Mai, 13; family visit to France and Italy, 19, 21, 22; visit to Geneva, 23; meets Miss Mary Clarke, 26; at Queen's birthday Drawing Room, 32; infatuated with Marianne Nicholson, 33; ill-health, 35, 50, 52, 61, 67, 79-81, 114, 115, 206, 220-22, 231, 235, 243, 244, 259, 264, 268, 283, 287, 298, 300-304, 306-8, 328, 329, 355, 361, 368, 377, 382, 387, 418, 428, 458, 469, 549, 561; studies mathematics, 37-9; meets Richard Monckton Milnes, 41; his marriage proposal rejected, 76; care for the sick and poor at Lea Hurst, 45; a disciple of her Aunt Hannah, 47; seeks Dr. Ward Howe's advice on nursing, 48, 49; rejects Henry Nicholson's marriage proposal, 52; loses Marianne Nicholson's friendship, 53; nurses her grandmother, Mrs. Shore, 54; family hostility to nursing plan, 56; studies sanitary conditions at home and abroad, 61; receives Kaiserswerth Year Book, 63; first visit to Kaiserswerth, 82; second visit, 89-91; her anonymous pamphlet on Kaiserswerth, 83; visit to Oxford, 64; friendship and visit to Rome with the Bracebridges, 65, 67, 68; meets Sidney Herbert, 69; acquaintance with Dr. Manning (later Cardinal), 71; meets Mary Stanley, 71; influence of Madre Santa Colomba, 72; nurses the poor of East Wellow; family discouragement, 74; visit with the Bracebridges to Egypt and Greece: diary of her secret agonies, 78-81; work at village school, 85; "butchered to make a Roman holiday": her indictment of family life, 93; writes description of her home life under title of Cassandra, 94-6; hospital experience in Dublin, 103; visits hospitals, infirmaries, almshouses and Institutions in Paris, 108; sees Lady Canning about Institution for care of sick gentlewomen, 110; enters the Maison de la Providence in Paris,

114; receives an allowance of £500 a year from her father, 112; takes a place of her own in Pall Mall, 115; assumes duties as Superintendent of Institution for sick gentlewomen in Harley Street, 116; her organising genius, 117-22; investigates conditions for hospital nurses, 124-6; proposed post at King's College Hospital, 126; her appearance, 127; nurses cholera patients at Middlesex Hospital, 127; prepares to go to Scutari, 136; her life and work at Scutari (*see* Crimean War); her return home from the Crimea, 256; public acclamation, 234-7; Nightingale Fund formed, 236; gift of brooch to F. N. by Queen Victoria, 236; reply to resolution by committee of Nightingale fund, 237; promise of India Office department for sanitary business, 256; her achievement for soldiers and nurses and her sense of failure, 256, 257; sets out to reform army health administration, 259-62; anticipates an early death, 262; her self-effacement, 262; prepares case for presentation to Queen Victoria, 264; received at Balmoral, 265; her impressions at Balmoral, 270; Lord Panmure promises to set up Royal Commission, 269; chooses name for Royal Commission, 270, 271; condemns plans for Netley Hospital, her pavilion design, 277; Lord Panmure asks for confidential report on sick and wounded, 279; threat to publish her experiences of Crimean campaign, 279; plan for equipment of troops for China, 280, 281; completes confidential report, 282, 294-7; strenuous days and nights writing and visiting hospitals, 283; protests to W. E. N. against mother's and sister's behaviour, 285, 286, 288; coaches Sidney Herbert on Royal Commission, 288, 289; convinced of her own early death, dismisses Sidney Herbert's ill-health as "fancies", 291; her evidence for Royal Commission, 293; describes report as "one of my works", 298; goes to Malvern seriously ill, 300; orders Dr. Sutherland to join her, 301; visit from W. E. N., 302; joined by Aunt Mai who forbids family visits, 302, 303; uses illness as protection from her family, 303, 304; declines offer of marriage by Sir Harry Verney, 305; convinced of approaching death, plans her funeral, 306, 307; her pamphlet on mortality in the army: statistics with pictorial charts, 310; press campaign on health of the army, 315; her anonymous *Contribution to the Sanitary History of the late War with Russia*, 316; offer to go to India, 316; seeks Royal Commission on health of the army in India, 317; consulted on War Office reform, 327; F. N. and her cats, 329, 355, 441, 442, 458, 521; her opinion of civil hospitals, 331, 332; her *Notes on Hospitals*, 332, 333; her advice sought on hospital construction, 333; designs hospital for Lisbon, 334; reform of hospital administration, 335; elected member of the Statistical Society, 335; scheme for uniform hospital statistics, 335; Nightingale Fund training school for nurses sub-committee appointed, 343 *et seq.*; school for nurses opened, 346; her new religion for intelligent artisans entitled *Suggestions for Thought*, 349; friendship with Benjamin Jowett, 351, 352, 431, 432, 488, 515, 521, 522, 523, 526, 538, 548; bitterness at losing Aunt Mai, 354, 355; gives the secret of her success, 360; refuses Queen's offer of apartment in Kensington Palace, 360; statuettes of F. N., 361-3; accused of hastening death of Arthur Hugh Clough, 381; aid asked in organising American Civil War hospitals, 380; advice sought on sanitary arrangements for Canadian expedition, 382; compares sympathy of women with that of men, 384-7; angered by "Woman's Rights" talk, 385; supervision of plans for barracks and hospitals, 398; consulted on colonial prisons, 398; her campaign for reform of army medical service, 399, 400; storm over Contagious Diseases Act, 400-402; work for Royal Commission on health of army in India, 404 *et seq.*; analysis of reports from India, 407; proposes a sanitary code for all India, 413; recognised as an expert on India, 418; presses for appointment of Sir John Lawrence

mother of Miss Florence Nightingale, 282; resentment at F. N.'s allowance of £500 a year, 285; too unwell to spend the winter in London, 303; visited in her old age by F. N. after an absence of nine years, 448; becomes an increasing anxiety to F. N., 517; her increasing childishness keeps F. N. at home, 518; her claim upon F. N., 527-8; in F. N.'s charge in London, 532; death, 547

Nightingale, Louis Shore, 588

Nightingale, Parthenope. *See* Verney, Lady

Nightingale, Peter, 4, 5

Nightingale, William Edward (W. E. N.), father of Florence: marriage to Fanny Smith, 1, 4; changes his name from Shore to Nightingale, 4; fondness of children, 9; candidate for Parliament, 14, 15; enquiries about hospital nursing, 96; distress over family conflicts, 111; makes F. N. an allowance of £500 a year, 112; accompanies F. N. to Scotland, 265; retreats to the peace of Embley, 269; visits F. N. at Malvern and is horrified by her condition, 302; long talks with F. N. on metaphysics, 503; old and ailing, an increased anxiety to F. N., 517; death, 526

Nightingale Fund to establish an institute for training of nurses, 236; St. Thomas's Hospital scheme, 338, 341; plans for establishing school, 343 *et seq.*; school for nurses opened, 346; school for midwives at King's College Hospital, 348-9, 437

Nightingale Nurses, 477, 537, 538; training of, 483-4; at Liverpool Workhouse Infirmary, 463

Nightingale Training School, 338, 477, 516, 517; reconstruction, 520-21; F. N.'s interest in probationers, 536, 537; hospitals and institutions with matrons and superintendents from, 567; school's Jubilee, 593

Nineteenth Century, 545

North London District Association, 567

Northbrook, Lord, 512, 540

Northcote, Sir Stafford, succeeds Lord Cranborne at India Office, 451; Memorandum from F. N., 454-5; meeting with F. N., promise of India Office department for Sanitary business, 455, 456; agrees to estab-

lish authority of Sanitary Committee in India, 457

Norton, Caroline, 320, 321

Notes on Hospitals, 332, 333

Notes on Lying-in Institutions, 504

Notes on Matters affecting the Health, Efficiency and Hospital Administration of the British Army, 282, 294-7

Notes on Nursing, 222, 338-41

Nurses, depravity of, 58

Nurses: F. N.'s reform of nursing profession, 256-7; hospital conditions, 124-5; Jubilee Institute for, 568; nurses, Nightingale, 536-8; register proposed, 570-73; Royal Charter petition before Privy Council, 572-574; training schools directed by Nightingale superintendents, 567

Nurses' Association, British, 570-74

Nurses in Bengal hospitals, 453-4

Nurses in Indian Military hospitals, 563

Nursing Reform, 125

Osborne, Hon. and Rev. Sidney Godolphin, 169-71, 174, 206

Paget, Lord George, 158

Paget, Sir James, 568

Palmerston, Lady, 125

Palmerston, Lord, 136, 203, 276, 277, 322, 392, 394, 395, 439

Panmure, Lord (later Earl of Dalhousie), 260, 394; sends Sanitary Commission to Scutari and the Crimea, 203; becomes Secretary for War; instructed to show consideration for F. N.'s wishes and opinions, 203; sets up Chelsea Board, 244; his despatch establishing F. N.'s position at Scutari, 249-50; character, 266-7; promises F. N. to set up a Royal Commission on health of the army, 269; discusses Royal Commission with F. N., 272, 273; sees trouble arising from F. N.'s criticisms of Netley hospital plans, 276; offers to incorporate improvements in Netley hospital, 277; asks F. N. for confidential report on care of sick and wounded and the Army's Sanitary requirements, 279; shows F. N. draft of instructions for Royal Commission, 280, 281; delays over sub-commissions; "wiping" sub-commission revoked and then reinstated, 309; succeeded as Secretary

organisation, 327, 353, 364, 365, 391-3, 586
Ward, Lord, 221
Ward, Mr. (Purveyor at Scutari), 153, 158
Wardroper, Mrs., Matron of St. Thomas's Hospital, 336; friendship with F. N., 338; her appearance and character, 344, 345; her supervision of training school probationers, 347, 348; retirement from St. Thomas's, 569
Weare, Miss, 224, 253
Wedderburn, Sir William, 488
Wellington, Duchess of, 270
Wellington, Duke of, 157
Westminster Hospital, 567
Wheeler, Sister Elizabeth, 179, 180
Whitfield, Mr., 336, 338, 345, 520
Wilbraham, Colonel, 479

Williams, Miss Rachael, 538, 539, 559, 567
Wolseley, Lord, 556, 558
Women, F. N.'s distrust of, 477
Women's Suffrage, 487, 488
Wood, Sir Charles, 417, 423
Wood, Sir Evelyn, 556
Woolner, Thomas, 363
Woolwich General Hospital, 478
Woolwich General Military Hospital, 379, 403
Workhouses, Association for improvement of London workhouses, 468; committee appointed to report on workhouses and workhouse Infirmaries, 470; nursing in Infirmaries, 462

Yule, Colonel, 541, 584

Zemindars, 546